EFFECTIVE PHYSICAL
SECURITY

EFFECTIVE PHYSICAL SECURITY

FIFTH EDITION

Lawrence J. Fennelly

AMSTERDAM • BOSTON • HEIDELBERG • LONDON
NEW YORK • OXFORD • PARIS • SAN DIEGO
SAN FRANCISCO • SINGAPORE • SYDNEY • TOKYO
Butterworth-Heinemann is an imprint of Elsevier

Butterworth-Heinemann is an imprint of Elsevier
The Boulevard, Langford Lane, Kidlington, Oxford OX5 1GB, United Kingdom
50 Hampshire Street, 5th Floor, Cambridge, MA 02139, United States

Notices

Knowledge and best practice in this field are constantly changing. As new research and experience broaden our understanding, changes in research methods, professional practices, or medical treatment may become necessary.

Practitioners and researchers must always rely on their own experience and knowledge in evaluating and using any information, methods, compounds, or experiments described herein. In using such information or methods they should be mindful of their own safety and the safety of others, including parties for whom they have a professional responsibility.

To the fullest extent of the law, neither the Publisher nor the authors, contributors, or editors, assume any liability for any injury and/or damage to persons or property as a matter of products liability, negligence or otherwise, or from any use or operation of any methods, products, instructions, or ideas contained in the material herein.

Library of Congress Cataloging-in-Publication Data
A catalog record for this book is available from the Library of Congress

British Library Cataloguing-in-Publication Data
A catalogue record for this book is available from the British Library

ISBN: 978-0-12-804462-9

For information on all Butterworth-Heinemann publications
visit our website at https://www.elsevier.com/

Working together
to grow libraries in
developing countries

www.elsevier.com • www.bookaid.org

Publisher: Todd Green
Acquisition Editor: Steve Merken
Editorial Project Manager: Nate McFadden
Production Project Manager: Stalin Viswanathan
Designer: Matthew Limbert

Typeset by TNQ Books and Journals

Dedication

It is with great happiness that we dedicate this book to our two very special daughters-in-law, Annmarie Carr Fennelly and Janet Mansfield Fennelly. Both of these strong women are working mothers, have three beautiful children each, and are wonderful Mothers, Wives, and our Daughters.

Larry and Annmarie Fennelly

Contents

Foreword

A manager designs and develops security, physical security, safety and investigative programs. **Louis A. Tyska, CPP**

This book is your road map to decoding and developing an effective security strategy beginning with the design build phase and addressing everything in between including life safety issues. Larry Fennelly and Marianna Perry have the knowledge and experience to see these complicated and ever-changing security challenges from a unique and multifaceted viewpoint. They both share their insight with the reader and that is why every security practitioner needs to read this book. Most security books focus on one topic, i.e., Risk Analysis or Security Surveillance Systems (CCTV) and access control and biometrics. I love this text because it has so much material in it that we need to address our everyday problems.

The baby boomers are retiring and the millennium generation is taking over. The face of security is also changing. Research is being done to advance the security profession to provide the highest level of protection while at the same time, increasing the bottom-line profitability of the organization. College courses are changing. Going forward, the combination of business as a major field of study and security or information technology as a minor is becoming the new norm. This change is being implemented to prepare security professionals to properly protect corporate assets.

The new "buzz words" from 2015 to 2020 will be the following:

1. What kind of "skill set" does the candidate/officer have?
2. What "certifications and specializations" does the candidate/officer have?
3. Both "physical security and informational security" will be merging with the move toward certifications.
4. "Career pathways" will be used by way of "internships."
5. Your "certifications" will be the bar for testing qualifications.
6. Education for a career in security is being "redesigned." Are you ready?
7. The holistic approach is preferred over independent components or "silos" as a logical approach to security systems.
8. 5.0 Megapixel cameras on phones and monitors with full (or true) HDTV—1080 are standard.

Do not be left behind! Plan for the future now!

The top crime threat problems according to recent reports are (1) cyber/communications security, (2) workplace violence, (3) business continuity, (4) insider threat, and (5) property crime.

We mention this because if you are going to be addressing crime problems you first need to know what they are. To make recommendations and solve problems, you first have to make sure that you have correctly identified the issue.

If a security assessment is not completed to determine the root causes of a security issue or vulnerability, the security practitioner may simply keep putting policies or procedures in place that address the symptoms and countermeasures of a problem and not the actual problem itself. This will be a frustrating (and sometimes costly) situation that can be avoided if, before any action is taken, an assessment is completed by a knowledgeable security professional to accurately identify security vulnerabilities. This will ensure that the true issues and concerns are being addressed, not just the *symptoms*.

The most demanding problem for managers and supervisors within a protection department is the physical security devices under his/her control. The supervisor's role should be to assist in enabling the manager to provide a level of support within the organization. Supervisors must take responsibility for corporate regulations, moral and ethical tone as well as providing the required level of security and customer service required.

Managers work with budgets and other resources (equipment, uniforms, technology, software, etc.) to ensure that the protective mission is achieved. Managers oversee processes (procedures) that accomplish organizational goals and objectives. Staff functions without a supervisory span of control over line employees may be performed by managers. Training, technical support, auditing, etc., are staff functions. A manager coordinates activities rather than supervises them. Turnover and job rotation can create overall improvement and a challenge. Staying current on industry trends and events by reviewing news sources, trade publications, and webinars and sources such as ASIS International and others.

Active shooter/active assailant's incidents, stabbings, and random unthinkable acts of violence are happening in our workplaces and on our televisions everyday. We cannot escape these mindless crimes and thefts that impact every segment of the security management operation. "Security Matters" now more than ever! Trying to decide which security concepts are right for your organization is a daunting full-time task. However, I suggest that you start off with a professional security assessment, so you can identify your security needs.

This book is your road map to decoding and developing an effective security strategy beginning with the design build phase and addressing everything in between including life safety issues. The authors have the knowledge and experience to see these complicated and ever-changing security challenges from a unique and multifaceted viewpoint. They both share their insight with the reader and that is why every security practitioner needs to read this book. Most security books focus on one topic, i.e., Risk Analysis or Security Surveillance Systems (CCTV) and access control. I love this text because it has so much material in it that we need to address our everyday problems.

Today's security books are more and more complicated and technical. We, as practitioners must stay ahead of the curve, to keep up. Books like this, and those of Thomas Norman, CPP, David Paterson, CPP, Sandi Davis (Women in Security), James F. Broder, CPP, Michael Fagel PhD, and Dr Jennifer Hestermann are security professionals and future educators along with Larry Fennelly and Marianna Perry. Writing a book listing 150 things…etc., is not an easy task. I commend these authors and those that I mentioned, for their vision and dedication that will keep us ahead of the curve.

Linda Watson, MA, CPP, CSC, CHS-V
Whirlaway Group LLC

Preface

We completed this book in about 6 months. Normally, this undertaking would take 18 months. We know that it is hard to believe, but it is true. We both know that the faster we could complete this book, get it published and into the hands of those who are responsible for those practitioners in security, then possibly the information will get out there and be of further help to our profession. This is basically a very hard book to finish. The first 35 are easy the next 35 are ok, then it gets harder and harder. We went through two drafts and then after having a strong handle on it, we keep adding and adding to the various pieces. A perfect example is the section on body cameras, I saw a report that was negative, then I found another report that was positive, so we add a piece I felt this was the best part of the book, because it was getting better and better.

Physical security is a big topic, cybercrimes and cyberterrorism, workplace violence, emergency management, and IT security issues will continue to be the top issues going forward.

Regulations and Compliances and security standards for your corporation will continue to be developed and aid in the improvement of your security assessment. Follow CPTED principles and security best practices and master plan development. After you have done so, call your local media to promote your accomplishments. Let the bad guys know that you take crime prevention and effective security at *your* school serious!

Times have changed and you must change as well, I was reading a deposition recently and the security manager said quote "We have been doing it this way for 30 years." Of course, you have that is why a man died and your being sued.

Social media need to monitored and included in your assessment process.

We are concerned because we know that many of you do not have good security and do not have adequate security in place to protect your assets. We are not advocating that you make your corporate or place of work a fortress into a cold, uninviting fortress. Instead, we want you to have not only a safe environment but also has effective security in place to address vulnerabilities and have continuous assessments to improve the process.

Enterprise risk management (ERM): (1) It looks at a holistic approach to ERM, which breaks down silos between physical and technological security and provides comprehensives risk management solutions. Eugene Ferraro recently said, (2) "We owe it not only to this country, but also to the free world, to think further ahead about future threats and what the solutions look like. And if we can reach consensus around these solutions, we will be in a better position to build them."

We wish to sincerely thank all of our contributors who made this book possible. We truly believe that compiling the knowledge of many security professionals is a more comprehensive approach to addressing the issue of physical security. We thank you for your professionalism as well as your contributions to our profession.

**Lawrence J. Fennelly
and Marianna A. Perry, CPP**

[1] Enterprise Security Risks and Workplace Competencies, ASIS, University of Phoenix & Apollo Education Group, 2016.
[2] Ibid.

Encompassing Effective CPTED Solutions in 2017 and Beyond: Concepts and Strategies

Lawrence J. Fennelly, CPOI, CSSI, CHS-III, CSSP-1,
Marianna A. Perry, MS, CPP, CSSP-1

Deterrence's, CPTED Design, Policies and Procedures, Training Programs and Security Awareness Programs. **Thomas L Norman, CPP, PSP, CSC 2016.**

INTRODUCTION

We are delighted to be a part of the series of white papers for School Dangers.Org. It is appropriate to say a few words about Tim Crowe and Crime Prevention through Environmental Design (CPTED), before you read our paper.

Tim Crowe wrote *Crime Prevention Through Environmental Design* (1991) based on a security assessment that he conducted for a school district in Florida. Tim's book (which was updated and modernized by Lawrence Fennelly in 2013) was and is still considered a primary resource for crime prevention practitioners in the security industry to help them better understand the relationship between design and human behavior. CPTED is a proactive approach to manipulate the physical environment and bring about the desired behavior of reduced criminal activity as well as reduced fear of crime. Tim Crowe and Larry Fennelly lectured for Rick Draper in Australia on the concepts of CPTED.

Tim Crowe's comprehensive set of guidelines were developed with one goal in mind—to reduce opportunities for crime in the built environment. His work is the "gold standard" for security practitioners and others who implement CPTED concepts as a crime prevention tool. Crowe's work is frequently used as a training tool for law enforcement, town planners, and architects. These guidelines have been used in hundreds of training sessions and cited in numerous publications.

Tim Crowe was a professor at the National Crime Prevention Institute (NCPI) at the University of Louisville in Louisville, Kentucky. Marianna Perry is the former Director of NCPI and together both she and Tim have presented training sessions on CPTED.

Effective Physical Security, Fifth Edition
http://dx.doi.org/10.1016/B978-0-12-804462-9.00001-4

We included this information because we want you to understand the origination of Tim Crowe's work on CPTED.

ENVIRONMENT

The conceptual thrust of a CPTED program is that the physical environment can be manipulated to produce behavioral effects that will reduce the incidence and fear of crime, thereby improving the quality of life. These behavioral effects can be accomplished by reducing the propensity of the physical environment to support criminal behavior. Environmental design, as used in a CPTED program, is rooted in the design of the human–environment relationship. It embodies several concepts. The term *environment* includes the people and their physical and social surroundings. However, as a matter of practical necessity, the environment defined for demonstration purposes is that which has recognizable territorial and system limits.

The term *design* includes physical, social, management, and law enforcement directives that seek to affect positively human behavior as people interact with their environment.

Thus, the CPTED program seeks to prevent certain specified crimes (and the fear attendant on them) within a specifically defined environment by manipulating variables that are closely related to the environment itself.

The program does not purport to develop crime prevention solutions in a broad universe of human behavior but rather solutions limited to variables that can be manipulated and evaluated in the specified human/environment relationship. CPTED involves design of physical space in the context of the needs of legitimate users of the space (physical, social, and psychological needs), the normal and expected (or intended) use of the space (the activity or absence of activity planned for the space), and the predictable behavior of both legitimate users and offenders. Therefore, in the CPTED approach, a design is proper if it recognizes the designated use of the space, defines the crime problem incidental to and the solution compatible with the designated use, and incorporates the crime prevention strategies that enhance (or at least do not impair) the effective use of the space. CPTED draws not only on physical and urban design but also on contemporary thinking in behavioral and social science, law enforcement, and community organization.

SPACE

The continuum of space within a residential complex (that is, a property consisting of one or more buildings containing dwelling units and associated grounds or, more broadly, a neighborhood consisting primarily of residential uses) may be divided into four categories:

- **Public**. Space that, whatever its legal status, is perceived by all members of a residential area or neighborhood as belonging to the public as a whole, which a stranger has as much perceived right to use as a resident.
- **Semipublic**. Space accessible to all members of the public without passing through a locked or guarded barrier. There is thought to be an implied license for use by the public, and strangers will rarely be challenged. This is generally associated with multifamily housing.
- **Semiprivate**. Space restricted for use by residents, guests, and service people on legitimate assignments. In multifamily housing, this is usually secured by protection officers (or doormen), locks, or other forms of physical barriers. Strangers can be expected to be challenged as potential trespassers.
- **Private**. Space restricted for use by residents of a single dwelling unit, their invited guests, and service people, with access

generally controlled by locks and other physical barriers. Unauthorized use is always challenged when the opportunity for challenge presents itself.

TARGET HARDENING

The emphasis on design and use deviates from the traditional target-hardening approach to crime prevention. Traditional target hardening focuses predominantly on denying access to a crime target through physical or artificial barrier techniques (such as locks, alarms, fences, and gates). Target hardening often leads to constraints on use, access, and enjoyment of the hardened environment. Moreover, the traditional approach tends to overlook opportunities for natural access control and surveillance. The term *natural* refers to deriving access control and surveillance results as a by-product of the normal and routine use of the environment. It is possible to adapt normal and natural uses of the environment to accomplish the effects of artificial or mechanical hardening and surveillance. Nevertheless, CPTED employs pure target-hardening strategies either to test their effectiveness as compared with natural strategies or when they appear to be justified as not unduly impairing the effective use of the environment.

As an example, a design strategy of improved street lighting must be planned, efficient, and evaluated in terms of the behavior it promotes or deters and the use impact of the lighted (and related) areas in terms of all users of the area (offenders, victims, other permanent, or casual users). Any strategies related to the lighting strategy (e.g., block-watch or neighborhood watch, 911 emergency service, police patrol) must be evaluated in the same regard. This reflects the comprehensiveness of the CPTED design approach in focusing on both the proper design and effective use of the physical environment. Additionally, the concept of proper design and effective use emphasizes the designed relationship among

strategies to ensure that the desired results are achieved. It has been observed that improved street lighting alone (a design strategy) is ineffective against crime without the conscious and active support of citizens (in reporting what they see) and of police (in responding and conducting surveillance). CPTED involves the effort to integrate design, citizen and community action, and law enforcement strategies to accomplish surveillance consistent with the design and use of the environment.

CPTED Strategies

There are three overlapping strategies in CPTED (as shown in Fig. 1.1):

1. Natural access control
2. Natural surveillance
3. Territorial reinforcement

Access control and surveillance have been the primary design concepts of physical design programs. At the outset of the CPTED program, access control and surveillance systems—preexisting as conspicuous concepts in the field of CPTED—received major attention. Access control and surveillance are not mutually exclusive classifications since certain

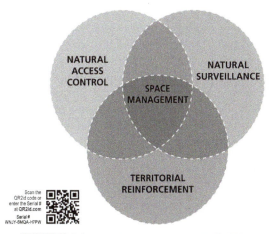

FIGURE 1.1 Overlapping strategies in CPTED.

strategies achieve both, and strategies in one classification typically are mutually supportive of the other. However, the operational thrust of each is distinctly different, and the differences must be recognized in performing analysis, research, design, implementation, and evaluation.

Access control is a design concept directed primarily at decreasing crime opportunity. Access control strategies are typically classified as organized (e.g., security officers), mechanical (e.g., locks, lighting, and alarms), and natural (e.g., spatial definition). The primary thrust of an access control strategy is to deny access to a crime target and to create a perception of risk in offenders. Surveillance is a design concept directed primarily at keeping intruders under observation. Therefore, the primary thrust of a surveillance strategy is to facilitate observation, although it may have the effect of an access control strategy by effectively keeping intruders out because of an increased perception of risk. Surveillance strategies are typically classified as organized (e.g., police patrol), mechanical (e.g., lighting, locks, and alarms), and natural (e.g., windows).

Photos 1.1–1.3 reflect good natural surveillance.

Traditionally, access control and surveillance, as design concepts (Fig. 1.2), have emphasized mechanical or organized crime prevention techniques while overlooking, minimizing, or ignoring attitudes, motivation, and use of the physical environment. More recent approaches to physical design of environments have shifted the emphasis to natural crime prevention techniques, attempting to use natural opportunities presented by the environment for crime prevention. This shift in emphasis led to the concept of territoriality.

The concept of territoriality (elaborated most fully to date in the public housing environment) suggests that physical design can contribute to a sense of territoriality. That is, physical design can create or extend a sphere of influence so that users develop a sense of proprietorship—a sense

PHOTO 1.1

PHOTO 1.2

PHOTO 1.3

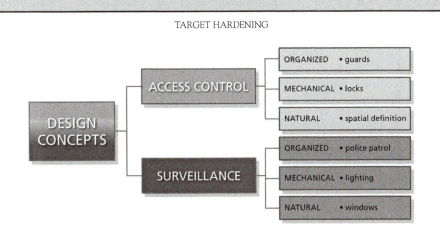

FIGURE 1.2 Typical access control and surveillance concepts as well as classifications.

PHOTO 1.4 Reflects physical design based on territoriality.

of territorial influence—and potential offenders perceive that territorial influence (Photo 1.4).

At the same time, it was recognized that natural access control and surveillance contributed to a sense of territoriality, making it effective for crime prevention. Natural access control and surveillance will promote more responsiveness by users in protecting their territory (e.g., more security awareness, reporting, and reacting) and promote greater perception of risk by offenders.

Maintenance

Finally, care and maintenance allow for the continued use of a space for its intended purpose, as well as contributing to territorial reinforcement. Deterioration and blight indicate less concern and control by the intended users of a site and indicate a greater tolerance of disorder. Proper maintenance protects the public health, safety, and welfare in all existing structures, residential and nonresidential, and on all existing premises by establishing minimum standards, best practices, as well as a master plan. Maintenance is the responsibility of the facilities manager, owners, and occupants.

Furthermore, the effort to achieve a balance between design for crime prevention and design for effective use of environments contributed to the shift in focus from organized and mechanical strategies per se to natural strategies. This was because natural strategies exploited the opportunities of the given environment both to naturally and routinely facilitate access control and surveillance and to reinforce positive behavior in the use of the environment. The concept reflects a preference, where feasible, to reinforce existing or new activities, or to otherwise reinforce the behavior of environment users so that crime prevention flows naturally and routinely from the activity being promoted.

The conceptual shift from organized and mechanical to natural strategies has

PHOTO 1.5 Reflects mechanical layout of mounted camera with street light and roof lighting.

PHOTO 1.6 Can you see the man hiding in the bushes?

oriented the CPTED program to develop plans that emphasize natural access control and surveillance and territorial reinforcement (Photo 1.5).

Although conceptually distinct, it is important to realize that these strategy categories tend to overlap in practice. It is perhaps most useful to think of territorial reinforcement as the umbrella concept, comprising all natural surveillance principles, which in turn comprises all access control principles. It is not practical to think of territorial reinforcement, natural surveillance, and access control as independent strategies because, for example, access control operates to denote transitional zones, not necessarily impenetrable barriers. If these symbolic or psychological barriers are to succeed in controlling access by demarcating specific spaces for specific individuals, potential offenders must perceive that unwarranted intrusion will elicit protective territorial responses from those who have legitimate access. Similarly, natural surveillance operates to increase the likelihood that intrusion will be observed by individuals who care but are not officially responsible for regulating the use and treatment of spaces. If people observe inappropriate behavior but do nothing about it, then the most carefully planned natural surveillance tactics are useless in terms of stopping crime and vandalism (Photo 1.6).

The Three-D Approach[1]

For CPTED to be a success, it must be understandable and practical for the normal users of the space. That is, the normal residents of a neighborhood and the people who work in buildings or commercial areas must be able to use these concepts. Why? Because these people know more about what is going on in that environment and they have a vested interest (their own well-being) in ensuring that their immediate environment operates properly. The technologist or specialist, who may be a traffic engineer, city planner, architect, or security specialist, should not be allowed to shoulder the responsibility alone for safety and security. The specialist needs to follow the dictates of the users of the space because he/she can often be swayed by misperceptions or by the conflicting demands of his professional competition.

The Three-D approach to space assessment provides a simple guide for the layperson to use in determining the appropriateness of how his/her space is designed and used. The Three-D concept is based on the three functions or dimensions of human space:

1. All human space has some designated purpose.

[1] Crowe TD, Fennelly LJ. Crime prevention through environmental design. 3rd ed. Elsevier Publishers; 2013.

2. All human space has social, cultural, legal, or physical definitions that prescribe the desired and acceptable behaviors.

3. All human space is designed to support and control the desired behaviors.

By using the Three Ds as a guide, space may be evaluated by asking the following types of questions.

Designation

- What is the designated purpose of this space?
- What was it originally intended to be used for?
- How well does the space support its current use and its intended use? Is there conflict?

Definition

- How is the space defined?
- Is it clear who owns it?
- Where are its borders?
- Are there social or cultural definitions that affect how that space is used?
- Are the legal or administrative rules clearly set out and reinforced in policy?
- Are there signs?
- Is there conflict or confusion between the designated purpose and definition?

Design

- How well does the physical design support the intended function?
- How well does the physical design support the definition of the desired or accepted behaviors?
- Does the physical design conflict with or impede the productive use of the space or the proper functioning of the intended human activity?
- Is there confusion or conflict in the manner in which the physical design is intended to control behavior?

The three CPTED strategies of territorial reinforcement, natural access control, and natural surveillance are inherent in the Three-D concept.

Does the space clearly belong to someone or some group? Is the intended use clearly defined? Does the physical design match the intended use? Does the design provide the means for normal users to naturally control the activities, to control access, and to provide surveillance? Once a basic self-assessment has been conducted, the Three Ds may then be turned around as a simple means of guiding decisions about what to do with human space. The proper functions have to be matched with space that can support them—with space that can effectively support territorial identity, natural access control, and surveillance and intended behaviors have to be indisputable and be reinforced in social, cultural, legal, and administrative terms or norms. The design has to ensure that the intended activity can function well and it has to directly support the control of behavior.

Examples of Strategies in Action

There are hundreds of examples of CPTED strategies in practice today. In each example, there is a mixture of the three CPTED strategies that is appropriate to the setting and to the particular security or crime problem. Some of the examples were created in the direct application of CPTED concepts. Others were borrowed from real-life situations. The common thread is the primary emphasis on naturalness—simply doing things that you already have to do but doing them a little better.

Some examples of CPTED strategy activities are:

- Providing clear border definition of controlled space;
- Providing clearly marked transitional zones that indicate movement from public to semipublic to private space;
- Relocating gathering areas to locations with natural surveillance and access control, or to locations away from the view of would-be offenders;

- Placing safe activities in unsafe locations to bring along the natural surveillance of these activities to increase the perception of safety for normal users and risk for offenders;
- Placing unsafe activities in safe spots to overcome the vulnerability of these activities with the natural surveillance and access control of the safe area;
- Redesignating the use of space to provide natural barriers to conflicting activities;
- Improving the scheduling of space to allow for effective use and appropriate critical intensity;
- Redesigning space to increase the perception or reality of natural surveillance;
- Overcoming distance and isolation through improved communication and design efficiencies.

Use of Information

It goes without saying that all important decisions should be based on good information. Especially where the design and use of the physical environment is at stake, it is imperative that at least five basic types of information be collected and used. Unless a rational basis is used to make informed decisions, the same mistakes that generated the original problem will continue to be made.

The five basic types of information needed for good CPTED planning are crime analysis information, demographic information, land use information, observations, and resident or user interviews. This information does not have to be sophisticated. It exists in a fundamental form in every community or location. Moreover, unless it can be presented in its most basic form, it is of little value. For instance, very little can be done with a statistical measure that says burglaries are up by 5%. Much more can be done with a crime map that shows a clustering of burglaries in a specific block.

Even more can be done when one finds that the burglar used an alleyway as his/her approach to a series of related offenses because it afforded a good cover for his vehicle.

The other bits of information that are needed should be available in simple, usable formats.

Following is a simple guide to each type of information:

- *Crime analysis*. This type of information is available in every police department; it is obtained by plotting offenses on a wall map and organizing the information on crime reports for the major purpose of identifying patterns of criminal activity. There are two basic types of patterns: geographic and similar offense.
- *Demographic*. This is information that describes the nature of the population for a given city, district, or neighborhood. It is available through city planning departments or the city manager's or mayor's office. Another source of this type of information is the Census Bureau and the city and county data books that may be found in most public libraries.
- *Land use*. City planning departments, zoning boards, traffic engineering councils, and local councils of government have information and maps that describe and depict the physical allocations and uses of land. Simple wall maps with colored sections showing residential areas, commercial areas, industrial areas, parks, schools, and traffic flows can be of immeasurable assistance in understanding the physical setting. Natural boundaries and neighborhoods are easier to visualize on such maps, especially in relation to land use and pedestrian and traffic flows.
- *Observations*. It is very helpful to conduct either formal or informal visual reviews of physical space to get first-hand knowledge of how, when, and by whom that space is used and where problems may arise.
- Environmental cues are the key to normal user and offender behavior.
- Observations may include pedestrian/vehicle counts, on- and off-street parking, maintenance of yards and fences, the degree of proprietary behaviors prohibited by residents and/or users, the presence of either controlling or avoidance behaviors,

and other potential indicators of territorial concern such as the percentage of window blinds drawn in homes and businesses overlooking parks or schools.

- *Resident or user interviews.* This source of information is needed to balance the other data sources. People's perceptions of where they feel safe and where they feel endangered often vary from the locations on crime maps where the most offenses occur. It is vital to determine the residents' or users' perceptions and extent of identity with the surrounding space, what affects their behavior or reactions as they move about, and what they think the needs are. Any attempt to skip the basics in favor of more complex forms of information gathering or analysis often obscures the picture. Professionals often suppress the active participation of residents or space users by relying on complex modes of analysis. This is dangerous because it can cause some very basic ideas or explanations to be overlooked. It is axiomatic that very little good will be accomplished without the full and active involvement of the users of space.

Some Benefits of CPTED Planning Activities

In addition to dealing with the reduction of crime and fear problems, other benefits of CPTED planning include the following:

- *Treatment of crime problems at various environmental scales.* The CPTED process for identifying crime/environment problems; selecting CPTED strategies; and initiating, implementing, and evaluating anticrime projects can be applied to entire neighborhoods or types of institutional settings within a city, such as secondary schools, or the process can be applied equally well to a small geographic area or to one particular institution.
- *Integration of prevention approaches.* CPTED principles are derived from an opportunity model of criminal behavior that assumes that

the offender's behavior can be accounted for by understanding how, and under what circumstances, variables in the environment interact to induce crime. Once an assessment of the opportunity structure is made, then appropriate strategies can be designed and integrated into a coordinated, consistent program.

- *Identification of short- and long-term goals.* Comprehensive broad-based programs like CPTED have ultimate goals that may take years to accomplish. Unlike CPTED, however, many programs fail to develop short-term or proximate goals and adequate ways to measure their success. The CPTED approach includes an evaluation framework that details proximate goals relating to increased access control, surveillance, and territorial reinforcement. The rationale is that the ultimate program success is directly related to its success in achieving the proximate goals.
- *Encouragement of collective responses to problems.* The CPTED emphasis is on increasing the capacity of residents to act in concert rather than individually. Strategies are aimed at fostering citizen participation and strengthening social cohesion.
- *Interdisciplinary approach to urban problems.* An explicit policy of interdisciplinary teaming ensures effective cooperation among diverse city departments such as public works, social services, economic development, police, and so forth. Each participant benefits from exposure to the responsibilities, jurisdiction, and skills of the others.
- *Encouragement of better police/community relations.* A key strategy is to coordinate law enforcement and community service activities with the result of improving police/community relations and developing an anticrime program that is not solely dependent on enforcement agencies.
- *Development of security guidelines and standards.* CPTED programming can lead to the creation of security criteria for newly constructed or

modified environments to avoid planning and design decisions that inadvertently provide opportunities for crime.

- *Assistance in urban revitalization.* Through its impact on physical, social, and economic conditions, CPTED can be instrumental in revitalizing communities including downtown areas. Once business leaders, investors, and other citizens perceive that a comprehensive effort is underway to reduce crime and fear, there will be an improvement in community identity and cohesiveness.
- *Acquisition of development funds.* The incorporation of CPTED into existing programs can provide additional jurisdiction for awarding grants, loans, and community development funds.
- *Institutionalization of crime prevention policies and practices.* CPTED projects can create a local management capability and expertise to maintain ongoing projects. This capability can be incorporated into existing citizen organizations or municipal agencies.

An Ounce of Prevention: A New Role for Law Enforcement Support of Community Development

Public/private sector partnerships enhance public safety by sharing information, making the community more aware of threats and involving them in the problem-solving process. Collaboration is a key word for partnerships because all partners must recognize that their goals or missions overlap and they work together to share resources and achieve common goals. The added value of public–private sector partnerships is the cross-transfer of skills, knowledge, and expertise between the public and the private sectors.[2] For a partnership to be successful, each partner has to understand the value they will gain from participating. Successful partnerships involve partners that

are committed to working together to achieve common goals—building the community. There are a number of compelling reasons for law enforcement to be involved in CPTED aside from the formulation of partnerships:

1. CPTED concepts have been proved to enhance community activities while reducing crime problems.
2. CPTED concepts are fundamental to traditional law enforcement values in terms of helping the community to function properly.
3. CPTED requires the unique information sources and inherent knowledge of the community that is endemic to the law enforcement profession.
4. CPTED problems and issues bear a direct relationship to repeat calls or service and to crime-producing situations.
5. CPTED methods and techniques can directly improve property values, business profitability, and industrial productivity, thereby enhancing local tax bases.

Law enforcement agencies, regardless of size, must be involved formally in the review and approval process of community and business projects. Their participation must be active and creative, rather than passive and reactive. Moreover, any such involvement should not be understood to expose the agencies to possible litigation, since it is the role of law enforcement in CPTED to provide additional information and concerns that may not have occurred to the persons who are responsible (and qualified) for making changes to the environment. The expression, "Pay me now, or pay me later," conveys the idea that the early involvement of a knowledgeable law enforcement agency in the conceptualization and planning of community projects can lead to improvements in the quality of life and to reductions in the fear and incidence of crime. This early involvement is one of the most cost-effective methods of crime prevention.[3]

[2] http://it.ojp.gov/documents/d/fusion_center_guidelines.pdf.

[3] Crowe TD, Fennelly LJ. Crime prevention through environmental design. 3rd ed. Elsevier Publishers; 2013.

CPTED ASSESSMENTS[4]

During a CPTED assessment, focus on the CPTED principles of:

Natural surveillance
Access management
Territoriality
Physical maintenance
Order maintenance
Activity support

Be sure that you notice positive attributes of the area while identifying needed changes or improvements. Logically organize your observations and recommendations.

QUESTIONS TO BE ANSWERED DURING AN ASSESSMENT

- Are there casual **surveillance** opportunities? If not, can they be added?
- Is there sufficient **lighting** for all vehicular and pedestrian pathways and activity areas used during hours of darkness (Photo 1.7)?
- Is there sufficient activity **lighting** indoors and is it supplemented by sources of natural light? Is there emergency lighting?

PHOTO 1.7 Reflects a lack of landscape maintenance.

- Is **access** managed? If not, what combination of strategies could be used to better manage access?
- Are all **spaces designated and delineated** for specific use? If not, can they be?
- Are there **conflicts** between uses?
- Is there sufficient **capacity**? Is **crowding** creating tension, fear, or potential dangers?
- Are there expressions of pride and ownership (**territoriality**)? Can they be increased?
- Are all areas well **maintained**—kept clean and functional with no needed repairs or replacements? If not, when were they last maintained?
- Are **rules of conduct** communicated? Enforced?
- Are there **supporting activities** that enhance surveillance, access management, and social order? If not, can they be added?
- Are the grounds **legible**? Is it easy to understand where you are at any given point? Is it obvious which path or direction you need to take to arrive at a desired location?
- Does the **landscaping** enhance the ability to read the site? Does it provide shade and buffering where needed? Does it provide an aesthetic quality? Is it accessible? Is it healthy and well maintained? Is it a problem?
- How do the site users **behave**? Is there respect for the environment? Are there areas where tensions and disorder are common?
- Is there **graffiti** or other signs of vandalism?
- Is there **CCTV or video surveillance**? If so, are they placed in prime locations? Are there other means of surveillance?
- Are there successful **CPTED applications** already in place? If so, take note and use them as positive examples.[5]

Surrounding Neighborhood

- Adjacent land uses
- Condition of adjacent streets and properties
- Traffic patterns and volumes on adjacent streets

[4] www.popcenter.org/tools/cpted/.

[5] http://cptedsecurity.com/cpted_design_guidelines.htm.

- Pedestrian crossing safeguards (marked crossings, traffic lights)
- Recommendations for improvements

Perimeter and Points of Entry

- First impressions on approaching the site/location
- Walls and/or fencing
- Type, location, hours of operation, and users
- Special staff and/or visitor access points
- Sign(s) that identify the site/location, welcome visitors, and information about special visitor parking and entry
- Signs and/or maps to guide visitors to special parking and entry
- Signs and/or pavement markings to guide vehicles
- Surveillance opportunities from interior spaces
- Landscaping and cleanliness (Photo 1.8)
- Lighting
- Recommendations for improvements.

Vehicular Travel Routes and Parking Facilities

- Motor vehicle traffic patterns, including bus and student drop-off/pickup loops in school applications (Photo 1.9)

- Signs and/or maps to guide visitors to appropriate parking and entry locations
- Sign(s) to identify visitor parking
- Surveillance of parking lots from interior spaces
- Lighting
- Recommendations for improvements.

Pedestrian Travel Paths and Gathering Areas

- Pedestrian routes to and from building(s)
- Pedestrian crosswalk markings or designated pedestrian routes
- Signage, landscaping, and/or landmarks to guide pedestrians
- Surveillance of walkways and exterior corridors
- Formal and informal gathering areas

PHOTO 1.8

PHOTO 1.9

- Lighting
- Recommendations for improvements.

Building Exteriors and Grounds

- Aesthetics, building design, location, and security of windows and doors
- Surveillance capability both natural and mechanical
- Hidden nooks and alcoves
- Use of mirrors and/or CCTV, security surveillance systems
- Cleanliness and landscaping
- Lighting
- Recommendations for improvements.

Building Interiors

- External and/or internal surveillance capability
- Access management (observed versus policy and procedure)
- Hidden nooks and alcoves in corridors, stairwells, and special use areas
- Use of mirrors and/or CCTV/video surveillance
- Restrooms
- Alarmed areas
- Cleanliness, maintenance, and other territorial reinforcement
- Natural, artificial, and emergency lighting
- Recommendations for improvements.

Maintenance and Delivery Areas

- Access doors, location, and surveillance opportunities
- Security and access management during delivery/maintenance
- Dumpster/trash location(s)
- Storage of fuels and chemicals
- After-hours use
- Recommendations for improvements.

CPTED SURVEY FOR COLLEGES AND UNIVERSITIES: 30 VULNERABILITIES BASED ON CPTED ASSESSMENTS

1. Poor visibility at entry to campus
2. Easy vehicular access onto campus
3. No clear boundary separating the campus from public property
4. Inadequate distance between campus buildings and neighbors
5. Exterior doors to buildings unlocked 24/7
6. Areas and buildings on campus hidden by landscaping or vegetation
7. School adjacent to traffic hazard
8. Portions of buildings or campus inaccessible to emergency vehicles
9. Secluded hangout areas on campus
10. No safety/security awareness program for students, faculty, and staff
11. Perimeter of campus not visible from streets
12. No barriers between parking and lawn
13. Gravel in parking area
14. Dangerous traffic routes or patterns on campus
15. Enclosed courtyard that offers concealment to criminals
16. High parapets on buildings that hide criminals
17. No security officers on site for access control or patrol duties
18. No "escort to vehicle" program during darkness
19. Inadequate lighting on campus
20. No lighting maintenance plan to repair or replace nonoperational lights
21. Crime magnet or hangout located close to campus
22. No vegetation/landscape planting and maintenance program
23. Benches on campus that can be used for sleeping by homeless individuals

24. Faculty, staff, and students not displaying ID badges
25. Bollards not used to prevent vehicles from driving on sidewalks
26. No cameras or video surveillance program
27. Exterior doors in dorms propped open
28. Courtesy desk at entrance to dorms not staffed 24/7
29. Parking areas that are not clearly visible from buildings
30. No signage on campus.

CPTED RECOMMENDATIONS

The following are some environmental problems and issues (as well as recommendations) that may be documented in part of a CPTED assessment:

- One-way street systems have been found not only to improve traffic flow but also to create dead zones for business, with resulting crime or fear of crime that deters development efforts.
- Through traffic in neighborhoods has been found to be detrimental to residential housing values, stability, and crime rates.
- Downtown projects continue to fail by making fundamental errors that reduce natural surveillance and natural access control, resulting in the loss of desired users and domination by unwanted users.
- Fortress effects are produced by designers of convention centers, hotels, banks, senior citizen housing, and parking lot structures. These destroy the surrounding land uses and create a "no-man's land."
- Bleed-off parking enhances conflict between commercial and residential uses; both lose.
- Design and management can actually reduce business and increase victimization of employees and customers.
- Mall and major event facility parking areas with poorly planned access control and layout can produce traffic congestion and become magnets for undesirable activity.
- School and institutional designs can inadvertently create dysfunctional areas where surveillance is impossible, resulting in increased behavioral and crime problems and overall impediments to successful operations (e.g., students' achievement in schools).
- Public housing and affordable housing can become projects that serve as magnets for transients, as opposed to local poor, with further detrimental effects on existing neighborhoods.

Nearly every environmental situation or location is amenable to the application of CPTED concepts. The law enforcement agency can assist in asking the right questions and supplying the right kind of information to help the community to make more informed decisions.

CPTED adds a new dimension by incorporating these elements into space design and management:

- Natural access control. Your space should give some natural indication of where people are allowed and are not allowed. Do not depend just on locks, alarms, surveillance systems, and security officers but make security part of the layout (see later section on landscape security).
- Natural surveillance. Again, traditional factors like good lighting are important, but do not overlook a natural factor such as a strategically placed window or the placement of an employee work station.
- Territorial reinforcement. This is an umbrella concept, embodying all natural surveillance and access control principles. It emphasizes the enhancement of ownership and proprietary behaviors.

CPTED proposes that the proper design and effective use of the built environment can lead to a reduction in the opportunity, fear, and incidence of predatory stranger-to-stranger-type crime, as well as result in an improvement of the quality of life (NCPI, 2008). Crime prevention design solutions should be integrated into the design and function of the buildings, or at least the location where they are being implemented.

In his writings on CPTED, Tim Crowe stated"… It is clear that light affects human behavior and too much or too little light will have different effects. It is now generally accepted that performance improves and fatigue levels drop in direct proportion to increased levels of light, but it also relates to the work or play environment."[6]

The ancient field of chromotherapy, or photobiology as it is now called, is making a comeback because many scientists believe that color and light can affect health and behavior. Richard J. Wurtman, a nutritionist at the Massachusetts Institute of Technology, states that light is the most important environmental input, after food in controlling bodily function.[7]

Many psychologists believe that light has a tremendous influence on human behavior. There is a level of light that people experience as the most pleasant. Brightly lit rooms are more arousing than dimly lit rooms. Light also influences the image of a retail store as shoppers look at and scrutinize merchandise to purchase.

CPTED principles were founded not only on social interactions, criminology, and architecture but also on the psychological impact of the principles. Colors have a physical aspect in security, i.e., assisting in way finding and moving people to safer locations, proper entrances, etc., and also a psychological impact. Security practitioners do well in applying the physical aspect of color such as using lighter colors to reflect more light but not very well at considering the emotions evoked from a particular color. Many security practitioners believe that the use of color may be one aspect to consider for preventing crime and may have a positive impact on workplace violence, school safety, and a number of other applications. Any designer or interior decorator can tell you how important color is for setting the mood for an environment. Experiments have shown that different colors affect blood pressure, pulse, and respiration rates, as well as brain activity and biorhythms.[8]

PSYCHOLOGICAL PROPERTIES OF COLORS[9]

Red—Red is a powerful color. Its effect is physical, strong, and basic. Red is stimulating and lively as well as friendly.

Positives: physical, courage, strength, warmth, energy, basic survival, fight or flight, stimulation, masculinity, excitement.

Negatives: defiance, aggressive and aggression, visual impact, strain.

Blue—Blue is the color of the mind and is essentially soothing. It affects us mentally, rather than like the physical reaction we have to red. Strong blues will stimulate clear thoughts and lighter, soft blues will calm the mind and aid concentration. The world's favorite color is blue, but it can be perceived as cold, unemotional, and unfriendly.

Positives: intellectual, communication, trust, efficiency, serenity, duty, logic, coolness, reflection, calm.

Negatives: coldness, aloofness, lack of emotion, unfriendliness.

Yellow—The yellow wavelength is relatively long and essentially stimulating. The wrong

---

[6] Crowe TD, Fennelly LJ. Crime prevention through environmental design. 3rd ed. Elsevier Publishers; 2013.

[7] http://www.nytimes.com/1982/10/19/science/color-has-a-powerful-effect-on-behavior-researchers-assert.html.

[8] Ibid.

[9] http://www.colour-affects.co.uk/psychological-properties-of-colours.

color scheme with yellow can cause fear and anxiety.

>*Positives*: emotional, optimism, confidence, self-esteem, extraversion, emotional strength, friendliness, creativity.
>
>*Negatives*: irrationality, fear, emotional fragility, depression, anxiety, suicide.

Green—If a green color scheme is used incorrectly it can indicate stagnation.

>*Positives*: harmony, balance, refreshment, universal love, rest, restoration, reassurance, environmental awareness, equilibrium, peace.
>
>*Negatives*: boredom, stagnation, blandness, enervation.

Violet—The excessive use of purple can bring about too much of the wrong tone faster than any other color if it communicates something cheap and nasty.

>*Positives*: spiritual awareness, containment, vision, luxury, authenticity, truth, quality.
>
>*Negatives*: introversion, suppression, inferiority.

Orange—Orange focuses our minds on issues of physical comfort—food, warmth, shelter, and sensuality. It is a fun color. Too much orange suggests a lack of serious intellectual values.

>*Positives*: physical comfort, food, warmth, security, sensuality, passion, abundance, fun.
>
>*Negatives*: introversion, decadence, suppression, inferiority.

Black—Black is all colors, totally absorbed. It creates barriers, as it absorbs all the energy coming toward you. Black is the absence of light. Many people are afraid of the dark. In cowboy movies, the good guys wear what color hats? The bad guys wear what color hats? We wear a black tie to a funeral. We wear black to look thinner; however, in 2016 a fashion designer stated multicolor clothing was the way to go. Black race horses look faster.

>*Positives*: sophistication, glamor, security, emotional safety, efficiency, substance.

>*Negatives*: oppression, coldness, menace, heaviness.

Gray—The heavy use of gray usually indicates a lack of confidence and fear of exposure.

>*Positives*: psychological neutrality.
>
>*Negatives*: lack of confidence, dampness, lack of energy, depression, hibernation.

Pink—Being a tint of red, pink also affects us physically, but it soothes rather than stimulates. Pink is a powerful color, psychologically.

>*Positives*: physical comfort, food, warmth, security, sensuality, passion, abundance, fun.
>
>*Negatives*: inhibition, emotional claustrophobia, emasculation, physical weakness.

White—White is total reflection. It reflects the full force of the spectrum to the eyes. White is purity, the negative effect of white on warm colors is to make them look and feel garish.

>*Positives*: hygiene, sterility, clarity, purity, cleanness, simplicity, sophistication, efficiency.
>
>*Negatives*: sterility, coldness, barriers, unfriendliness, elitism. White is total reflection.

Brown—Brown usually consists of red and yellow with a large percentage of black.

>*Positives*: seriousness, warmth, nature, earthiness, reliability, support.
>
>*Negatives*: lack of humor, heaviness, lack of sophistication.

At a local bank, we noticed the warm color scheme of the bank interior and the lighting levels were designed to help customers feel safe and comfortable. We could tell that someone had certainly done their homework. Additionally, the bank manager was in the lobby greeting customers. The comfort zone they were hoping for definitely worked. They earned an A+! Many hospitals and other medical facilities use green as an interior color to project calmness and relaxation to help patients feel less nervous and anxious.

When discussing the psychology of color, remember that blue and green have a relaxing effect, whereas red and orange are stimulating. Warm colors are perceived as being protective and clear and saturated colors are experienced as more pleasant. Dark colors are perceived as more dominant and more strongly suggest hostility and aggression. The psychology of color is complex. There are differing opinions about color as well as scientific research on colors and the combinations of colors.

CPTED involves the design of physical space in the context of the needs of legitimate users of the space (physical, social, and psychological needs), the normal and expected (or intended) use of the space (the activity or absence of activity planned for the space), and the predictable behavior of both intended users and offenders. Therefore, in the CPTED approach, a design is proper if it recognizes the designated use of the space, defines the crime problem incidental to and the solution compatible with the designated use, and incorporates the crime prevention strategies that enhance (or at least do not impair) the effective use of the space.

Kerry Kirpatrick, the Social Media Director for Buildings Magazine, stated that research has revealed that increased productivity is a benefit of green buildings through a study that was designed to reflect indoor environments encountered by large numbers of people every day. "These findings have far ranging implications for worker productivity, student learning, and safety."[10]

The ceiling of parking garages should be painted white as to get the best reflection possible from lighting. Consider LED lighting because it is the most cost-effective. Also, painting the walls white will enhance the effect and strength of not only the CPTED principle of surveillance but also that

of access control (due to visual sense of place) and maintenance, as related in the "broken windows theory"[11] of crime and disorder. Additionally, placement of lighting must be carefully considered in conjunction with video surveillance to avoid conflicting uses, obscuring or making images undetectable due to glare and possible "hot spots" when using warm lighting sources.

Street lighting can have an effect on perceived personal safety and reduce the fear of becoming victimized in a particular environment. Street lighting is generally seen as the most important physical feature of an environment to affect perceived personal safety. The general consensus is that adequate street lighting can reduce crime rates and also reduce the fear of crime. Consideration must again be given to the environment addressed and its intended use. Overlighting or too much light in a neighborhood may have a negative consequence on the surveillance principle of CPTED by resulting in residents closing their blinds to block out the offending, trespassing light and limiting natural surveillance.

CPTED LANDSCAPE SECURITY RECOMMENDATION

Utilizing adequate lighting, walkways and entryways to buildings should be clearly visible for members of the community. Landscape should be maintained to minimize obstacles to clear observability and places of concealment for potential assailants. This is achieved by trimming bushes to 36 inches in height and tree branches to 8 feet from the ground.

Sidewalks, streets, and parking lots must be clean (power washed) and free of graffiti. Ensure that there is proper signage and adequate lighting.

Parks should have a 360-degree view of the area and park benches should be designed

[10] http://energyalliancegroup.org/author/kerry/.

[11] http://www.britannica.com/topic/broken-windows-theory.

to not allow someone to sleep on the bench. Create a venue for after-school activities that encourage youth to take ownership of the space for socializing, such as small shelter areas with cell phone chargers and Wi-Fi access.

Signage plays an important role in park security. There should be signs indicating the hours the park is open and rules for those utilizing the space. Proper signage removes the excuses for unacceptable behavior, draws attention to the illegitimate activity, and legitimizes police involvement, thus making the violation of the information on the posted signs an excellent crime prevention tool.

There is a vast array of traffic calming devices, such as speed bumps and raised crosswalks. These areas should be painted yellow and proper signage posted. At the entrance to neighborhoods or communities, post neighborhood watch or block watch signs.

Eliminate "hot spots" by planting thorny bushes (barberry, holly, etc.) in problem areas. Use boulders or bollards to control vehicular access (see Photo 1.9). Consider adding community art or sculptures, which not only control access but also reinforce the purpose by giving implied ownership to the artists.

Perimeter fencing should be between 6 and 8 feet tall with three strands of barb wire on the top for a total of 7–9 feet in height. We would not recommend this unless it was a large property and the perimeter was a significant distance from the business or facility. Careful consideration to the type of fencing, the desired impact (boundary definition vs. security), and the location of the facility (rural vs. urban) must be taken into account and there should be at least 10 feet of clear space on both sides of the fence (Photo 1.10).

LED lighting is cost-effective and should meet lighting standards and guidelines for brightness but may not serve all applications best.

Bus stops should be located in an area where an open business is in clear observation of

PHOTO 1.10

PHOTO 1.11

the stop. Alternatively, this problem may be addressed by contacting the school or bus company to monitor the space via video surveillance.

Do not allow tagging or graffiti in public spaces. Consider the use of paint or coatings that will allow for easy removal of graffiti. All graffiti or tagging should be removed within 24h (Photo 1.11).

"Hot spots" need to be eliminated. If they cannot be completely eliminated, develop

[12] http://www.policechiefmagazine.org/magazine/index.cfm?fuseaction=display_arch&article_id=902&issue_id=52006.

a program to keep unauthorized users or unwanted individuals out of the area.

Community policing programs, including the formulation of public–private sector partnerships[12] can be used to fight disorder and crime.

Vacant lots are best monitored by citizens that we give "ownership" of them. One example is a place in Richmond, Virginia, where a community flower garden was placed. People who worked in the garden monitored the space. Another option is for the city to share the property via giving the lot to Habitat for Humanity to build a structure on within a given time frame, thus resulting in tax revenue. Inspections from local government agencies can also result in the owners of vacant property being held responsible for the upkeep of the property or pay fines for noncompliance.

Redesign properties using CPTED principles to make them more crime resistant by reducing the criminal opportunity within the community.

There are some properties, such as Health & Urban Development (HUD) properties, that may need a higher level of protection, such as additional lighting and surveillance systems. Law enforcement support is also needed as to address specific issues and to support a safe community.

Locate open spaces and recreational areas in neighborhoods so they are visible (natural surveillance) from nearby homes and the street. Avoid landscaping that might create blind spots or hiding places. Make sure there is effective lighting. Design streets to discourage cut through or high-speed traffic using "traffic calming" measures. Join or start a neighborhood watch in your neighborhood.

In apartment buildings, ensure that interior hallways are well lit with a secure front door. Install good-quality deadbolt locks and peepholes on unit doors. Provide a secondary locking device to any sliding glass doors, windows on ground floor, and fire escapes. Provide a common space in central locations to encourage tenant interaction. Join or start an apartment watch or neighborhood watch in your building.

For retail businesses, locate checkout counters near the front of the store, clearly visible from outside. Window signs should cover no more than 15% of the windows to provide clear visibility into and out of the store. Use shelving and displays no higher than 4 inches to help see who is in the store. Avoid creating outdoor spaces that encourage loitering. Install mirrors at strategic locations as well as a security surveillance system.

Measuring and Evaluation of CPTED

Very little has been written on how to measure the effectiveness of your CPTED program. Some work has been done in 2005—see references for this material.

Let us call the site in question "the complex" since CPTED covers the full spectrum.

You get 3 years of data from the local police department and from the complex. After a full assessment and review of the natural surveillance (landscape security) and natural access and territoriality, the complex hardens the target.

The job of security now must change to be more proactive. In the past crimes of the past 3 years are to be addressed and programs such as awareness or neighborhood are implemented followed by security making monthly reports on the status of aspects of physical security.

Awareness

- Become aware of your community and who the strangers are. The guy walking down the street with the black dog. Who is he?
- Look for signs of behavior that does not fit the normal pattern. "Can I help you?" you ask. Now evaluate the response.
- Ever go for a walk and see four newspapers on the lawn. What does that tell you? Thieves also do assessments and evaluate your complex.

Fear of Crime

- We have seen fear many times on television when a school is in lockdown and parents have been outside for an hour waiting to see their child. It is not a pretty sight.

CPTED Strategies

- The earlier discussion suggests a series of general design strategies that can be applied in any situation to improve natural access control, natural surveillance, and territorial behavior.
- Provide a clear border definition of controlled space.
- Provide a clearly marked transition from public to semipublic to private space.
- Locate gathering areas in places with natural surveillance and access control and away from the view of potential offenders.
- Place safe activities in unsafe locations and unsafe activities in safe locations.
- Provide natural barriers to conflicting activities.
- Improve the scheduling of space to provide the effective and critical intensity of uses.
- Design spaces to increase the perception of natural surveillance.
- Overcome distance and isolation through improved communications and design efficiencies, e.g., emergency telephones and pedestrian paths.
- Turn soft targets into hard targets.

Obtaining Results

After all of the above-mentioned strategies have been completed and security is maintained at the highest level, you should have a reduction in crime risks and crime as well as a reduction in fear of crime. Then after 3 years, you compare the data with the previous 3 years to see your results (Fennelly and Perry, 2016).

CONCLUSION

CPTED addresses the potential victim and the potential criminal's mindset in preventing crime through manipulating the built environment and better planning for its intended use.

A security assessment is the process of evaluating a site for security vulnerabilities and making recommendations to address said vulnerabilities. The goal is to either remove or reduce the potential vulnerability.

Reduce opportunities for crime and fear of crime by making open areas more easily observable and by increasing activity in the neighborhood.

Provide ways in which neighborhood residents, business people, and law enforcement can work together more effectively to reduce opportunities and incentives for crime.

Increase neighborhood identity, investor confidence, and social cohesion.

Provide public information programs that help schools, businesses, and residents protect themselves from crime.

Make the area more accessible by improving transportation services.

Improve the effectiveness and efficiency of governmental operations.

Encourage citizens to report crimes so they can be a part of the problem-solving process. The steps taken to achieve these objectives include:

- improved, cost-effective outdoor lighting
- sidewalk and landscaping improvements
- partnerships with law enforcement and other local officials
- neighborhood watch, business watch, and school watch programs
- neighborhood cleanups
- a campaign to educate businesses about safe cash handling procedures and how to discourage robberies
- improve and expand public transportation.

Basic improvements in neighborhoods and communities can enhance "quality of life" and provide an atmosphere of cohesiveness. The application of CPTED concepts has been used successfully throughout the country to reduce not only the incidence of crime but also the fear of crime, which leads to an improvement in the quality of life for everyone who lives, works, or visits the neighborhood or community.

Shown is a QR code material prepared by Diane Zahm, titled Using CPTED in Problem Solving Tool Guide No. 8 (2007) POP Guide. A special thanks to Rick Draper for designing the QR code for us.

Reference Material

[1] Risk Analysis and Security Countermeasure Selection, Thomas L. Norman, CPP, PSP, CSC, CRC Press 2016, p. 281.
[2] Measuring Crime Prevention through Environmental Design in a Gated Residential Area: A Pilot Survey 2012 Elsevier.
[3] Lawrence J. Fennelly, Marianna Perry lafenn@aol.com, mariannaperry@lpsm.us.
[4] www.litigationconsultants.com.

Introduction to Vulnerability Assessment*

Mary Lynn Garcia, CPP

This chapter provides a description of how to apply the principles and concepts of implementing a physical protection system (PPS) and how to identify the vulnerabilities of an installed PPS and propose effective upgrades if needed. It also discusses the additional key concepts of risk management, vulnerability assessment (VA), and systems engineering.

This text is a follow-on to the previously published *Design and Evaluation of Physical Protection Systems*. That book (hereafter referred to as the *Design* textbook) provided an overview of the principles and concepts that must be considered when implementing a PPS; this book is a description of how to apply those principles and concepts to identify the vulnerabilities of an installed PPS and propose effective upgrades if needed. This book is the basis of all VAs conducted by Sandia National Laboratories during the last 30 years for a wide spectrum of customers including the US Department of Energy, US Department of Defense, North Atlantic Treaty Organization, US Department of State, Government Services

Administration, dam and water systems, prisons, schools, communities, and chemical companies.

A VA is a systematic evaluation in which quantitative or qualitative techniques are used to predict PPS component performance and overall system effectiveness by identifying exploitable weaknesses in asset protection for a defined threat. After the VA identifies weaknesses, it is used to establish the requirements for an upgraded PPS design. In addition, a VA is also used to support management decisions regarding protection system upgrades. Risk assessment and VA are such closely related activities that many security professionals use the terms interchangeably. This may not present a huge problem in practice, but it does hinder communication between and among security service providers and customers.

The VA process can be broken into three distinct phases: planning, conducting the VA, and reporting and using the results. This process is part of the larger risk assessment process. Each of the phases will be described in detail in the

*Originally from Garcia, ML. Vulnerability assessment of physical protection systems. Boston: Butterworth-Heinemann, 2006. Updated by the editor, Elsevier, 2016.

remaining chapters of this text. The key points discussed in this chapter include:

- Risk management and VA
- Risk assessment and the VA process
- VA process overview
- VA and systems engineering

This text is concerned with the VA of a PPS, but the concepts can be applied to cyber protection, personnel protection, and overall security protection at a facility or across an enterprise. For clarity, throughout this text the term enterprise includes organizations, companies, agencies, governments, or any other entity with the need to manage security risks. The term asset includes people, property, information, or any other possession of an enterprise that has value.

It is important to differentiate security from safety when discussing a VA. Safety is defined as the measures (people, procedures, or equipment) used to prevent or detect an abnormal condition that can endanger people, property, or the enterprise. These include accidents caused by human carelessness, inattentiveness, and lack of training or other unintentional events. Security, on the other hand, includes the measures used to protect people, property, or the enterprise from malevolent human threats. This includes civil disturbances, sabotage, pilferage, theft of critical property or information, workplace violence, extortion, or other intentional attacks on assets by a human. A good security VA will consider safety controls because some safety measures aid in detection and response to security events (sprinklers will fight fires regardless of the cause), but some attacks require additional detection and response capability. For example, a disgruntled employee can sabotage critical manufacturing equipment and reduce production to a significant extent. Without security controls, it could be difficult to determine quickly enough whether this is an intentional act of sabotage and prevent a significant loss of revenue.

RISK MANAGEMENT AND VULNERABILITY ASSESSMENT

Risk management is the set of actions an enterprise takes to address identified risks and includes avoidance, reduction, spreading, transfer, elimination, and acceptance options. Good risk management programs will likely include a combination of these options. Risk avoidance is accomplished by removing the source of the risk; for example, a company may choose to buy a critical component from another company, rather than manufacture it. This removes the production line as a sabotage target. Risk reduction is achieved by taking some actions to lower risk to the enterprise to reduce the severity of the loss. This is the goal of many security programs—lower risk by implementing at least some security measures. Risk can also be spread among multiple locations, perhaps by having similar production capability at more than one enterprise facility. Then, loss of capability at one site may be managed by increasing production at the other locations. Another example of risk spreading is the distribution of assets across a large industrial facility. By separating the assets, fewer assets may be at risk during any given adversary attack. Risk transfer is the use of insurance to cover the replacement or other costs incurred as a result of the loss. This is an important tool in many security systems. Risk acceptance is the recognition that there will always be some residual risk. The key is to knowingly determine an acceptable level, rather than unwittingly accepting it. In security risk management, these decisions are based on the consequence of loss of the asset, the defined threat, and the risk tolerance of the enterprise. A trade-off analysis must be performed to ensure that the dollars spent on physical security provide a cost-effective solution to security issues. If other risk management options provide equal or better results at lower cost, the use of a PPS may not be justified.

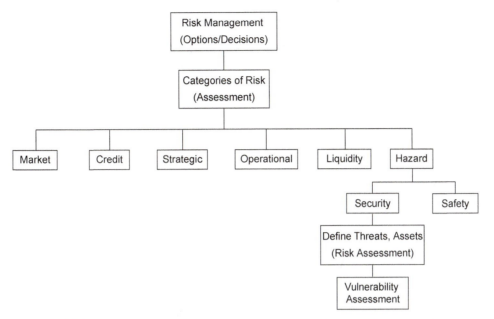

FIGURE 2.1 Relationship between risk management and vulnerability assessment.

Security is only one facet of risk; therefore, it must be considered in the context of holistic risk management across the enterprise, along with other categories such as market, credit, operational, strategic, liquidity, and hazard risks. The relationships among risk management, risk assessment, and VA are shown in Fig. 2.1. Risks across an enterprise must be managed holistically, and those identified as above an acceptable level must be addressed. VA is one of the constituent pieces of security risk assessment and is used to support risk management decisions.

To frame the relationship between risk assessment and risk management, consider definitions provided by Kaplan and Garrick, who state that in risk assessment, the analyst attempts to answer three questions: What can go wrong? What is the likelihood that it would go wrong? What are the consequences? The answers to these questions help identify, measure, quantify, and evaluate risks. Then, risk management builds on risk assessment by answering

a second set of questions: What can be done? What options are available? What are their associated trade-offs in terms of costs, benefits, and risks? What are the impacts of current management decisions on future options? The answer to the last question provides the optimal solution. Total risk management results from this process, where total risk management is defined as a systematic, statistically based, holistic process that builds on formal risk assessment and management by answering the two sets of questions and addressing the sources of system failures.

A security risk assessment is the process of answering the first three questions using threat, likelihood of attack, and consequence of loss as their benchmarks.

A thorough security risk assessment would consider risks in the component parts of a security system (cyber, executive, transportation protection, etc.) to facilitate informed risk decisions across the enterprise. As applied to the VA of a PPS, risk assessment is an evaluation of the

PPS supported by a number of analysis methodologies, including:

- threat analysis
- consequence analysis
- event and fault tree analyses
- vulnerability analysis

RISK ASSESSMENT AND THE VULNERABILITY ASSESSMENT PROCESS

Most facilities or enterprises routinely conduct risk assessments of their security systems to verify that they are protecting corporate assets and to identify areas that may need additional attention. These assessments are defined differently for different enterprises, but in general they include consideration of the likelihood of a negative event; in this case, it is a security incident and the consequence of that event. The *Design* textbook ended with a description of risk assessment and provided a formula that can be used to calculate risk, using qualitative or quantitative measures. That discussion, with one addition, is repeated here.

Security risk can be measured qualitatively or quantitatively through the use of the following equation:

$$R = P_A \times (1 - P_E) \times C$$

where R = risk to the facility (or stakeholders) of an adversary gaining access to, or stealing, critical assets. Range is 0–1, with 0 being no risk and 1 being maximum risk. Risk is calculated for a period of time, such as 1 year or 5 years; P_A = probability of an adversary attack during a period of time. This can be difficult to determine, but generally there are records available to assist in this effort. This probability ranges from 0 (no chance at all of an attack) to 1 (certainty of attack). Sometimes in the calculation of risk, we assume there will be an attack, which mathematically sets $P_A = 1$. This is called a conditional risk, where the condition is that the adversary attacks. This does not mean there will absolutely be an attack, but that the probability of attack is unknown or the asset is so valuable that it will be protected anyway. This approach can be used for any asset, but it is generally reserved for the most critical assets of a facility, where the consequence of loss is unacceptably high, even if P_A is low. For these assets, a PPS is generally required; $P_E = P_I \times P_N$, where P_I is the probability of interruption by responders and P_N is the probability of neutralization of the adversary, given interruption. P_N can include a range of tactics from verbal commands up through deadly force. The appropriate response depends on the defined threat and consequence of loss of the asset. P_E represents the vulnerability of the PPS to the defined threat; C = consequence value, or a value from 0 to 1 that relates to the severity of the occurrence of the event. This is a normalizing factor, which allows the conditional risk value to be compared with other risks across the facility. A consequence table of all events can be created that covers the loss spectrum, from highest to lowest. By using this consequence table, risk can be normalized over all possible events. Then, limited PPS resources can be appropriately allocated to ensure that the highest consequence assets are protected and meet an acceptable risk.

Note that this equation introduces the use of a new term—the *probability of neutralization* (P_N). This was discussed only briefly in the *Design* book, because many facilities do not have an immediate response to security events. It is included here because response is a part of VA at all facilities.

Using probabilistic risk assessment is more formal, scientific, technical, quantitative, and objective when compared with risk management, which involves value judgment and heuristics and is more subjective, qualitative, societal, and political. Ideally, the use of probabilities is based on objective likelihoods, but in security it is common to use more subjective likelihoods based on intuition; expertise; partial, defective, or erroneous data; and, occasionally, dubious theories. This is important because these are major sources of uncertainty, and uncertainty is a major element of risk. Additionally, these measures can reduce the credibility of the security risk assessment for senior management, who are used to seeing documented data in standard analysis models. In security systems, this uncertainty is even larger than normal, owing to the lack of dependable (i.e., quantifiable) data for all types of adversary attacks.

An additional use of the risk equation is that the security risk life cycle can be viewed in context. When considering security systems and the attack timeline, the attack can be broken into three discrete phases: preattack, which is the time the adversary takes to plan the attack; the attack phase, when the adversary actually shows up to attack the facility, and the attack has started; and postattack, when the adversary has completed the attack, and the consequences of a successful attack occur. If the problem is approached this way, each term in the equation is of primary importance during different phases of the attack. As such, P_A is most useful during the preattack phase. This is where intelligence agencies and deterrence have their biggest effect. Intelligence agencies gather information concerning threats and provide assessments about their likelihood of attack. These agencies may even develop enough information to disrupt an attack by collecting enough legal evidence to arrest the adversary, through tips from inside sources, or by alerting targeted enterprises, allowing them to increase security protection. All of these activities will have an effect on P_A. Heightened security responses to intelligence assessments indicating potential attacks on Citibank and the stock exchange in New York, and the World Bank in Washington, DC, are examples of preattack influences.

If a quantitative approach is used, the P_A and C terms can be calculated using historical data and consequence criteria, respectively. In a qualitative analysis, these terms can be represented using descriptors such as likely, very likely, or not likely for P_A and critical, severe, or minimal for the C term. This determination is based on the capability of the threat and the consequence of loss of the asset. If the likelihood of attack is high, but the consequence is low (think about shoplifting at one store in an enterprise), the problem to be solved is easier than if both P_A and C are high. (This ignores the cumulative effects of shoplifting across the enterprise. Many thefts of low-value items can add up to a high overall impact and this is part of the analysis.) There are times when either approach is appropriate, and the choice should be driven by the consequence of loss. This is based on the assumption that assets with a higher consequence of loss will attract more capable and motivated adversaries (threats), which in turn will require a PPS that is correspondingly more effective. Fig. 2.2 represents the transition from qualitative to quantitative analysis, using consequence as the discriminator. Qualitative analysis uses the presence of PPS components and adherence to PPS principles as system effectiveness measures. A quantitative analysis uses specific component performance measures derived from rigorous testing to predict overall system effectiveness. At any given facility either or both techniques may be used depending on the consequence of loss of the asset. Relative value of PPS components based on expert opinion is another form of analysis of system effectiveness; however, the outcome depends heavily on the knowledge and experience of the expert.

This section ends with a definition of terms that are used in risk assessments, particularly with respect to the probability of attack by an adversary. These are the proper definitions of these terms; some enterprises may use them differently. Probability is a number that is, by definition, between 0 and 1 and may or may not be time dependent. (As an example, the probability of snow on any given day in Ohio may be 0.25, but the probability of snow in Ohio is 1.0 over the next year.)

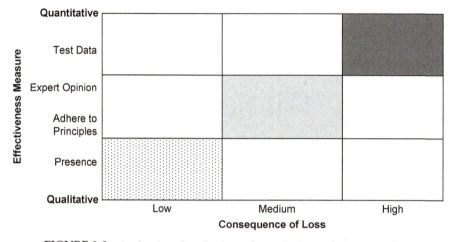

FIGURE 2.2　Application of qualitative and quantitative analysis approaches.

This is discussed further in the next section. Although probability of attack is routinely cited as a threat measure, it is important to note that there frequently is not enough data to support a true probability. For example, there is no statistical data to support the probability of terrorist attacks. That fact, however, has not prevented the massive expenditure of dollars by governments and commercial enterprises to increase security at airports, seaports, critical infrastructures, and other facilities since 9/11. This is a good example of high-consequence, low-probability events and the use of conditional risk. For some assets, the consequence of loss is unacceptably high, and measures are taken to prevent successful adversary attacks, regardless of the low likelihood of attack. Frequency refers to how many times an event has happened over a specified time and is also called a rate. Annual loss exposure is an example of a frequency often used in security risk assessments. Likelihood may be a frequency, probability, or qualitative measure of occurrence. This is more of a catchall term and generally implies a less rigorous treatment of the measure. Haimes has written a thorough discussion of risk modeling, assessment, and management techniques that can be used in security or general risk applications.

STATISTICS AND QUANTITATIVE ANALYSIS

In any discussion of quantitative security system effectiveness, the subject of statistics of security performance arises. To many, statistics is a subject that arouses suspicion and even dread; however, there are a few fairly simple concepts that form the basis of statistical analysis of security effectiveness. Most of these concepts are related to the possible outcomes of a security event. A security event occurs when a security component (people, procedures, or equipment) encounters a stimulus and performs its intended task, for example, when something, such as a human or small animal, enters the detection envelope of an intrusion sensor. There are four possible outcomes of this event:

1. The sensor successfully detects a human-size object.
2. The sensor fails to detect a human-size object.
3. The sensor successfully ignores a smaller-than-human-size object.
4. The sensor fails to ignore a smaller-than-human-size object.

The successes and failures are related such that when a human-size object is presented, there are two complementary results, and when a smaller-than-human-size object is presented, there are also two complementary results. This fact is used later in the discussion. Sensors are the example used here, but this principle applies to any of the probabilities used in this text—the success or failure of a PPS component or the system in performing its intended task can be measured.

Most statistical analysis of security performance is based on these four possible outcomes. The rate at which a sensor successfully detects objects is described as the detection rate. For example, if a sensor successfully detects a human-size object 9 times out of 10 events the detection rate for that group of 10 events is 0.9 or 90%. This is a statistic but is not yet a probability. The detection rate can be turned into a probability when coupled with a confidence level, which is established based on the number of events that are analyzed; the more the data available, the more the confidence there is in the probability. This is easily understood when considering a common example. If a person tosses a coin and the outcome is heads, it would be unwise to assume that every coin toss will result in heads. However, if that person tosses a coin 100 times and 49 results are heads and 51 results are tails, there is a fairly high confidence that the outcomes will be about 50/50. If the experiment is continued to include 1000 trials, the confidence in the estimate of the likely results is even higher. At this point the rate can be estimated with some statistical confidence, and this estimate is a probability. In other words, a probability is an estimate of predicted outcomes of identical trials stated with a confidence level. If 100% confidence is required, an infinite number of tests are required. In reality, when designing performance tests, a confidence level is chosen that requires performance of a reasonable number of trials.

It is not the intent of this section to teach readers how to calculate the statistics of security component effectiveness, but to familiarize them with the terminology and underlying concepts as applied to a PPS. For example, if a metal detector is tested by carrying a gun through it 20 times and it detects all 20 times, the probability of detection can be calculated at a specified confidence level. Often the confidence level used for security component testing is 95%. Using this confidence level, the probability calculated for the metal detector based on the 20 trials is 0.85 (it is often said that the probability is 85%, but in proper statistical terminology, a probability is always a number between 0 and 1). In simpler language, there is a 95% confidence that the metal detector will detect the gun at least 85% of the time. The actual detection rate may be higher, but this is what can be supported given the amount of data collected. If the metal detector is tested 30 times at the same 95% confidence, the probability is now 0.9. Again restating in simple language, there is a 95% confidence that the metal detector will detect the gun at least 90% of the time.

Sometimes it is more useful to classify PPS component performance into error rates rather than probabilities. These error rates are the mathematical complement of the success rates, which is the number of trials minus the number of successes (i.e., the number of failures). The error rates are stated as false accept and false reject rates. In the preceding sensor example, not detecting the human-size object is a false accept and detecting a smaller-than-human-size object is a false reject. This example is used to show that these are the same possible outcomes; however, error rates are seldom used when describing the performance of detection sensor devices. Error rates are much more useful when characterizing the performance of entry control devices, particularly when evaluating the performance of biometric identity verification devices. These devices measure some biological feature, such as a fingerprint, to verify the identity of an individual. In this case, false acceptance of a fingerprint from someone who should not be allowed into a security area and false rejection of someone who should be allowed to enter a secured area are useful ways to view the data.

Other factors of interest in security component evaluation include discrimination and susceptibility to noise. Discrimination describes a sensor's ability to ignore an object that is of the appropriate magnitude but is not the intended target. Often, this is beyond the technical capability of the device. In the preceding sensor example, a human-size object may or may not have specific characteristics that allow the sensor to discriminate between a human and a human-size animal like a small deer or large dog. When the sensor does not have the ability to discriminate between stimuli of equal magnitude, another statistic, the nuisance alarm rate (NAR), is used. A nuisance alarm is caused when the sensor detects an object that is of sufficient magnitude but benign in nature. Anyone who has had a belt buckle cause an alarm in an airport metal detector has experienced a nuisance alarm (assuming that person was not also carrying a gun!). The sources of nuisance alarms are easy to identify when the alarm is assessed by direct human observation or by viewing an image using a video camera. Understanding the causes of nuisance alarms is important in both design and analysis of a PPS. Installing a sensor that has low discrimination to an object or condition that is continually present in the sensor's operating environment will lead to a high NAR, thus lowering confidence in the system. In this scenario, human operators eventually discount alarms and may not pay sufficient attention to a real alarm when it occurs.

Some technologies are also susceptible to noise. Noise in the sensor includes sound, electromagnetic, or even chemical sources. This noise can be present in the background or be internal to the system. Whenever a sensor alarms on external or internal noise, this is defined as a false alarm. False alarms also reduce system effectiveness much the same way as nuisance alarms. Indeed, false alarms can further erode confidence in the PPS because there is no observable alarm source present.

Throughout the discussions of security component performance in this text, it is important to remember that the four possible outcomes of any event are considered. This information, together with the concepts of discrimination and susceptibility to noise, forms the basis of almost all security component performance evaluation. Combined with defeat analysis (which is discussed in other chapters), the full picture of PPS effectiveness emerges.

VULNERABILITY ASSESSMENT PROCESS OVERVIEW

The evaluation techniques presented in this text use a system performance-based approach to meeting the PPS objectives. Recall that the primary functions of a PPS are detection, delay, and response (see Fig. 2.3). Each of these functional subsystems is described in the following chapters and includes a description of both quantitative and qualitative methods of evaluating PPS components at a facility. Quantitative techniques are recommended for facilities with high-consequence loss assets; qualitative techniques can be used if there are no quantitative data available or if the asset value is much lower. It is important to determine before the start of the VA whether a qualitative or quantitative analysis technique will be used. This ensures that the VA team collects the appropriate data and reports the results in a form that is useful for the analysis.

When performing a VA, the general purpose is to evaluate each component of the PPS to estimate their performance as installed at the facility. Once this is done, an estimate of overall system performance is made. The key to a good VA is accurately estimating component performance. When using a quantitative approach, this is done by starting with a tested performance

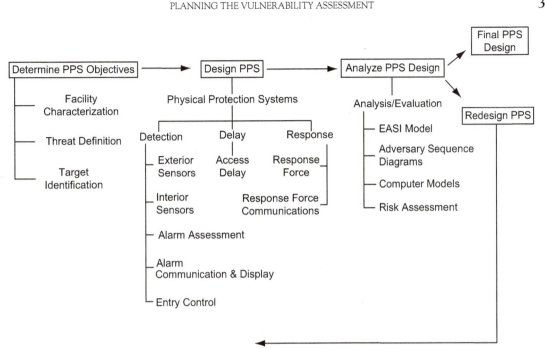

FIGURE 2.3 PPS evaluation process. As in the *Design* textbook, this process provides the framework for conducting a vulnerability assessment. Although frequently not part of the VA, the protection objectives must be known before evaluating the facility.

value for a particular PPS component, such as a sensor, and degrading its performance based on how the device is installed, maintained, tested, and integrated into the overall PPS. For qualitative analysis, performance of each component is degraded based on the same conditions, but the performance of the device is assigned a level of effectiveness, such as high, medium, or low, rather than a number. In addition, component performance must be evaluated under all weather conditions and facility states and considering all threats. The following sections introduce the various stages and activities of a VA.

PLANNING THE VULNERABILITY ASSESSMENT

Before a VA can be performed at a facility, a certain amount of preliminary work must be done to plan and manage the VA so that the customer is provided a useful product. The use of common project management principles and techniques provides a structure and a well-accepted method of approaching the technical, administrative, and business aspects of a VA. At a high level, a project can be broken into three major stages: planning, managing the work, and closeout.

Project Management

Projects, by their definition, have a defined start and end date. There is a point in time when the work did not exist (before the project), when it does exist (the project), and when it does not exist again (after the project). Many VA projects start with an initial customer contact, perhaps as a follow-on to existing work, a reference from another person or business, or as a result of a marketing activity. Project planning starts with understanding what the customer wants or needs. This stage of the project normally involves meetings with the customer to discuss what problems they are having or want to avoid, to understand why they are motivated to do this now, and to discover any specific constraints they may have. Defining the project includes determining the scope of work, as well as what needs to be done, over what period of time, and the cost of the final product. The project scope should state the project objectives and major constraints, such as dollars available or time to complete. Generally, the project is defined in a master document, statement of work, contract, memorandum of agreement, or some other equivalent document. This master document is usually supplemented by a requirements document, which is a summary of the technical specifications or performance required for the delivered product.

After the project has been approved, the customer has sent funding, the project team has been identified, and other administrative issues are set, the actual work can begin. Managing the project includes providing customer support; following the project plan; resolving major and minor project issues on a timely basis; and keeping the project on schedule, within budget and scope, and performing as expected. All of these aspects of the project are organized so that communication between the project leader and the customer and the project team occurs regularly, project risks are managed, product quality maintains an acceptable level, and all project metrics are monitored and remain in compliance.

At some point, all the direct project work is completed, all deliverables are in the customer's hands, the last status reports to the customer have been provided, and the project is complete; however, there are still some remaining issues that must be addressed before pronouncing the project complete. Project closeout can be broken into three areas: financial, administrative, and technical. Financial closeout of the project provides a final accounting of all project costs

and allocation of funds to complete the project. Administrative closeout tasks include collecting all project documentation, storing it in an archive, destroying drafts or working papers that are no longer needed, returning any customer-owned equipment or documents, and verifying that all sensitive information is properly marked and stored securely. The technical closeout of the project can include a project closeout meeting, a lessons learned review, and a closeout report to the customer or internal management.

The use of good project management principles, tools, and skills will help scope, define, manage, and complete a successful VA project for both the VA provider and the customer. A combination of project planning and management techniques minimizes the effects of inevitable project problems and provides a framework to work through major project hurdles.

Establish the Vulnerability Assessment Team

The functional responsibilities of a VA team require a project leader and appropriate subject matter experts (SMEs). Many VA teams will use only a few personnel to serve these roles. Each team member may perform multiple functions, but all appropriate functions must be performed for a thorough VA. The major roles and responsibilities of the VA team include:

- project lead
- systems engineer
- security system engineer
- SME—sensors
- SME—alarm assessment
- SME—alarm communication and display (AC&D)
- SME—entry control
- SME—delay
- SME—response
- SME—communication systems
- SME—analyst
- SME—on-site personnel

All members of the VA team should understand their roles and responsibilities, including what information or activities they are expected to contribute to the overall assessment.

Project Kickoff Meetings

Before starting the VA, it is helpful to have kickoff meetings with the project team and the customer. The project team kickoff meeting is meant to familiarize all team members with the project scope, deliverables, schedule, and funding and to answer any questions. The project leader should provide the team with a detailed description of the project including the customer's objectives, the project schedule and budget, a review of any travel arrangements that must be made, the deliverables and their format, and how customer contact will be managed. This meeting is also the time to start planning the VA. An overview of the facility layout, geography, weather, and operations can be presented, along with any information concerning threats and targets. Usually, the tools that will be used in the analysis are known, but if not, this is a good time to initiate discussion about appropriate analysis tools.

It can be useful to summarize all of the known information about the project and facility in a VA team guide. This guide serves as a means of communicating information to all project team members and as a living document that captures facility information. The guide is a reasonably detailed description of the planned activities but does not need to be extremely lengthy. It is expected that some portions of the guide will be common to all VAs and some portions will be unique to a specific facility. The team guide should include the background of the VA, how it will be conducted, team assignments, logistics, and administrative details.

Whatever the scope of the VA, a variety of site-specific data are required to complete the planning phase of the VA. This information is necessary to plan and carry out the VA in the most efficient and least intrusive manner

possible. The more this information is known before the team gets to the facility, the easier and faster the VA will be, thus limiting the cost and duration of the team visit. Typical information required includes drawings of the facility, number of employees, operational hours, locations of critical assets, existing PPS equipment, weather conditions, on-site personnel contact information, and location of a workspace for the VA team. If known, this information is included in the team guide.

Another important aspect of the VA project is a briefing to senior management of the facility that will be evaluated. The better the purpose of the VA is communicated to management, the easier the evaluation will be, with few objections to team activities. This briefing should be clear about the goals and objectives of the VA, how it will be used, when it will be completed, and how the results will be communicated. For some facilities, senior management will receive the report directly. For others, the report may be submitted to another group, who will then distribute the results to the facility. Once the VA team arrives on site, it may be necessary to have a kickoff meeting to explain the VA to lower level facility personnel. Senior management, facility points of contact, the facility security manager, operations and safety representatives, the entire VA team, and other stakeholders should be invited to this briefing. If facility management has already heard a briefing on the project, they may not attend, although it is probably good practice to invite them or a representative. It is always a welcome touch to invite the most senior manager at the facility to address the group and express his/her support of the process; at the very least, the security manager of the facility should be an active part of this briefing, especially if the VA team is from off-site. Every effort should be made to provide a kickoff meeting at the start of the VA, but if this is not possible, the project leader should be prepared to brief managers and staff at the facility before collecting data in each of the functional areas.

PROTECTION OBJECTIVES

To successfully complete a good VA, it is critical that protection system objectives are well understood. These objectives include threat definition, target identification, and facility characterization. Each enterprise defines VA and risk assessment differently, and as a result some facilities may not have defined threats or identified assets. At facilities where the threat and assets have not already been defined, this task must be included as part of the VA project, although this is generally part of a risk assessment. This will likely add cost and time to the project; therefore, it is critical to understand this before finalizing these details in the project plan.

Knowing the threat is one of the required inputs to a VA because the threat establishes the performance that is required from the PPS. We would not evaluate a PPS protecting an asset from vandals the same way we would for a system protecting an asset from terrorists. By describing the threat, the assumptions that were made to perform the assessment are documented and linked to the decisions that are made regarding the need for upgrades. As such, threat definition is a tool that helps facility managers understand how adversary capabilities impact asset protection and helps PPS designers understand the requirements of the final PPS.

In addition to threat definition, the VA team must also have an understanding of the assets to be protected at the facility. As with threat definition, some customers do not have their assets identified and prioritized before performing a VA. In this case, this must be accomplished before performing the VA. There are three methods for target identification including manual listing of targets, logic diagrams to identify vital areas for sabotage attacks, and use of consequence analysis to screen and prioritize targets. After threats have been defined and assets have been prioritized, a considerable amount of information will exist that is used to establish protection system objectives. The volume of information can be combined into a matrix that relates probability of attack, threat level and tactic, and consequence of loss of assets.

Facility Characterization

The major part of a VA is facility characterization, which consists of evaluating the PPS at the facility. The goal of a VA is to identify PPS components in the functional areas of detection, delay, and response and gather sufficient data to estimate their performance against specific threats. The PPS is characterized at the component and system level, and vulnerabilities to defeat by the threat are documented. Data collection is the core of PPS characterization; accurate data are the basis for conducting a true analysis of the ability of the PPS to meet its defined objectives. Accuracy, however, is only one of several factors to consider. The data gathered must be appropriate to the purpose and scope of the VA, and the quantity and form of the data must be sufficient based on available resources and desired confidence in the results.

A facility tour is usually conducted early in a VA. During the initial facility tour, the VA team begins to gather information regarding the general layout of the facility, the locations of key assets, information about facility operations and production capabilities, and locations and types of PPS components. Review of key documents and selected records are two important PPS characterization activities. These are useful in the evaluation of the effectiveness of a PPS and may begin during the planning phase of a VA. This step of a VA will also include interviews with key facility personnel. Interviews are critical to clarify information and to gain greater insight into specific facility operating procedures. Interviews with personnel at all organizational levels are recommended. Testing is the most valuable data collection method for evaluating the effectiveness of a PPS. Evaluation testing can determine whether personnel have the skills and abilities to perform their duties, whether procedures work, and whether equipment is functional and appropriate. Evaluation tests include functional, operability, and performance tests. Functional tests verify that a device is on, and that it is performing as expected (i.e., a sensor still has a probability of detection of 0.9). Operability tests verify that a device is on and working (i.e., a sensor is on and detects but has moved due to vibration so it is aimed at the wrong location). Performance testing is the characterization of a device by repeating the same test enough times to establish a measure of device capability against different threats. (A sensor is tested many times using crawling, walking, and running modes and under day, night, and varying weather conditions to fully characterize the probability of detection and NAR.) Because performance tests are fairly rigorous and require many repetitions over a period of time, they are generally impractical during a VA. Performance testing is typically performed in a laboratory or nonoperational facility.

One of the goals of the VA team before any system analysis is to identify the various facility states that can exist at the facility. A VA is used to establish vulnerabilities at a facility at all times of the day and at all times of the year. As such, the team must understand the various facility states, so they can determine if the PPS is more or less vulnerable at these times. If the team does not identify these states and determines system effectiveness during all of these different states, the VA will be incomplete and may lead to a false sense of protection. Examples of facility states include normal operating hours, nonoperational hours, a strike at the facility, emergencies such as fire or bomb threats, and shift changes. Once all project planning is complete and protection objectives are understood, the VA team is ready to visit the facility and start collecting data.

DATA COLLECTION—DETECTION

The detection function in a PPS includes exterior and interior intrusion sensors, alarm assessment, entry control, and the alarm communication and display subsystem all working together. Intrusion detection is defined as knowledge of a person or vehicle attempting to gain unauthorized entry into a protected area by someone who can authorize or initiate an appropriate response. An effective PPS must first detect an intrusion, generate an alarm, and then transmit that alarm to a location for assessment and appropriate response. The most reliable method of detecting an adversary intrusion is through the use of sensors, but this can also be accomplished by personnel working in the area or the on-site guard force. Exterior sensors are those used in an outdoor environment, and interior sensors are those used inside buildings.

Intrusion Sensors

Intrusion sensor performance is described by three fundamental characteristics: probability of detection (P_D), NAR, and vulnerability to defeat. These three fundamental characteristics are heavily dependent on the principle of operation of a sensor and the capability of the defined threat. An understanding of these characteristics and the principle of operation of a sensor is essential for evaluating the intrusion sensor subsystem at a facility. Different types and models of sensors have different vulnerabilities to defeat. Sensors can be defeated by spoofing or bypass, and consideration of these attack modes is part of the VA. Exterior sensors are grouped into three application types: freestanding, buried line, or fence-associated sensors. Interior sensors are grouped as boundary penetration, interior motion, and proximity sensors.

Exterior perimeters are generally found only in high-security applications such as prisons, military bases, research facilities, critical infrastructure facilities, and industrial hazardous facilities (i.e., chemical plants). With a large percentage of the critical infrastructure in the United States owned and operated by the private sector, there is more interest in using exterior sensors in private industry since 9/11. If exterior sensors are not in use at a facility, this is an implicit indication that assets are low value or that the expected threat is low and no evaluation is necessary. The overall evaluation of exterior sensors will include attention to details such as sensor application, installation, testing, maintenance, NAR, and performance against the expected threats. If the threat is able to cut, climb, or bridge fences, this must be considered during the VA. The goal of exterior sensor evaluation is to provide an estimate of sensor performance (P_D) against defined threats, along with supporting notes, pictures, and observations that support this estimate. This will help establish the baseline performance of the overall PPS and, if not acceptable, will provide opportunities for upgrade improvements. Factors that will cause performance degradation include NAR and ease of defeat of the sensor through bypass or spoofing.

Interior sensors are used to aid detection of intrusions inside buildings or other structures. Unlike exterior sensors, interior sensors are commonly used at all types of commercial, private, and government facilities. Just as with exterior sensors, there are several factors that contribute to overall sensor performance. The most common interior sensors are balanced magnetic switches, glass-break sensors, passive infrared (PIR) sensors, interior monostatic microwave sensors, video motion detectors, and combinations of sensors, usually PIR and microwave sensors, in dual technology devices.

Interior boundary penetration sensors should detect someone penetrating the enclosure or shell through existing openings (doors, windows, and ventilation ducts) or by destroying walls, ceilings, and floors. Early detection gives more time for the response team to arrive; detection should occur during entry rather than afterward. Volumetric detection uses sensors to detect an intruder moving through interior space toward a target. The detection volume is usually an enclosed area, such as a room or hallway. Most interior volumes provide little delay other than the time required to move from the boundary to the target. Common sensors used for volumetric sensing are microwave and passive infrared radiation. Point sensors, also known as proximity sensors, are placed on or around the target to be protected. In a high-security application, point sensors usually form the final layer of protection, after boundary penetration sensors and volumetric sensors. Capacitance proximity, pressure, and strain sensors are commonly used for point protection, but a number of sensors previously discussed as boundary penetration and volumetric sensors are readily applicable to point protection.

Use of technology is not the only means of sensing intrusions into a facility or area. Employees working in the area, guards on patrol, and video surveillance are other commonly used techniques. These may be effective against very low threats, but testing has shown that these methods will not be effective against more capable threats or when protecting critical assets. Humans do not make good detectors, especially over a long period of time. The lack of firm criteria for what is an adversary intrusion, and the difficulty in recognizing this in time to prevent the attack, as well as safety concerns for employees, all contribute to this problem. Reliable intrusion sensing is best achieved through the use of sensors and is also less expensive than hiring guards. Another weakness of human sensing of intrusions is that it is easier to divert attention away from intrusions, particularly if they are engaged in other activities, such as doing their primary job, answering phones, or assisting visitors. If the defined threat or asset value is significant, sensing through human observation should be degraded during the VA.

When evaluating interior sensors, the goal is to make a determination of how well installed devices will perform against the expected threat. If sensors are present, there is an implicit expectation that they will be effective in protecting assets. Consideration must be given to the principle of operation of the sensor and its operating environment, installation and interconnection of equipment, NAR, maintenance, and the defined threat. The environment associated with interior areas is normally controlled and is, therefore, predictable and measurable. Consequently, it is possible to evaluate sensors for their performance in a particular environment.

After tours, interviews, and testing are complete, the VA team should document intrusion sensing subsystem strengths and weaknesses. Remember that intrusion detection is just one part of the VA, and the analysis cannot be completed until similar information is collected about the other protection subsystems. This part of the VA concentrates on the probability of detection (P_D) for each sensing type—exterior or interior sensors or sensing by humans. Estimates may be made using qualitative or quantitative criteria.

Alarm Assessment

After an alarm is generated using sensors or human observation, the alarm must be assessed to determine the cause and decide what, if any, response is needed. The detection function is not complete without alarm assessment. There are two purposes of assessment. The first is to determine the cause of each alarm, which includes deciding whether the alarm is due to an adversary attack or a nuisance alarm. The second purpose of assessment is to provide additional information about an intrusion that can be provided to responders. This information includes specific details such as who, what, where, and how many. The best assessment systems use video cameras to automatically capture images that show the cause of an alarm and then display these images to an operator who can assess the alarm. Assessment may also be accomplished through human observation, but this is much slower and not as effective.

It is important to differentiate video assessment from video surveillance when conducting a VA. Alarm assessment refers to direct observation of alarm sources by humans or to immediate image capture of a sensor detection zone at the time of an intrusion alarm. This assessment zone and the captured image can be reviewed to determine the cause of the alarm and initiate the proper response to the alarm. Video surveillance uses cameras to continually monitor all activity in an area, without benefit of an intrusion sensor to direct operator attention to a specific event or area. Many surveillance systems do not use human operators but record activity on storage media for later review. The most effective security systems will use video assessment and not surveillance to determine causes of alarms.

A video assessment subsystem allows security personnel to rapidly determine whether an intrusion has taken place at a remote location. Major subsystem components include:

- digital camera and lens
- lighting system
- transmission system
- video recorder and/or storage
- video monitor
- video controller

At the end of this part of the VA, an estimate of the probability of assessment (P_{As}) must be provided for use in the system analysis. This probability is a result of the combined effects of video image quality and resolution, speed of capture of images, proper installation and maintenance of all components, and integration of sensor detection zones with camera field-of-view coverage. The most important factor in assessment subsystem evaluation is to verify that video images containing the alarm source provide enough detail to an operator to allow an accurate determination of the cause of the alarm.

Entry Control

The entry control subsystem includes all the technologies, procedures, databases, and personnel that are used to monitor movement of people and materials into and out of a facility. An entry control system functions in a total PPS by allowing the movement of authorized personnel and material through normal access routes and by detecting and delaying unauthorized movement of personnel and material. Entry control elements may be found at a facility boundary or perimeter, such as personnel and vehicle portals; at building entry points; or at doors into rooms or other special areas within a building. In addition to checks for authorized personnel, certain prohibited items or other materials may also be of interest on entry or exit. For evaluation purposes, entry control is defined as the physical equipment used to control the movement of people or material into an area. Access control refers to the process of managing databases or other records; determining the parameters of authorized entry, such as whom or what will be granted access; when they may enter; and where access will occur. Access controls are an important part of the entry control subsystem.

The primary objective of controlling entry to facilities or areas is to ensure that only authorized persons are allowed to enter and to log these events for documentation purposes. The objective of searching vehicles, personnel, and packages before entry into these areas is to prevent the introduction of contraband materials that could be used to commit sabotage or to aid in the theft of valuable assets. The primary objective of exit control is to conduct searches of personnel, vehicles, and packages to ensure that assets are not removed without proper authorization. A secondary objective of entry and exit control is to provide a means of accounting for

personnel during and after an emergency. There are several methods an adversary may use to defeat an entry control point. These include bypass, physical attack, deceit, and technical attacks. Any or all of these methods may be used by the defined threat, and consideration of this is an important prerequisite to entry control subsystem evaluation.

Under operational loads, the entry control subsystem's performance should not adversely impact security or user operations. The system can be divided into two areas with regard to performance—online and off-line functions. Online functions should be treated as a higher priority by the system. These include alarm annunciation, portal access requests, and alarm assessment that require an immediate response to the user. Off-line functions include generation of preformatted alarm history reports or ad hoc database queries.

In addition to the system software, the access control software that commands the entry control subsystem hardware and maintains and manages the data and logic necessary for system operation must be evaluated as part of the VA. In general, the software must receive electronic information from the installed entry control devices, compare this information to data stored in a database, and generate unlock signals to the portal locking device when the data comparison results in a match. Failure to achieve a successful data match will result in a signal that will not unlock the portal.

Many individual entry control technologies are available, as well as many combinations of them that are used in a PPS. In general, these devices are used to control personnel, contraband material, and vehicle entry or exit and include manual, machine-aided manual, and automated operation. The entry control subsystem uses probability of detection as the primary measure of effectiveness. In the security industry the terms false accept rate and false reject rate are also used to characterize entry control device performance. The false accept rate is the complement of the probability of detection and is equal to $1-P_D$. This is a key measurement of subsystem performance because it represents the probability of defeat of the device. The entry control subsystem can be broken into two major categories: personnel and vehicle control. Contraband material control, such as metal or explosives detection, is a subset of each of these categories.

Alarm Communication and Display

AC&D is the PPS subsystem that transports alarm and video information to a central location and presents the information to a human operator. The two critical elements of an AC&D subsystem are the speed of data transmission to specified locations and the meaningful presentation of that data. Most AC&D subsystems integrate the functions of detection (detect and assess a potential intrusion) and response (initiate either immediate or delayed response procedures), as well as other subsystems such as radio communications and entry control. Although an AC&D subsystem is a complex integration of people, procedures, and equipment, evaluation by the VA team can be reduced to a handful of performance indicators. Effective AC&D subsystems are robust, reliable, redundant, fast, secure, and easy to use.

The AC&D communications system moves data from collection points (sensor and tamper alarms, video, self-test signals) to a central repository (database, server) and then to a control room and display. If the central repository is physically located in the control room, it may consist of multiple computers or displays, and the communication system may also move data throughout the repository and control room. Alarm communication has several characteristics that compel the evaluation. These characteristics include the amount of alarm data, speed of delivery, and high system reliability.

The control and display interfaces of the AC&D subsystem present information to an operator and enable the operator to enter commands affecting the operation of the AC&D subsystem and its components. The ultimate goal of this subsystem is to promote the rapid evaluation of alarms. An effective control and display system presents information to an operator rapidly and in a straightforward manner. The subsystem also responds quickly to operator commands. The control and display system must be evaluated with the human operator in mind; therefore, operation under conditions not directly related to the AC&D subsystem must be observed during evaluations. The console design should facilitate the exchange of information between the system and the operator, such as alarm reports, status indications, and commands. A good human interface improves the mechanics of issuing commands and of deciphering the information presented. Thus, the amount of data displayed should be limited to only what is required by the operator.

The overriding evaluation principle for the AC&D subsystem must be operator first, and the operator must always be in command of the system. The primary purpose of any AC&D subsystem is to enhance facility security. This is accomplished by making operators more efficient and effective in their duties, thus providing the best protection for the cost of subsystem implementation. An easy-to-use system is much more likely to succeed than an unnecessarily complex one.

The primary performance measure for an AC&D subsystem is the probability of assessed detection (P_{AD}). It is a basic principle of an effective PPS that detection is not complete until an alarm has been assessed, which is why P_{AD} is used as the performance measure for the AC&D subsystem. Factors that contribute to this include time for alarm receipt, time to assess the alarm, ease of system use and control by the operator, and operator workload. This term is the product of probability of detection of the sensor subsystem and the probability of alarm assessment. This formula can be used qualitatively or quantitatively—the key is to verify that both sensors and assessment work together to protect assets. The VA team establishes performance of the intrusion sensing and alarm assessment subsystems individually and then evaluates the AC&D subsystem to show how all subsystems work as an integrated system. P_{AD} is then degraded further based on the results of the evaluation of individual AC&D components. These include:

- operator workload
- displays (input/output and ergonomics)
- video system integration
- maintenance
- communications systems for moving sensor data to a display
- processing systems (computers)
- other functions (such as entry control)
- physical infrastructure (power, environmental, cabling, etc.)
- system administration

Poorly integrated AC&D subsystems impact overall system effectiveness by causing decreases in performance in each of the individual components.

DATA COLLECTION—DELAY

The second function of an effective PPS is delay, which slows down the adversary and allows time for the desired assessment and response. This delay is effective only if it follows detection, which can take different forms. The most obvious form of detection is through the use of electronic sensor systems, which relay information back to a monitoring station. When dealing with truly massive delay barriers such as 15 ft of heavily reinforced concrete or underground bunkers, it may be perfectly acceptable to use humans as the one and only sensor system. Security patrols conducting scheduled or random inspections will be capable of detecting any manual entry attempt with sufficient time

to neutralize the adversaries. Increases in adversary task time are accomplished by introducing impediments along all possible adversary paths to provide sufficient delay for any suitable response. In general, estimates of delay times are made using literature searches, actual testing, or approximations made using data from the literature or tests. The delay time of any barrier depends on adversary tools and the barrier material. Adversaries have the option of using tactics of force, stealth, deceit, or combinations of these tactics during an attack. Delay evaluation during a VA is primarily directed toward adversary tactics of force or stealth; the entry control subsystem addresses deceit.

To aid alarm assessment and interruption of the adversary at predictable locations, consideration must be given to installing barriers and detection systems adjacent to each other so that the barrier is encountered immediately after the sensor. This delays the adversary at the point of an alarm, increases the probability of accurate assessment, and allows for an effective response. Barrier effectiveness is supported through the use of the principle of balance, which ensures that each aspect of a specific barrier configuration is of equal strength.

A barrier is normally considered as penetrated when an adversary reaches a point 3 ft beyond the barrier. In contrast, defeat is a much broader term, which implies that the barrier is no longer effective in delaying the adversary. This distinction is important because it is quite often easier to defeat a barrier via stealth or other means than it is to penetrate it. Most security barriers at industrial facilities are designed to deter or defeat sporadic acts of vandalism, inadvertent entry, or casual thievery. For more motivated or capable threats, however, these traditional fences, buildings, doors, and locks may present little deterrence or delay.

A close examination of the large variety of scenarios and tools an adversary can select to penetrate a given facility will likely indicate that existing barriers do not ensure that adversary delay time will always be sufficient for the system. Further, if the adversary has not been detected before encountering a particular barrier, or during penetration, the effectiveness of that barrier will be negligible. Most conventional barriers such as distance, fences, locks, doors, and windows provide short penetration delay against forcible (and perhaps stealthy) attack methods that use readily available hand or power tools. Against thick, reinforced concrete walls and other equally impressive-looking barriers, explosives become an effective, rapid, and more likely method of penetration by a determined adversary. An example is the use of vehicle bombs. In addition, recall that security guards are not an effective delay unless they are located in protected positions and are equipped as well as the adversary (i.e., armed adversary and unarmed guards).

An important concept in delay evaluation is that delay is a strong function of the defined threat and adversaries' skill. Stealth, cunning, and surprise can be valuable assets to any adversaries. The VA team should look not only at the physical delay elements present in a PPS but also at their condition and integration with the rest of the PPS. The team must consider unique ways that an adversary team could and most likely would exploit weaknesses in the PPS. One of the often overlooked aspects of a VA is how adversaries can, and will, use existing tools and materials within the facility to achieve their goals.

There are a variety of active or passive barriers that can be used to provide delay, and many are present in the normal course of building construction. Depending on adversary tools and capabilities, these barriers will have different delay times. Location of the barrier also plays an important role in the delay time and effectiveness of a barrier. A thick concrete wall on the exterior of a building may be susceptible to rapid breaching with explosives. The same wall, however, when incorporated into an interior underground vault may provide substantial delay, as the adversaries may not be able to use large quantities of explosives without collapsing the entire structure around them. Typical barriers include fences, gates, turnstiles, vehicle barriers, walls, floors, roofs, doors, windows, grilles, utility ports, and other barriers.

DATA COLLECTION—RESPONSE

Response is the third and final function of a PPS that is evaluated during a VA. There are many ways to respond to a security event; the appropriate response depends on the defined threat, the value of the asset, and the use of risk management options other than a PPS at the facility. At any given facility, one or more response strategies may be in use, and this will affect data collection activities accordingly. In addition to the response strategy, security communication is a critical part of any response function and must also be considered during the VA.

The key information collected during the VA relates to two important and interrelated factors. The first is the time it takes for the desired response to be placed into effect; the second is the effectiveness of that response. These aspects of response are facilitated by reliable communication among the responders and with others. A related matter is whether there is an immediate on- or off-site response. During the initial design and implementation of a PPS, each facility must decide if the response goal is to react after a successful attack or to stop the adversary from completing a successful attack. The misalignment of response goals and protection objectives at a facility will cause serious degradation of PPS effectiveness.

Response goals can be broadly categorized as delayed or immediate, respectively. Delayed response refers to any after-the-event reaction, where preventing a successful attack is less important than initiating asset recovery or investigation procedures, or where evacuation of the facility is the response to an attack. Examples of delayed response include review of surveillance tapes after an asset has been lost or damaged, incident investigation, asset tracking and recovery, criminal prosecution, or any combination of these. Immediate response refers to the timely deployment of any personnel to an intrusion to prevent undesirable events from occurring or to the immediate implementation of a mitigation procedure, such as evacuation, after a successful attack, to limit the effects of undesirable events. Generally speaking, if there is no immediate response to security events, there is a basic assumption that the asset can be lost and that this risk is acceptable. This may be true when the asset value is low, the threat is not very capable or motivated, the frequency of the event (i.e., the probability of attack) is low, or the asset is protected using another risk management alternative (i.e., insurance) rather than physical protection, or if liability concerns limit the use of an immediate response. For critical assets, however, the lack of an immediate response to a malevolent intrusion increases the risk of asset loss; therefore, it must be carefully considered during the VA.

The two measures of an immediate response are the time for arrival and neutralization. The time to arrive is used to establish interruption; neutralization is a measure of response effectiveness, given arrival. Interruption is a measure of the detection, delay, communication, and response functions of the PPS and is represented by the probability of interruption (P_I). Neutralization measures response force numbers, training, tactics, and use of any weapons or equipment and is represented by the probability of neutralization (P_N). In addition, the VA team must estimate the probability of communication (P_C), which is essential for an effective immediate response.

Several general response strategies can be used at any given facility; some high-security sites with multiple critical assets may use more than one strategy, and the response strategy plays a major role in how a facility is evaluated during a VA. Response strategies include deterrence, denial, containment, and recovery. Deterrence is used to discourage some low-level threats from attacking a facility by presenting the appearance of tight security, suggesting that an attack would not be successful. This strategy is used at almost all private and government facilities. Because this strategy relies on the adversary's perception that they are not likely to succeed, this approach will work only against less capable or motivated threats.

For some critical assets or production facilities, such as hazardous chemical, biological, and nuclear materials or toxic waste, where release of these agents into the environment through sabotage would cause many injuries, deaths, or contamination, a denial strategy is required. Denial refers to the protection of material by preventing adversary access to areas where materials are stored or to vital equipment used to process the material. For a successful sabotage event to occur, the adversary only has to complete the attack on the target and cause the release; capture of the adversary after a successful release does not prevent the consequence of the attack.

A containment strategy is generally used when the adversary goal is theft of an asset. Containment means that the adversary is not allowed to leave the facility with the asset; that is, they are contained on-site and the theft attempt is not successful. This strategy is usually reserved for facilities with high-value or high-consequence assets, such as mints that store large quantities of currency, museums, precious gem or metal repositories, or hazardous material storage locations. Prisons also use a containment strategy, but they are attempting to prevent inmates from leaving a facility, not the theft of assets.

In the event that deterrence or containment strategies fail, a backup approach is recovery of the stolen asset. In some recovery strategies, the recovery is immediate (i.e., hot pursuit of the adversary as he/she speeds away in a car). For most facilities, there is an acceptance that assets may be lost for a period of time, and recovery of the assets at some point in the future is the primary response. Recovery responses include investigation, tracking of assets, and follow-up using criminal prosecution.

Security communications consist of the people, procedures, and technology used to transmit communications among members of the response force during both normal and response operations. During normal operations, security communications may be required for conducting entry control, escort, patrols, and other security functions (for an on-site security group). During response to an attack, communications are essential for organizing responders, directing them to the scene of the emergency, and successfully interrupting or neutralizing the adversary. Accurate and reliable communication is required for interruption and neutralization. The overall performance measure used is the P_C, which is a measure of confidence that information will flow through the system, starting with alarm reporting and ending with deployment and engagement with the adversary. For a delayed response using video surveillance or assessment, P_C will depend on the transmission system used to capture and store alarm and video information for later review.

The actual performance measures and estimates used depend on the response strategy and the presence of an immediate response. For delayed responses, it is sufficient to ensure that there is timely and accurate detection, and that legally admissible and usable video information is captured as evidence. This requires a fully functional communication system, limited in this case to integrated sensing and video assessment, and transmission of this information to a storage location. This can be approximated using the probability of assessed detection. For any immediate response, response force time, neutralization capability, and the probability of communication will be the key aspects of the evaluation.

ANALYSIS

After all the appropriate data have been collected, analysis of the PPS can begin. There are two basic analysis approaches used in a VA: compliance or performance based. Compliance-based approaches depend on conformance to specified policies or regulations; the metric for this analysis is the presence of the specified equipment and procedures. Performance-based approaches actually evaluate how each element of the PPS operates and what it contributes to overall system effectiveness. The use of compliance- or feature-based systems is only effective against low threats, when assets have a low consequence of loss, or when cost-benefit analyses have been performed that document that physical protection measures are not the most cost-effective risk management option. A compliance-based analysis is easier to perform because the measure of system effectiveness is the presence of prescribed PPS equipment, procedures, and people. The analysis consists of a review of facility conformance to the compliance requirements, the use of checklists to document the presence or absence of components, and a deficiency report that notes where the facility is out of compliance. The VA report summarizes these findings and the facility makes improvements according to enterprise policy. Because the premise of this text is that overall system effectiveness is the goal of a VA, and that all dollars spent on PPS elements should result in improved protection while also complying with requirements, this text primarily addresses performance-based analysis. Performance-based analysis can use either qualitative or quantitative techniques.

When conducting either a qualitative or quantitative performance-based analysis, the following six-step process is used:

1. Create an adversary sequence diagram (ASD) for all asset locations.
2. Conduct a path analysis, which provides P_I.
3. Perform a scenario analysis.

4. Complete a neutralization analysis, if appropriate, which provides P_N.
5. Determine system effectiveness, P_E.
6. Develop and analyze system effectiveness upgrades, if system effectiveness (or risk) is not acceptable.

If desired, a facility may also choose to evaluate the PPS using risk as a metric, although this method is more commonly used in risk assessment and not in VA.

An ASD is a functional representation of the PPS at a facility that is used to describe the specific protection elements that are present. It illustrates the paths that adversaries can follow to accomplish sabotage or theft goals. Because a path analysis determines whether a system has sufficient detection and delay to result in interruption, it is conducted first. The path analysis uses estimated performance measures, based on the defined threat tools and tactics, to predict weaknesses in the PPS along all credible adversary paths into the facility, measured by the probability of interruption. This step is facilitated through the use of an ASD of the facility to be analyzed.

A scenario analysis is conducted to determine whether the system has vulnerabilities that could be exploited by adversaries using varying tactics, resulting in lower effectiveness of the PPS. Scenario analysis considers specific tactics along the path, as well as attacks on the PPS or on the response force. These tactics include stealth, force, and deceit, and they may be used individually or combined during a scenario. As in path analysis, an important aspect of scenario analysis is consideration of different operating states at the facility or near the asset. There are usually at least two facility states—open and closed. As a part of scenario analysis, an effort is made to identify the worst cases of attack scenarios. Although analysis is not limited to these situations, they are very useful because they define the adversary attacks that test the limits of PPS effectiveness.

After weak paths and suitable attack scenarios have been determined, a neutralization analysis can be performed. This part of the analysis is performed only at facilities where there is an immediate response resulting in a face-to-face confrontation with adversaries. Neutralization analysis provides information about how effective the response function will be under different scenarios and is a measure of response force capability, proficiency, training, and tactics.

At this point, PPS effectiveness can be calculated, using qualitative or quantitative techniques. System effectiveness is represented using only P_I (as in the case of a delayed response using review of video and investigation, when the mere presence of an immediate response will chase an adversary away, or when an adversary will surrender if interrupted), or through the use of both P_I and P_N (at facilities where an immediate response will engage with the adversary).

If the baseline analysis of the PPS shows that the system does not meet its protection objectives, the VA team can suggest upgrades that will address these issues. Usually, these upgrades are not specific technical recommendations but are functional improvements that can be achieved by increasing performance at certain locations. The analysis is then repeated using these performance increases to estimate the overall increase in the ability of the system to meet its objectives. These results are provided to security system designers who will determine which specific equipment or other upgrades will provide the required performance. Once the analysis is completed, it is important to present both the baseline and upgrade analyses to establish the need for improvements and show the return on investment (ROI) in upgrades.

REPORTING AND USING THE VULNERABILITY ASSESSMENT

After analysis of facility data is complete, the VA team reports the results in a manner that is useful to the managers at the facility. The goal of the report is to provide accurate, unbiased information that clearly defines the current effectiveness of the PPS, along with potential solutions if the current system is not effective. The VA informs facility management of the state of the PPS and supports upgrade decisions. In general, the VA report is then used in successive projects that address the identified vulnerabilities and improve the PPS at the facility.

Reporting can be formal or informal, verbal or written, and may take the form of a short overview, or a longer, more detailed approach. The choice of reporting form and content is an aspect of the project agreement and generally follows the conventions of the customer or facility being evaluated. Regardless of how reporting is presented and documented, certain content must be included to make the report understandable and useful to the facility. By its very nature, a VA report is a powerful document and should not be shared indiscriminately. Protection of the final report, as well as the appropriate distribution, should be defined as part of the master project agreement. It is recommended that one organization has final control of the document and who it is shared with, even though other organizations may have copies.

Once the VA report is completed, a variety of responses or next steps can take place. By far, the most common approach is for the facility to pursue improving the PPS and following the recommendations of the VA team. A VA can be thought of as the analysis of system requirements that must occur before system design and implementation. The same things that made a particular PPS weak can limit the effectiveness of any upgrades if they are not carefully considered. This process may be relatively short and easy if the recommendations involve only procedural or minor equipment changes, such as replacing one type of CCTV camera with another. If the system requires major equipment upgrades, however, the proper approach to the upgrade design will ensure a cost- and performance-effective result.

The goal of the design team is to create upgrades that meet the performance predicted in the upgrade analysis phase of the VA. This can be difficult to accomplish, and it can take several iterations between the designers and the facility to clarify goals and constraints and to create the best system that can be installed for the available funding. The three general stages of design activity include conceptual, preliminary, and final design. Although this discussion is focused on the VA of an existing facility, the same process is used for evaluation of a new facility. For new facilities, VA analysts and designers work together closely to model the proposed PPS at the facility and then iterate on which PPS elements will give the most cost-effective solution. Once they agree, the system designers work through the design stages to define how the final design will be implemented to meet the specified performance.

SYSTEMS ENGINEERING AND VULNERABILITY ASSESSMENT

This section introduces the systems engineering process and describes how this process is used in a VA. Before discussing this relationship, a few definitions and a brief introduction to systems engineering are provided.

In the *Design* textbook, a system was defined as "an integrated collection of components or elements designed to achieve an objective according to a plan." Systems may be small (a microwave oven) or large (a city), and all systems are composed of other smaller systems (or subsystems). In some applications, a collection of many systems into a functional whole is called a system of systems or a family of systems. Further, systems are not found only in engineering, but exist in other disciplines as well. For example, there is a criminal justice system that includes law enforcement, the courts, and corrections. Biological systems can be microorganisms, a pond, or a human. A social system includes the culture, behaviors, and mores of a society. Systems engineering

> ...is an interdisciplinary approach and means to enable the realization of successful systems. It focuses on defining customer needs and required functionality early in the development cycle, documenting requirements, and then proceeding with design synthesis and system validation while considering the complete problem. Systems engineering considers both the business and the technical needs of customers with the goal of providing a quality product that meets user needs.

It is concerned with the integration of functional, technical, and operational requirements within the business goals and environment of the customer. Integration refers not only to physical or electrical integration (although these are important aspects of system performance) but also to the integration of customer needs, technical performance, safety, reliability, procedures, personnel, maintenance, training, testing, and life cycle costs of the proposed solution. The systems engineering process flow is shown in Fig. 2.4. The process is iterative and should begin at the requirements stage. A VA fits into this stage of the cycle, which guides the other stages. The results of the VA are used to establish the requirements for an upgraded system design, which are validated through the use of analysis and testing. Once

installed, the system should be tested and maintained to optimize system performance and allow for some expansion. At some point, requirements may change or the system reaches the end of its usable lifetime, and replacement of the system or components must be addressed.

Systems engineering is not about being a good engineer—everyone is a systems engineer in his/her area of expertise. Rather, systems engineering is a logical and structured process that starts by defining the problem to be solved, considering multiple potential solutions, and then analyzing these solutions to support selection and implementation of the most balanced and robust design that meets requirements and goals. Implementation of the design includes proper installation, maintenance, testing, and training of personnel to preserve optimal system function. Systems engineering also addresses the final disposition, retirement, or replacement of the system after its useful lifetime has been reached. The information presented in this section is an overview of systems engineering based on principles developed by the International Council on Systems Engineering (INCOSE) and a text by Martin. An effective VA follows basic systems engineering principles.

A common model of systems development is one that considers both systems and component engineering. These two areas are science based, where science determines what is, component

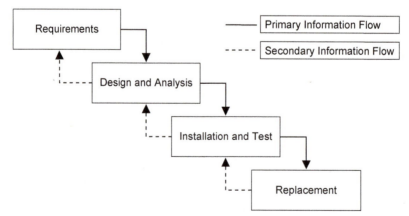

FIGURE 2.4 Systems engineering process.

engineering determines what can be, and systems engineering determines what should be. The systems engineering domain includes user requirements (define the problem) and system requirements (boundaries and constraints), which lead to the component engineering domain. This domain includes component selection, design, analysis, integration, and testing.

During a VA, the project leader generally serves as the systems engineer who ensures that the final product meets customer needs, although large projects may include a systems engineer as a separate team member. Component engineers are the SMEs on the VA team who bring technical depth in engineering, adversary and response tactics, explosives, analysis, and other areas to evaluation activities.

Because the VA process described in this chapter is performance based, it embraces all the areas of system development described previously: science, systems, and component engineering. The science-based nature of this approach cannot be ignored. An example may clarify the distinction between compliance- and performance-based approaches. A compliance-based approach might select a radar to provide exterior intrusion detection instead of other sensors, such as microwave, active infrared, fence-associated, or buried cable, based on past use, a large inventory of available devices, approved lists, or vendor-provided information. In contrast, a performance-based approach would begin by ensuring that all system requirements are identified and that the selected device is the one that best meets all requirements. Then, performance of the device is based solely on the trade-off analysis of which devices meet all requirements. Examples of exterior intrusion detection requirements include probability of detection, NAR, vulnerability to defeat by the defined threat, integration with other PPS components, expansion capability, and life cycle cost of implementation and operation. This example emphasizes the need for good systems engineering, so that the VA and any necessary upgrades provide the best PPS for the cost. As a result, customer desires often must be bound by explaining what realistically can and cannot be achieved using PPS components. This rationale is included in the requirements stage of systems engineering, which is described next and is a part of VA project management. A brief comparison of compliance- and performance-based approaches is shown in Table 2.1.

TABLE 2.1 Comparison of Compliance- and Performance-Based Vulnerability Assessment Approaches[a]

Criterion	Compliance-Based Approach	Performance-Based Approach
Asset value	Low	All assets
Requirement basis	Policy	Overall system performance
Component performance measure	Presence	Effectiveness and integration
Data collection methodology	Site survey	Site evaluation testing
Analysis	Checklist	System effectiveness
Reporting	Deficiency report	Path effectiveness and vulnerabilities
Upgrade design	Address deficiencies	Functional performance estimates
Component selection	Component engineering	Systems engineering
Underlying process	Satisfy policy requirement	Systems engineering

[a] *Compliance-based approaches are less rigorous and easier to perform than performance-based approaches. Compliance-based approaches are most appropriate for low-value assets, whereas a performance-based process can be used for assets of any value.*

Given this background, Fig. 2.3 illustrates the systems engineering process as applied in a VA, which will be discussed in other chapters. The remaining sections of this chapter describe the phases of systems engineering in more detail and how they relate to a VA, and include references to specific chapters in the book that contain further information. The purpose of this discussion is not to thoroughly describe the systems engineering process but to show how a VA is based on the process.

SYSTEM REQUIREMENTS

As shown in Fig. 2.3, evaluation of a PPS begins with an understanding of the problem that is to be solved. This includes facility characterization, defining the threat, and target identification. In systems engineering, these PPS objectives are a subset of system requirements, and they serve as the primary basis for appropriate PPS evaluation by SMEs from a variety of disciplines.

A requirement is a characteristic that identifies the levels needed to achieve specific objectives under a given set of conditions and is a binding statement in a contract or regulatory document. In formal systems engineering documents, requirements can be thresholds or goals; thresholds are something that must be achieved, whereas goals have some degree of usefulness or desirability, but are not necessarily mandatory. Requirements are generally stated as "shall," whereas goals are stated as "should." This is a major point to consider when establishing system requirements. There are many customer, user, and stakeholder wants, needs, and expectations. Early in the evaluation process, these imprecise statements must be reduced to an actionable and measurable set of mandatory requirements, so that the final product delivers what the customer expects. It is not uncommon to skip this step in the process and jump immediately into system evaluation. This approach

almost always leads to dissatisfied customers and incomplete products and should be avoided. There are three types of requirements in a system: functional, constraint, and performance.

A functional requirement describes the product and level of detail, including component interfaces and what the PPS will do. These requirements address the integration of people, procedures, and equipment that provide the desired end product. They also address stakeholder, customer, and user needs, desires, and expectations. There is a difference in the needs of stakeholders (those who have a role in or expectations of the product), customers (those who pay for the system), and users (those who will operate and maintain the final product). A requirements analysis considers these different needs. These questions are appropriate for customers and stakeholders: What needs are we trying to meet? What is wrong with the current system? Is the need clearly articulated? Other questions concerning who the intended users are, how they will use the product, and how this is different from the present operation are appropriate for users.

Constraint requirements include any external or internal compliance condition or stipulation that must be met. They include external laws and regulations, legal liabilities, standards, and enterprise policies and procedures. Examples are federal safety requirements, labor law, fire and electrical codes, enterprise-defined infrastructure, and project management processes. In a VA, additional constraints are a function of the specific site, such as terrain, weather, facility layout and footprint, the presence of a response force, and other unique conditions. These constraints are part of the operational environment that must be considered in the VA. Other constraints may be imposed by the limits of available technology, such as the previous radar example.

Performance requirements define how well a capability must operate and under what conditions. These are stated in clear, unambiguous, and measurable terms. Examples of performance measures are earned value, monthly financial status, milestones met, other business or administrative measures, and security performance measures such as probability of detection, delay times, probability of assessment, and probability of interruption. Performance requirements are derived from functional requirements and specify the metrics that are used to judge component and system effectiveness in meeting requirements.

There are many reasons to perform a VA, and these underlying needs must be understood by the VA team before beginning the evaluation. For example, periodic VAs may be required by an enterprise policy or regulatory agency (a constraint requirement), even though the system is still performing as required. Or, the facility may have recently been attacked and lost a critical asset, and there is a desire to improve protection of assets (a functional requirement). Since 9/11, many private companies and government agencies have issued new threat guidance concerning the use of weapons of mass destruction and need to perform VAs to verify that existing PPSs are still effective (a performance requirement). These examples emphasize the need to understand customer goals in asking for a VA. In addition, the customer's intended use of the VA must be considered. If the VA is performed only to satisfy a regulatory requirement, but there is no intention of implementing any changes in response to identified vulnerabilities, this is important for the VA team to understand. If the customer is unwilling or unable to allocate additional funding or other resources to improving the PPS if required, this is part of the operating environment that constrains the VA. Identifying customer needs, motivation, and desires is a part of VA project management.

In a VA, functional requirements can be equated to defining the protection objectives— what is to be protected (assets) and from whom (threat). A high-level functional requirement in security is to "protect the secret rocket fuel formula from theft by a competitor." In addition to these requirements, it is also important to characterize the enterprise in terms of its mission and the external and enterprise operating environments, particularly with respect to any compliance constraints that must be met. For example, since 9/11, a variety of laws and mandates have been enacted by the US government that have had a significant impact on security at airports and seaports. These new constraint requirements must be considered during VAs at these sites, so that their effect on overall system effectiveness is considered.

The performance requirements of the security system are related to the capability of the defined threat. For example, a PPS that protects assets from vandals requires lower performance than one against a group of highly motivated and well-equipped environmental activists. This is why it is so important to define protection objectives before starting the VA and not jump right into design, or worse, procurement, of PPS components. In many instances, an enterprise has responded to a security incident or regulatory requirement by buying more cameras, with no analysis of what capability the new cameras will add to the current system. This relates to the earlier point concerning thresholds and goals. As applied to a VA, a threshold is used to specify the minimum acceptable performance of the PPS that must be achieved (i.e., probability of detection must be 0.9 for running, walking, and crawling intruders). If the threshold cannot be met by an improved PPS within the constraints, the system is not implemented or requirements are reduced because analysis does not support making an additional investment in a system or upgrade that cannot meet the minimum functional requirements. Put in different terms, the ROI is zero—additional money was spent with no corresponding increase in the ability of the PPS to protect assets. This is not the traditional interpretation of ROI, where there is a direct financial gain as a result of system improvement. Rather, this ROI is the proactive protection of assets in a structured and reasoned manner. This may pay off indirectly in financial gain by protecting the enterprise's reputation, ensure business continuity in case of an attack, and show external auditors or agencies that reasonable steps were taken to protect high-value assets. If a PPS that meets customer needs and system requirements cannot be implemented, other risk management alternatives should be considered, perhaps in combination. There are often other ways to achieve the customer's goals that are cheaper and more effective than reducing risk using a PPS.

SYSTEM DESIGN AND ANALYSIS

At this point, a clear set of requirements exists and has been agreed to by the customer, and the VA can begin. The system is evaluated by SMEs (i.e., component engineers) considering the defined threats and identified assets, and all constraints are factored into the evaluation. A VA on a PPS considers the functions of detection, delay, and response and evaluates how well people, procedures, and equipment meet all requirements. It is implicit in this approach that the defined threat must physically enter the facility to attack. As a result, standoff attacks from off-site or cyber attacks on networks are not part of the VA of a PPS; these are legitimate security concerns that are addressed in the overall security system for the facility. During a VA, the current system is evaluated based on the system requirements, and analysis is used to show whether the system meets the requirements. If the baseline analysis shows that the system does not meet requirements, potential upgrades are analyzed, but only to a functional level (i.e., specific devices that achieve this performance are not identified). In this case, the VA then establishes a new set of system requirements that is passed to designers for upgrade improvements using the new functional and performance requirements. The upgrade design process is described later in this section.

VA analysis is supported through the use of evaluation tests on installed PPS components, which document PPS component performance and how this affects the overall system. Any performance deficiencies are documented and used in the analysis. These component deficiencies lead to system weaknesses that can be exploited by adversaries, which is the definition of a vulnerability. For many PPS components, historical test data already exist that are used in analysis. The principles and techniques used to evaluate the detection, delay, and response subsystems and components of the PPS form the core of this text.

The VA analysis process includes the use of trade-off analyses that consider the performance that can be expected for various combinations of PPS elements and assist in selection of performance options that best meet all requirements. A robust design will also look beyond the requirements (i.e., thresholds) and determine how effective the system is in meeting customer desires. For example, analysis of a PPS must show effectiveness against the defined threat; in addition, analyses showing how well the system will perform against higher threats can also be performed to give an indication of system effectiveness beyond requirements. This additional performance documents how effective the PPS will be as threats increase, and if this performance can be obtained for little increased cost, it can be a viable option. This is an example of a customer goal, as compared with a requirement. The analysis shows how an investment in the PPS can be leveraged to add system capability at a low cost, for example, installing larger, high-resolution CCTV monitors in the alarm-monitoring station. It may cost a little more to buy better monitors, but better monitors will make operators faster and more effective at assessing intrusion alarms caused by small objects. As a result, a small additional investment in better monitors will provide more effective alarm assessment capability. This relates to the earlier point about meeting customer goals—implementation of this option should be discussed with and approved by the customer, and consider all impacts to the PPS, such as any increased cost of installation, normal and backup power specifications, and operator viewing distance.

At the end of the VA, analysis shows either that the current PPS is effective in meeting requirements, or it is not. If not, the VA team will propose various functional and performance upgrades to the PPS that will meet requirements. At this point, the VA is complete, and the final report is written. If the facility chooses to follow the VA recommendations, and assuming that many equipment improvements are needed, another separate group of PPS designers is assigned to design the upgraded PPS. The design of a PPS is a complex subject that could easily fill another book; however, the process is summarized in the remainder of this section.

The design stage of the systems engineering process is often iterative, starting with conceptual design, proceeding to a preliminary design, and ending with the final system design that is deployed. As the design progresses, a multidisciplinary team (much like the team that performed the VA) reviews potential design options to converge on the best solution. In many cases, the existing requirements may not completely specify the performance required of the upgraded system, and this is part of the reason for an iterative design cycle. This process is facilitated by the use of design reviews, modeling and simulation tools, test data, and discussions with the customer to verify that the proposed solution is in alignment with their needs (shall requirements) and desires (should requirements). The final design ends in a detailed description of the product and how it is implemented (a detailed final drawing package). Before implementing the final design, the system components are analyzed to validate and verify system operation. Validation is the process of checking satisfaction of stakeholders (have we done the right job?) and verification checks that the design meets the specified technical requirements and the components are properly integrated (have we done the job right?).

Validation checks to ensure that no requirements were missed and that there are no extraneous requirements. This is called requirements traceability and is frequently used in large, costly systems (and may be required by some customers). Traceability shows that the product is just what the customer wanted, no more and no less. It also serves to document and explain selection of specific components during the system design stages and links requirements to these components and the overall system. If there is no link between a component and a requirement, the customer was given more than they needed. This is important because it clarifies for the customer why one device was used over another in the final design. Consider the example of specifying a camera in a PPS design. Many types of cameras are available, and selection of the appropriate camera depends on the functional, constraint, and performance requirements of the system. If the defined threat includes an adversary crawling across a perimeter at night, camera resolution, lighting, video recording, and storage must be specified to meet this performance requirement. Contrast this with a defined threat that includes a vehicle crashing the perimeter. The larger profile of a vehicle will not require the same camera resolution as a crawling attacker; thus the specific camera that is selected may be different. However, the vehicle will be moving at a faster rate of speed than a crawler, and this constraint will influence what other devices are incorporated into the system design. Validation often uses acceptance tests under local conditions to check that the system meets the needs and expectations of stakeholders. If formal documentation is needed, the use of traceability software, as noted previously, may be warranted (go to www.telelogic.com for an example). The software documents the link between requirements, system design, implementation, and test.

SYSTEM INSTALLATION AND TEST

At this stage of the upgrade process, the new design is implemented as described in the drawings and specifications of the final design package. Deviations from these specifications should be approved by knowledgeable experts who understand their effects on component and overall system performance. Some changes may be relatively transparent, but others may seriously affect system performance. For example, changing the distance between or height of light fixtures may change the amount of light that is available in an area. System installation is supplemented by on-site operational, functional, and performance tests to ensure that the system is working as predicted and the customer's needs are met. Operational tests confirm that an installed device is working (i.e., it sends a signal), and functional tests show that the device is working and performing as expected (i.e., a sensor still has the expected P_D). It is also recommended that final acceptance tests are performed before the customer accepts the delivered system. An acceptance test is the final stage of system delivery, and test results are used to either justify or withhold final payments to vendors, depending on whether the system passes or fails the test.

Because the PPS is expected to continue to perform after initial installation, proper maintenance and periodic testing of components and the system are required to maintain optimal system function. These are aspects of the overall system and system design also includes recommendations on the maintenance, testing, and training procedures that should be used to keep the system operating reliably and as expected. These details are aided by complete system documentation, a preliminary training program to acquaint users with the proper ways to maintain the system, and recommended procedures and processes that will ensure continued acceptable system performance. Component installation, maintenance, testing, and staff training procedures are evaluated during the VA and can have a significant effect on overall system performance. Procedural improvements can also be low-cost system upgrades.

SYSTEM REPLACEMENT

It is good systems engineering practice to include planning for the retirement and replacement of the system in the system design, after its expected lifetime has been reached. The final design that is implemented should allow for system expansion and growth, up to a certain point. Typically, this point allows for 50% expansion above the current capability. This advance planning allows for expansion of systems in response to changes without excessive cost or loss of protection. Examples of system expansion include the installation of fiber-optic cable bundles with more conductors than currently needed at initial installation. It only costs a little more to buy a fiber bundle with twice as many conductors; installation costs are the same. Alternatively, a conduit with a larger diameter could be used to allow room for additional wiring at a later date. In the same way, adding power drops or junction boxes will allow for rapid expansion of the PPS in the future. It is expected that technology will advance, threats will change, facilities may grow or shrink, or equipment will fail, any of which can create a need for new components that meet existing or new requirements. Although retirement and replacement are not part of a VA, expansion capability of the PPS is one criterion that is considered during a VA.

SUMMARY

This chapter described risk management, VA, and systems engineering and explained how these processes support security system evaluation. Risk management and risk assessment were reviewed. Both qualitative and quantitative techniques to measure system effectiveness in a VA were described, as well as when each technique is appropriate. The use of statistical measures was discussed to introduce this topic and to show how statistics are used to support system evaluation. The VA process was also introduced by dividing the process into three stages—planning, conducting, and reporting—and using the results. This chapter ended with a brief description of how the evaluation process described in this text follows a systems engineering process to enable the realization of successful systems. This process focuses on defining customer requirements and then evaluating the system while considering the complete problem. Systems engineering integrates disciplines and groups into a team effort, following a structured development process that proceeds from problem definition to evaluation and analysis to implementation of any required system upgrades, while considering both the business and the technical needs of customers with the goal of providing a quality product that meets user needs.

References

[1] Garcia ML. The design and evaluation of physical protection systems. Boston: Butterworth-Heinemann; 2001.

[2] Grose VL. Managing risk: systematic loss prevention for executives. Arlington, VA: Omega Systems Group; 1987.

[3] Kaplan S, Garrick BJ. On the quantitative definition of risk. Risk Anal 1981;1(1):11–27.

[4] Haimes YY. Risk modeling, assessment, and management. 2nd ed. Hoboken, NJ: Wiley and Sons; 2004.

[5] International Council on Systems Engineering (INCOSE). Definition available at: http://www.incose.org/practice/whatissystemseng.aspx; April 18, 2005.

[6] Martin JN. Systems engineering guidebook: a process for developing systems and products. Boca Raton, FL: CRC Press; 1987.

3

Influence of Physical Design

Marianna A. Perry, MS, CPP

This chapter discusses crime prevention through environmental design (CPTED) and how practitioners, designers, community members, and law enforcement activity can all collaborate to help make urban community housing developments safer. Individuals must realize that safe communities are formed with their interaction and involvement in partnership programs with law enforcement and other community agencies. Residents and those with a "vested" interest in the community join together and partner with law enforcement to reduce not only crime but also the fear of crime and change the perception of the community.

INTRODUCTION

The relationship between physical design and informal social control of crime is a new idea only in the sense of its systematic application to the modern urban scene. Prior to the development of the modern city, most societies took some precautions to relate security in the physical environment to a responsibility for security actions by the inhabitants themselves.

In the rush of modern urban development, however, economic and political priorities seem to far outweigh security priorities, with the result that many urban settings now seem deliberately designed to discourage informal social control. No colonial community would have done so, even when stockades were no longer needed for defense. New England towns continued to be constructed so that homes and stores formed a hollow square around a central common area where social activities could take place and where livestock could be kept in relative security. In this kind of environment, everyone knew everyone else's business. While this meant less personal privacy than the modern city dweller may enjoy, it also meant a high degree of shared responsibility for controlling undesirable behavior and unwanted intrusion.

Only recently have students of modern urban society begun again to take serious note of the relationship between physical design and informal social control. Jane Jacobs first applied the concept to modern cities in 1961. In her book *The Death and Life of Great American Cities* [1], she theorized that multiple land uses along residential streets provided an interaction between the physical design and the users (pedestrians and residents), which promoted natural and informal surveillance and, therefore, increased the safety of the streets.

Lee Rainwater, in an evaluation of a public housing project in St. Louis in 1966, discussed the effect of physical design on the attitudes of public housing residents, pointing out that inappropriate architectural design was directly related to antisocial behavior [2].

Effective Physical Security, Fifth Edition
http://dx.doi.org/10.1016/B978-0-12-804462-9.00003-8

Elizabeth Wood, writing in 1961, suggested that current design patterns in public housing projects appeared to discourage informal social relationships and gatherings, thereby preventing the development of social interactions through which residents could create informal social controls and self-policing [3].

Schlomo Angel, in 1968, found that variations in the level of pedestrian and vehicular traffic could either encourage or discourage crimes [4]. Too few users provided enough potential victims but not enough potential witnesses.

Gerald Leudtke and E. Lystad found, as the result of studies in Detroit, that

> many of the features of urban form and structure… could tend to facilitate or decrease the probability of crime. Such physical features include the condition and maintenance of buildings, streets, and alleys; evidence of recent construction; mixtures of land use; rates of pedestrian traffic and pedestrian accumulation within various land uses; location of structures on an urban grid pattern; and distance to adjacent structures. Other examples are types of parking facilities; visibility into structures from roads, sidewalks and adjoining buildings; concealment by trees, shrubs, parked automobiles, fences, signs, and advertising; the visibility of entrance points; building setbacks; and, the number and arrangement of entrance points in a building [5].

In 1969, Oscar Newman and George Rand [6] developed a theory of territoriality (now referred to as *defensible space*) that held that proper physical design of housing encourages residents to extend their social control from their homes and apartments out into the surrounding common areas. In this way, they change what previously had been perceived as semipublic or public territory into private territory. Upgrading the common areas in this way results in increased social control and an interaction between physical environment and its users that reduces crime.

As Newman himself defines it,

> Defensible space is a surrogate term for the range of mechanisms—real and symbolic barriers, strongly defined areas of influence, improved opportunities for surveillance—that combine to bring an environment under the control of its residents. A defensible space is a living residential environment that can be employed by inhabitants for the enhancement of their lives, while providing security for their families, neighbors, and friends. The public areas of a multifamily residential environment devoid of defensible space can make the act of going from street to apartment equivalent to running the gauntlet. The fear and uncertainty generated by living in such an environment can slowly eat away and eventually destroy the security and sanctity of the apartment unit itself. On the other hand, by grouping dwelling units to reinforce association of mutual benefit, by delineating paths of movement, by defining areas of activity for particular users through their juxtaposition with internal living areas, and by providing for natural opportunities for visual surveillance, architects can create a clear understanding of the function of a space, who its users are and ought to be. This, in turn, can lead residents of all income levels to adopt extremely potent territorial attitudes and policing measures, which act as a strong deterrent to potential criminals [7].

A study by Reppetto [8] in Boston indicated the need to expand the CPTED process to include whole neighborhoods and provide for comprehensive data collection efforts, which would both define the nature of crime patterns and suggest appropriate countermeasures.

Reppetto was also able to show that closely knit communities do tend to protect their members through informal social controls. This finding was further emphasized by John Conklin in *The Impact of Crime*:

> A tightly knit community can minimize the problem of street crime. However, informal social control also poses a threat to the diversity of behavior that exists in a pluralistic society, even though it may curb violent crime. Still, street crime would decline if interaction among the residents of a community were more frequent, and if social bonds were stronger. A sense of responsibility for other citizens and for the community as a whole would increase individuals' willingness to report crime to the police and the likelihood of their intervention in a crime in progress. Greater willingness of community residents to report crime to the police might also obviate the need for civilian police patrols. More interaction in public places and human traffic on the sidewalks would increase surveillance of the places where people now fear to go. More intense social ties would reinforce surveillance with a willingness to take action against offenders [9].

C. Ray Jeffrey, in his classic theoretical work *Crime Prevention Through Environmental Design* [10], written before Jeffrey became aware of the works of Newman and others, proposed a threefold strategy involving not only physical design but also increased citizen participation and the more effective use of police forces. He contended that the way to prevent crime is to design the total environment in such a manner that the opportunity for crime is reduced or eliminated.

Jeffrey contends that both the physical and social characteristics of an urban area affect crime patterns. Better physical planning is a key to unlocking the potential for improved physical security and the potential for development of informal social control. He also argues for high levels of precision in the analytical stages that precede physical planning for crime reduction:

> One of the major methodological defects in ecological studies of crime rates has been the use of large units and census tract data as a basis for analysis. The usual units are rural–urban, intricacy, intercity, regional, and national differences....Such an approach is much too gross for finding the physical features associated with different types of crimes. We must look at the physical environment in terms of each building, or each room of the building, or each floor of the building. Fine-grain resolution is required in place of the usual large-scale photographs....Whenever crime rates are surveyed at a micro level of analysis, it is revealed that a small area of the city is responsible for a majority of the crimes. This fact is glossed over by gross statistical correlation analysis of census tract data, which ignore house-by-house or block-by-block variations in crime rates. For purposes of crime prevention we need data that will tell us what aspects of the urban environment are responsible for crime, such as the concentration of homicide or robbery in a very small section of the city [11].

DEFENSIBLE SPACE

Oscar Newman and others have explored and further defined the defensible space concept in recent years through design studies and experiments involving existing and new public housing projects. The following summary of defensible space techniques will give the practitioner an initial understanding of this important application of physical design to the urban residential environment.

Design for defensible space involves attempts to strengthen two basic kinds of social behavior called *territoriality* and *natural surveillance*.

Territoriality

The classic example of territoriality is "a man's home is his castle" tradition of the American single-family home and its surroundings. In this tradition, the family lays claim to its own territory and acts to protect it. This image of the home as a castle reinforces itself "by the very act of its position on an integral piece of land buffered from neighbors and the public street by intervening grounds" [12].

As the urban setting has grown, the single-family home has become, to developers, an economic liability. Family housing has moved into the row house (townhouse), apartment complex, high-rise apartment structure, and massive public housing project. Whatever the benefits of this transition, the idea of territoriality has been largely lost in the process. The result is that "most families living in an apartment building experience the space outside their apartment unit as distinctly public; in effect, they relegate responsibility for all activity outside the immediate confines of their apartment to the public authorities" [13].

As residents are forced by the physical design of their surroundings to abandon claim to any part of the outside world, the hallways, stairways, lobbies, grounds, parking lots, and streets become a kind of no-man's land in which criminals can operate almost at will. Public and private law enforcement agencies (formal controls) attempt to take up the slack, but without the essential informal social control that a well-developed social sense of territoriality brings, law enforcement can do little to reduce crime.

Natural Surveillance

The increased presence of human observers, which territoriality brings, can lead to higher levels of natural surveillance in all areas of residential space. However, the simple presence of increased numbers of potential observers is not enough, because natural surveillance, to be effective, must include an action component. The probability that an observer will act to report an observed crime or intervene in it depends on the following:

- The degree to which the observer feels that his or her personal or property rights are violated by the observed act.
- The extent to which the observer is able to identify with the victim or property under attack.
- The level of the observer's belief that his or her action can help, on the one hand, and not subject him or her to reprisals on the other.

Obviously, the probability for both observation and action is greatly improved by physical conditions, which create the highest possible levels of visibility.

Design Guidelines

Defensible space offers a series of architectural guidelines that can be used in the design of new urban residential complexes to promote both the residential group's territorial claim to its surroundings and its ability to conduct natural surveillance [14].

- **Site design** can stress the clustering of small numbers of residential units around private hallways, courtyards, and recreation areas. In these restricted zones, children can play, adults can relax, and strangers can easily be identified and questioned. Such private spaces can be created by internal and external building walls and access arrangements and by the use of perceptual barriers such as a fence, shrubbery, and other boundary markers.

- **Site interrelationships design** can be used to create semiprivate connecting and common spaces between and among the private family clusters. Walkways, vehicle access ways, parking areas, recreational facilities, lobbies, and laundry and shopping areas can be designed so that each cluster relates to them much like each resident of a cluster relates to his or her common private space. Physical design can be used to further extend the sense of territoriality and the possibility for informal social control.

- **Street design** and the design of other public spaces can be engineered to make these spaces into semipublic extensions of the residential clusters and their connectors. Closing streets to through traffic, installing benches and play areas near the streets, providing adequate lighting, and placing perceptual barriers to indicate the semipublic nature of the area can help to define these spaces as part of the shared residential group territory.

- **Surveillance-specific design** can be used in each of the design areas mentioned here to increase general visibility by providing adequate lighting, by reducing or eliminating physical barriers to visibility, and by the visibility-promoting location of key areas (e.g., entrances, lobbies, elevator waiting areas, and recreational and parking areas) so as to be directly visible from as many viewpoints as possible.

Modifying Existing Physical Design

Cost limitations prevent substantial reconstruction of most existing urban residential facilities. However, a number of relatively low-cost techniques can be used to modify existing facilities so as to promote territoriality and natural surveillance. These include the following:

- Installing adequate security devices (locks, doors, and windows) in each residential unit.

- Dividing common lawn areas (front or back) into private yards and patios through the use of shrubbery, low fences, and other perceptual barriers.
- Improving the attractiveness and semiprivacy of pathways and other common outside areas by use of decorative paving and lighting: installing benches and other seating arrangements at strategic intervals; careful landscaping; and tying play areas, parking, and vehicle access ways to the overall design.
- Reducing the number of public access points and providing the remaining points with adequate lighting, visibility, and security.
- Establishing audio and video surveillance (monitored by residents or by security staff) in strategic internal areas.

It should be emphasized, in summary, that creating defensible space is not the same as creating a hardened security system (as might be found, for example, in a high-rise luxury apartment). In fact, it is almost the opposite: Defensible space operates on the premise that the living environment must be opened up and used by residents and others, not closed in. It is only in the open, used environment that people can be stimulated to establish the self-policing condition, which is informal social control. In this open living environment, opportunities for crime may continue to exist, but the probability for criminal activity is reduced.

It should also be emphasized that the physical design component of defensible space should always be accompanied by efforts to develop and sustain active citizen participation and by strategies for improved interaction between citizens and law enforcement agencies.

CRIME PREVENTION THROUGH ENVIRONMENTAL DESIGN

CPTED is still a rapidly growing field of study and experimentation. CPTED attempts to apply physical design, citizen participation, and law enforcement strategies in a comprehensive, planned way to entire neighborhoods and major urban districts, as well as to specific urban subsystems such as public schools and transportation systems.

Cautions

Before summarizing the CPTED approach, we suggest that the practitioner views CPTED developments with a healthy skepticism, at least for the present. There are several reasons why a sense of caution is in order:

- CPTED approaches have been conclusively demonstrated.
- There is some disagreement among crime prevention theorists as to the correctness of the assumptions on which current CPTED programs are based.
- The magnitude of the typical CPTED project may be well beyond the practitioner's current ability to plan, implement, and manage.
- The cost of a typical CPTED project can represent a major financial investment, and unless the investment can be justified on a research and demonstration basis, there is no guarantee that it will be cost-effective.

Despite these cautions, it is useful for the practitioner to be aware of the principles and current applications of the CPTED concept so that he or she can watch its developments and make appropriate use of the knowledge that it may produce.

Recent Projects

In a project combining the best of current community policing techniques with the principles of CPTED the city of Manchester, New Hampshire, proved the value of this integrated approach. In Manchester, the police department formed partnerships with community organizations and provided appropriate crime prevention training, including CPTED to all of the officers assigned to the project areas. By combining the concepts of community policing with the application of CPTED and other related crime prevention strategies, the community realized remarkable reductions in several crime categories. The area encompasses three areas of public housing in which CPTED principles were applied. The changes in community perceptions about crime were measured through surveys and the crime statistics were updated frequently to give the police department the best possible data. In this enterprise community area, drug activity reduced 57%, robbery reduced 54%, burglary reduced 52%, and police calls for service dropped 20%. Additionally, the perceptions of the area's citizens were markedly improved. This example demonstrates the levels of success possible when sound policing, crime prevention, and the concepts of CPTED are combined in the correct proportions. As a result of these levels of success the project was recognized by the Department of Housing and Urban Development (HUD) through the awarding of the John J. Gunther Award. This award recognizes the best practices and was awarded in this instance in the category of suitable living environment.

Territorial Defense Strategies

Territorial defense strategies emphasize prevention of property-related crimes such as breaking and entering, auto theft, and household larceny. Within this group, there are five related strategy areas: land use planning, building grounds security, building perimeter security, building interior security, and construction standards.

- **Land use planning strategies** involve planning activities aimed at avoiding land use mixtures that have a negative impact on neighborhood security through zoning ordinances and development plan reviews.
- **Building grounds security strategies** provide the first line of defense against unauthorized entry of sites and offer social control mechanisms to prevent dangerous and destructive behavior of visitors. The emphasis is on the access control and surveillance aspects of architectural design. The target environment might be a residential street, the side of a housing complex, or alleyways behind or between business establishments.
- **Building perimeter security strategies** provide a second line of defense for protecting site occupants and property by preventing unauthorized entries of buildings. They involve physical barriers, surveillance and intrusion detection systems, and social control mechanisms.
- **Building interior security strategies** provide the third line of defense for protecting site occupants and property by preventing unauthorized access to interior spaces and valuables through physical barriers, surveillance and intrusion detection systems, and social control mechanisms.
- **Construction standards strategies** involve building security codes that require construction techniques and materials that tend to reduce crime and safety hazards. These strategies deal both with code adoption and code enforcement.

It is important to be able to effectively evaluate territorial defense strategies and consider the three types of changes.

- Type one addresses design features such as locks, lights, fences, etc.
- Type two considers the impact of the implemented design features on the legitimate users of the property. Have they been inconvenienced by the changes in physical design and are they "on board" within the risk management process?
- Type three changes deal with the direct effect of the intervening factors on crime and the indirect influence of physical design on crime [16].

Personal Defense Strategies

The second basic strategic approach focuses on the prevention of violent or street crimes such as robbery, assault, and rape and the reduction of fear associated with these crimes. Specific strategies included safe streets for people, transportation, cash off the streets, and citizen intervention.

- **Safe streets for people strategies** involve planning principles derived primarily from the CPTED concepts of surveillance and activity support. Surveillance operates to discourage potential offenders because of the apparent risk of being seen and can be improved through various design modifications of physical elements of the street environment (e.g., lighting, fencing, and landscaping). Pedestrian traffic areas can be channeled to increase their use and the number of observers through such measures as creating malls, eliminating on-street parking, and providing centralized parking areas.
- **Transportation strategies** are aimed at reducing exposure to crime by improving public transportation. For example, transit waiting stations (bus, trolley) can be located near areas of safe activity and good surveillance, or the distance between stations can be reduced, which improves accessibility to specific residences, business establishments, and other traffic-generating points.
- **Cash off the streets strategies** reduce incentives for crime by urging people not to carry unnecessary cash and provide commercial services that minimize the need to carry cash.
- **Citizen intervention**, unlike the three previous strategies, consists of strategies aimed at organizing and mobilizing residents to adopt proprietary interests and assume responsibility for the maintenance of security.

Law Enforcement Strategies

The third general approach involves police functions that support community-based prevention activities. The two major activities are police patrol and citizen–police support.

- **Police patrol strategies** focus on ways in which police deployment procedures can improve their efficiency and effectiveness in responding to calls and apprehending offenders.
- **Citizen–police support strategies** consist of police operational support activities that improve citizen–police relations and encourage citizens to cooperate with the police in preventing and reporting incidents. Essentially, community members become the "eyes and ears" of law enforcement and are force multipliers to deter crime.

Community policing requires cooperation between members of the community and the police. Community members may be individual citizens, citizen groups, business associations, and government agencies and local offices that include health departments, building inspectors, and community development offices. Community members must be involved in not only calling the police to report a crime but also helping to identify and solve other problems in the community. The most important element of community policing is problem solving, and crime is simply identified as a symptom of other problems in the community. The main focus of community policing is to deal with the underlying cause of crime and not just react to the symptoms of the problem [17].

Confidence Restoration Strategies

This fourth general strategy for commercial and residential environments involves activities that are aimed primarily at mobilizing neighborhood interest and support to implement needed CPTED changes. Without such interest and support, it is unlikely that programs of sufficient magnitude could possibly be successful, particularly in many high-crime rate neighborhoods where people have lost hope. There are two specific strategy areas: investor confidence and neighborhood identities.

- **Investor confidence strategies** promote economic investment and, therefore, social and economic vitality.
- **Neighborhood identity strategies** build community pride and foster social cohesion.

Most of these specific strategies are discussed in this and other chapters (some under different names). As a whole, this list of strategies is well organized and provides a good framework with which to view the possible interaction of a variety of crime prevention efforts.

Demonstrations

To see how these strategies were applied, let us look briefly at the major changes described in the American Architecture Foundation's presentation, *Back from the Brink: Saving America's Cities by Design* [18]. This provides examples of CPTED applications, with very little mention of crime, as applied in Portland, Oregon, and some other locales. The principles applied are sound, workable redesign strategies that accomplish the goals of CPTED without overreliance on their direct crime prevention intent. Indeed, they are not presented as crime prevention, but redevelopment efforts, which consider the quality of life above most other considerations.

The CPTED applications in the featured cities achieve the following:

- Reduce opportunities for crime and fear of crime by making streets and open areas more easily observable and by increasing activity in the neighborhood.
- Provide ways in which neighborhood residents, businesspeople, and police can work together more effectively to reduce opportunities and incentives for crime.
- Increase neighborhood identity, investor confidence, and social cohesion.

- Provide public information programs that help businesspeople and residents protect themselves from crime.
- Make the area more accessible by improving transportation services.
- Improve the effectiveness and efficiency of governmental operations.
- Encourage citizens to report crimes.

The steps taken to achieve these objectives include the following:

- Outdoor lighting, sidewalk, and landscaping improvements.
- Block watch, safe homes, and neighborhood cleanups.
- A campaign to discourage people from carrying cash.
- A major improvement and expansion of public transportation.
- Improved street lighting.
- Public transportation hubs that are purpose-built.

These improvements have enhanced the quality of life and provided an atmosphere of improvement in each of the communities featured.

The application of CPTED to school design has been promoted in a number of locations through the work of local practitioners and in cooperation with school district personnel.

Additional CPTED case studies and information may be found in the text, written by Tim Crowe, *Crime Prevention through Environmental Design: Applications of Architectural Design and Space Management Concepts* [19]. This text offers CPTED as a specific topic and is widely used by students and practitioners.

The Future of Crime Prevention Through Environmental Design

The most consistent finding in evaluations of CPTED and related projects is that the users of space must be involved in design decisions. Their involvement ensures that the designs are realistic and that the users will comply with the behavioral objectives of the plans. Numerous applications of CPTED concepts have been tried successfully on a spot basis, which tends to support the idea that the more simplistic approaches are the most viable. That is, it seems reasonable to assume that the crime prevention practitioner may confidently use CPTED strategies in very specific, controlled environmental settings.

There are many hundreds of examples of CPTED strategies in practice today. It is unfortunate that most of the successful applications have not been publicized well, since they are usually part of ongoing field activities that do not come to the attention of evaluators or government agencies. However, it has been noted that most applications center on some mixture or interaction between the three basic CPTED processes of natural surveillance, natural access control, and territoriality. The most basic common thread is the primary emphasis on naturalness—simply doing things that you already have to do but doing them a little better.

The most productive uses of CPTED, in the foreseeable future, will center on the following simplistic strategies:

- Provide clear border definition of controlled space.
- Provide clearly marked transitional zones that indicate movement from public to semipublic to private space.
- Relocate gathering areas to locations with natural surveillance and access control or to locations away from the view of would-be offenders.
- Place safe activities in unsafe locations to bring along the natural surveillance of these activities (to increase the perception of safety for normal users and risk for offenders).
- Place unsafe activities in safe spots to overcome the vulnerability of these activities with the natural surveillance and access control of the safe area.
- Redesignate the use of space to provide natural barriers to conflicting activities.

- Improve scheduling of space to allow for effective use, appropriate "critical intensity," and the temporal definition of accepted behaviors.
- Redesign or revamp space to increase the perception or reality of natural surveillance.
- Overcome distance and isolation through improved communication and design efficiencies.

The future of CPTED rests with the persons who shape public and private policy. Crime prevention practitioners will have to communicate CPTED concepts in terms that relate to the overall priorities of their organizations or communities. Productivity, profitability, and quality of life are concerns that affect policy-makers, not specifically security or crime prevention for its own sake. Accordingly, chief executives, builders, architects, planners, engineers, and developers will have to embrace CPTED design objectives. Elected officials and legislative bodies will have to be held accountable for assuring that CPTED is considered in capital improvement and development plans. Property owners and residents of neighborhoods and commercial areas need the opportunity to question planning, zoning, and traffic signalization decisions. Finally, strategic plans that encompass 20-year community development periods require an assessment of crime prevention needs and programs.

The United States federal government initiated physical design criteria to ensure appropriate protection for federal buildings and occupants after the 2001 terrorist attacks at the World Trade Center and the Pentagon and the 1995 bombing of the Murrah Federal Building in Oklahoma. These guidelines consider not only physical security, but also CPTED.

CONCLUSION

The application of environmental design concepts by the crime prevention practitioner can be as cost-effective as the design of crime risk management systems for individual place managers. Such an application must be based, however, on sound analysis of particular crime patterns and the physical and social conditions that are related to those patterns. It should stress innovative solutions that are appropriate to the particular circumstances, that are cost-effective, and that will not create more problems than they solve. It should stress working with "things as they are," rather than with "things as they ought to be."

The practitioner needs, above all, to become well acquainted with the people and organizations responsible for physical development and redevelopment in his or her community. The best opportunities for applying CPTED occur when buildings, street layouts, street lighting programs, new subdivisions, shopping centers, and housing projects are still in the planning stages, and crime prevention principles can be incorporated before construction starts. It has been proven that it is more cost efficient to design security into the planning of a project rather than to retrofit a building or space after completion. Good security design can help prevent crime. It is important to remember that the premise behind CPTED is the physical design and the use of space. It is not the typical target-hardening approach to crime prevention [20].

In keeping with the theory that the quality of the physical environment impacts human behavior, we think that crime prevention and community development go hand in hand. Physical design that enhances the environment from a balanced economic–social–political standpoint can also discourage criminal activity, and the concept of CPTED can be used in any situation—high-density urban areas, small cities and towns, and even rural areas. The essential role of the practitioner is to see the "whole picture" or a holistic approach to see to it that physical design, citizen participation, and police activities fit together. In reality, we need to get back to the basics of what it takes to have a strong community—involvement, interaction,

and partnership programs with a shared responsibility for safety.

In June 2009, ASIS International published a guideline entitled "Facilities Physical Security Measures, ASIS GDL, FPSM-2009" [21]. This publication includes CPTED along with typical physical security countermeasures as a major component in any crime prevention program. The physical design of an environment is an important element to consider and the major task of the crime prevention practitioner is to analyze existing and planned physical design, to determine how it relates to existing or potential crime patterns, and to recommend physical design countermeasures to the proper person or organization.

References

[1] Jacobs J. The death and life of great American cities. New York: Vintage Books; 1961.
[2] Rainwater L. Fear and the home-as-haven in the lower class. J Am Inst Plan January 1966:23–37.
[3] Wood E. Housing design: a social theory. New York: Citizens' Housing and Planning Counsel of New York, Inc.; 1961.
[4] Angel S. Discouraging crime through city planning. Berkeley: University of California Press; 1968.
[5] Leudtke G, Lystad E. Crime in the physical city. Final Report. LEAA Grant No. NI. 1970. p. 69–78.
[6] Newman O, Rand G. Defensible space. Published by Oscar Newman. New York Publishing: Macmillan; 1972.
[7] National Institute of Law Enforcement and Criminal Justice. Urban design, security, and crime. In: Proceedings of a seminar held April 12–13, 1972. Published by the Law Enforcement Assistance Administration (LEAA); 1972. p. 15.
[8] Reppetto TA. Residential crime. Cambridge, MA: Ballinger Publishing; 1974.
[9] Conklin J. The impact of crime. New York: Macmillan Publishing; 1975. p. 299.
[10] Jeffrey CR. Crime prevention through environmental design. Beerly Hills, CA: Sage Publications; 1971.
[11] Jeffrey CR. Behavior control techniques and criminology. In: Ecology youth development workshop. Honolulu: University of Hawaii School of Social Work; 1975.
[12] Op cit., Newman, pp. 51–52.
[13] Ibid.

[14] Ibid.

[15] Newman O. Design guidelines for creating defensible space. Washington, DC: LEAA; 1976.

[16] Robidas RL. Reports on activity in project area for the Manchester (NH) police department. 1996.

[17] Lab SP. Crime prevention: approaches, practices and evaluations. OH: Bowling Green State University; 2007. Anderson Publishing.

[18] American Architecture Foundation. Back from the brink: saving America's cities by design, videocassette. Washington, DC: American Architecture Foundation; 1996.

[19] Crowe TD. Crime prevention through environmental design: applications of architectural design and space management concepts. Stoneham, MA: Butterworth. 1991.

[20] Atlas RI. 21st century security and CPTED. Boca Raton, FL: Auerbach Publications; 2008.

[21] ASIS International. Facilities physical security measures guideline. Alexandria, VA: ASIS International; 2009. ASIS GDL, FPSM-2009.

Approaches to Physical Security*

Richard Gigliotti, Ronald Jason

This chapter discusses the theory and concepts of how to approach physical security, and the idea that the best way to approach this is to base the security level on the physical protection required to meet the need. There is also a detailed discussion of different methods of physical security, and in what situations each level would apply.

Protection of one's person and possessions is natural and universally accepted. Unfortunately, there are those who have made it their objective to deprive some of us of one or both of these. In the battle against the criminal element, our resourcefulness in designing and developing more and better methods of protecting our life, property, and livelihood has been unbounded. No system, however, can be made completely secure. Any system conceived can be defeated.

In other words, no physical protection system is 100% defeat proof. If it can be designed to eliminate most threats, it will have its weak links, for example, with a perimeter fence or an alarm system. In any event, if a system cannot fully protect against a threat, it must be at a minimum offer enough protection to delay the threat until the system can be upgraded, at least temporarily, to the point at which the threat can be defeated (e.g., the arrival of local law enforcement authorities or

on-site guard force, the implementation of contingency measures such as additional physical barriers, or the release of noxious gases).

Maximum security is a concept. Physical barriers, alarm systems, security forces, and all the other components of a security system do not individually achieve maximum security. The parts of the system cannot realize the ultimate aim unless they are combined in the right proportions.

LEVELS OF PHYSICAL SECURITY

How would one categorize a particular security system? Would one consider protection minimum, medium, or maximum, and what criteria would be used in making this determination? Would a facility be compared to a prison, nuclear reactor, department store, or the average American home? While the initial question may appear to be answered easily, arriving at an intelligent and impartial assessment becomes much more difficult simply because there are no known universally accepted standards by which the security professional may evaluate a security system.

This lack of standards often deludes responsible individuals into believing that the protection

---

*Originally from Security design for maximum protection. Boston: Butterworth-Heinemann, 2000. Updated by the editor, Elsevier, 2016.

they provide (or are paying for) is of a higher level than is actually the case. Because of the confusion and lack of cohesive opinion on the subject, this chapter considers the following five levels of security systems (also see Fig. 4.1):

Level 1: minimum security
Level 2: low-level security
Level 3: medium security
Level 4: high-level security
Level 5: maximum security

Minimum Security

Such a system would be designed to *impede* some unauthorized external activity. Unauthorized external activity is defined as originating outside

the scope of the security system and could range from simple intrusion to armed attack.

By virtue of this definition, a minimum security system would consist of simple physical barriers such as regular doors and windows equipped with ordinary locks. The average American home is the best example of a site protected by a minimum security system.

Low-Level Security

This refers to a system designed to *impede* and *detect* some unauthorized external activity. Once simple physical barriers and locks are in place, they can be supplemented with other barriers such as reinforced doors, window bars and grates, high-security locks, a simple lighting

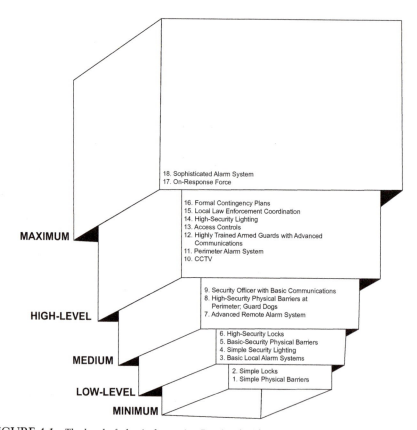

18. Sophisticated Alarm System
17. On-Response Force

16. Formal Contingency Plans
15. Local Law Enforcement Coordination
14. High-Security Lighting
13. Access Controls
12. Highly Trained Armed Guards with Advanced Communications
11. Perimeter Alarm System
10. CCTV

9. Security Officer with Basic Communications
8. High-Security Physical Barriers at Perimeter; Guard Dogs
7. Advanced Remote Alarm System

6. High-Security Locks
5. Basic-Security Physical Barriers
4. Simple Security Lighting
3. Basic Local Alarm Systems

2. Simple Locks
1. Simple Physical Barriers

MAXIMUM

HIGH-LEVEL

MEDIUM

LOW-LEVEL

MINIMUM

FIGURE 4.1   The level of physical security. *Reprinted with permission from Security Management.*

system that could be nothing more elaborate than normal lighting over doors and windows, and a basic alarm system that would be an unmonitored device at the site of the intrusion that provides detection capability and local annunciation. Small retail stores, storage warehouses, and even older police stations are examples of sites that could be protected by low-level security systems.

Medium Security

A system of this type would be designed to *impede*, *detect*, and *assess* most unauthorized external activity and some unauthorized internal activity. Such activity could range from simple shoplifting to conspiracy to commit sabotage. When a system is upgraded to the medium level, those minimum and low-level measures previously incorporated are augmented with impediment and detection capability as well as assessment capability. To reach the medium level of security, it is necessary to:

1. Incorporate an advanced intrusion alarm system that annunciates at a staffed remote location.
2. Establish a perimeter beyond the confines of the area being protected and provide high-security physical barriers such as penetration-resistant fences at least 6–8 ft high and topped with multiple strands of barbed wire or barbed tape at that perimeter, or use guard dogs in lieu of perimeter protection.
3. Use an unarmed security officer (with basic training) equipped with the means for basic communication (e.g., cell phones) to off-site agencies.

Medium-security facilities might include bonded warehouses, large industrial manufacturing plants, some large retail outlets, and National Guard armories.

High-Level Security

A system of this sort would be designed to *impede*, *detect*, and *assess* most unauthorized

external and *internal activity*. After those measures previously mentioned have been incorporated into the system, high-level security is realized with the addition of the following:

1. State-of-the-art equipment installed.
2. Security surveillance systems (CCTV) with digital state-of-the-art components and installation.
3. A perimeter alarm system, remotely monitored, at or near the high-security physical barriers.
4. High-security lighting, (LED), which at a minimum provides at least 0.05 foot-candles of light around the entire facility.
5. Highly trained armed security officers or unarmed security officers who have been screened for employment (background checks and drug tested) and who are equipped with advanced means of communications, such as dedicated cell phones, two-way radio links to police, and duress alarms.
6. Controls designed to restrict access to or within a facility to authorized personnel such as using access control and/or biometrics.
7. Formal plans prepared with the knowledge and cooperation of police dealing with their response and assistance in the event of specific contingencies at the protected site.
8. Varying degrees of coordination with local law enforcement authorities.
9. Annual assessment or security audits conducted.
10. All systems checked on a monthly basis.

Examples of high-level security sites include certain prisons, defense contractors, pharmaceutical companies, and sophisticated electronics manufacturers.

Maximum Security

Such a system is designed to *impede*, *detect*, *assess*, and *neutralize* all unauthorized *external* and *internal activity*. In addition to those measures already cited, it is characterized by the following:

1. A sophisticated, state-of-the-art alarm system too strong for defeat by a lone individual, remotely monitored in one or more protected locations, tamper indicating with a backup source of power, and access control and biometrics
2. On-site response force of highly screened and trained individuals armed 24h a day, equipped for contingency operations, and dedicated to neutralizing or containing any threat against the protected facility until the arrival of off-site assistance.

The highest level of physical security protection will be found at nuclear facilities, some prisons, certain military bases and government special research sites, and some foreign embassies.

To upgrade a security system to the next highest level, all criteria for that level must be met (see Fig. 4.1). Remember that individual criteria from a higher level can be met without upgrading the total system. For example, if a medium-security facility institutes access controls and installs a digital CCTV system, the overall level of security has not been upgraded to a high level. In reality, what results in a medium-security system with some high-level characteristics. Depending on its capabilities, a high-level system could achieve maximum security by the addition of a neutralizing capability. By using modern methods, materials, and technology, a maximum security system can be developed or an existing system upgraded.

This chapter focuses on several examples of components that could result in maximum security. When the term *maximum security* is used, it denotes the high level of physical security offered by the total system. There is a little discussion of less than high-security components, such as wooden doors, local alarm systems, and simple fences, because their presence in a maximum security environment is incidental and does not significantly contribute to the maximum security concept.

Maximum security is security in-depth—a system designed with sufficient diversity and redundancy to allow the strength of one particular component to offset the weakness of another. There is no set rule regarding the number of protective layers; again, it depends on the material being protected. As a general rule, however, the more layers, the more difficult it is to defeat the total system. For years the Nuclear Regulatory Commission has inspected nuclear facilities on a component-specific basis. Such an evaluation certainly can point out weaknesses in any component but by no means does it attest to the effectiveness of the total system. Maximum security depends on the total system not on its individual components.

The Psychology of Maximum Security

The concept of maximum security is as much psychological as it is physical. To the casual criminal, a maximum security facility is a target to be given up in favor of a minimum (or zero) security facility. To the security director, maximum security accurately describes the system of protection designed to allow him or her to go home at night with the conviction, real or imagined, that the assets entrusted for protection will still be there in the morning. To the average citizen, maximum security is a state of mind more than physical components. Plus you do not want to be a soft target.

When designing a protection system, one can capitalize on the psychological aspects of maximum security. If a system can create the appearance of impenetrability, then it has succeeded in deterring some lesser adversaries. The same principle can be seen when one compares a threat dog to an attack dog. The former has been trained to put on a show of aggression, while the latter has been trained to carry out the threat—a case of bite being worse than bark.

While the concept of maximum security may deter those not up to the challenge, it will not turn aside those who are. Whenever the value of the protected assets exceeds the degree of perceived risk, there will always be takers. For a criminal to act and, for that matter, a crime to be committed, there must be desire and opportunity; the criminal must want to commit the act and must have the opportunity. The effectiveness of the system can be measured in terms of eliminating the opportunity, and the psychology of the system can be measured in terms of eliminating the desire.

The desire to commit a crime can be eliminated or reduced in different ways. The result is that the criminal feels the risk outweighs the treasure and moves on to another target. The strongest reason for a criminal to lose desire is the threat of getting caught. The possibility of apprehending the criminal may be increased by the use of lighting for observation capabilities, barriers that delay intrusion, alarms that signal an intrusion, and a security force that can neutralize intrusion. For the maximum psychological effect to be achieved the capabilities of the protection system must be known to the criminal, that is, they must convince the criminal that the odds of getting caught are high. This can be accomplished by posting signs in and around the facility advertising its protection. The capabilities of the system should be announced, but details should be considered proprietary information and safeguarded accordingly. This is the primary reason that certain details of maximum security (e.g., communication, access controls, locks, and CCTV) are changed whenever key personnel terminate their employment. It is far simpler and cheaper to attempt to eliminate a criminal's desire than it is to eliminate the opportunity.

There are those who disagree on the value of advertising a security system's capabilities. They feel that maintaining a low profile somehow contributes to the overall effectiveness of the system and that criminals will not know that an attractive target exists. This philosophy can be called the *ostrich syndrome*; it may have been true before the advent of mass media and multimedia, but it certainly is not today. A security director who plans to maintain so low a profile that a criminal will be fooled is merely risking the assets he or she has been entrusted to protect. Rather, anyone scrutinizing a protected facility, passively or actively, will understand that he or she will have to plan carefully and more than likely enlist additional help.

It is important, therefore, that consideration be given to the psychological aspects of maximum security when designing or maintaining a system. An implied presence can do wonders in dissuading criminals from targeting a facility.

THE VALUE OF PLANNING

When setting up a maximum security system, the best results come from a careful and detailed plan. Two basic questions must first be answered:

1. What is being protected? What assets?
2. How important is it? (This is measured in terms of political and economic impact, corporate commitment to its protection, and health and safety of the public.)

A third question is sometimes asked: Do the costs of protecting it outweigh its value? This may be a consideration when planning for a security system less than maximum, but it is tacitly implied that something calling for maximum security is worth the cost to someone. Once these questions have been answered, planning can commence.

One of the best approaches to take is to list the basic prerequisites of the security system. As was previously stated, maximum security is designed to impede, detect, assess, and neutralize all unauthorized external and internal activity. Under each prerequisite are listed those components that would accomplish these tasks. If the system includes a capability to neutralize, this is stated and provided for accordingly:

- Security force
- Response force
- Coordination and partnership with local law enforcement authorities and fire departments

Next, decide which components are going to be used to impede (Table 4.1), detect (Table 4.2), assess (Table 4.3), and (if necessary) neutralize (Table 4.4).

Once it is decided which components will be used to make up the maximum security system, attention should be directed to developing a design-reference threat.

TABLE 4.1   Components to Impede

Physical Barriers	Locks
Perimeter fence	Perimeter fence
High-security doors	Openings
High-security windows	Designated doors
Vault	

Security force	Access controls
Manning levels	Protected areas
Training	Vital areas
	Equipment

TABLE 4.2   Components to Detect

Alarm Systems
Doors
Perimeter
Protected areas
Vital areas

TABLE 4.3   Components to Assess

Lighting	Communications	CCTV
Perimeter	On-site	Perimeter
Protected areas	Off-site	Protected areas
Vital areas		Vital areas

TABLE 4.4   Components to Neutralize

Security Force	Response Force	LLEA Coordination
Manning levels	Manning levels	Contingency planning
Training	Training	Training drills
Equipment	Equipment	

Design-Reference Threat

The design-reference threat defines the level of threat with which the facility's physical protection system could contend (or is designed to defeat). This is a most important consideration when designing or upgrading a system and is essential for cost-effective planning.

The security director should list all possible threats and risks to a particular facility. For example, a hospital's security director might list the following as conditions or situations the system should be able to defeat:

- Emergency room coverage and emergency procedures
- Pharmacy coverage effective security application
- Disorderly conduct of patience's
- Internal theft or diversion
- Assaults on employees/doctors or visitors inside and outside
- Armed attack on facility or guns inside the complex
- Burglary and theft
- Robbery, theft of drugs
- Kidnapping, rape
- Auto theft from parking lot
- Hostage incident
- Infant kidnapping
- Biohazardous and radiological waste storage
- Power loss and backup system
- Violent storms and bad weather

The next step is to evaluate these threats in descending order of credibility, that is, which threats are the most credible based on past experience, loss rates, crime statistics, and so on. The hospital in this example could list, going from the most credible to the least, the following:

1. Internal theft or diversion
2. Auto theft from parking lot
3. Disorderly conduct
4. Assaults on employees or visitors on property
5. Burglary
6. Robbery
7. Hostage incident
8. Kidnapping
9. Armed attack
10. Workplace violence

In this example, internal theft or diversion is considered a very real possibility (probably based on past experience) followed by theft of automobiles from the hospital's parking lot. Although possible, the threat of armed attack carries low credibility; therefore, it is of far less concern when deciding on the design of and money to be invested in the security system. Once the credible, realistic threats have been identified and given higher priority, this information can be used to arrive at the design-reference threat.

The types of adversaries that would likely encounter the security system is another area of consideration when determining the design-reference threat. The Nuclear Regulatory Commission describes six generic categories of adversaries as follows:

1. Terrorist groups
2. Organized sophisticated criminal groups
3. Extremist protest groups
4. Disoriented persons (psychotic, neurotic)
5. Disgruntled employees or patents
6. Miscellaneous criminals

The security director should now assess these potential adversary groups in terms of likelihood of encounter, from most likely to least. The hospital's list would probably look like this:

1. Miscellaneous criminals
2. Disgruntled employees and workplace violence
3. Disoriented persons
4. Organized sophisticated criminal groups
5. Extremist protest groups
6. Terrorist groups

The most likely threat group would include petty thieves from within the hospital's workforce.

Time, location, and circumstance influence the likelihood of a threat from a particular group. For example, labor disputes could lead to threats by disgruntled employees; hospitalizing an unpopular political figure could lead to threats by terrorists. In any case, extraordinary circumstances should not influence the determination of likely adversaries but should be considered during contingency planning.

Once the likely threats and adversaries have been determined, it becomes necessary to correlate the two and establish a specific design-reference threat. The process begins by comparing the most credible threats with the most likely adversaries for a particular facility (in this case, the hospital).

1. Internal theft or diversion
   a. Miscellaneous criminals
   b. Disgruntled employees
   c. Organized sophisticated criminals
2. Auto theft
   a. Miscellaneous criminals
   b. Organized sophisticated criminals
3. Disorderly conduct
   a. Disoriented persons
   b. Miscellaneous criminals
4. Assaults
   a. Miscellaneous criminals
   b. Disoriented persons
   c. Organized sophisticated criminals
5. Burglary
   a. Organized sophisticated criminals
   b. Miscellaneous criminals

6. Robbery
   a. Disoriented persons
   b. Miscellaneous criminals
7. Hostage incidents
   a. Disoriented persons
   b. Miscellaneous criminals
   c. Disgruntled employees
   d. Extremist protesters
8. Kidnapping
   a. Organized sophisticated criminals
   b. Terrorists
   c. Extremist protesters
   d. Miscellaneous criminals
9. Armed attack
   a. Terrorists
   b. Extremist protesters/disgruntled employees
   c. Workplace violence

There is always overlap among adversary groups, and this fact must be kept in mind when preparing a threat-versus-adversary analysis. In the example here, the hospital's security director has defined the primary threat to the facility as internal theft or diversion and the most likely adversaries in this area as miscellaneous criminals followed by disgruntled employees and organized sophisticated criminals. The protection system must be designed or upgraded to counter the most real threat. The most worthy adversary, however, appears to be an organized sophisticated criminal, probably because of the hospital's drug supply. Although the least likely adversary in this threat, this is the most capable (in terms of desire, resources, and capability); therefore, the system must be designed to defeat him or her. At the same time, adversaries of lesser capability will also be defeated. A very simple analogy illustrates this principle: A screened door, if properly installed, keeps out flies; it also keeps out wasps, butterflies, and birds.

Continuing the process of determining the adversary most capable of carrying out the most credible threats, the hospital's security director probably comes up with the following results:

1. Internal theft—organized sophisticated criminals
2. Auto theft—organized sophisticated criminals
3. Disorderly conduct—disoriented persons
4. Assaults—organized sophisticated criminals
5. Burglary—organized sophisticated criminals
6. Robbery—miscellaneous criminals
7. Hostage incident—terrorists
8. Kidnapping—terrorists
9. Armed attack—terrorists
10. Workplace violence

Planning a system to address a realistic security concern as well as the adversary most capable of causing that concern allows the system's architect to prepare for the worst possible case and least capable adversary alike.

Establishing the design-reference threat, therefore, is contingent on determining the groups to which the specific threats or adversaries belong:

- Internal theft (crimes against property)
- Auto
- Burglary
- Violent conduct (crimes against persons)
- Robbery armed
- Disorderly conduct
- Assaults/Rape
- Hostage incidents
- Kidnapping
- Armed attack

On this basis, the hospital's security director knows where to channel resources and the degree of protection needed. Since internal theft or diversion has been defined as the most credible threat, the system should be designed to counter this crime as it would be perpetrated by an organized sophisticated criminal. This is where a great deal of budget money is used.

The next most credible threat is auto theft from the parking lot. Again, resources have to be directed to counter auto theft perpetrated by an organized sophisticated criminal. At the other end of the scale, an armed attack on the facility is a very remote possibility. If it were to happen, chances are the act would be perpetrated by terrorists. Since the possibility is quite low, attention and resources (and budget money) are minimal if any in this area, and they more than likely consist of contingency planning or local law enforcement coordination.

The design-reference threat and its supporting analysis become the basis for planning the measures to be instituted to preclude its occurrence or counter its effects.

EXAMPLE 4.1: A NUCLEAR FUEL CYCLE FACILITY

Determining the design-reference threat for a nuclear fuel cycle facility, for example, would follow the same process.

1. Possible threats
   a. Internal theft or diversion
   b. Armed attack
   c. Hostage incident
   d. Burglary
   e. Civil disturbance
   f. Auto theft
   g. Sabotage
   h. Employee pilferage
   i. Kidnapping
   j. Robbery
   k. Assaults
2. Credible threats (most to least)
   a. Internal theft or diversion of nuclear material
   b. Sabotage (including threats)
   c. Armed attack (as a prelude to other action)
   d. Civil disturbance (including antinuclear demonstrations)
   e. Employee pilferage (of non-nuclear material)
   f. Assaults
   g. Auto theft (from parking lot)
   h. Kidnapping
   i. Hostage incident
   j. Burglary
   h. Robbery

3. Potential adversaries (most to least)
   a. Terrorist groups
   b. Disoriented persons
   c. Disgruntled employees
   d. Extremists or protesters
   e. Miscellaneous criminals
   f. Organized sophisticated criminals
4. Matchup of threats and adversaries
   a. Internal theft or diversion
      i   Disgruntled employees
      ii Disoriented persons
      iii Terrorists
   b. Sabotage
      i   Terrorists
      ii Disoriented persons
      iii Disgruntled employees
   c. Armed attack
      i   Terrorists
   d. Civil disturbance
      i   Extremists or protesters
   e. Pilferage
      i   Miscellaneous criminals
   f. Assaults
      i   Disoriented persons
   g. Auto theft
      i   Miscellaneous criminals
   h. Kidnapping
      i   Terrorists
      ii Disoriented persons

Continued

EXAMPLE 4.1: A NUCLEAR FUEL CYCLE FACILITY—*(cont'd)*

i. Hostage incident
  i   Terrorists
  ii   Disoriented persons
  iii Disgruntled employees
j. Burglary
  i   Miscellaneous criminals
k. Robbery
  i   Miscellaneous criminals
l. Most credible threat—most capable adversary
  i   Internal theft or diversion—terrorists
  ii   Sabotage—terrorists
  iii Armed attack—terrorists
  iv   Civil disturbance—extremists or protesters
  v   Pilferage—disgruntled employees
  vi   Assault—disoriented persons
  vii Auto theft—miscellaneous criminals
  viii Kidnapping—terrorists
  ix   Hostage incident—terrorists
  x   Burglary—miscellaneous criminals
  xi   Robbery—miscellaneous criminals
5. Basic generic threats
  a. Theft
    i   Internal and external
    ii   Pilferage
    iii Auto
    iv   Burglary
  b. Violence
    i   Sabotage
    ii   Armed attack
    iii Civil disturbance
    iv   Assault
    v   Kidnapping
    vi   Hostage incident
    vii Robbery

We can see that a nuclear fuel cycle facility's prime security concern is the theft or diversion of nuclear material. The most capable adversary (although the least likely) is a terrorist group. Although theft may be the most serious concern, other violent actions, including sabotage and armed attack, are very real possibilities. The chance of a fuel cycle facility being burglarized or robbed (in the traditional sense) is negligible due to the heavy protection provided. The security director must therefore base this system on a design-reference threat that reflects the most serious concerns. The Code of Federal Regulations requires that nuclear fuel cycle facilities "must establish and maintain…a physical protection system…designed to protect against…theft or diversion of strategic special nuclear material and radiological sabotage." The Code describes the threats the system must be able to defeat:

1. Radiological or biological sabotage. (1) A determined violent external assault, attack by stealth, or deceptive actions, of several persons with the following attributes, assistance, and equipment: (A) well trained, (B) inside assistance, which may include a knowledgeable individual who attempts to participate in a passive role, an active role, or both, (C) suitable weapons, up to and including handheld automatic weapons, equipped with silencers and having effective long-range accuracy, (D) hand-carried equipment, including incapacitating agents and explosives; (2) an internal threat of an insider, including an employee (in any position).

2. Theft or diversion of formula quantities of strategic special nuclear material. (1) A determined, violent, external assault, attack by stealth, or deceptive actions by a small group with the following attributes, assistance, and equipment: (A) well trained, (B) inside assistance, which may include a knowledgeable individual who attempts to participate in a passive role, an active role, or both, (C) suitable weapons, up to and including handheld automatic weapons, equipped with silencers and having effective long-range accuracy, (D) hand-carried equipment, including incapacitating agents and explosives, (E) the ability to operate as two or

Layering for Protection

The designer must remember the principle of security in-depth. Protection must be layered to provide diversity and redundancy (Fig. 4.2). Whenever and wherever possible, components are layered. Conduct a walk-through of the facility and likely threat routes. Start either at a point outside and work in, or start at the most sensitive point within the facility and work out.

PHYSICAL BARRIERS

Physical barriers should be checked at the area considered the most sensitive, such as the vault, cell block, tool crib, or shipping department. This area is called the objective.

1. Provide a high-security barrier around the objective.
2. Enclose a high-security barrier within another high-security barrier.
3. Surround the outer barrier with a penetration-resistant fence.
4. Establish isolation zones on either side of the penetration-resistant fence.
5. Surround the outer isolation zone with yet another penetration-resistant fence and isolation zone.
6. Establish an isolation zone on the outside of the outermost fence.

Entry and exit points should be identified and those vital to the effectiveness of the total system

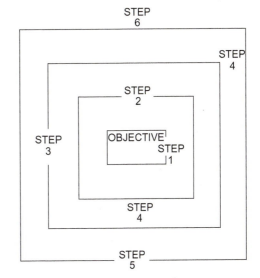

FIGURE 4.2 Layering. *Reprinted with permission from Security Management.*

determined. High-security doors and windows must be installed or upgraded where appropriate. As a general rule, if a window is not needed at a particular location, it should be eliminated. The area containing the objective should be a vault or other such strong room, depending on cost considerations and the effectiveness of the total system. It is important to evaluate the structural components of the facility, including walls, ceilings, and floors, and determine their ability to withstand a threat equivalent to the design-reference threat.

Physical barriers are not exclusively for keeping someone out. They can also be used to keep someone in.

Locks

After deciding which openings require locks (high security and otherwise), the types of locks are selected. The use of a single grand master combination for any mechanical locking system is not considered a sound security practice.

Access Controls

Protected and vital areas are designated and a decision made as to who will be admitted to the facility and who will be allowed unrestricted access within it. Generally, the protected area includes the facility and the outside area around it, up to the first penetration-resistant fence. Vital areas include the vault or strong room and could include the alarm stations, emergency generator buildings, or other areas that could be considered vital to the protection of the objective and the facility. (One must not overlook the possibility that the facility, rather than its contents, could be the target of an action.)

Security Force

Appropriate staffing levels of the security force for each shift are established with the amount of training necessary and desirable. (Some states have mandated training levels for security officers.) The force is equipped with resources to handle the design-reference threat.

Alarm Systems

A maximum security system should have a state-of-the-art perimeter alarm system capable of detecting an intrusion anywhere on the perimeter. Additionally, all vital areas should be equipped with alarms capable of detecting the presence of an intruder. All doors that contribute to the protection system should have alarms that are continuously monitored by a person in a remote location on-site. Alarm circuits should be supervised so that tampering with the system or its components causes an alarm.

Lighting

The value of lighting should be considered for impeding as well as for assessing. In deciding where security lighting should be directed, it should be kept in mind that proper placement avoids silhouetting security personnel. High-intensity glare lighting, positioned to illuminate the isolation zone outside of the protected area, is always appropriate in a maximum security environment. Also, inside areas can be illuminated to facilitate the use of state-of-the-art and digital CCTV, thus saving money on expensive low-light cameras, energy costs (LED lights) notwithstanding.

Communications

The ability to communicate on-site is of vital importance to the security force. Consider the alternatives for communications. In addition to commercial telephones, the security force should be equipped with at least one dedicated and supervised hotline to LLEAs and a two-way radio network. Each officer should have a two-way radio and the system should have at least a two-channel capability. Additionally, the facility should be able to communicate with the law enforcement by radio or cell phone.

SECURITY SURVEILLANCE SYSTEM (CCTV)

The CCTV digital cameras should be placed to ensure proper surveillance and assessment. Depending on the type and quality of equipment, the perimeter and protected and vital areas can be effectively monitored.

Response Force

If the nature of the security system requires it to neutralize a threat, attention must be directed toward establishing a response force of security personnel properly trained and equipped for that purpose. The number of personnel constituting a response force should be sufficient to counter the design-reference threat.

Law Enforcement Partnerships

When a system has been designed or upgraded to safeguard something that requires protection of this magnitude, local law enforcement authorities should be brought into the picture. It always helps to establish a liaison very early in the game. Once the cooperation is secured, it is helpful to consult with them on contingency planning to meet the design-reference threat and, if possible, schedule joint training sessions and drills to exercise the plans.

Once the process of analysis has been completed, it is time to plan the security system. It is much easier to incorporate security features when a facility is constructed. In this respect, corporate support is essential. The security director should work with the architects and contractors throughout the construction. When this is not possible and an upgrade to an existing facility is necessary, the security director more often than not becomes the chief architect of the upgrade. Whenever this happens, the value of planning as discussed becomes evident, as it is the basis for the formal security setup.

THE SECURITY OR MASTER PLAN AND COUNTERMEASURES

The security or master plan is frequently contracted out to a consultant who works with the security director. Before system implementation, it is a necessary building document; after implementation, it becomes a necessary reference document. Needless to say, the plan should be treated as proprietary, and access to it should be restricted to those who have a *need to know*.

The plan can take many forms and contain a great deal of information. In its basic sense, it is a description of the protection system and its components. Detail can be as much or as little as desired by the security director. For use as a building document, however, it should be quite detailed. Information can be deleted after implementation, but if the facility is regulated by an agency that requires safeguards, the plan may require many details. If this is the case, the document should be treated as sensitive.

The security plan should contain, but not necessarily be limited to, the following information:

1. A description of the facility and its organizational structure.
2. The security organization of the facility.
3. A discussion of the physical barriers used in the system.
4. A discussion of the alarm system used.
5. A description of access controls used to restrict access to or within the facility.
6. A discussion of security lighting at the facility.
7. A description of the communications capability.
8. A description of the security surveillance systems (CCTV) capability and its use.
9. A breakdown of the security force, its organization, training, equipment, capabilities, resources, and procedures.
10. A discussion of outside resources including law enforcement and others as appropriate.
11. Annual assessments and design and upgrade of your master plan.

Depending on the nature of the facility and its commitment to regulatory agencies, or if the security director so desires, other plans can be developed, such as contingency, training, and qualifications plans.

Justification

When it finally comes down to selling a security design or upgrade to the people who have to pay for it, the job can be made somewhat easier by following a few basic principles.

Most security directors have heard that, "Security contributes nothing to production, is an overhead item, and is a necessary evil." Dealing with the "necessary evil syndrome" has been the subject of much discussion since the business of assets protection started. Good security holds losses to a minimum and keeps down costs, resulting in increased profits. Fulfillment of the security mission can be called negative profit, compared with the positive profit generated by production. Accordingly, security management personnel must justify many, if not all, systems, expenditures, programs, personnel, approaches, and, at times, their own existence.

Most facilities cut costs for security before anything else; therefore, a planned, systematic approach is necessary to keep this practice to a minimum and secure the resources necessary for efficient security operation. Justification should be based on the following steps:

1. Convincing oneself that a proposal is justified
2. Convincing others that it is justified
3. Formulating the approach
4. Presenting the approach.

CONVINCING ONESELF THAT A PROPOSAL IS JUSTIFIED

It has been said that a good salesperson believes in the product. So, too, must the security director believe in the proposal. Before it can be justified to anyone, it has to be justified in his or her mind. In some cases, this takes only a few minutes and consists of a mental evaluation of the issue. In others, it is a lengthy, detailed examination of alternatives.

As a first step, it is necessary to define the issue—just what is wanted: personnel, equipment, policy, and so on. Then, consider the pros and cons: Do the results justify the expense? Is there a cheaper way to accomplish the same thing? Is it really necessary and what happens if it is not done? Is there enough money available to finance it?

Next, consider the benefit to the company: Will this increase profits? Not likely. Will this

reduce overhead? Possibly. Will this make the job easier? Probably.

Turnaround time must be considered, that is, the time it will take to gain a return or realize a benefit from the expenditure or approach.

The security director must rely somewhat on gut feeling. If it is felt that the proposal is logical and rational but there is a negative gut feeling, set the proposal aside and reconsider it at a later date. Circumstances could change and the whole proposal could become moot.

Convincing Others That It Is Justified

Once the proposal is sound, it has to be sold to others, who may see everything involving security printed in red ink. Generally, any money that can be saved, no matter what the percentage, a plus is when justifying a proposal. Money saved is negative profit and should be sold as such.

Before an attempt is made to convince others of the soundness of an approach, the security director must research the whole issue, investing the time and effort proportional to the expense and importance of the issue. Research is based on the company's past experience, personal experience, supporting documentation, and others' perceptions.

Company's Experience

The company may have encountered problems in this area in the past and therefore could be receptive to the idea. An existent policy could support the proposal or eliminate it from the start.

The security director should consider any adverse publicity that could result from implementation of, or failure to implement, the approach. Tarnished company image is perhaps one of the most overlooked areas of corporate concern. If a company is in the midst of a problem that threatens its image, its executives and public relations officers often go to great lengths to preserve its image; however, the inclination to spend money to counter bad press diminishes as time goes by. The tendency to prevent recurrence of an unfavorable situation diminishes as more time elapses. An idea is best promoted hard on the heels of a situation it would have prevented.

Personal Experience

A security director has probably dealt with the same issue before or is familiar with others' handling of a similar issue. Draw on previous experience to define and analyze possible short- and long-term ramifications and positive and negative results.

It is advisable to pay particular attention to idiosyncrasies that could provide necessary direction to the approach and, if possible, capitalize on them. For example, if the approving authority has a liking for gadgets and the approach calls for the use of gadgetry, this affinity could be parlayed into a successful acquisition.

Formulating the Approach

Armed with the raw data accumulated up to this point, it is necessary to adopt a strategy for communicating arguments in a convincing manner.

Formulation of the approach is based on personal knowledge and experience with the approving authority. If charts and transparencies are generally well received, they should be used; however, the amount of time spent should be in proportion to the magnitude of the project.

If personal experience shows that a concise approach is best, the security director should formulate accordingly. Decide on the format, written or verbal, and prepare for both. Consistency is important; the odds increase in favor of subsequent approvals if credibility has been established. Make a list of areas to

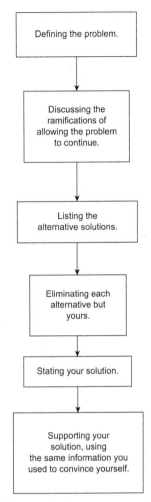

FIGURE 4.3 The justification process. *Reprinted with permission from Security Management, pp. 30–34.*

be covered by priority (Fig. 4.3). Certain basic information must be communicated regardless of the format:

1. Definition of the problem
2. Ramifications
3. Alternatives
4. Elimination of each alternative (except the one proposed)
5. The solution
6. Support for the solution

Presenting the Approach

Once the issue has been researched and an approach formulated, it must be presented. (It is always a good idea to send a memo regarding the issue beforehand.) If a formal presentation is required, it is recommended that the presentation be tested on affected individuals who should be encouraged to offer their critiques.

The first consideration in this report should be timing. Once the presentation commences, the approach should be presented as formulated and included the basic information already discussed. The security director must be concise and consistent, anticipate any questions, and be prepared to answer them. Depending on time and importance, audiovisual aids can be effective, as can handouts; it may be no more than a single-page outline, but it helps to leave something for later reference. Above all, do not oversell.

If, after this effort, the proposal is not approved and you wish to protect yourself, do so with memos to file and other such correspondence, so that if problems result from the proposal's disapproval, it can be shown that you tried.

DESIGNING SECURITY AND LAYOUT OF SITE

Designing security into a new complex should begin with interior security. Work your way out to the exterior and then to the outer perimeter. Keep in mind these points before you sit down with the architects:

1. Elimination of all but essential doors and windows.
2. Specification of fire-resistant material throughout the interior.
3. Installation of fire, intrusion, and environmental control systems.
4. Separation of shipping and receiving areas if possible.
5. Provisions for the handicapped/disabled.
6. Adequate lighting around the perimeter, before, during, and after construction.
7. Review architectural design plans and layout.
8. Site assessment/site survey planned.
9. Interior/exterior detection systems.
10. Natural surveillance and CPTED principles and strategies.
11. Security protection officers/supervision.
12. Employee awareness/policy and procedures.
13. Education of physical security programs.
14. Budget planning and five-year plan.
15. Audits/assessment/future needs.
16. The conclusion of your report should reflect every aspect of the security operation.

Deterrents

By definition—"Serving to Deter Relating to Deterrence"

Category A

- Security surveillance system used to prevent crime in private and public locations
- CPTED principles and concepts
- Defensible space principles and concepts
- Situational crime prevention principles and concepts
- Lighting that meets standards and design by increased visibility
- Biometrics and access control to specific areas
- CPTED design
- CPTED landscape principles
- Signage or visible security signs
- Padlocks and door locks and peepholes
- Intrusion alarms and signage of alarm
- Security surveillance systems (CCTV)
- Security awareness programs
- Planters and thorny bushes
- Bollards or barricades closing down streets
- Barking dog, inside or outside

- Vehicle in driveway
- Area traffic and escape route available
- Policy and procedures
- Training programs

Category B

- Security officers armed and unarmed in private function, i.e., hotel door man, bus drivers, tickets sellers or ticket takers, and conductors.
- Police officers in uniform and armed security who may deduce that a crime is about to be committed and deter the incident in their presence.
- Security officer patrolling the parking lots of hotels, hospitals, and retail locations, protecting corporate assets and customer protection.
- Guardian angels patrolling streets, neighborhoods, and subways.
- People in the area.

Crime displacement theory: by target hardening and soft target moving to another location.

CPTED Strategies

1. Natural access control
2. Natural surveillance
3. Territorial reinforcement (Crowe and Fennelly 2013)

Defensible space—This concept was developed in the public housing environment. It is similar to CPTED strategies (Crowe and Fennelly 2013).

Environmental security differs from CPTED in that it uses a broader range of crime control strategies including social management, social media, target hardening activity support, and low enforcement.

CPTED security landscape principles:

1. For natural surveillance but back bushes to a height of 3 ft.
2. Cut back the tree branches to 8 ft from the ground.

3. Chain link fence height between 6 and 8 ft plus three strands of barbed wire.
4. Height of a stone wall between 6 and 8 ft.
5. A least 10 ft of clear space both sides of the fence and wall.[1]

Situation crime prevention incorporates other crime prevention and law enforcement strategies in an effort to focus on place-specific crime problems.

Results and Objectives

- Reduce violent crime
- Reduce property crime
- Displacement of crime
- Eliminate the threats and risk
- Reduce the likelihood of more incidents
- Eliminate vulnerabilities and protect assets

Risk management defined[2] as the process by which an entity identifies its potential losses and then decides what is the best way to manage these potential losses.

- Risk: Exposure to possible loss (i.e., fire, natural disasters, product obsolescence, shrinkage, work stoppages).
- Security managers are primarily interested in crime, shrinkage, accidents, and crises.
- Risk managers generally are more focused on fire and safety issues.
- Pure risk: Risk in which there are no potential benefits to be derived (i.e., earthquake, flood).
- Dynamic risk: Risk that can produce gain or profit (i.e., theft, embezzlement).
- Possible maximum loss: Maximum loss sustained if a target is *totally destroyed*.
- Probable maximum loss: Amount of loss a target is *likely to sustain*.

[1] Broder JF. CPP risk analysis and the security survey. 3rd ed. Elsevier; 2006.

[2] Ibid

SUMMARY

This chapter was updated and reviewed in 2017 by the editor. The theory and concepts laid out apply generically across the board. The approaches to physical security are based on the physical protection required to meet the need. Through the use of the risk equation, various proposed upgrades in physical protection at a facility can be compared.

The options that give the best cost/benefit to the facility can be implemented. The risk is normalized to the consequence of loss of the asset and thus the allocation of scarce physical protection resources is appropriately applied to keep all risks at an acceptable level.

References

[1] Gigliotti RJ, Jason RC, Cogan NJ. What is your level of physical security? Secur Manag 1980:46–50.

[2] U.S. Nuclear Regulatory Commission. Generic adversary characteristics summary report. Washington, DC: The Commission; 1979.

[3] United States Code of Federal Regulation, Title 10, Part 73.1. 1982.

[4] Gigliotti RJ. The fine art of justification. Secur Manag 1980:30–4.

[5] Garcia ML. The design and evaluation of physical protection of systems. Boston: Butterworth-Heinemann; 2001.

[6] Fennelly LJ, Perry M. 150 Things You Need To Know about Physical Security. Elsevier; 2017.

Security Lighting

Joseph Nelson, CPP, Philip P. Purpura, CPP, Lawrence J. Fennelly, CPO, CSS, CHL III, CSSP-1, Gerard Honey, James F. Broder, CPP

Adequate light not only helps people recognize and avoid danger, but also in many cases deters criminals by creating in them the fear of detection, identification and apprehension. **Randy Atlas, CPP (1993).**

INTRODUCTION

In this chapter, the concept of lighting as it relates to crime and crime prevention is discussed. The two major purposes of lighting, to create a psychological deterrent to intrusion and to aid in detection, are put to the test involving natural and constructed light.

From a business perspective, lighting can be justified because it improves sales by making a business and merchandise more attractive, promotes safety and prevents lawsuits, improves employee morale and productivity, and enhances the value of real estate. From a security perspective, two major purposes of lighting are *to create a psychological deterrent to intrusion* and *to enable detection*. Good lighting is considered such an effective crime control method that the law, in many locales, requires buildings to maintain adequate lighting.

One way to analyze lighting deficiencies is to go to the building at night and study the possible methods of entry and areas where inadequate lighting aids a burglar. Before the visit, contract local police as a precaution against mistaken identity and recruit their assistance in spotting weak points in lighting.

What lighting level aids an intruder? Most people believe that, under conditions of darkness, a criminal can safely commit a crime. But this view may be faulty, in that one generally cannot work in the dark. Three possible levels of light are bright light, darkness, and dim light. *Bright light* affords an offender plenty of light to work but enables easy observation by others; it deters crime. Without light, in *darkness*, a burglar finds that he or she cannot see to jimmy a good lock, release a latch, or do whatever work is necessary to gain access. However, *dim light* provides just enough light to break and enter while hindering observation by authorities. Support for this view was shown in a study of crimes during full-moon phases when dim light was produced.

This study examined the records of 972 police shifts at three police agencies over a 2-year period to compare nine different crimes during full-moon and nonfull-moon phases. Only one crime, breaking and entering, was greater during full-moon phases. Although much case law supports lighting as an indicator of efforts to provide a safe environment, security specialists are questioning conventional wisdom about lighting. Because so much nighttime lighting goes unused, should it be reduced or turned off? Does an offender look more suspicious under a light or in the dark with a flashlight? Should greater use be made of motion-activated lighting? How would these approaches affect safety and cost-effectiveness? These questions are ripe for research.

David G. Aggleton, CPP, stated in a recent article in *Security Technology Executive* (March 2011) that "A quick rule of thumb for minimum reflected light is: (A) Detection: 0.5 fc, (B) Recognition: 1.0 fc, (C) Identification: 2.0 fc are required."

Maintenance and bulb replacement ensure high-quality lighting.

ILLUMINATION [3]

Lumens (of light output) per watt (of power input) is a measure of lamp efficiency. Initial lumens per watt data are based on the light output of lamps when new; however, light output declines with use. *Illuminance* is the intensity of light falling on a surface, measured in foot-candles (English units) or lux (metric units). The *foot-candle* (fc) is a measure of how bright the light is when it reaches 1 foot from the source. One lux equals 0.0929 fc. The light provided by direct sunlight on a clear day is about 10,000 fc, an overcast day would yield about 100 fc, and a full moon gives off about 0.01 fc. A sample of outdoor lighting illuminances recommended by the Illuminating Engineering Society of North America are as follows: self-parking area, 1 fc; attendant parking area, 0.20–0.90 fc; covered parking area, 5 fc; active pedestrian entrance, 5 fc; and building surroundings, 1 fc. It is generally recommended that gates and doors, where identification of persons and things takes place, should have at least 2 fc. An office should have a light level of about 50 fc.

Care should be exercised when studying fc. Are they horizontal or vertical? Horizontal illumination may not aid in the visibility of vertical objects such as signs and keyholes. (The preceding fc are horizontal.) The fc vary depending on the distance from the lamp and the angle. If you hold a light meter horizontally, it often gives a different reading that if you hold it vertically. Are the fc initial or maintained?

TYPES OF LAMPS [4]

The following lamps are applied outdoors:

- **Incandescent**. These are commonly found at residences. Passing electrical current through a tungsten wire that becomes white-hot produces light. These lamps produce 10–20 lumens per watt, are the least efficient and most expensive to operate, and have a short lifetime of 9000 h.
- **Halogen and quartz halogen lamps.** Incandescent bulbs filled with halogen gas (like sealed-beam auto headlights) provide about 25% better efficiency and life than ordinary incandescent bulbs.
- **Fluorescent lamps**. These pass electricity through a gas enclosed in a glass tube to produce light, yielding 40–80 lumens per watt. They create twice the light and less than half the heat of an incandescent bulb of equal wattage and cost 5–10 times as much. Fluorescent lamps do not provide high levels of light output. The lifetime is 9000–20,000 h. They are not used extensively outdoors, except for signs. Fluorescent lamps use one-fifth to one-third as much electricity as incandescent with a comparable lumen rating and last up to 20 times longer. They are cost-effective with yearly saving per bulb of $9.00–$25.00.
- **Mercury vapor lamps**. They also pass electricity through a gas. The yield is 30–60 lumens per watt and the life is about 20,000 h.

- **Metal halide lamps**. They are also of the gaseous type. The yield is 80–100 lumens per watt, and the life is about 10,000 h. They often are used at sports stadiums because they imitate daylight conditions and colors appear natural. Consequently, these lamps complement closed-circuit TV (CCTV) systems, but they are the most expensive lights to install and maintain.
- **High-pressure sodium lamps**. These are gaseous, yield about 100 lumens per watt, have a life of about 20,000 h, and are energy efficient. These lamps are often applied on streets and parking lots, and through fog are designed to allow the eyes to see more detail at greater distances. They also cause less light pollution then mercury vapor lamps.
- **Low-pressure sodium lamps**. They are gaseous, produce 150 lumens per watt, have a life of about 15,000 h, and are even more efficient than high-pressure sodium. These lamps are expensive to maintain.
- **LED (light-emitting diodes)**. LED lighting is cost-effective and should meet lighting standards and guidelines for brightness but may not serve all applications best.

These are small lights, such as Christmas bulbs and spotlights. They use very low energy consumption and are long lasting up to 50,000–80,000 h. This rapidly growing light source may be the light of the future. Currently, they are used in many applications such as in garages, street lighting, and rear taillights in motor vehicles.

- **Quartz lamps**. These lamps emit a very bright light and snap on almost as rapidly as incandescent bulbs. They are frequently used at very high wattage—1500–2000 W is not uncommon in protective systems—and they are excellent for use along the perimeter barrier and in troublesome areas.
- **Electroluminescent lights**. These lights are similar to their fluorescent cousins; however, they do not contain mercury and are more compact.

Each type of lamp has a different *color rendition index* (CRI), which is the way a lamp's output affects human perception of color. Incandescent, fluorescent, and halogen lamps provide an excellent CRI of 100%. Based on its high CRI and efficiency the preferred outdoor lamp for CCTV systems is metal halide. Mercury vapor lamps provide good color rendition but are heavy on the blue. Low-pressure sodium lamps, which are used extensively outdoors, provide poor color rendition, making things look yellow. Low-pressure sodium lamps make color unrecognizable and produce a yellow-gray color on objects. People find they produce a strange yellow haze. Claims are made that this lighting conflicts with aesthetic values and affects sleeping habits. In many instances, when people park their vehicles in a parking lot during the day and return to find their vehicle at night, they are often unable to locate it because of poor color rendition from sodium lamps; some even report their vehicles as stolen. Another problem is the inability of witnesses to describe offenders accurately.

Mercury vapor, metal halide, and high-pressure sodium take several minutes to produce full light output. If they are turned off, even more time is required to reach full output because they first have to cool down. This may not be acceptable for certain security applications. Incandescent, halogen, and quartz halogen have the advantage of instant light once the electricity is turned on. Manufacturers can provide information on a host of lamp characteristics including the "strike" and "restrike" time.

The following sources provide additional information on lighting:

- National Lighting Bureau (http://www.nlb.org): Publications.
- Illuminating Engineering Society of North America (http://www.iesna.org): Technical materials and services, recommended practices and standards, many members are engineers.

- International Association of Lighting Management Companies (http://www.nalmco.org): Seminars, training, and certification programs.

Cost and Return on Investment

Cost is broken down into three categories: (1) 88% energy cost, (2) 8% capital cost, and (3) maintenance cost. Return on investment (ROI) is broken down into (1) efficiency and energy savings payback, (2) reduce costs by shutting off unnecessary units, and (3) the concept of going green.

Lighting Equipment

Incandescent or gaseous discharge lamps are used in streetlights. Fresnel lights have a wide flat beam that is directed outward to protect a perimeter and glares in the faces of those approaching. A floodlight "floods" an area with a beam of light, resulting in considerable glare. Floodlights are stationary, although the light beams can be aimed to select positions. The following strategies reinforce good lighting:

1. Locate perimeter lighting to allow illumination of both sides of the barrier.
2. Direct lights down and away from a facility to create glare for an intruder. Make sure the directed lighting does not hinder observation by the patrolling officer.
3. Do not leave dark spaces between lighted areas for burglars to move in. Design lighting to permit overlapping illumination.
4. Protect the lighting system. Locate lighting inside the barrier, install protective covers over lamps, mount lamps on high poles, bury power lines, and protect switch boxes.
5. Photoelectric cells enable light to go on and off automatically in response to natural light. Manual operation is helpful as a backup.

6. Consider motion-activated lighting for external and internal areas.
7. If lighting is required in the vicinity of navigable waters, contact the U.S. Coast Guard.
8. Try not to disturb neighbors by intense lighting.
9. Maintain a supply of portable emergency lights and auxiliary power in the event of a power failure.
10. Good interior lighting also deters burglars. Locating lights over safes, expensive merchandise, and other valuables and having large clear windows (especially in retail establishments) lets passing patrol officers see in.
11. If necessary, join other business owners to petition local government to install improved street lighting.

TWENTY-FIVE THINGS YOU NEED TO KNOW ABOUT LIGHTING [7]

1. **Watts**: Measures the amount of electrical energy used.
2. **Foot-candle**: Measure of light on a surface 1 square foot in area on which one unit of light (lumen) is distributed uniformly.
3. **Lumen**: Unit of light output from a lamp.
4. **Lamp**: Term that refers to light sources that are called *bulbs*.
5. **Lux**: Measurement of illumination.
6. **Illuminare**: Intensity of light that falls on an object.
7. **Brightness**: Intensity of the sensation from light as seen by the eye.
8. **Foot-lambert**: Measure of brightness.
9. **Glare**: Excessive brightness.
10. **Luminaire**: Complete lighting unit; consists of one or more lamps joined with other parts that distribute light, protect the lamp, position or direct it, and connect it to a power source.

11. **Ballast**: Device used with fluorescent and high-intensity discharge (HID) lamps to obtain voltage and current to operate the lamps.
12. **HID**: Term used to identify four types of lamps—mercury vapor, metal halide, and high- and low-pressure sodium.
13. **Coefficient of utilization**: Ratio of the light delivered from a luminaire to a surface compared to the total light output from a lamp.
14. **Contrast**: Relationship between the brightness of an object and its immediate background.
15. **Diffuser**: Device on the bottom or sides of a luminaire to redirect or spread light from a source.
16. **Fixture**: A luminaire.
17. **Lens**: Glass or plastic shield that covers the bottom of a luminaire to control the direction and brightness of the light as it comes out of the fixture or luminaire.
18. **Louvers**: Series of baffles arranged in a geometric pattern. They shield a lamp from direct view to avoid glare.
19. **Uniform lighting**: Refers to a system of lighting that directs the light specifically on the work or job rather than on the surrounding areas.
20. **Reflector**: Device used to redirect light from a lamp.
21. **Task or work lighting**: Amount of light that falls on an object of work.
22. **Veiling reflection**: Reflection of light from an object that obscures the detail to be observed by reducing the contrast between the object and its background.
23. **Incandescent lamps**: Produce light by passing an electric current through a tungsten filament in a glass bulb. They are the least efficient type of bulb.
24. **Fluorescent lamps**: Second most common source of light. They draw an electric arc along the length of a tube. The ultraviolet light produced by the arc activates a phosphor coating on the walls of the tube, which causes light.
25. **HID lamps**: Consist of mercury vapor, metal halide, and high- and low-pressure sodium lamps. The low-pressure sodium is the most efficient but has a very low CRI of 5.

ENERGY MANAGEMENT

The efficiency and management of lighting is becoming a high priority in commissioning new buildings and upgrading existing systems. Indeed, the subject of energy management is expected to become one of the most important considerations within the building regulation documents and has a tremendous impact on the way the construction industry looks at energy. It is apparent that serious measures must now be taken to reduce energy use and waste. This will have an impact on security lighting and the way it is applied. Lighting experts show an increasing urge to work alongside electrical contractors and installers to help them increase their business opportunities by identifying the roles and applications in which energy-efficient lighting should be installed. Electrical contractors are becoming better educated in lighting design that is effective and energy efficient.

Lighting design personnel need to

- Recognize inefficient installations.
- Appreciate the environmental, cost, and associated benefits of energy-efficient lighting schemes.
- Estimate energy cost savings and calculate the payback period.
- Recognize the situations in which expert and specialist knowledge are needed in the design of management systems.
- Think in terms of increasing business while trying to preserve the environment.

At certain points in time, it was said that lighting any system brighter was advantageous.

However, we are now seeing a trend away from large floodlights illuminating the night sky with a strong white glare, as exterior lighting is becoming much more focused on the minimum lux levels required. We are also seeing a move toward directional beams.

The lighting industry wants to remove itself from a proliferation of public and private external lighting schemes to counter the light pollution problem and become more energy and cost conscious in its makeup. There must be a mechanism to tackle the problem of countless floodlights, up lighters, spotlights, decorative installations, and an array of security lighting forms that are badly installed and specified, create light pollution, and use high energy levels.

Lighting pollution is now at the forefront of debates for two main reasons:

1. Light pollution spoils the natural effect of the night skies.
2. The greater the light pollution, the greater the power consumption.

Unfortunately, a certain degree of light pollution is needed to satisfy safety and security applications. Equally, there is always the desire to have purely decorative lighting installations, so the answer lies in a compromise. Systems must be designed with a degree of thought given to the avoidance of light pollution and energy waste. External lighting must provide minimal light pollution, a safe environment, and an attractive feature. For attractive features, we can see a greater use of fiber optic solutions with color-changing effects and lighting engineered to direct the illumination downward. Bollards or recessed ground luminaries can be set into walkways so there is no spill into the night sky. Intelligently, designed schemes can ensure that lighting is reflected only in a downward direction so that pedestrians are better guided and the lighting has a pleasing effect with little overspill.

Therefore, within the lighting industry, there is a need to raise standards in all aspects associated with light and lighting, in particular when it comes to energy management and light pollution. We need to define and harness the pleasures of lighting but at the same time promote the benefits of well-designed energy-efficient schemes among the public at large. There must also be miniaturization and increased lamp life. Energy management must therefore be a part of security lighting.

LIGHTING CHECKLIST

1. Is all of the perimeter lighted?
2. Is there a strip of light on both sides of fence?
3. Is the illumination sufficient to detect human movement easily at 100 yards?
4. Are lights checked for operation daily prior to darkness?
5. Is extra lighting available at entry points and points of possible intrusion?
6. Are lighting repairs made promptly?
7. Is the power supply for lights easily accessible (for tampering)?
8. Are lighting circuit drawings available to facilitate quick repairs?
9. Are switches and controls
   a. Protected?
   b. Weatherproof and tamper resistant?
   c. Accessible to security personnel?
   d. Inaccessible from outside the perimeter barrier?
   e. Equipped with centrally located master switch(es)?
10. Is the illumination good for guards on all routes inside the perimeter?
11. Are the materials and equipment in receiving, shipping, and storage areas adequately lighted?
12. Are bodies of water on the perimeter adequately lighted?
13. Is an auxiliary source of power available for protective lighting?

Protective Lighting Checklist

1. Is protective lighting adequate on the perimeter?
2. What type of lighting is it?
3. Is the lighting of open areas within the perimeter adequate?
4. Do shadowed areas exist?
5. Are outside storage areas adequately lighted?
6. Are inside areas adequately lighted?
7. Is the guard protected or exposed by the lighting?
8. Are gates and boundaries adequately lighted?
9. Do lights at the gates illuminate the interior of vehicles?
10. Are critical and vulnerable areas well illuminated?
11. Is protective lighting operated manually or automatically?
12. Do cones of light on the perimeter overlap?
13. Are perimeter lights wired in series?
14. Is the lighting at shipping and receiving docks or piers adequate?
15. Is the lighting in the parking lots adequate?
16. Is an auxiliary power source available with backup standby units?
17. Is the interior of buildings adequately lighted?
18. Are top secret and secret activities adequately lighted?
19. Are guards equipped with powerful flashlights?
20. How many more and what types of lights are needed to provide adequate illumination? In what locations?
21. Do security personnel report light outages?
22. How soon are burned-out lights replaced?
23. Are open areas of a campus sufficiently lighted to discourage illegal or criminal acts against pedestrians?
24. Are any areas covered with high-growing shrubs or woods where the light is insufficient?
25. Are the outsides of buildings holding valuable or critical activities or materials lighted?
26. Are interiors of hallways and entrances lighted when buildings are open at night?
27. Are areas surrounding women's dormitories well lighted? Within a college setting?
28. Are campus parking lots lighted sufficiently to discourage tampering with parked cars or other illegal activities?
29. Are areas where materials of high value are stored well lighted? Safes, libraries, bookstores, food storage areas, and so forth?
30. Lamp life versus efficiency?
31. Lamp CRI?
32. Continuous levels of light at night?
33. Provide specific levels of light for CCTV units? We are in the age of HD cameras and HD television monitors as well as low-light cameras, all of which are crime deterrents in some cases.
34. Required light for evening patrols?
35. Complex should have an even and adequate distribution of light?

Lighting Levels

By definition a foot-candle is a unit of illuminance or light falling onto a surface. It stands for the light level on a surface 1 foot from a standard candle. One foot-candle is equal to one lumen per square foot.

- 0.5 fc for perimeter of outer area
- 0.4 fc for perimeter of restricted area
- 10 fc for vehicular entrances
- 5 fc for pedestrian entrance
- 0.5–2 fc for roadways
- 0.2 fc for open years
- 0.2–5 fc for decks on open piers
- 10–20 fc for interior sensitive structures

Open parking light levels are a minimum of 0.2 fc in low-level activity areas and 2 fc in high-vehicle activity areas. If there is cash collection, the light level is a minimum of 5 fc.

- Loading docks—15 fc
- Loading docks interior—15 fc
- Shipping and receiving—5 fc
- Security gate house —25–30 fc
- Security gate house interior—30 fc

For pedestrians or normal CCTV cameras the minimum level of light for

- Detection—0.5 fc
- Recognition—1 fc
- Identification—2 fc
- Parking structures—5 fc
- Parking areas or open spaces—2 fc
- Loading docks—0.2–5 fc
- Loading dock parking areas—15–30 fc
- Piers and dock—0.2–5 fc

LIGHTING DEFINITIONS

Lumens

The quantity or flow of light emitted by a lamp is measured in lumens. For example, a typical household bulb rated at 100 W may output about 1700 lumens.

Illuminance is the concentration of light over a particular area and is measured in lux, representing the number of lumens per square meter or foot-candles. One foot-candle is equal to 10.76 lux (often approximated to a ratio of 1:10).

Note: When evaluating the amount of light needed by a particular CCTV camera (or the eye) to perceive a scene, it is the amount of light shining over the area of the lens iris (camera or eye), or its luminance, that is critical.

Reflectance

When we see an object, our eyes are sensing the light reflected from that object. If there is no light reflected from the object, we only see a silhouette in contrast to its background. If the object is illuminated by other than white light we will see the object in colors that are not true.

The color of the surface also impacts reflectance; a light surface, such as a parking lot paved in concrete, will have higher reflectance than a dark surface (a parking lot paved in asphalt or blacktop). The measure of reflectance of an object is the ratio of the quantity of light (measured in lumens) falling on it to the light reflected from it, expressed as a percentage.

Color Rendition Index

The ability of a lamp to faithfully reproduce the colors seen in an object is measured by the CRI. Security personnel need the ability to accurately describe color. It is an important aspect in the apprehension of criminals who are caught on CCTV displays and recordings. CRI is measured on a scale of 1–100. A CRI of 70–80 is considered good, above 80 is considered excellent, and 100% is considered daylight.

Corrected Color Temperature

A measure of the warmth or coolness of a light is the corrected color temperature. It has a considerable impact on mood and ambiance of the surroundings.

Lighting Systems

A lighting system consists of a number of components, all of which are important to the effectiveness of a lighting application. Following is a list of the major components and their functions:

- **Lamp (also known as a lightbulb).**
  Manufactured light source that includes the filament or an arc tube, its glass casing, and its electrical connectors. Types of lamps include incandescent and mercury vapor, which describe the types of technologies used to create the light.
- **Luminary (also known as fixture).** Complete lighting unit consisting of the lamp, its

holder, and the reflectors and diffusers used to distribute and focus the light.

- **Mounting hardware**. Examples are a wall bracket or a light pole used to fix the correct height and location of the luminary.
- **Electrical power**. Operates the lamp, ballasts, and photocells. Some lamp technologies are sensitive to reduced voltage, in particular the HID family of lamps (metal halide, mercury vapor, and high-pressure sodium).

References

[1] Purpura P. Police activity and the full moon. J Police Sci Adm 1979;7(3):350.
[2] Berube H. New notions of night light. Secur Manage 1994:29–33.
[3] National Lighting Bureau. Lighting for safety and security. Washington, DC: National Lighting Bureau; n.d. p. 1–36; Smith MS. Crime prevention through environmental design in parking facilities. Washington, DC: National Institute of Justice; 1996. p. 1–4; Bowers DM. Let there be light. Secur Manage; 1995. p. 103–111; Kunze DR, Schiefer J. An illuminating look at light. Secur Manage 1995. p. 113–116.
[4] Fischer RJ, Halibozek E, Green G. Introduction to security. 8th ed. Boston: Butterworth-Heinemann; 2008.
[5] Fennelly LJ, Perry M. 150 Things You Need To Know about Physical Security. Elsevier; 2017.

Websites

National Lighting Bureau: www.nlb.org.
Illuminating Engineering Society: www.iesna.org.
International Association of Light Management Companies: www.nalmco.org.

APPENDIX 5.A LIGHTING DESCRIPTION

TABLE 5.1 Lighting Types

Type	CRI (Color Rendition Index)	Light Color
Incandescent	100	White
		Reflects all light
Fluorescent	62	Bluish/white
		Good color rendition
Mercury vapor	15	Blue/green
		Fair color rendition
		When used as a streetlight, there will be a blue label indicating wattage
High-pressure sodium	22	Golden/white
		Poor color rendition
		When used as a streetlight, there will be a yellow label indicating wattage
Low-pressure sodium	44	Yellow
		Very low color rendition
Metal halide	65–90	Bright white
		Very high color rendition
		When used as a streetlight, there will be a white label indicating wattage
Halogen/quartz halogen	100	White
LED	95–98	White
Induction	80–100	White

TABLE 5.2   Operation Costs (10 years)

Technology	Wattage	Lamp Changes	Energy	Maintenance	Material	Operation Cost
High-pressure sodium	70	3.7	$927	$201	$73	$1201
High-pressure sodium	150	3.7	$1971	$201	$73	$2245
High-pressure sodium	250	3.7	$3154	$201	$73	$3427
High-pressure sodium	400	3.7	$4878	$201	$73	$5151
High-pressure sodium	1000	3.7	$11,563	$201	$224	$11,988
Induction	40	0	$429	$0	$0	$429
Induction	80	0	$858	$0	$0	$858
Induction	100	0	$1072	$0	$0	$1072
Induction	120	0	$1287	$0	$0	$1287
Induction	200	0	$2144	$0	$0	$2144
Metal halide (V)	150	5.8	$1971	$321	$187	$2479
Metal halide (V)	175	8.8	$2263	$482	$278	$3022
Metal halide (V)	250	8.8	$3101	$482	$280	$3863
Metal halide (V)	400	8.8	$4793	$482	$280	$5556
Metal halide (V)	1000	7.3	$11,248	$402	$365	$12,014
Metal halide (H)	150	7.8	$1971	$428	$249	$2648
Metal halide (H)	175	11.7	$2263	$642	$370	$3275
Metal halide (H)	250	11.7	$3101	$642	$374	$4117
Metal halide (H)	400	11.7	$4793	$642	$374	$5810
Metal halide (H)	1000	9.7	$11,248	$535	$487	$12,270
Low-pressure sodium	180	5.5	$2308	$301	$345	$2954
Low-pressure sodium	135	5.5	$1873	$301	$257	$2432
Low-pressure sodium	90	5.5	$1306	$301	$203	$1809
Low-pressure sodium	55	4.9	$838	$268	$161	$1267
Low-pressure sodium	35	4.9	$629	$268	$161	$1057

U.S. Energy Technologies, 2007.

6

Electronics Elements: A Detailed Discussion*

Thomas L. Norman, CPP, PSP, CSC

INTRODUCTION

This chapter includes a detailed discussion of design elements for alarm/access control systems, system servers, workstations, advanced elements, CCTV and digital video systems, wireless digital video, security communications systems, command/control and communications (C3) consoles, console guard functions, and communications systems.

ALARM/ACCESS CONTROL SYSTEMS

The basic elements of most current alarm and access control systems are discussed in the sections that follow.

Identification Devices

Identification devices include card/key/barcode[1]/radio frequency identification readers, keypads, and biometric[2] readers. Access control systems can determine your identity by what you know, by what you have, or by who you are.

The most basic types of identification (ID) readers are keypads. Basic keypads are simple 12-digit keypads that contain the numbers 0–9 and * and # signs (Fig. 6.1). The most desirable attributes of keypads are that they are simple to use and they are cheap. The most undesirable attribute of the keypad is that it is relatively easy for a bystander to read the code as it is being entered, and then you have been duplicated in the access control database (i.e., now two people know your code so now no one is sure if the person who used the code is really you). Also, the pizza delivery guy usually knows a code because there is usually someone in the organization who gives out his or her code for such things. This defeats the purpose of access control because now management has no idea who has the codes. Although shrouds for keypads are available, they are cumbersome and

---

[1] Barcode is a machine-readable array of lines that due to their spacing and line width contain a unique identity that is assigned to an asset. Barcodes can also be in the form of patterns of dots, concentric circles, and hidden in images. Barcodes are read by optical scanners called barcode readers.

[2] Biometric identification devices identify the user by some unique physical attribute, typically including fingerprints, retinas, iris patterns, hand geometry, ear patterns, and voices. Biometric algorithms can also be used to identify people by their walking gate, facial patterns, and handwriting.

*Originally from Integrated Security Systems Design. Thomas Norman: Butterworth-Heinemann, 2015. Updated by the editor, Elsevier, 2016.

FIGURE 6.1 Alarm keypad.

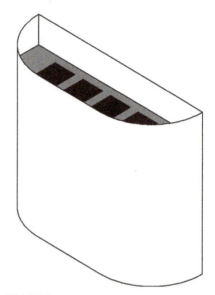

FIGURE 6.2 Early access control keypad.

FIGURE 6.3 Hirsch Scramble Pad. *Image used with permission of Hirsch Electronics, Inc.*

do not seem to be well accepted, and the pizza delivery guy still knows the code.

Two other variants are the so-called "ashtray" keypad, which conceals the code quite well (Fig. 6.2), and the Hirsch keypad, which works very well. The Hirsch keypad displays its numbers behind a flexible, transparent cover using seven-segment LED modules. Then, to confuse the guy across the room with the binoculars, it scrambles the position of the numbers so that they almost never show up in the same location on the keypad twice. This ensures that even though the guy with binoculars can see the pattern of button pressing, it will be useless because that pattern does not repeat often (Fig. 6.3). We have also found that in many organizations, there is something about the high-tech nature of the Hirsch keypad systems that seems to make its users more observant of the need not to give out the code to unauthorized people.

One step up the scale of sophistication from keypads are ID cards and card readers. Access control cards come in several variants, and there are a number of different card reader types to

FIGURE 6.4 Magnetic stripe card.

match both the card type and the environment. Common card types include the following:

- Magnetic stripe
- Wiegand wire
- Passive proximity
- Active proximity
- Implantable proximity
- Smart cards (both touch and touchless types)

Increasingly rare types include the following:

- Barcode
- Barium ferrite
- Hollerith
- Rare-earth magnet

Magnetic Stripe Cards

Magnetic stripe cards (Fig. 6.4) have a magnetic band (similar to magnetic tape) laminated to the back of the card. These were invented by the banking industry to serve automatic teller machines. Typically, there are two or three bands that are magnetized on the card. The card can contain a code (used for access control identification), the person's name, and other useful data.

Usually in access control systems, only the ID code is encoded. There are two types of magnetic stripe cards: high and low coercivity (how much magnetic energy is charged into the magnetic stripe). Bank cards are low coercivity (300 Oersted) and most early access control cards were high coercivity (2750 or 4000 Oersted). However, as clients began to complain that their bank cards failed to work after being in a wallet next to their access card, many manufacturers switched to low coercivity for access cards as well. Magnetic stripe cards are desirable attributes that they are easy to use and inexpensive. Undesirable attributes are that they are easy to duplicate and thus not suitable for use in any secure facility.

Wiegand Cards/Keys

The Wiegand effect is named after its discoverer, John R. Wiegand. This effect occurs when a specially made wire is moved past a magnetic field, causing it to emit a very fast magnetic pulse in response (10 µs) to the magnetic field. Wiegand wires are placed into cards and keys in a pattern of north/south such that they create ones and zeros when read by a Wiegand card/key reader. In the early days of access

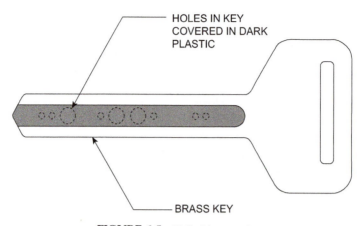

FIGURE 6.5   Hollerith access key.

control, a wiring protocol was established to accommodate Wiegand effect readers called the Wiegand wiring scheme for card readers. Today, manufacturers refer to their proximity card readers to be wired with this Wiegand wire interface.

Barcode Cards

Barcode cards use any of several barcode schemes, the most common of which is a conventional series of lines of varying thicknesses. Barcodes are available in visible and infrared types. The visible type looks similar to the UBC barcode on food articles. Infrared barcodes are invisible to the naked eye but can be read by a barcode reader that is sensitive to infrared light. The problem is that either type can be easily read and thus duplicated; so barcodes are also not suitable for secure environments.

Barium Ferrite Cards

Barium ferrite cards are based on a magnetic material similar to that used in magnetic signs and refrigerator magnets. A pattern of ones and zeros is arranged inside the card, and because the material is essentially a permanent magnet, it is very robust. Barium ferrite card readers can be configured for insertion or swipe type. For swipe types, these are often in the form of an aluminum plate placed within a beveled surface. The user simply

touches the card to the aluminum surface and the card is read. Swipe and insertion barium ferrite cards and keys are almost nonexistent today, relegated only to legacy systems. The aluminum touch panel is still common in some locales.

Hollerith

The code in Hollerith cards is based on a series of punched holes. The most common kind of Hollerith card is that which is used in hotel locks. Some Hollerith cards are configured such that their hole patterns are obscured by an infrared transparent material. One brand of Hollerith is configured into a brass key (Fig. 6.5). Hollerith cards are not commonly used in secure facilities.

Rare-Earth Magnets

An extremely rare type of access credential is the rare-earth key. The rare-earth magnets are set in a pattern of four wide by eight long and each can be positioned so that north is pointing left or right, making a pattern of ones and zeros. Such keys are very difficult to duplicate and are suitable for high-security facilities, although their cost is high because each key must be handmade.

Photo Identification Elements

Access cards grant access and identification cards provide visual evidence that the bearer is authorized to be in the area. Identification badges can have many visual attributes, including a photo of the bearer, a logo of the organization (not necessarily a wise thing), the bearer's name, and a color scheme that may identify areas where the person is authorized. Sometimes, a color or code may designate if the bearer is a contractor or vendor.

To help verify the authenticity of the card, it is common to laminate a holographic overlay that provides a visual indication that the card has not been tampered with.

Some organizations use separate access cards and identification cards, but most have combined the two functions into a single credential.

Multitechnology Cards

As organizations grow, it is common for some employees to need to travel to multiple offices and facilities where different card technologies may be used. There are three solutions to this problem. One solution is to have the traveling employees carry a different card for each facility they visit. Another is to convert the entire organization's access control system to a single card standard, which can be expensive. Finally, technology can come to the rescue by creating a card that contains codes that are readable by two or more access control systems. Multitechnology cards can include magnetic stripes, Wiegand, proximity, and even smart cards all in one card. Implantable chips can provide access to very high-security facilities with an assurance that the credential has not found its way into the wrong hands.

Card Readers

Card readers have been configured in a number of different ways. Early card readers were of the insertion type (Fig. 6.6). These were prone to getting dirty and thus reading intermittently. Swipe readers came next (Fig. 6.7). These were easier to keep clean and more reliable. These mostly eliminated the problem of chewing gum and coins being inserted and were also easy to use. However, reliability was still a problem.

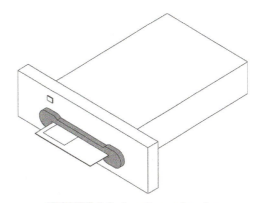

FIGURE 6.6 Insertion card reader.

Proximity card readers date back to the early 1970s, and they continue to evolve (Fig. 6.8). Reliability issues have been virtually eliminated for all but intentional abuse. Proximity card readers have been designed for many unique environments, including normal interior walls (for mounting to single-gang electrical box) (Fig. 6.9) and door frames (mullion readers) (Fig. 6.10). There are also long-range readers for use in car parks and garages so that the user does not need to roll down the car window and be exposed to the weather (Fig. 6.11).

Proximity cards and readers work by passing a handshake set of radio frequency signals (traditionally in the 60–150 kHz range). Basically, the reader is always transmitting a low power signal through one of two antennas in the card reader. When a card comes into the radio energy field, the radio frequency energy is picked up by one of two antennas on the card and is used to charge a capacitor. When the capacitor voltage reaches a critical level, it "dumps" its energy into an integrated circuit (chip) on the card, which is programmed with a unique card number.

The chip also has a radio frequency transmitter, and it transmits the unique card number through a second antenna on the card. All this occurs in milliseconds. When the card reader picks up the transmission from the card, it passes the card number to the reader input board of the access control system, where a grant/deny access decision is made based on the facility code and card number, which

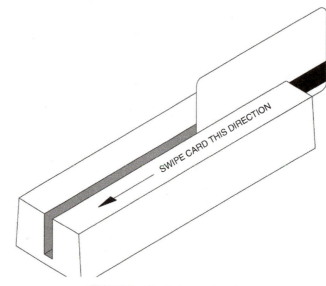

FIGURE 6.7   Swipe card reader.

FIGURE 6.8   Proximity card reader. *Image used with permission of HID Global.*

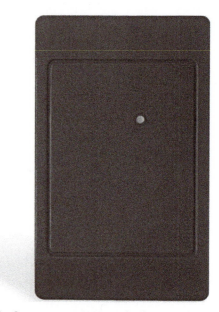

FIGURE 6.9   One-gang proximity reader. *Image used with permission of HID Global.*

together make up the unique card number code, and the day and time of presentation of the card.

Newer proximity cards and readers use smart-card technology that can also receive, store, and process information from the card reader back to the card, allowing more complicated transactions. For example, the card can be used like a credit card to purchase food in a vending machine or gas at a gas pump. The card can store a history of transactions, such as where the user has gone and with what readers he or she has interacted. Some transactions may be unknown to the user such that it is possible to

FIGURE 6.12 VeriChip implantable access control credential. *Used with permission from VeriChip Corporation.*

FIGURE 6.10 Mullion proximity reader. *Image used with permission of HID Global.*

FIGURE 6.11 Long-range proximity reader. *Image used with permission of HID Global.*

track a user's position in a facility at any given time or for other special purposes. One exotic access control credential is the implantable chip. Only slightly larger than a grain of rice, the chip can be implanted in a user's arm and can provide access to high-security areas. These chips have been implanted in agricultural animals and pets for many years to help track an animal's health and locate its owner when lost. It is the closest thing to biometrics (Fig. 6.12).

TWIC Cards

The U.S. Transportation Security Agency (TSA) has implemented the Transportation Worker Identification Credential (TWIC) program. The TWIC card can be used for all personnel who require unrestricted physical or computer access to TSA-controlled facilities. TWIC credentials are used at facilities that are under the jurisdiction of the Aviation and Transportation Security Act and the Maritime Transportation Security Act.

TWIC cards include a photo, biometric credential, and standard access card credentials all in a single card. TWIC positively ties the person to his or her credential and to the person's threat assessment. The credential can then be used to allow unrestricted access to the cardholder for appropriate areas of the facility. TWIC cards will help ensure that cardholders who travel from facility to facility can be recognized with a single card.

Biometric readers come in many forms, but all share the function of identifying a person by his or her unique physical attributes. Common biometric readers include fingerprint readers, hand geometry readers, iris scanners, voice recognition systems, handwriting recognition systems, and finger blood vessel pattern recognition systems.

Other Field Devices

These include electrified locks, door position switches, request-to-exit (REX) devices, and gate operators.

There are a nearly infinite number of types and applications of electrified locks. This is one of the areas that set the master designer apart from the journeyman. It pays to learn electrified locks exceptionally well because many codes stipulate how certain types of electrified locks can be applied. Also, each project has a unique set of security requirements that combined with door types, directions of travel, fire exit paths, and codes, makes for an infinite combination of lock types. There are several basic types of locks.

Electrified Strikes

Electrified strikes replace the conventional door strike into which a typical door latch closes. Unlike a conventional door strike, which requires that the door latch be retracted for it to open, the electric strike unlocks the door by simply folding back to release the door latch as the user pulls the door open. It springs back instantly as the door latch clears the strike so that it is ready to receive the latch as the door closes again. There are many types of electric strikes, but they all operate in the same way. A few electric strikes are strong enough to be considered security devices, but most should not be relied on for high-security environments. Unfortunately, most electric strikes are not rated for their strength, which makes it difficult to determine whether one should rely on it to resist a forced attack. Any strike that does not list its physical strength should be assumed to be incapable of resisting a forced attack. One of the favorable attributes of electric strikes is that they do not draw power except when they unlock. This makes them suitable for environments in which power availability is a concern.

Electrified Mortise Locks

A mortise lock is a lock that is built into a routed pocked or "mortise" in the door. These locks are very strong because the lock is sizable relative to the latch and dead bolt and the lock is effectively part of the door, so it is essentially as strong as the door. When a mortise lock is placed in either a solid-core door or a hollow metal door, it is placed into a hollow metal frame. The result is a very strong door and lock. Mortise locks are available in different configurations, the most common being office and storeroom types. The office lock is equipped with only a latch bolt, and the storeroom type is equipped with both a latch bolt and a dead bolt. Electrified mortise locks are simply normal mortise locks in which the latch bolt has been attached to a solenoid within the lock body so that upon triggering the solenoid the latch bolt retracts, unlocking the door. There are a few electrified storeroom mortise locks, but most are of the office type.

Magnetic Locks

Often considered the staple of electrified locks, the magnetic lock is little more than just an electromagnet attached to a door frame, and there is an armature attached to the door. When the electromagnet is energized and the armature on the door is against the lock, the lock engages. These are typically very strong locks, usually having 800–1500 lbs. of holding force. This lock is sometimes stronger than the door to which it is attached. Magnetic locks should be used with a redundant means of unlocking to ensure that a person inside the locked area can always exit. A "push to exit" button or crash bar that interrupts power to the magnetic lock is always advised.

Electrified Panic Hardware

Where a door is located in the path of egress, panic hardware is often used, depending on the occupancy rating. Panic hardware is required on any door where there could be a large number of people needing exit in an emergency. Panic hardware is easily identified by the push bar (formerly called a crash bar) that the users press as they push through the door. Panic hardware facilitates a single exit motion because users have only to push on the door as they are moving through it. This facilitates the rapid exit of large numbers of people because no one has to wait behind anyone else while they stop to turn a door handle. In a severe emergency such as a fire, such momentary delays can compound to cause a crush of people behind a door that is unlocked but that can become a barrier if someone has difficulty with the door handle. There are several basic types of panic hardware configurations, depending on the requirements of the door to which the panic hardware is mounted. Panic hardware is electrified by one of several methods, usually involving a solenoid that releases a latch on the door.

Specialty Locks

Most people pay little attention to doors and locks; they just use them. However, there are a remarkable number of variations of doors, frames, locks, and electrification methods. Some unusual locks have been developed for special needs.

Switches

Door and gate position switches (DPSs) sense if the door or gate is opened or closed. A variant of the DPS is the monitor strike, which determines if the door is not only closed but also whether a latch bolt or dead bolt is in fact engaged. The typical DPS is composed of a magnetically sensitive switch and a magnet placed close to the switch.

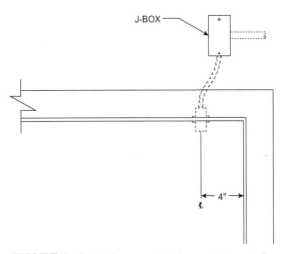

FIGURE 6.13 Surface-mounted door position switch.

Typically, the switch is placed on the door frame and the magnet is placed on the door or gate. When the door or gate is opened, the switch also opens, sending a signal to the alarm system. Variants of DPSs include surface and concealed mounting versions (Figs. 6.13 and 6.14), wide- and narrow-gap sensing areas, and conventional or balanced bias types. Wide-gap DPSs were developed to prevent accidental triggering by nuisance conditions, such as when the wind blows against a sliding glass door.

To prevent an intruder from simply placing a magnet against the DPS while opening the door, balanced-bias switches were developed that place the switch in a closely controlled magnetic field. If another magnet is brought near the switch when the door is closed, that act alone will trigger an alarm even before the door is opened.

Other types of DPSs include plunger type, Hall effect, and mercury switches. These are sometimes used in areas where it is not possible to place a magnet in the door or gate or where a device must be alarmed if it is moved. The plunger switch alerts when the object that is pushed against it is moved. These are often mechanical switches and can be unreliable for high-security applications. Hall effect switches rely on the presence of a magnetic field within a

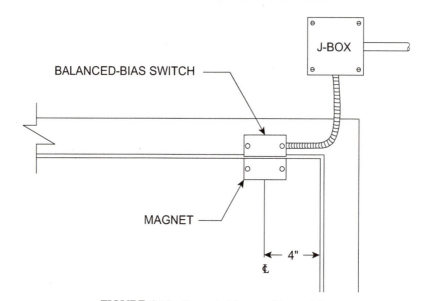

FIGURE 6.14   Concealed door position switch.

confined area to alert. They also work by moving the object. Mercury switches are sometimes placed inside an object that should not be moved in any dimension and can be made to alert to the slightest movement. These are often used with radio frequency transmitters.

Duress Switches

Duress switches are usually placed under a desk or counter to alert security if the person at the counter feels threatened. The two most common types are finger activated and foot switch activated. If the person believes he or she needs assistance, he or she can either push a shrouded button (or two buttons together to prevent false alarms) or place a toe under and lift a foot switch. Another type used in cash drawer applications is the bill trap. This type activates when the last bill in a drawer is removed, indicating a robbery.

Request-to-Exit Sensors

It is good that a security system can alert when a door is opened, but what about a DPS at a door equipped with a card reader? When a person is exiting that door legally, there must be some way to sense that the exit is not an alarm and bypass the DPS for the duration of the door opening. This is what a REX sensor does.

There are two common types of REX sensors, infrared and push switch. An infrared REX sensor is placed above the door on the secure side and constantly monitors the door handle searching for human motion. When motion is sensed in the approach area to the door, the sensor activates and thus alerts the access control electronics that the pending door opening is a legal exit, not an alarm.

The push switch type is configured either as a labeled button near the door (required in most municipalities for magnetic locks) or can be a switch that is configured into the handle of a mortise lock or the electrified panic hardware push bar. These are more intuitive.

Even when other types of REX sensors are used on magnetically locked doors, it is still important to configure a labeled "push to unlock" button near the door. This button should be wired both to the access control system electronics to signal a legal exit and to the lock through a timer to ensure that if the access control system electronics should fail, the user may still exit the door. It is not only embarrassing brutal so can be legally costly and even deadly if a user is ever trapped inside a building with no way to exit.

Door and Gate Operators

Door and gate operators are mechanical devices that automatically open and close doors and gates in response to a command. Door operators are common in public buildings and assist in the movement of large numbers of people with little effort or assist handicapped persons through the door. Gate operators are commonly used to automatically open vehicle gates in response to a command.

Door operators are often used with magnetic locks such that the access control system may both unlock and then open a door. This is common at main public and commercial building doors, and this combination is also frequently used where there is a requirement to assist the handicapped. Wherever door operators are used with magnetic locks, it is imperative to sequence the operation such that the door unlocks first and then opens. If this sequencing is not built into the design, the automatic operator may fail after a short period of time. Better door operator companies have incorporated a special circuit for this purpose, but it must be specified. I designed one of the first such interfaces for a major door operator manufacturer. Doors that are in the path of egress must be equipped with safety devices to ensure that a person can exit in an emergency with no special knowledge. This typically means that there must be a labeled push button or some other type of code-approved method of egress. Codes will always prevail on any magnetically locked door. Do not assume that a code from one city is acceptable in another. Know your codes.

Gate operators that are electrically locked must also be interfaced to function correctly.

Revolving Doors and Electronic Turnstiles

Revolving doors and electronic turnstiles are sometimes used to provide a positive access control. That is, each person must enter and leave using an access credential, and only one person may transit the portal at a time for accountability purposes.

Revolving doors (Fig. 6.15) can be equipped with a special operator that will allow only one person at a time through a rotating (X) pane. Like door operators, revolving doors can be locked between uses, but even when unlocked, they can be controlled by the operator so that only one rotation is permitted. Early revolving door operators were sometimes problematic. However, modern operators by major manufacturers are well developed, and most work well. It is wise to coordinate directly with the manufacturer of the revolving door operator to achieve the desired functions. These may include the following:

- Card reader controlled
- Remote bypass from a security console
- Autoreverse if two or more people enter on one card use
- Autoreverse if an unauthorized person attempts to use the door at the same time as an authorized user but from the opposite side of the revolving door
- Audio alert of improper use with instructions

Such doors are also available with status alerts on alarm, on reverse, with user count, and other options.

Revolving doors for access control should be configured to the "X" rather than "+" configuration when waiting for next use.

Electronic turnstiles (Fig. 6.16) are similar to the old-fashioned turnstiles used at subways and ballparks, except that the rotating member is replaced by an infrared photo beam that detects when someone passes through. There is also a type of electronic turnstile that uses paddle arms or glass wings to act as a physical barrier. These devices

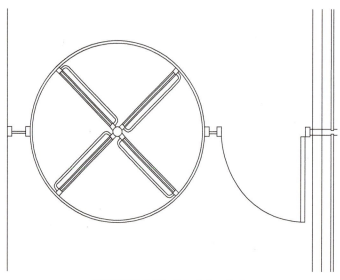

FIGURE 6.15   Revolving door.

FIGURE 6.16   Electronic turnstiles with paddle barriers.

are designed to control access to a commercial or government building with a high degree of speed (throughput) and elegance. Electronic turnstiles must be used with an access control system that can deliver speedy card executions to be accepted by the users. As for revolving doors, the designer should coordinate the specifications carefully with the turnstile manufacturer.

Electronic Processing Components

Electronic processing components include reader interface boards, alarm input boards, output relay boards, and controllers. Every alarm and access control system made today uses some form of controller between the workstations/servers and the field devices (Fig. 6.17).

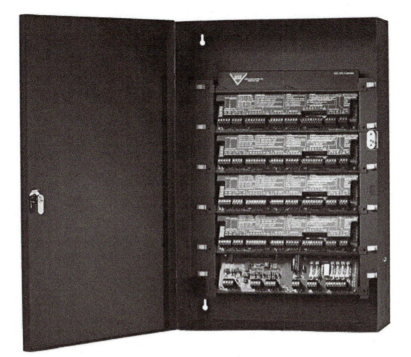

FIGURE 6.17 Alarm/access control panel. *Image used with permission of DSX Access Systems, Inc.*

These vary slightly from manufacturer to manufacturer, but the theme is the same. Each has three basic elements:

- A microprocessor with connectivity to the server and other controllers
- Memory
- Field device interface modules (reader interface boards, alarm input boards, and output relay boards)

The configuration may vary (some systems combine these elements together into one board, whereas in others they are components that can be distributed or wired together in one electrical box), but all systems use these same elements. However, that will change soon.

When I began writing this book in 2006, the concept of microcontrollers, which I had long proposed, was scoffed at by most in the industry. However, by the time this book was published in its first edition, at least one manufacturer was making small microcontrollers that control a single door, with some auxiliary inputs and outputs. At that time, I said that newer generations of microcontrollers will contain their own memory and microprocessor. They will fit in a small box above the door. All that has come to pass. I also said that they will eventually incorporate a mini data switch connected by Ethernet. So far that has not happened, although I understand it to be under discussion as the second edition of this book goes to press.

I said then that this design would revolutionize the industry. The alarm and access control industry has been based for years on metal bending—that is, on the sale of hardware. This is about to become a software industry. It is part of the sea change mentioned previously.

Soon, it will be possible to connect a card reader, DPS, REX, and lock, together with an intercom outstation and a video camera, into a single small electronic smart switch that will contain its own central processing unit (CPU) and memory. I have been predicting this for more than a decade, and now as the second edition goes to press, it is occurring.

SERVER (AND BUSINESS CONTINUITY SERVER)

All enterprise-class alarm and access control systems depend on servers to store and manage the master databases on which all system operations rely. Smaller systems may incorporate the server functions directly into the system's workstation. Servers operate basically two kinds of services: system operation and archiving. On simple systems, these are both contained within a single server. On larger, more complex systems, these functions may be separated into separate boxes.

On larger systems, it is common to have a backup server that duplicates the database and functions of the primary server. This second server is usually configured to take over in the event the primary server experiences some unexpected failure or planned shutdown. Smart designers place the backup server in another building or even in another state to act as a business continuity server, not just a failover server. There are two basic functions on backup servers: mirrored operation and failover operation. Mirrored backup servers are used to maintain a constant and instantaneous backup of archived data (both alarm/access control data and video image data). Failover servers wait until the primary server fails, then they take control of the system instantaneously or, in simpler systems, by having the operator switch to the failover server. These servers should be used for system operating services and for archiving where the backup server is in the same physical area as the primary server. For true business continuity servers, the backup servers should be located off-site and all archiving should be mirrored to ensure that if a catastrophic event occurs at the primary server location, no data are lost.

WORKSTATIONS

Workstations are the human interface that manage and communicate with the controllers and servers. In simple systems, one workstation may do it all—server, card programming, system programming, report printing, identification badging, and alarm monitoring. However, on enterprise-class alarm and access control systems, these functions are divided among different workstations.

On a system, I designed for a corporate headquarters of a major petrochemical company, a single building had five workstations—one for card and system programming, one to capture pictures and program data for the photo identification system, one at the main lobby desk to monitor alarms and the electronic turnstiles access, and two for alarm monitoring in the security command center. The same system used five servers in two different buildings. All these workstations and servers resided on just one campus. This system is capable of monitoring hundreds of sites in multiple countries. There can be multiple workstations at each site, resulting in dozens to hundreds of workstations.

The point is that there is no practical limit to the number of workstations in a system. Workstations can be connected directly to the server, to the Ethernet backbone, to a controller, or to the Internet using a web browser so that a security manager can make decisions remotely while on vacation or during a weekend. Enterprise-class systems provide infinite choice.

Data Infrastructure Basics

When the user presents a card to a card reader and the card reader passes that information to a controller, a decision is made to unlock the door. That information, along with alarm detection information, is transmitted along a data infrastructure to the server, and then it is distributed to appropriate workstations. The data infrastructure is the backbone of the system. In older systems, there was a unique data infrastructure for the alarm and access control system, but most modern systems have converted to an Ethernet communications protocol. Older protocols included RS-485, Protocol A, Protocol B, 20-ma current loop, and other methods. The newer Ethernet protocol supports worldwide systems architectures that can be connected in many different ways to meet the special needs of each client, each site, and each security environment. Additionally, Ethernet protocols can also communicate CCTV and voice technologies all on a single data infrastructure. Ethernet can be easily converted to fiber optics, 802.11a/b/g/n, laser, or geostationary satellite and even on SCADA systems to facilitate unique environmental requirements where normal wired infrastructures present design challenges. It would be easy to write an entire book(s) on the subject of security system data infrastructures, and it is a difficult subject to boil down to its basics. More information on this subject is presented here and in the System Commissioning section of this book.

Interfaces to Other Building Systems

Alarm and access control systems begin to perform wonders when they are interfaced to other building systems. Typical interfaces include fire alarm systems, elevators, parking control systems, lighting control systems, signage, roll-down doors, private automatic branch exchange systems, paging systems, water features, irrigation control systems, and even escalators. The primary purposes for interfacing alarm and access control systems to other building systems are to control access to things other than doors and gates, enhance safety or convenience to building users, automate building functions that would otherwise be handled manually or by numerous other systems, or insert a delay into the path of an intruder.

ADVANCED ELEMENTS

Legacy Systems Integration

One of the key challenges facing enterprise security systems designers is how to integrate the new technology into older, legacy systems. Typically, government entities and large corporations have developed their security systems in a somewhat haphazard fashion. This resulted from the fact that electronic security was initially addressed at the local level in almost all large organizations, and only later did they come to realize that there was a value to having a single standard across the entire organization. The result was that most organizations had many different types of products across various sites that were difficult to blend into a single contiguous system. To complicate this problem, the security industry has a long tradition of proprietary systems that are not based on any single standard (with the exception of CCTV systems, which had to conform to the preexisting NTSC standard). Virtually every alarm and access control system and every major security intercom system used components that could not be interchanged.

This problem was compounded by the early introduction of digital video systems that were based on proprietary compression technologies, which again ensured that the stored data could not be shared with their competitors' products. The first piece of good news is that the entire suite of enterprise security system components connects to Ethernet data infrastructures.

There are three bad news, not entirely small problems:

- Older and current alarm and access control systems still use proprietary software interfaces that in most cases are not intended to link their data with other competing systems. Manufacturers still seem to hope against all logic that their clients will gleefully abandon all installations made by other manufacturers and replace them with equipment made by them.

- Different digital CCTV manufacturers have adopted varying video compression technologies, making interfacing to a single standard difficult. Some manufacturers have even modified existing compression algorithms to become proprietary to them alone.
- As security intercom manufacturers move to digital products, they are also adopting numerous different compression protocols, again making a single platform more difficult.

Now the second piece of good news: Computers are very good at operating multiple protocols together on the same platform. This means that unless the compression protocol is truly unique, it is possible to combine multiple protocols into a single operational platform.

The third piece of good news is that some of the alarm and access control system manufacturers are beginning to make uniform interfaces to create multisystem interoperability.

The fourth piece of good news is that, in almost all cases, it is not necessary to fully interface different systems together to get them to cooperate in truly meaningful ways.

Data Versus Hardware Interfaces

Alarm and access control systems are often interfaced to other building systems, such as elevators and building automation systems. There are two ways to accomplish these interfaces. They can be realized either by exchanging data information or by handshaking with dry contacts between the two systems. There are advantages and disadvantages to both approaches.

Data interfaces have wonderful advantages. First, a single data interface (one little wire) can last a lifetime, no matter how many times the systems are expanded, adapted, and upgraded. Once the original data interface is connected and the software is interfaced, the systems can be adapted repeatedly to expand the quantity and functions of the interfaces.

Second, the single wire can control an empire. Once an interface is conducted on a network, it is global. It is not necessary to interface each and every site if the systems can communicate by a data interface.

Although data interfaces are wonderful, because they rely on software and they are vulnerable to software upgrades. When software is upgraded, it is not uncommon for software programmers to forget the little details of the last issue that almost nobody used. Nobody used it; it cannot be important enough to keep updated while we are under a tight schedule to meet the upgrade release date. We can pick that up in a patch later. Thus, the poor unsuspecting client eagerly waits for his or her new software upgrade to install it and the interface does not work anymore—instant software data interface vulnerability. There are indeed organizations that have had to reinstall obsolete software to maintain an old data interface.

Likewise, there are advantages and disadvantages to hardware interfaces. Hardware interfaces are accomplished by connecting the dry contact of a relay in one system to the input point of another system. This allows the first system to signal the second system that some condition has changed and the second system should do something about it. This simple principle is multiplied to accommodate as many individual connections as each system needs. Relays can be combined to perform logic (and, or, not, and if), and they are reliable. Once a relay interface is set up and tested, it does not matter how many times the software is updated on either system. It will always work.

The disadvantage of hardware interfaces is that they are generally site specific and they are entirely inflexible. If the system is expanded, and more interface points are needed, more relays and more inputs will be required—more expense every time there is a change or expansion. Thus, it is a trade-off. Each system requires an individual decision as to what is in the best interest of the organization.

CCTV AND DIGITAL VIDEO SYSTEMS

Evolution of Analog Video Systems

The Bookends of Time

There was once a time when video cameras were a very rare element in security systems. Any system that had even one video camera was considered the pinnacle of high technology security systems. Now security video cameras are available for under $100. In the old days, the ability to see outside the building was considered extraordinary. Today, cameras are used to determine if a particular person in a crowd of 50 is acting suspiciously without human intervention and then alert a security officer to that fact for further analysis. This kind of automation can be occurring across 1000 cameras over an entire subway system, vastly increasing the value of the security organization to the city it serves.[3]

How Analog Video Works

Television video was invented by Philo Farnsworth, who was an employee of Thomas Edison. This inventive genius worked out that if you could control the movement of a directed electronic beam against a phosphorus surface affixed to glass within a vacuum tube, you could "paint" the phosphor with a luminous line. Vary the intensity of the beam and you can make it glow brighter and darker. Cause the beam to return to its origin and shift it down a bit over and over again and you can paint a picture on the phosphorus screen. Carefully select the phosphor so that it glows for exactly the time it takes to write one complete frame and time that to be slightly faster than the persistence of the sensitivity of the human retina and you have moving images. Television—what a concept!

[3] The designer is cautioned to select intelligent video systems with great caution. Like buying a bar at retirement, the dream is often sweeter than the reality unless careful research, testing, and selection occur before the system is implemented.

The earliest security video systems hardly qualified to fit the term, having only one or two tube-type (black-and-white Vidicon) cameras, some coaxial cable, and one or two black-and-white video monitors. Vidicon's tubes and monitors required annual replacement. A huge advance in sophistication occurred when RCA invented the sequential video switcher. This handy box connected up to 16 video cameras and displayed them on two video monitors. One sequenced through all the cameras, and the second displayed one's favorite camera view.

The Branch

Then video evolution took a branch that still continues today. On one branch was the development of a device called a "quad." This device displayed four video cameras on a single screen and recorded them all on a single tape. On the other branch was an extension of the old sequencer, the video matrix switch. The video switch allowed the connection of many cameras (as few as 16 and as many as 64 in the early days) and could display them on up to four (or eight) video monitors. A keyboard gave the user the ability to program any camera to any monitor and could also sequence cameras to one or more monitors.

Videotape

It was at approximately this time that videotape recorders became useful for security projects. Prior to that, videotape recorders used reel-to-reel tape, with early recorders using 2-in. tape to record only 1h of video, and the recorders were the size of a small chest of drawers. Recorders did not become practical for any security application until RCA invented the enclosed 3/4-in. U-matic videotape cartridge. The U-matic tape recorder was the size of a piece of luggage but would record up to 2h. Soon after, Phillips invented the VHS tape recorder and the U-matic was history. The VHS tape recorder was small and could record up to 6h of video. Then in the early 1990s, a company called Robot introduced a VHS recorder that was able to record up to 24 h in combination with a totally new device, the video multiplexer.

The major problem was that at that time it was not common to break video images down, which stream at a rate of 30 frames per second, to a series of individual frames at a rate of 4 frames per second.[4] Such a device would have to be able to store one image from each camera and discard the next three.

The multiplexer was specifically made to work with the new 24-h recorder and vice versa. What was truly unique about this new pair was that it worked in a totally new way to achieve the remarkable result of 24-h recording. A Robot researcher determined that although the VHS recorder could not record a continuous stream of any video slower than 6 h, it could nonetheless record a huge number of individual frames of video if they were sequenced to the recorder in individual images. This approach resulted in its ability to record almost exactly 2 frames per second for 16 cameras. VHS recorders were designed to record a single stream of video that fed at a rate of 30 frames per second. The new multiplexer sampled a frame from each camera for every half second and fed that frame as a still image to the video recorder. Thus, the new 24-h VHS recorder stored one frame from each camera in sequence until all were recorded and then began again with the first camera. The new multiplexer passed a single frame of video from each of 16 cameras in sequence to the video recorder and then started all over again. To do this, the

multiplexer had to do something completely new. It converted the analog scanned video into a series of digitized single frames. It was then possible to store digital frames individually on tape moving much slower than one could store an analog frame. At the time, the digitization of video was a footnote to the achievement of the multiplexer. Hardly anyone took notice. However, a few of us in the industry took note and began predicting the future. I began talking about the coming digital revolution as early as 1993.

HOW DIGITAL VIDEO DIFFERS FROM ANALOG

Capturing and Displaying Analog Video

Analog video is created in a video camera by scanning an electron beam across a phosphor. The beam intensity is determined by the amount of light on each small area of the phosphor, which itself responds to the light being focused on it by a lens. That beam is then transmitted to a recording, switching, or display device. Analog switchers simply make a connection between devices by closing a relay dry contact. Recorders simply record the voltage changes of the electron beam onto tape and display devices convert the voltage back into an electron beam and aim it at another phosphorus surface, which is the display monitor that is viewed.

Capturing and Displaying Digital Video

Digital video images are captured entirely differently. Light is focused by a lens onto a digital imager. This is an integrated circuit in which the "chip" is exposed rather than covered by the plastic body of the chip, as in a normal integrated circuit. It is a little known fact that virtually all integrated circuits respond to light. Early electronic programmable read-only memory chips were in fact erased of their programming

---

[4] There were a few selected examples of "frame grabbers" that created digital images from analog video signals. A typical implementation included a circuit to select the horizontal and vertical synchronization pulses from the video signal, an analog-to-digital converting circuit, a color decoder circuit, memory to store the acquired image (frame buffer), and a data interface that the computer could use to control the acquisition of the video signal. Early frame grabbers had only enough memory to acquire and store a single frame, hence the name. Modern streaming video systems derive from this early technology.

by "flashing" them with light. This phenomenon was utilized to make an integrated circuit that comprised hundreds of thousands (today millions) of individual light-sensitive chips. When light was focused on this chip, it responded by creating a different voltage in each individual picture element (pixel) in direct proportion to the amount of light striking that particular element. A matrix was formed from the output voltages of each row and column of chips, and this lattice was then scanned to replicate the voltage of a conventional tube-type video imager. The result was the world's first digital imager. Video can be displayed in much the same way as it is gathered. The most common technologies today are liquid crystal displays (LCDs) and plasma displays for directly viewed displays and digital light processor (DLP) devices for projected video. All of these are variations of the same basic concept. A semitransparent color pixel (blue, green, red) is arrayed in front of an illuminator. The video image is fed to the display and the pixels do their job, displaying the video images. LCDs have become the de facto standard for smaller displays, and both plasma displays and LCDs are common for large screens. DLP projectors accommodate most displays over 60 in. diagonal, except for video walls, which are composed by grouping arrays of LCD, plasma, or projected video box displays.

Archiving Analog and Digital Video

Analog video is transmitted as a fluctuating voltage with codes embedded for color, hue, and gamma. This fluctuating voltage is processed and fed to a recording head. The basic analog recording head for video works on the same principle as an analog audiotape recorder; that is, current is fed to a specially formed electromagnet, which is formed to present a smooth surface to the tape that is being swept across the head by a pair of rotating reels. The electromagnet has a very tiny gap, across which a magnetic flux is developed in response to the fluctuating current. As the tape is rolled across the tiny gap in the recording head, the tape is magnetized in direct proportion to the current in the electromagnetic head. To play the tape back, the same tape is moved past another playback head, and the magnetic signals recorded on the tape are converted back to electrical currents, corresponding to the originally recorded signal. Videotape differs from audiotape in that the heads are slightly tilted and spun to record a series of diagonal stripes, each corresponding to a field of a video frame (Fig. 6.18). There are two fields for each video frame, and these are interlaced such that the first field records or displays 525 stripes of video. The beam is then shifted down to an area between the first and second stripes of the first field, and then the process is

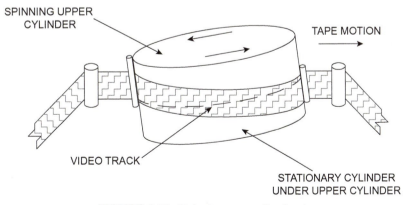

FIGURE 6.18   Helical scan recording head.

repeated for the second field of 525 stripes. When both fields are displayed together, the result is that the two fields are combined together to form a single video frame. Two fields are used because by painting the entire screen twice and by shifting the second field slightly down from the first field so that its lines lie in between the lines on the first field, the image is of higher resolution than that of just one field and they are interlaced so that the eye does not catch the time difference from the first stripe at the top of the screen to the last stripe at the bottom.

Digital video is transmitted instead by a string of data packets. Each packet is composed of ones and zeros in a designated format. The packet has a header, footer, data, and, sometimes, encryption.[5] The header has the packet address (where it comes from and where it is going, what kind of data are in the packet, how much data are in the packet, the camera identifier, date and time, and other information). The footer has information that closes the packet so that the destination device knows it has received the whole packet. Each packet of video is stored on digital disk or digital tape, and the video can be retrieved based on its time code, camera number, the alarm condition that the video is recording, or any other criteria that may have been stored in the header.

Digital Transmission Systems

Digital video packets are transmitted in either of two basic protocols: Transport Control Protocol (TCP) or User Datagram Protocol (UDP)/RDP. TCP is a one-to-one communication relationship—one sending device and other receiving device. Well, that is not entirely true.

---

[5] Encryption is a process of replacing clearly written text language (clear text) with a substitute of mixed-up characters (or even pixels of an image) so that the meaning of the text is concealed. The intended recipient will have a key to unlock the clear text from the garbled letters, numbers, or pixels so that the message can be read.

TCP packets can in fact be broadcast to many destination addresses, but it requires opening an individual one-to-one session for each destination device. Where many cameras and several monitoring stations are involved, this can consume so much of the network's resources that the entire system can freeze from data overload. For these situations, the network designer selects UDP or RDP protocols.

Digital Basics

One cannot really understand digital video without understanding digital systems. To understand digital systems, one must understand the TCP/Internet Protocol (IP), on which all digital video systems are based. Protocols are the basic language and culture of digital systems. In the beginning, there were numerous noncompeting digital protocols and languages. Each was developed by scientists and engineers for a specific purpose and application. There were two challenges: how to get computers to talk the same language regardless of the operating system or program language and how to get the signals from here to there in the physical world. These were separate problems, but both had to be solved for networks to work at all. Basically, the early data communication solutions broke down into methods that were specific to either military or academia. In fact, the military funded most early digital communication efforts, and academia began working on the problem for the military (the beginning of a long and prosperous funding relationship for academia). Soon after the first viable computer was built, at which time there existed only several computers in several universities and military research agencies, the idea of networking these computers occurred to the users. The Applied Research Programs Agency (ARPA; a branch of the US military) funded a program to develop a network that would network the various computers together. ARPANET was born. Now, early in the development of any new technology, there are competing ideas that are developed to solve the unique problems of the organization that it serves. Some of these turn out to be really good ideas, but most do not. They might have gotten the job done for the specific application, but networking requires a simple, robust way of getting many different computers to exchange communications through a common language. It is necessary to make sure that the communication has actually occurred and that only the intended recipients get the message. There were many challenges. Just getting signals across the nation was a major task because only telephone lines existed to get the job done. ARPANET did just that, along with the development of the digital modem, which converted digital pulses into audio tones and then reassembled the tones back to data at the receiving end. ARPANET later evolved into the World Wide Web.[6] At the same time that ARPANET was evolving into the World Wide Web, other scientists were struggling with how to get the signals from here to there in the physical world. Basically, three ways evolved. The first worked for point-to-point communications, connecting any two computers together, and this involved the invention of modems. The second and third ways involved connecting many computers together in a true network and two approaches developed, from which a truly rich tapestry of interconnections has evolved. The first is a ring network and the second is a line, hub, and tree family of networks. Both approaches functioned by connecting individual digital devices (nodes) onto a network. In early ring networks, a token (thus the term token ring) was passed from node to node like a baton in a relay race. Whoever has the token can talk. Everybody else gets ready to listen.[7] When the node with the token is done

dumping data on the ring, the token is passed onto the next node on the ring. It examines the data to determine if it is the addressee and, if it is, it downloads the data; otherwise, it passes it onto the next node, after adding its own message to the data. Token rings are robust because there can be no collisions of data messages on the network. They work well as long as the data being sent is relatively small. When the data movement becomes large, token rings break down under the weight of all the data, and the ring moves slower and slower as each node processes what it does not want and adds its own to the message. Remember, however, there is never a collision because only one node can be on the ring at any given time.

The other method that was developed was collision based. The earliest of these were line communication systems in which each node attached to a common communication line, such as a coaxial wire. Any node could get on the line at any time and transmit, and every node was in listen mode if it was not transmitting. The great idea of this approach was that nodes did not have to wait for a token to be passed to them to listen; they were pretty much always listening. This greatly reduced total traffic on the network. The problem was that if two nodes tried to transmit at the same time, there was a collision and no other node could hear because the data turned into noise, like a room full of people arguing where no one can be understood. This approach required a protocol that could handle the collisions. Two methods were used to handle the collisions. The first was that the single long data streams of token rings were broken down into smaller individual packets of data that would be transmitted and then reassembled at the receiving end. The second was an embedded code that told the receiving node that it had in fact received all the packets of the message to which the packet belonged. So if a message consisted of 25 packets and only 23 were received, the receiving node would call out on the network for the two missing packets,

[6]Griffiths, R. T. 11 October 2002 From ARPANET to the World Wide Web. Leiden University, Leiden, The Netherlands. Available at www.let.leidenuniv.nl/history/ivh/chap2.html.

[7]Cisco Education, available at www.cisco.com/univercd/cc/td/doc/cisintwk/ito_doc/tokenrng.html.

and the sending node would resend only those two packets. When all the packets of the message were received, the receiving node would call back to the sending node with a message that all packets had been received and that communication was over. This approach took some working out for several years until the highly robust and reliable TCP/IP protocol suite was developed and refined. Along the way, the network protocols developed virtual local area networks (VLANs), virtual private network (VPN) subnets, and even so-called supernets. In theory, there is no practical limit to the number of nodes that can be connected to a TCP/IP network. Today, we are working on IP version 6 (IPv6), which has a potential limit in the trillions of connected nodes, all communicating together on a common backbone, the Internet. After the pure line network came hub or star networks. The hub was simply a line network in which there was a single central point to which all the nodes connected. That device was called a hub. Hubs work well for a few nodes, for example, up to 256 nodes, depending on traffic. However, as the number of nodes increases, so does the number of collisions of data packets. A collision is when two data devices try to send a data packet on the same line at the same time. It is a funny thing about physics: It always works. For anyone who wondered if the data world somehow is more mysterious than the physical world, collisions prove the fact that the same rules work everywhere. As in any other kind of collision, things get broken. So when a data collision occurs, neither packet can get through intact. Neither packet gets to its destination; both must be sent again until each one is on the data bus alone to find its destination. Until then, both data devices may send the same packet repeatedly until one of them makes it, and then the other packet will have no competition for the data bus and it can find its destination too. Thus, with increasing collisions comes increasing traffic. In fact, there is a critical mass beyond which there are more requests to resend information than there can

be new information being sent. That is a system crash.

This problem can be resolved by analyzing the data traffic on a typical network, which will almost always prove that most traffic across the network does not in fact have to be sent across the entire network but only to nodes[8] that are logically (and often physically) grouped together—for example, nodes within a specific building or a campus. By limiting that kind of traffic to just the nodes within that group and making exceptions for traffic that specifically asks to go outside the group, we can vastly reduce the amount of traffic, again making more overall traffic a reality. The device that does this is a data switcher. The data switcher is capable of switching traffic only to the devices to which the data are being addressed, based on a logical group so that most traffic is unencumbered by the other traffic that does not need to go out to the overall network. Fewer connections, fewer collisions, and more traffic. So a switch is a device that determines where data go.[9] As many nodes connect together using switches, they form a local area network (LAN).

There is a higher level of restriction than that of switches. Routers can do the same job for entire buildings and a campus, making sure that traffic that does not really need to go from

---

[8] Node is a common term meaning a network drop—that is, a computer, printer, server, or other device that feeds data to/from the network.

[9] People who are learning about network architecture are often confused by the terms hub, switch, router, and firewall. A simplified but easy way to remember these is that a hub connects nodes together, a switch determines where data go, a router determines what kind of data go, and a firewall blocks malicious data traffic. These devices can be combined elegantly to construct a network that sends data exactly where and to whom it should go and denies malicious data from ever landing on the network. Modern data devices can combine the functions of switch, router, and firewall into a single device called a network gateway.

Chicago to New York stays on the Chicago campus. Routers connect individual LANs into wide area networks (WANs). Routers can even be used to create logical subnetworks (subnets) that can ensure that the security system is inaccessible on the company's administrative network. A subnet is essentially a VLAN (a network within a network). Routers are also capable of creating a VPN, which is essentially a tunnel within a network or Internet connection that shields the session from prying eyes on the network or Internet. This is useful when a remote user is compelled to use the Internet for private company work. Think of it as a wormhole through which you could operate your laptop at home as though you were actually connected by hardware directly to your network at work. This is different than an Internet session that can easily be hacked. A VPN shields the communication between your laptop and your network within a force field of encryption. VLANs and VPNs are used to facilitate communications between segments of an enterprise security system across a corporation's WAN or across the Internet.

Routers also route data not just based on its intended address but also based on what kind of data they are. For example, certain types of data can be "zipped right past" other switches and ports on the network if those ports have no need to see that kind of data. This is an important principle for security systems that we will understand better as we begin to discuss unicast and multicast data types later. Digital video systems sometimes use multicast-type data to conserve the bandwidth of the LAN. However, many devices cannot coexist with multicast data, so a router is used to ensure that those devices never see the multicast data.

Remember the ring? Did you think it was dead with line and tree networks? Oh, not so! One critical element of enterprise security systems is that they need to be reliable, redundant, and robust. By connecting a line of switches together and closing the two ends of the line,

we get a loop or ring again. By adroit switch programming, we can configure the system such that it communicates not just one way to home but both ways around the loop. Again by adroit switch and router programming, we can configure the loop so that if one switch or node is lost, for example, if the loop is cut, the others will communicate left and right from the cut in the loop so that only the node and not the entire tree is lost in the pruning. Routers and switches can be programmed so that the loop heals itself and reports the lost node so repairs can be made in a timely manner. I recommend designing all enterprise-class security systems as a dual-redundant self-healing loop wherever possible.

WIRELESS DIGITAL VIDEO

Conduit and wiring are expensive. It can represent up to 70% or more of the total cost of outdoor systems. However, conventional wisdom is that wired reliability is not possible in wireless systems. That is not so. If the goal is to replicate a dual-redundant self-healing wired loop, it is indeed possible and practical to do so at lower cost compared to that of conduit and wire. However, there are a few problems, which will be discussed here.

Wireless Approaches and Frequencies

There are usually many ways to do things, and that is certainly true for wireless video. Following is a list of the most common ways of transmitting video wirelessly:

- Laser: Although becoming more difficult to find, laser transmitters and receivers have several advantages over other methods. The system typically comprises a laser transmitter and receiver pair, with optical lenses and weatherproof enclosures. The system is normally one-directional, so it is not well suited for pan/tilt/zoom cameras that need control signals. Laser video transmitters are immune to radio frequency noise but are affected by heavy fog or rain or blowing objects (Fig. 6.19).

- Microwave: Microwave wireless systems can transmit either analog signals or data. Unlike laser and many radio systems, virtually all microwave systems require a license. Properly applied microwave systems can transport signals at considerable distances, typically up to 20 miles. Microwave systems can be bidirectional and require careful, permanent placement. Although temporary systems exist, those are usually deployed by the military, not for civilian use. Microwave systems are subject to different interference factors, including fog, rain, lightning, and other microwave signals. However, when fiber is not practical and radio frequencies are a potential problem due to other radio frequency interference, microwave is often a sure thing (Fig. 6.20).
- Radio: Most wireless video today is transmitted over radio waves. These can be either analog or digital. Radio-based wireless systems are of two types: licensed and unlicensed. It is often more reliable to use licensed systems for permanent installations because interference is less likely.
- Frequencies: The following are common frequencies for radio video transmitters/receivers:

  440 MHz (FM TV–analog)
  900 MHz (FM TV–analog and digital)
  1.2 GHz (FM TV–analog)
  2.4 GHz (FM TV–analog and 802.11 digital)
  4.9 GHz (public safety band)
  5.0–5.8 GHz (802.11 digital)
  10–24 GHz (digital)

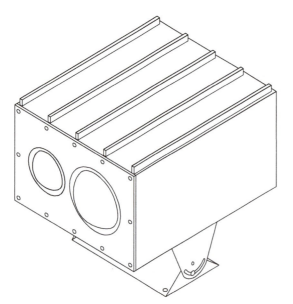

FIGURE 6.19   Laser communicator.

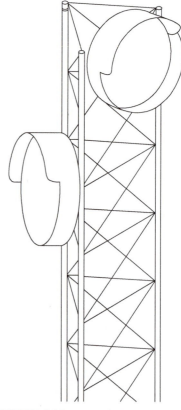

FIGURE 6.20   Caption Microwave tower.

Analog

There are very few analog transmitters and receivers available today. Most of them are in the UHF frequency band. Analog transmitter/receiver pairs suffer from radio frequency noise and environmental conditions more so than do digital systems, and their signal becomes weaker with distance, affecting their image quality. Analog radio systems directly transmit the analog PAL/NTSC video signal over the air. Most of these systems require a license if their power is more than 50 MW.

NTSC is a transmission standard named after the National Television Standards Committee, which approved it for use in the United States. It transmits a scan rate of 525 at 60 Hz and uses a video bandwidth of 4.2 MHz and an audio carrier of 4.5 MHz.

PAL stands for phase-alternating line. PAL is used in many countries throughout Europe, Africa, the Middle East, South and Southeast Asia, and Asia. PAL signals scan 625 lines at 50 Hz. The video bandwidth is 5.0 MHz and the audio carrier is 5.5 MHz. Some countries use a modified PAL standard called PAL N or PAL M. PAL N has a video bandwidth of 4.2 MHz and audio carrier of 4.5 MHz. PAL M has a scan rate of 525 lines at 50 Hz, video bandwidth of 4.2 MHz, and audio carrier of 4.5 MHz.

Analog frequencies were shown previously as FM TV (see the list earlier).

Digital

Digital radio frequency systems transmit IP (TCP/IP or UDP/IP) signals over the air. Typically, to transmit video, either the video signal is sourced directly from an IP-enabled video camera, or an analog video signal (PAL/NTSC format) is converted to UDP/IP through a video codec.

Transport Control Protocol or User Datagram Protocol

The main difference between TCP/IP and UDP/IP is that, although both are IP, TCP is a method for ensuring that every packet reaches its destination. When one does not, the destination computer makes a request to the transmitting computer to resend the missing packet. This results in more traffic. For data such as video or audio, which are dynamic and constantly changing, there is no point in going back for a packet because the image will already have been displayed or the audio will have been heard. Thus, UDP/IP is used. UDP is a connectionless protocol that, like TCP, runs on top of IP networks. Unlike TCP/IP, UDP/IP provides very few error recovery services, offering instead a direct way to send and receive data over an IP network. It is used primarily for broadcasting video and audio over a network.

Frequencies

Common digital radio frequencies are 2.4, 5.0, 5.8, and 10–24 GHz. Some of these frequencies are unlicensed and others require a license. Generally, 802.11a/b/g/i does not require a license, whereas other protocols do.

Latency Problems

Digital signals insert circuit delays called latency. Latency is normally measured in milliseconds (ms), microseconds (µs), or nanoseconds (ns). Cabled wire inserts zero millisecond latency. High-quality digital switch latency is measured in the microsecond range. The very best switches measure latency in nanoseconds. Latency becomes a significant problem above 150 ms. You should strive to design systems that have latency under 50 ms. Long latency times have three potential effects: First, you are not seeing the video in real time, but instead you are seeing a delay of the actual image. Second, you are not controlling a pan/tilt/zoom camera in real time. This is a major problem. Imagine trying to pan/tilt/zoom a camera to look at a license plate in a parking lot. Now imagine that each time you adjust its position, it overshoots its target because you are looking at the image later than the camera is sending it. This requires a constant adjustment until you can finally, and with much frustration, target the license plate. Following a moving target is utterly hopeless. Last, very long latencies (>1s) can on many systems cause the TCP/IP processing to lose track of packets, resulting in the sending of many duplicate video packets or the loss of video packets. The loss of packets results in very bad or totally useless video, and the sending of additional packets can result in even slower (possibly useless) transmission that is so full of duplicate packets that no entire image can be received in a timely fashion. This is especially true of satellite transmissions. Low latency is good. The best digital wireless systems insert less than 1 ms per node. Some common system design approaches can inject up to 35 ms per node.

SATELLITE

Video can also be sent via satellite. There are two common methods.

Satellite Dish

Satellite dish transmission uses either a fixed or a portable satellite dish to uplink and downlink to a geosynchronous satellite. In the fall of 1945, a Royal Air Force electronics officer and member of the British Interplanetary Society, Arthur C. Clarke [the famed author of 2001: A Space Odyssey (1968)], wrote a short article positing that if a satellite's orbit positioned directly over the equator could be configured such that it rotated at exactly the same speed as the rotation of the earth, then it would appear to "hang" motionless in orbit above a fixed position over the earth. This would allow for continuous transmissions to and from the satellite. Previous early communication satellites (Echo, Telstar, Relay, and Syncom) were positioned in low Earth orbits and could not be used for more than 20 min for each orbit.

Satellite video is fraught with four major problems: precise positioning, weather interference, latency delays exceeding 240 ms and the expense of a fixed IP address on a satellite dish. The time to set up precise dish positioning can be up to one-half hour, depending on skills (some people never get it). We have seen satellite latency of up to 2500 ms. That kind of latency is almost impossible to deal with.

Satellite Phone

Satellite phones can also be used to transmit video. Unlike satellite dishes, no precise positioning is required. Simply turn on the radio, connect the video camera, establish the communication, and send. Satellite phones are very expensive, as is their satellite time, but for reporters in the field and offshore oil platforms, they make a great backup to satellite dish communications.

Latency Problems

All satellite communications insert very high latency, typically more than 240 ms. This is useless for pan/tilt/zoom use, and the insert delay makes voice communications tricky. However, if you cannot get communications there any other way, it is a real blessing. For unmanned offshore oil platforms, when connected to an alarm system, the video can confirm that a fishing vessel has moored itself out 100 miles from shore and that a break-in on the platform is occurring. Combined with voice communications, those intruders can be ordered off the platform in virtual real time with an indication that the vessel number has been recorded. During high-security levels, the video system allows for a virtual "guard tour" of the platform, without the need to dispatch a helicopter at a cost of thousands of dollars for each sortie.

WIRELESS ARCHITECTURES

There are three basic wireless architectures, and they are an analog of the wired networks.

Point-to-Point

Point-to-point wireless networks are composed of two nodes, and they communicate wirelessly between the two. It is analogous to a modem connection. Wireless point-to-point connections require a line-of-sight signal or a good reflected signal.

Point-to-Multipoint

Point-to-multipoint connections are networks in which a single wireless node makes connection to several or many other wireless nodes. The single wireless node serves all the others, and all of them communicate to each other through the same single node. This is analogous to a hub or switch or router connection. Wireless point-to-multipoint connections also require line-of-sight signals or absolutely reliable reflected signals.

Wireless Mesh

Wireless mesh systems are like the Internet. That is, each node connects onto the matrix of the mesh and finds as many connections as it can. It selects a primary connection based perhaps on best signal strength or rules set for the least number of nodes between the source and destination node. If the node cannot talk directly to the destination node, then that signal will "hop" through other nodes until it finds the destination node. A wireless mesh is like the Internet. You may not know how you got to a server in Europe, but you sure can see the web page. Wireless meshes can let signals hop several times, so even if there is no line-of-sight connection available, you can almost certainly hop around that oil tank, tree, or building by jumping across several other nodes that do have line-of-sight connections to each other. A well-designed wireless mesh network will automatically and continuously search for the best available connection or shortest available path for each and every node from its source to its destination.

It will do this every time, all the time, making sure that you always have a good, solid signal.

Full-Duplex Wireless Mesh

Old radio-heads like me know that there are two ways of talking over the air: half-duplex and full-duplex. The difference is critical for digital video systems, and if the reader learns anything about wireless systems in the book, this is the thing to understand. In half-duplex systems, each node (transceiver) can either listen or talk but cannot do both at the same time. So when it is talking, it is not listening. When it is listening, it cannot talk. For a digital video system, the bandwidth of the transceiver is effectively cut in half, not because it has in fact less bandwidth but because it is communicating bidirectionally only half the time. For a 54-GHz system, it starts out of the box as a 27-GHz system. Subtract network overhead and encryption and you are left with approximately 22 or 23 GHz less available bandwidth. OK, you say, I can live with 22 GHz. However, if you understand that the purpose of wireless mesh networks is to use the mesh to retransmit video from node to node, it takes on new meaning. That loss of half of the bandwidth occurs with each retransmission. From the first node to the second, bandwidth is 22 GHz minus the video signal (e.g., 2 GHz), leaving 20 GHz. From the second node to the third, it is halved again from 20 to 10 GHz, and now we subtract the second video camera's signal load too. That is another 2 GHz, leaving only 8 GHz. There is not enough bandwidth left to safely add a third camera because we need to reserve at least 6 GHz of overhead for communication snafus. We are effectively out of bandwidth after only two camera nodes.

On the other hand, full-duplex wireless nodes communicate both directions (transmit and receive) all the time. That is because a full-duplex wireless mesh system uses two radios in each node (one transmitter and one receiver). By careful antenna selection, we can transmit and receive continuously at each wireless node. Considering our example again, we can communicate digital video effectively across up to 10 nodes, assuming a 2-GHz drop for each camera (I use a standard of four hops). Another trick is antenna selection. There are basically two types of antennas for all radio systems: directional and omnidirectional. An omnidirectional antenna transmits or receives in a pattern like an apple. There is a slight pinch at the top and bottom of the pattern, but the rest of the radiation pattern is spherical, at least in the horizontal plane. Directional antennas narrow their "view" by restricting the view that its designer does not want. By "pinching" the part of the spherical radiation pattern that is unwanted, the part that is desired is lengthened, sometimes considerably. This creates "gain." Useful signals can be derived from either a line-of-sight connection or a single reflected signal. However, that reflected signal can be a problem if the receiver can see both the original and the reflected signal. Reflected signals arrive later than line-of-sight signals because they are traveling a longer distance from source to destination. All antennas suffer from a phenomenon called multipath. Multipath signals are signals that originate from the transmitting source but from at least two sources, at least one of which may be a reflected signal. There is another type of antenna that is little known (at least until now) called a multiphased omnidirectional antenna.

VIDEO ANALYTICS

Video analytics is a technology that processes a digital video signal using a special algorithm to perform a security-related function. There are three common types of video analytics:

- Fixed algorithm analytics
- Artificial intelligence learning algorithms
- Facial recognition systems

The first two of these try to achieve the same result. That is, they try to determine if an unwanted or suspicious behavior is occurring in the field of view of a video camera and the algorithm notifies the console operator of the finding. However, each takes a dramatically different route to get to its result. Fixed algorithm analytics use an algorithm that is designed to perform a specific task and look for a specific behavior. For example, common behaviors that fixed algorithm analytics look for including the following:

- Crossing a line
- Moving in the wrong direction down a corridor
- Leaving an article
- Picking up an article
- Loitering
- Floating face down in a swimming pool

Each fixed algorithm looks for a very specific behavior. The client must pay for each individual algorithm for each individual video camera in most cases.

Artificial intelligence learning algorithms operate entirely differently. Learning algorithm systems begin as a blank slate. They arrive completely dumb. After connecting to a given camera for several weeks, they begin to issue alerts and alarms. During that time period the system is learning what is normal for that camera's image during the day, night, weekday, weekend, and hour by hour. After several weeks, the system begins to issue alerts and alarms on behavior in the screen that it has not seen before or that is not consistent with what it has seen during that time period for that day of week.

An example illustrates the usefulness of this approach. In one early installation at a major international airport that was intended to spot children climbing on a baggage carousel, the system alerted on a man who picked up a small bag from the carousel and placed it inside an empty larger bag. The man was intercepted and interrogated only to discover that the luggage inside his did not belong to him and that he was part of a ring who came to the airport regularly to steal baggage in this way. The airport had no idea this was even occurring, so there was no way they could have purchased a fixed behavior algorithm for this, even if such existed (which it did not). This approach to video analytics is most useful.

The third type of analytic is facial recognition. Facial recognition systems can be used for access control or to help identify friend or foe. Facial recognition systems can also be used to further an investigation.

Typical facial recognition systems match points on a face with a sample stored in a database. If the face does not match a record, it will try to create a new record from the best image of that person available. These are capable of making real-time matches of one image against many. The latest version of facial recognition systems constructs 3-D maps of faces in real time and compares those to a truly vast database. One manufacturer claims to be able to match individuals in real time against a country-sized database of images (millions of records).

Traditional facial recognition systems require well-lit scenes and fairly static backgrounds. The latest versions are reported to work under fair to poor lighting and with dynamic backgrounds.

LENSES AND LIGHTING

Lenses are to video what loudspeakers are to audio systems. Just as there is a dramatic difference in the quality of audio depending on the quality of the loudspeaker playing the music, so also the quality of lenses directly determines the quality of the video image. For many years, security installers used to place cheap plastic lenses on otherwise good video cameras to present a price advantage against their competition. The result was very poor and sometimes virtually useless video images. With the introduction of megapixel video cameras as expectations of better quality images increased, many users were very disappointed to see poor images from

very expensive cameras when the installers fitted them with standard quality lenses.

It is very important to use only good lenses on every video camera. And it is especially important to use only megapixel quality lenses on megapixel video cameras. A good lens will be all glass, coated to reduce flare, and should be an achromatic design, which brings red and blue to focus at the same point on the focal plane. Manufacturers of cheap plastic lenses often use euphemisms to conceal their poor construction, calling them something such as "optical resin."

Lenses should be back-focused in the camera to assure that its focus is exactly fitted to the camera. The designer should pay attention to be sure that this has been done and quiz the installer on how it is done so that one can be certain the required skills are present in the installer.

Likewise good lighting is essential for a good quality image. Good lighting has three main components: lighting level, lighting contrast, and lighting color temperature.

Lighting Level

Adequate lighting is needed for good video. I suggest reading *Guide to Security Lighting for People, Property, and Public Spaces*, prepared by Illuminating Engineering Society of North America (IESNA) Security Lighting Committee. A 73-page report is available as a free download on the Internet.[10]

A minimum lighting level is at least 1 ft-candle, measured at 1 m above the ground with a quality "incident-type" light meter. Incident-type light meters measure light on a white translucent surface on the meter itself. Reflected-type light meters measure light reflected from the scene. The light reading should be taken in the scene with an incident-type meter, not at the video camera with a reflected-type meter. While 1 ft-candle can provide a minimally acceptable

[10] http://www.smsiinc.com/pdfs/security-lighting-guide.pdf.

lighting level for a walkway or parking lot, a level of 5 ft-candles or greater is required for a truly good image. Specifications should require 5 ft-candles around building entrances, walkway nexus points, and undercover parking (including parking structures). The more light the better. By way of comparison, the range of typical outdoor daylight is about 6000 ft-candles.

Light level terminology can be confusing. Light sources are measured in lumens. Light on a surface is measured in both foot-candles and lux. Although the math can be tedious, the practitioner can roughly convert 1 ft-candle to 10 lux. One foot-candle is the amount of light on a surface exactly one foot from a candle.

Lighting Contrast

Lighting contrast is the difference in light level between lightest and darkest areas in the scene. If everything were lit at exactly the same level and the subject wore clothing similar to his or her skin color, it would be difficult to identify the subject. Illumination uniformity ratios should be about 4:1 (average/minimum). Ideally, there should be good contrast between the subject and the surrounding scene. Lighting should facilitate clear identity of the subject's clothing, face, and other identifying features.

Lighting Color Temperature

Lighting color is measured in color temperature (Kelvin). The low end of the Kelvin spectrum is red, and the high end of the spectrum is blue. Right in the middle is daylight. Daylight for video is approximately 5600 K. Lamps with color temperatures lower than this will appear yellow to red and lamps with color temperatures higher than this will appear green to blue. Incandescent and sodium vapor lamps make the video image to appear as yellow, while some LED lamps can cause video to present as blue. Both cause difficulty in the identification of subjects' clothing and can result in completely wrong descriptions being given by the console

operator to his or her guard staff. This can lead to the release of guilty subjects because their clothes do not match the description.

Other Lighting Issues

Protect lighting from vandalism with protective covers, protected power lines (buried or in conduit), and with mounts too high to reach easily. Assure emergency lighting in case of power outages. Emergency lighting should cover all paths of egress including stairwells.

SECURITY COMMUNICATIONS

Security communications are the root of response. Communications involves the following categories:

- Communications between security officers and the public they serve.
- Communications between security officers and other security officers.
- Communications between security officers and the public via telephones.
- Communications between security officers and public agencies (fire/police, etc.).

Security communications serve several purposes:

- Receiving information and direction to do the job.
- Assisting the public with access or information.
- Directing subjects to comply with established security policies.
- Coordinating emergency responders.

Two-Way Radios

Two-way radios are the heart of communications for any security staff. They provide the ability for security officers to communicate with each other and with other facility personnel, including management and maintenance/cleaning staff.

Two-way radios are used for communications from the security console to field officers and from officer to officer in the field.

Two-way radios have varying frequencies. Common spectrum sections include the 150- and 450-MHz bands. Radios with 800 MHz are a blend of traditional two-way radio technology and computer-controlled transmitters. The system's main advantage is that radio transmitters can be shared among various departments or users with the aid of computer programming. Virtual radio groups, called "talk groups," are created in software to enable private departmental conversations. This gives the system the look and feel of one having many different "frequencies" when in fact everyone is sharing just a few. A quick reference of public and private radio frequencies can be found at http://www.bearcat1.com/freer.html.

Cell Phones

Cell phones can provide an inexpensive means of communications, particularly cell phones with a two-way radio function. They provide in a single unit both a two-way radio and the ability to call the police directly when needed, as well as managers.

Cell phones have limits, however. Before deciding on using a cell phone as a primary means of communication, it is important to conduct a test with the type of cell phone planned for use in every dark recess of the building, parking structure, stairwell, restroom, storage room, and throughout the entire facility. Otherwise, you may discover a dead spot in exactly the place where the worst possible emergency is occurring, exactly when it occurs. Cell phones are particularly valuable for patrol officers in vehicles because of their wide geographical reach, allowing the officer to be reached both on and off the property.

Intercoms

Security intercoms enable console officers to talk to anyone near a field intercom station (typically another officer or a member of the public).

Calls can usually be initiated either from the console or from the intercom field station by pressing a "call" button. Most intercoms are hands-free devices, although handsets are sometimes used. ADA (Americans with Disability Act)-compliant intercoms also provide a visual indicator that the call has been sent and acknowledged, in case the user is hearing impaired.

Other types of intercoms include call-out only stations and intercom bullhorns. Callout stations are similar to standard intercoms but are not equipped with call buttons. The console officer always originates the call for this type. Intercom bullhorns are similar to call-out stations but are equipped with a horn that acoustically amplifies the audio so that the console officer and subject can communicate at farther distances (usually up to 100 ft). Intercom bullhorns usually also require an auxiliary amplifier to provide adequate power to be heard at that distance. The horn gathers the voice of the subject, although it is more difficult for the officer to hear the subject than it is for the subject to hear the officer. Bullhorns are often used only for directions to the subject and not back to the officer.

Emergency Phones

Emergency phones (also called assistance phones) are intercoms that are also equipped with flashing lights or strobes to help a responding officer find the subject who is calling and to deter a crime against that subject because the strobe calls attention to the area, making a crime of violence less probable.

Paging Systems

Paging systems are strictly for communication from the console officer to the field. Paging systems can be specific to a single paging speaker or horn or to a field of speakers and horns to cover a large area. Paging systems are useful for making announcements to large numbers of people simultaneously, such as to order an evacuation or to issue directions in an emergency.

ANALOG VERSUS DIGITAL

Analog

Intercom and voice systems historically used analog communications—that is, a microphone was connected to an amplifier and a speaker. For larger systems, a matrix switcher was used to manage one or a few console communication paths out to many field intercoms. This is called a circuit-switched network. Traditional telephone systems are also circuit-switched networks. Each circuit can carry only one communication and there must be a continuous wire connection from speaker to subject. This approach is fine for a single site, but it has drawbacks, including the fact that the wiring is of a fixed architecture, so one intercom master station wires to many field stations. If one wants to add more master stations, one must wire from master to master. There is a single point of failure at the main master where the field intercom stations are first wired. Also, when the organization wants to move the location of the main master station, much costly rewiring is necessary.

Digital

For enterprise systems, the drawbacks of circuit-switched networks present major problems. How do you maintain a circuit from New York to California? The cost of leased lines is too high, so digital intercoms are used. As digital video systems become more prevalent, it is also easier to "piggyback" voice communications on that digital path. Digital systems use packet-switched networks instead of circuit-switched networks for communications. Therefore, their path can be dynamic. If the organization wants to move its console, it only has to connect the new console to the nearest digital switch.

Digital intercoms have certain drawbacks too. For security, audio is more important than any other communication. Dropped audio could mean a lost life. So audio communications must be configured as the priority communication to ensure that no communication is lost as, for example, a new screen of video cameras is loading from one guard tour to the next. This is a programming element and cannot be configured in software if it is not written into the code. Audio compression protocols commonly include the G.7xx series, including G.711, G.721, G.722, G.726, G.728, and G.729. Another common protocol is the MPEG protocol, including MP-3. These are all UDP protocols. The software designer must ensure that the audio protocol is given priority of communications over the digital and data protocols. Where this is not done, the security officer can find it difficult to talk while video is loading. This condition is unacceptable, although at the time of this writing several video software manufacturers publish software with this flaw. Their common workaround is to require an additional client workstation just for audio. This is one of those design flaws that no one would buy if he or she knew about it ahead of time.

Digital audio has many advantages. Additional intercom stations can be added on anywhere an extra switch port exists, dramatically reducing wired infrastructure costs. Additional switches can be added at little cost in new infrastructure. For enterprise systems, the Internet or asynchronous transfer mode networks permit communications across state and national boundaries, making possible a monitoring center in one state that monitors sites throughout the world.

Wireless Digital

Any digital communication can be configured to operate wirelessly as well as on a wired network. This enables communications to remotely located emergency phones across an endless expanse of park or parking lot. All one needs is power and that can sometimes be obtained via solar panels and batteries. Emergency phones are an ideal application for solar panels and batteries because they draw power only when in use, except for a small amount of power for the radio frequency node. This is usually very low, typically less than 25 W for a well-designed system.

Communication System Integration

It is also possible to integrate two-way radios, cell phones, land phones, and intercoms into a consolidated communications system (CCS). Typically, there are only one or two security officers at a console, but there may be many communications systems. In the worst case I have seen, at a high-rise building in Los Angeles, there were 10 separate intercoms for elevators, 4 intercom systems for security, 4 two-way radio systems, 2 paging systems, 8 telephone lines, and cell phones. All this was (barely) manageable until an earthquake struck. Then, chaos broke loose in the security console room. Remember, that was 29 separate communications systems for a console room with one or two officers. That does not work very well.

In an ideal configuration, the systems have been coordinated such that there is no more than one of each type of system (interdiscipline coordination-instilled design flaws) and those few systems are further coordinated into a "CCS." The CCS assembles the various communication platforms into a single piece of software that manages the communications to a single (or multiple) console officer station. Calls that cannot be taken are queued.

Queued calls go to an automated attendant that provides feedback to waiting parties. In the earthquake example, people in a stopped elevator would hear an automated message from the intercom speaker when they press the help button advising them that an earthquake has just struck the building and that there is a heavy demand on the security console officer and advising them that their call is in a queue. They would be advised to push the help button for a second time if there is a medical emergency,

advancing their call in the queue. In the meantime, there would be a digitized ringtone and recorded message with enough variation to keep their anxiety level low. The system could also advise them of the expected wait time.

COMMAND/CONTROL AND COMMUNICATION CONSOLES

Monitoring Consoles

Consoles and workstations provide a means to instruct the security system on how to behave and interact with its environment and users, to provide a face for the security system to its human user (viewing cameras, using the intercom, responding to alarms, etc.), and to obtain system reports. There are a limited number of common implementations of these types of workstations. System size dictates the type.

Small Systems

Single-site systems are often designed with a common workstation that will provide all system services together in a single computer. The system may separate alarm/access control, video monitoring, and the intercom master station into three separate units and may commonly be designed as an analog video/intercom system rather than digital. However, this trend will change over time toward digital video and intercom as these systems become more prevalent in the smaller systems. In any event, the alarm/access control system will likely comprise field devices (card readers, locks, etc.), field device controllers, and a single computer to manage them.

System interface and automation will likely be limited to activating video cameras in response to alarms, and this interface may well be accomplished using dry contacts.

Thus, the small system will likely comprise a single computer workstation for the alarm/access control system, a video multiplexer and perhaps a pair of analog video monitors for the few video cameras, and an intercom master station to answer intercoms. These will likely be located at a lobby desk, security office, or manager's office.

Medium-Sized Systems

Medium-sized systems will typically incorporate a higher level of system integration and possibly more than one workstation or console. Medium-sized systems may well separate system functions into those that will exist on a server and those that will operate on a client workstation. These systems may be designed as analog video/intercom, or they may be digital. It is possible that the client workstations will include a separate workstation for the lobby desk or security office and another one for administration of the system by a manager.

Enterprise-Class Systems

Any enterprise-class system (multiple buildings and/or multiple sites) that is not designed initially with a digital video/digital intercom infrastructure will be a costly system to upgrade, expand, and maintain as time goes by.

These systems routinely incorporate a high level of integration to other building systems and routinely have both local and remote or centralized system monitoring and/or administration.

All enterprise-class systems are built around a client/server model and may involve many clients and many servers, including servers acting as local and/or central archivers, local and/or centralized guard workstations, and local and/or centralized administrative workstations including photo identification and identity verification workstations.

WORKSTATION AND CONSOLE SPECIFICS

Command, Control, and Communications Consoles

The most sophisticated of all security consoles, the C3 console, is the operational heart of an enterprise-class alarm monitoring and management system. Usually, having more than one console (sometimes up to a dozen), the C3 approach is the ultimate in centralized corporate oversight for safety, security, and sometimes even operational efficiency.

Incidents such as major refinery explosions can be effectively prevented if health, safety, and efficiency (HSE) monitoring is augmented centrally. This method of centralized monitoring can advise local on-site HSE personnel of unsafe practices in conflict with established corporate safety or security policies that may be occurring without the knowledge of local managers. For every employee who might complain about the intrusion of centralized authority, lives can truly be saved by avoiding unsafe industrial practices that would otherwise go unnoticed.

A C3 console normally incorporates one or more workstations, and each workstation includes a number of LCD monitors. Typically, two to four monitors display video, one displays alarm and control maps, one may display alarm/access control system activity, and an additional monitor may be used for an application package such as a report writer, spreadsheet, or word processor. On some systems, email service and voice communication software may be used. C3 consoles may also have one or more large screen displays that anyone in the room can easily see. These are typically run from one of the workstations in the console. The C3 console generally also incorporates situational analysis software to help the console officers understand what is being displayed in the system in the context of locations of buildings, avenues, and waterways in the real world.

One consideration regarding C3 consoles (and others as well, but especially C3 consoles) is the issue of workstation processing power. Every program and process requires CPU, memory, and video card-processing cycles, and there are a finite number for each individual workstation, based on its processor, clock speed, and video card. It is possible to crash a workstation that is overloaded with requests for processing cycles. That is a bad thing. So it is important to design workstations in a manner that ensures that it will not happen. The good news is that Moore's law indicates that processing power will grow by a factor of two approximately every year and a half. The bad news is that the processing power of any workstation is determined by its weakest link, which could be the processor, the video card, memory type and capacity, the operating system, or the software. There is not a single, simple formula to calculate how much processing power is required for a given application. However, there is a simple way to make a useful calculation:

- Find a machine that is roughly similar to the type of machine you intend to specify. Generally, the manufacturer of the digital video software will have several machines to select from in its lab.
- Ask the lab technician to start up the machine with only the operating system and the digital video application running (displaying no cameras at this time). Load the task manager and note the CPU usage in percentage of utilization.
- Now display one camera at the resolution and frame rate to be viewed. Again, look at the task manager and note the difference in CPU processing percentage of utilization.
- Then display 4 and then 16 cameras and note the percentage of utilization of CPU.
- Next, open a browser window on top of the video that is already open and again note the CPU utilization figures.
- Last, load on top of this a standard spreadsheet or word-processing application and again note the CPU utilization, with all this running.

From the previous information, you can calculate how much CPU utilization will occur when the computer is fully loaded with all intended camera signals and ancillary browsers programs. This will be a real-world number that is meaningful.

The system should be designed so as not to ever exceed 60% of CPU utilization. Exceeding 60% of continuous duty will result in overheating and shortening of the life of the CPU. It may result in the inability of the computer to adequately process video, causing observably bad images and possibly crashing the computer. This condition can also occur if the image specifications are exceeded. For example, if the computer's capacity is based on the display of 32 2-CIF images at 15 fps, and the console user reprograms the resolution to 4-CIF and the frame rate to 30 fps, these results could occur. The user must be instructed as to the design limitations of the workstation.

Important elements of any security console workstation include the processor, memory, the video card, and the quality of monitor. It is unwise to skimp on servers and workstations. They do the heavy lifting in the system. Unlike other parts of the system in which scale equals dollars (more units ¼ more money), a significant investment in servers and workstations does not usually equal a significant increase in the overall cost of the system. It is a wise investment for the designer to recommend and for the client to make.

Ergonomics for C3 consoles are also a major consideration. The console design may comprise any of a number of configurations, including a wraparound design in which the console is nestled into a corner or side wall or a cluster of individual workstation desks facing a large screen display or video wall at one end of the room. Special attention should be paid to the quality of lighting; keyboard, mouse, and monitor position; and the quality of chairs. All these factors have a bearing on the ability of the console officer to observe video over a period of many hours.

There has also been much discussion regarding how many cameras should be displayed on a console, and like everyone else, I have an opinion. First, let us state the various cases made. The many-is-better argument goes like this: If many cameras are displayed, then the console officer can observe the video of any camera at his or her pleasure. He or she can quickly scan all the available views and may see something that he or she would never observe if the cameras were not otherwise displayed. The fewer-is-better argument goes like this: Some scientific studies have shown that an officer cannot view more than approximately six images with any precision of observation over any long time period. Having more monitors may create complacency on the part of the observing officer, and in any event it is better if most video views respond to some kind of alarm or event indicator if possible. For this reason, it is better to use many cameras and fewer monitors and have the cameras triggered by alarms where possible.

I am in the second camp. However, there is a caveat. I am also an advocate of creating a series of scene views using related video cameras—for example, all the cameras on the first level of a parking structure, second level, and so on. These related camera groups can be assembled to create a "virtual guard tour" that allows the console officer to "walk" the facility by sequentially selecting the groups of related cameras. Additionally, any alarms can also be programmed to select the related group of cameras, not just the single camera that is nearest to the alarm event. A superset of guard tour groups is video pursuit, which is discussed later in the book.

C3 Console Use in Public Agency Settings

C3 consoles are of particular use for mass transit facilities where the responding officer will almost always be a sworn police officer. For such installations, it is important to use the C3 console as a vetting console, staffed by civilians, not by a police dispatcher. This is to ensure that the dispatch officer is not swamped by nuisance alarms, of which there may be many in such installations.

After vetting the alarm through the C3 console, real events needing the dispatch of a sworn officer can be passed to the dispatch console for appropriate action.

A well-designed C3 console scheme should permit the civilian console officer to be able to "pass off" the event to a sworn officer at a different console simply by moving an icon

representing the civilian monitor to an icon representing the sworn officer's monitor.

When this is done, the video should queue at the sworn officer's monitor, sounding an alarm to direct his or her attention to the event and keeping the civilian online to hand off the audio.

Lobby Desk Consoles

Security workstations are often placed at lobby desks where the public is assisted. Here, the security designer is often requested to design the workstation into a highly aesthetic environment.

Careful coordination with the interiors architect is required to determine the ergonomic elements required. The architect will need to closely coordinate the design of the console with the measurements of the lobby desk security components.

Dispatch Consoles

Similar to C3 consoles, dispatch consoles also may have many workstations. In addition to the security video, alarm/access control, and intercom elements, radio dispatch will be a major element. Computer-aided dispatch (CAD) software will likely be implemented, and this must also be coordinated to display locations of cars, personnel, and activities. The video system can be integrated with CAD software to achieve this result, and the security intercom may also be integrated with the two-way radio system, telephone system, and even cellular/radio phone system to facilitate communications. In all other respects, dispatch consoles are similar in requirements and design to C3 consoles, except that the designer is often burdened with very limited space, sometimes requiring more functions be added into a very small existing space.

Administrative Workstations

Administrative workstations facilitate the programming of cards, system software, hardware and firmware configuration changes, and the creation and reviewing of system reports. Administrative work stations are generally limited to no more than two monitors and may be combined with other duties on the security manager's or site manager's desk.

Administrative workstations are the simplest and least demanding of security work stations. As always, observe processor, memory, and video card requirements. Administrative workstations include the computer, monitors, keyboard, and mouse and report printer.

Identification Badging Consoles

Virtually every medium and large system involves photo identification badges. These are usually bonded on or printed directly onto an access credential.

Photo identification credentials typically display a photo of the credential holder, a logo of the organization or some other identifying logo, the name and department of the person, and may also display a color or pattern scheme that is an identifying feature of the person's access privileges. This function presents the human readable portion of an access credential that facilitates an organization's staff to easily identify people wearing badges, the organization or department to which they belong, and whether they are allowed unescorted access to the area in which they are found.

Photo identification systems comprise an identification badging console (workstation), a digital camera, lights, background, posing chair, and a credential printer.

Based on badging volume and the organization's human resources processes, the system may be centralized or distributed across several sites, and the credential printers may be attached to either the workstation or a network in which they are shared by several photo identification workstations.

Identity Verification Workstations

Although rare, identity verification workstations facilitate absolute verification of a credentialed person through an access portal. These are used in high-security environments such as nuclear and weapons storage facilities, research and design facilities, and other places where critical proprietary information or assets that could present harm to the public are housed.

The identity verification workstation is typically used with a revolving door, optical turnstile, or mantrap to provide a means to verify with certainty that the person holding an access credential is who he or she claims to be.

The workstation is part of the overall identity verification portal, which includes a credential reader; a movement-pausing mechanism (revolving door, physical or electronic turnstile, mantrap, or in the simplest form, an electrically locked door); and a visual recognition system, usually in the form of a video camera and computer software, that displays a live image of the person next to an image retrieved from the photo identification database corresponding to the one stored for the access credential that was just presented at the portal. After making the comparison, the security officer staffing the identity verification portal verifies that the credential is valid for the portal (authorized for the portal and the date and time of use) and that the credential holder is the person who is authorized to carry the credential (the live video image of the person matches the photo ID image). After verification, the security officer manually unlocks the door using a remote electronic release, allowing the credential holder into the restricted area.

GUARD CONSOLE FUNCTIONS

Guard consoles are used to manage the security of the facility. The guard console is the aircraft control tower of the security operation. From this location, it should be possible for the console guard to keep an eye on all the major access control and intrusion events occurring in the building. Basic guard console functions include the following:

- Vetting alarms for appropriate response
- Granting access remotely
- Video surveillance

- Video guard tours
- Video pursuit
- Building system interfaces

Vetting Alarms

Any alarm that occurs anywhere in the security system will report to the guard console. The console software should be integrated to extend its eyes, ears, and mouth into the depths of the facility, wherever an alarm occurs. The guard should receive immediate notification of the alarm and immediately be able to verify the alarm from the console. Often, the best way to do this is by the presence of a video camera near the alarm. If the alarm is verified as an intrusion, the console guard must then take some action, either dispatching an officer to respond (radio) or confronting the subject via security intercom. For this reason, good design principles indicate that, where possible, every alarm should have a camera nearby to permit alarm verification. Ideally, there should also be a field intercom station or field talk station near the camera to direct the subject away from the area of the intrusion. Additionally, the software should be configured such that for every alarm a camera is programmed to queue for display automatically, and that camera image should be recorded. For digital video systems, a preevent record period is also recommended. That is, even if the camera is not programmed for continuous archiving, the system should be archiving every camera continuously for 2 min such that in the event of an alarm for which that camera may respond, that 2 min being recorded before the alarm becomes part of the alarm video event archive. Otherwise, it is recorded over continuously.

Granting Access Remotely

Another common function of guard consoles is the remote granting of access to authorized visitors, contractors, and vendors. Typically, one or more remote doors may facilitate such access.

If there is a constant flow of people through the door, it may be appropriate to locate a guard there to facilitate authorization and access granting. However, often the flow does not warrant the cost of a full-time guard. For such cases, it is ideal if there can be configured a vestibule for access granting to include a card reader for authorized users, a camera, and an intercom to facilitate a gracious granting of access privileges. These designs take two common forms.

Finished Visitor Lobby

A finished visitor lobby may be used for remote access granting after normal business hours—for example, in a multitenant high-rise building environment. The vestibule provides a secure means of granting access without putting anyone in the building at risk, including the lobby desk guard.

Visitor vestibules can be under the control of the console guard and/or may also be under the control of a tenant via use of a building directory and intercom system. In such cases, the visitor looks up the tenant and places a call using the code next to the tenant's name. Upon answering, the tenant can enter a telephone code unlocking the inner door and permitting access into the building.

Where the control is exclusive to the console guard, the guard may also have control over the elevator system to ensure that the visitor actually goes to the floor he or she has requested and for which he or she is authorized by the tenant.

Delivery Lobby

Delivery lobbies can be created at a loading dock to reduce guard force count. In such cases, again a vestibule is created and the system is activated as an event whenever the vestibule is occupied, when the outer door is opened.

An assumption is made that the delivery person is unfamiliar with the building, so its use is in the hands of the guard, making the delivery person's knowledge level unimportant.

The guard console will display the delivery lobby camera upon opening of the outer door, and the delivery lobby intercom will be queued. The console guard will initiate a call to the delivery person asking him or her to whom he or she is making a delivery. After answering, the guard will ask the delivery person to present his or her driver's license and delivery company identification face up on a credential camera reader. The credential reader is a lighted box with a platen for placing the identification papers for viewing.

After recording the delivery person's identification, the guard instructs the delivery person to place his or her delivery papers on the platen to record the location of the package for delivery. After this is done, the guard will then enable the elevator–hall call buttons and may also direct the elevator to the proper floor if he or she has been given elevator floor select control on his or her console.[11]

Video Surveillance

Video surveillance involves the act of observing a scene or scenes and looking for specific behaviors that are improper or that may indicate the emergence or existence of improper behavior.

Common uses of video surveillance include observing the public at the entry to sports events, public transportation (train platforms, airports, etc.), and around the perimeter of secure facilities, especially those that are directly bounded by community spaces.

The video surveillance process includes the identification of areas of concern and the identification of specific cameras or groups of cameras that may be able to view those areas. If it is possible to identify schedules when security trends have occurred or may be likely to occur, that is also helpful to the process. Then, by viewing the selected images at appropriate times, it

[11] With thanks to Chuck Hutchinson, Senior Security Manager, Crescent Real Estate Equities, Ltd.

is possible to determine if improper activity is occurring.

One such application is for train platforms. Following a series of reports of intimidating behavior at a particular train platform, the use of video cameras and intercoms was found to reduce the potential for such events as the perpetrators began to understand that their behavior could be recorded and used to identify them to police. Furthermore, the act of getting on a train did not deter the police who boarded at the next station and apprehended the criminals. Word got around and the behavior was reduced dramatically.

Video Guard Tours

The use of correlated groups of video cameras programmed to be viewed as a group allows the console officer to see an entire area at once. He or she can then step through the spaces of the facility, each time viewing the entire area as though he or she were walking through a guard tour.

It is much faster to perform a virtual video guard tour than a physical guard tour, thus allowing more frequent reviews of the spaces. Additionally, because the cameras are always in place, people behaving improperly are unaware that they are being viewed by authorities until a response occurs, either by dispatched officer or by intercom intervention, either of which can be effective in deterring improper behavior.

Video guard tours are especially effective at managing very large facilities, such as public transportation facilities in which the spaces can be vast and the time to travel between areas can be significant.

Video Pursuit

The guard tour cameras can also be set up to create a "video pursuit" that will allow a console officer in an environment such as an airport or casino to follow a subject as he or she walks through the space by selecting the camera in the group into which the subject has walked. With each selection, a new group will be displayed where the new display includes the selected camera and other cameras displaying views into which the subject might walk if he or she leaves the area under display. As the subject moves from camera to camera, video pursuit keeps the subject centered in a cocoon of cameras. A corresponding display of maps will show the console officer where the subject is located by highlighting the central camera and those around it where the subject might walk.[12]

COMMUNICATION SYSTEMS

Security communication systems facilitate rapid information gathering, decision-making, and action taking.

Security System Intercoms

Security intercoms provide a convenient way for visitors to gain information or access at remote doors. They may be used either to facilitate remote access granting or to direct the visitor to a visitor lobby. They visit or can query the console security officer by pressing a call button on the intercom, thus initiating a call. Likewise, the console security officer can also initiate a call directly from the console.

A second type of intercom is the officer-controlled security intercom. Similar to a conventional intercom station but without the call button, these are often placed next to a video camera for use in directing a subject after verifying an alarm.

The third type of security intercom is the intercom bullhorn. It is similar to the officer-controlled intercom but has the ability to reach farther distances due to the bullhorn.

---

[12] Video pursuit was invented jointly by the author and his protégé, Mr David Skusek.

Elevator and Parking System Intercoms

Security intercoms are often located in elevators and elevator lobbies and at parking entrances.

Emergency Call Stations

A security intercom coupled with a blue strobe and emergency signage, this intercom is a welcome point of help in areas where an assault could occur, such as in parking structures and walkways on a college campus. Reports indicate that assault crimes can diminish from historical norms where emergency call stations are used.

Digital intercom systems utilize a codec from the field intercom station to the digital infrastructure. The digital video software often accommodates the communication path and can also automatically queue the intercom for use whenever the camera viewing the intercom is on screen. That can be accomplished automatically in response to an alarm.

Analog intercoms use either two-wire or four-wire field intercom stations. Four-wire intercom stations use two wires for the speaker, two for the microphone, and sometimes two for the call button, whereas two-wire intercoms use only two wires for all three functions. Four-wire intercoms can operate in full-duplex mode (simultaneous talk/listen), whereas two-wire intercoms can only operate in half-duplex mode, although this is often more advisable because it allows the console security officer to control the conversation and ensures that conversations in the console room will not be unintentionally overheard at the field intercom station.

Direct Ring-Down Intercoms

These are telephones that ring to a specific number when the receiver is lifted or the call button is pressed (hands-free version). These are commonly used in elevators and emergency call stations. Direct ring-down phones are available in both CO (central office line connection) and non-CO versions (non-CO versions create their own ring-down voltage and need only a pair of wires connected to an answering phone station set). These are frequently used for remote parking gates. Both types are also usually equipped with remote control over a dry contact relay at the ring-down station, permitting remote access through a parking gate or door.

Two-Way Radio

Two-way radio systems facilitate constant communications among a dispatcher, console security officer, security management, security guards, and building maintenance personnel.

Two-way radio systems can comprise an assembly of handheld radios with no master station or may be equipped with a master station at the security command center. In any event, a charging station will need to be accommodated in the space planning of the security command center.

Two-way radio systems can be integrated via communications software with other communication systems to create a CCS that can integrate radio, telephone, pagers, and intercoms into a single communication platform.

Pagers

Pagers can be used to notify roving security officers of an alarm or can discretely notify an officer of a condition requiring his or her attention. Many alarm/access control systems can connect directly to a paging system transmitter for local broadcast within a building or on a campus. The systems can also be connected to a telephone dialer to broadcast a page across a city or the country. At a minimum, the security console can be configured to utilize paging software to key in messages independent of any other interface.

Wireless Headsets

For security consoles and lobby security desks that require the console officer to move about considerably, it is useful to equip the intercom/telephone or two-way radio with wireless headphones. These free the console officer from the common tether of a standard headset. Wireless headsets can be connected to various ways depending on the manufacturer and model, including to a headphone plug, USB, or RS-232.

SUMMARY

The basics of alarm/access control systems include identification devices (card readers, keypads, and biometric systems). Keypads can be simple or complex, the most advanced of which scrambles the numbers for each use and limits the view of adjacent users. Card reader types include magnetic stripe, Wiegand, passive and active proximity, and smart cards. Many organizations use multitechnology cards, which allow the user to access various facilities, each of which may require a different card technology.

Access cards are commonly used with photo identification systems such that the access card and identification together form the credential. Photo identification cards help identify users by sight, showing what areas they have access to and displaying their photo, name, and department.

Other devices include locks, door position switches, and request to exit devices. Common electrified lock types include electrified strikes, electrified mortise locks, magnetic locks, electrified panic hardware, and specialty locks. DPS can be either surface mounted or concealed. Other devices include door and gate operators and revolving doors and turnstiles. Access control system field elements are controlled by electronic processing boards, which include a microprocessor, memory, and field interface modules. All these devices are managed by servers and workstations.

The different subsystems of an integrated security system can be blended together into a single system. The system can also be interfaced with other systems to achieve advanced automated functions.

Early analog video systems included only cameras, cable, and monitors. As demand increased, more cameras were displayed on a few monitors using a sequential switcher. As the technology progressed, sequential switchers grew to become digital matrix switchers, and quads and multiplexers promised to display and record multiple cameras onto a single tape. Analog video was recorded by using a helical-scan spinning record head. Early recorders used 2-in. reel-to-reel tape, which was later replaced by cartridges, notably the VHS cassette.

Digital video records and transmits the video as a series of ones and zeros rather than as a voltage on a coaxial cable, as does analog video.

Digital systems transmit their information in packets. To truly understand digital video systems, or networks, one must fully understand how the TCP/IP protocol works. It is also important to understand how network switching and routing work. Other issues that are important to understand include both wired and wireless networks. Wired networks utilize cable, switchers, and routers. Wireless networks utilize lasers, microwave, and radio links, including land- and space-based radio. Typical radio-based networks connect via point-to-point, point-to-multipoint, and with wireless mesh networks.

Video analytics include fixed algorithm analytics, artificial intelligence learning algorithms, and facial recognition algorithms.

Security communications are the root of response. Common technologies include two-way radios, cell phones, and intercoms. Intercoms can also be related to emergency phones and paging systems.

Command and communications consoles vary greatly depending on the needs of the facility they serve. Small systems often have simple consoles, providing only basic functions. Medium-sized systems generally include some system integration elements, whereas enterprise-class systems often use extensive

integration. Console types include lobby desk consoles, dispatch consoles, administrative workstations, identification badging consoles, and identity verification consoles. Guard consoles vet alarms for appropriate response, grant access remotely, conduct video surveillance and video guard tours, utilize video pursuit, and manage building system interfaces.

QUESTIONS AND ANSWERS

1. Identification devices identify by
   a. What you know
   b. What you have
   c. Who you are
   d. All of the above
2. Other access control field devices include
   a. Electrified locks, door position switches, REX devices, and gate operators
   b. Mechanical locks, magnetic tape, signal lights, and pushbutton switches
   c. Pushbutton switches, locks of all types, fiber optic cable, and cameras
   d. None of the above
3. Biometric readers read
   a. Characteristics of a card
   b. Characteristics of a key code
   c. Characteristics of a person
   d. None of the above
4. Common electrified lock types include
   a. Electrified mortise locks
   b. Magnetic locks
   c. Electrified panic hardware
   d. All of the above
5. It is common to use two servers for access control
   a. Primary and business continuity server
   b. Primary and secondary
   c. Primary and ordinary
   d. Primary and a second server that is never turned on unless it is needed
6. Security system designers must often interface new system elements with
   a. Systems from antiquity

    b. Nonautomated security systems
    c. Legacy security systems
    d. None of the above
7. Digital security systems may use
    a. TCP/IP protocol
    b. UDP protocol
    c. RDP protocol
    d. All of the above
8. Wireless signals may include
    a. Radio, laser, and microwave
    b. Radio, fiber optic, and laser
    c. Fiber optic, unicast, and multicast
    d. None of the above
9. Video analytics may include
    a. Fixed algorithm analytics

    b. Artificial intelligence learning
      algorithms
    c. Facial recognition systems
    d. All of the above
10. Security communications systems may
    include
    a. Emergency phones
    b. Intercoms and paging systems
    c. Two-way radio and cell phones
    d. All of the above

Answers

    1: d, 2: a, 3: c, 4: d, 5: a, 6: c, 7: d, 8: a, 9: d, 10: d.

Use of Locks in Physical Crime Prevention*

James M. Edgar, CPP, PSP, William D. McInerney,
Eugene D. Finneran, John E. Hunter

This chapter discusses the use of locks in physical crime prevention. The terminology of locks and lock components is detailed, as well as a way of critically looking at locks in terms of crime prevention and security.

LOCK TERMINOLOGY AND COMPONENTS

The effectiveness of any locking system depends on a combination of interrelated factors involved in the design, manufacture, installation, and maintenance of the system. A prevention specialist needs to understand the weaknesses and strengths of the various systems, and know how each must be used to achieve maximum benefit from its application. This requires a thorough understanding of the inner workings of the various types of locks. It is not sufficient to know what a good lock is in someone else's opinion. A good lock today may not be as good tomorrow as technology improves and manufacturers

alter their designs and production techniques. A lock that is excellent in some applications may be undesirable in others. Knowledge of the basic principles of locking systems will enable a preventions specialist to evaluate any lock and determine its quality and its effectiveness in a particular application.

KEY-OPERATED MECHANISMS

A key-operated mechanical lock uses some sort of arrangement of internal physical barriers (wards, tumblers) that prevent the lock from operating unless they are properly aligned. The key is the device used to align these internal barriers so that the lock may be operated. The lock is ordinarily permanently installed. The key is a separate piece, which is designed to be removed from the lock to prevent unauthorized use.

Three types of key-operated locks will be introduced in this section: disc or wafer tumbler, pin tumbler, and lever.

---

*Originally from The Use of Locks in Physical Crime Prevention. James M. Edgar, William D. McInerney, Joe A. Mele: Butterworth-Heinemann, 1987. Updated by the editor, Elsevier, 2016.

Effective Physical Security, Fifth Edition
http://dx.doi.org/10.1016/B978-0-12-804462-9.00007-5

Tumbler Mechanisms

A tumbler mechanism is any lock mechanism having movable, variable elements (the *tumblers*) that depend on the proper key (or keys) to arrange these tumblers into a straight line, permitting the lock to operate. The tumbler, which may be a disc, a lever, or a pin, is the lock barrier element that provides security against improper keys or manipulation. The specific key that operates the mechanism (called the *change key*) has a particular combination of cuts, or bitings, which match the arrangement of the tumblers in the lock. The combination of tumblers usually can be changed periodically by inserting a new tumbler arrangement in the lock and cutting a new key to fit this changed combination. This capability provides additional security by protecting against lost or stolen keys.

Tumbler mechanisms and the keys that operate them are produced to specifications that vary with each manufacturer and among the different models produced by each manufacturer. These specifications are known as the *code* of the lock mechanism. The coding for each mechanism provides specifications for both the fixed and variable elements of the lock assembly. Fixed specifications include:

- the dimensions of each of the component parts of the lock and the established clearance between each part (e.g., the size and length of the key must match the size and depth of the keyway);
- the spacing of each tumbler position and their relation to each other (Fig. 7.1);
- The depth intervals or increments in the steps of each cut or biting (Fig. 7.2).

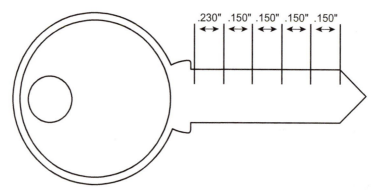

FIGURE 7.1　The spacing or position of each cut on the key is a fixed dimension corresponding to the position of each tumbler in the lock.

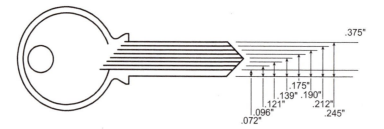

FIGURE 7.2　The depth interval (increment) of the steps of each cut or biting is a fixed dimension.

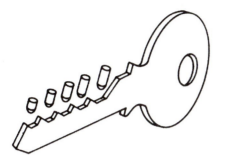

FIGURE 7.3 The depth of each cut corresponds to the length of each tumbler in the lock.

The relationship between the dimensions of the tumblers and the biting on the key is shown for a typical pin tumbler mechanism in Fig. 7.3. These codes provide a locksmith with dimensions and specifications to produce a specific key to operate a particular lock or to key additional locks to the combination of a particular key.

The different arrangements of the tumblers permitted in a lock series are its *combinations*. The theoretical or mathematical number of possible combinations available in a specific model or type of lock depends on the number of tumblers used and the number of depth intervals or steps possible for each tumbler. If the lock had only one tumbler, which could be any of 10 lengths, the lock would have a total of 10 combinations. If it had two tumblers, it would have a possible total of 100 (10×10) combinations. With three tumblers, 1000 (10×10×10) combinations are possible. If all five tumblers were used, the lock would have a possible 100,000 combinations. The number of mathematically possible combinations for any lock can be determined by this method.

Due to a number of mechanical and design factors, however, not all of these theoretically possible (implied) combinations can actually be used. Some combinations allow the key to be removed from the lock before the tumblers are properly aligned (shedding combinations)—something that should not be possible with a properly combinated tumbler lock. Others, such as equal depth combinations, are avoided by the manufacturers.

Some combinations result in a weakened key that is prone to break off in the lock. Others are excluded because the space from one cut in the key erodes the space or positioning of adjacent cuts. The combinations that remain after all of these possibilities have been removed are called *useful combinations*. The useful combinations, which are actually employed in the manufacture of the lock series, are the basis for the *biting chart* that lists the total combinations used in a particular type of model or lock. When other factors are equal, the more the combinations that can actually be used in a lock, the greater the security of the lock. Total useful combinations range from one for certain types of warded locks to millions for a few high-security tumbler key mechanisms.

Disc or Wafer Tumbler Mechanisms

Disc tumbler mechanisms consist of three separate parts: the keys, the cylinder plug, and the cylinder shell (or housing; Fig. 7.4). The plug contains the tumblers, which are usually spring-loaded flat plates that move up and down in slots cut through the diameter of the plug. Variably dimensioned key slots are cut into each tumbler. When no key is inserted or an improper key is used, one or more tumblers will extend through the sides of the plug into the top or bottom locking grooves cut into the cylinder shell, firmly locking the plug to the shell. This prevents the plug from rotating in the shell to operate the lock. The proper change key has cuts or bitings to match the variations of the tumblers. When inserted, the key aligns all of the tumblers in a straight line at the edge of the cylinder plug (the *shear line*) so that no tumbler extends into the shell. This permits the plug to rotate.

Disc mechanisms generally provide only moderate security with limited key changes or combinations. Depth intervals commonly used are from 0.015 to 0.030 inches, which permit no more than four or five depths for each tumbler position. Some models use as many as six tumblers. The more commonly found five-tumbler mechanism, which allows five depth increments

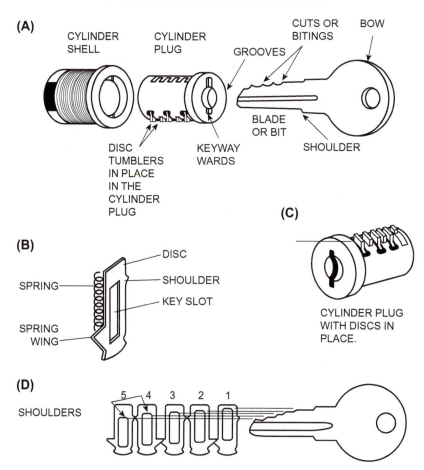

FIGURE 7.4   The key slots in the discs correspond to the cuts, or bitings, in the key. Note how each cut in the key will align its corresponding disc in a straight line with the others.

for each tumbler position, would have a maximum of 3125 implied combinations. The number of useful combinations would, of course, be considerably fewer for the reasons indicated earlier. Some added security is provided by the common, although not universal, use of warded and paracentric keyways, which help protect against incorrect keys and manipulation. Nevertheless, most of these locks may be manipulated or picked fairly easily by a person with limited skills. In addition, the variations cut into the tumblers can be *sight read* with some practice while the lock is installed. Sight reading involves

manipulating the tumblers with a thin wire and noting the relative positions of each tumbler in the keyway. Since each lock has only a limited number of possible tumbler increments, the correct arrangement of these increments can be estimated with fair accuracy, permitting a key to be filed or cut on the spot to operate the lock.

Pin Tumbler Mechanisms

The pin tumbler mechanism is the most common type of key-operated mechanism used in architectural or builders' (door) hardware in

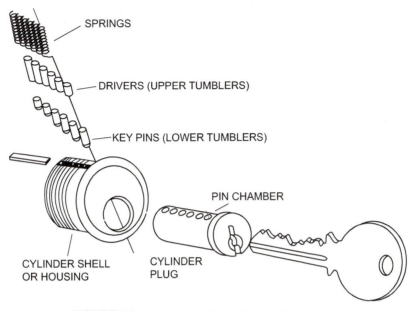

FIGURE 7.5 Basic pin tumbler cylinder lock mechanism.

the United States. The security afforded by this mechanism ranges from fair in certain inexpensive cylinders with wide tolerances and a minimum of tumblers to excellent with several makes of high-security cylinders, including those that are listed by Underwriters Laboratories (UL) as manipulation- and pick-resistant.

The lock operates very much like disc tumbler mechanisms (Fig. 7.5). The locking system consists of a key, a cylinder plug, and a cylinder shell or housing. Rather than using discs, the mechanism uses pins as the basis interior barrier. Each lock contains an equal number of upper tumbler pins (drivers) and lower tumbler pins (key pins). The proper key has cuts or bitings to match the length of the lower pins. When it is inserted, the tops of the key pins are aligned flush with the top of the cylinder plug at the shear line. The plug may then rotate to lock or unlock the mechanism. When the key is withdrawn, the drivers are pushed by springs into the cylinder plus, pushing the key pins ahead of them until the key pins are seated at the bottom

of the pin chamber. The drivers extending into the plug prevent it from rotating (Fig. 7.6).

If an improper key is inserted, at least one key pin will be pushed into the shell, or one driver will extend into the plug. In either case, the pin extending past the shear line binds the plug to the shell. One or more key pins may be aligned at the shear line by an incorrect key, but all will be aligned only when the proper key is used.

Depth intervals commonly used for pin tumbler cylinders vary from 0.0125 to 0.020 inches. These intervals allow between 5 and 10 depths for each tumbler position. The number of pins used ranges from three to eight—five or six is the most common number. Maximum useful combinations for most standard pin tumbler cylinders (assuming eight tumbler depth increments) are as follows:

Three pin tumblers, approximately 130 combinations
Four pin tumblers, approximately 1025 combinations

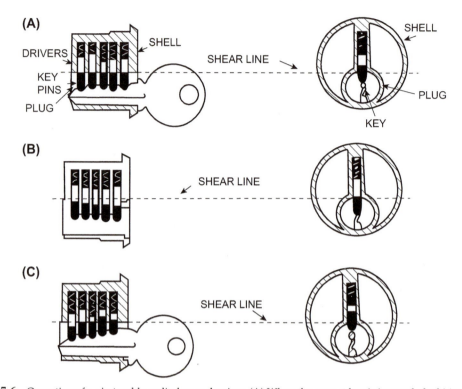

FIGURE 7.6 Operation of a pin tumbler cylinder mechanism: (A) When the correct key is inserted, the bitings in the key align the tops of the lower tumblers (key pins) with the top of the cylinder plug at the shear line. The plug may then be rotated in the shell to operate the lock. (B) When the key is withdrawn, the springs push the upper tumblers (drivers) into the cylinder plug. With the pins in this position, the plug obviously cannot be turned. (C) When an incorrect key is used, the bitings will not match the length of the key pins. The key will allow some of the drivers to extend into the plug, and some of the key pins will be pushed into the shell by high cuts. In either case, the plug cannot be rotated. With an improper key, some of the pins may align at the shear line, but only with the proper key will all five align so that the plug can turn.

Five pin tumblers, approximately 8200 combinations
Six pin tumblers, approximately 65,500 combinations.

These estimates assume that the useful combinations amount to no more than 23% of the mathematically possible combinations. Many common pin tumbler locks use fewer than eight increments, so the number of useful combinations for a specific lock may be much lower than the figures given in the table. Master keying will also greatly reduce the number of useful combinations.

Pin tumbler mechanisms vary greatly in their resistance to manipulation. Poorly constructed, inexpensive cylinders with wide tolerances, a minimum number of pins, and poor pin chamber alignment may be manipulated quickly by persons of limited ability. Precision-made cylinders with close tolerances, a maximum number of pins, and accurate pin chamber alignment may resist picking attempts even by experts for a considerable time.

Most pin tumbler lock mechanisms use warded keyways for additional security against incorrect keys and manipulation. The wards projecting into the keyway must correspond to

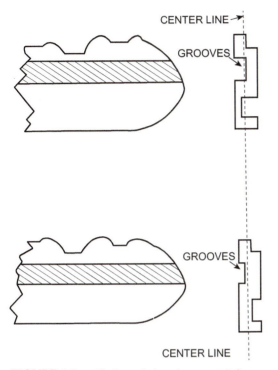

CENTER LINE

GROOVES

GROOVES

CENTER LINE

FIGURE 7.7   Milled, warded, and paracentric keys.

tumbler cylinders with either type of modified driver, special techniques must be used.

There are a number of variations of the pin tumbler cylinder on the market. One, which is seeing increasingly widespread use, is the *removable core cylinder* (Fig. 7.9). These locks were originally produced by the Best Universal Lock Company, whose initial patents have now expired. Most major architectural hardware manufacturers now have them available in their commercial lock lines. This type of cylinder uses a special key called the *control key* to remove the entire pin tumbler mechanism (called the *core*) from the shell. This makes it possible to quickly replace one core with another having a different combination and requiring a different key to operate. Because of this feature, removable core cylinders are becoming increasingly popular for institutional use and in large commercial enterprises where locks must be changed often.

Removable core cylinders do not provide more than moderate security. Most systems operate on a common control key, and possession of this key will allow entry through any lock in the system. It is not difficult to have an unauthorized duplicate of the control key made. If this is not possible, any lock, particularly a padlock, of the series may be borrowed and an unauthorized control key made. Once the core is removed from a lock, a screwdriver or other flat tool is all that is necessary to operate the mechanism. Additionally, the added control pins increase the number of shear points in each chamber, thus increasing the mechanism's vulnerability to manipulation.

Another variation that has been in widespread use for many years is *master keying*. Almost any pin tumbler cylinder can easily be master keyed. This involves the insertion of additional tumblers called *master pins* between the drivers and key pins. These master pins enable a second key, the *master key*, to operate the same lock (Fig. 7.10). Generally, an entire series of locks is combinated to be operated by the same master key. There may also be levels of master keys, including submasters, which open a portion, but not all, of a

grooves cut into the side of the key, or the key cannot enter the lock. When the wards on one side of the keyway extend past the center line of the key, and wards on the other side also extend past the center line, this is known as a *paracentric* keyway (Fig. 7.7). Although warded keyways are commonly used on most pin tumbler mechanisms, paracentric keyways are usually restricted to the better locks. They severely hinder the insertion of lock picks into the mechanisms and the ability of the manipulator to maneuver the pick once it is inserted.

Modifications have been made to the drives in better locks to provide increased security against picking (Fig. 7.8). The usual modified shapes are the *mushroom* and the *spool*. Both of these shapes have a tendency to bind in the pin chamber when picking is attempted, making it more difficult to maneuver them to the shear line. To be consistently successful in picking pin

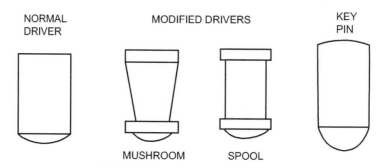

FIGURE 7.8   Pin tumbler modification.

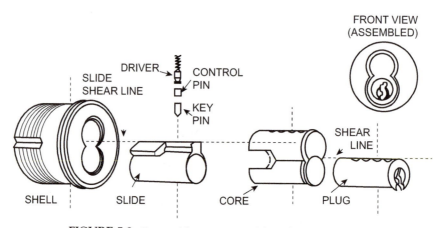

FIGURE 7.9   Removable core, pin tumbler, cylinder mechanism.

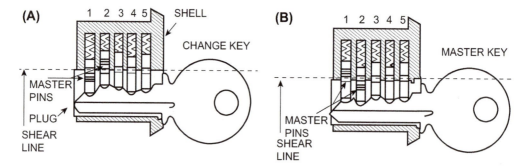

FIGURE 7.10   Master-keyed pin tumbler cylinder mechanism: (A) This is a simple master-keyed system using master pins in the first and second tumbler positions. When the change key is inserted, note that the top of the first master pin aligns with the top of the cylinder plug. The remaining positions show the key pins aligned with the top of the plug. This arrangement permits the plug to turn. (B) With the master key inserted, the first position aligns the top of the key pin with the cylinder plug. The master pin is pushed farther up the pin cylinder. The second position shows the master pin aligning at the top of the plug. The master pin has dropped farther down the pin hole in the plug. The remaining three positions are unchanged. This arrangement also allows the plug to rotate.

series; master keys that open a larger part; and grand masters that open the entire series. In very involved installations, there may even be a fourth level (great grand master key).

There are a number of security problems with master keys. The most obvious one is that an unauthorized master key will permit access through any lock of the series. Less obvious is the fact that master keying reduces the number of useful combinations that can be employed since any combination used must not only be compatible with the change key, but with the second, master key. If a submaster is used in the series, the number of combinations is further reduced to those that are compatible with all three keys. If four levels of master keys are used, it should be obvious that the number of useful combinations becomes extremely small. If a large number of locks are involved, the number of locks may exceed the number of available combinations. When this occurs, it may be necessary to use the same combination in several locks, which permits one change key to operate more than one lock (*cross keying*). This creates an additional security hazard.

One way of increasing the number of usable combinations and decreasing the risk of cross keying is to use a *master sleeve* or ring. This sleeve fits around the plug, providing an additional shear line similar to the slide shear line in a removable core system. Some of the keys can be cut to lift tumblers to sleeve shear line and some to the plug shear line. This system, however, requires the use of more master pins. Any increase in master pins raises the susceptibility of the lock to manipulation, since the master pins create more than one shear point in each pin chamber, increasing the facility with which the lock can be picked.

Thus, although master-keyed and removable core systems are necessary for a number of very practical reasons, you should be aware that they create additional security problems of their own.

The basic pin tumbler mechanism has been extensively modified by a number of manufacturers to improve its security. The common features of high-security pin tumbler cylinder mechanisms are that they are produced with extremely close tolerances and that they provide a very high number of usable combinations. Additional security features include the use of very hard metals in their construction to frustrate attacks by drilling and punching.

Lever Tumbler Mechanisms

Although the lever lock operates on the same principles as the pin or disc tumbler mechanism, its appearance is very different. Fig. 7.11 illustrates a typical lever mechanism. Unlike pin or

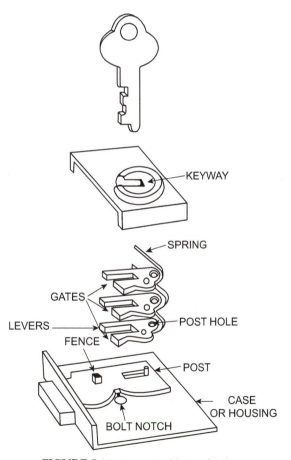

FIGURE 7.11   Lever tumbler mechanism.

disc tumbler devices, the lever lock does not use a rotating core or plug, and the bolt is usually an integral part of the basic mechanism thrown directly by the key. The only other type of mechanism in which the key directly engages the bolt is the warded mechanism. You will recall that the bolt in pin or disc tumbler systems is usually directly operated by the *cylinder plug*, not the key. The key is used to rotate the plug but never comes into direct contact with the bolt.

Despite these somewhat deceptive appearances, the lever lock operates very much like the other tumbler mechanisms. Each *lever* is hinged on one side by the *post*, which is a fixed part of the case. The *leaf springs* attached to the levers hold them down in a position that overlaps the *bolt notch* as shown in Fig. 7.12. In this position, the *bolt* is prevented from moving back into a retracted position by its *fence*, which is trapped by the front edges (*shoulder*) of the levers. When the key is inserted and slightly rotated, the bitings on the key engage the *saddle* of the lever, raising it to a position where the fence aligns with the slot in the lever (called the *gate*). In this position, the fence no longer obstructs the movement of the bolt to the rear, and the bolt can be retracted.

The retraction is accomplished by the key engaging the shoulder of the bolt notch. While the bitings of the key are still holding the levers in an aligned position, the key contacts the rear shoulder of the bolt notch, forcing the bolt to retract as the key is rotated. As the bolt is retracted, the fence moves along the gate until the bolt is fully withdrawn. When the key has rotated fully, completely retracting the bolt, it can be withdrawn.

If an improperly cut key is inserted and rotated in the lock, either the levers will not be raised far enough to align all of the gates with the fence or one or more levers will be raised too high, so that the bottom edge of the lever obstructs the fence (Fig. 7.12). In either case, the bolt is prevented from being forced to the rear, thus opening the lock.

Fig. 7.13A shows one version of the basic lever. A number of variations are on the market.

Some levers are made with projections built into the gate designed to trap the fence in various positions (Fig. 7.13B). The front and rear traps prevent the fence from being forced through the gate when the bolt is in the fully extended or fully retracted position. Fig. 7.13C shows another variation: serrated (sawtooth) front edges. These serrations are designed to bind against the fence when an attempt is made to pick the lock. They are commonly found on high-security lever tumbler mechanisms.

Lever mechanisms provide moderate to high security depending on the number of levers used, their configuration, and the degree of care used in the construction of the lock mechanism. Any mechanisms using six or more tumblers can safely be considered a high-security lock. Some mechanisms use a double set of levers, requiring a double-bited key. The levers are located on both sides of the keyway. This configuration makes the lock very difficult to pick or manipulate.

Lever locks are commonly found in applications where moderate to high security is a requirement, including safe deposit boxes, strong boxes, post office boxes, and lockers. The lever mechanisms available in the United States, because of the integrated, short-throw bolt, are not ordinarily used as builders' hardware. But they are commonly used in that application in Europe, and some of these locks have found their way into the United States.

COMBINATION LOCKS

In principle, a combination lock works in much the same way as a lever mechanism. When the tumblers are aligned, the slots in the tumblers permit a fence to retract, which releases the bolt so that the bolt can be opened. The difference is that where the lever mechanism uses a key to align the tumblers, the combination mechanism uses numbers, letters, or other symbols as reference points that enable an operator to align them manually. Fig. 7.14 shows a simplified view of a

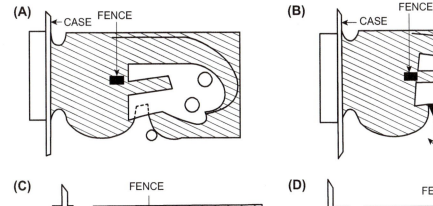

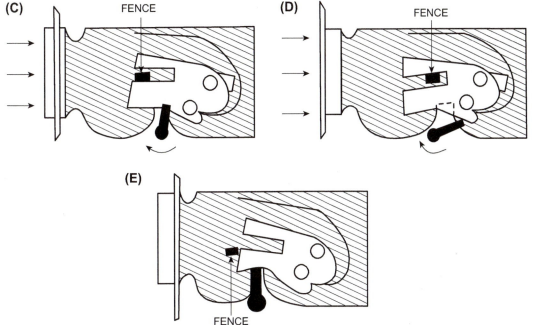

FIGURE 7.12 Operation of a typical lever tumbler mechanism: (A) The bolt is in the fully extended locked position and the key has been withdrawn from the keyway. In this position, the spring forces the lever down toward the bolt notch, trapping the fence against the forward edge (shoulder) of the lever. This prevents the bolt from being forced back. (B) The key has been inserted and the biting on the key has lifted the lever against the spring tension, aligning the gate with the fence. The bolt can now be moved back into the retracted position. (C) The key has begun to force the bolt back into a retracted position by engaging a shoulder of the bolt notch at the same time it is keeping the lever suspended at the correct height to allow the fence to pass into the gate. (D) The bolt is now fully retracted and the key can be withdrawn. (E) If an improper key is inserted the biting either will not lift the lever high enough for the fence to pass through the gate or the lever will be raised too high and the fence will be trapped in front of the lower forward shoulder of the lever. From this position, the bolt cannot be forced back into the retracted position.

typical three-tumbler combination lock mechanism. The tumblers are usually called *wheels*. Each wheel has a slot milled into its edge, which is designed to engage the *fence* when the slot has been properly aligned. This slot is called a *gate*. The fence is part of the lever that retracts the bolt. The gates are aligned with the fence by referring to letters, numbers, or other symbols on the dial.

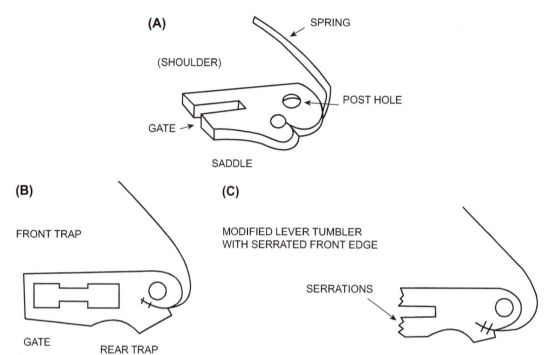

FIGURE 7.13   Lever tumblers. To operate the lock, the key contacts the lever at the saddle, lifting it until the fence is aligned with the gate. The saddles on the various tumblers are milled to different depths to correspond to different cuts on the key.

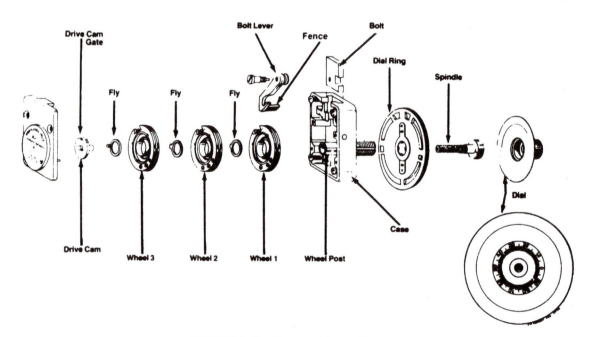

FIGURE 7.14   Three-tumbler combination.

The sequence of symbols that permits the lock to operate is its *combination*. A typical combination sequence using numbers is 10–35–75. The fact that three numbers are used in the combination indicates that the lock contains three tumblers. The number of tumblers in a lock always corresponds to the number of symbols used in its combination. Few modern combination locks use more than four tumblers because combinations of five or more symbols are unwieldy and hard to remember. Older models, however, used as many as six.

Both *drive cam* and dial are fixed to the *spindle* so that as the dial is rotated, the drive cam will also rotate in an identical fashion. The drive cam has two functions. It is the means by which motion of the dial is transferred to the wheels, and when all wheels are properly aligned and the fence retracted, it is the mechanism by which the bolt lever is pulled to retract the bolt.

The wheels are not fixed to the spindle but ride on a *wheel post* that fits over the spindle. These wheels are free floating and will not rotate when the dial is turned unless the *flies* are engaged. The flies are designed to engage pins on the wheels at predetermined points (determined by the combination of that particular lock). When the flies engage these pins, the wheels pick up the rotating motion of the dial. When the flies are not engaged, the wheels will remain in place when the dial is rotated.

To operate a typical three-wheel combination lock, the dial is first turned four times in one direction to allow all of the flies to engage their respective wheels so that as the dial is being turned, all of the wheels are rotating with it. At this point the wheels are said to be *nested*. The object is to disengage each wheel at the spot where its gate will be aligned with the fence. To do this, the operator stops the dial when the first number of the combination reaches the index mark on the dial ring. This first stop aligns the gate of wheel 1 with the fence.

The operator then reverses direction to disengage wheel 1, which remains stationary, and

rotates the dial three turns to the second number in the combination. When this number is under the index mark, wheel 2 is aligned. Again reversing direction to disengage wheel 2, the operator makes two turns to the last number of the combination. This aligns wheel 3. At this point all of the gates are aligned with the fence. The operator then reverses direction once again and turns the dial until it stops.

This last operation has two functions. It aligns the gate on the drive cam with the fence, which permits the fence to retract into the space provided by the three gates in the wheels and the fourth gate in the drive cam. The bolt lever is now engaged with the wheels and drive cam. As the operator continues rotating the dial, the drive cam pulls the bolt lever to retract the bolt. When the dial will no longer rotate, the bolt is fully retracted, and the lock is open.

The security afforded by combination mechanisms varies widely. The critical elements are the number of tumblers used in the lock, the number of positions on the tumbler where the gate can be located, and the tolerances in the width of the gate and fence. Wide tolerances allow the fence to enter the gates even when they are not quite completely aligned, so that, although the proper combination may be 10–35–75, the lock may also operate at 11–37–77.

Until the 1940s, it was often possible to open many combination locks by using the sound of the movement of the tumblers and feeling the friction of the fence moving over the tumblers as indicators of tumbler position. (Tumblers in combination locks do not click despite Hollywood's contentions to the contrary.) Skilled operators were often able to use sound and feel to determine when each tumbler came into alignment. Modern technology has all but eliminated these possibilities, however, through the introduction of sound baffling devices, nylon tumblers, improved lubricants to eliminate friction, false fences, and cams that suspend the fence over the tumblers so that they do not make contact until after the gates are already aligned (Fig. 7.14).

Another manipulation technique of recent vintage utilized the fact that the tumbler wheels with gates cut into them are unbalanced: more weight is on the uncut side than on the cut side. By oscillating the dial, these cut and uncut sides could be determined, and the location of the gates estimated. The introduction of counterbalanced tumblers has virtually eliminated this approach to the better mechanisms.

Radiology has also been used to defeat combination locks. A piece of radioactive material placed near the lock can produce ghost images of the tumblers on sensitive plates, showing the location of the gates. Nylon and Teflon tumblers and shielding material that are opaque to radiation are used to defeat this technique.

LOCK BODIES

Most lever tumbler and warded mechanisms contain an integrated bolt as a part of the mechanism. The key operates directly to throw the bolt, thereby opening and locking the lock. This is not true of pin and disc tumbler locks. These consist of two major components. The cylinder plug, the shell, the tumblers, and springs are contained in an assembly known as the *cylinder*. The other major component is the *lock body*, which consists of the bolt assembly and case or housing. The *bolt assembly* consists of the bolt, a *rollback*, and a *refractor*. This assembly translates the rotating motion of the cylinder plug to the back-and-forth motion that actually operates the bolt. When the cylinder is inserted into the lock body, it is typically connected to the bolt assembly by a *tail piece* or cam. A cylinder can be used in a number of different lock bodies. Here we will be primarily concerned with the types of bodies used on standard residential and light commercial doors. The pin tumbler is the usual mechanism used in these locks, although some manufacturers offer door locks using disc tumbler cylinders (such as the Schlage Cylindrical Lock).

Bolts

There are two types of bolts used for most door applications: the *latch bolt* and the *dead bolt*. Examples of these are illustrated in Fig. 7.15. They are easily distinguished from each other. A latch bolt always has a beveled face, whereas the face on a standard dead bolt is square.

Latch Bolt

This bolt, which is sometimes called simply a latch, a locking latch (to distinguish it from nonlocking latches), or a spring bolt is always spring-loaded. When the door on which it is mounted is in the process of closing, the latch bolt is designed to automatically retract when its beveled face contacts the lip of the strike. Once the door is fully closed, the latch springs back to extend into the hole of the strike, securing the door.

A latch bolt has the single advantage of convenience. A door equipped with a locking latch will automatically lock when it is closed. No additional effort with a key is required. It does not, however, provide very much security.

The throw on a latch bolt is usually $\frac{3}{8}$ inch but seldom more than $\frac{5}{8}$ inch. Because it must be able to retract into the door on contact with the lip of the strike, it is difficult to make the throw much longer. But, because there is always some space between the door and the frame, this means that a latch may project into the strike no more than $\frac{1}{4}$ inch (often as little as $\frac{1}{8}$ inch on poorly hung doors). Most door jambs can be spread at least $\frac{1}{2}$ inch with little effort, permitting an intruder to quickly circumvent the lock.

Another undesirable feature of the latch bolt is that it can easily be forced back by any thin shim (such as a plastic credit card or thin knife) inserted between the face plate of the lock and the strike. Antishim devices have been added to the basic latch bolt to defeat this type of attack. They are designed to prevent the latch bolt from being depressed once the door is closed. Fig. 7.16A shows a latch bolt with antishim device. These are

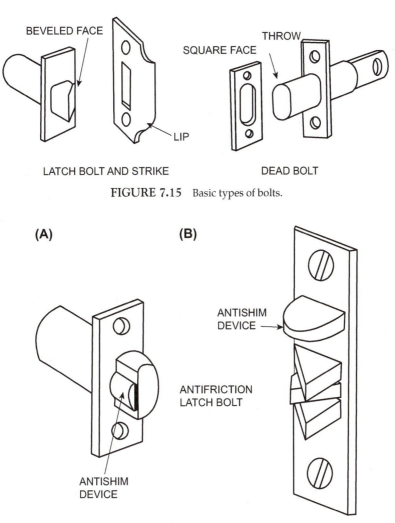

FIGURE 7.15 Basic types of bolts.

FIGURE 7.16 Modified latch bolts: (A) latch bolt with antishim device and (B) antifriction latch bolt with antishim device.

often called *deadlocking latches*, a term that is mildly deceptive since these latches do not actually deadlock and they are not nearly as resistant to jimmying as deadlocks. Often a thin screwdriver blade can be inserted between the face plate and the strike and pressure applied to break the antishim mechanism and force the latch to retract.

Another type of latch bolt, shown in Fig. 7.16B, is called an *antifriction latch bolt.* The antifriction device is designed to reclosing pressure required to force the latch bolt to retract. This permits a

heavier spring to be used in the mechanism. Most modern antifriction latches also incorporate an antishim device. Without it, the antifriction latch is extremely simple to shim.

Dead Bolt

The dead bolt is a square-faced solid bolt that is not spring-loaded and must be turned by hand into the locked and unlocked position. When a dead bolt is incorporated into a locking mechanism, the result is usually known

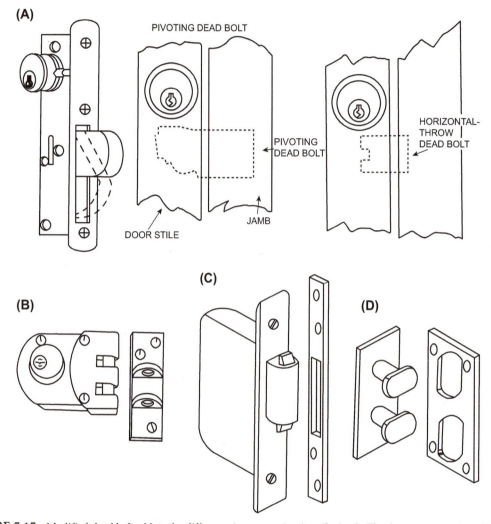

FIGURE 7.17 Modified dead bolts. Note the difference in penetration into the jamb. The deeper penetration afforded by the pivoting bolt increases protection against jamb spreading.

as *deadlock*. The throw on a standard dead bolt is also about ½ inch, which provides only minimal protection against jamb spreading. A *long-throw dead bolt*, however, has a throw of 1 inch or longer. One inch is considered the minimum for adequate protection. Properly installed in a good door using a secure strike, this bolt provides reasonably good protection against efforts to spread or peel the jamb.

The ordinary dead bolt is thrown horizontally. On some narrow-stile doors, such as aluminum-framed glass doors, the space provided for the lock is too narrow to permit a long horizontal throw. The *pivoting dead bolt* is used in this situation to get the needed longer throw (Fig. 7.17A). The pivoting movement of the bolt allows it to project deeply into the frame, at least 1 inch, usually more. A minimum of 1 inch is recommended. When used with a reinforced strike, this bolt can provide good protection against efforts to spread or peel the frame.

Increased security against jamb spreading is provided by a number of different types of dead bolts that collectively are known as *interlocking dead bolts*. These are specifically designed to interlock the door and the strike so that the door jamb cannot be spread. The most common of these is the *vertical-throw dead bolt* shown in Fig. 7.17B. This is usually a rim-mounted device. The other two devices shown in Fig. 7.17C–D (the *expanding dead bolt* and the *rotating dead bolt*) are meant to be mounted inside the door. These locks require a securely mounted strike or they are rendered ineffective.

DOOR LOCK TYPES

Five basic lock types are used on most doors in the United States: mortise, rim-mounted, tubular, cylindrical, and unit. Each of these has a number of advantages and disadvantages from the point of view of the protection offered. Each, however, with the single exception of the cylindrical lockset, can offer sound security when a good lock is properly installed.

Mortise

It was but a few years ago that almost all residential and light commercial locks were mortise locks. A mortise lock, or lockset, is installed by hollowing out a portion of the door along the front or leading edge and inserting the mechanism into this cavity. Suitable holes are then drilled into the side of the door in the appropriate spot for the cylinders and door knob spindle (where the door knob is part of the unit, as is usually the case). Fig. 7.18A shows a typical mortise lockset. These mechanisms require a door that is thick enough to be hollowed out without losing a great deal of its strength in the process. One of the major weaknesses of mortise locks is that the cylinder

is usually held in the lock with a setscrew, which provides very little defense against pulling or twisting the cylinder out of the lock with a suitable tool. Cylinder guard plates can be used to strengthen the lock's resistance to this threat. On some mortise locks, the trim plate acts as a cylinder guard.

Rim Mounted

A rim-mounted mechanism is simply a lock that is installed on the surface (rim) of the door (Fig. 7.18B). Most are used on the inside surface, since outside installation requires a lock that is reinforced against direct attacks on the case. These are usually supplementary locks installed where the primary lock is not considered enough protection. These may or may not be designed for key operation from the outside. If they are, a cylinder extends through the door to the outside where it can be reached by a key.

Tubular

This lock (sometimes called a bore-in) is installed by drilling a hole through the door to accommodate the cylinder (or cylinders) and a hole drilled from the front edge of the door to the cylinder for the bolt assembly (Fig. 7.18C). This type of installation has virtually replaced the mortise lock in most residential and light commercial applications because it can be installed quickly and by persons of limited skill.

Cylindrical Lockset

The cylindrical lockset ordinarily uses a locking latch as its sole fastening element (Fig. 7.18D). It is installed like the tubular lock by drilling two holes in the door. The cylinders are mounted in the doorknobs, rather than in a case or inside the door, which makes them vulnerable to just about any attack (hammering, wrenching, etc.) that can knock or twist the knob off the door. Unfortunately, because it is inexpensive and simple to install,

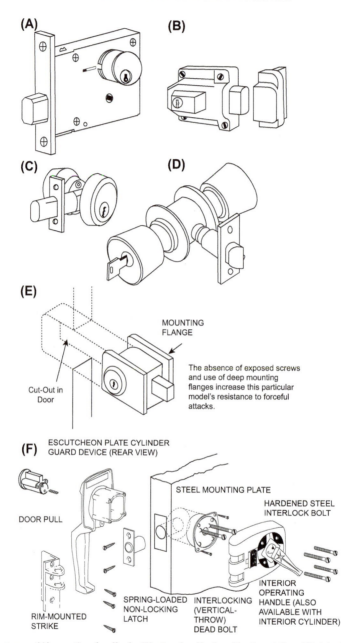

FIGURE 7.18 Lock types: (A) mortise deadlock, (B) rim deadlock with rim strike, (C) tubular deadlock, (D) cylindrical (lock-in-knob) lockset, (E) unit lock, (F) Ideal Superguard Lock II. Note washers must be used for additional protection against cylinder pulling. These are not supplied with the lock.

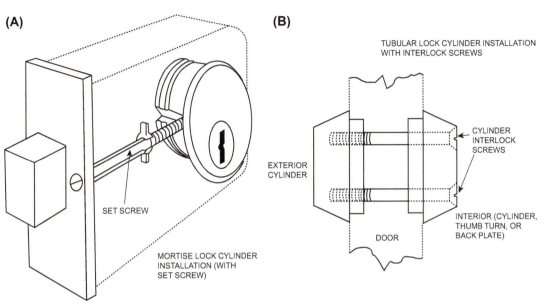

(A)

SET SCREW

MORTISE LOCK CYLINDER
INSTALLATION (WITH
SET SCREW)

(B)

TUBULAR LOCK CYLINDER INSTALLATION
WITH INTERLOCK SCREWS

EXTERIOR
CYLINDER

CYLINDER
INTERLOCK
SCREWS

DOOR

INTERIOR (CYLINDER,
THUMB TURN, OR
BACK PLATE)

FIGURE 7.19   Mortise lock cylinder installation: (A) with setscrew and (B) with interlock screws.

about 85% of all residential locks currently used in new construction in the United States are of this type. It provides virtually no security whatsoever. There is perhaps no harder or faster rule in lock security than the rule that all cylindrical locks should be supplemented by a secure, long-throw dead bolt. Or, better yet, they should be replaced. A number of more secure locks designed to replace the cylindrical lock are now on the market. One of these is illustrated in Fig. 7.18D.

Unit Locks

A unit lock is installed by making a U-shaped cutout in the front edge of the door and slipping the lock into this cutout (Fig. 7.18E). This type of lock usually has the advantage of having no exposed screws or bolts. It is ordinarily used in place of mortise locks where the door is too narrow to mortise without considerable loss of strength. A good unit lock properly installed on a solid door provides excellent protection against attempts to remove the cylinder or to pry or twist the lock off the doors.

Cylinders

Cylinders are mounted in the lock body in a number of ways. Most mortise cylinders are threaded into the lock and secured with a small setscrew (Fig. 7.19). Tubular and rim locks use cylinder interlock screws inserted from the back of the lock. Better mechanisms use ¼-inch or larger diameter hardened steel screws for maximum resistance to pulling and wrenching attacks (Fig. 7.19). Better cylinders incorporate hardened inserts to resist drilling.

Two basic cylinder configurations are available. *Single-cylinder* locks use a key-operated cylinder on the outside, and a thumb turn or blank plate on the inside (Fig. 7.20). *Double-cylinder* locks use a key-operated cylinder on both sides of the door (Fig. 7.20). This prevents an intruder from breaking a window near the door, or punching a hole through the door, reaching in, and turning the lock from the inside. The disadvantage of double cylinders is that rapid exit is made difficult since the key must first be located to operate the inside

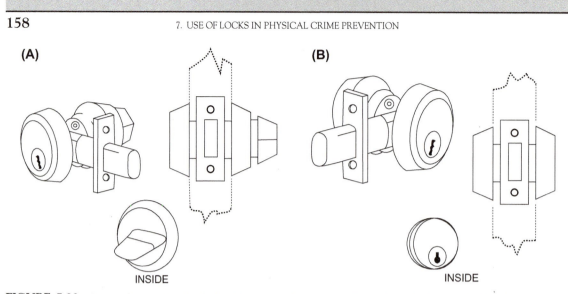

FIGURE 7.20   (A) Single cylinder deadlock with interior thumb turn. (B) Double-cylinder deadlock with interior key cylinder.

cylinder. If a fire or other emergency makes rapid evacuation necessary, a double-cylinder lock could pose a considerable hazard.

Padlocks

The distinguishing feature of padlocks is that they use a shackle rather than a bolt as the device that fastens two or more objects together (Fig. 7.21). The shackle is placed through a hasp, which is permanently affixed to the items to be fastened. Three methods are commonly used to secure the shackle inside the lock body. The simplest and least secure method is to press a piece of flat spring steel against an indentation in the shackle. When the key is inserted, it rotates to spread the spring releasing the shackle (Fig. 7.22). This is a locking method commonly found on warded padlocks. It is found more rarely on tumbler-type locks, but it is found occasionally on the less expensive models.

A slightly more secure method uses a locking dog. The dog is spring-loaded and fits into a notch cut into the shackle (Fig. 7.22). The key is used to retract the dog, permitting the shackle to be withdrawn. Both of these spring-loaded mechanisms are vulnerable to attacks that take advantage of the fact that the locking device can be forced back against the spring by a suitable tool. Shimming and rapping are common techniques used to open them. Often a stiff wire can be pushed down the shackle hole to engage and force back the spring or locking dog. Spring-loaded padlocks should not be used where reasonable security is required.

Positive locking techniques do much to reduce the vulnerability of padlocks to these types of attacks. The most common positive locking method uses steel balls inserted between the cylinder and the shackle. In the locked position, the ball rests half in a groove in the cylinder and half in a notch cut into the shackle. In this position the shackle cannot be forced past the steel ball. When the cylinder is turned to the unlocked position, the groove deepens, permitting the ball to retract into the cylinder when pressure is put on the shackle. This releases the shackle and opens the lock. These locks are designed so that the key cannot be removed unless the lock is in the locked position.

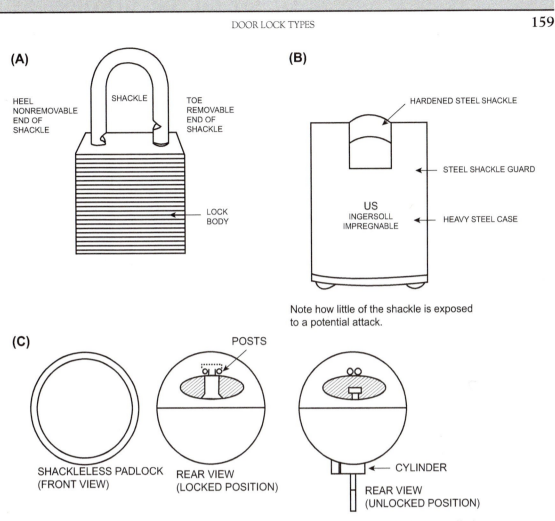

FIGURE 7.21   (A) Warded padlock. (B) High-security padlock. (C) Shackleless padlock.

Padlocks are vulnerable to attacks at several points. The shackle can be pried out of the lock by a crowbar or jimmy, or it can be sawed or cut by bolt cutters. The casing can be crushed or distorted by hammering. Modifications have been incorporated into better padlocks to reduce their vulnerability to these approaches. Heavy, hardened steel cases and shackles are used to defeat cutting and crushing. Rotating inserts and special hardened materials are used to prevent the sawing of shackles. Toe and heel locking is used to prevent prying (Fig. 7.22).

High-security padlocks are large and heavy, using hardened metals in the case, and a thick, hardened, and protected shackle. Positive locking methods are always used. As little of the shackle is exposed to attack as possible in the locked position. A typical high-security padlock is shown in Fig. 7.21. This is the shackleless padlock, which is designed so that a locking bar that is contained entirely inside the case is used in the place of an exposed shackle. This is sometimes called a hasp lock rather than a padlock.

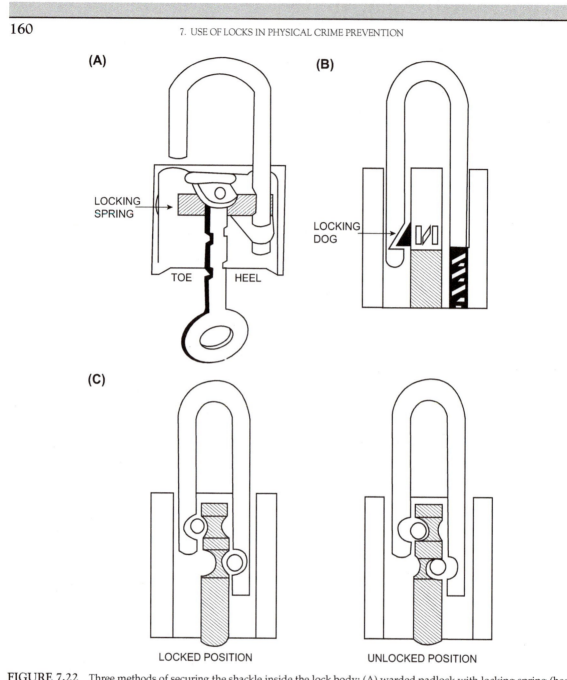

FIGURE 7.22   Three methods of securing the shackle inside the lock body: (A) warded padlock with locking spring (heel locking), (B) padlock with locking dog (toe locking), and (C) positive locking padlock (heel and toe locking).

A padlock is, however, no better than the hasp it engages. Hasps offering reasonable security are made of hardened metals. They must be properly mounted on solid materials so that they cannot be pried off. In the locked position, no mounting screw or bolt should be accessible. Padlocks and hasps should always be considered as a unit. There is no point in mounting a high-security padlock on an inferior hasp. The hasp and lock should always be about the same quality. Where they are not, the complete device is only as good as its weakest member.

STRIKES

Strikes are an often overlooked but essential part of a good lock. A dead bolt must engage a solid, correctly installed strike, or its effectiveness is significantly reduced. The ordinary strike for residential use is mounted with two or three short (usually less than 1 inch) wood screws on a soft wood door frame. It can be easily pried off with a screwdriver. High-security strikes are wider and longer and often incorporate a lip that wraps around the door for added protection against jimmying and shimming (Fig. 7.23). Three or more offset wood screws at least 3½ inches long are used to mount the strike. These screws must extend through the jamb and into the studs of the door frame. This provides added protection against prying attacks. Additionally, none of the fastening screws should be in line. In-line screws tend to split soft wood when they are screwed in. Strikes designed for installation on wood frames should always use offset screws as fasteners.

Reinforced steel should be used on metal-framed doors, especially aluminum frames. Aluminum is an extremely soft metal and, unless a reinforced strike is used, the jamb can be peeled away from the strike area, exposing the bolt to a number of attacks or allowing it to clear the jamb thereby freeing the door to open.

Bolts should be used to mount strikes in metal frames. If the bolt does not penetrate a substantial steel framing member, then a steel plate should be used to back the bolt (very large steel washers may be an acceptable substitute). This prevents the strike from being pried out of aluminum or thin steel frames.

ATTACKS AND COUNTERMEASURES

There are two basic methods of attacking locks: surreptitious techniques and force. There are also a number of ways of circumventing a lock by assaulting the objects to which it is fastened. This chapter will be concerned only with techniques used to defeat locks and the measures that can be used to forestall those techniques.

No lock is completely invulnerable to attack. A lock's effectiveness is determined by how long it will resist the best effort of an intruder. An expert can pick an average pin tumbler cylinder in seconds, and no lock can survive strong force applied for a sufficient length of time. The sole object of using any lock at all is to *delay* an intruder. A good lock makes entry riskier or more trouble than it is worth, and that is the objective. Fortunately, most potential intruders are not experts, thus most moderately secure locks can survive for a reasonable amount of time against common attack techniques.

The proper use of countermeasures will significantly reduce a locking system's vulnerability to breaching by an unauthorized person. However, not all of the countermeasures suggested in the following sections will be appropriate for every application. There is always the necessity of striking a suitable compromise between the expense and inconvenience of a locking system and the value of the items it is designed to protect. Complex and expensive very-high-security systems are simply not appropriate for most residential applications.

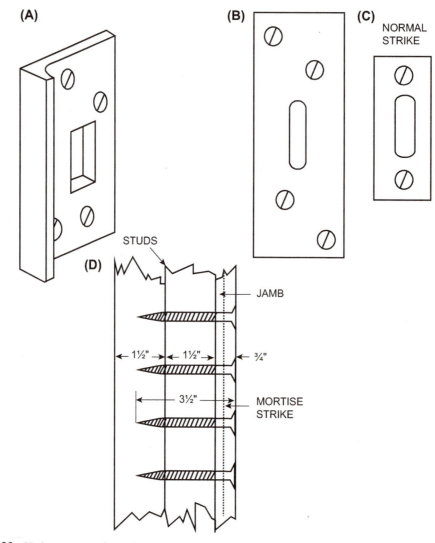

FIGURE 7.23 High-security strikes: (A) security strike with reinforced lip to prevent jimmying and shimming, (B) security strike for wood frames with offset screws, (C) normal strike, and (D) proper installation of a strike on a wood frame.

On the other hand, a cheap padlock on a warehouse containing valuable merchandise is an open invitation for someone to break in and steal it. The objective should always be to ensure reasonable protection in the circumstances surrounding a particular application. With locks, overprotection is often more harmful than insufficient protection. If the user is faced with a more complex security system than is really necessary, she or he simply will not use it. A great many unlawful entries are still made through *unlocked* doors and windows. The temptation to avoid the inconvenience of constantly locking and unlocking barriers seems to be insurmountable for some people. Contributing to this temptation by insisting on more protection than the user actually needs simply aggravates the problem.

Surreptitious Attacks

Four basic surreptitious approaches are used to breach locking devices: illicit keys, circumvention of the internal barriers of the lock, manipulation of the internal barriers, and shimming. The susceptibility of any locking device to these approaches cannot be eliminated but can be minimized through the use of commonsense countermeasures.

Illicit Keys

The easiest way of gaining entry through any lock is by using the proper key for that lock. Thousands of keys are lost and stolen every year. A potential intruder who can determine which lock a lost or stolen key fits has a simple and quick means of illicit entry. If an intruder cannot get hold of the owner's key, quite often he or she can make a duplicate. The casual habit of leaving house keys on the key ring when a car is left in a commercial parking lot or for servicing provides a potential intruder with a golden opportunity to duplicate the house keys for later use. One can also find out the owner's address very quickly by examining the repair bill or tracing the automobile license number.

The risk of lost, stolen, or duplicated keys cannot be eliminated entirely, but certain steps can be taken to minimize it.

Maintain Reasonable Key Security

- Under some circumstances, it is almost impossible to avoid leaving at least the ignition key with a parked car or one to be serviced. But all other keys should be removed.
- When keys are being duplicated, the owner should ensure that no extra duplicates are made.
- Many locks, particularly older locks, have their key code stamped on the front of the case or cylinder. This permits anyone to look up the code in a locksmith's manual and find the proper combination for that lock (or for that combination lock). Codebooks are

readily available for most makes of locks, so if the code appears anywhere on the lock where it can be read after the lock is installed and locked, it should be removed by grinding or over stamping. If removal is not possible, the lock or its combination should be changed.

- Managers and owners of commercial enterprises should maintain strict control over master keys and control keys for removable-core cylinders. The loss of these keys can compromise the entire system, necessitating an extensive and expensive system-wide recombination. Too often in large institutions just about everyone can justify a need for a master key. This is nothing more than a demand for convenience that subverts the requirements of good security. The distribution of master keys should be restricted to those who literally cannot function without them.

Since it is impossible to prevent people from losing keys no matter how careful they are, the next precaution is to *ensure that the lost key cannot be linked to the lock it operates.*

- The owner's name, address, telephone number, or car license number should never appear anywhere on a key ring. This has become common practice to ensure the return of lost keys, but if they fall into the wrong hands, the address provides a quick link between the keys and the locks they fit. The proper protection against lost keys is to always have a duplicate set in a secure place.
- For the same reasons, keys stamped with information that identifies the location of the lock should not be carried around. This used to be a common practice on locker keys, safety deposit box keys, and some apartment building keys. It is no longer as common as it once was, but it still exists. If the keys must be carried, all identifying information should be obliterated, or they should be duplicated on a clean, unmarked key blank.

Recombinate or Replace Compromised Locks

If all these precautions fail and the owner reasonably believes that someone has obtained keys to her or his locks, the combinations of these locks should be changed immediately. Where this is not possible, the locks may have to be replaced. When only a few locks are involved, recombinating cylinders is a fairly quick and inexpensive operation well within the competence of any qualified locksmith.

Another common attack method using a key against which there is less direct protection is the *try-out key*. Try-out key sets are a common locksmith's tool and can be purchased through locksmith supply houses, often by mail. These sets replicate the common variations used in the combination of a particular lock series. In operation, they are inserted into the lock one at a time until one is found that will operate the lock.

Try-out keys are commercially available only for automotive locks. There is nothing, however, to prevent a would-be intruder from building a set for other locks. In areas where one contractor has built extensive residential and commercial developments, most of the buildings will often be fitted with the same lock series. If it is an inexpensive series with a limited number of useful combinations, a homemade try-out key set that replicates the common variations of this particular lock series could be very useful to the potential intruder.

The defense against try-out keys is simply to use a lock with a moderate to high number of available combinations. Any lock worth using has at least several thousand useful combinations. No intruder can carry that many try-out keys, so the risk that he or she will have the proper key is minimal.

Circumvention of the Internal Barriers of the Lock

This is a technique used to directly operate the bolt *completely bypassing* the locking mechanism that generally remains in the locked position throughout this operation. A long, thin stiff tool is inserted into the keyway to bypass the internal barriers and reach the bolt assembly. The tool (often a piece of stiff wire) is then used to maneuver the bolt into the retracted, unlocked position. Warded locks are particularly vulnerable to this method (as was indicated earlier), but some tumbler mechanisms with an open passageway from the keyway to the bolt assembly are also susceptible. Some older padlocks and cylindrical mechanisms had an open passageway of this sort. Few of these are manufactured anymore, but some of the older models are still in use. Any lock that has this type of an opening should be replaced with a better device if reasonable security is a requirement.

Manipulation

The term manipulation covers a large number of types of attacks. At least 50 discrete techniques of manipulating the mechanism of a lock without the proper key have been identified. Fortunately, however, they all fall rather neatly into four general categories: *picking, impressioning, decoding, and rapping*. Regardless of the specific technique used, its purpose is to maneuver the internal barriers of a tumbler mechanism into a position where they will permit the bolt to be retracted. In a disc or pin tumbler mechanism, this means that the cylinder plug must be freed to rotate; in a lever lock, the levers must be aligned with the fence.

The basic countermeasures against all forms of manipulation are the use of close tolerances in the manufacture of the mechanism and increasing the number of pins, discs, or levers. Close tolerances and a large number of tumblers make manipulation a time-consuming process. A number of specific defenses to the various forms of manipulation have also been developed. These will be presented in some detail in the following sections.

Picking

Lock picking is undoubtedly the best known method of manipulation. It requires skill developed by dedicated practice, the proper tools, time, and often a small dose of good luck. No lock is pick proof, but the high-security locks are so difficult to pick that it takes even an expert a long time to open them. One definition of a high-security mechanism, in fact, is one that cannot be picked by an expert in less than half a minute.

The techniques involved in picking the three basic types of tumbler mechanisms are very similar that an example using the pin tumbler cylinder will serve to illustrate the rest.

All picking techniques depend on the slight clearances that must necessarily exist in a mechanism for it to function. The basic technique requires slight tension to be placed on the part of the mechanism that retracts the bolt (which is the cylinder plug in pin tumbler mechanisms) by a special tension tool designed for that purpose (Fig. 7.24). The result of this tension is shown in Fig. 7.25. The pin chamber in the plug has moved slightly out of alignment with the pin chamber in the cylinder shell, creating two *lips* at points A and B. When the key pin is pushed up by the pick, it tends to catch at the shear line because the lip at point A permits it to go no farther. This pushes the driver above the shear line where the lip at point B prevents it from falling down into the cylinder plug once more. As long as tension is maintained, it will stay above the shear line.

This operation is facilitated by the fact that, as shown in Fig. 7.26, the pin chambers in a cylinder plug are seldom in a perfectly straight line. Consequently, the pin closest to the direction of tension will be more tightly bound than the rest of the pins when tension is applied. It can easily be located because it will offer the most resistance to being maneuvered by the pick. Each pin is tested by lifting it with the pick. The pin that is most resistant is picked first. When this pin reaches the shear line, often the cylinder plug will move slightly. The picker receives two important benefits from this very small

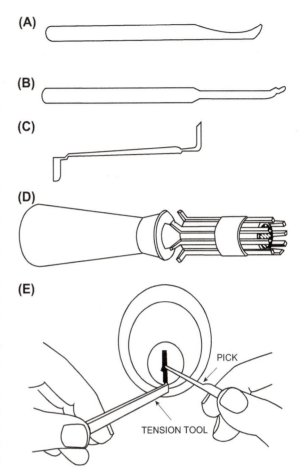

FIGURE 7.24 Lock picks: (A) standard pick, (B) rake pick, (C) tension tool, (D) special pick for tubular mechanisms, and (E) pick and tension tool in use.

movement: first it indicates that the pin has indeed been lifted to the shear line, and second, the movement of the cylinder increases the misalignment between the pin chamber in the plug and the one in the shell, making it even less likely that the driver will drop down into the plug (Fig. 7.27). Once this pin has been picked, the next pin nearest the direction of tension will be the most tightly bound. It is located and picked next. The cylinder plug will again move a very small amount. This operation continues until all of the pins are picked above the shear line and the cylinder plug is free to rotate.

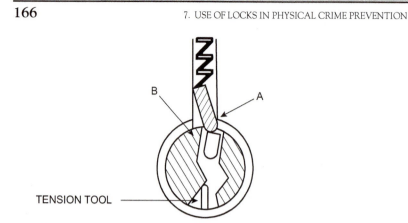

FIGURE 7.25 Illustration of the misalignment caused in a pin tumble cylinder when tension is applied.

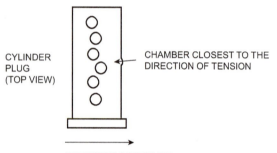

FIGURE 7.26 Pin chamber misalignment. Pin chambers on even the best cylinders are not in a perfectly *straight line*. The misalignment in this illustration is highly exaggerated for clarity.

There are endless variations of this basic picking technique. One of the most common is the use of a *rake pick*. When this pick is used, very slight tension is applied to the plug, and then the rake is run along the tumblers lifting them slightly each time until all of them reach the shear line. Raking increases the chance that one or more key pins will inadvertently be pushed up into the cylinder shell, which will not allow the plug to rotate. It is often necessary to release the tension applied to the plug and start over again several times. Nevertheless, it is a very fast technique and very popular. With luck, an expert using a rake can pick an average pin tumbler in a few seconds.

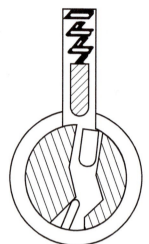

FIGURE 7.27 Increased misalignment occurs as each pin is picked.

Most of the improvements in lock technology made over the last few thousand years have been devoted to increasing the resistance of locks to picking. The major defense is the use of very close tolerances in the mechanism during manufacture. This makes the forced misalignment between the plug and shell necessary for successful picking more difficult to achieve. The addition of more tumblers is also some protection against picking, since it takes the operator more time to pick all of the tumblers in the mechanism. The Sargent Keso mechanism and the Duo disc tumbler use this basic approach. The 12 pins in the former and 14 (soon to be 17) discs in the high-security (UL listed) Duo take a reasonably long time for one to pick successfully. In addition, the unusual configurations of these tumblers make picking even more difficult.

The unusual arrangement of tumblers is also a basic security feature of Ace (tubular) mechanisms. These cannot be picked using ordinary picks, but there are special tools available that facilitate picking this lock. The Ace lock also requires special skills, but these are not too difficult to achieve once basic picking techniques have been mastered.

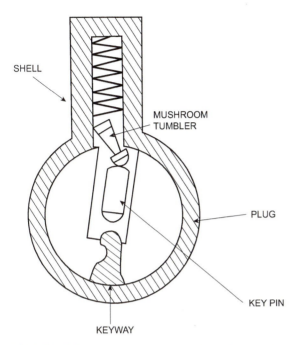

SHELL

MUSHROOM
TUMBLER

PLUG

KEY PIN

KEYWAY

FIGURE 7.28 Mushroom and spool tumblers tend to bind in the pin hole when manipulation is attempted.

make it extremely difficult to pick the key pin to the shear line, since, when interlocked, the two pins act as if they were one solid pin. The key pin and driver will not split at the shear line unless the pins are first rotated to the correct position.

Fewer such embellishments are possible with discs and levers. Most high-security lever locks, however, do use levers that have a front edge cut in a sawtooth design (serrated). These serrations tend to catch on the fence as it is pushed back to provide pressure on the levers. This often makes it necessary for the operator to release tension and start over again, which increases the time spent picking the lock. The use of two sets of levers with two corresponding fences also increases a lever mechanism's resistance to picking attempts.

Impressioning

Impressioning is a technique used to make a key that will operate the lock. It cannot ordinarily be used against high-security mechanisms, but against the average lock it can be very successful.

To make a key by impressioning, a correct key blank is inserted into the lock. It is then securely gripped by a wrench or pliers (there are also special tools available for this purpose) and a strong rotational tension is applied to the plug. While this tension is applied, the key is moved up and down in the keyway. Since the tumblers are tightly bound in the lock by the tension applied to the plug, they will leave marks on the blank. The longest key pin will leave the strongest impression. The key is then removed and a slight cut is filed in the blank. The top of the key is smoothed down with a file or abrasive paper, and the key is again inserted to pick up the impression of the next longest pin. As long as the pin leaves an impression, the cut is deepened. When the pin will no longer leave a mark, the cut is at the right depth. When all of the cuts are to the right depth, the key will operate the lock and permit entry.

Modifications of pin design for increased resistance to picking (and other forms of manipulation) are becoming increasingly important as a basic means of precluding this form of attack. As shown in Fig. 7.28, mushroom, spool, and huck pins tend to bind in the pin chamber when tension is applied to the cylinder plug, preventing the key pin from reaching the shear line. The use of these pins does not provide an absolute defense against picking attempts, but a steady hand and a great deal of skill are required to pick them successfully.

Pins that must be rotated provide what is perhaps the maximum protection currently available against picking. The Medeco and the new Emhart interlocking mechanism both require pins to be lifted to the shear line and rotated to a certain position before the lock will operate. It is very, very difficult to consistently rotate these pins into the correct position. The interlocking pins on the Emhart also

Certain types of lock mechanisms are more susceptible to impressioning than others. Warded locks are easily defeated by this method since the fixed wards can be made to leave strong impressions, and, as previously stated, the depth of the cut on a warded key is not critical. Lever locks are probably the most immune to this technique, since it is difficult to bind the levers in such a manner that they will leave true impressions on the key blank. The use of serrated levers greatly increases this difficulty.

The average pin and disc tumbler mechanism is vulnerable to this approach, but some of the better high-security mechanisms, because of their unusual keys, are not. The Medeco and Emhart interlocking mechanisms are highly resistant. The correct angles of the slant cuts necessary on these keys cannot be determined by impressioning. The special design of the pins in the BHI Huck-Pin cylinder makes the pins bind almost anywhere in the pin hole except at the shear line. All of the impressions that appear on the key blank are, therefore, likely to be false impressions. So, although this mechanism uses a fairly standard paracentric key, it is still very difficult to defeat by impressioning. Modified spool and mushroom tumblers in any pin tumbler mechanism also tend to increase the difficulty of getting good impression marks.

Decoding

Another method of making a key for a particular lock is through decoding. It was mentioned earlier that most disc tumbler mechanisms can be sight read fairly easily. Sight reading involves the manipulation of the tumblers with a thin wire while noting their relative positions in the keyway. Since each mechanism has only a limited number of possible tumbler increments, the correct alignment of these increments can be estimated with fair accuracy, permitting a key to be filed or cut on the spot to rotate the lock. This is one method of decoding.

A more common method is to insert a decoding tool or a specially marked key blank for a short distance into the keyway of a pin or disc tumbler mechanism. Using the key, rotational tension is applied to the plug, which causes misalignment between the pin chambers in the plug and shell. The key is then slowly inserted into the keyway until it has forced the first tumbler to the shear line (Fig. 7.29). The length of this first key pin is determined by the distance the blank (or special tool) enters the keyway. The blank is then moved to the second tumbler, and so on until the length of all of the tumblers is determined and a key can be cut.

Pin tumbler cylinders have wide tolerances, which are the mechanisms that are most susceptible to this particular decoding method. Disc tumblers are less so, although most can easily be sight read. (The Duo, however, is very resistant to sight reading.) Lever locks require special equipment to decode.

The special features offered on some high-security pin tumbler systems dramatically

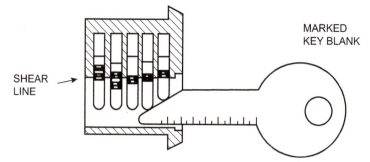

FIGURE 7.29   Decoding using a marked key blank.

increase their resistance to this technique. Some are almost immune. The Ace can be decoded, but it usually requires special tools. The use of mushroom or spool tumblers in almost any mechanism increases its resistance to decoding. And, of course, the close tolerances of any of the better mechanisms are a basic defense against decoding as well as impressioning and picking.

Rapping

This approach relies on the fact that pins in a tumbler mechanism can move freely in the pin chambers. Tension is applied to the plug, resulting in the usual misalignment between the core and shell pin bores. The lock is then struck with a sharp tap just above the tumblers. This causes the pins to jump in their bores. As each key pin reaches its shear line, it pushes the driver before it into the shell where it tends to bind, unable to drop back down into the plug because of the lip caused by the misalignment. Not all of the drivers will be pushed over the shear line by one rap. Several may be required.

Theoretically, almost any lock may be defeated by rapping, but in practice it is a method that is used primarily on padlocks. Since padlocks are not encased in a door, they respond more freely to rapping. Modified, manipulation-resistant pins make rapping very difficult, but not impossible; it is, nevertheless, not a practical approach to high-security padlocks, which use close tolerances and modified pins.

Shimming

Any part of a locking mechanism that relies on spring pressure to hold it in place is vulnerable to shimming unless it is protected. Spring-loaded latch bolts can be shimmed by a thin plastic or metal tool unless they are protected by antishim devices. The locking dogs in padlocks are susceptible to a shim inserted into the shackle hole. The shim acts to force the dog back against the spring pressure releasing the shackle.

Padlocks that use heel and toe locking are more difficult to shim, but the safest course to use is a nonsprung, positive locking system that cannot be threatened by shimming.

Forceful Attacks

If a potential intruder does not have the skills necessary to decode, impression, or pick a lock, the only course is to find a key or use force against the lock to disable and breach it. Comparatively few intruders have developed manipulative skills, so it is not surprising that the large majority of attacks on locks employ force of one kind or another. Locks can be punched, hammered, wrenched, twisted, burned, pulled, cut, exploded, and pried. Given the right tools and a sufficient amount of time, any lock can be defeated by force. But the nature of forceful attacks entails a number of real disadvantages to an intruder who is trying to gain entry without being discovered in the process. First, large and cumbersome tools that are difficult to carry and conceal are often required. This is especially true if one of the better protected locks is being attacked. Second, forceful attacks usually make a considerable amount of noise. Noise, especially unusual noise, tends to prompt people to investigate. Third, it is always immediately evident to even a casual observer that the lock has been attacked. When surreptitious techniques are used, the lock can be opened without damage and relocked, and no one will be able to tell that an unlawful entry has taken place. This often permits the intruder to thoroughly cover tracks even before an investigation is started.

The object of countermeasures against forceful attacks is to increase these hazards. Generally, more force will have to be applied to stronger, better protected locks, requiring larger and more sophisticated tools, taking more time, making more noise, and leaving more evidence that the lock has been defeated.

Although it is sometimes possible to wrench, pry, or pull an entire lock out of a door, most attacks are directed at either the bolt or the cylinder. If the bolt can be defeated, the door is open. If the cylinder can be defeated, the bolt can be maneuvered into an unlocked position. The common type of attack will be presented in the next section, along with measures that can be taken to strengthen a lock against them. It bears repeating that no lock is absolutely immune to forceful attacks. The object is to make its defeat more difficult, noisier, and more time-consuming, increasing the chances that an intruder will be detected or simply give up before successfully breaching the lock.

Attacks on Bolts

Bolts can be pried, punched, and sawed. The object of these attacks is to disengage the bolt from the strike.

Jimmying and Prying

A jimmy is by definition a short prying tool used by burglars. It is a traditional and well-known burglary tool, but other, more lawful, prying tools will work just as well if not better. These include pry bars, crowbars, nail pullers, and large screwdrivers.

The easiest prying attack is against latch bolts with antishim devices. A screwdriver or similar tool with a flat blade is inserted between the strike and latch bolt. Pressure is applied until the antishim mechanism inside the lock breaks. The latch is then easily pushed into the retracted position and the door is open. A supplementary long-throw or interlocking dead bolt is the best defense against this attack. No interlocking, long-throw dead bolts are theoretically vulnerable to jimmying, but it takes a much larger tool, more time, and the destruction or spreading of part of the door jamb so that the end of the dead bolt can be reached with the prying tool. Even then, a great deal of force is required to push the bolt back into the lock and free the door. These combined disadvantages make direct jimmying attacks against long-throw dead bolts very impractical. They are even more impractical

against interlocking dead bolts. If the lock and strike are properly installed, the whole strike would have to be pried loose. This would ordinarily entail the destruction of a considerable portion of the jamb around the strike.

A dead bolt also can be attacked indirectly by prying. An attempt is made to spread the door frame so that the bolt is no longer engaging the strike (Fig. 7.30). An average man can apply about 600 inch-pounds of force using a pry bar 30 inches long. This is usually more than enough to spread a door jamb to clear the normal 72-inch bolt, but a 1-inch (or longer) bolt is more difficult to clear. Interlocking bolts are almost impossible to defeat with this method since they, in effect, anchor the door to the door frame. To spread the frame, the entire strike would have to be pried out. A properly installed security strike is very difficult to remove. Interlocking dead bolts were designed to resist just this type of attack. By and large, they

FIGURE 7.30 Jamb spreading by prying with two large screwdrivers.

are successful. When properly installed, they are, as a practical matter, virtually immune.

Automobile bumper jacks (or similar tools) can also be used to spread a door jamb and release the bolt (Fig. 7.31). Most American jacks are rated at 1 ton. It is probably safe to say that most wooden door frames will succumb to that much force. Reinforced metal frames are more resistant. Long-throw and interlocking dead bolts provide some protection. They may even provide enough protection in most circumstances, since a jamb can only be spread so far by the jack before it buckles outward releasing the jack. The best defense against jamb spreading, however, is a properly constructed and reinforced door frame.

Fortunately, this type of attack is fairly rare. An automobile jack is an awkward tool, hard to carry and conceal, and it requires some time to set up and operate.

Punching

The California Crime Technological Research Foundation (CCTRF) identified punching as a possible direct attack on a dead bolt (Fig. 7.32). The attacker would have to punch through the wall and framing members to reach the bolt. It would be fairly easy to miss the bolt on the first few tries, so several attempts may be necessary. In essence, the punch and hammer are used to force the bolt back into the body of the lock, allowing it to clear the strike. CCTRF determined that an average man can apply a force of 125 inch-pounds with a 1-pound hammer.

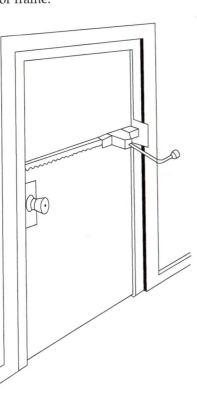

FIGURE 7.31 Use of an automobile bumper jack to spread the door frame. Standard bumper jacks are rated to 2000 pounds. The force of the jack can be applied between the two jambs of a door to spread them and overcome, by deflection, the length of the latch throw.

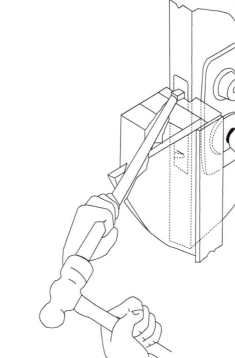

FIGURE 7.32 Forcing the dead bolt with a drift punch and hammer.

Most bolts will probably succumb to a determined punching attack. But it is a noisy approach, and rather hit or miss since it is somewhat difficult to tell if the punch is actually engaging the bolt, and the punch has a tendency to be a serious disadvantage to an intruder, making this an attack of last resort.

Sawing

Bolts can be sawed by inserting a hacksaw or hacksaw blade between the face plate and the strike. (A portion of the jamb will usually be removed or the jamb spread to allow easy access.) Better locks now use hardened bolts or hardened inserts inside the bolt to resist sawing. An even better defense are free-wheeling rollers placed inside the bolt. When the saw reaches these rollers, the sawing action rolls them back and forth but will not cut them. Modified bolts are present in almost all relatively secure locks, and they are virtually immune to sawing attacks.

Peeling

Another way to expose the bolt in metal-framed doors is by peeling. Thin sheet steel and aluminum can be easily peeled. The normal countermeasure against this attack is to use a reinforced strike. Peeling may also be used with prying in an attempt to force the bolt back into the lock.

Attacks on Cylinders

Like bolts, cylinders can be pried and punched. They also can be drilled, pulled, wrenched, or twisted. The usual objective of such attacks is to completely remove the cylinder from the lock. Once it has been removed, a tool can be inserted into the lock to quickly retract the bolt.

Cylinder Pulling

The tool usually used for cylinder pulling is a slam hammer or dent puller—a common automobile body shop tool ordinarily used to remove dents from car bodies. The hardened self-tapping screw at the end of the puller is screwed into the keyway as far as it will go. The hammer is then slammed back against the handle. More often than not, an unprotected cylinder will be yanked entirely out of the lock with one or two slams. CCTRF determined that 200 inch-pounds of force could be applied to a cylinder by a dent puller using a 2½-pound hammer having an 8-inch throw.

Many cylinders are vulnerable to this kind of attack because they are poorly anchored in the lock. Mortise cylinders, for example, are ordinarily threaded into the housing and held in place with a small setscrew. The threads are usually soft brass or cast iron. A good yank shears both these threads and the setscrew.

Most tubular and rim cylinders are held in place by two (or more) bolts inserted from the rear of the lock. This is a much more secure method of retaining the cylinder and one that resists pulling. Retaining bolts of at least ¼ inch in diameter made of hardened steel are good protection against most pulling attempts.

The threat of pulling can be significantly reduced by the addition of a cylinder guard. Some better lock assemblies are offered with built-in guards. Locks that do not have a built-in guard can be protected with a bolt-on guard. These are bolted over the cylinder using carriage bolts that extend completely through the door (Fig. 7.33). They offer the maximum available resistance to pulling. The cylinder guard, when correctly mounted, cannot be pried off without virtually destroying the entire door.

Cylindrical (lock-in-knob) locksets are extremely vulnerable to pulling. Often the doorknob will be pulled off with the cylinder, exposing the entire internal mechanism to manipulation. There is no method of reinforcing a cylindrical lockset against the threat of pulling. The best measure is to replace it or add a good supplementary deadlock with a cylinder guard.

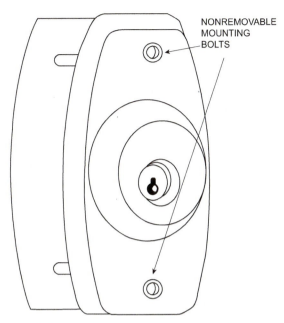

FIGURE 7.33 Bolt-on cylinder guard with back plate. This commercially available plate is of heavy aluminum and is mounted from the inside of the door with hardened steel bolts that enter threaded holes in the guard. It combines good protection with good appearance.

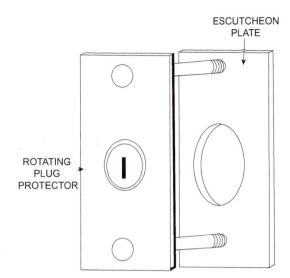

FIGURE 7.34 Cylinder guard with rotating plug protector.

Lug Pulling

If the cylinder is protected against pulling, an attacker may turn to the cylinder plug. The plug is much harder to pull and requires a special tool that looks something like a gear puller. A hardened self-tapping screw is engaged in the keyway and pressure is slowly exerted on the plug until the tumblers snap and the plug can be pulled from the cylinder shell. The bolt mechanism can then be operated by a tool inserted through the shell. The ordinary cylinder guard is no protection against this attack. A special guard is available, however, which is designed to prevent the plug from being pulled (see Fig. 7.34).

Wrenching, Twisting, and Nipping

Most cylinders project from the surface of the door sufficiently to be gripped by a pipe wrench or pliers. Twisting force is applied to the cylinder by the wrench, which is often sufficient to snap or shear the setscrews or bolts that hold the cylinder in the lock. If the cylinder does not project enough for a wrench to be used, a ground-down screwdriver can be inserted in the keyway and twisting force applied to the screwdriver with a wrench. CCTRF found that an 18-inch-long pipe wrench could apply a maximum torque of 3300 inch-pounds to a protruding cylinder housing, and a screwdriver turned with a wrench could produce 600 inch-pounds.

The proper protection against this threat once again is a cylinder guard. Some of the built-in guards are free-wheeling, which prevents a twisting force from being successfully applied. Those that are not free-wheeling are still made of hardened steel, which does not allow the wrench to get a good bite, but more important, it prevents the wrench from reaching the actual cylinder. If a screwdriver and wrench are used, the cylinder might be twisted loose, but it cannot be pulled out. Although the lock might be damaged, it will not be defeated.

Bolt nippers also can be used to remove protruding cylinders by prying and pulling. Cylinder guards also forestall this type of attack.

Cylindrical locksets are very susceptible to wrenching, twisting, and nipping attacks. Some of the better cylindrical devices have free-wheeling doorknobs that provide some protection against wrenching and twisting. Some incorporate breakaway knobs, which do not expose the internal mechanism of the lock when the knob is twisted off. Nevertheless, combinations of twisting, pulling, and hammering attacks usually quickly defeat these devices. The best remedy is to replace cylindrical mechanisms or supplement them with guarded deadlocks.

Drilling

Cylinder plugs can be drilled out using a fairly large drill bit, but the most common drilling attack is centered on the shear line between the plug and shell (Fig. 7.35). A smaller bit is used to drill through the pins, creating a new shear line and releasing the plug, which can then be rotated using a screwdriver or key blank in the keyway. Most of the better locks incorporate hardened inserts to frustrate drilling. Any lock receiving UL approval incorporates these features. Hardened materials do not prevent drilling, but drilling through tempered steel is a long and slow process, which greatly increases the chances of detection.

BHI's Huck-Pin cylinder has an added protection against drilling. When most cylinders are drilled at the shear line, the drivers will fall out of the shell into the plug, releasing the plug

to rotate. BHI's drivers are flanged, which prevents them from falling out, so they still effectively lock the mechanism after it is drilled. This does not prevent the entire cylinder from being drilled out, but this is an even longer and slower process than drilling along the shear line.

Punching

Rim-mounted deadlocks are particularly vulnerable to punching. These are ordinarily mounted on the back of a door with wood screws. But, since most of the currently available doors are made with particle board cores under a thin veneer overlay, screws are seldom able to take much pressure. Several good blows with a hammer and punch on the face of the cylinder will often drive it through the door, pulling the screws out, so the entire lock body is dislodged.

Correctly mounting the lock using bolts that extend through the door and engage an escutcheon plate (or even large washers) on the front side generally frustrates punching attacks.

Cylindrical locksets are vulnerable to combination punching and hammering attacks. The knob is first broken off, then the spindle is punched through the lock, exposing the latch bolt assembly to manipulation.

Hammering

Hammering, as well as pulling, wrenching, and twisting, is a quick and very effective way to disable cylindrical locksets. It is not as effective against cylinders, particularly those that

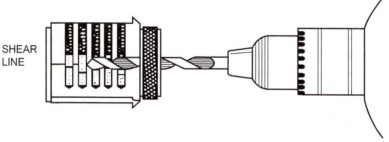

FIGURE 7.35 Drilling.

are protected by cylinder guards. Ordinarily the knob on a cylindrical mechanism can be quickly broken off by one or two strong blows. There is no direct defense against this type of attack. Again, the only viable solution is a supplementary guarded deadlock or replacement of the cylindrical lockset with a more secure lock.

LOCKS AND THE SYSTEMS APPROACH TO SECURITY

Locks are an essential part of most security systems. They are, however, only one part. The effectiveness of a lock cannot be considered apart from the effectiveness of the entire system. A lock is no better than the door it is on, or the frame in which the door is mounted. The strongest lock available on a substandard door does not prevent the door from being defeated, even though the lock cannot be.

The degree of protection required from any security system reflects the value of the items to be protected. Most residences require only a modest degree of security—sufficient to thwart the casual or opportunistic intruder. Jewelry stores, banks, and other establishments, which must keep valuable items on the premises, attract a more determined attacker. The degree of protection for these places must, therefore, necessarily be greater. But whatever the degree of protection required, the actual protection offered by any system is no greater than the vulnerability of its weakest member. A good lock on a poor door provides no more protection than the strength of the door. A good lock on a solid door in a substandard wall is as vulnerable as the wall is weak.

The locks employed in any protection system must complement the system. If a moderate degree of security is required (as in a residential application), a good cylinder properly installed in a secure lock body must be correctly mounted on a good, solid door. The door must be correctly hung, using good hardware, on a properly constructed door frame. The frame must be strongly braced and secured to the wall. The wall must be at least as strong as the door system installed in it. If the lock, the door, the frame, or the wall is significantly weaker than the rest of the system, it is the point most likely to be successfully attacked.

A good lock is essential to a good security system. It is often the point at which an intruder will focus an attack. But good locks are not synonymous with good security. Always examine the system as a whole.

APPENDIX 7A: KEY CONTROL*
Eugene D. Finneran

Before an effective key control system can be established, every key to every lock that is being used in the protection of the facility and property must be accounted for. Chances are good that it will not even be possible to account for the most critical keys or to be certain that they have not been copied or compromised. If this is the case, there is but one alternative—rekey the entire facility.

Once an effective locking system has been installed, positive control of all keys must be gained and maintained. This can be accomplished only if an effective key record is kept. When not issued or used, keys must be adequately secured. A good, effective key control system is simple to initiate, particularly if it is established in conjunction with the installation of new locking devices. One of the methods used to gain and maintain effective key control is outlined as follows:

1. **Key cabinet**. A well-constructed cabinet will have to be procured. The cabinet will have to be of sufficient size to hold the

*Originally from Finneran, ED. Security supervision: A handbook for supervisors and managers. Stoneham (MA): Butterworths; 1981.

original key to every lock in the system. It should also be capable of holding any additional keys that are in use in the facility but are not a part of the security locking system. The cabinet should be installed in such a manner so as to be difficult, if not impossible, to remove from the property. It should be secured at all times when the person designated to control the keys is not actually issuing or replacing a key. The key to the key cabinet must receive special handling, and when not in use it should be maintained in a locked compartment inside a combination-type safe.

2. **Key record**. Some administrative means must be set up to record key code numbers and indicate to whom keys to specific locks have been issued. This record may take the form of a ledger book or a card file.

3. **Key blanks**. Blanks used to cut keys for issue to authorized personnel must be distinctively marked for identification to ensure that no employees have cut their own keys. Blanks will be kept within a combination-type safe and issued only to the person authorized to cut keys and then only in the amount that has been authorized by the person responsible for key control. Such authorization should always be in writing, and records should be maintained on each issue, which will be matched with the returned key. Keys damaged in the cutting process must be returned for accountability.

4. **Inventories**. Periodic inventories will have to be made of all key blanks, original keys, and all duplicate keys in the hands of the employees to whom they have been issued. This cannot be permitted to take the form of a phone call to an employee, supervisor, or executive asking if they still have their key. It must be a personal inspection of each key made by the person who has been assigned responsibility for key control.

5. **Audits**. In addition to the periodic inventory, an unannounced audit should be made of all key control records and procedures by a member of management. During the course of these audits a joint inventory of all keys should be conducted.

6. **Daily report**. A daily report should be made to the person responsible for key control from the personnel department, indicating all persons who have left or will be leaving the employ of the company in the near future. A check should be made, upon receipt of this report, to determine whether the person named has been issued a key to any lock in the system. In the event a key has been issued, steps should be initiated to ensure that the key is recovered.

Security force personnel will normally be issued master keys, when such a system is in effect, or they will be issued a ring of keys permitting them to enter any part of the guarded facility. Keys issued to the security force should never be permitted to leave the facility. They should be passed from shift to shift and must be receipted for each time they change hands. The supervisor must ensure that all security personnel understand the importance of not permitting keys to be compromised.

A lost master key compromises the entire system and results in a breakdown of the security screen. Such compromise will necessitate the rekeying of the entire complex, sometimes at a cost of thousands of dollars.

If rekeying becomes necessary, it can most economically be accomplished by installing new locking devices in the most critical points of the locking system and moving the locks removed from these points to less sensitive areas. Of course, it will be necessary to eventually replace all of the locks in the system, but by using the procedure just described the cost can be spread over several budgeting periods.

NEW STANDARD SET FOR EXIT DEVICES, LOCKS, AND ALARMS [1]

The Builders' Hardware Manufacturer's Association (BHMA) has announced a new American National Standard for exit locks and exit alarms for the safety and security of building occupants.

Developed by BHMA, the new standard was recently approved by the American National Standards Institute (ANSI).

In effect, the new standard recognizes the increased importance of locks, alarms, and other devices that control egress from a building. The standard establishes general requirements as well as operational tests and finish tests for these products. In addition, it gives descriptions and type numbers of exit locks and exit alarms.

Revisions include increased performance requirements with respect to the recommended tests and a slam test not part of the earlier standards has been added. Testing of products in accordance with this standard allows for certification to the ANSI/BHMA standard to be established by third-party testing laboratories.

For more information, or to purchase copies of the ANSI/BHMA A156.29 Standard, please visit http://www.buildershardware.com.

ELECTRIFIED PANIC HARDWARE [2]

Where a door is located in the path of egress, panic hardware is often used, depending on the occupancy rating. Panic hardware is required on any door where there could be a large number of people needing exit in an emergency. Panic hardware is easily identified by the push bar (formerly called a crash bar) that the users press as they push through the door.

Panic hardware facilitates a single exit motion because users have only to push on the door as they are moving through it. This facilitates the rapid exit of large numbers of people because no one has to wait behind anyone else while they stop to turn a door handle. In a severe emergency such as a fire, such momentary delays can compound to cause a crush of people behind a door that is unlocked but that can become a barrier if someone has difficulty with the door handle. There are several basic types of panic hardware configurations, depending on the requirements of the door to which the panic hardware is mounted. Panic hardware is electrified by one of several methods, usually involving a solenoid that releases a latch on the door.

Specialty locks. Most people pay little attention to doors and locks; they just use them. However, there are a remarkable number of variations of doors, frames, locks, and electrification methods. Some unusual locks have been developed for special needs.

Switches. Door and gate position switches (DPS) sense if the door or gate is opened or closed. A variant of the DPS is the monitor strike, which determines if the door is not only closed but also whether a latch bolt or dead bolt is in fact engaged. The typical DPS is composed of a magnetically sensitive switch and a magnet placed close to the switch. Typically, the switch is placed on the door frame and the magnet is placed on the door or gate. When the door or gate is opened, the switch also opens, sending a signal to the alarm system. Variants of DPSs include surface and concealed mounting versions, wide- and narrow-gap sensing areas, and conventional or balanced bias types. Wide-gap DPSs were developed to prevent accidental triggering by nuisance conditions, such as when the wind blows against a sliding glass door. To prevent an intruder from simply placing a magnet against the DPS while opening the door, balanced-bias switches were developed that place the switch in a closely controlled magnetic field. If another magnet is brought near the switch when the door is closed, that act alone will trigger an alarm even before the door is opened. Other types of DPSs include plunger type, Hall effect, and mercury switches. These are sometimes used in areas where it is not possible to place a magnet in the door or gate or where a device must be alarmed if it is moved. The plunger switch alerts when the object that is pushed against it is moved. These are often mechanical switches and can be unreliable for high-security applications. Hall effect switches rely on the presence of a magnetic field within a confined area to alert. They also work by moving the object. Mercury switches are sometimes placed inside an object that should not be moved in any dimension and can be made to alert to the slightest movement. These are often used with radio frequency transmitters.

REFERENCES

[1] Security Beat [weekly newsletter by publisher of Access Control and Security Systems] 2, no. 7, February 19, 2002.
[2] Electronics Elements a Detailed Discussion, Thomas L. Norman, CPP, PSP, CSC.

APPENDIX 7B: KEY CONTROL AND LOCK SECURITY CHECKLIST*

John E. Hunter

1. Has a key control officer been appointed?
2. Are locks and keys to all buildings and entrances supervised and controlled by the key control officer?
3. Does the key control officer have overall authority and responsibility for issuance and replacement of locks and keys?
4. What is the basis for the issuance of keys, especially master keys?

* Prepared by John E. Hunter, U.S. National Park Service.

5. Are keys issued only to authorized personnel? Who determines who is authorized? Is the authorization in writing?
6. Are keys issued to other than installation personnel? If so, on what basis? Is it out of necessity or merely for convenience?
7. Are keys not in use secured in a locked, fireproof cabinet? Are these keys tagged and accounted for?
8. Is the cabinet for duplicate keys regarded as an area of high security?
9. Is the key or combination to this cabinet maintained under appropriate security or secrecy? If the combination is recorded, is it secured?
10. Are the key locker and record files in order and current?
11. Are issued keys cross-referenced?
12. Are current records maintained indicating
    a. Buildings and/or entrances for which keys are issued?
    b. Number and identification of keys issued?
    c. Location and number of duplicate keys?
    d. Issue and turn in of keys?
    e. Location of locks and keys held in reserve?
13. Is an audit ever made, asking holders to actually produce keys, to ensure that they have not been loaned or lost?
14. Who is responsible for ascertaining the possession of key?
15. Is a current key control directive in effect?
16. Are inventories and inspections conducted by the key control officer to ensure compliance with directives? How often?
17. Are keys turned in during vacation periods?
18. Are keys turned in when employees resign, are transferred, or are fired?
19. Is the removal of keys from the premises prohibited when they are not needed elsewhere?

20. Are locks and combinations changed immediately upon loss or theft of keys or transfer or resignation of employees?

21. Are locks changed or rotated within the installation at least annually regardless of transfers or known violations of key security?

22. Are current records kept of combinations to safes and the dates when these combinations are changed? Are these records adequately protected?

23. Has a system been set up to provide submasters to supervisors and officials on a need basis with facilities divided into different zones or areas?

24. If master keys are used, are they devoid of markings identifying them as master keys?

25. Are master keys controlled more closely than change keys?

26. Must all requests for reproduction or duplication of keys be approved by the key control officer?

27. Are key holders ever allowed to duplicate keys? If so, under what circumstances?

28. Where the manufacturer's serial number on combination locks and padlocks might be visible to unauthorized persons, has this number been recorded and then obliterated?

29. Are locks on inactive gates and storage facilities under seal? Are seals checked regularly by supervisory or key control personnel?

30. Are measures in effect to prevent the unauthorized removal of locks on open cabinets, gates, or buildings?

31. Are losses or thefts of keys and padlocks promptly reported by personnel and promptly investigated by key control personnel?

32. If the building was recently constructed, did the contractor retain keys during the period when construction was being completed? Were locks changed since that time? Did the contractor relinquish all keys after the building was completed?

33. If removable-core locks are in use, are unused cores and core change keys given maximum security against theft, loss, or inspection?

34. Are combination lock, key, and key control records safeguarded separately (i.e., in a separate safe or file) from keys, locks, cores, and other such hardware?

35. Are all locks of a type that offers adequate protection for the purpose for which they are used?

Internal Threats and Countermeasures*

Philip P. Purpura

INTRODUCTION

A **threat** is a serious, impending or recurring event that can result in loss, and it must be dealt with immediately. **Internal loss prevention** focuses on threats from inside an organization. Crimes, fires, and accidents are major internal loss problems. Catrantzos [12] points to the insider, trusted employee who betrays their allegiance to their employer and commits workplace theft, violence, sabotage, espionage, and other harmful acts. The workplace can be subject to infiltration by spies, gangs, organized crime, and terrorists. Losses can result from full-time, part-time, and temporary employees; contractors; vendors; and other groups who have access to the worksite both physically and remotely.

Productivity losses also illustrate the range of internal losses. Such losses can result from poor plant layout or substance abuse by employees. Other productivity losses result from employees who loaf, arrive at work late, leave early, abuse coffee breaks, socialize excessively, use the Internet for nonwork-related activities, and prolong work to create overtime; these abuses are called **theft of time**.

Faulty measuring devices, which may or may not be known to employees, are another cause of losses. Scales or dispensing devices that measure things ranging from truck weight to copper wire length are examples.

We can see that the spectrum of internal threats is broad. Although this chapter concentrates on internal theft and associated countermeasures, the strategies covered also apply to many internal and external (e.g., burglary and robbery) threats.

INTERNAL THEFT

How Serious Is the Problem?

Internal theft also is referred to as *employee theft, pilferage, embezzlement, fraud, stealing, peculation,* and *defalcation*. **Employee theft** is stealing by employees from their employers. **Pilferage** is stealing in small quantities. **Embezzlement** occurs when a person takes money or property that has been entrusted to his or her care; a breach of trust occurs. *Peculation* and *defalcation* are synonyms for embezzlement. Whatever term is used, this problem is an insidious menace to the survival of businesses, institutions, and

* From Purpura, PP. Security and loss prevention 6e. Boston: Butterworth-Heinemann; 2013. Updated by the editor, Elsevier, 2016.

organizations. This threat is so severe in many workplaces that employees steal anything that is not "nailed down."

The total estimated cost of employee theft varies from one source to another, mainly because theft is defined and data are collected in so many different ways. An often-cited statistic, from the U.S. Chamber of Commerce, is that 30% of business failures result from employee theft. The Association of Certified Fraud Examiners ([2]: 4–5) conducted research that found that the typical organization loses 5% of its annual revenue to **occupational fraud**, defined as follows: "The use of one's occupation for personal enrichment through the deliberate misuse or misapplication of the employing organization's resources or assets." They claim that if this figure were applied to the Gross World Product, global losses would translate to about $2.9 trillion annually. These figures may be higher when direct and indirect costs are combined. Indirect costs can include damage to brand, a slowing of production, lower employee morale, investigative expenses, and an insurance premium hike after a claim. The mean loss per case was about $160,000 and each crime lasted about 18 months before detection.

Why Do Employees Steal?

Two major causes of employee theft are employee personal problems and the environment. Employee personal problems often affect behavior on the job. Financial troubles, domestic discord, drug abuse, and excessive gambling can contribute to theft. It is inappropriate to state that every employee who has such problems will steal, but during trying times, the pressure to steal may be greater. Research by the Association of Certified Fraud Examiners ([2]: 4–5) revealed that the most common behavioral "red flags" of offenders were living beyond their means (43%) and financial difficulties (36%). A wise employer should be alert to troubled employees and suggest referral to an employee assistance program.

The environment also affects internal theft (Fig. 8.1). Blades ([8]: 35) writes that an individual's differences (e.g., ethnicity, accent, or hobbies) can result in bullying or tormenting by coworkers that can lead to alienation and thoughts of revenge, such as theft and violence. Management must ensure that the corporate culture facilitates respect for individual difference. A system of policies, procedures, awareness, and training are essential. Otherwise, litigation can result, besides other losses.

Politicians, corporate executives, and other "pillars of society" are constantly being found guilty of some form of crime, resulting in inadequate socialization. In other words, poor examples are set: employees may observe managerial illegalities and then act similarly. In many businesses, because so many people are stealing, those who do not steal are the deviants and outcasts; theft becomes normal and honesty becomes abnormal. Some managers believe that employee theft improves morale and makes boring jobs exciting. In certain workplaces, employees are actually instructed to be dishonest. This can be seen when receiving department workers are told by their supervisor to accept overages during truck deliveries without notifying the vendor.

Edwin Sutherland, a noted criminologist, offered his theory of **differential association** to explain crime. Simply put, criminal behavior is learned during interaction with others, and a person commits crime because of an excess of definitions favorable to violation of law over definitions unfavorable to violation of law. The implication of this theory for the workplace is that superiors and colleagues in a company are probably a more important determinant of crime than is the personality of the individual. Conklin ([17]: 278–279) writes in his criminology textbook that a former head of the Securities and Exchange Commission's Division of Enforcement stated bluntly, "Our largest corporations have trained some of our brightest young people to be dishonest."

A study of college student knowledge of how to commit computer crimes found that threat

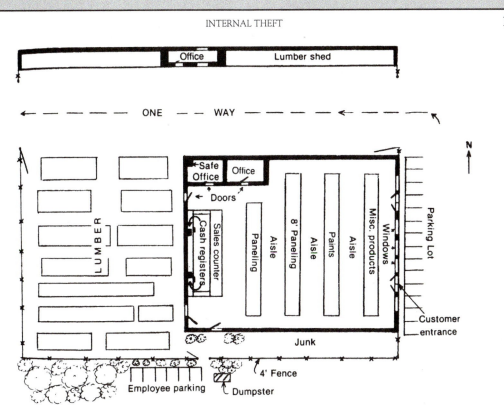

FIGURE 8.1 Woody's Lumber Company. Woody's Lumber Company has suffered declining profits in recent years. A recently hired manager quickly hired six people to replace the previous crew, which was fired for internal theft. Four additional people were quickly hired for part-time work. The process for conducting business is to have customers park their cars in the front of the store, walk to the sales counter to pay for the desired lumber, receive a pink receipt, drive to the rear of the store, pick up the lumber with the assistance of the yard crew, and then depart through the rear auto exit. At the lumber company, loss prevention is of minimal concern. An inoperable burglar alarm and two fire extinguishers are on the premises.

of punishment had little influence on their misdeeds. In this study, the strongest predictor of computer crime was differential association with others who presented definitions favorable to violation of the law ([56]: 495–518).

The implications for security from differential association theory point to the importance of ethical conduct by top management, who should set a good example in the socialization of all employees. In addition, since criminal laws can be impotent, preventive security strategies are essential.

When employees steal, a hodgepodge of rationalizations (excuses) is mentally reviewed to relieve guilt feelings. Some of these rationalizations are "Everybody does it," "It's a fringe benefit,"

and "They aren't paying me enough." Research by Klenowski et al. [38] found through interviews of white-collar offenders that they rely on gender themes of masculinity and femininity to justify their criminal behavior. The researchers show that men and women account for their crimes in different ways. Generally, both seek to minimize guilt and maintain a positive self-image; however, men used *self-reliance* (e.g., accomplish goals in the business world at the expense of all else) to rationalize criminal behavior, while women relied on *necessity* (e.g., self-defined distressed financial situation). The researchers concluded that it is easier for men to deny harm, condemn accusers, and argue that the behavior is normal than it is for women.

Donald R. Cressey [18], in his classic study, analyzed thousands of offenders to ascertain common factors associated with inside thievery. He found three characteristics that must be present before theft would be committed. Cressey's **employee theft formula** is

Motivation + Opportunity + Rationalization = Theft

Motivation develops from a need for money to finance a debt or a drug problem or to win approval from others. Opportunity occurs at many unprotected locations, such as a loading dock. Cressey observed that embezzlers' financial problems are "nonshareable" because of embarrassment or shame, and they rationalize their illegal behavior. This formula illustrates the need for security and an honest environment.

Deterrence has its limitations because following a crime, the certainty of both swift action by authorities and punishment often do not occur. *Prevention* seeks proactive security methods to reduce the probability of harmful events and to mitigate losses if harmful events occur. *Rational choice theory*, related to deterrence theory, points out that a person studies the consequences of a crime against the benefits prior to committing a crime and chooses a criminal act if the rewards offset the consequences. *Routine activity theory* notes that crime occurs when three elements converge (1) a motivated offender, (2) a suitable target, and (3) the absence of a capable guardian. Rational choice theory and routine activity theory are sometimes viewed as opportunity theories that seek to reduce opportunities for crime by changing physical features of the environment, implementing security strategies, and changing behavior. *Situational crime prevention* techniques offer practical strategies to reduce *opportunities* for crime. Examples include increasing the effort and risks confronting the offender. These theories have practical application to the employee theft problem.

Speed ([57]: 31–48) offers insights into the complexity of employee dishonesty, what deters and motivates employee thieves, and management countermeasures. He focused his research on a major retailer in the United Kingdom to learn how loss prevention could be better targeted. Speed studied company records of employee offenders and surveyed attitudes of a sample of employees. He proposed a management strategy that divides employees into four groups, based on age and length of service, and then he designed loss prevention strategies for each group. The four groups and the strategies for each are summarized next:

- *First group*: Employees 20 years of age or younger, new to the company.
- *Second group*: Employees in their 20 years of age employed with the company for about 2 years.
- *Third group*: Employees with greater length of service and experience than the first two groups.
- *Fourth group*: Employees with considerably greater length of service or are much older.

Speed's research shows that the first group presents great risk of theft because they are less likely to be deterred by disapproval by others or by losing their job. However, more of them fear being caught than the slightly more experienced employees. The first group commits the simplest types of offenses with the lowest values. Strategies for this group include restricted access to high-risk operations and ensuring they are complying with systems. The second group also presents great risk of theft because they are confident that they will avoid detection. They commit high value offenses but are influenced more than the first group by the possibility of losing their job. The recommended strategy for this group is to portray the risks of criminality and the possibility of prosecution. Theft among the third group is less common but more complex and less easy to detect. This group is more likely to be deterred by disapproval by others.

Controls that remove opportunities are less likely to be successful with this group. A more successful strategy is to remind them of the status and benefits they maintain within the company and the financial impact of offending. The fourth group represents the lowest risk but the greatest confidence of not being caught. This group is similar to the third group on other characteristics.

How Do Employees Steal?

The methods used to steal from employers are limited by employee imagination. Employees often pilfer items by hiding them under their clothing before leaving the workplace. Methods that are more sophisticated may involve the careful manipulation of computerized accounting records. Collusion among employees (and outsiders) may occur. Research by the Association of Certified Fraud Examiners ([2]: 5) noted that asset misappropriation schemes were the most common form of fraud by employees. Some employee theft methods follow:

1. Wearing items while leaving the workplace. For example, wearing pilfered underwear or wearing scrap lead that has been molded to one's body contours
2. Smuggling out pilfered items by placing the item in a lunchbox, pocketbook, computer, bundle of work clothes, umbrella, newspaper, legitimate purchase, hat, or even one's hair
3. Hiding merchandise in garbage pails, dumpsters, or trash heaps to be retrieved later
4. Returning to the workplace after hours and helping oneself to goods
5. Truck drivers turning in fictitious bills to employers for fuel and repairs and then splitting the money with truck stops
6. Collusion between truck drivers and receiving personnel
7. Executives padding expense accounts
8. Purchasing agents receiving kickbacks from vendors for buying high-priced goods
9. Retail employees pocketing money from cash sales and not recording the transaction
10. Padding payrolls as to hours and rate of pay
11. Maintaining nonexistent or fired employees on a payroll and then cashing the paychecks
12. Accounts payable employees paying fictitious bills to a bogus account and then cashing the checks for their own use

Possible Indicators of Theft

Certain factors *may* indicate that theft has occurred:

1. Inventory records and physical counts that differ
2. Inaccurate accounting records
3. Mistakes in the shipping and receiving of goods
4. Increasing amounts of raw materials needed to produce a specific quantity of goods
5. Merchandise missing from boxes (e.g., every pallet of 20 boxes of finished goods has at least two boxes short a few items)
6. Merchandise at inappropriate locations (e.g., finished goods hidden near exits)
7. Security devices found to be damaged or inoperable
8. Windows or doors unlocked when they should be locked
9. Workers (e.g., employees, truck drivers, repair personnel) in unauthorized areas
10. Employees who come in early and leave late
11. Employees who eat lunch at their desks and refuse to take vacations
12. Complaints by customers about not having their previous payments credited to their accounts
13. Customers who absolutely have to be served by a particular employee

14. An unsupervised, after-hours cleaning crew with their own keys
15. Employees who are sensitive about routine questions concerning their jobs
16. An employee who is living beyond his or her income level
17. Expense accounts that are outside the norm

MANAGEMENT COUNTERMEASURES

Management Support

Without management support, efforts to reduce losses are doomed. *A good management team sets both a foundation for strategies and an atmosphere in which theft is not tolerated.* Support for budget requests and appropriate policies and procedures are vital.

Effective Planning and Budgeting

Before measures are implemented against internal theft, a thorough analysis of the problem is essential. What are the losses and cost-effective countermeasures? What types of losses are occurring, where, how, by whom, when, and why?

Internal and External Relations

Good internal and external relations can play a role in preventing employee theft. Employees respect loss prevention practitioners who are professional and are often more willing to provide information and cooperate. With a heightened loss prevention atmosphere within a workplace, an external reputation is sure to follow.

Job Applicant Screening and Employee Socialization

The screening of job applicants is a major theft-prevention technique (Fig. 8.2). Although screening is often touted as an effective strategy to prevent internal theft, research by the

Association of Certified Fraud Examiners ([2]: 5) found that 85% of offenders had not been previously charged or convicted of a fraud offense. Thus, infinity screening is vital.

Accountability, Accounting, and Auditing

Accountability defines a responsibility for and a description of something. For example, John Smith is responsible (i.e., is held accountable) for all finished products in a plant, and he maintains accurate records of what is in stock. **Accounting** is concerned with recording, sorting, summarizing, reporting, and interpreting business data. **Auditing** is an examination or check of a system to uncover deviations. Personnel audit physical security by checking intrusion alarm systems, closed-circuit television (CCTV), and so on. An auditor audits the accounting records of a company to see if the records are reliable and to check for fraud.

Policy and Procedural Controls

Policy and procedural controls coincide with accountability, accounting, and auditing. In each of these three functions, policies and procedures are communicated to employees through manuals and memos. *Policies* are management tools that control employee decision-making and reflect the goals and objectives of management. *Procedures* guide action to fulfill the requirements of policies.

As an example, a company policy states that before trash is taken to outside dumpsters, a loss prevention officer must be present to check for stolen items. Procedures point out that, to conform to this policy, the head of the cleaning crew must call the loss prevention office and wait for an officer to arrive before transporting the trash outside.

Signs

Placing messages about loss prevention on the premises is another method. The message

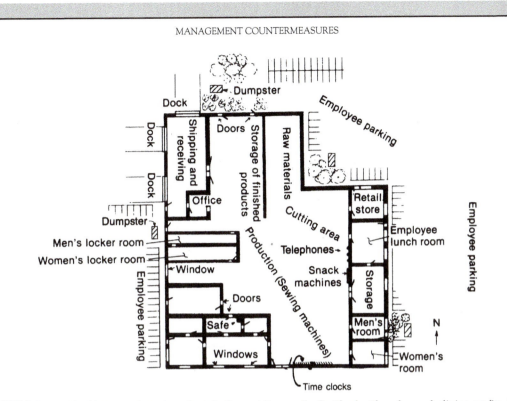

FIGURE 8.2   Smith shirt manufacturing plant. In the past 2 years, the Smith plant has shown declining profits. During this time, managers believed that employee theft might be the cause, but they were unsure of what to do and were worried about additional costs. Employees work one shift from 8 a.m. to 5 p.m. 5 days per week and are permitted to go to their cars to eat lunch from noon to 1 p.m. A total of 425 employees are divided as follows: 350 sewing machine operators, 15 maintenance personnel, 20 material handlers, 20 miscellaneous workers, 2 retail salespeople, 5 managers, and 13 clerical support staff members. A contract cleanup crew works from 6 to 8 a.m. and from 5 to 7 p.m. on Monday, Wednesday, and Friday; Sunday cleanup is from 1 to 4 p.m. The crewmembers have their own keys. Garbage dumpster pick up is 7 a.m. and 7 p.m. Monday, Wednesday, and Friday. The plant contains a fire alarm system and four fire extinguishers. One physical inventory is conducted each year.

must be brief, to the point, and in languages for diverse readers. An example of a message is "Let's all work together to reduce losses and save jobs." Boba and Santos ([9]: 257) reported that crime prevention signage at construction sites is cost-effective and shows management commitment to reduce theft.

Loss Reporting and Reward System

Numerous organizations have established loss reporting through such avenues as a toll-free number, suggestion box, website, or intranet. A reward system is a strategy to reinforce reporting; one method is to provide the anonymous informant with a secret number that is required to pick up reward money at a bank.

The Sarbanes-Oxley (SOX) Act of 2002 requires publicly traded companies to provide a system of reporting anonymously, with penalties for noncompliance. Research shows that the best avenue to encourage reporting is through a confidential, 24-h hotline operated by a third party (Fig. 8.3) [29].

Research by Scicchitano et al. ([53]: 7–19) found that, among the large retailers they surveyed, management encouraged employees to report dishonesty that they observed in the workplace. A hotline with rewards was effective in encouraging employees to report losses.

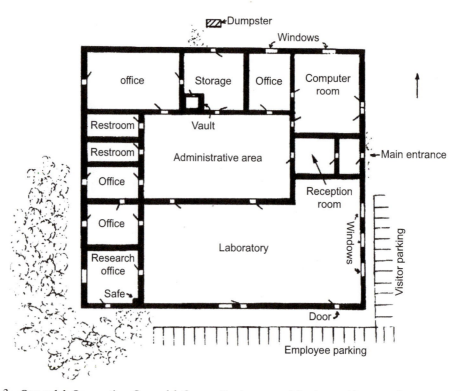

FIGURE 8.3   Compulab Corporation. Compulab Corporation is a research business with tremendous potential. However, it seems that whenever it produces innovative research results, a competitor claims similar results soon afterward. Compulab employs 33 people, including a research director, 2 assistants, 10 scientist–researchers, 8 computer specialists, and an assortment of office staff. The facility is open 24 h a day, 7 days per week, and employees work a mixture of shifts each month and remotely from their homes and other locations. Almost every employee has his or her own key for entrance into the building.

The researchers emphasized that corporate climate plays an important role in facilitating peer reporting. Boba and Santos ([9]: 255) found through their study that hotlines were cost-effective in controlling theft; employees are less likely to steal when they believe the probability of apprehension is high; and employee offenders fear coworker sanctions more than management sanctions.

Investigations

Employee thieves often are familiar with the ins and outs of an organization's operation and can easily conceal theft. In addition, a thorough knowledge of the loss prevention program is common to employee thieves. Consequently, an undercover investigation is an effective method to outwit and expose crafty employee thieves and their conspirators.

Businesses subject to theft should partner with police to investigate and disrupt stolen goods markets. Investigations should focus on pawnshops, flea markets, suspect wholesalers and retailers, online sites, fences, and organized crime groups.

Another investigative approach is **graph-based anomaly detection** that consists of mining of data sets, such as employee information, network activity, e-mail, and payroll that contain possible interconnected and related data for analysis and plotting on a graph to expose unusual activities that may indicate an insider threat. Eberle et al. [24] explain that if we know what is normal behavior, deviations from that behavior could be an anomaly; however, they note that graph-based anomaly detection is challenging because an offender will try to act as close to legitimate actions as possible.

Property Losses and Theft Detection

To remedy property losses within an organization, several strategies are applicable. CCTV, both overt and covert, and radio frequency identification (RFID) are popular methods discussed in other parts of this book. In addition, for high-value assets, a global positioning satellite locator chip can be imbedded in an asset to notify security or police and to track the movement of an asset via computer when it is moved without authorization. Here, an emphasis is placed on inventory system, marking property, and use of metal detectors. An **inventory system** maintains accountability for property and merchandise. For example, when employees borrow or use equipment, a record is kept of the item, its serial number, the employee's name, and the date. On return of the item, both the clerk and the user make a notation, including the date. Automated systems can include a microchip on the item that is read by a scanner for a digital record. Inventory also refers to merchandise for sale, raw materials, and unfinished goods.

Marking property (e.g., tools, computers, and furniture) serves several useful purposes. When property is marked with a serial number, a special substance, or a firm's name is etched with an engraving tool, thieves are deterred because the property can be identified, it is more difficult to sell, and the marks serve as evidence. Marking also helps when locating the owner. Publicizing the marking of property reinforces the deterrent effect. Police departments have operated a program known as "operation identification" for many years in an effort to recruit citizens to mark their property in case of loss.

Besides the popular use of a pinhole lens camera for covert surveillance to catch a thief, another investigative technique is to use fluorescent substances to mark property. An ultraviolet light (black light) is necessary to view these invisible marks, which emerge as a surprise to the offender. To illustrate, suppose an organization's petty cash is not adequately secured and money is missing. To expose the offender, fluorescent substances, in the form of powder, crayon, or liquid, are used to mark the money. A few employees who work after-hours are the suspects. Before these after-hour employees arrive, the investigator handling the case places bills previously dusted with invisible fluorescent powder in envelopes at petty cash locations. The bills can be written on with the invisible fluorescent crayon. Statements such as "marked money" can be used to identify the bills under ultraviolet light. Serial numbers from the bills are recorded and retained by the investigator. Before the employees are scheduled to leave, the "planted" bills are checked. If the bills are missing, then the employees are asked to show their hands, which are checked under an ultraviolet light. Glowing hands expose the probable thief, and identification of the marked money carried by the individual strengthens the case. The marked money should be placed in an envelope because the fluorescent substances may transfer to other objects and onto an honest person's hands. A wrongful arrest can lead to a false-arrest suit. A check of a suspect's bills, for the marked money, helps avoid this problem. Many cleaning fluids appear orange under an ultraviolet light. The investigator should analyze all cleaning fluids on the premises and select a fluorescent color that is different from the cleaning substances. Other items that may fluoresce include lotions, plastics, body fluids, and some drugs.

Another method of marking property is by applying microdots. Microdots contain a logo or ID number, and the dots are painted or sprayed on property. A microscope is used to view the dots that identify the owner of the property. One utility company, for example, suffered millions of dollars of losses from the theft of copper wire and equipment, so it applied the dots to copper assets to help identify company property during investigations and recovery [11].

Walk-through **metal detectors**, similar to those at airports, are useful at employee access points to deter thefts of metal objects and to identify employee thieves. Such detectors also uncover weapons being brought into an area. Handheld metal detectors are also helpful. It is important to note that metal detectors may be overrated because certain firearms, knives, and other weapons are made primarily of plastic. Consequently, X-ray scanners are an expensive option to identify contraband. (The next chapter covers contraband detection.)

Insurance, Bonding

If insurance is the prime bulwark against losses, premiums are likely to skyrocket and become too expensive. For this reason, *insurance is best utilized as a supplement to other methods of loss prevention that may fail.* Fidelity bonding is a type of employee honesty insurance for employees who handle cash and perform other financial activities. Bonding deters job applicants and employees with evil motives. Some companies have employees complete bonding applications but do not actually obtain the bond.

Confronting the Employee Suspect

Care must be exercised when confronting an employee suspect. Maintain professionalism and confidentiality. The following recommendations, in conjunction with good legal assistance, can produce a strong case. The list of steps presents a *cautious approach*. Many locations require approval of management before an arrest.

1. Never accuse anyone unless absolutely certain of the theft.
2. Theft should be observed by a reliable person. Do not rely on hearsay.
3. Make sure you can show intent: the item stolen is owned by the organization, and the person confronted removed it from the premises.
   In steps 4–14, an arrest has not been made.
4. *Ask* the suspect to come to the office for an interview. Employees do not have a right to have an attorney present during one of these employment meetings. If the suspect is a union employee and requests a union representative, comply with the request.
5. Without accusing the employee, he or she can be told, "Some disturbing information has surfaced, and we want you to provide an explanation."
6. Maintain accurate records of everything. These records may become an essential part of criminal or civil action.
7. Never threaten a suspect.
8. Never detain the suspect if the person wants to leave. Interview for less than 1 h.
9. Never touch the suspect or reach into the suspect's pockets.
10. Request permission to search the suspect's belongings. If left alone in a room under surveillance, the suspect may take the item concealed on his or her person and hide it in the room. This approach avoids a search.
11. Have a witness present at all times. If the suspect is female and you are male, have another woman present.
12. If permissible under the Employee Polygraph Protection Act of 1988, ask the suspect to volunteer for a polygraph test and have the suspect sign a statement of voluntariness. Follow EPPA guidelines.
13. If a verbal admission or confession is made by the suspect, have him or her write it out, and have everyone present sign it. Do not correct the suspect's writing errors.
14. Ask the suspect to sign a statement stipulating that no force or threats were applied.

15. For the uncooperative suspect, or if prosecution is favored, call the public police, but first be sure you have sound evidence as in step 3.
16. Do not accept payment for stolen property because it can be construed as a bribe and it may interfere with a bond. Let the court determine restitution.
17. Handle juveniles differently from adults; consult public police.
18. When in doubt, consult an attorney.

Prosecution

Many feel strongly that prosecution is a deterrent, whereas others maintain that it hurts morale and public relations and is not cost-effective. Whatever management decides, it is imperative that an incident of theft be given considerable attention so that employees realize that a serious act has taken place. Establish a written policy that is fair and applied uniformly.

PHYSICAL SECURITY COUNTERMEASURES

Integration and Convergence

The physical security strategies covered in subsequent pages are being increasingly combined into what is called integrated systems. Keener ([36]: 6) offers this definition: "An **integrated system** is the control and operation by a single operator of multiple systems whose perception is that only a single system is performing all functions." These computer-based systems include access controls, alarm monitoring, CCTV, electronic article surveillance, fire protection and safety systems, HVAC, environmental monitoring, radio and video media, intercom, point-of-sale transactions, and inventory control. Traditionally, these functions existed separate from each other, but increasingly they are integrated and installed within facilities worldwide, controlled and monitored by operators and management at a centralized workstation or from remote locations.

The benefits of integrated systems include lower costs, a reduction in staff, improved efficiency, centralization, and reduced travel and time costs. For example, a manufacturing executive at corporate headquarters can monitor a branch plant's operations, production, inventory, sales, and loss prevention. Likewise, a retail executive at headquarters can watch a store and its sales floor, special displays, point-of-sale transactions, customer behavior, inventory, shrinkage, and loss prevention. *These "visits" to worldwide locations are conducted without leaving the office!*

Integration requires careful planning and clear answers to many questions, such as the following:

- Will the integrated system truly cost less and be easier to operate and maintain than separate systems?
- Does the supplier truly have expertise across all the applications?
- Is the integration software listed or approved by a third-party testing agency such as Underwriters Laboratories?
- Do authorities prohibit integration of certain systems? Some fire departments prohibit integrating fire alarm systems with other systems.

Robert Pearson ([48]: 20) writes,

"When attending a conference or trade show, it becomes obvious that every vendor and manufacturer claims to have the "total integrated solution." It would appear that one would only need to place an order at any number of display booths and all the security problems at a user's facility would simply vanish. The vendors and manufacturers freely use terms such as integrated systems, enterprise systems and digital solutions in an effort to convince end users to purchase systems and components."

Pearson goes on to describe a typical security alarm system composed of sensors that connect to a data-gathering panel connected to a computer at a security control center. Integration would mean that sensors, card readers, and other functions would connect to the same data-gathering panel that reports to the same computer. Which multiple functions are integrated depends on the manufacturer. Some manufacturers began with energy management and added security alarm systems in later years; others began with security alarm systems and added access control. Pearson points out that integrating functions among different manufacturers via a single computer is often challenging and produces various approaches. However, integration firms exist that specialize in application-specific software that combines systems for a specific client.

Convergence of IT and physical security means that both specializations and related technologies unite for common objectives. Efforts to secure access to databases, e-mail, and organizational intranets are merging with access controls, fire and burglar alarm systems, and video surveillance. Physical security is increasingly relying on IT systems and related software. Both IT systems and physical security systems have sensors that generate data that are managed. As examples, an IT system will have an antivirus program and a physical security system will have motion detectors.

Bernard ([6]: 34–37) notes that convergence continues to evolve and he distinguishes between technology convergence and organizational convergence. He writes **technology convergence** whereby voice, data, and video devices and systems interact with each other and require a cable and wireless communications infrastructure with enough bandwidth to hold the enhanced level of data throughput. A second type of security convergence is **organizational convergence**, which aims to integrate IT and physical security. Bernard illustrates this type by explaining that IT security protects information and physical security protects information;

organizations should include both simultaneously when planning information security.

Brenner [10] offers scenarios of how the IT security side and the physical security side can work together:

> An offender steals a computer in the workplace. A security incident event management technology system detects a resource change (missing computer). A physical security information management system checks door access records and other physical security. All of the systems "talk to each other" (i.e., compare data) and notification technology triggers an alarm and response. Security practitioners have enhanced data to assist investigations.

> In another scenario, data loss prevention (DLP) technology detects a threat to a spouse on a company computer. A corporate physical security investigator checks the insider's background and finds that the insider is a domestic violence offender. IT security technology (e.g., telephony monitoring and DLP systems) is applied and security personnel monitor the case closely for action.

Bernard ([7]: 28–32) refers to another aspect of convergence known as **identity management system** (IDMS). It is used to manage identities and privileges of computer systems and people. Bernard touts the benefits of IDMS by explaining, for example, the following: "Physical security can leverage the HR enrollment of employees by integrating the physical access control system with the IDMS, so the access control privileges are managed automatically along with IT privileges as HR enrolls, re-assigns and terminates employees." Bernard notes that the federal government is aware of the importance of IDMS in its personal identity verification (PIV) systems mandated by **Homeland Security Presidential Directive (HSPD) 12**. This mandate points to a single smart access card to be used for both physical and IT security among federal agencies.

Advantages of the convergence of IT and physical security include enhanced data, remote monitoring, and less travel time and expenses. Disadvantages include a virus that may affect physical security when sharing a single server; downtime (from various causes, such as maintenance, a threat or hazard), and an organization's bandwidth may reach its limit from the requirements of video surveillance. Sources for planners are best practice IT security standards, such as those from the International Organization for Standardization (ISO) and the International Electrotechnical Commission (IEC).

IT specialists in organizations are playing a larger role in physical security decisions. They want to ensure that physical security technology is compatible with the network. Physical security purchasing decisions in organizations often consist of a committee of personnel from security or loss prevention, IT, and operations. If IT managers can convince senior management that cybercrime is a greater threat than physical crime, then this also will influence the direction of the security budget.

Another player in corporate management change is the facility manager. This individual, often an engineer, ensures that the company's infrastructure, which houses people and operations, functions at optimum efficiency to support business goals. The traditional security department is likely to feel a "pull" toward IT or the facility manager because its boundaries are dissolving due to information and communications technology. The process of management is increasingly dependent on information, who controls it, what is done with it, and its dissemination ([26]: 10).

There are those who may claim the demise of the traditional security manager, who will be replaced by the IT manager or facility manager. The argument is that if an offender enters a facility and steals a computer, this crime is minor in comparison to, say, the potential harm from a hacker accessing a company's IT system. Such reasoning misses the broad, essential functions performed by the traditional security manager and staff. Examples are preventing crimes against people, responding to crimes, rendering first aid, conducting investigations, working with public police to arrest offenders, life safety, and fire protection. At the same time, traditional security practitioners must be put on notice to become involved in lifelong learning of IT systems, which touch all aspects of their traditional duties.

Access Controls

Access controls regulate people, vehicles, and items during movement into, out of, and within a building or facility. With regulation of these movements, assets are easier to protect. If a truck can enter a facility easily, back up to the shipping dock so the driver can load valuable cargo without authorization, and then drive away, that business will not survive. However, access controls such as the following prevent losses: the truck must stop at a gate, a security officer records identifying information on the truck and driver and runs a check through corporate IT for authorization to access, a pass is then issued, and documents are exchanged at the shipping dock under the watchful eyes of another officer. RFID technology can be applied whereby information in ID tags on the truck is uploaded (wireless) to a reader/access control system at the gate. If the truck is authorized to enter, the gate opens. As the truck enters, the reader automatically collects identifying information on the driver and the truck; when the truck departs, information is updated. Other options include CCTV and vehicle license plate recognition (the plate is scanned and then checked in a database for problems).

Controlling Employee Traffic

Access control varies from simple to complex. A simple setup for employees includes locks and keys, officers checking identification badges, and written or digital logs of entries and exits. Systems that are more complex use a "smart card" containing computer memory that interacts with a reader for a host of functions and records; biometrics are used to deny or grant access. A person holding a card-containing RFID can be monitored by readers throughout a facility, and if the person enters a sensitive area without authorization, security is notified and physical security features activated (e.g., alarm sounded, doors locked, and camera zoomed in on person). A prime factor influencing the kind of system employed is need. A research laboratory developing a new product requires strict access controls, whereas a retail business would require minimal controls.

The fewest entrances and exits are best for access control and lower costs. If possible, employees and others should be routed to the entrance closest to their destination away from valuable assets.

Unauthorized exits locked from within create a hazard in case of fire or other emergency. To ensure safety yet fewer losses, emergency exit alarms should be installed as required by codes. These devices enable quick exit, or a short delay, when pressure is placed against a horizontal bar that is secured across the door. An alarm is sounded when these doors are activated, which discourages unauthorized use.

Searching Employees

Management can provide in the contract of employment that reasonable detentions are permissible; that reasonable searches may be made to protect people and company assets; and that searches may be made at any time of desks, lockers, containers carried by employees, and vehicles ([33]: 47 and 68; [44]: 84). Case law has permitted an employer to use a duplicate key, known to the employee, to enter a locker at will. On the other hand, an employee who uses a personal lock has a greater expectation of privacy, barring a written condition of employment to the contrary that includes forced entry. When a desk is assigned to a specific employee, an expectation of privacy exists, unless a contract states otherwise. If employees jointly have access to a desk to obtain items, no privacy exists.

Policies and procedures on searches should consider input from management, an attorney, employees, and a union if on the premises. Also, consider business necessity, what is subject to search, signed authorization from each employee, signs at the perimeter and in the workplace, and searches of visitors and others.

Visitors

Visitors include customers, salespeople, vendors, service people, contractors, and government employees. Any of these people can steal or cause other losses. Depending on need, various techniques are applicable to visitor access control. An appointment system enables preparation for visitors. When visitors arrive without an appointment, the person at reception should lead him or her to a waiting room. Lending special equipment, such as a hard hat, may be necessary. A record or log of visits is wise. Relevant information would be name of the visitor, driver's license number and state, date of visit, time entering and leaving, purpose, specific location visited, name of employee escorting visitor, and temporary badge number. These records aid investigators. A kiosk with touch screen directory features (Fig. 8.4) offer options such as visitor check in, printing a customized map, and creating a temporary access badge. Whenever possible, procedures should minimize employee–visitor contact. This is important, for instance, in the shipping and receiving department, where truck drivers may become friendly with employees and conspiracies may evolve. When restrooms and vending machines are scattered throughout a plant, truck drivers and other visitors who are permitted easy access may cause losses. These services should be located at the shipping and receiving dock, and access to outsiders should be limited.

Controlling the Movement of Packages and Property

The movement of packages and property also must be subject to access controls. Some

FIGURE 8.4 Interactive kiosk that manages a variety of visitors. *Courtesy Honeywell Security.*

Employee Identification System

The use of an employee identification (card or badge) system will depend on the number of employees that must be accounted for and recognized by other employees. An ID system not only prevents unauthorized people from entering a facility but also deters unauthorized employees from entering restricted areas. For the system to operate efficiently, clear policies should state the use of ID cards, where and when the cards are to be displayed on the person, who should collect cards from employees who quit or are fired, and the penalties for noncompliance. A lost or stolen card should be reported so that the proper information reaches all interested personnel. Sometimes ID systems become a joke and employees refuse to wear the badges, or they decorate them or wear them in odd locations on their persons. To sustain an ID system, proper socialization is essential.

Simple ID cards contain employer and employee names. A more complex system would include an array of information: name, signature, address, employee number, physical characteristics (e.g., height, weight, hair, and eye colors), validation date, authorized signature, location of work assignment, thumbprint, and color photo. ID cards often serve as access cards and for many other purposes.

Contractors, visitors, and other nonemployees require an ID card that should be clearly distinguishable from employee ID cards. Temporary ID badges can be printed with a chemical that causes the word *void* to appear after a set period. If the ID card is an access card, an expiration date and time can be entered into the computer system.

A protective laminate coating increases the life of cards. It also discourages tampering; if an attempt is made to alter the card, it will be disfigured. Anticounterfeiting measures are always improving to counter offenders and include various holographic (image) techniques, secret symbols or letters on the badge, and invisible alphanumeric type viewed by a laser.

locations require precautions against packaged bombs, letter bombs, and other hazards. Clear policies and procedures are important for incoming and outgoing items. To counter employee theft, outgoing items require both scrutiny and accountability. RFID tags on assets, in union with readers placed strategically at a facility, signal an alarm when an asset is moved to an unauthorized location. Uniformed officers can check outgoing items, while a property pass system serves the accountability function. At one distribution center, an employee was given permission and a property pass to take home cardboard. He or she tied the flat cardboard with string and while he or she exited, a security officer asked to search the cardboard. Although the employee strongly objected to the search because he or she had a property pass, a flat screen television was found.

The area where ID cards are prepared, and relevant equipment and supplies, must be secure. In addition, the equipment and software should be password protected.

Automatic Access Control

The Security Industry Association traces the development of automatic access control systems as described next (D'Agostino, 2005 [19]: 1–2). Traditionally, access control systems have been at the center of electronic security systems at buildings that include access control, ID badges, alarm systems, and CCTV. **Authentication** (i.e., verifying identity) and **authorization** (i.e., verifying that the identified individual is allowed to enter) have typically occurred as a single-step process in access control. Depending on security needs, access control has been designed for one-factor authentication (e.g., card or personal identification number or biometric), two-factor authentication (e.g., card-plus-PIN or card-plus-biometric), or three-factor authentication (e.g., card-plus-PIN and biometric).

Cryptography (i.e., the study of coded or secret writings to provide security for information) became part of access control systems with the use of **encryption** (i.e., hardware or software that scrambles data, rendering it unintelligible to an unauthorized person intercepting it) to protect passwords and other information. Encryption is essential under the requirements of HSPD-12 [31]: 39). It continues in importance as Ethernet networks (i.e., a trademark for a system of communications between computers on a local area network) replace proprietary equipment connections and as security systems increasingly rely on Internet protocol (IP) messages and shared networks with other businesses. Traditionally, because no security standards existed for these systems, manufacturers applied their own designs. However, according to the Security Industry Association,

standards are now in place because of the following drivers:

- The convergence of physical and IT security.
- **Common user provisioning** that permits a single point of employee registration and dismissal (usually in a human resources system) with assignment of physical and IT privileges.
- Large customers (e.g., the federal government) require their facilities to be **interoperable** (i.e., products or systems working with other products or systems).
- Access controls enabling a single credential (i.e., smart card) to be used across an enterprise at buildings, facilities, and computer networks. This refers to HSPD-12, the federal government PIV program, and standards for cryptography that all serve as a model for the private sector [39]: 58).
- **Digital certificate systems**, which are the electronic counterparts to driver licenses and other ID, are used to sign electronic information and serve as part of the foundation of secure e-commerce on the Web, and are essential for physical access control system integration with IT.

The traditional lock-and-key method of access control has its limitations. For instance, keys are difficult to control and easy to duplicate. Because of these problems, the need for improved access control and technological innovations, a huge market has been created for electronic card access control systems. These systems contain wired and wireless components. The benefits of these systems include the difficulty of duplicating modern cards and cost savings because security officers are not required at each access point.

Modern access control systems are also Internet-based and offer numerous features for employees, visitors, and management. For example, employees can report a lost or stolen card, visitors can preregister, management can see detailed reports of those who enter and leave, and CCTV other physical security can be integrated into the system to aid investigations.

Before an automatic access control system is implemented, several considerations are necessary. *Safety must be a prime factor to ensure quick exit in case of emergency.* Another consideration deals with the adaptability of the system to the type of door presently in use. Can the system accommodate all traffic requirements? How many entrances and exits must be controlled? Will there be an annoying waiting period for those who want to gain access? Are additions to the system possible? What if the system breaks down? Is a backup source of power available (e.g., generators)?

Tailgating and pass back are other concerns. **Tailgating** means an authorized user is followed by an unauthorized user. To thwart this problem, a security officer can be assigned to each access point, but this approach is expensive when compared to applying CCTV, revolving doors, and turnstiles. Revolving doors can be expensive initially, and they are not an approved fire exit. Optical turnstiles contain invisible infrared beams to count people entering and leaving to control tailgating and pass back. These sensors can be installed in a door frame and connected to an alarm system and CCTV. **Pass back** refers to one person passing an opening and then passing back the credential so another person can pass through the opening.

A summary of cards used in card access systems follows:

- *Smart cards* contain computer memory within the plastic that records and stores information and personal identification codes. Security is increased because information is in the card, rather than the reader. Zalud ([66]: 86) writes that because of the memory in the card, it can require the user to supply a PIN or biometric to the reader before the card interacts with the reader; this feature prevents unauthorized use. In addition, cryptography features secure communications between the reader and the card. Smart cards permit a host of activities from access control to making purchases, while almost eliminating the need for keys or cash. This type of card is growing in popularity as its applications expand.

- *Proximity cards* (also referred to as RFID) need not be inserted into a reader but placed in its "proximity." A code is sent via radio frequency, magnetic field, or microchip-tuned circuit. This card is in wide use today.

- *Contact memory buttons* are stainless-steel buttons that protect an enclosed computer chip used for access. The information in the button can be downloaded or updated with a reader like other systems. These buttons are known for their durability, serve to ensure accountability of security officers on patrol, and are applied as an asset tag. The buttons are used widely.

- *Magnetic stripe cards* are plastic, laminated cards (like credit cards) that have a magnetic stripe along one edge onto which a code is printed. When the card is inserted, the magnetically encoded data are compared to data stored in a computer and access is granted on verification. This card is wide used but easy to clone.

- *Wiegand cards* employ a coded pattern on a magnetized wire within the card to generate a code number. To gain access, the card is passed through a sensing reader. Other technologies have reduced the popularity of this type of card.

- *Bar-coded cards* contain an array of tiny vertical lines that can be visible and vulnerable to photocopying or invisible and read by an infrared reader. Other technologies have reduced the popularity of this vulnerable card.

- *Magnetic dot cards* contain magnetic material, often barium ferrite, laminated between plastic layers. The dots create a magnetic pattern that activates internal sensors in a card reader. This card is easy to clone and rarely used.

Access card systems vary in terms of advantages, disadvantages, and costs. Each type of card can be duplicated with a sufficient amount of knowledge, time, and equipment. For example, a magnetic stripe is easy to duplicate. A piece of cardboard with a properly encoded magnetic stripe functions with equal efficiency. The Wiegand card has the disadvantage of wear and tear on the card that passes through a slot for access. Proximity cards have the advantage of the sensing element concealed in a wall, and the card typically can be read without removing it from a pocket. Smart cards are expensive, but they can be combined with other card systems; also, they are convenient because of the capability of loading and updating the card applications over the Web ([43]: 28; [5]: 75; [27]: 156–157; [28]: 18; [62]: 23).

Near-field communication (NFC) is a technology with wide applications ([34,46]: S-10). It is short-range (less than 4 inches), wireless (radio) communications between two devices by touching them together or placing the devices in close proximity. NFC evolved from RFID; the difference is that whereas RFID is one-way, NFC is two-way—an NFC-enabled device can send and receive information. A smart phone containing NFC capabilities can serve as a credit or debit card. A device with NFC can serve as a library card, transit pass, and access card to a secure door, computer or network, among other applications. A wallet and keys may someday become obsolete. NFC communication is subject to hacking. The RF signal can be captured with an antenna; information can be stolen or modified. Security includes use of a password, encryption, keypad lock, and antivirus software.

Biometric Technologies

Biometric security systems have been *praised as a major advance in access control because such*

FIGURE 8.5 Verifying identity through hand geometry. *Courtesy HID Corporation.*

systems link the event to a particular individual, whereas an unauthorized individual may use a key, card, PIN, or password. Di Nardo ([22]: 195) defines biometrics as "the automated use of physiological or behavioral characteristics to determine or verify identity." He adds that it can also be defined as "the study of measurable biological characteristics."

These systems seek to verify an individual's identity through fingerprint scan, hand geometry (shape and size of hand) (Fig. 8.5), iris scan (the iris is the colored part around the pupil of the eye), facial scan, retinal scan (capillary pattern), voice patterns, signature recognition, vascular (vein) pattern recognition, palm print, ear shape, gait, and keystroke dynamics. The biometric leaders are fingerprint, hand geometry, iris, and face recognition ([22]: 194–216; [52]: 41–55).

Biometric security systems have disadvantages and can be circumvented. As examples, retinal can be affected by diseases, vascular is expensive and requires bulky equipment, drugs can affect gait, and keystroke has high error rates. Iris was defeated by using a glass eyeball, contact lenses, or high-resolution photos ([22]: 194–216).

Fingerprint can be circumvented by collecting an authorized person's latent fingerprint by lifting it with tape. Terrorists cut off the thumb of a bank manager to gain entry through a fingerprint-based access control system. Researchers constructed fake fingers by taking casts of real fingers and molding them into Play-Doh. The researchers developed a technique to check for moisture as a way to reduce this ploy [4].

Spence [58] writes in *Locksmith Leger* that certain locksmiths are hesitant to become involved with biometric fingerprint systems. One quipped, "They're 1 percent of my sales and 10 percent of my service calls." Failure rates were between 3% and 20%.

Research continues to improve biometrics. In the near term, we will not see facial scan pick a known terrorist out of a crowd, but the technology is evolving. Digitized photos shot at angles or in poor light can be flawed. The challenge with facial scan is identifying a person on the move ([51]: 16–21).

Biometric systems operate by storing identifying information (e.g., fingerprints, photos) in a computer to be compared with information presented by a subject requesting access. Access controls often use multiple technologies, such as smart card and biometrics. One location may require a card and a PIN (Fig. 8.6), whereas another requires scanning a finger and a PIN. Many systems feature a distress code that can be entered if someone is being victimized. Another feature is an alarm that sounds during unauthorized attempted entry. Access systems can be programmed to allow select access according to time, day, and location. The logging capabilities are another feature to ascertain personnel location by time, date, and the resources expended (e.g., computer time, parking space, cafeteria). These features provide information during investigations and emergencies.

We are seeing an increasing merger of card access systems and biometric technology, and thus, missing or stolen cards is less of a concern. We will see more point-of-sale readers that accept biometric samples for check cashing, credit cards, and other transactions. As

FIGURE 8.6 Card reader and keypad. *Courtesy Diebold, Inc.*

research continues to improve biometrics, these systems will become universal—banking, correctional facilities, welfare control programs, and so forth.

Locks and Keys

The basic purpose of a lock-and-key system is to hinder unauthorized entry. Attempts to enter a secure location usually are made at a window or door to a building or at a door somewhere within a building. Consequently, locks deter unauthorized access from outsiders and insiders. *Many see a lock only as a delaying device that is valued by the amount of time needed to defeat it.* Zunkel ([67]: 32) notes, "… it is important that designers know that a lock by itself is only part of a larger system that includes the door, the wall, the perimeter and a security plan." An offender may decide to avoid a high-security lock and break through a weak door, wall, ceiling, floor, roof, or window.

Standards related to locking systems include those from American National Standards Institute (ANSI), American Society for Testing and Materials (ASTM), Underwriters Laboratories (UL), and the Builders Hardware Manufacturers Association (BHMA). Local ordinances may specify requirements for locks.

Two general ways to classify locks are mechanical and electromechanical. **Mechanical locks** include the common keyed lock and the push button lock that contains a keypad to enter an access code to release the lock. **Electromechanical locks** include an electronic keypad that is connected to an electric strike, lock, or magnetic lock. When the access code is entered, the strike or lock is released to open the door ([21]: D-5).

There are many types of locks and locking systems that range from those that use simple, ancient methods to those that apply modern technology, including electricity, wireless components, computers, and the Internet. Here, we begin with basic information as a foundation for understanding locks.

Locking devices are often operated by a key, numerical combination, card, or electricity. Many locks (except padlocks) use a dead bolt and latch. The **dead bolt** (or bolt) extends from a door lock into a bolt receptacle within the door frame. Authorized entry is made by using an appropriate key to manually move the bolt into the door lock. **Latches** are spring loaded and less secure than a dead bolt. They are cut on an angle to permit them to slide right into the strike when the door is closed (Fig. 8.7). Unless the latch is equipped with a locking bar (deadlatch), a knife can possibly be used to push the latch back to open the door.

The **cylinder** part of a lock contains the keyway, pins, and other mechanisms that permit the dead bolt or latch to be moved by a key for access (Fig. 8.8). Double-cylinder locks, in which a cylinder is located on each side of a door, are a popular form of added security as compared to single-cylinder locks. *Double-cylinder locks*

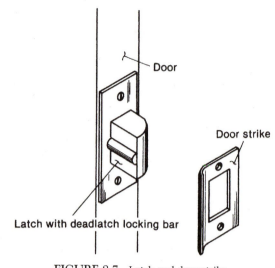

FIGURE 8.7   Latch and door strike.

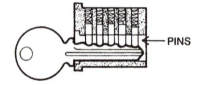

FIGURE 8.8   Cylinder.

require a key for both sides; however, fire codes may prohibit such locks. With a single-cylinder lock, a thief may be able to break glass or remove a wood panel and then reach inside to turn the knob to release the lock. For safety's sake, locations that use double-cylinder locks must prepare for emergency escape by having a key readily available.

Key-in-knob locks are used universally but are being replaced by key-in-the-lever locks (Fig. 8.9) to be ADA compliant. As the name implies, the keyway is in the knob or lever. Most contain a keyway on the outside and a button on the inside for locking from within.

Entrances for Handicapped

The Internal Revenue Service offers a tax credit to eligible businesses that comply with

FIGURE 8.9 Mechanical lock with lever requiring no wiring, electronics, or batteries. *Courtesy Ilco Unican.*

provisions of the ADA to remove barriers and promote access for individuals with disabilities [25]. The door hardware industry offers several products and solutions to aid the disabled (Fig. 8.10). Electrified door hardware such as magnetic locks and electromechanical locks retracts the latch when energized.

Attacks and Hardware

The Internet, including YouTube, offers a wealth of information on attacking locks. In addition, lock picking has become a sport with club members and chapters in multiple countries [41]. Google queries for "attacks on locks," "lock picking," and "lock bumping" result in millions of sources. These methods are explained next.

There are several ways to attack locks. One technique, as stated earlier, is to force a knife between the door frame (jamb) and the door near the lock to release the latch. However, when a deadlatch or dead bolt is part of the locking mechanism, methods that are more forceful are needed. In one method, called "springing the door," a screwdriver or crowbar is placed between the door and the door frame so that the bolt extending from the door lock into the bolt receptacle can be pried out, enabling the door to swing open (Fig. 8.11). A 1-inch bolt will hinder this attack.

In "jamb peeling," another method of attack, a crowbar is used to peel at the door frame near the bolt receptacle so that the door is not stopped from swinging open. Strong hardware for the door frame is helpful. In "sawing the bolt," a hacksaw is applied between the door and the door frame, similar to the placement of the screwdriver in Fig. 8.11. Here again, strong hardware, such as a metal bolt composed of an alloy capable of withstanding a saw blade, will impede attacks. Some offenders use the cylinder-pulling technique: the cylinder on the door is actually ripped out with a set of durable pliers or tongs. A circular steel guard surrounding the cylinder (Fig. 8.11) will frustrate the attacker. Offenders also are known to use automobile jacks to pressure door frames away from a door.

Both high-quality hardware and construction will impede attacks, but the door itself must not be forgotten. If a wood door is only 1/4-inch thick, even though a strong lock is attached, the offender may simply break through the door. A solid wood door 1 3/4 inches thick or a metal door is a worthwhile investment. Wood door frames at least 2 inches thick provide durable protection. When a hollow steel frame is used, the hollow area can be filled with cement to resist crushing near the bolt receptacle. An L-shaped piece of iron secured with one way screws will deter attacks near the bolt receptacle for doors swinging in (Fig. 8.12). When a padlock is used in conjunction with a safety hasp, the hasp must be installed correctly so that the screws are not exposed (Fig. 8.13).

Many attacks are by forced entry, which is easier to detect than when the use of force is

Lever trim reduces force required to unlatch a door.

Push/Pull Latch

Push/Pull latches are popular on institutional doors because of ease of operation.

Proximity Card

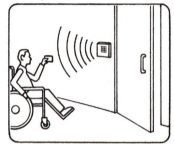

Proximity card reader requires only close presence of the user's card to activate door's automatic opener.

Presence detectors are popular with automatic exit doors and require no physical action.

FIGURE 8.10   Entrances for handicapped. *Courtesy Von Duprin Division of Ingersoll-Rand Company.*

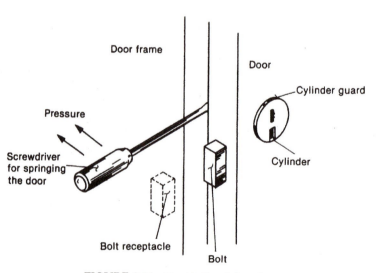

FIGURE 8.11   Dead bolt and door frame.

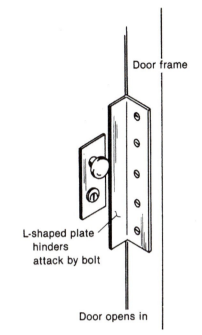

FIGURE 8.12   L-shaped plate.

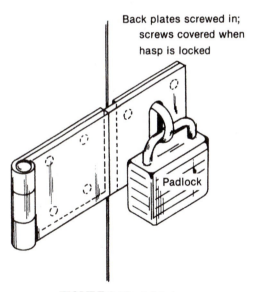

FIGURE 8.13   Safety hasp.

minimal. Lock picking is one technique needing a minimum amount of force. It is used infrequently because of the expertise required, although picks are available on the Internet.

Lock picking is accomplished by inserting a tension wrench (an L-shaped piece of metal) into the cylinder and applying tension while using metal picks to align the pins in the cylinder as a key would to release the lock (Fig. 8.8). The greater the number of pins, the more difficult it is to align them. A cylinder should have at least six pins. **Lock bumping** is touted as an easy method of picking a pin tumbler lock by inserting a specially designed bump key into the keyway and applying a slight force while turning the key. Another type of attack (more difficult) utilizes a blank key, matches, and a file. The blank key is placed over a lighted match until carbon is produced on the key. Then the key is inserted into the cylinder. The locations where the pins have scraped away the carbon signify where to file. Needless to say, this method is time-consuming and calls for repeated trials. Offenders sometimes covertly borrow a key, quickly press it into a bar of soap or wax, return the key, and then file a copy on a blank key. This method illustrates the importance of key control.

After gaining access, an offender may employ some tricks to make sure nobody enters while he or she is busy. This is accomplished, for instance, by inserting a pin or obstacle in the keyway and locking the door from the inside.

Whatever hardware is applied, the longer it takes to attack a lock, the greater is the danger for the offender. One further point: most burglary insurance policies state that there must be visible signs of forced entry to support a claim.

Offenders may use other methods of entry. A thief may simply use a stolen key or a key (or access card) borrowed from another person. Unfortunately, intruders often enter restricted areas because somebody forgot to use a locking device. This mistake renders the most complex locks useless.

The methods of defeating lock-and-key systems do not stop here. Innovative thieves and various kinds of locks, keys, and access systems create a hodgepodge of methods that loss prevention practitioners should understand.

Types of Locks

Volumes have been written about locks. The following briefly summarizes simple and more complex locks:

- *Warded (or skeleton key tumbler) lock*: This older kind of lock is disengaged when a skeleton key makes direct contact with a bolt and slides it back into the door. It is an easy lock to pick. A strong piece of L-shaped metal can be inserted into the keyway to move the bolt. Warded locks are in use in older buildings and are recognized by a keyway that permits seeing through. Locks on handcuffs are of the warded kind and can be defeated by a knowledgeable offender.
- *Disc tumbler lock*: The use of this lock, originally designed for the automobile industry, has expanded to desks, file cabinets, and padlocks. Its operation entails flat metal discs, instead of pins, that align when the proper key is used. These locks are mass produced, inexpensive, and have a short-life expectancy. More security is offered than warded locks can provide, but disc tumbler locks are subject to defeat by improper keys or being jimmied.
- *Pin tumbler lock*: Invented by Linus Yale in 1844, the pin tumbler lock is used widely in industry and residences (Fig. 8.8). Its security surpasses that of the warded and disc tumbler kinds.
- *Lever tumbler lock*: Lever locks vary widely. These locks disengage when the proper key aligns tumblers. Those found in luggage, cabinets, chests, and desks often provide minimal security, whereas those found in bank safe deposit boxes are more complex and provide greater security. The better quality lever lock offers more security than the best pin tumbler lock.
- *Combination lock*: This lock requires manipulating a numbered dial(s) to gain access. Combination locks usually have three or four dials that must be aligned in the correct order for entrance. These locks provide greater security than key locks because a limited number of people probably will know the lock combination, keys are unnecessary, and lock picking is obviated. They are used for safes, bank vaults, and high-security filing cabinets. With older combination locks, skillful burglars are able actually to listen to the locking mechanism to open the lock; more advanced mechanisms have reduced this weakness. A serious vulnerability results when an offender watches the opening of a combination lock with either binoculars or a telescope. Retailers sometimes place combination safes near the front door for viewing by patrolling police; however, unless the retailer uses his or her body to block the dial from viewing, losses may result. This same weakness exists where access is permitted by typing a PIN.
- *Combination padlock*: This lock is similar in operation to a combination lock. It is used on employee or student lockers and in conjunction with safety hasps or chains. Some of these locks have a keyway so they can be opened with a key.
- *Padlock*: Requiring a key, this lock is used on lockers or in conjunction with hasps or chains. Numerous types exist, each affording differing levels of protection. More secure ones have disc tumbler, pin tumbler, or lever characteristics. Serial numbers on padlocks are a security hazard similar to combination padlocks.

Other kinds of locks include devices that have a bolt that locks vertically instead of horizontally. Emergency exit locks with alarms or "panic alarms" enable quick exit in emergencies while deterring unauthorized door use. Sequence locking devices require locking the doors in a predetermined order; this ensures that all doors are locked because the outer doors will not lock until the inner doors are locked.

The use of interchangeable core locks is a method to deal with the theft, duplication, or loss of keys. Using a special control key, one core (that part containing the keyway) is simply replaced by another. A different key then is needed to operate the lock. This system, although more expensive initially, minimizes the need for a locksmith or the complete changing of locks.

Automatic locking and unlocking devices also are a part of the broad spectrum of methods to control access. Digital locking systems open doors when a particular numbered combination is typed. If the wrong number is typed, an alarm is sounded. Combinations can be changed when necessary. Electromagnetic locks use magnetism, electricity, and a metal plate around doors to hold doors closed. When the electricity is turned off, the door can be opened. Remote locks enable opening a door electronically from a remote location.

Trends taking place with locks and keys include increasing use of electronics and microchip technology. For example, hybrids have been developed whereby a key can serve as a standard hardware key in one door and an electronic key in another door. "Smart locks" have grown in popularity. These locks combine traditional locks with electronic access control; read various types of access cards for access; use a tiny computer to perform multiple functions, including holding data (e.g., access events); and can be connected to an access control system for uploading and downloading data. Aubele [3] refers to "intelligent key systems" whereby keys are programmable like access control cards to limit access according to specific times and doors. In addition, these keys store data on use.

Wireless locking systems and RF online locking systems make use of modern technology, although care must be exercised in the evaluation and purchasing process. A pilot project helps to ensure reliability. Signals are hindered by metallic materials (e.g., steel buildings).

Master Key Systems

In most instances, a lock accepts only one key that has been cut to fit it. A lock that has been altered to permit access by two or more keys has been *master keyed*. The **master key system** allows a number of locks to be opened by the master key. This system should be confined to high-quality hardware utilizing pin tumbler locks. A disadvantage of the master key system is that if the master key is lost or stolen, security is compromised. A *change key* fits one lock. A *submaster key* will open all locks in, for instance, a wing of a building. The master key opens locks covered by two or more submaster systems.

Key Control

Without adequate key control, locks are useless and losses are likely to climb. Accountability and proper records are necessary, as with access cards. Computerized, online record-keeping programs are available for key control, similar to software used in electronic card access control systems ([63]: 79–85). Keys should be marked with a code to identify the corresponding lock; the code is interpreted via a record stored in a safe place. A key should never be marked, "Key for room XYZ." When not in use, keys should be positioned on hooks in a locked key cabinet or vault. The name of the employee, date, and key code are vital records to maintain when a key is issued. These records require continuous updating. Employee turnover is one reason why precise records are vital. Departing employees will return keys (and other valuables) if their final paycheck is withheld. Policies should state that reporting a lost key would not result in punitive action; an investigation and a report will strengthen key control. If key audits check periodically, who has what key, control is further reinforced. To hinder duplication of keys, "do not duplicate" may be stamped on keys, and company policy can clearly state that key duplication will result in dismissal. Lock changes are wise every 8 months and sometimes at shorter intervals on an irregular basis. Key control also is important for vehicles such as autos, trucks, and forklifts. These challenges and vulnerabilities of traditional lock and key systems have influenced organizations in switching to modern access control and biometric systems.

Intrusion Detection Systems

An **intrusion detection system** detects and reports an event or stimulus within its detection area. A response to resolve the reported problem is essential. The emphasis here is on interior sensors. Sensors appropriate for perimeter protection are stressed in Chapter 9. We must remember that intrusion detection systems are often integrated with other physical security systems and rely on IT systems with Internet capabilities.

What are the basic components of an intrusion detection system? Three fundamental components are sensor, control unit, and annunciator. **Sensors** detect intrusion by, for example, heat or movement of a human. The **control unit** receives the alarm notification from the sensor and then activates a silent alarm or **annunciator** (e.g., a light or siren), which usually produces a human response. There are various intrusion detection systems, and they can be wired or wireless. Several standards exist for intrusion detection systems from UL, ISO, the Institute of Electrical and Electronics Engineers, and other groups. Types of interior sensors are explained next ([27]: 104–122; [30]: 48–94).

Interior Sensors

In the electronics field, a "switch" is a component that can interrupt an electrical circuit (e.g., as with a light switch). A *balanced magnetic switch* consists of a switch mounted to a door (or window) frame and a magnet mounted to a moveable door or window. When the door is closed, the magnet holds the switch closed to complete an electrical circuit. An alarm is triggered when the door is opened and the circuit is interrupted.

An ordinary magnetic switch is similar to the balanced type, except that it is simpler, is less expensive, and provides a lower level of security. Switches can be visible or hidden and afford good protection against opening a door; however, no security method is ever "foolproof."

Mechanical contact switches contain a push button-actuated switch that is recessed into a surface. An item is placed on it that depresses the switch, completing the alarm circuit. Lifting the item interrupts the circuit and signals an alarm.

Pressure-sensitive mats contain two layers of metal strips or screen wire separated by sections of foam rubber or other flexible material. When pressure is applied, as by a person walking on the mat, both layers meet and complete an electrical contact to signal an alarm. These mats are applied as internal traps at doors, windows, and main traffic points, as well as near valuable assets. The cost is low, and these mats are difficult to detect. If an offender detects the mat, he or she can walk around it.

Grid wire sensors are made of fine insulated wire attached to protected surfaces in a grid pattern consisting of two circuits, one running vertical, the other horizontal, and each overlapping the other. An interruption in either circuit signals an alarm. This type of sensor is applied to grill work, screens, walls, floors, ceilings, doors, and other locations. Although these sensors are difficult for an offender to spot, they are expensive to install, and an offender can jump the circuit.

Trip wire sensors use a spring-loaded switch attached to a wire stretched across a protected area. An intruder "trips" the alarm (i.e., opens the circuit) when the wire is pulled loose from the switch. If an offender spots the sensor, he or she may be able to circumvent it.

Vibration sensors detect low-frequency energy resulting from the force applied in an attack on a structure (Fig. 8.14). These sensors are applied to walls, floors, and ceilings. Various sensor models require proper selection.

Capacitance sensors create an electrical field around metallic objects that, when disturbed,

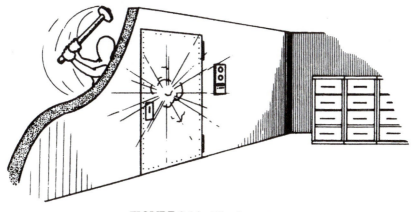

FIGURE 8.14 Vibration sensor.

FIGURE 8.15 Capacitance sensor.

signals an alarm (Fig. 8.15). These sensors are applied to safes, file cabinets, grills at openings (e.g., windows), fences, and other metal objects. One sensor can protect many objects; however, it is subject to defeat by using insulation (e.g., heavy gloves).

Infrared photoelectric beam sensors activate an alarm when an invisible infrared beam of light is interrupted (Fig. 8.16). If the system is detected, an offender may jump over or crawl under the beam to defeat it. To reduce this vulnerability, tower enclosures can be used to stack sensors.

Ultrasonic motion (UM) detectors focus on sound waves to detect motion. Active UM detectors create a pattern of inaudible sound waves that are transmitted into an area and monitored by a receiver. This detector operates on the *Doppler Effect*, which is the change in frequency that results from the motion of an intruder. Passive UM detectors react to sounds (e.g., breaking glass). These

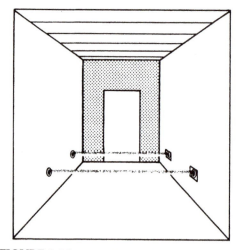

FIGURE 8.16   Infrared photoelectric beam system.

detectors are installed on walls or ceilings or used covertly (i.e., disguised within another object). The sensitive abilities of these detectors result in many false alarms, which limit use.

Microwave motion detectors also operate on the Doppler frequency-shift principle. An energy field is transmitted into an area and monitored for a change in its pattern and frequency, which results in an alarm. Because microwave energy penetrates various construction materials, care is required for placement and aiming. However, this can be an advantage in protecting multiple rooms and large areas with one sensor. These sensors can be defeated (like UM) by objects blocking the sensor or by fast or slow movement.

Passive infrared (PIR) intrusion sensors are passive in that they do not transmit a signal for an intruder to disturb. Rather, moving infrared radiation (from a person) is detected against the radiation environment of a room. When an intruder enters the room, the level of infrared energy changes and an alarm is activated. Although the PIR is not subject to as many nuisance alarms as ultrasonic and microwave detectors, it should not be aimed at sources of heat or surfaces that can reflect energy. The PIR can be defeated by blocking the sensor so it cannot pick up heat.

Passive audio detectors listen for noise created by intruders. Various models filter out naturally occurring noises not indicating forced entry. These detectors can use public address system speakers in buildings, which can act as microphones to listen to intruders. The actual conversation of intruders can be picked up and recorded by these systems. To enhance this system, CCTV can provide visual verification of an alarm condition, video in real time, still images digitally to security or police, and evidence. The audio also can be two-way, enabling security to warn the intruders. *Such audiovisual systems must be applied with extreme care to protect privacy, confidentiality, and sensitive information, and to avoid violating state and federal wiretapping and electronic surveillance laws.*

Fiber optics is used for intrusion detection and for transmission of alarm signals. It involves the transportation of information via guided light waves in an optical fiber. This sensor can be attached to or inserted in many things requiring protection. When stress is applied to the fiber optic cable, an infrared light pulsing through the cable reacts to the stress and signals an alarm.

Trends

Two types of sensor technologies often are applied to a location to reduce false alarms, prevent defeat techniques, or fill unique needs. The combination of microwave and PIR sensors is a popular example of applying **dual technologies** (Fig. 8.17). Reporting can be designed so an alarm is signaled when both sensors detect an intrusion (to reduce false alarms) or when either sensor detects an intrusion. Sensors are also becoming "smarter" by sending sensor data to a control panel or computer, distinguishing between humans and animals, and activating a trouble output if the sensor lens is blocked. *Supervised wireless sensors* have become a major advancement because sensors can be placed at the best location without the expense of running a wire;

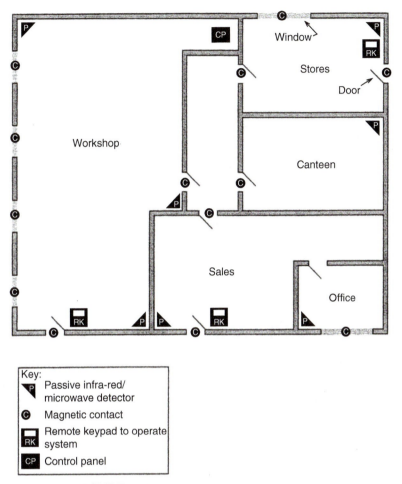

FIGURE 8.17 Commercial intrusion alarm system.

these sensors are constantly monitored for integrity of the radio frequency link between the sensor and panel, status of the battery, and whether the sensor is functioning normally ([27]: 104; [47]: 36–48).

Operational Zoning

Operational zoning means that the building being protected has a segmented alarm system, whereby the alarm can be turned on and off within particular zones depending on usage. For example, if an early morning cleaning crew is in the north end of a plant, then that alarm is turned off while other zones still have the alarm on. Furthermore, zoning helps to pinpoint where an intrusion has occurred.

Alarm Monitoring

Today, many entities have an alarm system that is monitored by an in-house station (e.g., a console at a secure location) or from a central station (contract service) located off the premises. These services easily can supply reports of unusual openings and closings, as well as those of the regular routine. Chapter 9 covers alarm signaling systems.

Closed-Circuit Television

CCTV (Fig. 8.18) assists in deterrence, surveillance, apprehension, and prosecution. This technology is also helpful in civil cases to protect an organization's interests. The applications go beyond security and justice. For instance, CCTV can yield a greater ROI by serving as a tool to understand production problems or customer behavior. Although it may be costly initially, CCTV reduces personnel costs because it allows the viewing of multiple locations by one person. For instance, throughout a manufacturing plant, multiple cameras are installed, and one security officer in front of a console monitors the cameras. Accessories include pan (i.e., side-to-side movement), tilt (i.e., up-and-down movement), and zoom lenses, referred to as "PTZ" in the industry, which are mechanisms that permit viewing mobility and opportunities to obtain a close look at suspicious activity. Additional system capabilities include recording incidents and viewing when limited light is present. Modern technology has greatly altered CCTV capabilities, as described in subsequent paragraphs.

Standards for CCTV systems are from several sources. These include ANSI, SIA, National Electrical Manufacturers Association, American Public Transportation Association, government agencies, ISO/International Electrotechnical Commission, and the International Code Council. England and Australia are especially active preparing CCTV standards.

During the 1950s, CCTV began its development. The traditional CCTV system that came into greater use in the 1970s consisted of analog recording systems, solid-state cameras, and coaxial cable ([55,59]: 114). This older technology applied multiple cameras connected through cabling to a camera control unit and a multiplexer that fed several videocassette recorders (VCRs) in a central control room. The images were viewed real time via several monitors. The disadvantages of this technology include the following: the control room is a single point of failure within the security infrastructure; if a camera is moved, cable is required for the connection; the use of VCRs results in numerous cassette tapes requiring storage space; and humans are necessary to change and store tapes.

Older technology, such as the VCR that could record for a limited number of hours, was followed by time-lapse recorders (i.e., single frames of video are stored at intervals over an extended period of time) with recording capabilities up to several hundred hours, plus an alarm mode in which the recorder reverts to real time when an alarm condition exists. Real-time setting records 30 frames a second; time-lapse video may record between 1 frame a second and 1 frame every 8 s. Time-lapse recorder features included a quick search for alarm conditions during playback,

FIGURE 8.18   Closed-circuit television (CCTV) sign. Camera at top.

the playing of recorded video frames according to the input of time by the user, and the interface with other security systems such as access controls to ensure a video record of all people entering and departing.

A new generation CCTV system developed with unshielded twisted-pair cabling (i.e., a cable with multiple pairs of twisted insulated copper conductors in a single sheath) that enabled cameras to run on the existing infrastructure. **Digital video recorders** (DVRs) were introduced in the mid-1990s, and with them, several advantages over analog, including recording on hard disk drives, as a file is stored on a personal computer. Other advantages are avoiding tape storage, remote viewing, easy playback and searches, improved quality of images, and longer life of recordings. Another advance is digital recording in networking, which is referred to as **network video recorder** (NVR). Rather than many DVRs networked together, an NVR is the camera system. An NVR is digital cameras managed by specially designed computer operating software designed to manage video surveillance [1]: 8).

IP-based network cameras permit IP networking of video to be shared where the network reaches, including offsite storage. IP video can be controlled and viewed from a PDA, phone, laptop computer, or other mobile device. It is also encrypted. IP-based CCTV systems, including IP cameras, IP video servers, and IP keyboards can be located almost anywhere. In addition, the IP keyboard can control the PTZ and other management functions such as recording and searching. When the existing infrastructure in a building is used, a building can become automated on one cable system and include not only CCTV but also access control, fire/safety systems, voice, network traffic, and other systems.

Not everyone is happy with IP-based network cameras. Pfeifle, L. [50] reports of one retail security practitioner who argued that with IP a lot of coordination is required, especially with IT employees, installation is difficult,

enough bandwidth must be available, and with several cameras, a platform to manage them is necessary.

It is important to distinguish between the older **analog technology** and the newer **digital technology**. Analog signals are used in their original form and placed, for example, on a tape. Most earlier electronic devices use the analog format (e.g., televisions, record players, cassette tape recorders, and telephones). Analog technology is still applied today. With digital technology, the analog signals are sampled numerous times, turned into numbers, and stored in a digital system. Today, many devices contain digital technology (e.g., high-definition TV, CDs, fiber-optic telephone lines, and digital telephones).

Even with the shift to IP-based network systems for CCTV, video is still transmitted over coaxial cable, twisted pair wire, fiber-optic cable, microwave, radio frequency, and telephone lines. What we have is the opportunity (as with other electronic security systems) for, say, an executive in New York to monitor inside a business in Hong Kong.

The choice of wireless video transmission (e.g., microwave or radio frequency) is an option under certain circumstances. Examples include flexible deployment whereby cameras must be moved periodically (e.g., changing exhibition hall), covert surveillance requiring quick and easy installation, at emergency sites, and historical buildings where a cable route is not possible. Careful planning is required prior to the installation of transmitters and receivers to prevent the radio signal from being blocked. *Line of sight* is an important issue. Interference can result from environmental conditions such as metallic buildings, aluminum siding, solar flares, lightning, heavy rain, snow, and high wind ([13]: 46–48).

When IT personnel are approached about including CCTV on a network, they are often concerned about how much bandwidth the video will use. To allay fears, one option at a multibuilding facility is to maintain a DVR at every building for storage of video so all video is not transmitted to the central computer.

For those end users using traditional analog technology while moving toward an IP-based retrofit, options include using "hybrid" products that accommodate both analog and IP-based signals. Lasky ([40]: 38) advises against a full IP retrofit unless there is a clear understanding of the amount of bandwidth required on a network with numerous IP cameras.

Organizations that employ CCTV systems may consider streaming video surveillance from remote sites to regional centers. Although this approach can be challenging, it can also reduce plant and personnel costs. A key factor in this decision is compression because bandwidth limitations affect the amount of video that can be exchanged between transmitting and receiving sites. Similar to a roadway tunnel, only a certain number of vehicles can enter the tunnel at any one time. However, if the vehicles are made smaller, more can fit. **Compression** is the amount of redundant video that can be stripped out of an image before storage and transmission, and there are various compression techniques ([42]: 34).

Another concern, as physical security personnel increasingly rely on a network, is access to the network for various security-related information. In this case, the IT personnel have the option of placing such security information on a subnet to prevent access to the whole network.

Changing technology has brought about the **charged coupled device (CCD) or "chip" camera**, a small, photosensitive unit designed to replace the tube in the closed-circuit camera. CCD technology is found in camcorders. CCD cameras have certain advantages over tube cameras: CCD cameras are more adaptable to various circumstances, they have a longer life expectancy, "ghosting" (i.e., people appearing transparent) is less of a problem, there is less intolerance to light, less power is required, and less heat is produced, thereby requiring less ventilation and permitting installation in more locations.

Another technology for capturing images digitally is the complementary metal oxide semiconductor (CMOS). Teledyne DALSA [61], a global leader in digital imaging, offering both CCD and CMOS, notes that each has a bright future and there are advantages and disadvantages depending on application. Both types convert light into electric charge and process it into electronic signals. CCD costs less and is not as complex as CMOS.

Digital cameras are replacing analog cameras. Although analog signals can be converted into digital signals for recording to a PC, quality may suffer. Digital cameras use digital signals that are saved directly to hard drive, but space on a hard drive is limited for video. Network cameras are analog or digital video cameras connected to the Internet with an IP address.

Megapixel and high-definition (HD) security cameras are part of the more recent evolution of video surveillance ([45]: 40–43). Both provide an enhanced picture image over analog. **Megapixel** refers to the number of million pixels in an image. We often identify this term with still picture photography. A greater number of pixels result in increased image detail. This is especially helpful during investigations if, as examples, a person needs to be positively identified or in a casino when a playing card requires identification. Keys ([37]: 27) extols the benefits of megapixel cameras. He notes that with megapixel technology, by zooming in on a recorded image that may initially appear useless, it can show important details. Keys concedes that there are lighting issues with these cameras. He also writes that they are "memory hogs" and planners must study the memory needed to archive data. **HD** could be considered a subset or type of megapixel camera. It complies with industry standards to ensure excellent color and it produces a wider image than megapixel. If campus police were seeking disorderly students in a large crowd, HD would be appropriate over megapixel. Which camera is better depends on the application.

Combining megapixel, HD, and other types of cameras can result in an effective, multipurpose IP-based network video system.

Increasing "intelligence" is being built into CCTV–computer-based systems. **Multiplex** means sending many signals over one communication channel. Video multiplex systems minimize the number of monitors security personnel must watch by allowing numerous cameras to be viewed at the same time on one video screen. The pictures are compressed, but a full view is seen of each picture. If an alarm occurs, a full screen can be brought up. The digital multiplex recorder enables users to record events directly to a hard drive, reducing storage space.

The prolonged watching of CCTV monitors (i.e., screens) by personnel, without falling asleep, has been a challenge since the origin of these systems. Personnel that are not rotated periodically become fatigued from watching too much TV. This serious problem is often overlooked. People may "test" the monitoring of the system by placing a bag or rag over a camera or even spraying the lens with paint. If people see that there is no response, CCTV becomes a hoax. The use of dummy cameras is not recommended because, when people discover the dummy, CCTV can be perceived as a deceitful farce.

Users of CCTV systems are especially interested in the recording capabilities of their systems, knowing their personnel are often occupied with multiple tasks (e.g., answering questions for customers, providing information over the telephone) and unable to watch monitors continuously. When an event does occur, these systems permit a search of recordings by date, time, location, and other variables.

CCTV capabilities can be enhanced by using **video motion detection** (VMD). A video motion detector operates by sending, from a camera, a picture to a memory evaluator. The memory evaluator analyzes the image for pixel changes. Any change in the picture, such as movement, activates an alarm. These systems assist security officers in reacting to threats and reduce the problem of fatigue from watching monitors. Tse ([64]: 42) refers to a study by an Australian firm that found that after 12 min of continuous watching of monitors, an operator would often miss up to 45% of scene activity, and after 22 min, up to 95% is overlooked.

The integration of VMD and **video analytics**, also referred to as intelligent video systems (IVS), is a technology that offers different functions that aim to precisely define alarm conditions, enhance the capabilities of CCTV systems, and reduce the problem of humans missing important events on monitors. These systems enable the user to preselect actions that are programmed into the digital video system, and this software signals an alarm when such an event takes place. Examples of events triggering an alarm include stopped or moving vehicles, objects that are abandoned or removed, and loitering of people ([3]: 48–53; [23]: 48–50).

Cameras commonly are placed at public streets, access points, passageways, shipping and receiving docks, merchandise storage areas, cashier locations, parts departments, overlooking files, safes, vaults, and production lines. In the workplace, the location of cameras requires careful planning to avoid harming employee morale. A key restriction on the placement of cameras is that they must not be applied to an area where someone has a reasonable expectation of privacy (e.g., restrooms, locations where individuals change clothes).

The extent of the use of hidden surveillance cameras is difficult to measure, especially because many individuals are unaware of the existence of these cameras in workplaces. Pinhole lenses are a popular component of hidden surveillance cameras. They get their name from the outer opening of the lens, which is 1/8–1/4 inch in diameter and difficult to spot. Cameras are hidden in almost any location, such as in clocks, file cabinets, computers, sprinkler heads, and mannequins.

SECURITY OFFICERS

Security officers play an important role in countering internal losses. They must be integrated with technology, and this entails quality training and supervision. When uniformed officers patrol on foot inside a facility—through production, storage, shipping, receiving, office, and sales floor areas—an enhanced loss prevention atmosphere prevails. Unpredictable and irregular patrols deter employee theft (among other losses). A properly trained officer looks for deviations such as merchandise stored or hidden in unusual places and tampered security devices. Thoroughly searching trash containers deters employees from hiding items in that popular spot. Losses also are hindered when officers identify and check people, items, and vehicles at access points.

Safes, Vaults, and File Cabinets

Safes

Protective containers (Fig. 8.19) secure valuable items (e.g., cash, confidential information). These devices generally are designed to withstand losses from fire or burglary. Specifications vary, and an assessment of need should be carefully planned. Management frequently is shocked when a fire-resistive safe in which valuable items are "secured" enables a burglar to gain entry because the safe was designed only for fire. The classic **fire-resistive (or record) safe** often has a square (or rectangular) door and thin steel walls that contain insulation. During assembly, wet insulation is poured between the steel walls; when the mixture dries, moisture remains. During a fire, the insulation creates steam that cools the safe below 350°F (the flash point of paper) for a specified time. The FBI maintains safe insulation files to assist investigators. Record safes for computer media require better protection because damage can occur at 125°F, and these records are more vulnerable to

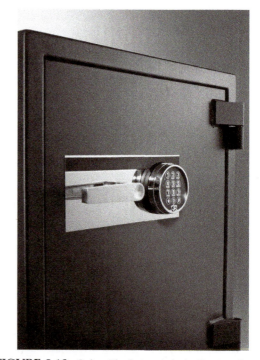

FIGURE 8.19 Safe with electronic lock. *Courtesy Sargent & Greenleaf, Inc.*

humidity. Fire safes are able to withstand one fire; thereafter, the insulation is useless.

The classic **burglary-resistive (or money) safe** often has a thick, round door, and thick walls. Round doors were thought to enhance resistance, but today many newer burglary-resistive safes have square or rectangular doors. The burglary-resistive safe is more costly than the fire-resistive safe.

Better quality safes have the Underwriters Laboratories (UL, a nonprofit testing organization) rating. This means that manufacturers have submitted safes for testing by UL. These tests determine the fire- or burglary-resistive properties of safes. For example, a fire-resistive container with a UL rating of 350-4 can withstand an external temperature to 2000°F for 4h while the internal temperature will not exceed 350°F. The UL test actually involves placing a safe in an increasingly hot furnace to simulate a fire. In reference to burglary-resistive containers, a UL rating of TL15, for example, signifies weight of at least 750 pounds and resistance to an attack on its door by common tools for a minimum of 15 min. UL-rated burglary-resistive safes also contain UL-listed combination locks and other UL-listed components. When selecting a safe, consider recommendations from insurance companies and peers, how long the company has been in business, and whether or not safe company employees are bonded.

Attacks

Before a skilled burglar attacks a safe, he or she studies the methods used to protect it. Inside information (e.g., a safe's combination) is valuable, and scores of employees and former employees of attacked firms have been implicated in burglaries. Listed next are major attack techniques of two types: with force and without force. Attack methods using force include the following:

- *Rip or peel*: Most common, this method is used on fire-resistive safes that have lightweight metal. Like opening a can of sardines, the offender rips the metal from a corner. The peel technique requires an offender to pry along the edge of the door to reach the lock.
- *Punch*: The combination dial is broken off with a hammer. A punch is placed on the exposed spindle, which is hammered back to enable breakage of the lock box. The handle then is used to open the door. This method is effective against older safes.
- *Chop*: This is an attack of a fire-resistive safe from underneath. The safe is tipped over and hit with an ax or hammer to create a hole.
- *Drill*: A skillful burglar drills into the door to expose the lock mechanism; the lock tumblers are aligned manually to open the door.
- *Torch*: This method is used against burglar-resistive safes. An oxygen–acetylene cutting torch melts the steel. This equipment is brought to the safe, or the offender uses equipment from the scene.
- *Carry away*: The offender removes the safe from the premises and attacks it in a convenient place.

Attack methods using no force include the following:

- *Office search*: Simply, the offender finds the safe combination in a hiding place (e.g., taped under a desk drawer).
- *Manipulation*: The offender opens a safe without knowing the combination by using sight, sound, and touch—a rare skill. Sometimes the thief is lucky and opens a safe by using numbers similar to an owner's birth date, home address, or telephone number.
- *Observation*: An offender views the opening of a safe from across the street with the assistance of binoculars or a telescope. To thwart this, one should place the numbers on the top edge of the dial, rather than on the face of the dial.
- *Day combination*: For convenience, during the day, the dial is not completely turned each time an employee finishes using the safe. This facilitates an opportunity for quick access. An offender often manipulates the dial in case the day combination is still in effect.
- *X-ray equipment*: Metallurgical X-ray equipment is used to photograph the combination of the safe. White spots appear on the picture that helps to identify the numerical combination. The equipment is cumbersome, and the technique is rare.

The following measures are recommended to fortify the security of safes and other containers:

1. Utilize alarms (e.g., capacitance and vibration), CCTV, and adequate lighting.
2. Secure the safe to the building so it is not stolen. (This also applies to cash registers that may be stolen in broad daylight.) Bolt

the safe to the foundation or secure it in a cement floor. Remove any wheels or casters.

3. Do not give a burglar an opportunity to use any tools on the premises; hide or secure all potential tools (e.g., torch).

4. A time lock permits a safe to be opened only at select times. This hinders access even if the combination is known. A delayed-action lock provides an automatic waiting period (e.g., 15 min) from combination use to the time the lock mechanism activates. A silent signal lock triggers an alarm when a special combination is used to open a safe.

5. At the end of the day, turn the dial several times in the same direction.

6. A written combination is risky. Change the factory combination as soon as possible. When an employee who knows the combination is no longer employed, change it.

7. Maintain limited valuables in the safe through frequent banking.

8. Select a safe with its UL rating marked on the inside. If a burglar identifies the rating on the outside, an attack is made easier.

9. Consider modern features of safes: remote access management, reports of cash flow, and traceable deposits.

Vaults

A walk-in vault is actually a large safe; it is subject to similar vulnerabilities from fire and attack. Because a walk-in vault is so large and expensive, typically, only the door is made of steel, and the rest of the vault is composed of reinforced concrete. Vaults are heavy enough to require special support within a building. They commonly are constructed at ground level to avoid stress on a building.

File Cabinets

Businesses that sustain loss of their records from theft, fire, flood, or other threats or hazards face serious consequences, such as the possibility of business failure and litigation. Certain types of records require protection according to law. Some vital records are customer-identifying information, accounts receivable, inventory lists, legal documents, contracts, research and development, and human resources data. Records help to support losses during insurance claims.

File cabinets that are insulated and lockable can provide fair protection against fire and burglary. The cost is substantially lower than that of a safe or vault, but valuable records demanding increased safety should be placed in a safe or vault and copies stored off-site. Special computer safes are designed to protect against forced entry, fire, and moisture that destroys computer media.

References

[1] Alten J. Shhh… don't tell anyone that DVRs are becoming obsolete. Secur Dir News 2005;2. [March].

[2] Association of Certified Fraud Examiners. Report to the nations on occupational fraud and abuse, 2010. 2010. www.acfe.com.

[3] Aubele K. Checking out security solutions. Secur Manag 2011;55. [December].

[4] Aughton S. Researchers crack biometric security with play-Doh. PC PRO 2005. www.pcpro.co.uk/news/81257.

[5] Barry J. Don't always play the cards you are dealt. Secur Technol Des 1993. [July–August].

[6] Bernard R. The state of converged security operations. Secur Technol Exec 2011;21. [April].

[7] Bernard R. Web services and identity management. Secur Technol Des 2006;16. [January].

[8] Blades M. The insider threat. Secur Technol Exec 2010;20. [November/December].

[9] Boba R, Santos R. A review of the research, practice, and evaluation of construction site theft occurrence and prevention: directions for future research. Secur J 2008;21. [October].

[10] Brenner B. How physical, it security sides can work together. Computerworld 2010. [September] www.computerworld.com.

[11] Canadacom. Hydro lost millions from theft, damage last year. Vanc Sun 2007. [February 7] www.canada.com.

[12] Catrantzos N. No dark corners: a different answer to insider threats. Homel Secur Aff 2010;6. [May] www.hsaj.org.

[13] Chan H. Overcoming the challenges of wireless transmission. Secur Technol Des 2005;15. [October].

[14] Coleman J. Trends in security systems integration. Secur Technol Des 2000;10. [August].

[15] Computer Security Institute/FBI. CSI/FBI computer crime and security survey. 2005. www.GoCSI.com.

[16] Computer Security Institute/FBI. CSI/FBI computer crime and security survey. 2006. www.GoCSI.com.

[17] Conklin J. Criminology. 7th ed. Boston: Allyn & Bacon Pub; 2001.

[18] Cressey D. Other People's money: a study in the social psychology of embezzlement. Belmont (CA): Wadsworth; 1971.

[19] D'Agostino S, et al. The roles of authentication, authorization and cryptography in expanding security industry technology. 2005. www.siaonline.org.

[20] Dean R. Ask the expert. Secur Prod 2005;9. [September].

[21] Department of Defense. User's guide on controlling locks, keys and access cards. Port Hueneme (CA): Naval Facilities Engineering Service Center; 2000.

[22] Di Nardo J. Biometric technologies: functionality, emerging trends, and vulnerabilities. J Appl Secur Res 2009;4.

[23] Duda D. The ultimate integration—video motion detection. Secur Technol Des 2006;16. [June].

[24] Eberle W, et al. Insider threat detection using a graph-based approach. J Appl Secur Res 2011;6(1).

[25] EEOC. How to comply with the American with disabilities act: a guide for restaurants and other food service employers. 2011 (January 19) www.eeoc.gov.

[26] Freeman J. Security director as politician. Secur Technol Des 2000. [August].

[27] Garcia M. Vulnerability assessment of physical protection systems. Burlington (MA): Butterworth-Heinemann; 2006.

[28] Gersh D. Untouchable value. iSecurity 2000. [November].

[29] Greene C. Hang up on fraud with confidential hotlines. Fraud Alert 2004. [Chicago (IL): McGovern & Greene].

[30] Honey G. Intruder alarms. 2nd ed. Oxford (UK): Newnes; 2003.

[31] Hulusi T. Creating a trusted identity. Secur Technol Exec 2011;21. [May].

[32] Hunt S. Integrated security solutions: getting to know it. Secur Prod 2006;10. [February].

[33] Inbau F, et al. Protective securitly law. 2nd ed. Boston: Butterworth-Heinemann; 1996.

[34] Jarvis B. The next generation of access control: virtual credentials. Access Control Trends Technol 2011. [June].

[35] Jordan B. Telework's growing popularity. Homel Def J 2006;4. [June].

[36] Keener J. Integrated systems: what they are and where they are heading. Secur Technol Des 1994. [May].

[37] Keys R. What is intelligent video?. Law Off Manazine 2010;6. [March].

[38] Klenowski P, et al. Gender, identity, and accounts: how white collar offenders do gender when making sense of their crimes. Justice Q 2011;28. [February].

[39] Kosaka M. Public goes private. Secur Prod 2010;14. [March].

[40] Lasky S. Video from the top. Secur Technol Des 2006;16. [June].

[41] Loughlin J. Security through transparency: an open source approach to physical security. J Phys Secur 2009;3(1).

[42] Mellos K. A choice you can count on. Secur Prod 2005;9. [October].

[43] Morton J. Top smart card blunders. Buildings 2011;105. [April].

[44] Nemeth C. Private security and the law. Burlington (MA): Elsevier Butterworth-Heinemann; 2005.

[45] Nilsson F. The resolution to your confusion. Secur Technol Exec 2011;21. [March].

[46] Nosowitz D. Everything you need to know about near field communication. Popular Sci 2011. [March] www.popsci.com.

[47] O'Leary T. New innovations in motion detectors. Secur Technol Des 1999;9. [November].

[48] Pearson R. Integration vs. Interconnection: it's a matter of semantics. Secur Technol Des 2000;11. [November].

[49] Pearson R. Open systems architecture: are we there yet. Secur Technol Des 2001;11. [January].

[50] Pfeifle L. McDonald's, Saks begin first install of HDCCTV. Secur Dir News 2010. [January 25] www.securitydirectornews.com.

[51] Philpott D. Physical security—biometrics. Homel Def J 2005;3. [May].

[52] Piazza P. The smart cards are coming… really. Secur Manag 2005;49. [January].

[53] Scicchitano M, et al. Peer reporting to control employee theft. Secur J 2004;17. [April].

[54] Shaw E, et al. Managing the threat from within. Inf Secur 2000;3. [July].

[55] Siemon Company. Video over 10G ip™. 2003. www.siemon.com.

[56] Skinner W, Fream A. A social learning theory analysis of computer crime among college students. J Res Crime Delinquency 1997;34. [November].

[57] Speed M. Reducing employee dishonesty: in search of the right strategy. Secur J 2003;16. [April].

[58] Spence B. Advances in fingerprint biometric technology. Locksmith Ledger 2011. [June] www.locksmith-ledger.com.

[59] Suttell R. Security monitoring. Buildings 2006;100. [May].

[60] Swartz D. Open Architecture systems: the future of security management. Secur Technol Des 1999;9. [December].

[61] Teledyne DALSA. CCD vs. CMOS. 2011. www.teledynedalsa.com.

[62] Toye B. Bar-coded security ID cards efficient and easy. Access Control 1996. [March].

[63] Truncer E. Controlling access system performance. Secur Manag 2011;55. [March].

[64] Tse A. The real world of critical infrastructure. Secur Prod 2006;10. [May].

[65] U.S. Department of Homeland Security, Science and Technology Directorate and the Executive Office of the President, Office of Science and Technology Policy. The National plan for research and development in support of critical infrastructure protection. 2004. www.dhs.gov.

[66] Zalud B. Higher level credentials leave footprint on card printers. Security 2010;47. [October].

[67] Zunkel D. A short course in high-security locks. Secur Technol Des 2003;13. [February].

External Threats and Countermeasures*

Philip P. Purpura

INTRODUCTION

External loss prevention focuses on threats from outside an organization. This chapter concentrates on countermeasures to impede unauthorized access from outsiders. If unauthorized access is successful, numerous losses are possible from such crimes as assault, burglary, robbery, vandalism, arson, and espionage. Naturally, employees as well as outsiders or a conspiracy of both may commit these offenses. Furthermore, outsiders can gain legitimate access if they are customers, repair technicians, and so on.

Internal and external countermeasures play an interdependent role in minimizing losses; a clear-cut division between internal and external countermeasures is not possible because of this intertwined relationship. In addition, as explained in the preceding chapter, we are in an era of universal threats. This means that because of telework, employees and organizations face the same threats whether work is accomplished on or off the premises.

The IT perspective is important to produce comprehensive security. IT specialists use terms such as *denial of access* and *intrusion detection*, as do physical security specialists; however, IT specialists apply these terms to the protection of information systems. As IT and physical security specialists learn from each other, a host of protection methods will improve, examples being integration of systems, investigations, and business continuity planning.

METHODS OF UNAUTHORIZED ENTRY

One avenue to begin thinking about how to prevent unauthorized entry is to study the methods used by offenders. Both management (to hinder penetration) and offenders (to succeed in gaining access) study the characteristics of patrols, fences, sensors, locks, windows, doors, and the like. By placing yourself in the position of an offender (i.e., *think like a thief*) and then that of a loss prevention manager, you can see, while studying Woody's Lumber Company, the Smith Shirt manufacturing plant, and Compulab Corporation (discussed in Chapter 8), that a combination of both perspectives aids in the designing of defenses. (Such planning is requested in a case problem at the end of this chapter.) Furthermore, keep in mind these theories and practical applications of the theories; these include rational choice and routine activity

---

*From Purpura PP. Security and loss prevention 6e. Boston: Butterworth-Heinemann; 2013 Updated by the editor, Elsevier, 2016.

theories and situational crime prevention techniques to reduce opportunities for crime.

Forced entry is a common method used to gain unauthorized access, especially at windows and doors. Offenders repeatedly break or cut glass (with a glass cutter) on a window or door and then reach inside to release a lock or latch. To stop the glass from falling and making noise, an offender may use a suction cup or tape to remove or hold the broken glass together. A complex lock may be rendered useless if the offender is able to go through a thin door by using a hammer, chisel, and saw. Forced entry also may be attempted through walls, floors, ceilings, roofs, skylights, utility tunnels, sewer or storm drains, and ventilation vents or ducts. Retail stores may be subject to **smash and grab attacks**: a store display window is smashed, merchandise is quickly grabbed, and the thief immediately flees.

Atlas ([3]: 52) describes burglars who targeted a retail chain by rattling storefronts to create false alarms; this resulted in slow police response and retail management turning off the burglar alarm systems to avoid fines. Police and retail management "bit the bait" and the burglars, disguised with masks and gloves, shattered drive-through windows with a tire iron, climbed in, and stole unsecured cash boxes prepared for morning business.

Berube ([5]: 326–381) writes of conflicting research results on the deterrent effect of burglar alarm systems. Certain burglars do not care if they activate an alarm because they only spend one or 2 min at the crime scene and police are unlikely to respond quickly to make an arrest. Because of the false alarm problem, police may be hesitant to respond quickly or not respond at all. When we consider rational choice and routine activity theories, slow police response to alarm activations reduce risk for burglars and increase opportunities. Berube also cites research that supports the deterrent effect of alarm systems.

Unauthorized access also can be accomplished *without force*. Wherever a lock is supposed to be used, if it is not locked properly, access is possible. Windows or doors left unlocked are a surprisingly common occurrence. Lock picking or possession of a stolen key or access card renders force unnecessary. Dishonest employees are known to assist offenders by unlocking locks, windows, or doors and by providing keys and technical information. Offenders sometimes hide inside a building until closing and then break out following an assault or theft. Tailgating and pass back are other methods of gaining access without force, as covered in the preceding chapter. Sly methods of gaining entry are referred to as **surreptitious entry**.

COUNTERMEASURES

Countermeasures for external (and internal) threats can be conceptualized around the five "Ds":

- *Deter*: The mere presence of physical security can dissuade offenders from committing criminal acts. The impact of physical security can be enhanced through an **aura of security**. An aura is a distinctive atmosphere surrounding something. Supportive management and security personnel should work to produce a professional security image. They should remain mum on such topics as the number and types of intrusion detection sensors on the premises and security system weaknesses. Security patrols should be unpredictable and never routine. Signs help to project an aura of security by stating, for example, Premises Protected By High-Tech Redundant Security. Such signs can be placed along a perimeter and near openings to buildings. The aura of security strives to produce a strong psychological deterrent so offenders will consider the success of a crime to be unlikely. It is important to note that no guarantees come with deterrence. (Criminal justice policies are in serious trouble because deterrence is faulty; criminals continue to commit crimes even while facing long sentences.) In the security realm, deterrence must be backed up with the following four "Ds."

- *Detect*: Offenders should be detected and their location pinpointed as soon as they step onto the premises or commit a violation on the premises. This can be accomplished through observation, closed-circuit television (CCTV), intrusion sensors, duress alarms, weapons screenings, protective dogs, and hotlines.
- *Delay*: Security is often measured by the time it takes to get through it. **Redundant security** refers to two or more similar security methods (e.g., two fences; two types of intrusion sensors). **Layered security** refers to multiple security methods that follow one another and are dissimilar (e.g., perimeter fence, strong doors, a safe). Both redundant and layered securities create a time delay. Thus, the offender may become frustrated and decide to depart, or the delay may provide time for a response force to arrive to make an apprehension.

Nunes-Vaz et al. ([29]: 372) favor distinguishing between "layered security" and "security-in-depth" to enhance research and to guide investments in security. They write, "Risk minimization is best achieved by strengthening the layer that may already be the most effective, and by focusing on the weakest function within that layer." In addition, they argue that "security-in-depth" aims to produce not only effective layers but also coherent integration of layers.

- *Deny*: Strong physical security, often called *target hardening*, can deny access. A steel door and a safe are examples. Frequent bank deposits of cash and other valuables extend the opportunity to deny the offender success.
- *Destroy*: When you believe your life or another will be taken, you are legally permitted to use deadly force. An asset (e.g., proprietary information) may require destruction before it falls into the wrong hands.

Environmental Security Design

When a new facility is planned, the need for a coordinated effort by architects, fire protection and safety engineers, loss prevention practitioners, local police and fire officials, and other specialists cannot be overstated. Furthermore, money is saved when security and safety are planned before actual construction rather than accomplished by modifying the building later.

Years ago, when buildings were designed, loss prevention features were an even smaller part of the planning process than today. Before air conditioning came into widespread use, numerous windows and wide doors were required for proper ventilation, providing thieves with many entry points. Today's buildings also present problems. For example, ceilings are constructed of suspended ceiling tiles with spaces above the tiles that enable access by simply pushing up the tiles. Once above the tiles, a person can crawl to other rooms on the same floor. Roof access from neighboring buildings is a common problem for both old and new buildings. Many of these weak points are corrected by adequate hardware such as locks on roof doors and by intrusion sensors.

Architects are playing an increasing role in designing crime prevention into building plans. **Environmental security design** includes natural and electronic surveillance of walkways and parking lots, windows and landscaping that enhance visibility, improved lighting, and other architectural designs that promote crime prevention. Additionally, dense shrubbery can be cut to reduce hiding places, and grid streets can be turned into cul-de-sacs by using barricades to reduce ease of escape.

An illustration of how CPTED is applied can be seen with the design of Marriott hotels ([23]: 84–88). To make offenders as visible as possible, traffic is directed toward the front of hotels. Lobbies are designed so that people walking to guest rooms or elevators must pass the front desk. On the outside, hedges are emphasized to produce a psychological barrier that is more appealing than a fence. Pathways are well lit and guide guests away from isolated areas. Parking lots are characterized by lighting, clear lines of sight, and access control. Walls of the garage are painted white to enhance lighting. On the inside of hotels, the swimming pool, exercise room, and vending and laundry areas have glass doors and walls to permit maximum witness potential. One application of CCTV is to aim cameras at persons standing at the lobby desk and install the monitor in plain view. Since people can see themselves, robberies have declined. CPTED enhances traditional security methods such as patrolling officers and emergency call boxes.

Research from the United Kingdom has extended the reach of CPTED. The UK Design Against Crime (DAC) Program seeks a wide group of design professionals to develop creative and often subtle design solutions to combat crime and fear of crime. The DAC is a holistic, human-centered approach that facilitates crime prevention without inconveniencing people or creating a fortress environment. Examples include the following: a fence with a top rail that is angled to discourage young people from sitting on the fence and "hanging out"; the playing of classical music to prevent youth from congregating in certain areas; and the "antitheft handbag" that has a short strap, a carefully located zipper, thick leather, and an alarm ([10]: 39–51).

CPTED is enhanced through the "Broken Windows" **theory** of James Q. Wilson and George Kelling [48]. This theory suggests that deteriorated buildings that remain in disrepair and disorderly behavior attract offenders and crime while increasing fear among residents. If someone breaks a window and it is not repaired, more windows may be broken, and a continuation of dilapidated conditions may signal that residents do not care. Minor problems, such as vandalism, graffiti, and public intoxication, may grow into larger problems that attract offenders and destroy neighborhoods. However, residents can increase safety and security when they take pride in the conditions of their neighborhood.

Perimeter Security

Perimeter means outer boundary, and it is often the property line and the first line of defense against unauthorized access (Fig. 9.1). Building access points such as doors and windows also are considered part of perimeter defenses at many locations. Typical perimeter security begins with a fence and gate and may include

FIGURE 9.1   Perimeter security. *Courtesy of Wackenhut Corporation. Photo by Ed Burns.*

multiple security methods (e.g., card access, locks, sensors, lighting, CCTV, and patrols) to increase protection (Fig. 9.2). Technology can extend security surveillance beyond the perimeter, as illustrated with radar that is applied at a facility near a waterway (Fig. 9.3).

The following variables assist in the design of perimeter security:

1. Whatever perimeter security methods are planned, they should interrelate with the total loss prevention program and business objectives. In addition, green security should be considered.
2. Perimeter security needs to be cost-effective. When plans are presented, management is sure to ask: "What type of return will we have on our investment?"
3. Although the least number of entrances strengthens perimeter security, the plan must not interfere with normal business and emergency events.
4. Perimeter security has a psychological impact on potential intruders. It signals a warning to outsiders that steps have been taken to block intrusions. Offenders actually "shop" for vulnerable locations (i.e., opportunities).
5. Even though a property line may be well protected, the possibility of unauthorized entry cannot be totally eliminated. For example, a fence can be breached by going over, under, or through it.
6. Penetration of a perimeter is possible from within. Merchandise may be thrown over a fence or out of a window. Various things are subject to smuggling by persons walking or using a vehicle while exiting through a perimeter.
7. The perimeter of a building, especially in urban areas, often is the building's walls. An offender may enter through a wall (or roof) from an adjoining building.
8. To permit an unobstructed view, both sides of a perimeter should be kept clear of vehicles, equipment, and vegetation. This allows for what is known as **clear zones**.
9. Consider integrating perimeter intrusion sensors with landscape sprinkler systems. Trespassers, protesters, and other intruders will be discouraged, and, when wet, they are easier to find and identify.
10. Perimeter security methods are exposed to a hostile outdoor environment not found indoors. Adequate clothing and shelter are necessary for security personnel. The selection of proper security systems prevents false alarms from animals, vehicle vibrations, and adverse weather.
11. Perimeter security should be inspected and tested periodically.

Barriers

Post and Kingsbury ([34]: 502–503) state, "the physical security process utilizes a

FIGURE 9.2 Multiple security methods increase protection.

FIGURE 9.3   Radar extends security surveillance beyond the perimeter at a facility near a waterway. *Courtesy of Honeywell Security.*

number of barrier systems, all of which serve specific needs. These systems include natural, structural, human, animals, and energy barriers" **Natural barriers** are rivers, hills, cliffs, mountains, foliage, and other features difficult to overcome. Fences, walls, doors, and the architectural arrangement of buildings are **structural barriers. Human barriers** include security officers who scrutinize people, vehicles, and things entering and leaving a facility. The typical **animal barrier** is a dog. **Energy barriers** include protective lighting and intrusion detection systems.

The most common type of barrier is a *chain-link fence* topped with barbed wire (Fig. 9.1). A search of the Web shows many industry standards for fences from ASTM, UL, ISO, and other groups from the United States and overseas. For example, ASTM F567 focuses on materials specifications, design requirements, and installation of chain-link fencing.

One advantage of chain-link fencing is that it allows observation from both sides: a private security officer looking out and a public police officer looking in. Foliage and decorative plastic woven through the fence can reduce visibility and aid offenders. Opposition to chain-link fencing sometimes develops because management wants to avoid an institutional-looking environment. Hedges are an alternative.

It is advisable that the chain-link fence be made of at least 9-gauge or heavier wire with 2″ × 2″ diamond-shaped mesh. It should be at least 7 ft high. Its posts should be set in concrete and spaced no more than 10 ft apart. The bottom should be within 2 inches of hard ground; if the ground is soft, the fence can become more secure if extended a few inches below the ground. Recommended at the top is a *top guard*—supporting arms about 1 or 2 ft long containing three or four strands of taut barbed wire 6 inches apart and facing outward at 45 degrees.

FIGURE 9.4 Anticlimb fence with vulnerability.

Anticlimb fences (Fig. 9.4) are an alternative to the chain-link fence. Applied in Europe, with growing interest and application in the United States, these fences are more attractive and more difficult to climb than the chain-link fence. The mesh openings are small which prevents fingers and shoes from being inserted into the fence to climb. As with all other security measures, anticlimb fences have vulnerabilities.

Barbed wire fences are used infrequently. Each strand of barbed wire is constructed of two 12-gauge wires twisted and barbed every 4 inches. For adequate protection, vertical support posts are placed 6 ft apart, and the parallel strands of barbed wire are from 2 to 6 inches apart. A good height is 8 ft.

Concertina fences consist of coils of steel razor wire clipped together to form cylinders weighing about 55 pounds. Each cylinder is stretched to form a coil-type barrier 3 ft high and 50 ft long. The ends of each 50-foot coil need to be clipped to the next coil to obviate movement. Stakes also stabilize these fences. This fence was developed by the military to act as a quickly constructed barrier. When one coil is placed on another, they create a 6-foot-high barrier. One coil placed on two as a base provides a pyramid-like barrier that is difficult to penetrate. Concertina fences are especially helpful for quick, temporary repairs to damaged fences.

Razor ribbon and *coiled barbed tape* are increasing in popularity. They are similar to concertina fencing in many ways. Every few inches along the coil are sharp spikes, looking something like a small-sharpened bow tie.

Gates are necessary for traffic through fences. The fewer gates, the better because, like windows and doors, they are weak points along a perimeter. Gates usually are secured with a chain and padlock. Uniformed officers stationed at each gate and fence opening increase security while enabling the observation of people and vehicles.

Vehicle barriers control traffic and stop vehicles from penetrating a perimeter. The problems of vehicle bombs and drive-by shootings have resulted in greater use of vehicle barriers. These barriers are assigned government-certified ratings based on the level of protection; however, rating systems vary among government agencies. One agency, for example, tests barriers against 15,000-pound trucks traveling up to 50 miles per hour, while another agency tests 10,000-pound trucks traveling the same speed. **Passive vehicle barriers** are fixed and include decorative bollards, large concrete planters, granite fountains, specially engineered and anchored park benches, hardened fencing, fence cabling, and trees. An alternative to bollards is a *plinth wall*—a continuous low wall of reinforced concrete with a buried foundation ([45]: 2–33). Moore [20] notes alternatives to bollards, including *tiger traps* (i.e., a path of paving stones over a trench of low-density concrete that will collapse under a heavy weight) and *NOGOs* (i.e., large, heavy bronze blocks). **Active vehicle barriers** are used at entrances and include gates, barrier arms, and pop-up-type systems that are set underground and, when activated, spring up to block a vehicle ([44]: 49–53). Factors to consider when planning vehicle barriers include frequency of traffic, type of road (e.g., a curved road slows vehicles), aesthetics, and how the barrier is integrated with other physical security and personnel ([21]: 30). As we know, no security method is foolproof, and careful security planning is vital, including ADA requirements. In 1997, to protest government policy, the environmental group Greenpeace penetrated government security in Washington, DC, and dumped 4 tons of coal outside the Capitol building. The driver of the truck drove the wrong way up a one way drive leading to the building!

Walls are costly and a substitute for fences when management is against the use of a wire fence. Attractive walls can be designed to produce security equal to fences while blending into surrounding architecture. Walls are made from various materials: bricks, concrete blocks, stones, or cement. Depending on design, the top of walls 6 or 7 ft high may contain barbed wire, spikes, or broken glass set in cement. Offenders often avoid injury by throwing a blanket or jacket over the top of the wall (or fence) before scaling

it. An advantage of a wall is that outsiders are hindered from observing inside. However, observation by public police during patrols also is hindered; this can benefit an intruder.

Hedges or shrubbery are useful as barriers. Thorny shrubs have a deterrent value. These include holly, barberry, and multiflora rose bushes, all of which require a lot of watering. The privet hedge grows almost anywhere and requires minimal care. A combination of hedge and fence is useful. Hedges should be less than 3 ft high and placed on the inside to avoid injury to those passing by and to create an added obstacle for someone attempting to scale the fence. Any plants that are large and placed too close to buildings and other locations provide a climbing tool, cover for thieves, and a hiding place for contraband.

Municipal codes restrict the heights of fences, walls, and hedges to maintain an attractive environment devoid of threatening–looking barriers. Certain kinds of barriers may be prohibited (e.g., barbed wire) to ensure conformity. Planning should encompass research of local standards.

The following list can help a security manager eliminate weak points along a perimeter or barrier.

1. Utility poles, trees, boxes, pallets, forklifts, tools, and other objects outside a building can be used to scale a barrier.
2. Ladders left outside are an offender's delight. Stationary ladders are made less accessible via a steel cage with a locked door.
3. A **common wall** is shared by two separate entities. Thieves may lease and occupy or just enter the adjoining building or room and then hammer through the common wall.
4. A roof is easy to penetrate. A few tools, such as a drill and saw, enable offenders to cut through the roof. Because lighting, fences, sensors, and patrols rarely involve the roof, this weakness is attractive to thieves. A rope ladder often is employed to descend from the roof, or a forklift might be used to lift

items to the roof. Vehicle keys should be hidden and other precautions taken.

5. Roof hatches, skylights, basement windows, air conditioning and other vent and duct systems, crawl spaces between floors and under buildings, fire escapes, and utility covers may need a combination of locks, sensors, steel bars, heavy mesh, fences, and inspections. A widely favored standard is that any opening greater than 96 square inches requires increased protection.

Protecting Buildings Against Terrorism

To help justify security and loss prevention expenditures, executives should refer to the *Reference Manual to Mitigate Potential Terrorist Attacks against Buildings* ([45]: iii), here referred to as FEMA 426. This publication notes that building designs can serve to mitigate multiple hazards. For example, hurricane window design, especially against flying debris, and seismic standards for nonstructural building components apply also to bomb explosions. Next, Purpura [36] describes protection methods from FEMA 426.

FEMA 426 refers to site-level considerations for security that include land use controls, landscape architecture, site planning, and other strategies to mitigate risks of terrorism and other hazards. **Land use controls**, including zoning and land development regulations, can affect security because they define urban configurations that can decrease or increase risks from crime and terrorism. For instance, managing storm water on-site can add security through water retention facilities that serve as a vehicle barrier and blast setback. This reduces the need for off-site pipes and manholes that can be used for access or to conceal weapons. FEMA 426 offers several building design suggestions to increase security (Fig. 9.5).

A **target-rich environment** is created when people, property, and operations are concentrated in a dense area. There are advantages and disadvantages to a dense cluster. An advantage is the possibility to maximize standoff (i.e., protection when a blast occurs) from the perimeter. Additional security benefits are a reduction in the number of access and surveillance points and a shorter perimeter to protect. A dense cluster of buildings can possibly save energy costs through, for instance, heat transfer from heat-producing areas to heat-consuming areas. In addition, external lighting would not be dispersed over a large area, requiring more lights and energy. In contrast, dispersed buildings, people, and operations spread the risk. However, dispersal can increase the complexity of security (e.g., more access points), and it may require more resources (e.g., security officers, CCTV, lighting perimeter protection).

FEMA 426 recommends that designers consolidate buildings that are functionally compatible and have similar threat levels. For instance, mail rooms, shipping and receiving docks, and visitor screening areas, where people and materials are often closely monitored prior to access, should be isolated and separated from concentrations of people, operations, and key assets.

The design of open space with protection in mind offers several benefits: the ease with which to monitor and detect intruders, vehicles, and weapons; standoff value from a blast; pervious open space that permits storm water to percolate back into the ground, reducing the need for pipes, manholes, and other covert access points and weapon concealment sites; and wetland or vegetated area to improve aesthetic value while hindering vehicle intrusion.

Keep out zones help to maintain a specific distance between vehicles or people and a building. This is accomplished through perimeter security. If terrorists plan to attack a specific building, they will likely use surveillance to study security features, look for vulnerabilities, and try to penetrate access controls and defenses through creative means; security planning should include surveillance and other methods to identify individuals who may be gathering such information from off or on the premises.

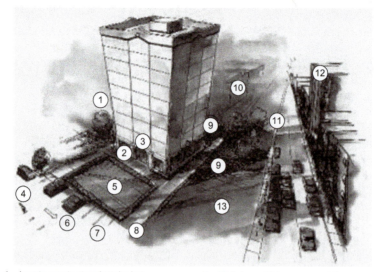

1. Locate assets stored onsite but outside of the facility within view of occupied rooms in the facility

2. Eliminate parking beneath facilities

3. Minimize exterior signage or other indications of asset locations

4. Locate trash receptacles as far from the facility as possible

5. Eliminate lines of approach perpendicular to the building

6. Locate parking to obtain stand-off distance from facility

7. Illuminate building exteriors or sites where exposed assets are located

8. Minimize vehicle access points

9. Eliminate potential hiding places near facility; provide an unobstructed view around facility

10. Site facility within view of other occupied facilities on the installation

11. Maximize distance from facility to installation boundary

12. Locate facility away from natural or man-made vantage points

13. Secure access to power/heat plants, gas mains, water supplies, and electrical service

FIGURE 9.5 Summary of site mitigation measures. *U.S. Department of Homeland Security. Reference manual to mitigate potential terrorist attacks against buildings, FEMA 426. Washington (DC): FEMA; December 2003.*

Here are other suggestions for buildings from FEMA 426:

- Provide redundant utility systems to continue life safety, security, and rescue functions in case of an emergency.
- Since hardened glazing may cause windows not to blow out in a blast, a system for smoke removal is essential.
- When possible, elevate fresh air intakes to reduce the potential of hazardous materials entering a building from ground level. The intakes should be sloped down and have screens in case a device is thrown toward the opening.
- Manipulation of the HVAC system could minimize the spread of a hazardous agent. Filtration systems are another option, although expensive.

Mitigation for Explosive Blasts

Standoff distance is the distance between an asset and a threat. FEMA 426 views *distance* as the most effective and desirable strategy against a blast because other methods may vary in effectiveness, be more costly, and result in unintended consequences. A blast wall can become a part of the fragmentation if a bomb is detonated close to it. Urban environments create challenges when designing standoff distance because land is often expensive and it may be unavailable. There is no ideal standoff distance; numerous variables take part in planning, such as the type of threat or explosive, construction characteristics and target hardening, and desired level of protection.

Blast and antiramming walls provide an expensive option for protecting buildings, especially in urban areas. Revel ([38]: 40) writes that a test of a blast wall conducted by the U.S. Government's Technical Support Working Group (TSWG) showed the effectiveness of this security method. The blast wall sustained an explosion more powerful than the one that destroyed the Murrah Federal Building (Oklahoma City bombing) and the effects on the test building behind the blast wall were reduced by about 90%. The blast wall was constructed by first inserting in the ground 18-foot blast posts, with 9 ft extending above the ground. Then steel-jacketed concrete and rebar-filled panels were lowered between the posts in an interlocking pattern. When the explosion occurred, the posts twisted and deflected the blast above and back from the panels, directing the force up and beyond the lower structural steel of the building and around the ends of the wall. The blast wall is also capable of absorbing large vehicle impact at high speeds.

Although several building design features can mitigate explosive blasts, many factors enter into the design of buildings, including cost, purpose, occupancy, and location. A high-risk building should incorporate more mitigation features than a low-risk building. Significant changes to existing buildings may be too expensive; therefore, lower cost changes must be sought. Bollards and strong gates are less expensive than making major structural changes to a building. In addition, trees, vegetative groupings, and earth berms offer some degree of blast shielding. Examples of mitigation features from FEMA 426 are as follows:

- Avoid "U-" or "L-" shaped building designs that trap the shock waves of a blast. Circular buildings reduce a shock wave better than a rectangular building because of the angle of incidence of the shock wave.
- Avoid exposed structural elements (e.g., columns) on the exterior of a facility.
- Install as much glazing (i.e., windows) as possible away from the street side.
- Avoid locating doors across from one another in interior hallways to limit the force of a blast through the building.
- High-security rooms should be blast- and fragment-resistant.
- Provide pitched roofs to permit deflection of launched explosives.

Glazing

Annealed glass, also called *plate glass*, is commonly used in buildings. It has low strength, and upon failure, it fractures into razor sharp pieces. *Fully thermally tempered glass* (TTG) is four to five times stronger than annealed glass, and upon failure, it will fracture into small cube-shaped fragments. Building codes generally require TTG anywhere the public can touch (e.g., entrance doors). *Wire-reinforced glass* is made of annealed glass with an embedded layer of wire mesh. It is applied as a fire-resistant and forced entry barrier. All three types of glass present a dangerous hazard from a blast [45].

Traditionally, window protection focused on hindering forced entry. Today, we are seeing increasing designs that mitigate the hazardous effects of flying glass from various risks, besides explosion. Experts report that 75% of all damage and injury from bomb blasts results from flying and falling glass. Vendors sell *shatter-resistant film*, also called *fragment retention film*, which is applied to the glass surface to reduce this problem. Conversely, a report on the 1993

World Trade Center attack claimed that the destroyed windows permitted deadly gases to escape from the building, enabling occupants to survive. A balanced design (i.e., type of glass, glass frame, and frame to building) means that all the window components have compatible capacities and fail at the same pressure levels. The U.S. General Services Administration publishes glazing protection levels based on how far glass fragments would enter a space and cause injuries. It is important to note that the highest level of protection for glazing may not mitigate the effects from a large explosion [45].

Blast curtains are window draperies made of special fabrics designed to stop glass window shards that are caused by explosions and other hazards. Various designs serve to catch broken glass and let the gas and air pressure dissipate through the fabric mesh. The fibers of these curtains can be several times as strong as steel wire. The U.S. General Services Administration establishes criteria for these products ([30]: 143–144).

Glass can be designed to block penetration of bullets, defeat attempted forced entry, remain intact following an explosion, and protect against electronic eavesdropping. The Web shows many standards for glazing from the American Architectural Manufacturers Association (AAMA), ANSI, UL, ASTM, Consumer Product Safety Commission, ISO, and overseas groups. Security glazing should be evaluated on comparative testing to an established national consensus standard such as ASTM F1233, Standard Test Method for Security Glazing Materials and Systems. Important issues for glazing include product life cycle, durability, installation, maintenance, and framing [39].

Underwriters Laboratories classifies *bullet-resistant windows* into eight protection levels, with levels 1 to 3 rated against handguns and 4 to 8 rated against rifles. Level 4 or higher windows usually are applied by government agencies and the military. Protective windows are made of either glass or plastic or mixtures of each.

Laminated glass absorbs a bullet as it passes through various glass layers. The advantage of glass is in its maintenance: it is easy to clean and less likely to scratch than plastic. It is less expensive per square foot than plastic but heavier, which requires more workers and stronger frames. Glass has a tendency to spall (i.e., chip) when hit by a bullet. UL752-listed glass holds up to three shots, and then it begins to shatter from subsequent shots.

Two types of plastic used in windows are acrylic and polycarbonate. Both vary in thickness and are lighter and more easily scratched than glass. *Acrylic windows* are clear and monolithic, whereas glass and polycarbonate windows are laminates consisting of layers of material bonded one on top of another. Acrylic will deflect bullets and hold together under sustained hits. Some spalling may occur. *Polycarbonate windows* are stronger than acrylics against high-powered weapons. Local codes may require glazing to pop out in an emergency.

In addition to protective windows, wall armor is important because employees often duck below a window during a shooting. These steel or fiberglass plates also are rated.

Burglar-resistant windows are rated (UL 972, Burglary Resisting Glazing Material); available in acrylic and polycarbonate materials; and protect against hammers, flame, "smash and grab," and other attacks. Combined bullet- and burglar-resistant windows are available. Although window protection is an expense that may be difficult to justify, insurers offer discounts on insurance premiums for such installations.

Electronic security glazing, containing metalized fabrics, can prevent electromagnetic signals inside a location from being intercepted from outside, while also protecting a facility from external electromagnetic radiation interference from outside sources. Standards for this type of glazing are from the National Security Agency, NSA 65–8.

Window Protection

Covering windows with grating or security screens is an additional step to impede entrance by an intruder or items being thrown out by a dishonest employee. *Window grating* consists of metal bars constructed across windows. These bars run horizontally and vertically to produce an effective form of protection. Although these bars are not aesthetically pleasing, they can be purchased with attractive ornamental designs. *Security screens* are composed of steel or stainless-steel wire (mesh) welded to a frame. Screens have some distinct advantages over window grating. Employees can pass pilfered items through window bars more easily than through a screen. Security screens look like ordinary screens, but they are much heavier in construction and can stop rocks and other objects.

When planning window protection, one must consider the need for emergency escape and ventilation. To ensure safety, certain windows can be targeted for the dismantling of window protection during business hours.

Window Locks

Businesses and institutions often contain windows that do not open. For windows that do open, a latch or lock on the inside provides some protection. The *double-hung window*, often applied at residences, is explained here as a foundation for window protection. It consists of top and bottom windows that are raised and lowered for user convenience. When the top window is pushed up and the bottom window pushed down, a crescent sash lock containing a curved turn knob locks both parts of the whole window in place (Fig. 9.6). By inserting a knife under the crescent sash lock where both window sections meet, an offender can jimmy the latch out of its catch. If an offender breaks the glass, the crescent sash lock can be unlocked by reaching inside. With such simple techniques known to offenders, defenses that are more complicated are necessary. Nails can be used to facilitate a quick escape while maintaining good window security: one drills a downward-sloping hole into the right and left sides of the window frame where the top and bottom window halves overlap and inserts nails that are thinner and longer than the holes. This enables the nails to be quickly removed during an emergency escape. If a burglar attacks the window, he or she cannot find or remove the nails (Fig. 9.6). Another method is to attach a window

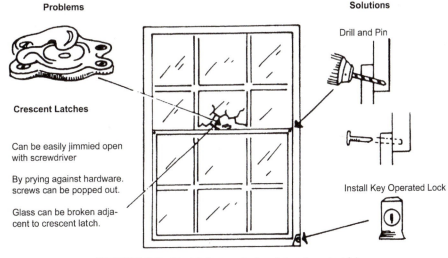

Problems

Crescent Latches

Can be easily jimmied open with screwdriver

By prying against hardware, screws can be popped out.

Glass can be broken adjacent to crescent latch.

Solutions

Drill and Pin

Install Key Operated Lock

FIGURE 9.6 Double-hung window (view from inside).

lock requiring a key (Fig. 9.6). These locks are capable of securing a window in a closed or slightly opened position. This can be done with the nail (and several holes) as well. The key should be hidden near the window in case of emergency.

Electronic Protection for Windows

Four categories of electronic protection for windows are foil, vibration, glass-breakage, and contact-switch sensors. *Window foil*, which has lost much of its popularity, consists of lead foil tape less than 1-inch wide and paper thin that is applied directly on the glass near the edges of a window. In the nonalarm state, electricity passes through the foil to form a closed circuit. When the foil is broken, an alarm is sounded. Window foil is inexpensive and easy to maintain. One disadvantage is that a burglar may cut the glass without disturbing the foil. *Vibration sensors* respond to vibration or shock. They are attached directly on the glass or window frame. These sensors are noted for their low-false alarm rate and are applicable to fences, walls, and valuable artwork, among other things. *Glass-breakage sensors* react to glass breaking. A sensor the size of a large coin is placed directly on the glass and can detect glass breakage several feet away. Some types operate via a tuning fork, which is tuned to the frequency produced by glass breaking. Others employ a microphone and electric amplifier. *Contact switches* activate an alarm when opening the window interrupts the contact. In Fig. 9.7, this sensor protects a door and roof opening.

Additional ideas for window protection follow:

1. A strong window frame fastened to a building prevents prying and removal of the entire window.
2. First floor windows are especially vulnerable to penetration and require increased protection.
3. Consider tinting windows to hinder observation by offenders.

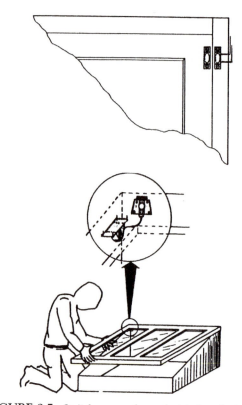

FIGURE 9.7 Switch sensors have electrical contacts that make or break an electrical circuit in response to a physical movement.

4. Windows (and other openings) that are no longer used can be bricked.
5. Expensive items left near windows invite trouble.
6. Cleaning windows and windowsills periodically increases the chances of obtaining clear fingerprints in the event of a crime.

Doors

Many standards apply to doors, from the AAMA, ANSI, ASTM, BHMA, National Association of Architectural Metal Manufacturers (NAAMM), NFPA, Steel Door Institute (SDI), UL, and ISO. In addition, other countries have standards. Aggleton ([1]: 24) writes that because of life safety issues (e.g., quick egress in case of emergency), door hardware and locks are subject to more stringent codes and standards than other physical security, such as intrusion sensors.

Doors having fire ratings must meet certain frame and hardware requirements. Decisions on the type of lock and whether electronic access will be applied also affect hardware. Decisions on doors are especially crucial because of their daily use and the potential for satisfying or enraging users and management ([40]: 40).

Businesses and institutions generally use aluminum doors. Composed of an aluminum frame, most of the door is covered by glass. Without adequate protection, the glass is vulnerable, and prying the weak aluminum is not difficult. The all-metal door improves protection at the expense of attractiveness.

Hollow-core doors render complex locks useless because an offender can punch right through the door. Thin wood panels or glass on the door are additional weak points. More expensive, *solid-core doors* are stronger; they are made of solid wood (over an inch thick) without the use of weak fillers. To reinforce hollow-core or solid-core doors, one can attach 16-gauge steel sheets via one way screws.

Whenever possible, door hinges should be placed on the inside. Door hinges that face outside enable easy entry. By using a screwdriver and hammer, one can raise the pins out of the hinges to enable the door to be lifted away. To protect the hinge pins, it is a good idea to weld them so they cannot be removed in this manner. Another form of protection is to remove two screws on opposite sides of the hinge, insert a pin or screw on the jamb side of the hinge so that it protrudes about half an inch, and then drill a hole in the opposite hole to fit the pin when the door is closed. With this method on both top and bottom hinges, even if the hinge pins are removed, the door will not fall off the hinges (Fig. 9.8).

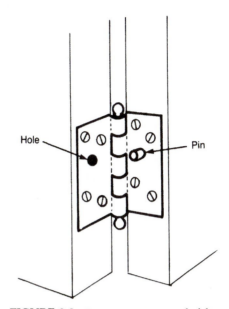

FIGURE 9.8 Pin to prevent removal of door.

Contact switches applied to doors offer electronic protection. Greater protection is provided when contact switches are recessed in the edges of the door and frame. Other kinds of electronic sensors applied at doors include vibration sensors, pressure mats, and various types of motion detectors aimed in the area of the door.

More hints for door security follow:

1. A wide-angle door viewer within a solid door permits a look at the exterior prior to opening a door.
2. Doors (and windows) are afforded extra protection at night by chain closures. These frequently are seen covering storefronts in malls and in high-crime neighborhoods.
3. To block "hide-in" burglars (those who hide in a building until after closing) from easy exit, require that openings such as doors and windows have a key-operated lock on the inside as well as on the outside.
4. Almost all fire departments are equipped with power saws that cut through door locks and bolts in case of fire. Many firefighters can gain easy access to local buildings because building

owners have provided keys that are located in fire trucks. Although this creates a security hazard, losses can be reduced in case of fire.

5. All doors need protection, including garage, sliding, overhead, chain-operated, and electric doors.

Intrusion Detection Systems

Standards for intrusion detection systems are from UL, the Institute of Electrical and Electronics Engineers (IEEE), and ISO, plus other groups in the United States and overseas. UL, for example, "lists" installation companies that are authorized to issue UL Certificates on each installation. This means that the installer conforms to maintenance and testing as required by UL, which conducts unannounced inspections.

Intrusion detection systems; these systems have gone through several generations, leading to improved performance. Not in the table is *magnetic field*, which consists of a series of buried wire loops or coils. Metal objects moving over the sensor induce a current and signal an alarm. Research shows that the vulnerability to defeat (VD) for magnetic field and infrared photo beam is high. Microwave, electric field, fence disturbance, seismic sensor cable, taut wire, and video motion systems all have a medium VD. The VD for ported coaxial cable systems is low. Visible sensors are relatively easy to defeat but cost-effective for low-security applications. Multiple sensors, and especially covert sensors, provide a higher level of protection ([8]: 57–61; [37]: 36–42; [41]: 80–82).

Fiber optics is a growing choice for intrusion detection and transmission. **Fiber optics** refers to the transportation of data by way of guided light waves in an optical fiber. This differs from the conventional transmission of electrical energy in copper wires. Fiber optic applications include video, voice, and data communications. Fiber optic data transmission is more secure and less subject to interference than older methods.

Fiber optic perimeter protection can take the form of a fiber optic cable installed on a fence.

When an intruder applies stress on the cable, an infrared light source pulsing through the system notes the stress or break and activates an alarm. Optical fibers can be attached to or inserted within numerous items to signal an alarm, including razor ribbon, security grills, windows, and doors, and it can protect valuable assets such as computers.

Dibazar, et al. [11] writes of their research on the development and deployment of "smart fence" systems consisting of multiple sensor technologies. Their research illustrates the direction and capabilities of "smart fence" systems. Included in their design are "(a) acoustic based long range sensor with which vehicles' engine sound and type can be identified, (b) vibration based seismic analyzer which discriminates between human footsteps and other seismic events such as those caused by animals, and (c) fence breaching vibration sensor which can detect intentional disturbances on the fence and discriminate among climb, kick, rattle, and lean."

Garcia ([13]: 83–84) views intrusion sensor performance based on three characteristics: probability of detection of the threat, nuisance alarm rate, and VD. The *probability of detection* depends on several factors including the desired threat to be detected (e.g., walking, tunneling), sensor design, installation, sensitivity adjustment, weather, and maintenance/testing. According to Garcia, a *nuisance alarm rate* results from a sensor interacting with the environment, and a sensor cannot distinguish between a threat and another event (e.g., vibration from a train). A *false alarm rate* results from the equipment itself, and it is caused by inadequate design, failure, or poor maintenance. VD varies among systems. **Bypass** means the adversary circumvented the intrusion detection system. **Spoofing** means the adversary traveled through the detection zone without triggering an alarm; depending on the sensor, one strategy is by moving very slowly. Garcia emphasizes the importance of proper installation and testing of intrusion detection systems.

No one technology is perfect; many protection programs rely on dual technology to strengthen intrusion detection. In the process of selecting a system, it is wise to remember that manufacturers' claims often are based on perfect weather. Security decision-makers must clearly understand the advantages and disadvantages of each type of system under various conditions.

Applications

Intrusion detection systems can be classified according to the kind of protection provided. There are three basic kinds of protection: point, area, and perimeter. **Point protection** (Fig. 9.9) signals an alarm when an intrusion is made at a special location. It is also referred to as **spot or object protection**. Files, safes, vaults, jewelry counters, and artwork are targets for point protection. Capacitance and vibration systems provide point protection and are installed directly on the object. These systems often are used as a backup after an offender has succeeded in gaining access. **Area protection**

(Fig. 9.10) detects an intruder in a selected area such as a main aisle in a building or at a strategic passageway. Microwave and infrared systems are applicable to area protection. **Perimeter protection** (Fig. 9.11) focuses on the outer boundary of the premises. If doors and windows are part of the perimeter, then contact switches, vibration detectors, and other devices are applicable.

Alarm Signaling Systems

Alarm signaling systems transmit data from a protected area to an annunciation system. Local ordinances and codes provide guidelines and restrictions on these systems.

Local alarm systems notify, by sound or lights, people in the hearing or seeing range of the signal. This includes the intruder, who may flee. Typically, a siren or bell is activated outside a building. Often, local alarms produce no response—in urban areas, responsible action may not be taken, and in rural areas,

FIGURE 9.9   Point protection.

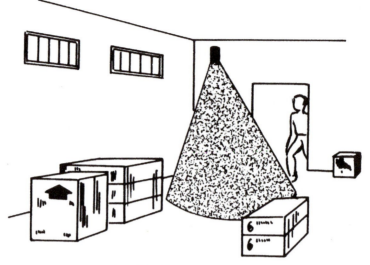

FIGURE 9.10   Area protection.

FIGURE 9.11   Perimeter protection.

nobody may hear the alarm. These alarms are less expensive than other signaling systems but are easily defeated. If a local alarm is used during a robbery, people may be harmed. Research from the United Kingdom ([9]: 53–72) points to the benefits of delayed-audible alarms during a burglary that are triggered as the offender enters the premises but sound a few minutes later so cameras have an opportunity to record the offender and police still have time to respond prior to the offender's escaping if they are notified promptly. Combining these strategies with an immediate silent alarm to a central station increases the opportunity for an arrest.

A **central station** alarm system receives intrusion, fire, medical, and environmental signals at a computer console located and monitored a distance away from the protected location. When an alarm signal is received, central station personnel contact police, firefighters, or other responders. Central station services employ sales, installation, service, monitoring, and response personnel. Proprietary monitoring systems are similar to central station systems, except that the former does the monitoring and the system is operated by the proprietary organization. Resources for central station design are available from UL, NFPA, and the Security Industry Association ([32]: 80).

Technology drives advances in central station capabilities. Remote video monitoring enables a central station operator to view what triggered an alarm to verify the need for a human response. Global positioning system (GPS) permits real-time tracking (e.g., location, direction, and speed) and archiving of moving assets and people. Off-site video storage, especially at a UL-listed central station, affords increased protection and backup for video recordings. It also helps to prevent the problem of offenders taking recording equipment with them as they leave the crime scene and, thus, destroying evidence ([12]: 44–46).

WeGuardYou [47], a security vendor, describes how its technology is applied to shopping mall security as explained next. Each security vehicle functions as a central station that offers real-time local and remote video, alarm, and data monitoring while transferring information over a secure wireless system. In one scenario, a woman leaves a mall one evening, packages and pocketbook in hand. Suspected muggers are in the parking lot. Cameras follow the woman in real time as the images are sent to mobile units (i.e., security vehicles), besides showing on TV monitors inside the mall central station control room. Mobile units containing emergency lights, loudspeaker, and enhanced lighting converge on the "hot spot" to prevent victimization. If an emergency occurs, security officers take action, all security personnel are notified via radio, police and EMS are notified, and fixed cameras and those on mobile units record the incident with images remotely accessible.

Various data transmission systems are utilized to signal an alarm. Here, the older technology is covered first before the modern technology. As with fire alarm systems, security alarm systems are using less traditional phone lines to transmit an alarm as digital systems involving cellular networks, fiber optics, and voice over IP are advancing ([22]: 32).

Automatic telephone dialer systems include the tape dialer and digital dialer. Tape dialer systems are seldom used today. They deliver a prerecorded or coded message to an interested party (e.g., central station, police department) after that party answers the telephone. Digital dialers use coded electronic pulses that are transmitted and an electronic terminal decodes the message. Digital dialers, often called digital communicators, are still applied today, although the technology is more advanced than in earlier years. Local codes typically prohibit tape dialers or similar automatic devices connected to authorities (e.g., police and fire) because of false alarms, wasted resources, and the need for authorities to ask questions about the emergency. The central station evolved to serve as a buffer between the site of the emergency and authorities so information can be gathered and verified prior to contacting authorities.

Today, there are different automatic voice/pager dialer systems on the market that contact a central station or individual when a sensor is activated. The technology is also applied in sales, such as the use of software enabling calls through a computer.

Radio frequency and *microwave* data transmission systems often are applied where telephone lines are not available or where hardwire lines are not practical. The components include transmitter; receiver; and repeaters to extend range, battery backup, and solar power.

Fiber optic data transmission systems, as discussed earlier, transport data by way of light waves within a thin glass fiber. These cables are either underground or above ground. The components include transmitter, receiver, repeaters, battery backup, and solar power. Fiber optic systems are more secure than direct wire.

Signals should be backed up by multiple technologies. Options for off-site transmission of activity include satellite, local area network, wide area network, cellular, and the Internet. Cellular is especially useful for backup, since it is more likely to remain in operation in certain disasters. It can also be used as a primary transmission method ([50]: 74–83).

Among the advances in alarm monitoring is **remote programming**. Using this method, a central station can perform different functions without ever visiting the site. Capabilities include arming and disarming systems, unlocking doors, performing diagnostics and corrections, and, with access systems, adding or deleting cards.

Alarm systems also may be multiplexed or integrated. *Multiplexing* is a method of transmitting multiple information signals over a single communications channel. This single communications channel reduces line requirements by allowing signal transmission from many protected facilities. Two other advantages are that information that is more detailed can be transmitted, such as telling which detector is in an alarm state, and transmission line security is enhanced with encoding. *Integrated systems*, as covered in Chapter 8, combine multiple systems (e.g., alarm monitoring, access controls, and CCTV).

Closed-Circuit Television

CCTV allows one person to view several locations (Fig. 9.12). This is a distinct advantage when protecting the boundaries of a facility, because it reduces personnel costs.

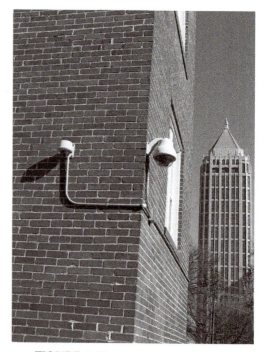

FIGURE 9.12   Closed-circuit television.

Television programs and movies sometimes portray an intruder penetrating a perimeter barrier by breaking through when a CCTV camera had momentarily rotated to another location. Usually, the camera just misses the intruder by returning to the entry point right after the intruder gains access. Such a possibility can be averted via overlapping camera coverage. If cameras are capable of viewing other cameras, personnel can check on viewing obstructions, sabotage, vandalism, or other problems. Smoked domes prevent an offender from identifying the direction of the camera. In addition, covert CCTV surveillance should be considered for outdoor applications in conjunction with overt CCTV surveillance.

Tamperproof housings will impede those interested in disabling cameras. Different models are resistant to vandalism, bullets, explosion, dust, and severe weather. Housings are manufactured with heaters, defrosters, windshield wipers, washers, and sun shields.

Low-light-level cameras provide the means to view outside when very little light is available. When no visible light is available, an infrared illuminator creates light, invisible to the naked eye, but visible to infrared-sensitive cameras. Another option is *thermal imaging cameras*, which sense heat from an intruder and are especially helpful to spot them in darkness, fog, smoke, foliage, and up to several miles away ([43]: 56–66; [33]: 24–28). An essential aspect of CCTV usage is proper monitoring. Although video motion detection and video analytics (Chapter 8) apply technology to identify anomalies that human observers may miss, security management should take action to reduce fatigue and ensure good-quality viewing. Suggestions include rotating personnel every 2h, limit TV monitors to fewer than 10, arrange monitors in a curved configuration in front of the viewer, control the lighting over the console to avoid glare on the monitor screens or tilt the monitors if necessary, place the monitors in an order that permits easy recognition of camera locations, provide a swivel chair that hampers the opportunity for sleeping, and assign tasks to the viewer (e.g., communications and logging).

Lighting

From a business perspective, lighting can be justified because it improves sales by making a business and merchandise more attractive, promotes safety and prevents lawsuits, improves employee morale and productivity, and enhances the value of real estate. From a security perspective, three major purposes of lighting are *to create a psychological deterrent to intrusion, to enable detection, and to enhance the capabilities of CCTV systems*. Good lighting is considered such an effective crime control method that the law, in many locales, requires buildings to maintain adequate lighting.

Painter and Farrington [31] conducted a major study on the effect of lighting on the incidence of crime in England. Three residential areas

were selected. One was the experimental area that contained improved lighting. The second was labeled the adjacent area. In addition, the third served as the control area. Lighting in the adjacent and control areas remained unchanged. The research included the question of whether improved lighting might result in a reduction of crime in the adjacent area. The research results showed a marked reduction in different crimes in the experimental area, whereas crime in the adjacent and control areas remained the same.

One way to study lighting deficiencies is to go to the premises at night and study the possible methods of entry and areas where inadequate lighting will aid an offender. Before the visit, one should contact local police as a precaution against mistaken identity and to recruit their assistance in spotting weak points in lighting.

Three sources for information on lighting are the Illuminating Engineering Society of North America (IESNA), the National Lighting Bureau, and the International Association of Lighting Management Companies. The IESNA provides information on recommended lighting levels for various locations.

What lighting level will aid an intruder? Most people believe that under conditions of darkness a criminal can safely commit a crime. However, this view may be faulty, in that one generally cannot work in the dark. Three possible levels of light are *bright light*, *darkness*, and *dim light*. Bright light affords an offender plenty of light to work but enables easy observation by others; it will deter crime. Without light—in darkness—a burglar finds that he or she cannot see to jimmy a door lock, release a latch, or perform whatever work is necessary to gain access; a flashlight is necessary, which someone may observe. However, dim light provides just enough light to break and enter while hindering observation by authorities. Support for this view was shown in a study of crimes during full-moon phases, when dim light was produced. This study examined the records of 972 police shifts at three police agencies, for a 2-year period, to compare nine different crimes during full-moon and nonfull-moon phases. Only one crime, breaking and entering, was greater during full-moon phases ([35]: 350–353). Although much case law supports lighting as an indicator of efforts to provide a safe environment, security specialists are questioning conventional wisdom about lighting ([6]: 29–33). Because so much nighttime lighting goes unused, should it be reduced or turned off? Should greater use be made of motion-activated lighting? How would these approaches affect safety and cost-effectiveness? These questions are ripe for research.

Illumination

Lumens (of light output) per watt (of power input) are a measure of lamp efficiency. Initial lumens per watt data are based on the light output of lamps when new; however, light output declines with use. **Illuminance** is the intensity of light falling on a surface, measured in foot-candles (English units) or lux (metric units). The **foot-candle (FC)** is a measure of how bright the light is when it reaches 1 ft from the source. One **lux** equals 0.0929 FC. For measures of illuminance, values not labeled as vertical are generally assumed to be horizontal FC (or lux). The light provided by direct sunlight on a clear day is about 10,000 FC; an overcast day would yield about 100 FC; and a full moon, about 0.01 FC. A sample of outdoor lighting illuminances recommended by the Illuminating Engineering Society of North America [16] are as follows: guarded facilities, including entrances and gatehouse inspection, 10 FC (100 lux); parking facilities, garages, and covered parking spaces, 6 FC (60 lux) on pavement and 5 FC (50 lux) for stairs, elevators, and ramps; and for fast-food restaurant parking, general parking at schools and hotels/motels, and common areas of multifamily residences and dormitories, 3 FC (30 lux).

Care should be exercised when studying illuminance. Horizontal illuminance may not aid in the visibility of vertical objects such as signs and keyholes. FC vary depending on the distance from the lamp and the angle. If you hold a light meter horizontally, it often gives a different reading than if you hold it vertically. Are the FC initial or maintained? Maintenance and bulb replacement ensure high-quality lighting ([27]: 1–36; [42]: 1–4).

Lamps

The following lamps are applied outdoors ([24]: 12–13; [27]: 1–36; [42]: 1–4):

- *Incandescent* lamps are at residences. Electrical current passes through a tungsten wire enclosed in a glass tube. The wire becomes white-hot and produces light. These lamps produce 17–22 lumens per watt, are the least efficient and most expensive to operate, and have a short lifetime of from 500 to 4000 h. *Compact fluorescent light bulbs* are replacing incandescent bulbs because they are "earth friendly," useless energy, last longer (10,000 h), and generate less heat.
- *Halogen* and *quartz halogen* lamps are incandescent bulbs filled with halogen gas (like sealed-beam auto headlights) and provide about 25% better efficiency and life than ordinary incandescent bulbs.
- *Fluorescent* lamps pass electricity through a gas enclosed in a glass tube to produce light, producing 67–100 lumens per watt. They create twice the light and less than half the heat of an incandescent bulb of equal wattage and cost 5–10 times as much. Fluorescent lamps do not provide high levels of light output. The lifetime is from 9000 to 17,000 h. They are not used extensively outdoors, except for signage.
- *Mercury vapor* lamps also pass electricity through a gas. The yield is 31–63 lumens per watt, and the life is over 24,000 h with good efficiency compared to incandescent lamps. Because of their long life, these lamps are often used in street lighting.
- *Metal halide* lamps are also of the gaseous type. The yield is 80–115 lumens per watt, and the efficiency is about 50% higher than

mercury vapor lamps, but the lamp life is about 6000 h. They often are used at sports stadiums because they imitate daylight conditions, and colors appear natural. Consequently, these lamps complement CCTV systems, but they are the most expensive light to install and maintain.

- *High-pressure sodium* lamps are gaseous, yield about 80–140 lumens per watt, have a life of about 24,000 h, and are energy efficient. These lamps are often applied on streets, parking lots, and building exteriors. They cut through fog and are designed to allow the eyes to see more detail at greater distances.
- *Low-pressure sodium* lamps are gaseous, produce 150 lumens per watt, have a life of about 15,000 h, and are even more efficient than high-pressure sodium. These lamps are expensive to maintain.

Each type of lamp has a different **color rendition**, which is the way a lamp's output affects human perceptions of color. Incandescent, fluorescent, and certain types of metal halide lamps provide excellent color rendition. Mercury vapor lamps provide good color rendition but are heavy on the blue. High-pressure sodium lamps, which are used extensively outdoors, provide poor color rendition, making things look yellow. Low-pressure sodium lamps make color unrecognizable and produce a yellow-gray color on objects. People find sodium vapor lamps, sometimes called *anticrime lights*, to be harsh because they produce a strange yellow haze. Claims are made that this lighting conflicts with aesthetic values and that it affects sleeping habits. In many instances, when people park their vehicles in a parking lot during the day and return to find their vehicle at night, they are often unable to locate it because of poor color rendition from sodium lamps; some report their vehicles as being stolen. Another problem is the inability of witnesses to describe offenders accurately.

Mercury vapor, metal halide, and high-pressure sodium take several minutes to produce full light output. If they are turned off, even more time is required to reach full output because they first have to cool down. This may not be acceptable for certain security applications. Incandescent, halogen, and quartz halogen have the advantage of instant light once electricity is turned on. Manufacturers can provide information on a host of lamp characteristics including the "strike" and "restrike" time.

Lighting Equipment

Fresnel lights have a wide flat beam that is directed outward to protect a perimeter, glaring in the faces of those approaching. A floodlight "floods" an area with a beam of light, resulting in considerable glare. Floodlights are stationary, although the light beams can be aimed to select positions. The following strategies reinforce good lighting:

1. Locate perimeter lighting to allow illumination of both sides of the barrier.
2. Direct lights down and away from a facility to create glare for an intruder. Make sure the directed lighting does not hinder observation by patrolling officers.
3. Do not leave dark spaces between lighted areas for offenders to move within. Design lighting to permit overlapping illumination.
4. Protect the lighting system, locate lighting inside the barrier, install protective covers over lamps, mount lamps on high poles, bury power lines, and protect switch boxes.
5. Photoelectric cells will enable lights to go on and off automatically in response to natural light. Manual operation is helpful as a backup.
6. Consider motion-activated lighting for external and internal areas.
7. If lighting is required near navigable waters, contact the U.S. Coast Guard.
8. Work to reduce light pollution, such as wasting energy and disturbing neighbors with light trespass.

9. Maintain a supply of portable, emergency lights and auxiliary power in the event of a power failure.
10. Good interior lighting also deters offenders.
11. If necessary, join other business owners to petition local government to install improved street lighting.

Parking Lot and Vehicle Controls

Employee access control at a building is easier when the parking lot is on one side of a building rather than surrounding the building. Vehicles should be parked away from shipping and receiving docks, garbage dumpsters, and other crime-prone locations.

Employees should have permanent parking stickers, whereas visitors, delivery people, and service groups should be given a temporary pass to be displayed on the windshield. Stickers and passes allow uniformed officers to locate unauthorized vehicles.

Parking lots are more secure when these specific strategies are applied: CPTED, access controls, signs, security patrols, lighting, CCTV, and panic buttons and emergency phones. Crimes often occur in parking lots, and these events can harm employee morale and result in lawsuits, unless people are protected. Hospitals, for example, supply an escort for nurses who walk to their vehicles after late shifts. Employee education about personal safety, locking vehicles, and additional precautions prevent losses.

Certain types of equipment can aid a parking lot security/safety program. Cushman patrol vehicles, capable of traveling through narrow passageways, increase patrol mobility. Bicycles are another option. A guardhouse or security booth is useful as a command post in parking lots (Fig. 9.13).

FIGURE 9.13   Access controls at a parking lot.

Various technologies can be applied to controlling vehicles at access points. One example is *automatic license plate recognition systems* that apply image-processing technology that reads a vehicle's license plate and uses infrared light to illuminate a plate in the dark. A high-speed camera is used to photograph a plate, and then the recorded information is compared to a database. Besides access controls, the applications include fleet management, locating stolen vehicles, and border security ([26]: 1).

The threat of terrorism has influenced the design of parking lots and vehicle controls. Different types of parking lots present various security issues. Surface lots keep vehicles away from buildings, consume large amounts of land, and may add to storm water runoff volume. On-street parking provides no setback. A garage may require blast resistance. If the garage is under a building, a serious vulnerability exists, since an underground bomb blast can be devastating.

A designer can propose minimizing vehicle velocity because, for example, a bollard that can stop a 15,000-pound truck moving at 35 MPH may not be able to stop the same truck moving at 55 MPH (FEMA 426). *The road itself can become a security measure by avoiding a straight path to a building*. A straight road enables a vehicle to gather speed to ram a barrier, penetrate a building, and then detonate a bomb. Approaches should be parallel to the building and contain high curbs, trees, or berms to prevent vehicles from leaving the road. Curving roads with tight corners offer another strategy.

Traffic calming strategies are subtler and communicate appropriate speed. Examples are speed humps and raised crosswalks. A speed hump is not as rough as a speed bump. The latter is often used in parking lots. All these strategies reduce speed and liability while increasing safety. Drawbacks are that the response time of first responders increases and snow removal may become difficult.

Security Officers

Officers normally are assigned to stationary (fixed) posts or to patrol. A **stationary post** is at a door or gate where people, vehicles, and objects are observed and inspected. Stationary posts also involve directing traffic or duty at a control center where communications, CCTV, and alarms are monitored. **Foot or vehicle patrols** conducted throughout the premises, in parking lots, and along perimeters identify irregularities while deterring offenders. Examples of unusual or harmful conditions that should be reported are damaged security devices, holes in perimeter fences or other evidence of intrusion, hidden merchandise, unattended vehicles parked inappropriately, keys left in vehicles, employees sleeping in vehicles or using drugs, blocked fire exits, cigarette butts in no-smoking areas, accumulations of trash, and odors from fuels or other combustibles. In contrast to public police officers, private security officers act in primarily a preventive role and *observe and report*.

Before security officers are employed, farsighted planning ensures optimum effectiveness of this service. What are the unique needs and characteristics of the site? How many people and what assets require protection? What are the vulnerabilities? How many hours per day is the facility open? How many employees? How many visitors and vehicles enter and exit daily? What are the specific tasks of security officers, how much time will be expended on each task, and how many officers are required?

Security officers are expensive. Costs include wages, insurance, uniforms, equipment, and training. If each officer costs $40,000 per year for a proprietary force and five officers are required for the premises at all times, to maintain all shifts 7 days per week requires approximately 20 officers. The cost would be about $800,000 per year. To reduce costs, many companies switch to contract security services and/or consider technological solutions.

Several specific steps can be taken to improve the effectiveness of officers. Three of the most critical are *careful applicant screening, sound training*, and *proper supervision*. Management should ensure that officers know what is expected of them. Policies, procedures, and day-to-day duties are communicated via verbal orders, memos, and training programs. Courtesy and a sharp appearance command respect that enhances security.

Policies should ensure that supervisors check on officers every hour. Rotating officers among duty assignments reduces fatigue while familiarizing them with various tasks. Providing inspection lists for adverse conditions will keep them mentally alert. The formal list should be returned with a daily report. Miller [18], in an ASIS CRISP Report entitled, "Fatigue Effects and Countermeasures in 24/7 Security Operations," offers shift work strategies to counter fatigue, such as "smart" scheduling and ensuring adequate time between schedule changes for proper sleep.

Armed versus Unarmed Officers

The question of whether to arm officers is controversial. Probably the best way to answer this question is to study the nature of the particular officer's assignment. If violence is likely, then officers should be armed. Officers assigned to locations where violent crimes are unlikely do not need firearms, which, if worn by officers, could be offensive. The trend is toward unarmed officers because of liability issues and costs for training and equipment. If weapons are issued to officers, proper selection of officers and training are of the utmost importance. Training should include use of force and firearms safety, as well as practice on the firing range every 4 months.

Monitoring Officers

Lower burglary and fire insurance premiums result from monitored patrols and insurance personnel subject the records to inspection. Early technology used *watch clocks* to monitor officer patrols along preplanned routes. The officer on patrol carried this old technology, consisting of a timepiece that contained a paper tape or disc divided into time segments. A watch clock was operated by an officer via keys mounted in walls at specific locations along a patrol route. These keys were often within metal boxes and chained to walls. When inserted into the watch clock, the key made an impression in the form of a number on the tape or disc. Supervisors examined the impressions to see whether the officer visited each key location and completed the scheduled route. Keys were located at vulnerable locations (e.g., entry points, flammable storage areas). Good supervision prevented officers from disconnecting all the keys at the beginning of the shift, bringing them to one location for use in the watch clock (and, thus, avoiding an hourly tour), and returning the keys at the end of the shift.

Automatic monitoring systems are another way to monitor patrols and keep records. Key stations are visited according to a preplanned time schedule and route. If an officer does not visit a key station within a specific time, a central monitoring station receives a transmitted signal, and if contact cannot be made, personnel are dispatched.

Bar code or *touch button* technology provides other avenues for monitoring patrols. A security officer carries a wand that makes contact with a bar code or touch button to record data that are later downloaded into a computer. Bar codes or buttons are affixed at vulnerable locations for a swipe by the wand to record the visit by the officer, who can also swipe bar codes or buttons that represent various conditions (e.g., fire extinguisher needs recharging). Supervision of these systems ensures that officers are patrolling properly and conditions are being reported ([2]: 48–58). To improve the efficiency of a security officer, the officer can use a wireless tablet PC (Fig. 9.14), which enables the officer to leave a monitoring post and take the workstation with him or her. If, for example, an officer must leave a control center to investigate an incident, the officer can bring the tablet PC and continue to

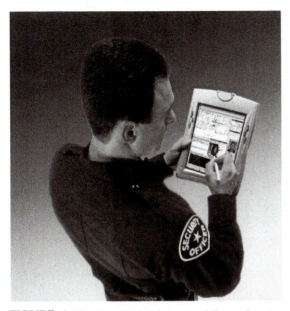

FIGURE 9.14 The tablet PC is a mobile workstation enabling a security officer to leave a post and do many things while mobile that are done from a desktop PC such as view closed-circuit television, monitor alarms, and open doors. *Courtesy of Hirsch Electronics, Santa Ana (CA).*

watch CCTV, monitor alarms, and open doors for employee access. Levine ([17]: 35) describes a customized PDA system that grew into a digital incident-reporting tool, then into a mobile phone with GPS tracking, as well as containing a camera, e-mail and text messaging functions, a panic alarm, time and attendance recording, and the means to read bar codes for monitoring patrols. He explained that in one case a client at a meeting complained about never seeing a security officer on patrol, so the security executive took out his computer, accessed the website, pulled up the previous day, and showed the client the tracking of the officer on patrol.

Contraband Detection

Contraband is an item that is illegal to possess or prohibited from being brought into a specific area. Examples are weapons, illegal drugs, and explosives. *Security officers and government personnel play a crucial role in spotting contraband at many locations.* They use special devices and canine services to locate contraband, and *these devices and services are as good as the personnel behind them.*

Various types of devices detect contraband. *Metal detectors* transmit a magnetic field that is disturbed by a metallic object, which sets off a light or audio signal. Two types of metal detectors are handheld and walkthrough. *X-ray scanners* use pulsed energy to penetrate objects that are shown on a color monitor. These devices are mobile and stationary and can inspect such things as mail, packages, loaded trucks, and shipping containers. Since the 9/11 attacks, ports, border checkpoints, airports, and other locations have intensified efforts to detect contraband, research and development and businesses selling detection devices have increased. Although vendors are prone to over promise and under deliver, contraband detection technology is improving. Reputable research groups applying scientific research methodologies improve the likelihood that devices operate as touted. For example, the National Institute of Standards and Technology [25] focuses on customer needs (e.g., police and military) and conducts research on various technologies. The focus of this group's research includes real-time imaging systems to detect large concealed objects for identifying suicide bombers and microwave electromagnetic signatures to identify dangerous liquids.

Protective Dogs

Besides serving to detect contraband and protect people, canine (K-9) is classified as an animal barrier that can strengthen security at a protected site. An *alarm dog* patrols inside a fenced area or building and barks at the approach of a stranger but does not attempt to attack. These dogs retreat when threatened but continue to bark. Such barking may become so alarming to an intruder that he or she will flee. A *guard or attack dog* is similar to an alarm dog, with an added feature of attacking an intruder. To minimize the possibility of a lawsuit, a business should selectively apply and adequately fence in these dogs, and warning signs should be posted. An experienced person on call at all times is needed to respond to emergencies. Another type of attack dog is the *sentry dog*. This dog is trained, kept on a leash, and responds to commands while patrolling with a uniformed officer. The advantages are numerous. These animals protect officers. Their keen senses of hearing and smell are tremendous assets when trying to locate a hidden offender (or explosives or drugs). Dogs can discern the slightest perspiration from people under stress, enabling the dogs to sense individuals who are afraid of them. An ingredient in stress perspiration irritates dogs, which makes frightened persons more susceptible to attack. When an "attack" command is given, a German shepherd has enough strength in its jaws to break a person's arm.

In addition to the possibility of a lawsuit if a dog attacks someone, there are other disadvantages to the use of dogs. If proprietary dogs are part of the protection team, personnel and kennel facilities are needed to care for the dogs. These costs and others include the purchase of dogs and their training, medical care, and food. Using a contract service would probably be more feasible. Another disadvantage is the possibility that dogs may be poisoned, anesthetized, or killed. An offender also may befriend a dog. Dogs should be taught to accept food only from the handler. Neighbors near the protected premises often find dogs noisy or may perceive them as offensive for other reasons.

Since the 9/11 attacks, interest in canines has increased. At the same time, there is a need for consistent standards for training, quality assurance, kenneling, selection of handlers, and presentation of evidence. Definitions also present a problem. For example, there is no consistent definition as to what constitutes an explosive detection canine. The Bureau of Alcohol, Tobacco, Firearms and Explosives has developed the National Odor Recognition Testing initiative, which could be a standard to which dogs could be certified. Research is being conducted on the use of chemical warfare agent detector dogs and GPS technology in conjunction with remote commands for searches, surveillance, and tracking of persons ([15]: 36–38).

Communications and the Control Center

As emergency personnel know, the ability to communicate over distance is indispensable. Every officer should be equipped with a portable two-way radio; this communication aid permits officers to summon assistance and notify superiors about hazards and impending disasters. Usually, officers on assignment communicate with a control center that is the hub of the loss prevention program. FEMA 426 ([45]: 3–45) recommends redundant communications. The control center is the appropriate site for a console containing alarm indicators, CCTV monitors, door controls, the public address system, and an assortment of other components for communication and loss prevention (Fig. 9.15).

Because of the convergence of IT and physical security, the traditional security control center may be within a network operations center. Some organizations may choose to outsource a portion of operations. Since these operations are critical, they must be secure both electronically and physically [19].

Because personnel will seek guidance from a control center in the event of an emergency, that center must be secure and operational at all times. A trend today is automated response systems programmed into the control center because so many decisions and actions are required for each type of emergency ([32]: 76–81). The control center is under increased protection against forced entry, tampering, or disasters when it contains a locked door; is located in a basement or underground; and is constructed of fire-resistant materials. An automatic, remotely operated lock, released by the

FIGURE 9.15 Security officer at console managing access control, closed-circuit television, alarm monitoring, and video imaging. *Courtesy of Diebold, Inc.*

console operator after identifying the caller also enhances security. Bullet-resistant glass is wise for high-crime locations. FEMA 426 ([45]: 3–47) recommends a backup control center, possibly at an off-site location. Whoever designs the control center should be well versed in ergonomics, which deals with the efficient and safe partnership between people and machines.

References

[1] Aggleton D. The latest innovations in door hardware. Secur Technol Exec 2010;20. [May].

[2] Arnheim L. A tour of guard patrol systems. Secur Manag 1999. [November].

[3] Atlas R. Fast food, easy money. Secur Manag 2010;54. [December].

[4] Bernard R. The security industry World has changed. Secur Technol Exec 2010;20. [May].

[5] Berube H. An examination of alarm system deterrence and rational choice theory: the need to increase risk. J Appl Secur Res 2010;5(3).

[6] Berube H. New notions of night light. Secur Manag 1994. [December].

[7] Burton R. A new standard for high-performance green buildings. Buildings 2010;104. [March].

[8] Clifton R, Vitch M. Getting a sense for danger. Secur Manag 1997. [February].

[9] Coupe T, Kaur S. The role of alarms and CCTV in detecting non-residential burglary. Secur J 2005;18.

[10] Davey C, et al. Design against crime: extending the reach of crime prevention through environmental design. Secur J 2005;18.

[11] Dibazar A, et al. Intelligent recognition of acoustic and vibration threats for security breach detection, close proximity danger identification, and perimeter protection. Homel Secur Aff 2011. [March] www.hsaj.org/?special:article=supplement.3.4.

[12] Evans R. Remote monitoring. Secur Prod 2005;9. [March].

[13] Garcia M. Vulnerability assessment of physical protection systems. Burlington (MA): Butterworth-Heinemann; 2006.

[14] Gips M. A pharmacopoeia of protection. Secur Manag 1999;43. [March].

[15] Harowitz S. Dog use dogged by questions. Secur Manag 2006;50. [January].

[16] Illuminating Engineering Society of North America. Guideline for security lighting for people, property, and public spaces. New York (NY): IESNA; 2003.

[17] Levine D. Armed and ready. Secur Technol Exec 2010;20. [October].

[18] Miller J. Fatigue effects and countermeasures in 24/7 security operations (CRISP report). 2010. www.asisonline.org.

[19] Milne J. Build your own security operations center. Secure Enterp 2005. [August 1] www.secureenterprisemag.com.

[20] Moore M. Defensive devices designed to blend in with New York. USA Today 2006. [July 31] www.usatoday.com/news/nation/2006-07-31-ny-security_x.htm.

[21] Morton J. Access denied. Buildings 2011;105. [May].

[22] Morton J. Upgrade your fire alarms with IP reliability. Buildings 2012;106. [March].

[23] Murphy P. Grounds for protection. Secur Manag 2000;44. [October].

[24] National Fire Protection Association. NFPA 730, guide for premises security, 2006 edition. Quincy (MA): NFPA; 2005.

[25] National Institute of Standards and Technology. Concealed weapon and contraband detecting, locating, and imaging. 2010. www.nist.gov/oles/diet-conceal.cfm.

[26] National Law Enforcement and Corrections Technology Center. No license to steal. TECHbeat 2006. [Spring].

[27] National Lighting Bureau. Lighting for safety and security. Washington (DC): National Lighting Bureau; n.d.

[28] Newman O. Defensible space. New York: Macmillan; 1972.

[29] Nunes-Vaz R, et al. A more rigorous framework for security-in-depth. J Appl Secur Res 2011;6(3).

[30] Owen D. Building security: strategies & cost. Kingston (MA): Reed; 2003.

[31] Painter K, Farrington D. Street lighting and crime: diffusion of benefits in the stoke-on-trent project. In: Painter K, Tilly N, editors. Crime prevention studies. Monsey (NY): Criminal Justice Press; 1999.

[32] Patterson D. How smart is your setup?. Secur Manag 2000;44. [March].

[33] Pierce C. Thermal video for the mainstream?. Secur Technol Des 2006;16. [May].

[34] Post R, Kingsbury A. Security administration: an introduction. 3rd ed. Springfield (IL): Charles C. Thomas; 1977.

[35] Purpura P. Police activity and the full moon. J Police Sci Adm 1979;7. [September].

[36] Purpura P. Terrorism and homeland security: an introduction with applications. Burlington (MA): Elsevier Butterworth-Heinemann; 2007.

[37] Reddick R. What you should know about protecting a perimeter. Secur Prod 2005;9. [April].

[38] Revel O. Protective blast and anti-ramming wall development. Secur Technol Des 2003. [November].

[39] Saflex, Inc. Architectural glazing. 2007. www.saflex.com.

[40] Schumacher J. How to resolve conflict with proper systems integration. Secur Technol Des 2000;10. [October].

[41] Shelton D. The new and improved moat. Secur Technol Des 2006;16. [March].

[42] Smith M. Crime prevention through environmental design in parking facilities. Washington (DC): National Institute of Justice; 1996. [April].

[43] Spadanuta L. How to improve your image. Secur Manag 2011;55. [March].

[44] True T. Raising the ramparts. Secur Manag 1996. [October].

[45] U.S. Department of Homeland Security. Reference manual to mitigate potential terrorist attacks against buildings, FEMA 426. Washington (DC): FEMA; 2003. [December].

[46] U.S. Environmental Protection Agency. Sustainability. 2011. www.epa.gov.

[47] WeGuardYou. Mall security scenario. 2011. http://weguardyou.com/applications-mallsecurity.html.

[48] Wilson J, Kelling G. Broken windows: the police and neighborhood safety. Atl Mon 1982. [March].

[49] Wroblaski K, et al. The great debate: 2011's key sustainability issues. Buildings 2011;105. [January].

[50] Zwirn J. Alarm design that rings true. Secur Manag 2003. [April].

Biometrics in the Criminal Justice System and Society Today

Dr. Thomas J. Rzemyk, Ed.D., CHPP, CAS

INTRODUCTION

This chapter will briefly discuss the history of biometrics in the United States and abroad. It will also provide an in-depth analysis on emerging trends and technology in the biometrics sector today as it relates to society, private organizations, and the law enforcement community to include local, state, and federal government agencies. Biometrics is defined as the process by which a person's unique physical and other traits are detected and recorded by an electronic device or system as a means of confirming identity.[1] In today's era, biometric data are considered to be a metric which directly relates to independent human characteristics through a form of independent proof of identification and access control. The features of biometric metrics and data can be used to categorize data in individuals and groups of individuals who may or may not be under direct surveillance. These specific features include voice, eye, and fingerprint data.

Evolution has proven that each human being was created differently from a physical and behavioral perspective. Each individual's fingerprints, iris', facial features, and body types are completely different from one another. Applying effective and efficient biometric technologies can be used to determine the identity of individuals from around the globe. Additionally, biometric technology tends to use automated methods of identifying or authenticating the identity of a living person based on a *physiological* or *behavioral* characteristics. Although primarily automated, there are many instances when this type of technology also requires *manual* intervention as well to ensure efficiency and accuracy. This chapter will conclude by discussing the challenge of collecting biometric information from private citizens, which has proven to be a controversial and highly discussed topic in today's era.

HISTORY OF BIOMETRICS AND FINGERPRINTING IN THE UNITED STATES

The law enforcement community and private security industry has been using biometric technology for decades to include voice and fingerprints. The first instances of biometrics

[1] Definition of "Biometrics", 2016. Retrieved from: http://www.dictionary.com/browse/biometrics.

Effective Physical Security, Fifth Edition
http://dx.doi.org/10.1016/B978-0-12-804462-9.00010-5

took place centuries ago in ancient China, when artists would engrave fingerprints on clay sets and artwork. In the early 1900s to the mid-1950s is when the art and skill of fingerprinting was established in the United States. Since implementation, verification of one's identity has been based upon the *authentication* of attributed and biographical human body characteristics to include human fingerprints. After small- and large-scale societies, industrial societies, globalization represents the third period of personal identification and the growth of independent biometric data collection.[2]

Since 1924, the Federal Bureau of Investigation (FBI) has been keeping formal *written* records of fingerprints from various individuals over time. By the late 1960s, the FBI fingerprint catalog had grown into the millions, and they knew that an automated system would need to be developed to manage the large number of records on file. Finally in 1986, the FBI developed the Automated Fingerprint Identification System (AFIS), which combined *manual* and *automated* *processes* into one computerized central database. However, this new system did not come without its difficulties and issues. It took several years and private vendors to improve AFIS and the speed at which it could match an inputted fingerprint match.

September 11, 2001 prompted the United States federal government to pass the United States Patriot Act and the Department of Homeland Security (DHS). The provisions of the United States Patriot Act required that federal agencies that had been operating independently since inception, now had to come together under the DHS umbrella. After the migration of several agencies, the independent databases could now be shared among each of the parties to improve communication and collaboration relationships.

By 2005, a small number of companies had developed universal standard applications to bring together national databases for comprehensive libraries of prints, making the selection of software upon which to run the AFIS database easier for agencies.[3] Additionally, even though automated systems may exist, it still takes at least one to two latent print fingerprint examiners to match a record for legality purposes.

BIOMETRICS USAGE TODAY

Biometrics in today's era has been growing, trending, and improving at a very rapid rate for both the public and private sectors. There are several private and public local state and federal agencies involved with biometrics activities today. However, one of the largest agencies involved is the FBI. Biometric technology is important because it is seen by many as a solution to a lot of the user identification and security problems in today networks.

THE FEDERAL BUREAU OF INVESTIGATION'S BIOMETRIC CENTER OF EXCELLENCE

The FBI has a data center and campus in Clarksburg, West Virginia called the Biometric Center for Excellence (BCOE). The purpose of the BCOE is to collaborate and improve information sharing and to advance the adoption of optimal biometric and identity management solutions, within and across the law enforcement and private security community. Each and every day, industry leading experts and scientists explore new and enhanced biometric technologies for integration into operations.

---

[2] Mordini E. Biometrics, human body, and medicine: a controversial history. Ethical, Legal, and Social Issues in Medical Informatics. Medical Information Science Reference (IGI Global); 2008.

[3] "Automated Fingerprint Identification System (AFIS)". World of Forensic Science 2005. Retrieved March 23, 2016 from: http://www.encyclopedia.com/doc/1G2-3448300049.html.

The FBI and the BCOE established and formalized the following biometric priorities[4]:

- Extend biometric technical capabilities
- Strengthen forensic science and advance biometrics
- Drive national biometrics
- Improve national security by developing and deploying biometric technologies.

BIOMETRIC MODALITIES AND TECHNOLOGY

Commonly implemented or studied biometric modalities by the FBI and other public and private agencies include the following:

Palm Print

The human palm and the fingerprint are not only very similar in nature but also contain several differences. As stated by the FBI, palm identification, just like fingerprint identification, is based on the aggregate of information presented in a friction ridge impression.[5] Palm prints used ridge flow, ridge characteristics, and raised structures to differentiate from one to another. Palm recognition has been used for decades, but it has been more of a manual process rather than an automated process due to slow technology enhancements in this area.

Fingerprint

The human fingerprint contains very unique characteristics such as circles, wavy lines, arcs,

and swirls. Fingerprinting is the most common method of collecting biometric information from human subjects. Since the FBI and other agencies began keeping records of millions of fingerprints, none have been proven to be exactly identical. There have been several that are similar, which can occur in the same genetic pools and in very rare instances, outside of the gene pool. Current AFIS technology permits fingerprints to be electronically categorized, scanned, and organized according to specific classifications and characteristics. Improvements in recent technologies have allowed for automated cross-referencing to take place. Previously, latent print examiners would verify the final results of a fingerprint inquiry (in many local, state, and federal jurisdictions, this still takes place for civil and criminal proceedings).

Hand Scanner and Finger Reader Recognition Systems

These measure and analyze the overall structure, shape, and proportions of the hand, such as length; width; thickness of the hand, fingers, and joints; and characteristics of the skin surface such as creases and ridges.

Facial Recognition

Facial recognition technology has had several enhancements over the past decade post 9/11. In the mid-21st century, facial recognition was limited to characteristics related to the eyes, ears, nose, mouth, jawline, and cheek structure. Several private organizations have released updated technologies to both government and the public. Newly enhanced technologies permit both verification and identification (open-set and closed-set).[6] Facial recognition technology today

---

[4] Federal Bureau of Investigations—BCOE, 2016. Retrieved March 23, 2016 from: https://www.fbi.gov/about-us/cjis/fingerprints_biometrics/biometric-center-of-excellence/about/about-the-biometric-center-of-excellence.

[5] Federal Bureau of Investigations—Biometrics (Palm Prints), 2016. Retrieved March 23, 2016 from: https://www.fbi.gov/about-us/cjis/fingerprints_biometrics/biometric-center-of-excellence/modalities/palm-print.

[6] Federal Bureau of Investigations—Biometrics (Facial Recognition), 2016. Retrieved from: https://www.fbi.gov/about-us/cjis/fingerprints_biometrics/biometric-center-of-excellence/modalities/facial-recognition.

uses complex mathematical representations and matching processes to compare facial features to several data sets using random (*feature-based*) and photometric (*view-based*) features. It does this by comparing structure, shape, and proportions of the face; distance between the eyes, nose, mouth, and jaw; upper outlines of the eye sockets; the sides of the mouth; the location of the nose and eyes; and the area surrounding the cheek bones. The main *facial recognition* methods are feature analysis, neural network, eigen faces, and automatic face processing. Although facial recognition technology has come a long way, there is still a need for enhancements to prove accuracy and reliability.

Iris Scan and Recognition

There are several technologies used today that are used to collect iris characteristics from human beings. It is a newer type of technology as compared to some of the older biometric tools. This technology uses complex mathematical patterns to document the human eye fingerprint. It then compares and contrasts the results of others in several proprietary and government databases for viable matches.

Voice Recognition

Voice recognition biometrics has evolved greatly in recent times in collaboration with speech therapists and other occupational related fields. As the FBI outlines, the speaker recognition process relies on features influenced by both the physical structure of an individual's *vocal tract* and the individual's *behavioral* characteristics.[7] There are several proprietary pieces of software that have

proven to be reliable but not always accurate. The United States government uses a technology called the Speaker Verification Application Program Interface or SVAPI. This specific technology is an interface that integrates with specific voice recognition programs, improves consistency-based practices, and permits for compatibility and interoperability between various vendors and networks. Different speech creates different shapes on the graph. Spectrograms also use color or shades of gray to represent the acoustical qualities of sound.

Deoxyribonucleic Acid

DNA is perhaps one of the most important biometrics today as it has been used to solve thousands of crimes around the globe. The technology surrounding DNA is always evolving and new enhancements are being applied to the law enforcement community. One of the most recent improvements has been the development of the *Rapid DNA Program Office* established in 2010 by the FBI. Rapid DNA, or Rapid DNA Analysis, describes the fully automated (hands-free) process of developing a CODIS Core STR profile from a reference sample buccal swab. The "swab in—profile out" process consists of automated extraction, amplification, separation, detection, and allele calling without human intervention.[8] The FBI's Imitative is to improve the process and the time that it takes to complete DNA testing by integrating technologies into CODIS and other DNA-related systems. In sum, the benefit of using DNA as a biometric identifier is the level of accuracy offered. Similar to fingerprint data, it is nearly impossible for two human subjects to share the same DNA structure.

[7] Federal Bureau of Investigations—Biometrics (Voice Recognition), 2016. Retrieved from: https://www.fbi.gov/about-us/cjis/fingerprints_biometrics/biometric-center-of-excellence/modalities/voice-recognition.

[8] Federal Bureau of Investigations—Biometrics (DNA), 2016. Retrieved from:https://www.fbi.gov/about-us/lab/biometric-analysis/codis/rapid-dna-analysis.

Writer Recognition

There are typically two types of handwriting and writer biometric recognition to include static and dynamic. In the static method, individuals write directly on paper and it is then scanned into a computer system for analysis.[9] Dynamic biometrics records handwriting in real time through the use of digitizers, tablets, and other devices. The handwriting examples can then be scanned through an automated system or independently by handwriting experts. This is equivalent to a traditional *handwritten* signature in many respects since if the signature is properly implemented, it is more difficult to forge than the traditional type. Digital signature schemes are *cryptographically* based and must be implemented properly to be effective. Digital signatures can be used for e-mail, contracts, or any message sent via some other *cryptographic protocol*.

Palm Veins

Vein matching and palm vein biometrics has been in place since the 1980s. It is considered a controversial type of biometric because of its accuracy and record history because it uses blood vessel patterns that exist to the naked eye. However, although highly debated, and not officially adopted by criminal laboratories, several government agencies such as the FBI, CIA, and DEA have been using it for years in several different formats. Vascular technology uses scanners to determine vessel and blood patterns in a nonautomated format. Advancements are currently underway to make these processes to become automated.

Behavioral Biometrics

Based on the manner in which people conduct themselves, such as writing style, walking rhythm, typing speed, and so forth.

[9] Chapran J. "Biometric Writer Identification: Feature Analysis and Classification". International Journal of Pattern Recognition & Artificial Intelligence 2006;483–503.

As stated in a previous edition of this chapter, for any of these characteristics to be used for sustained identification encryption purposes, they must be reliable, unique, collectable, convenient, long term, universal, and acceptable.

INTERNATIONAL BIOMETRICS: INDIA'S PRIVATE USAGE OF BIOMETRICS ON SOCIETY

The country of India encourages that all citizens of the nation to register their fingerprints and other biometric data to obtain a national identification card (ID). The fingerprints and other data are held in the largest national encrypted database in the world called *Aadhaar*. This database is shared among internal intelligence government agencies within India.[10] The system was designed to document all citizens in the country and to also help identify missing persons, criminals, to solve crimes, etc. Additionally, it was also developed to change the retail market. Custom *Aadhaar* numbers now permit some transactions within India to be completed based solely on biometric data. There has been a resistance by many in the country believing that it is a civil liberties infraction and a strict invasion of one's right to privacy. Although it is currently a volunteer-based program, this will most likely change moving forward. To date, about 50% of the country has *Aadhaar* numbers, and it is estimated that each and every citizen will have one in 3–5 years' time. The question is, *"How many other nations in the global community will move towards this type of classification system"*.

[10] Muralidharan K, Niehaus P, and Sukhtankar S. Building state capacity: Evidence from biometric smartcards in India (No. w19999). National Bureau of Economic Research 2014.

FUTURE ADVANCEMENTS OF BIOMETRICS

There will be several biometric enhancements over the next few years. To date, many of us have witnessed biometrics being integrated into our daily lives when using technology equipment. Smartphones, mobile devices, computers, workstations, communication systems, home security systems, entry systems, and other several pieces of equipment are now using fingerprints for authentication purposes. Also, as time moves, forward biometrics will be integrated into back-end technology systems to counter cybersecurity attacks. Finally, biometrics will be used for authentication and access control features as well.

Access Control Systems and Identification Badges

Dr. Joshua Sinai

This chapter discusses two types of access controls for security-based facilities: access control systems and protocols and access badges for personnel. These two types of access mechanisms are employed as comprehensive preventative measures to keep these facilities' external and internal perimeters secure from potential malicious physical intrusions, whether from the outside or, if they manage to bypass the initial access control point(s) and enter these facilities, once they are inside and unsupervised. This chapter's concluding section also discusses some of the latest trends in access control technologies as part of the continuous effort to address new vulnerabilities that malicious adversaries may be continuously trying to exploit.

It is important to note that in this discussion access control refers to control of the physical movement in and out of facilities but not the control of the transfer of proprietary or classified information via the Internet. Thus, the control of physical devices that might contain proprietary or classified information such as CDs or USB drives in and out of facilities is considered in this definition but not the deployment of protective access control mechanisms to manage Internet security.

Finally, the extent, magnitude, and tightness of access control security systems need to be established relative to a facility's assessed threat level.[1] Thus, risk management principles need to govern the nature of access control systems in facilities that is determined to be high threat, while security at facilities that face some degree of potential threat should be implemented relative to their assessed threat levels.

ACCESS CONTROL SYSTEMS AND PROTOCOLS

Perimeter barriers, intrusion detection devices, and protective lighting provide important physical security safeguards; however, they alone are not sufficient to protect a facility from intentional or accidental unauthorized access. For complete access security, access control system and protocols must be established and

---

[1] The author would like to acknowledge the peer review by Jeff Fuller, the President of Security Risk, Inc., of Fairfax, VA, a leading authority on risk management, who also suggested adding a threat assessment and risk management component to this chapter.

Effective Physical Security, Fifth Edition
http://dx.doi.org/10.1016/B978-0-12-804462-9.00011-7

maintained to preclude an unauthorized entry into a facility. Effective access control systems and protocols also serve to prevent the introduction of espionage devices (such as cameras, smartphones, and USB devices), dangerous materiel (such as firearms/IEDs), and other spycraft components (such as unobtrusive electronic bugs). Upon exit from a facility, by establishing proper access control systems and protocols, they also prevent the possible misappropriation, pilferage, or compromise of materiel or recorded information, whether intentional or accidental, by controlling the transport of outgoing packages, materiel, and other properties out of such facilities. In addition, access control rosters, personnel recognition systems such as ID cards, badge-exchange/drop-off procedures, and personal escorts for visitors all contribute to an effective facility access control system.

In this section, the governing principle in establishing access control is based on protecting two general circles around a facility in question: an inner circle and an outer circle.[2] The inner circle is defined as the facility "that is being protected, along with its immediate exterior".[3] The outer circle is the entire area around the facility, "stretching as far as a security officer can realistically visually control (1–3 blocks on average, depending on the surroundings)".[4]

Inner Circle Access Control

Designated Restricted Areas

One of the first steps in establishing an access control system is for a security manager to designate and establish the restricted areas that

require security protocols to safeguard them. In general, a restricted area is defined as any area that is subject to special restrictions or controls for security reasons. This does not necessarily include a facility's entrance lobby or cafeteria, if they are outside a restricted area, although entry into such areas may still require a certain degree of access control. Restricted areas may be established for the following:

- The enforcement of security measures and the exclusion of unauthorized personnel.
- Intensified access controls in areas requiring special protection.
- The protection of classified information or critical equipment or materials.

Determine the Required Degree of Security

The most important step in considering access control system requirements is to work through a risk = threat × vulnerability × consequence analysis to ensure that the access control system design addresses the specific threat profile challenging a facility and consider its consequences and vulnerabilities to a range of potential threat scenarios. By conducting such a collaborative risk analysis, a facility's security department will ensure that the access control system design addresses the threats, fits within the larger security system, and provides the best return on investment.[5] The access control requirements, therefore, should be driven by an assessment of the threats facing the facility. These assessments can include insider threats, disgruntled employees, criminal theft, vandals, and terrorists. The security-based/access control system should then be evaluated against each threat profile that the security department identifies as a potential threat. While it may

[2] Toben A. The inner and outer circle relationship – part I: access control, https://protectioncircle.wordpress.com/2016/02/25/the-inner-and-outer-circle-relationship-part-1-access-control/; February 25, 2016.

[3] Ibid.

[4] Ibid.

[5] Fuller J. Risk management from a county of city Perspective, Security Risk Newsletter, http://www.securityriskinc.com/wp-content/uploads/2015/03/SRI-Newsletter-5-Risk-Management-at-the-County-Level-Oct-2014.pdf; October 2014.

not be necessary to delve into great detail in this article on the processes and methods that support effective risk analysis and risk management, as with most risk assessments, the important point is that "an ounce of analysis is worth a pound of solutions."

The degree of security required to control access depends therefore on the nature, sensitivity, or importance of a facility's security level. Restricted areas are classified as controlled, limited, or exclusion areas.

- A controlled area is that portion of a restricted area usually near or surrounding a limited or exclusion area. Entry to the controlled area is restricted to personnel with a need for access. The controlled area is provided for administrative control, for safety, or as a buffer zone for in-depth security for the limited or exclusion area. The security director is responsible for establishing the control of movement within such an area.
- A limited area is restricted to authorized persons, with access granted via escorts and other internal restrictions.
- An exclusion area is the most secure area in a facility, with access granted under the most restrictive conditions.

Access Controls of Packages, Personal Property, and Vehicles

An effective access control system for physical items is also essential to prevent or minimize pilferage, sabotage, and other types of espionage.

PACKAGES/PERSONAL PROPERTY

A facility's standard operating procedure (SOP) may allow the entry of packages with proper authorization into restricted areas without inspection. A package checking system is also used at the entrance gate. When practical, all outgoing packages except those properly authorized for removal should be inspected. When a 100% security inspection is not possible,

security forces should conduct frequent unannounced spot checks of incoming or outgoing packages. An effective package-control system thus provides for a comprehensive management of the movement of authorized packages, material, and property, as well as mitigating the potential for the movement of unauthorized packages.

Property controls are not limited to packages carried openly, as they include the control of anything that could be used to conceal property or material. A facility's personnel should not be routinely searched except in unusual situations that warrant it. Searches must be performed according to a facility's SOP.

Outer Circle Access Control

As discussed earlier, the outer circle is defined as the entire area around the facility that can "realistically [be] visually controll[ed]".[6]

Vehicles

In a facility's outer circle, to manage the movement of vehicles, physical protective measures, such as fences, gates, and window bars need to be installed, where appropriate, to ensure that parking areas for privately owned vehicles (POVs) are established outside of restricted areas. Moreover, vehicle entrances should be kept at a minimum for the safe and efficient control of incoming traffic. Also, personal vehicles parked at a facility's garage or outdoor parking may be required to be registered with a facility's security office. In the case of visitors, security personnel should assign a temporary decal or other temporary ID tag for their vehicles to indicate authorized parking. The decal or the tag should be distinctly different from that of regular facility personnel.

The movement of delivery trucks and other commercial vehicles into and out of restricted

[6] See footnote 5

areas may be required to be supervised and inspected. Depending on the threat, vulnerability, and consequences analysis, delivery entrances should be controlled by locked gates when not in use and manned by security personnel when unlocked. In some cases, ID cards/badges could be issued to driver operators to ensure proper ID and registration for access to specific loading and unloading areas.

When necessary, delivery trucks and should be assigned escorts before they are permitted to enter designated limited or exclusion areas.

IDENTIFICATION BADGING SYSTEM

Whether for the outer or inner circles, an identification (ID) badging system is established at a facility to provide a method of identifying personnel authorized to use the premises. The ID system provides for personal recognition and the use of security ID cards or badges to aid in the control and movement of personnel activities in and out of a facility.

There are two types of ID cards: standard and security. Standard ID cards provide access into areas that are unrestricted and do not pose a security requirement. Security ID cards or badges provide for personnel requiring access to restricted areas. The design of each type of the card/badge must be simple for easy recognition and management by the monitoring security personnel.

Identification Methods

Four of the most common access control ID methods are the personal recognition system, the single-card/badge system, the card or badge-exchange system, and the multiple-card/badge system.

Personal Recognition System

In the personal recognition system, a security officer manning the access control area visually checks the person requesting entry to the facility. The criteria-determining entry is based on the need for entry being established by having the person listed in the access control roster and the individual being recognized.

Single-Card/Badge System

In this system, permission to enter a specific area is based on specifically designated and recognized letters, numbers, or particular colors (e.g., green or blue).

Card/Badge-Exchange System

In this system, two cards/badges contain identical photographs. Each card/badge has a different background color, or one card/badge has an overprint. One card/badge is presented at the entrance to a specific area and exchanged for the second card/badge, which is worn or carried while in that area. Individual possession of the second card/badge occurs only while the bearer is in the area for which it was issued. When leaving the area, the second card/badge is returned and maintained in the security area. This method provides a greater degree of security and decreases the possibility of forgery, alteration, or duplication of the card/badge.

Multiple-Card/Badge System

This system provides the greatest degree of security because instead of having specific markings on the cards/badges denoting permission to enter various restricted areas, the multiple-card/badge system provides an exchange at the entrance to each security area. Exchange cards/badges are maintained at each area only for individuals who have designated access to the specific area.

Mechanized/Automated Systems

An alternative to using security officers to visually check cards/badges and access rosters is to use building card-access systems or biometric-access readers. These systems can control the flow of personnel entering and exiting a complex. Included in these systems are the following:

- Coded devices such as mechanical or electronic keypads or combination locks.
- Credential devices such as magnetic stripe or proximity card readers.
- Biometric devices such as fingerprint readers or retina scanners.

Access control and ID systems base their judgment factor on a remote capability through a routine-discriminating device for a positive ID. These systems do not require security officers at entry points; they identify an individual in the following manner:

- The system receives physical ID data from an individual.
- The data are encoded and compared to stored information.
- The system determines whether access is authorized.
- The information is translated into readable results.

Access Control Rosters

Admission of personnel to a restricted area is granted to those identified and listed on an access control roster. Rosters are maintained at access control points. They are kept current, verified, and accounted for by an individual designated by a manager, who authenticates the rosters. Admission of persons other than those on the rosters is subject to specific approval by the security manager or another specific manager. These personnel may require an escort according to the local SOP.

Status of Badges

An important consideration in badging a facility's personnel is their role in an employee's career, whether at the beginning or termination of their service. Thus, for example, badges

with color coding can be used for various reasons that may include designating years of service, clearance levels, departments, and/or locations. In addition, a video badging can be deployed, which displays a corporate logo or a special design and may be color coded, and there are badges incorporating digitized data or a photograph.

When badges are initially introduced to a facility's security system, the following considerations need to be taken into account:

- If an employee loses their badge, specify a cost for its replacement. Some employers may allow one "free" replacement initially.
- When an employee is fired, determine who retrieves the badge, keys, or other company property. Ensure that all company badges are deleted if not used in the past 30 days.
- If a badge is stolen, determine the process to render it useless.
- If a badge is borrowed or used by an unauthorized person(s), determine the data associated with it, such as the holder's height, weight, and color of eyes and hair, which might be included on both sides of a card.
- Ensure there is a database for all facility badges, including approvals by authorized managers before access is granted.
- Identify access levels and authorization processes for all issued badges.
- Consider all potential vulnerabilities and the risk of threats that might arise if a badge is lost or stolen.

Control Methods

As discussed earlier, a number of methods are available to manage the movement and control of personnel in limited, controlled, and restricted areas. The following paragraphs discuss the use of escorts and the two-person rule.

Escorts

Escorts are selected because of their ability to accomplish access control tasks effectively and properly due to their training and knowledge of the areas being visited. Escorts may be guardforce or personnel from the area being visited. A facility's security regulations and SOPs determine if a visitor requires an escort while in the restricted area. Personnel on the access list may be admitted to restricted areas without an escort.

Two-Person Rule

The two-person rule is designed to prohibit access to sensitive areas or equipment by a lone individual. Two authorized persons are considered present when they are in a physical position from which they can positively detect incorrect or unauthorized procedures with respect to the task or operation being performed. The team is familiar with applicable safety and security requirements, and they are present during any operation that affords access to sensitive areas or equipment that requires the two-person rule. When the application of the two-person rule is required, it is enforced constantly by the personnel who constitute the team.

The two-person rule is applied in many other aspects of physical security operations, such as the following:

- When uncontrolled access to vital machinery, equipment, or materiel might provide an opportunity for intentional or unintentional damage that could affect the installation's mission or operation.
- When uncontrolled access to a facility's funds could provide opportunity for diversion by falsification of accounts.
- When uncontrolled delivery or receipt for materials could provide an opportunity for

pilferage through "short" deliveries and false receipts.

The two-person rule is governed by the authority and discretion of the facility's security manager. An electronic entry control system may be used to enforce the two-person rule. The system can be programmed to deny access until two authorized people have successfully entered their codes or swiped their cards.

Visitor Identification and Control

In classified facilities, to effectively control access by authorized visitors, appropriate procedures and systems must be implemented to control their movement. Approval for visitors should be obtained at least 24 h in advance (if possible) to assure proper vetting. Once their visits are authorized, visitors should be provided with cards/badges that will then be presented to the guards at the various entrances that are established at the restricted areas. Throughout their visit, guards at the initial access points must ensure that visitors stay in areas relating to their visit, where appropriate, by staying with their assigned escort at all times.

Individual or group visitors that are authorized to enter a restricted area must meet specific prerequisites before being granted access. Such access to a restricted area is granted in accordance with the following guidelines.

Employees Assigned to Work After Normal Operating Hours

Designated employees who are assigned to work in restricted areas after normal operating hours need to be approved by their supervisors, under established internal controls based on coordination with the security manager. Supervisors also need to notify security personnel of the workers' presence, authorization for their work, and duration of their work under such circumstances.

CONTRACTORS WORKING IN RESTRICTED FACILITIES

To allow contractor personnel to work as full-time, part-time, or as temporary consultants in restricted areas, the security manager must coordinate with the procurement office for their access badging. The security manager must also identify and coordinate the movement-control procedures for these contract personnel.

CLEANING TEAMS

Facility supervisors employing contractor cleaning teams must seek technical advice from the physical security office on internal controls for their operations in restricted areas. This may include providing escorts.

VISITORS

Before allowing designated visitors into a restricted area, the security office needs to be in contact with the employee or activity (such as a meeting) being visited. After verifying the visitor's identity and completing the registration forms, they will be issued a badge and assigned an escort (if required). Visitors may include public utility and commercial service representatives required to fulfill a service function.

VERY IMPORTANT PERSONS IN RESTRICTED FACILITIES

The procedures for admitting very important persons (VIPs), especially foreign nationals, into a facility's restricted areas are another important component of access control. Special considerations and coordination between a facility's protocol office and security office are required for facilitating and managing such visits. A 24-h (or longer) advance notice is desirable for these requests, along with an agenda for a visit and the designation of an escort, if appropriate. In case of VIPs from foreign countries of concern, a longer advance notice may be necessary so that such visits are coordinated with relevant local and national counterintelligence agencies.

Enforcement Measures

The most vulnerable link in any ID system is its enforcement. Security forces must be proactive in performing their duties. Some of these measures may include the following:

- Designating alert and tactful security personnel at entry control points.
- Ensuring that personnel possess quick perception and good judgment.
- Requiring entry control personnel to conduct frequent irregular checks of their assigned areas.
- Formalizing standard procedures for conducting guard mounts and posting and relieving security personnel. These measures will prevent posting of unqualified personnel and a routine performance of duty.
- Prescribing a uniform method of handling or wearing security ID cards/badges. If carried on the person, the card must be removed from the wallet (or other holder) and handed to security personnel. When worn, the badge will be worn in a conspicuous position to expedite inspection and recognition from a distance.
- Designing entry and exit control points of restricted areas to force personnel to pass in a single file in front of security personnel. In some instances, the use of turnstiles may be advisable to assist in maintaining a positive control.
- Providing lighting at control points. The lighting must illuminate the area to enable security personnel to compare the bearer with the ID card/badge.
- Enforcing access control measures by educating security forces and employees. Enforcement of access control systems rests primarily with the security forces;

however, it is essential that they have the full cooperation of the employees. Employees must be instructed to consider each unidentified or improperly identified individual as a trespasser. In restricted areas where access is limited to a particular zone, employees must report unauthorized individuals to the security force.

- Positioning ID card/badge racks or containers at entry control points so they are accessible only to guardforce personnel.
- Appointing a responsible custodian to accomplish control procedures of cards/badges according to policy manual. The custodian is responsible for the issue, turn in, recovery, and renewal of security ID cards/badges as well as monthly verification of individuals in various areas and the deletion of terminated employee badges.

The degree of risk management in the ID access control system is dependent on the degree of security risk toleration required. The following control procedures are recommended for preserving the integrity of a card/badge system:

- Maintenance of an accurate written record or log listing (by serial number) all cards and badges and showing those on hand, to whom they are issued, and their disposition (lost, mutilated, or destroyed).
- Authentication of records and logs by the custodian.
- A periodic inventory of records by a manager or auditors.
- The prompt invalidation of lost cards/badges and the conspicuous posting at security control points of current lists of lost or invalidated cards/badges.
- The establishment of controls within restricted areas to enable security personnel to determine the number of persons within the area.
- The establishment of the two-person rule (when required).

- The establishment of procedures to control the movement of visitors. A visitor control record will be maintained and located at entry control points.

Duress Code

In case of a potential security violation in a facility, a duress code should be issued. It is a commonly known and exercised word or phrase used during a normal conversation to alert other security personnel that an authorized person is either observing or might be under duress. A duress code requires planning and rehearsal to ensure that response protocols to an appropriate response are seamlessly employed. This code should be revised regularly to minimize possible compromise or misuse.

Leveraging Security System Technologies

For a large and complex facility that faces a range of threats, integration of security functions and cards, and cameras, a multilevel employees' tailored access requires leveraging an array of modern security technologies. The importance of understanding the features and capabilities of modern security technologies is crucial since, for example, the difference between old camera surveillance systems and their modern "smart camera" system successors is its exponentially greater order of magnitude effectiveness. The same is true in the management of security and access control systems, with modern systems capable of integrating access control into a facility's overall security system. By leveraging modern technology, therefore, the allocation of security personnel can be reduced in certain areas or be refocused on more pressing tasks. The overall effectiveness of the access control system can thus be improved dramatically by employing risk management principles to evaluate the best fit of a security system against its assessed threat, vulnerability, and consequence of a range of potential attacks.

In sum, some of the considerations for selecting an access control system should include the following: security functions, system features, reporting features, and help and support. Security functions should include video surveillance, card control management, Internet-based monitoring, 24/7 monitoring, systems and protocols to limit access to authorized individuals, door scheduling management, holiday schedule management, and biometric scan options. System features should include maximum number of doors, maximum number of users, alarm capabilities, professional installation, and automatic upgrades. Reporting features should include scheduled reports, customizable reports, email notifications, and reports available on smartphone. Finally, help and support features should include email, telephone, educational documents, video tutorials, and FAQs (frequently asked questions).[7]

Future Trends in Access Control

In terms of future trends, a facility's disparate access control systems will ultimately become increasingly networked, with information and data generated from them fused to produce predictive analytics, thereby upgrading reactive security to one that is more proactive.[8] Such integrative access control systems will provide users with "a single control platform to monitor the state of a facility or location and include data from video surveillance, video management, visitor management, time and attendance, alarms, photo imaging, badging, elevator control, building control, and many other systems".[9]

[7] Tripp N. Access control systems reviews, Top-10 reviews, http://access-control-systems-review.toptenreviews.com/; 2016.

[8] Laughlin R. 9 Emerging trends to watch in access control, Security InfoWatch, http://www.securityinfowatch.com/article/12090850/9-emerging-trends-to-watch-in-access-control; July 8, 2015.

[9] Ibid.

Risk and Other Considerations

There are important considerations concerning the establishment of effective access controls. These considerations include the following:

- **A security risk survey**. It should be performed prior to the installation. This should consider the internal and external threats to be managed as well as the assets to be protected. This can determine immediate and anticipated needs that require protection. Anticipated needs can be determined at the same time however should be considered from conducting risk surveys on a reasonable reoccurring basis to maintain current risk information as well as alignment to future organizational needs.
- **The size and nature of the security interest being protected**. The nature of the assets is also important to consider. For example, within the access control plans, consideration for additional security measures should be made. For example, areas with classified documents and high-value small items may need additional separation or compartmentalization with safes or other means.
- **Some security interests are more sensitive to compromise than others**. Brief observation or a simple act by an untrained person may constitute a compromise in some cases. In others, detailed study and planned action by an expert may be required.
- **All security interests should be evaluated according to their importance**. This may be indicated by a security classification such as confidential, secret, or top secret.
- **A restricted area**. It is any area that is subject to special restrictions or controls for security reasons. Restricted areas may be established for the following:
  - The enforcement of security measures and the exclusion of unauthorized personnel.

- Intensified controls in areas requiring special protection.
- The protection of classified information or critical equipment or materials.
- **Designated restricted areas**. While the security manager is typically responsible for designating and establishing restricted areas, those using the areas should be involved.

Degrees of Security

The degree of security and controls required depends on the risk nature, and sensitivity or importance of the security interest. While all controlled areas are restricted, restricted areas are generally classified by security management by the degree of security control over the access to the area. Some examples of the degrees involved can be expressed in categories of restriction such as "limited," "restricted," and "highly restricted."

- The security manager establishes the degree of control of movement and entry to a controlled area by designing and implementing access controls that will limit access to only those personnel with an organizational need.
- A standoff or limited area is generally a restricted area within close proximity of a security interest. Uncontrolled movement within this area may permit unacceptable risk to the asset(s). When appropriate, additional security elements to control movement in a limited area should also be considered. Escorts and other restrictions may prevent risks from occurring within limited areas.
- Generally, the restricted or highly restricted area is the exclusion area containing a security interest.
- Parking areas for POVs are established outside of restricted areas. Vehicle entrances must be kept at a minimum for safe and efficient control.
- Physical protective measures (such as fences, gates, and window bars) must be installed.[10]

[10] Nelson J. CPP, 150 things you need to know about security; 2017.

12

Chain-Link Fence Standards

Chain-Link Fence Manufacturers Institute*

This chapter discusses security fences including the different types of fences and the standards for security fences. The design features and material specifications are laid out, as well as resources for installation and inspection.

RECOMMENDATIONS

Chain-link fencing has been the product of choice for security fencing for over 60 years because of its strength, corrosion resistance, "see-through capabilities," ease of installation, versatility, different product selection, and value. A chain-link fence is one of the primary building blocks for a facility's perimeter security system.

The physical security barrier provided by a chain-link fence provides one or more of the following functions:

- Gives notice of a legal boundary of the outermost limits of a facility.
- Assists in controlling and screening authorized entries into a secured area by deterring entry elsewhere along the boundary.
- Supports surveillance, detection, assessment, and other security functions by providing a zone for installing intrusion detection equipment and closed-circuit television (CCTV).
- Deters casual intruders from penetrating a secured area by presenting a barrier that requires an overt action to enter.
- Demonstrates the intent of an intruder by their overt action of gaining entry.
- Causes a delay to obtain access to a facility, increasing the possibility of detection.
- Creates a psychological deterrent.
- Reduces the number of security guards required and frequency of use for each post.
- Optimizes the use of security personnel while enhancing the capabilities for detection and apprehension of unauthorized individuals.
- Demonstrates a corporate concern for facility security.
- Provides a cost-effective method of protecting facilities.

*Note: The information in this chapter has been provided as a public service to assist in the design of appropriate security fencing. The Chain-Link Fence Manufacturers Institute disclaims any responsibility for the design and operation of specific security fence systems. Permission obtained to be reproduced in 2012.

Effective Physical Security, Fifth Edition
http://dx.doi.org/10.1016/B978-0-12-804462-9.00012-9

SECURITY PLANNING

Chain-link fence enhances the goals of good security planning. In-depth security planning takes into consideration the mission and function, environmental concerns, threats, and the local area of the facility to be secured. This can be translated into an A-B-C-D method that points out the values of chain-link fencing to a security program.

A. Aids to security. Chain-link fencing assists in the use of other security equipment, such as the use of intrusion detectors, access controls, cameras, and so forth. Chain-link fences can be employed as aids to protection in an exterior mode or an internal protected property, as a point protection, and for general protection as required.
B. Barriers for security. These can be buildings, chain-link fences, walls, temporary checkpoints, and so on.
C. Controls. They support the physical security chain-link fences and barriers, such as an access control system tied into vehicle gates and pedestrian portals, various level identification badges and temporary badges, security escorts, and internal procedures.
D. Deterrents. A chain-link fence, guards, lighting, signage, and checkpoint control procedures are a few of the deterrents that ensure intruders will consider it difficult to successfully gain access.

When properly used, the aspects of the A-B-C-D method reinforce and support each other. Thus a chain-link fence is also a deterrent, and a barrier, if need be. By combining A-B-C-D, sufficient obstacles are created to prevent an intruder from obtaining information that is being worked on during the day in the controlled access area and then is protected at night, on weekends, and on holidays through the implementation of the security in-depth concept.

More important, keep in mind that a chain-link fence is the common denominator of the A-B-C-D system and will reduce overall risk, secure the environment, and reduce security costs if designed and installed properly. However, believing that a fence will eliminate all illegal access is not prudent. A fence system will only delay or reduce intrusion.

To ensure the effectiveness of the facility security fence program, it is recommended that a maintenance program be developed for the proper maintenance of the fence system, gates, gate operators, and related access controls.

MATERIAL SPECIFICATIONS

Material specifications for chain-link fence are listed in the following:

- *Chain-Link Fence Manufacturers Institute Product Manual* (CLFMI)
- American Society of Testing Materials (ASTM), volume 01.06
- Federal Specification RR-F-191K/GEN, May 14, 1990
- ASTM F 1553, "The Standard Guide for Specifying Chain-Link Fence," provides the appropriate information to develop a specification document.

Framework

The framework for a chain-link fence consists of the line posts; end posts; corner posts; gateposts; and, if required, a top, mid, bottom, or brace rail. The Federal Specification and the CLFMI "Wind Load Guide for the Selection of Line Post Spacing and Size" provide recommended post sizes for the various fence heights. However, the latter document also provides choices of line post types, sizes, and spacings to accommodate selected fence heights and fabric sizes for wind loads at various geographical project locations. The *CLFMI Product Manual*,

ASTM F1043, and ASTM F1083, as well as the Federal Specification, list the material specifications for the framework.

Chain-Link Fabric

The material specifications for chain-link fabric are thoroughly spelled out in the *CLFMI Product Manual*, ASTM, and Federal Specifications. The choice of chain-link fabric will govern the desired security level, and the various fabric-coating choices will govern the corrosion resistance. Light-gauge residential chain-link fabric will not be considered in this document. Provided are only those chain-link fabrics that offer a level of security, thus the gauge of wire and mesh size has been narrowed down to the following:

11 gauge (0.120 inches diameter)—minimum break strength of 850 lbf
9 gauge (0.148 inches diameter)—minimum break strength of 1290 lbf
6 gauge (0.192 inches diameter)—minimum break strength of 2170 lbf.

Mesh sizes to consider (mesh size is the minimum clear distance between the wires forming the parallel sides of the mesh) are 2-inch mesh, 1-inch mesh, and ⅜-inch mesh. Consider the following regarding mesh size:

- The smaller the mesh size, the more difficult it is to climb or cut.
- The heavier the gauge wire, the more difficult it is to cut.

The various mesh sizes available in the three previously discussed gauges are listed in the order of their penetration resistance/security:

1. Extremely high security: ⅜-inch mesh 11 gauge
2. Very high security: 1-inch mesh 9 gauge
3. High security: 1-inch mesh 11 gauge
4. Greater security: 2-inch mesh 6 gauge
5. Normal industrial security: 2-inch mesh 9 gauge.

Gates

Gates are the only moveable part of a fence and therefore should be properly constructed with appropriate fittings. Chain-link gate specifications are listed in the *CLFMI Product Manual*, ASTM, and Federal Specifications.

Limiting the size of the opening increases vehicular security and reduces the possibility of one vehicle passing another, and the smaller opening reduces the open–close cycle time. The cantilever slide gate is the most effective for vehicle security, especially one that is electrically operated and tied into an access control system. High-speed cantilever slide gate operators are available for certain applications.

Pedestrian/personnel gates can be constructed using a basic padlock or designed with an electrical or mechanical lock or a keypad/card key system tied into an access control system. Prehung pedestrian gates/portals installed independent of the fence line are available to isolate the gate from fence lines containing sensor systems thus reducing possible false alarms.

DESIGN FEATURES AND CONSIDERATIONS

Some basic design features to consider that enhance security:

- **Height**. The higher the barrier, the more difficult and time-consuming it is to broach.
- **Eliminating top rail**. Omission of a rail at the top of the fence eliminates a handhold, thus making the fence more difficult to climb. A seven-gauge coil spring wire can be installed in place of the top rail.
- **Adding barbwire**. Addition of three or six strands at the top of the fence increases the level of difficulty and time to broach. When using the three-strand 45-degree arm, it is recommended to angle the arm out from the secured area.

- **Bolt or rivet barbwire arms to post**. Barbwire arms are normally held to the post by the top tension wire or top rail. For added security, they can be bolted or riveted to the post.
- **Adding barbed tape**. Stainless-steel barbed tape added to the top and in some cases the bottom of the fence greatly increases the difficulty and time to broach.
- **Adding bottom rail**. Addition of a bottom rail that is secured in the center of the two line posts using a ⅜-inch diameter eye hook anchored into a concrete footing basically eliminates the possibility of forcing the mesh up to crawl under the fence. The bottom of the fence, with or without a bottom rail, should be installed no greater than 2 inches above grade.
- **Bury the chain-link fabric**. Burying the fabric 12 inches or more will also eliminate the possibility of forcing the mesh up.
- **Colored chain-link fabric**. One of the security features of a chain-link fence is visibility, allowing one to monitor what is taking place inside or outside of the fence line more efficiently. Color polymer-coated chain-link fabric enhances visibility, especially at night. Complete polymer-coated systems including coated fabric, fittings, framework, and gates increase visibility and provide greater corrosion resistance, especially for use in areas adjacent to the seacoast.
- **Double row of security fencing**. It is not uncommon to add an additional line of internal security fencing 10–20 feet inside the perimeter fence. In many cases, double rows of fencing are used with sensors and detectors, or with a perimeter patrol road in the area between the fences.
- **Clear zone**. In wooded or high grass areas, it is advisable to clear and grub a clear zone on either side of the fence to aid surveillance.
- **Internal security fencing**. Many situations require the need of a separate interior fence to add another level of security for a particular building, piece of equipment, or location.

- **Peen all bolts**. This eliminates the removal of the bolt nut.
- **Addition of a sensor system**. This adds another level of security to the fence system.
- **Addition of lighting**. Increases visibility as well as raises the level of psychological deterrent.
- **Signage**. Installed along the fence line, signs are important to indicate private secured areas (violators may be subject to arrest) and possibly note the presence of alarms and monitoring systems.

TYPICAL DESIGN EXAMPLE

We have chosen for our example to list the referenced specifications separately to help identify the various items that need to be specified. The specification writer may use this format or the standard construction specifications institute (CSI) format in developing their document.

In developing specifications for a typical chain-link fence, the design could be described as follows:

> 8′0″ high chain-link fence plus 1′0″, three strands of barbwire at top for a total height of 9′0″, consisting of 2 inches mesh 6-gauge chain-link fabric, *_____ o.d. or *_____ "C" line posts spaced a maximum of 10′0″ o.c., 7-gauge coil spring wire at top, secured to the chain-link fabric with 9-gauge hog rings spaced not greater than 12 inches, ⅝-inch o.d. bottom rail secured in the center with a ⅜-inch diameter galvanized steel eye hook anchored into a concrete footing, chain-link fabric secured to line post and rail at a maximum of 12 inches o.c. using 9-gauge tie wire.

> *_____ o.d. end and corner posts complete with ⅝-inch o.d. brace rail, ⅜-inch truss assembly, 12-gauge tension bands secured at a maximum of 12-inch o.c., tension bar, necessary, fittings, nuts, and bolts.

> Chain-link fabric shall comply with ASTM ____.*

> Post and brace rail shall comply with ASTM ____.*

> Barbwire shall comply with ASTM ____.*

> Fittings, ties, nuts, and bolts shall comply with ASTM ____.*

> Coil spring wire shall comply with ASTM ____.*

*Reference is made to ASTM as an example. All chain-link specifications, fabric, posts, fittings gates, and so forth are referenced in ASTM F 1553, Standard Guide for Specifying Chain-Link Fence.

A typical design/specification for gates would be listed as follows:

Pedestrian/personnel swing gates shall have a 4'0" opening by 8'0" high plus 1'0", and three strands of barbwire on top. Gate frames shall be fabricated from 2-inch o.d. or 2-inch square members, welded at all corners. Chain-link fabric shall be installed to match the fence line unless otherwise specified. Gateposts shall be *_____ o.d. complete with 1⅝-inch o.d. brace rail, ⅜-inch diameter truss assembly, 12-gauge tension bands secured a minimum of 12 inches apart, necessary tension bar, fittings, and nuts and bolts.

Chain-link fabric shall comply with ASTM ____.

Swing gates shall comply with ASTM ____.

Gateposts size, o.d., shall comply with ASTM ____.

Gateposts shall comply with ASTM ____.

Fittings shall comply with ASTM ____.

Cantilever slide gates shall be of the opening sizes as indicated on the drawings, having a height of 8'0" plus 1'0', and three strands of barbwire. (The construction and design of cantilever slide gates vary; therefore, it is best to list the specific specification.) Cantilever slide gates shall be constructed per ASTM F 1184, Class *____. Chain-link fabric shall match the fence line unless otherwise specified. (Cantilever slide gates require 4-inch o.d. gateposts; larger or smaller posts are not recommended.) The 4-inch o.d. gate-posts shall be complete with 1⅝-inch o.d. brace rail, ⅜-inch diameter truss assembly, 12-gauge tension bands secured a minimum of 12 inches apart, necessary tension bar, fittings, and nuts and bolts.

4-inch o.d. gatepost and 1⅝-inch o.d. brace rail shall comply with ASTM ____.

Fittings shall comply with ASTM ____.

Chain-link fabric shall comply with ASTM ____.

Installation

Installation for the fence line, terminal posts, and gates varies depending on the security level required, site conditions, geographical location, and soil and weather conditions. The best documents to assist you in this process are ASTM F 567, "Standard Practice for Installation of Chain-Link Fence," and the CLFMI "Wind Load Guide for the Selection of Line Post Spacing and Size."

Project Inspection

Improper material or installation can have a dramatic effect on the required security. It is important to verify that the project materials are in compliance with the contract specifications and that the fence has been installed properly. Procurement or facility managers may want to consider a mandatory requirement of their reviewing material certifications and shop drawings prior to the start of the project. This will ensure that proper products will be installed and that specific installation guidelines have been provided. CLFMI offers a *Field Inspection Guide* document to assist in this process.

Reference is made to various fence specifications; complete information can be obtained by contacting the following:

Chain-Link Manufacturers Institute
10015 Old Columbia Road, Suite B-215, Columbia, MD 21046; Phone: 301-596-2583; http://www.chainlinkinfo.org/

Standardization Documents Order Desk
Federal Specification RR-191K/GEN Bldg. 4D, Robbins Ave., Philadelphia, PA 19120-5094.

ASTM 100 Barr Harbor Drive West, Conshohocken, PA, 19428; Phone: 610-832-9500; http://www.astm.org/

Construction Specifications Institute 99 Canal Center Plaza, Suite 300, Alexandria, VA 22314; emembcustsrv@csinet.org.

In addition to information available from the previously listed organizations, design and engineering assistance is available through a number of CLFMI member firms. To find these firms, click on "Product/Services Locator" and select "All United States" and "Security Chain-Link Fence Systems" from the product listing. Then click "GO" and the firms who can assist you will be listed.

Conclusion. Chain-link fencing has been the product of choice for security fencing for over 60 years because of its strength, corrosion resistance, "see-through capabilities," ease of installation, versatility, different product selection, and value. A chain-link fence is one of the primary building blocks for a facility's perimeter security system. The physical security barrier provided by a chain-link fence gives one or more of the following functions:

- Gives notice legal boundary of the outermost limits of a facility.
- Assists in controlling and screening authorized entries into a secured area by deterring entry elsewhere along the boundary.
- Supports surveillance, detection, assessment, and other security functions by providing a zone for installing intrusion detection equipment and CCTV.

- Deters casual intruders from penetrating a secured area by presenting a barrier that requires an overt action to enter.
- Demonstrates the intent of an intruder by their overt action of gaining entry.
- Causes a delay to obtain access to a facility, thereby increasing the possibility of detection.
- Creates a psychological deterrent.
- Reduces the number of security guards required and frequency of use for each post.
- Optimizes the use of security personnel while enhancing the capabilities for detection and apprehension of unauthorized individuals.
- Demonstrates a corporate concern for facility security.
- Provides a cost-effective method for protecting facilities.

FIGURE 12.1

FIGURE 12.2

FIGURE 12.3

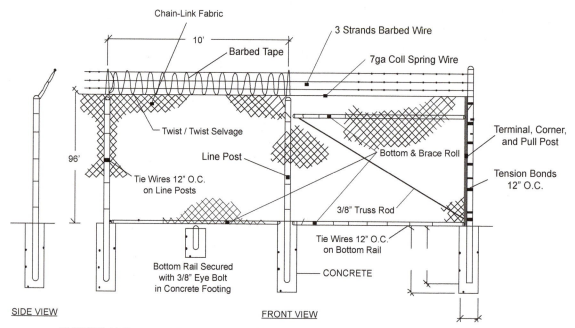

FIGURE 12.4

FIGURE 12.5 Typical detail of an 8-foot-high fence with 1-foot, three-strand barbed wire security.

Doors, Door Frames, and Signage

*Lawrence J. Fennelly, CPO, CSS, CHS III, CSSP-1,
Marianna A. Perry, MS, CPP, CSSP-1*

INTRODUCTION

No book on physical security would be complete without talking about doors. If you have never been to a place like Home Depot you know doors come in all sizes and shapes—hung on the right, hung on the left, 1-inch dead bolts, a mortise lock, etc., or it's hollow core, solid core, wood, or metal. Without getting too technical, we will discuss the many types of doors and hardware attached.

There are two types of flush doors: hollow core and solid core. A hollow core door is literally nothing more than two sheets of a thin substance overlaying hollow cardboard strips. A solid core door has a substantial security advantage over a hollow core door. Continuous block cores, a common type of solid core construction, are composed of wood blocks bonded together with end joints staggered and sanded to a smooth, uniform thickness.

Strictly from a security perspective, a metal, steel-sheathed door is superior to any type of wood door. A flush metal door comes with a metal frame, usually reinforced by interior formed sections. Metal doors are, however, less attractive and offer less insulation than wood doors.

A door system includes the door, frame, and anchorage to the building. As part of a balanced design approach, exterior doors in high-risk buildings should be designed to withstand the maximum dynamic pressure and duration of the load from an explosive blast. Other general door considerations are the following:

- Provide hollow steel doors or steel clad doors with steel frames.
- Provide blast-resistant doors for high threats and high levels of protection.
- Limit normal entry/egress through one door, if possible.
- Keep exterior doors to a minimum while accommodating emergency egress. Doors are less attack-resistant than adjacent walls because of functional requirements, construction, and method of attachment.
- Ensure that exterior doors open outward from inhabited areas. In addition to facilitating egress, the doors can be seated into the door frames so that they will not enter the buildings as hazardous debris in an explosion.
- Replace externally mounted locks and clasps with internally locking devices because the weakest part of the door system is the latching component.
- Install doors, where practical, so that they present a blank, flush surface to the outside to reduce their vulnerability to attack.

Effective Physical Security, Fifth Edition
http://dx.doi.org/10.1016/B978-0-12-804462-9.00013-0

- Locate hinges on the interior or provide concealed hinges to reduce their vulnerability to tampering.
- Install emergency exit doors so that they facilitate only exiting movement; if these doors have portable alarms remember to change batteries and check on systems annually.
- Equip any outward-opening double door with protective hinges and key-operated mortise-type locks.
- Provide solid doors or walls as a backup for glass doors in foyers.
- Strengthen and harden the upright surfaces of door jambs.

RESIDENTIAL BUILDINGS

Exterior Doors

1. All exterior doors, except sliding glass doors or metal doors, with or without decorative moldings, should be either solid core wood doors or stave, or solid wood flake doors and should be a minimum of $1^3/_4$ inches in thickness. No hollow core door or hollow core door filled with a second composition material, other than just mentioned, is considered a solid core door.
2. All exterior door hinges should be mounted with the hinge on the interior of the building, except where a nonremovable pin hinge or stud bolt is used (such hinges may be installed with the hinge facing the exterior of the building).
3. The shim space between the door buck and door frame should have a solid wood filler 12 inches above and below the strike plate area to resist spreading by force applied to the door frame. Screws securing the strike plate area should pass through the strike plate and door frame and enter the solid wood filler; a minimum of 3- or 4-inch screws should be used to secure a door

frame. The screws should also enter the solid wood filler at least ¼ inch.
4. No glazing may be used on any exterior door or window within 40 inches of any lock, except
   a. That glass should be replaced with the same thickness of polycarbonate sheeting of an approved type. (Plexiglass should not be used to replace glass.)
   b. That door locks should be a double-cylinder keyed lock with a mortised dead bolt that extends into the strike plate a minimum of 1 inch.
   c. *French doors* should have a concealed header and threshold bolt in the stationary, or first/closed door, on the door edge facing.
   d. *Dutch doors* should have a concealed header-type securing device interlocking the upper and lower portions of the door in the door edge on the door strike side provided that a double-cylinder lock with a 1-inch dead bolt is provided on the upper and lower sections of the door and the header device is omitted. You should also check about ADA compliance on doors as well as with the Builders Manufactures Hardware Association (BHMA) for changes in door standards. In addition, you should check before double-cylinder dead bolts are installed in residential buildings that it is in compliance with local fire safety and life safety codes.
   e. *Sliding glass doors*
      i. Sliding glass doors should be installed so as to prevent the lifting and removal of either glass door from the frame or from the exterior of the building. Consider secondary locking systems.
      ii. Fixed-panel glass doors (nonsliding) should be installed so that the securing hardware cannot be removed or circumvented from the exterior of the building.

iii. Each sliding panel should have a secondary locking or securing device in addition to the original lock built into the panel. The secondary device should consist of a Charley bar–type device, a track lock, a wooden or metal dowel, or inside removable pins or locks securing the panel to the frame.

iv. All "glass" used in exterior sliding glass doors and fixed glass panels is to be laminated safety glass or polycarbonate sheeting. Plexiglass or single-strength glass does not qualify for this program.

How to secure doors that have glass panels

1. Install a clear, unbreakable polycarbonate panel over the glass on the inside of the door or use the pane to replace the existing glass. Fasten the panel securely on the inside of the door.
2. Install grated wire mesh, a wrought iron grille, or decorative wire grate over the glass. Make sure there is no access through the grate.
3. Install a clear antipenetration film over the glass.

Pet doors—convenient, but may be an easy point of entry for a burglar.

Garage doors—if you use an automatic door opener, change the code from the factory setting. When you go on vacations, disable the opener and place a padlock through the track.

Storm door—offers minimal security protection—cannot rely on for security unless they are reinforced with steel and dead bolt lock.

Doors and Door Frames

Make sure the doors and frames are strong and in good condition. Exterior wooden doors should be solid and at least 44 mm (13/4") thick. Fit deadlocks to all outside doors, including French doors. All the exterior doors should have an equal resistance to forced entry. The front door is the most obvious, usually the easiest to get to, and is the first one tried by a burglar. The quality of the door is equally as important as the lock installed. Steel doors or solid core wooden doors provide satisfactory resistance against forced entry. Any hollow core door should be replaced or at least reinforced by adding exterior grade plywood on the outside of the door. A hollow core door is filled with corrugated cardboard and is easily broken through. A stile and rail door has stiles and rails as part of the face of the door; the remainder is composed of inset glass or wooden panels, which can easily be forced.

The panel edge is the weak point in a style and rail door and should be reinforced with exterior grade plywood.

Model Door Numbering System

Exterior number position, all numbers should be of the following:

- Placed at the top right of the door.
- Where a multiple bank of doors (3 or more) is present, it is a good practice to center the number or put the same number at both ends of the bank.
- Each door may be numbered separately as follows: 3-1, 3-2, etc.
- Some facilities/organizations choose to mark each door with an individual number when they face different directions (north and east).

EXTERIOR NUMBER SIZING

According to the International Fire Code § 505 requirements, all numbers should be the correct size in correlation with how far from the street or fire department access (Ord. 2010–17 § 1 (part), 2010; Ord. 2007–15 § 1, 2007):

- Structures up to 36 feet away, numbers are a minimum of 4 inches high and a minimum of 0.5 inch stroke width

- If the structure is 36–50 feet away, numbers are a minimum of 6 inches high and a minimum of 0.5 inch stroke width.
- When the structure is more than 50 feet away, numbers are a minimum of 9 inches high and a minimum of 1 inch stroke width. Some facilities/organizations have chosen to use 12 inch numbers for increased visibility. Obviously the larger the number, the greater the distance it will be visible by responders.

Exterior Doors in Commercial or Business Applications

- Should be numbered on the interior and exterior so they can be easily identified in the event of an emergency. Use clockwork numbering.
- Should have signage indicating whether the door is to be used for an emergency exit, employee entrance, authorized personnel only, or directing all visitors to enter through a specific door. People accessing the building need to be directed to the appropriate door.

Mechanical Locking Devices

Locks come in various shapes and sizes, each having a specific purpose, for example, warded locks, lever locks, pin tumbler locks, multiple axes tumblers, wafer tumbler locks, interlocking pins, electromagnetic locks, electronic locks (crash bars), electromechanical locks (breakaway strikes), and combination locks.

Strike Plates

A strike plate comes with every door lock. Many times strike plates are cosmetic and not intended to provide much security. The strike plate's attachment to the door frame is usually the weakest point in the entire door/door frame/lock system.

High-security strike plates are available. They sometimes come with a heavy gauge metal-reinforcing plate that mounts under the cosmetic strike plate and come with 3-inch long screws that secure the strike to the wall framing, not just to the door frame jamb. The screw holes are staggered so the screws do not penetrate into the same grain of wood. The concept of screwing into different wood grains in the door frame and wall framing is to make it more difficult to split the wood door frame or wall framing when the door is impacted. *This feature should be considered at every exterior door and at doors coming from attached garages.*

THE FUNCTION OF A DOOR

The modern equivalent to the cave dwellers' animal skin is the door. The function of a door in physical security is to provide a barrier at a point of entry or exit. The function of a door in maximum security is still to provide such a barrier, however, the barrier must also be impenetrable by ordinary means and offer the maximum delay time before penetration by extraordinary means (i.e., by the use of cutting tools, hand-carried tools, and some explosives).

During construction of a maximum security facility, it is necessary to define the function of all doors and their relationship to the total protection system. When an existing door is evaluated, the function must again be defined and include the area or material protected.

It is not necessary to make all doors maximum security—only those that are essential to the effective functioning of the total security system. Once a particular door is designated to be incorporated into the overall system, it must be upgraded to provide maximum security. There are two options in this respect: one can replace the door with a commercially available, penetration-resistant model or upgrade it to provide the necessary resistance. Obvious areas of concern when dealing with maximum security doors are door hinges and hardware.

Case Analysis

The Chula Vista, California, police department undertook an extensive study of the factors that attracted burglars to specific homes, as well as those protective devices that were most effective at preventing burglaries. Researchers and sworn police staff interviewed more than 300 victims and suspects, conducted more than 100 street-view environmental assessments, and reviewed over 1000 incident reports of burglaries committed against single-family homes. Key findings from the analysis phase included the following:

- Doors without dead bolt locks were targeted.
- Windows with single panes were targeted.
- Windows with simple stock latches were easily defeated.
- Sliding glass doors without specialized pin locks were easily rocked off their tracks.
- Almost all targeted properties had numerous hidden points of entry concealed by high shrubbery or solid fencing.

Chula Vista negotiated with the five major home developers in the city to make small, but significant, design changes to address the key risk factors and protective elements for residential burglary identified in the analysis phase. These changes were made in every new home built in the city after February 1999. Developers also agreed to distribute antiburglary literature tailored to Chula Vista residents at the point of sale.

TERMINOLOGY

Dead bolt On a multipoint lock, the deadbolt is located at the center of the lock to add increased security. It is normally of rectangular shape but can also be in the shape of a hook.

Electric strike An electrical device that permits releasing of the lock in the door from a remote control.

Flag hinge A door hinge system used on PVCu doors that allows for easy installation and adjustment.

Levers Levers are used in some mortise locks and padlocks. The higher the number of levers a lock contains, the higher the level of security it offers.

Mortise lock The lock fits into a mortise that has been "cut out" of a timber door edge. The locking action is achieved by a bolt that shoots out of the lock into the striker plate when the key is turned.

Rim lock Night latches are still sometimes referred to by their traditional name, "rim locks," although a rim lock usually now refers to a basic security lock for use on internal doors, gates, or outbuildings.

Thumbturn cylinder A knob fitted to one end of a cylinder that allows the door to be unlocked without a key from one side only.

STANDARDS FOR DOORS

Standards that apply to doors have been implemented or produced and supported by the Architectural Manufacturers Association (AAMA); ANSI; American Society for Testing and Materials (ASTM); National Association of Architectural Metal Manufacturers (NAAMM); NFPA 80, 2007, and NFPA 101, 2009; the Steel Door Institute (SDI); Underwriters Laboratory 305 (UL); and the International Standards Organization (ISO).

References

[1] http://www.nj.gov/education/schools/security/resources/DoorNumbering.pdf.
[2] Fennelly LJ, editor. Handbook of loss prevention and crime prevention. 5th ed. 2011. Waltham, MA, Ch. 9.
[3] The Chula Vista, CA, Residential Burglary Reduction Project: Chula Vista Police Department. 2001.

Glass and Windows

Lawrence J. Fennelly, CPOI, CSSI, CHS-III, CSSP-1,
Marianna A. Perry, M.S., CPP, CSSP-1

INTRODUCTION

The purposes of windows, aside from aesthetics, are to let in sunlight, allow visibility, and provide ventilation. When you research the types of windows and glass available, you start to see terms like *weather ability, durability, thermal performance, triple-insulating glass, thermal barriers,* and *solar windows.* Everyday another building is going "green," such as by diffusing light that enters a building, which cuts down on cooling costs, and the technology goes on and on from there.

"Healthy" buildings using current and innovative technology are contributing to healthier people through the use of proper cleaning chemicals and green cleaning. All of this creates a better environment and reduced energy costs.

TYPES OF GLASS

There are five main types of glass: laminated, sheet, tempered, bullet-resistant, and float.

Laminated glass. This is a type of safety glass that contains polyvinyl butyral or a similar substance and therefore holds together when shattered. It comes in high-performance laminated glass for structurally efficient glazing.

Sheet glass. This is least expensive and most vulnerable to breakage with a thickness of typically 3–4 mm.

Float glass/annealed glass. It has the quality of plate glass combined with the lower production cost associated with sheet glass manufacturing and is virtually distortion and defect free.

Tempered glass. This is treated to resist breakage and is three to five times stronger than sheet glass because it is 10 mm tempered.

Bullet-resistant glass. It is constructed using a strong, transparent material such as polycarbonate thermoplastic or by using layers of laminated glass. The polycarbonate layer is often sandwiched between layers of regular glass, and since the glass is harder than the plastic, the bullet is flattened and prevents penetration. It can be designed for both bullet and blast resistance. It will let in light and keep out trouble.

GLASS AND SECURITY

Take, for example, a police department recommends to a company that for tighter security, a glass wall and counter need to be added

Effective Physical Security, Fifth Edition
http://dx.doi.org/10.1016/B978-0-12-804462-9.00014-2

to create a barrier between the general public and the receptionist. In addition, a glass door is also installed that works off an access control, and if a visitor needs access, he or she would be escorted inside by a personnel member. Some people might not like this inconvenience, but it is the trade-off for security.

The following are factors to be considered for the selection of the type and size of a window:

- Energy efficiency and quality of unit
- Amount of sunlight, ventilation, and visibility
- Material and desired finish
  - Wood
  - Metal, aluminum, stainless steel
  - Finish color and "green" products.

Window hardware should have durability, function, and lock fitting. Consider the following:

- Type of glazing available for effectiveness of weather-stripping and wind pressure, explosion blasts, and fire;
- The size and shape to prevent access, and the cost to replace if vandalized;
- The use of grills or bars inside or outside.
- There are three types of glass:
  - Plate glass
  - Sheet glass
  - Float glass.

Window glass types are the following:

- Float glass
- Annealed glass
- Heat-strengthened glass
- Fully tempered glass
- Heat-soaked tempered glass
- Laminated glass
- Wire glass
- Insulated glass unit
- Low-emissivity (Low-E) glass.

In addition, the following are other considerations to keep in mind:

- Whether to use tempered glass, laminated glass, wired glass, bullet-resistant glass, and plastic glazing (e.g., polycarbonate or acrylic);
- Visibility requirements;
- The thickness; by altering thickness and composition, such as adding layers of glass or polycarbonate, security glass laminates can be customized to meet your requirements for specific risks/threats;
- The solution to security problems is to identify risk factors through assessment, use laminated glass with a thicker vinyl interior layer, and use compression operating window frames, awnings, and casements;
- Float glass can be broken with an average rock and toughened glass will shatter when it breaks;
- A crowbar can break or destroy standard window frames;
- Standard laminated glass (6.38 mm thick) can be broken with several blows from a hammer;
- Energy savings;
- Hardware, such as glass door hinges, locks, sliding glass door systems, and clamp supports, are available online or at any hardware store;
  - Sliding glass doors should be installed so as to prevent the lifting and removal of the glass door from the frame from the exterior of the building;
  - Fixed panel glass door (nonsliding) should be installed so that the securing hardware cannot be removed or circumvented from the exterior of the building;
  - Each sliding panel should have a secondary locking or securing device in addition to the original lock built into the panel.

The secondary device should consist of the following:

- Charlie bar–type device, secondary locking device
- Track lock, wooden or metal dowel
- Inside removable pins or locks securing the panel to the frame

- All "glass" used in exterior sliding doors and fixed glass panels should be made of laminated safety glass or polycarbonate sheeting. Plexiglas or single-strength glass will not qualify
- Doors should open on the inside track not the outside track.

The following are factors to consider when selecting the type and size of windows:

1. Requirements for light, ventilation, and view
2. Material and desired finish—wood, metal, aluminum, steel, stainless steel
3. Window hardware—durability, function
4. Types of glazing: sheet, plate, or float
5. Effectiveness of weather stripping
6. Appearance, unit size, and proportion
7. Method of opening (hinge or slider), choice of line of hinges
8. Security lock fittings
9. Accessible louver windows
10. Ground floor—recommend lower windows, large fixed glazing, and high windows, small openings
11. Size and shape to prevent access
12. Size because of cost due to vandalism
13. Use of bars or grills on inside
14. Glass
    a. Double glazing deterrent
    b. Types of glass
       - Acrylic glass also known as Plexiglas or polycarbonate
       - Tempered glass and laminated glass
       - Wired glass and bullet-resistant glass
       - Mirrors and transparent mirrors
    - Electrically conductive glass
    - Rough or patterned glass
    c. Vision requirements
    d. Thickness
    e. Secured fixing to frame
    f. Laminated barrier glass—uses
    g. Use of plastic against vandalism
    h. Fixed, obscure glazing for dwelling house garages
    i. Shutters, grilles, and louvers for sun control and visual barriers as well as security barriers.

Window Ironmongery

- Security window locks built-in during manufacture
- Security window locks fitted after manufacture
- Transom window locks
- Locking casement stays
- Remote-controlled flexible locks

Double Hung Wood

1. All locking devices to be secured with ¾-inch full-threader screws.
2. All window latches must have a key lock or a manual (nonspring-loaded or flip-type) window latch. When a nonkey-locked latch is used, a secondary securing device must be installed. Such secondary securing devices may consist of the following:
   a. Each window drilled with holes at two intersecting points of inner and outer windows and appropriate-sized dowels inserted in the holes. Dowels should be cut to provide minimum grasp from inside the window.
   b. A metal sash security hardware device of an approved type may be installed in lieu of doweling.

Note: Doweling is less costly and of a higher security value than more expensive hardware.

3. Follow balanced design principle. The glass falls first approach; that is, the walls are stronger than the anchors, the anchors are stronger than the frame, and the frame is stronger than the glazing.

Windows require protection when they

- Are less than 18 feet from ground level
- Are less than 14 feet from trees
- Have openings larger than 96 square inches.

Bullet-Resistant Materials, Bullet-Resistant Glazing for a Secure Workplace

Total Security Solutions offers a full line of bullet-resistant glass in acrylic, polycarbonate, and glass-clad polycarbonate. These products are available at UL protection levels 1–8, providing protection against guns ranging from a 9 mm to a 12 gauge. These bullet-resistant products are typically used in banks, credit unions, gas stations, and convenience stores but are appropriate for any business with cash on hand that wants to provide their employees with a secure work environment.

In addition to providing bullet-resistant products to glaziers and mill shops, Total Security Solutions provides custom milling and installation of secure barrier systems. Typical materials used in construction or sold directly include the following:

- Interior/exterior transaction windows
- Bulletproof doors
- Ballistic counters
- Package passers
- Bullet-resistant barriers and framing
- Bullet-resistant transparencies and fiberglass.

Bullet-Resistant Fiberglass Wall Panels

These are used to provide bullet-resistant protection to the walls of corporate executive offices, boardrooms, conference rooms, lobbies, reception area counters, customer service counters, and safe rooms. This bullet-resistant fiberglass can be installed by the manufacturer or even by a general contractor. Once installed, this product will never be seen but will provide high-quality ballistic protection and peace of mind for years and years to come.

Bullet-Resistant Doors

Along with protection for the walls and lobbies of offices, there are a wide variety of bullet-resistant doors to meet different needs, for example, solid executive style-veneered doors to match existing doors but with bullet-resistant protection. Again, this is invisible bullet-resistant protection, therefore, nobody will know it is there. In addition, there are also full-vision clear doors, half-vision clear doors, plastic laminate no-vision doors, and bullet-resistant steel doors. All of these doors are prehung, so any contractor can install them within minutes.

Bullet-Resistant Windows

Bullet-resistant windows can be custom built for the needs of each individual client. Office windows can be replaced with bullet-resistant windows ranging from levels 1–5, or existing windows can be left in place and a second bullet-resistant window can be added behind the existing window in such a way that it will be virtually invisible to the general public.

Bullet-Resistant Executive Office Products

The following can be used for offices, boardrooms, and conference rooms:

- High-quality executive style bullet-resistant doors
- Bullet-resistant wall armor to line all the walls of an office
- Bullet-resistant custom-made windows to protect all existing window locations
- High-security electronic maglocks to lock doors in the event of an attack.

Bullet-Resistant Transaction or Reception Area

- Bullet-resistant transaction window systems
- Package exchange units
- Bullet-resistant reception door with electric strike
- Bullet-resistant fiberglass for reception counter die wall
- Stainless-steel deal trays for small transactions.

Residential High-Level Security for Corporate Executives

- Provide bullet-resistant protection at point of entry (garage, front doors, front windows, etc.)
- Build safe room including walls, doors, windows, high-security locksets
- Convert closet into a high-level safe room
- Convert master bedroom into a high-level safe room (add invisible bullet-resistant protection to all walls, doors, and windows)

Finally, be advised that there are standards that apply to these installations and products.

WINDOW FILM

Window film is not bulletproof and there is *no* film product out there that is. Window film can be resistant to small arms and shotguns, however. LLumar window film products have a bomb blast proof film product.

Window film comes in four categories:

1. **Security or safety film**. The benefits are an outer pane of glass may break but the inner will stay intact. It is used to protect retail, commercial, and residential buildings and other types of window structures from the damages of flying glass due to earthquakes, windstorms, attacks, vandalism, theft, and accidents.
2. **Decorative film**. This makes glass surfaces clear and visible, enhances safety in public spaces, and allows you to customize your space with a corporate logo.
3. **Antigraffiti window film**. This is a protective film that helps prevent scribbling or other defacing a base surface. The film is easy to peel off and replace, eliminating graffiti, and the cost to replace glass.
4. **Solar film**. This has many benefits, such as it reflects and absorbs heat and light and it increases energy efficiency, reduces HVAC cost, protects furniture and carpets, and provides greater temperature stability.

Reference

[1] Stegbor, Security data sheet, V1.

Additional Web Resources

[1] International Window Film Association. www.iwfa.com.
[2] Extreme Window Solutions. www.extremewindowsolutions.com.
[3] Ace Security Laminates. www.acelaminate.com.
[4] Total Security. www.securityfilm.biz/index.htm.
[5] Pacific Bullet Proof. www.pacificbulletproof.com.

The Legalization of Marijuana and the Security Industry

Marianna A. Perry, M.S., CPP, CSSP-1, Lawrence J. Fennelly, CPOI, CSSI, CHL-III, CSSP-1

MARIJUANA—THE PROS AND CONS

Marijuana is the dried leaves, flowers, stems, and seeds from the hemp plant, *Cannabis sativa*. The plant contains the mind-altering chemical, *delta-9-tetrahydrocannabinol* (THC). Extracts with high amounts of THC can also be made from the cannabis plant. The THC in marijuana is the chemical responsible for most of marijuana's psychological effects because it acts much like the cannabinoid chemicals made naturally by the human body. The cannabinoid receptors are concentrated in the areas of the brain associated with thinking, pleasure, coordination, and time perception. The THC in marijuana attaches to these receptors and activates them and affects a person's memory, pleasure, movements, thinking, concentration, coordination, and sensory and time perception.

Marijuana is the third most popular recreational drug in the United States, behind alcohol and tobacco, according to the marijuana reform group NORML, and they state that marijuana is less dangerous than alcohol or tobacco because approximately 50,000 people die each year from alcohol poisoning and more than 400,000 deaths

each year are attributed to tobacco use. By comparison, marijuana is nontoxic and cannot cause death by overdose. The organization supports a legally controlled market for marijuana where consumers can buy marijuana for recreational use from a safe legal source.

The legalization of marijuana—whether it is for medical use or recreational use is a controversial subject. There are pros and cons on both sides of the argument and each side cites research data supporting their stance on the subject that the other calls "low quality." Proponents say that marijuana helps an economy and the job market and others say that it causes more crime and puts people at risk. The bottom line is that marijuana use can be good or bad, depending upon who you ask. For these reasons, the debate over marijuana continues.

SHOULD MARIJUANA BE LEGAL FOR MEDICINAL AND/OR RECREATIONAL PURPOSES?

Voters in several states across the nation have been asked to decide whether marijuana should be legal for use as a medicine, but the National Cancer Institute states that marijuana has been used for medicinal purposes for over 3000 years. Voters made their decisions about the legalization of marijuana for medicinal purposes on the basis of medical anecdotes, beliefs about the dangers of illicit drugs, and a smattering of inconclusive science. To help policy-makers and the public make better-informed decisions, the White House Office of National Drug Control Policy asked the Institute of Medicine (IOM) to review the scientific evidence and assess the potential health benefits and risks of marijuana.

The IOM report, *Marijuana and Medicine: Assessing the Science Base*, released in March 1999, found that the THC in marijuana is potentially effective in treating pain, nausea and vomiting and AIDS-related loss of appetite. They add that additional research involving clinical trials need to be conducted. The report also states that the therapeutic effects of smoked marijuana are modest and there may be medicines that are more effective. The report acknowledges that there are some patients that do not respond well to other medications they may "have no effective alternative to smoking marijuana."

The IOM report stated the following findings:

> The profile of cannabinoid drug effects suggests that they are promising for treating wasting syndrome in AIDS patients. Nausea, appetite loss, pain, and anxiety are all afflictions of wasting, and all can be mitigated by marijuana. Although some medications are more effective than marijuana for these problems, they are not equally effective in all patients. A rapid-onset (that is, acting within minutes) delivery system should be developed and tested in such patients. Smoking marijuana is not recommended. The long-term harm caused by smoking marijuana makes it a poor drug delivery system, particularly for patients with chronic illnesses. Terminal cancer patients pose different issues. For those patients the medical harm associated with smoking is of little consequence. For terminal patients suffering debilitating pain or nausea and for whom all indicated medications have failed to provide relief, the medical benefits of smoked marijuana might outweigh the harm.

Most research studies on both sides of the issue do agree that smoked marijuana is not a completely safe substance. It is a drug that when used, various effects can be produced. However, except for the harm associated with smoking, the adverse effects of marijuana use are within the range tolerated for other medications. The OEM has cautiously endorsed the medical use of marijuana, but smoked marijuana is a crude way to deliver THC because it also delivers harmful substances. Based on this information, it does appear as though marijuana does have medical value, but its therapeutic components must be used in conjunction with conventional therapy to be safe and useful.

The Food and Drug Administration (FDA) has not approved smoked marijuana as a safe and effective drug but recognizes that patients are looking for treatment options for some conditions such as nausea and vomiting caused by chemotherapy. Even though the FDA has not approved *botanical* marijuana because they have not found it safe and effective, they do however, recognize the interest in using marijuana for medicinal purposes. The FDA has approved the drug, dronabinol, which is a medicine made from THC, a light yellow resinous oil, which is extracted from the marijuana plant. It is used to treat or prevent the nausea and vomiting associated with chemotherapy to increase the appetites of patients with AIDS.

The American Lung Association (ALA) does encourage continued research into the benefits, risks, and safety of marijuana use for medicinal purposes. They recommend that any patient who is considering marijuana for medicinal purposes makes an informed decision by consulting with their doctor and also considers other methods of administration other than smoking.

In 2014, Colorado was the first state to allow the sale of marijuana for recreational use to anyone age 21 or older. Marijuana sold at retail stores carries a 25% state tax, plus the Colorado state sales tax of 2.9%, which makes recreational marijuana one of the most heavily taxed consumer products in Colorado.

As of June 19, 2015, 23 states and the District of Columbia currently had laws legalizing marijuana use in some form. Four states and the District of Columbia have legalized marijuana for recreational use. Many states have decriminalized the possession of small amounts of marijuana for recreational use, while others have passed medical marijuana laws allowing for limited use. Some medical marijuana laws are broader than others and list specific medical conditions that allow for treatment, but this varies from state to state. There are some states that have passed laws allowing residents to possess cannabis oil if they suffer from certain medical illnesses. For example, Virginia has laws that allow the possession of marijuana as long as the individual has a prescription from a doctor. Federal law prohibits doctors from prescribing marijuana, so basically the state laws are not valid. This means that doctors can write a recommendation for medical marijuana but not a prescription. While possession, sale, and consumption of marijuana remain illegal at the federal level, it is permitted for recreational use in four US states: Alaska, Colorado, Oregon, and Washington plus the US capital, Washington.

It is common knowledge that smoke is harmful to lung health. It does not matter whether the smoke is from burning wood, tobacco, or marijuana because toxins and carcinogens are released from combustion. Smoke from marijuana combustion has been shown to contain many of the same toxins, irritants, and carcinogens as tobacco smoke. Because marijuana smokers tend to inhale more deeply and hold their breath longer than cigarette smokers, there is greater exposure. Marijuana smoke injures the cell lining of the large airways and many marijuana smokers have symptoms such as a chronic cough, phlegm production, wheezing, and acute bronchitis.

Smoking marijuana affects the immune system and the body's ability to fight disease, especially for individuals with weakened immune systems or those taking immunosuppressive drugs. Smoking marijuana also kills the cells in the lungs that help remove dust and germs, which may lead to an increased risk of lower respiratory tract infections.

THE SHORT-TERM EFFECTS OF MARIJUANA

The THC in marijuana passes from the lungs into the bloodstream and stimulates the receptors in the parts of the brain. This causes the "high" that users feel. Other effects include the following:

- Altered senses (for example, seeing brighter colors)
- Altered sense of time
- Changes in mood
- Impaired body movement
- Difficulty with thinking and problem-solving
- Impaired memory.

THE LONG-TERM EFFECTS OF MARIJUANA

Marijuana also affects brain development. When teenagers use marijuana, it may permanently affect their thinking, memory, and learning functions.

Long-term marijuana use has also been linked to mental illnesses and mental health problems, such as follows:

- Temporary *hallucinations*—sensations and images that seem real though they are not
- Temporary *paranoia*—extreme and unreasonable distrust of others
- Worsening symptoms in patients with *schizophrenia* (a severe mental disorder with symptoms such as hallucinations, paranoia, and disorganized thinking)

- Depression
- Anxiety
- Suicidal thoughts among teens.

IS MARIJUANA ADDICTIVE?

Marijuana can be addictive. Research suggests that about 1 in 11 users becomes addicted to marijuana (Anthony, 1994; Lopez-Quintero, 2011). This number increases among those who start as teens (to about 17% or 1 in 6) (Anthony, 2006) and among people who use marijuana daily (to 25–50%) (Hall and Pacula, 2003).

SECURITY FOR MARIJUANA FARMS AND DISPENSARIES

For those who either cultivate or sell marijuana, it is important that they know how to protect their investment—equipment, inventory, products, and above all, their employees. The marijuana industry certainly comes with its own security challenges.

The legalization of recreational marijuana in Colorado and Washington introduced a new element for the cannabis industry in the United States—effective security that "fits" with this industry. Medicinal marijuana is legal in 23 states but is still considered a Schedule 1 controlled substance by the US government, which makes growing and selling marijuana illegal under federal law. This elevates the security situation for marijuana farms and dispensaries to a new level because many banks are reluctant to accept money that is generated from the sale of marijuana, so this has forced the industry to be an all-cash business. This has led to the development of "specialty" security companies for a niche market. Not only do these "specialty" security companies protect product and cash on hand, they are also responsible for securing the perimeter of the property, access control in and out of areas and buildings, monitoring video surveillance and response, monitoring the intrusion detection systems, and providing ongoing consulting services, they have to constantly monitor the temperature and lighting within the growing facilities. It is important that marijuana farms and dispensaries consider all possible threats and have state-of-the-art technology as a part of their security master plans, and that the security operation is efficient and either minimizes or eliminates any security vulnerability.

CNN reports that there are now big-box stores, named "weGrow," that offer marijuana growing equipment, supplies, and services (including recommendations for security) and they are being called the "Walmart of Weed." None of the "weGrow" stores actually sell marijuana, but they advertise that their services and products are designed especially for cultivating marijuana. This is a perfect example of the premise, supply, and demand.

"weGrow" also offers a "Dispensary Security Plan" that covers facility as well as operational security that is touted as something that "…every dispensary or cultivation owner must have! Essential document for anyone that plans to own a marijuana dispensary." It includes a sample security plan and advertises that custom plans are also available. The security plans are designed to "minimize security exposure and prevent breaches before they even occur. However, in the event that preventative measures fail, the operational security plan is designed to quickly observe, monitor, protect, counter and report any situations that do occur."

The facility security plan includes the following:

- Location and site security
- Secured employee parking
- Around the clock coverage
- Security surveillance systems (CCTV)
- Maintenance of security systems
- Access control/ingress and egress and biometrics
- Perimeter security

- Product security
- Fire alarm system
- Intrusion alarm system.

The operational security plan includes the following:

- Security threats and countermeasures
- Transactional security
- Delivery security
- Hazardous weather
- Human resource policies and protocols
- Employee security training
- Inventory control
- Guest, media, and visitor procedures
- Neighborhood involvement
- Emergency response
- Contingency planning.

The "specialty" security companies are meeting the needs of the marijuana industry because some dispensary owners have stated that ADT, the largest security provider in the nation has dropped or is refusing to accept customers in the marijuana industry. ADT told CNN, "Money it won't sell security services to businesses engaged in the marijuana industry because it is still illegal under federal law."

Owners in the marijuana cultivation and dispensary business state that they are concerned not only with thieves but also with federal authorities who are eager to see them put out of business.

With demand for security services to protect the marijuana industry, there is certainly not a shortage of opportunities for security professionals.

Endnotes

http://www.drugabuse.gov/publications/drugfacts/marijuana.

http://www.livescience.com/24553-what-is-thc.html.

http://norml.org.

http://www.livescience.com/24553-what-is-thc.html.

http://medicalmarijuana.procon.org/view.answers.php?questionID=255.

http://www.fda.gov/NewsEvents/PublicHealthFocus/ucm421163.htm.

http://www.livescience.com/24553-what-is-thc.html.

http://www.lung.org/stop-smoking/smoking-facts/marijuana-and-lung-health.html.

http://www.cnn.com/2013/12/28/us/10-things-colorado-recreational-marijuana/.

http://www.governing.com/gov-data/state-marijuana-laws-map-medical-recreational.html.

http://www.taipeitimes.com/News/biz/archives/2016/03/06/2003640899.

http://www.lung.org.

https://www.drugabuse.gov/publications/drugfacts/marijuana.

http://www.securityinfowatch.com/article/11601437/booming-cannabis-industry-presents-wealth-of-opportunities-to-security-system-installers-manufacturers.

http://www.cnn.com/2011/US/05/31/arizona.marijuana.superstore/index.html?iref=allsearch.

http://wegrowstore.com/index.php?page=shop.product_details&flypage=flypage.tpl&product_id=35&vmcchk=1&option=com_virtuemart&Itemid=262.

http://money.cnn.com/2013/04/29/smallbusiness/marijuana-security/.

Designing Security and Working With Architects

Lawrence J. Fennelly, CPPI, CSSM, CHL III, CSSP-1,
Ron Hurley, DSc., CPP

Architecture is not just a matter of style, image and comfort. It can create encounter—and prevent it. **Oscar Newman (1972).**

LEADERSHIP IN ENERGY AND ENVIRONMENTAL DESIGN

Today, it is critical to include security designers at the beginning of any new construction project or the renovation of an existing structure. Doing so will save your organization a great deal of money and time in doing what could have been done in the early stages of a project. Architects are experts in building design and construction but often do not consider the security needs of population the building will ultimate serve. Different groups have different needs and must be considered during the planning stages, so that the building does not have to be retrofitted with physical security measures not previously considered. All of which cause extra time, material, and money to complete. And, all of which ultimately be integrated with existing systems, which are not always compatible.

As with crime prevention through environmental design (CPTED), some of the leadership in energy and environmental design (LEED) concepts complement security concerns, whereas others conflict with physical security principles. The LEED Green Building Rating System represents the U.S. Green Building Council's (USGBC) effort to provide a national standard for what constitutes a "green building." Through its use as a design guideline and third-party certification tool, it aims to improve occupant well-being, environmental performance, and economic returns of buildings using established and innovative practices, standards, and technologies [1]. LEED is a voluntary building assessment tool that is most applicable to commercial, institutional, and high-rise residential construction. Owners, architects, and engineers must work together to strike a balance between building design objectives.

LEED looks at six basic categories: sustainable sites, water efficiency, energy and atmosphere, materials and resources, indoor environmental quality, and innovation and design process. Within each category, points are awarded for achieving specific goals. A total of 69 points is possible. A score of 26–32 points achieves basic certification, 33–38 achieves silver, 39–51 achieves gold, and 52–69 points achieve platinum certification. The LEED rating is awarded after the project has been documented by the USGBC.

Another goal in the LEED effort is to encourage more sustainable construction practices. LEED encourages manufacturers to provide materials that are as follows:

- Contain high recycled content and sustainable use raw materials
- Are manufactured close to the construction site
- Have low-volatile organic compound emissions
- Are designed to minimize energy consumption and packaging.

CRIME PREVENTION THROUGH ENVIRONMENTAL DESIGN PLANNING AND DESIGN REVIEW[2]

Again, the primary principles of CPTED are the following:

Natural surveillance—focusing on designing space, which enhances visibility. It also promotes social interaction of legitimate users. Examples include the following:

- Improved lighting
- Cutting overgrown hedges and bushes for better visibility
- Designing streets to encourage more pedestrian traffic
- Adding additional social space for legitimate users.

Natural access control—delineating public space from private space by strategically placing entrances, pathways, roadways, fencing, bollards, landscaping, along with other methods to define and accessible space.

Territoriality—defines ownership and responsibility for the defined space.

Maintenance—expresses ownership and care of the defined space.

One of the first priorities for implementing CPTED is to place it in the planning process of the organization or jurisdiction. School districts, housing authorities, transportation systems, and local government all have fundamental responsibilities for public safety. It is necessary that a formal relationship between crime prevention and planning be established. Private companies and public utilities control extensive properties and huge labor forces. Each has a process for making decisions about new development and investment. The CPTED concept and process must be incorporated into these ongoing processes. Research has shown that it is the multidisciplinary team that creates a greater value when working on CPTED projects. These multidisciplinary teams include architects, law enforcement, community stakeholders, planners, security professionals, and code enforcement officials to name but a few.

For communities and organizations, the CPTED process relates to and must be part of the following functions:

- **Comprehensive plans.** These determine the future patterns of land use and development. Comprehensive plans present the values of a community and a vision of what it will look like in the future. These plans establish goals and objectives for up to 50-year time periods. Crime prevention elements are clearly necessary in a community's comprehensive plan. Day-to-day decisions about problems and needs are improved by ensuring that they are consistent with comprehensive plans.
- **Zoning ordinances.** These are established to promote the health, safety, and welfare of the people by formally identifying the locations of land uses to ensure that activities are compatible and mutually supportive.

Zoning regulations affect land uses, development densities, yard setbacks, open space, building height, location and amount of parking, and maintenance policies. These, in turn, will affect activities and routines that concern exposure to crime, surveillance opportunities, and the definition of space for territorial control.

- **Subdivision regulation.** This includes lot size and dimension, street and right-of-way locations, sidewalks, amenities, and location of utilities. These elements directly influence access to neighborhoods, reduction of pedestrian and vehicle conflict, street lighting, and connections with other parts of the community.
- **Landscape ordinances.** These govern the placement of fences, signs, and plant materials. They may be used to improve spatial definition, surveillance, access control, and wayfinding. Hostile landscaping can make unwanted access to parking lots and private property less desirable. Landscape planting materials may also help to reduce graffiti by making large areas of walls inaccessible. Good horticulture improves the quality of life and helps to reduce exposure to crime.
- **Architectural design guidelines.** These guidelines specify goals and objectives for site and building performance. They will affect the location of activities and the definition of public and private space. The site decisions and plans for a building will directly affect opportunities for natural surveillance, pedestrian and vehicle access, wayfinding, and links to adjacent neighborhoods or land uses.
- **Access for physically and mentally challenged persons.** These requirements generally improve accessibility and wayfinding but rarely consider the risk of victimization that may be created by the use of out-of-the-way doors, hallways, or elevators.

Review Process

The work of builders, designers, and planners has long been affected by codes that govern nearly every aspect of a structure, except for security. Historically, a few jurisdictions enacted security ordinances, but most of these related to windows, doors, and locking devices. It is now becoming more common to find a local law or procedure calling for a full security or crime prevention review of plans before they are finalized. Nevertheless, it is still generally true that more attention is placed on aesthetics, drainage, fire safety, curb cuts, and parking access than on gaining an understanding of how a building or structure will affect the area in terms of security. A CPTED design review process must be established within communities and organizations to ensure that good planning is being conducted.

The manner in which physical space is designed or used has a direct bearing on crime or security incidents. The clear relationship between the physical environment and crime is now understood to be a cross-cultural phenomenon, as recent international conferences on CPTED have disclosed the universal nature of human/environment relations. That is, despite political and cultural differences, people basically respond the same way to what they see and experience in the environment. Some places make people feel safe and secure, while others make people feel vulnerable. Criminals or other undesirables pick up on the same cues. They look at the environmental setting and at how people are behaving. This tells them whether they can control the situation or run the risk of being controlled.

Someone has to question design, development, and event planning decisions. Do you think that anyone from the police department, or fire department for that matter, asked the builder of a major hotel in Kansas City whether they had extra steel-reinforcing rods leftover when they built the crossbridge that fell and resulted in many deaths and injuries? Did anyone ask the planners what effect the downtown pedestrian malls would have when the fad swept the country in early 2000–05? No! Major planning mistakes were made then and now because no one is asking hard questions.

Nine security points to remember with CPTED are as follows:

1. **General purpose of the building (i.e., residence, classroom, office).** Consider the hours of use, people who use the building, people who have access, key control, and the maintenance schedule. Who is responsible for maintenance? Is the building used for public events? If so, what type and how often? Is the building normally opened to the public? Identify the significant factors and make recommendations. Who is the facility manager and who has overall responsibility for crime prevention and security?

2. **Hazards involving the building or its occupants.** List and assign priorities (e.g., theft of office equipment, wallet theft, theft from stockrooms). Identify potential hazards that might exist in the future.

3. **Police or security officer applications.** What can these officers do to improve the response to the building and occupants from a patrol, investigation, or crime prevention standpoint? Would the application of security officers be operationally effective or cost-effective?

4. **Physical recommendations.** Inspect doors, windows, lighting, and access points. Recommend physical changes that would make the building more secure, such as pinning hinges on doors and fences.

5. **Locks, equipment to be bolted down, potential application of card control, and key control.** Make specific recommendations.

6. **Alarms.** Would an alarm system be cost-effective? Would the use of the building preclude the use of an alarm? Are the potential benefits of an alarm such that the building use should be changed to facilitate it? Consider all types of alarms, building-wide, or in specific offices. Consider closed circuit television and portable or temporary alarm devices.

7. **Storage.** Does the building have specific storage problems, such as expensive items that should be given special attention, petty cash, stamps, calculators, or microscopes? Make specific recommendations.

8. **Trespassing.** Are adequate "No Trespassing" signs posted? Are other signs needed such as "No Solicitation" or "No Skateboarding"?

9. **Custodians.** Can custodians be used in a manner that would be better from a security standpoint?

Personality of the Complex

Each project will have a distinctive personality. Let us take an average building, which is open from 9 a.m. to 5 p.m. The traffic flow is heaviest during this period. During the span from 5 p.m. to 12 a.m., the building is closed to the public. Some staff members may work late. Who secures the building? At 12 a.m., the cleaning crew arrives and prepares the building for another day. The whole personality of the complex must be considered before your report is completed.

Let us take a further example of building personality. The complex is 100×100 ft and it has two solid-core doors, one large window at the front of the building, and is air conditioned.

Case 1. The complex is a credit union on the main street next door to the local police department versus the same credit union on the edge of town.

Case 2. This is a large doctor's office. The doctor is an art buff and has half a million dollars in art in the office versus a doctor who has no art but has a small safe with about $200 worth of Class A narcotics inside.

Case 3. This building houses different stores that close at 6 p.m. versus a liquor store that is open until 2 a.m.

In these cases, I give six examples of the personality of a complex. As I stated, your recommendations must be tailored to fit the lifestyle and vulnerabilities of these buildings.

Positive and Negative Aspects of Making Recommendations

In making your recommendations for security improvements, you must consider the consequences of your suggestion in the event the property owner implements it. Negative as well as positive aspects are involved. Take, for example, a housing complex that has a high crime rate from outsiders and within. Your recommendation is, "Build a 10-foot high fence around the complex."

Positive Aspects

Crime is reduced—The environment can be designed so that the individual considering a criminal act feels that there is a good chance to be seen by someone who will take action and call the police. Another meaningful positive aspect is the fear of crime and if present, it also must be addressed.

Vandalism is less—The target of attack can be made to appear so formidable that the person does not feel able to reach the target. It adds to the physical aesthetics of the area through environmental design.

The visual impact is negative—This ensures the property of the residents, adding to their secure environment. Limiting the number of points of entry and establishing access control primarily decreases crime opportunity and keeps out unauthorized persons.

Negative Aspect

A fortress environment may create more of a psychological barrier than a physical one. It is socially undesirable and yet is replicated throughout our country at an increasing rate.

Community Reaction

This cannot be disregarded. Furthermore, vandalism at the time of early installation should be considered. Get the residents, occupants, employees, etc., involved in the early planning process.

Consciousness of fear may develop by those tenants whose apartments face the fence; but as the tenants come and go, it will eventually be accepted.

All fences are subject to being painted by groups with a cause. Consider using cyclone fencing or other see-through fencing to discourage visible graffiti from being applied to the fence. An eye-pleasing architectural CPTED feature would be to recommend the following: stones, gardens, terraces, etc., to improve the physical appearance and avoid the stigma of a fortress environment.

Crime Analysis

It is not necessary for you to be a statistician, but the more you know about and understand the local crime problems, the better equipped you are to analyze the potential crime risk loss in surveying a business or a home.

Crime analysis collection is simply the gathering of raw data concerning reported crimes and known offenders. Generally, such information comes from crime reports, arrest reports, and police contact cards. This is not to say that these are the only sources available for collecting crime data. Police reports, security officers' reports, reports from the fire department, Googling the location on the Internet, and newspapers are all sources available to obtain added data.

The analysis process as applied to criminal activity is a specific step-by-step sequence of five interconnected functions: crime data collection, crime data collation, data analysis, dissemination of analysis reports, and feedback and evaluation of crime data.

Crime analysis of the site you survey supplies you with specific information to enable you to further harden the target in specific areas where losses have occurred. It is a means of responding "after the fact," when a crime has been committed.

Deterrents

By definition—"Serving to Deter Relating to deterrence".

Category A

- Security surveillance system used to prevent crime in private and public locations
- CPTED principles and concepts
- Defensible space principles and concepts
- Situational crime prevention principles and concepts
- Lighting that meets standards and design by increased visibility
- Biometrics and access control to specific areas
- CPTED design
- CPTED landscape principles
- Signage or visible security signs
- Padlocks and door locks and peepholes
- Intrusion alarms and signage of alarm
- Security surveillance systems (CCTV)
- Security awareness programs
- Planters and thorny bushes
- Bollards or barricades closing down streets
- Barking dog, inside or outside
- Vehicle in driveway
- Area traffic and escape route available
- Policy and procedures
- Training programs.

Category B

- Security officers armed and unarmed in private function, i.e., hotel door man, bus drivers, tickets sellers or ticket takers, conductors;
- Police officers in uniform and armed security who may deduce that a crime is about to be committed and deter the incident in their presence;

- Security officer patrolling the parking lots of hotels, hospitals, and retail locations, and protecting corporate assets and customer protection;
- Guardian angels patrolling streets, neighborhoods, and subways;
- People in the area.

Crime displacement theory by target hardening and soft target moving to another location.

Category C

Guard shacks if occupied are a deterrent.

CPTED strategies

1. Natural access control
2. Natural surveillance
3. Territorial reinforcement (Crowe and Fennelly, 2013).

Defensible space—This concept was developed in the public housing environment. It is similar to CPTED strategies (Crowe and Fennelly, 2013).

Environmental security differs from CPTED in that it uses a broader range of crime control strategies including social management, social media, target-hardening activity support, and low enforcement.

CPTED landscape principles are the following:

1. For natural surveillance but back bushes to a height of 3 ft.
2. Cut back the tree branches to 8 ft from the ground.
3. Chain-link fence height 8 ft plus three strands of barbed wire.
4. Height of a stone wall—8 ft.
5. A least 10 ft of clear space both sides of the fence and wall.[1]

Situation crime prevention incorporates other crime prevention and law enforcement strategies in an effort to focus on place-specific crime problems.

---

[1] James F. Broder. CPP risk analysis and the security survey. 3rd ed. Elsevier; 2006.

Results and Objectives

- Reduce violent crime
- Reduce property crime
- Displacement of crime
- Eliminate the threats and risk
- Reduce the likelihood of more incidents
- Eliminate vulnerabilities and protect assets.

Risk management defined[2] as the process by which an entity identifies its potential losses and then decides what is the best way to manage these potential losses.

- Risk: Exposure to possible loss (i.e., fire, natural disasters, product obsolescence, shrinkage, work stoppages).
- Security managers are primarily interested in crime, shrinkage, accidents, crises.
- Risk managers generally are more focused on fire and safety issues.
- Pure risk: Risk in which there are no potential benefits to be derived (i.e., earthquake, flood)
- Dynamic risk: Risk that can produce gain or profit (i.e., theft, embezzlement)
- Possible maximum loss: Maximum loss sustained if a target is totally destroyed.
- Probable maximum loss: Amount of loss a target is likely to sustain.

Security Measures to Consider

Doors [3]

A door system includes the door, frame, locking hardware, and anchorage to the building; the doors might also be electronically controlled. As part of a balanced design approach, exterior doors in high-risk buildings should be designed to withstand the maximum dynamic pressure and duration of the load from the design threat explosive blast. These threats should be

[2] James F. Broder. CPP risk analysis and the security survey. 3rd. ed. Elsevier; 2006.

reexamined (more effective explosives), delivery mechanisms (canisters, backpacks, vehicles by size and type) to continue to design and redesign an environment to be responsive to changing threat conditions. Other general door considerations are as follows:

- Provide hollow steel doors or steel clad doors with steel frames.
- Provide blast-resistant doors for high threats and high levels of protection.
- Limit normal entry/egress through one door, if possible.
- Keep exterior doors to a minimum while accommodating emergency egress. Doors are less attack-resistant than adjacent walls because of functional requirements, construction, and method of attachment.
- Ensure that exterior doors open outward from inhabited areas. In addition to facilitating egress, the doors can be seated into the door frames so that they will not enter the buildings as hazardous debris in an explosion.
- Replace externally mounted locks and hasps with internally locking devices because the weakest part of the door system is the latching component.
- Install doors, where practical, so that they present a blank, flush surface to the outside to reduce their vulnerability to attack.
- Locate hinges on the interior or provide concealed hinges to reduce their vulnerability to tampering.
- Install emergency exit doors so that they facilitate only exiting movement. It is suggested that the handles on exit-only exterior doors be removed to further inhibit re-entry into the building through unauthorized openings.
- Equip any outward-opening double door with protective hinges and key-operated mortise-type locks. Consider protecting all electronic and electrical wiring inside the doorjamb or place in protection jacketing to protect against vandalism.

- Provide solid doors or walls as a backup for glass doors in foyers.
- Strengthen and harden the upright surfaces of doorjambs.

General Guidelines for Windows and Glazing

General guidelines for windows and glazing include the following:

- Do not place windows adjacent to doors because, if the windows are broken, the doors can be unlocked.
- Minimize the number and size of windows in a façade. If possible, limit the amount of glazed area in building façades to 15%. The amount of blast entering a space is directly proportional to the amount of openings on the façade. Consider placing fewer windows on the lower floors to reduce the impact of blast on the structure of the building; the notion of reducing all windows on façades above blast vulnerability area seems excessive.
- Consider using burglary- and ballistic-resistant glazing in high-risk buildings.
- Consider using laminated glass in place of conventional glass.
- Consider window safety laminate (such as Mylar) or another fragment retention film over glazing (properly installed) to reduce fragmentation.
- Consider placing guards, such as grilles, screens, or meshwork, across window openings to protect against covert entry. Affix protective window guards firmly to the structure.
- Consider installing blast curtains, blast shades, or spall shields to prevent glass fragments from flying into the occupied space.
- Consider curtains, blinds, and shades to limit entry of incendiary devices.
- Consider narrow recessed windows with sloped sills because they are less vulnerable than conventional windows.

- Consider windows with key-operated locks because they provide a greater level of protection than windows with simple latches. Stationary, nonoperating windows are preferred for security.
- Position the operable section of a sliding window on the inside of the fixed section and secure it with a broomstick, metal rod, or similar device placed at the bottom of the track.

Building design to achieve a desired protection level. The assessment process determines the level of protection sought for the building structure and defines the threat/hazard specific to the facility. Explosive blast threats usually govern building structure design for high-risk buildings. A structural engineer should determine the building design features needed to achieve the desired level of protection against the design blast threat, considering collapse of the building, as well as incipient injuries and fatalities.

PHYSICAL SECURITY SYSTEMS

Physical security concerns the physical measures designed to safeguard people; prevent unauthorized access to equipment, installations, material, and documents; and safeguard against terrorist attacks. As such, all security operations face new and complex physical security challenges across the full spectrum of operations. Challenges relative to physical security include the control of populations, information dominance, multinational and interagency connectivity, antiterrorism, and the use of physical security assets as a versatile force multiplier.

A *physical security systems infrastructure* is a network of electric security systems and devices that is configured, operated, maintained, and enhanced to provide security functions and services (such as operational and emergency communications and notification, intrusion detection, physical access control, video surveillance, visitor management, officer patrol tour management, and security administration) to achieve specific risk mitigation objectives [3].

50 Things You Should Know—Checklist

- Ensure that exterior doors into inhabited areas open outward. Ensure emergency exit doors only facilitate exiting.
- Secure room access hatches from the interior. Prevent public access to building roofs.
- Restrict access to building operation systems.
- Conduct periodic training of HVAC operations and maintenance staff.
- Evaluate HVAC control options.
- Install empty conduits for future security control equipment during initial construction or major renovation.
- Do not mount plumbing, electrical fixtures, or utility lines on the inside of exterior walls.
- Minimize interior glazing near high-risk areas.
- Establish written plans for evacuation and sheltering in place.
- Integrating multiple security systems in a layered effect including CPTED.
- Illuminate building access points.
- Restrict access to building information.
- Secure HVAC intakes and mechanical rooms.
- Limit the number of doors used for normal entry/egress.
- Lock all utility access openings.
- Provide emergency power for emergency lighting in restrooms, egress routes, and any meeting room without windows.
- Install a modern public address system that will direct individuals where to go in case of an emergency.
- Stagger interior doors and offset interior and exterior doors.
- Eliminate hiding places.
- Install a second and separate telephone service.
- Install radio telemetry distributed antennas throughout the facility.

- Use a badge identification system for building access.
- Install a CCTV security surveillance system.
- Install an electronic security alarm system.
- Install rapid response and isolation features into HVAC systems.
- Use interior barriers to differentiate levels of security.
- Locate utility systems away from likely areas of potential attack.
- Install call buttons at key public contact areas.
- Install emergency and normal electric equipment at different locations.
- Avoid exposed structural elements.
- Reinforce foyer walls.
- Use architectural features to deny contact with exposed primary vertical load members.
- Isolate lobbies, mail rooms, loading docks, and storage areas.
- Locate stairwells remotely. Do not discharge stairs into lobbies, parking, or loading areas.
- Elevate HVAC fresh air intakes.
- Create "shelter-in-place" rooms or areas.
- Separate HVAC zones. Eliminate leaks and increase building air tightness.
- Install blast-resistant doors or steel doors with steel frames.
- Physically separate unsecured areas from the main building.
- Install HVAC exhausting and purging systems.
- Connect interior nonload bearing walls to structure with nonrigid connections.
- Use structural design techniques to resist progressive collapse.
- Treat exterior shear walls as primary structures.
- Orient glazing perpendicular to the primary façade facing uncontrolled vehicle approaches.
- Use reinforced concrete wall systems in lieu of masonry or curtain walls.
- Ensure active fire system is protected from single-point failure in case of a blast event.
- Install a backup control center.

- Avoid eaves and overhangs or harden to withstand blast effects.
- Establish group floor elevation 4 ft above grade.
- Secure with greater purpose and hardware all openings to building within 14 ft of ground level or 14 ft of access to roof.

Integrating multiple security systems in a layered effect—including CPTED and environmental security, critical infrastructure protection, building designs, interior/exterior layout, detection systems, structural barriers, access controls, communications, and CCTV assessment—contributes to the protection of assets as well as the control and reduction of losses.

References

[1] US Green Building Council. LEED green building z rating system for new construction and major renovation version 2.1. November 2002. Available from: http//www.usgbc.org.
[2] Crowe TD. CPTED. Boston: Butterworth-Heinemann; 2000. p. 3–54.
[3] Bernard R. What is a security infrastructure? Secur Technol Exec 2010:6.

CHAPTER

17

Standards, Regulations, and Guidelines Compliance and Your Security Program, Including Global Resources

Roderick Draper

This chapter explores security compliance standards, regulations, and guidelines. It also discusses the resources available to organizations through regulatory agencies, standards bodies, and industry associations, ensuring that a security program is able to respond to changes in the regulatory environment.

INTRODUCTION

While the nature of the risks to which organizations are exposed vary widely, the need to have a clearly defined and defensible approach to risk management is common to all private and public sector enterprises. But where do you start?

Some industries are heavily regulated in the areas of physical and information security and the regulations provide direction for those responsible for risk management. For example, the Nuclear Regulatory Commission is responsible for defining and enforcing compliance with security requirements at commercially operated nuclear power stations in the United States

and as part of its mandate publishes a range of guidelines to support regulatory compliance. Similarly, but on a very different scale, workplace health and safety regulations in Queensland, Australia, require employers within the retail industry to develop risk management strategies relating to the threat of robbery. To assist organizations with managing their robbery-related risks and associated regulatory compliance, the Department of Industrial Relations publishes a guide that includes a range of strategies.

Notwithstanding the context within which a security program may exist, the strategies for understanding and managing security-related risks can be divided into two core groups:

1. Mandatory practices
2. Benchmark (minimum) practices

Mandatory practices are essential to meet legislative, regulatory, licensing, registration, or similar compliance requirements. These may be applicable to the activities in which the enterprise is engaged and/or be specific to risk management programs. For example, Bill 168 in Ontario, Canada, amended the Occupational

Effective Physical Security, Fifth Edition
http://dx.doi.org/10.1016/B978-0-12-804462-9.00017-8

Health and Safety Act (OHSA) to incorporate strict new standards in an attempt to reduce violence and harassment in the workplace. These requirements apply to all workplaces with five employees or more, and the Ministry of Labor has published guidelines to assist organizations with understanding the requirements and implementing appropriate strategies. Similarly, in-house security officers in some jurisdictions are required to receive specified training and hold licenses issued by a local regulatory authority. Any organization operating within such a jurisdiction must incorporate into its security program and all practices necessary to ensure compliance with the security licensing requirements.

Benchmark (minimum) practices are those approaches that in legal terms could "reasonably" be expected to be followed, given the specific circumstances that apply. For example, standards such as ISO 31010:2009, "Risk Management—Risk Assessment Techniques," provide generic guidance with respect to assessing a wide range of risks, but compliance with the process described in the standard is not necessarily mandatory. Strategies defined in standards published by recognized standards bodies only become mandatory where those standards are specified for compliance (e.g., electrical wiring standards specified in electrical safety regulations). However, where a published standard or guideline has clear application in the management of security-related risks, it should be carefully considered by the enterprise as a potential benchmark to be followed. Such recognized standards and guidelines provide a defensible basis for security management decisions. Taken in context, they can be used to support a business case for security expenditure or support a policy position.

Implementation of strategies can, of course, depart from those described in nonmandatory standards and guidelines; however, such decisions need to be made in an informed manner so that they are clearly supported by all the factors that should be considered. If decisions are made not to follow published standards and guidelines that are applicable to the management of security-related risks within the enterprise, it is important to reflect on how defensible those decisions would be in litigation or under scrutiny by the media or an aggrieved party to a risk event.

For example, there was a decision of the Supreme Court of Victoria, Australia, in 2009 relating to a robbery that occurred at a hotel (Ogden v. Bell Hotel Pty Ltd. [2009] VSC 219). The court held that the hotel's failure to implement reasonable security measures had contributed and led to the opportunity for the robbery. Although the hotel tried to argue that they had informal measures and expectations relating to security, they simply did not have a structured and defensible approach to security risk management. The hotel's failure to properly consider all of the risks and ensure that policies and procedures were developed in accordance with reasonable and expected practices contributed to the plaintiff being awarded $825,000 in damages.

STANDARDS

In this context the term standard means a document published by a recognized standards body for the purpose of specifying requirements and/or an approach to a specific subject area. There are literally hundreds of recognized standards bodies around the world operating within geographic or industry/technology boundaries. At an international level, there are numerous organizations that develop and publish standards for universal consumption. One of the largest is the International Organization for Standardization (ISO; www.iso.org).

In recent years the ISO has published a number of standards that have been derived from those published by national standards bodies. Subsequently, these new ISO standards have been adopted by the countries concerned in favor of or in addition to the originating local standard. For example, the Canadian Standards Association (CSA; www.csa.ca) developed and published its standard CAN/CSA-Q850-97, "Risk Management: Guideline for Decision Makers," in 1997. While Q850 remains a current Canadian standard, in 2010 CSA also adopted the ISO standard ISO 31000:2009, "Risk Management—Principles and Guidelines," and now publishes this under the title CAN/CSA-ISO 31000-10, "Risk Management—Principles and Guidelines." Similarly, the Australian and New Zealand standards bodies had initially published their risk management standard in 1995 and revised it several times until it was last published in 2004. When the ISO standard was published in 2009, it was adopted for use in Australia and New Zealand under the title AS/NZS ISO 31000:2009, "Risk Management—Principles and Guidelines." Unlike Q850 in the Canadian context where the original standard remains valid, the local standard (AS/NZS 4360) was superseded by the international standard (AS/NZS ISO 31000).

It is important to note that while not all ISO standards are adopted by regional or national standards bodies, they may still have application for security programs within those geographic locations. For example, the ISO standard for risk assessment mentioned in the introduction to this chapter has been widely adopted by standards bodies including the CSA, Asociación Española de Normalización y Certificación (AENOR; www.aenor.es), European Committee for Electrotechnical Standardization (CENELEC; www.cenelec.eu), Association française de normalization (AFNOR; www.afnor.org), British Standards Institution (BSI; www.bsigroup.com), and Österreichisches Normungsinstitut (ON, Austrian Standards Institute; www.as-institute.at), just to name a few. In contrast, the ISO risk management standard has not been embraced by the Australian and New Zealand standards bodies that adopted the ISO 31000 standard.

The application of any published standard must be considered in context with the benefits that will be derived through its adoption. While mandated regulatory requirements may be more likely to be drawn from national or international standards, those developed and published by industry bodies tend to be more specific in nature and underpin benchmark or minimum accepted practices. Apart from traditional participation on standard development committees, a number of recognized industry associations have developed working relationships with standards bodies to jointly develop and publish standards and guidelines. For example, ASIS International (www.asisonline.org) worked with the BSI to develop the standard ASIS/BSI BCM.01-2010, "Business Continuity Management Systems: Requirements with Guidance for Use." This joint industry/national standard is based on a BSI standard that is adapted for consideration within the security risk management context. Similarly, BSI has partnered with the Institute of Electrical and Electronics Engineers (IEEE; www.ieee.org) in the development of joint standards, and the North American Security Products Organization (NASPO) collaborated with the American National Standards Institute (ANSI; www.ansi.org) to produce ANSI/NASPO-SA-2008, "Security Assurance Standards for the Document and Product Security Industries."

The range of national, international, and industry standards that may be applicable to the management of individual security programs is far too extensive and dynamic to be listed in a volume such as this. It is important to consider standards covering both mandatory and benchmark practices, including those developed and published by national standards bodies and industry organizations. Where there are no locally applicable standards within a particular area of the security program, it is worthwhile reviewing those that may apply within other jurisdictions. Ultimately, and notwithstanding regulatory obligations, the application of provisions within a standard can be used to provide a structured approach to a given issue, deliver defensibility for decisions, and establish consistency across a security program.

REGULATIONS

Almost universally, all security programs must consider regulatory compliance with respect to workplace safety and life safety. However, there are many other areas where legislative, regulatory, licensing, registration, or similar compliance requirements are met through, or have a direct impact on, the security program. For example, the use of closed-circuit television (CCTV) as a security strategy is widespread. But deploying and operating a camera within any given space may come with a number of compliance requirements that may not be applicable in another location. Some of the regulatory considerations for deploying a CCTV camera might include the following:

- Licensing of the installer (e.g., as required in the Canadian Province of British Columbia; www.pssg.gov.bc.ca).
- Licensing of the camera operator (e.g., as required in the United Kingdom; www.sia. homeoffice.gov.uk).
- Conditions for installation (e.g., as required in workplaces in the Australian State of New South Wales; http://www.austlii.edu.au/ au/legis/nsw/consol_act/wsa2005245/s11. html).
- Registration of the CCTV system (e.g., as in Western Australia; https://blueiris.police. wa.gov.au/).
- Training for operators (e.g., as nominated in the Australian capital territory for bus cameras; http://www.tams.act.gov.au).
- Privacy management (e.g., in line with the Privacy Act in New Zealand; www.privacy. org.nz, and Standards for the Protection of Personal Information in Massachusetts;

http://www.mass.gov/Eoca/docs/ idtheft/201CMR1700reg.pdf).
- Documentation (e.g., in accordance with the requirements of the Commission d'accès à l'information du Québec, Canada; http:// www.cai.gouv.qc.ca/06_documentation/01_ pdf/new_rules_2004.pdf).

Notwithstanding specific laws with respect to firearms, the private security industry worldwide is impacted by escalations in regulatory obligations as authorities come under pressure to address community concerns about the training, competence, and suitability of security personnel to perform their assigned duties. In some jurisdictions, licensing and training requirements are only imposed on security contractors and do not apply to in-house security personnel (i.e., those employed directly by the company whose assets they are protecting). Whereas in other regulatory settings, licensing and training obligations are applied equally to in-house and contracted personnel.

In a situation where in-house staffs are not legally required to be licensed, an organization may wish to consider the benefits of employing licensed personnel. While there are clearly cost implications in meeting the licensing requirements, the decision to do so may mitigate risks associated with the actions or inactions of security personnel. For example, obtaining and maintaining a security-related license in most jurisdictions incorporate criminal background checks and basic training requirements. In effect, the regulator provides a foundational level of assurance with respect to the license holder's suitability to perform the functions for which he or she is licensed.

History has shown that holding a security industry license does not guarantee that security personnel will act appropriately and lawfully in performing their duties. It does, however, provide a level of defensibility for the decision to deploy a person in a role for which the industry regulator deems him or her to be suitable. This must, of course, be reinforced with robust poli-cies, procedures, standing orders, training, and awareness strategies to ensure that security per-sonnel are made aware of and accept their roles and responsibilities.

While the title of this chapter has the secu-rity program as its focus, security-related risks should not be considered in isolation and a holistic approach to risk management is critical to avoiding the pitfalls associated with manage-ment "silos." Regulatory compliance can, in fact, be the catalyst for greater cooperation across lines of demarcation that might otherwise be a hindrance to the effective management of speci-fied risks.

As noted in the introduction to this chap-ter, some industries are heavily regulated in the areas of physical and information security. There are lessons that can be learned by study-ing the requirements imposed on those indus-tries within the context of your own operations. Regulations are generally implemented to pro-tect the community from identified risks. By judiciously drawing motivation from regulatory controls in related fields, a security program can be significantly enhanced and made far more defensible from litigious actions.

GUIDELINES

While there are a range of published guide-lines available to support the implementation of aspects of security programs within specific settings, there are many more that have been developed and remain largely unknown or inac-cessible. In the context of this chapter, the term *guidelines* should be taken to include other types of publications with similar purposes, such as manuals, specifications, protocols, practices, templates, aide-memoires, checklists, and fact sheets.

The Federal Emergency Management Agency within the U.S. Department of Homeland Security (FEMA; www.fema.gov) publishes guidelines covering many aspects of physical security. Some of the more popular FEMA resources include the following:

- FEMA 426, "Reference Manual to Mitigate Potential Terrorist Attacks Against Buildings." This manual provides guidance to the building science community of architects and engineers and to reduce physical damage to buildings, related infrastructure, and people caused by terrorist assaults. The manual presents incremental approaches that can be implemented over time to decrease the vulnerability of buildings to terrorist threats. Many of the recommendations can be implemented quickly and cost effectively (http://www.fema.gov/library/viewRecord.do?id=1559).
- FEMA 452, "A How-To Guide to Mitigate Potential Terrorist Attacks Against Buildings." This how-to guide outlines methods for identifying the critical assets and functions within buildings, determining the threats to those assets, and assessing the vulnerabilities associated with those threats. The methods presented provide a means to assess risks and to make decisions about how to mitigate them. The scope of the methods includes reducing physical damage to structural and nonstructural components of buildings and related infrastructure, and reducing resultant casualties during conventional bomb attacks, as well as attacks involving chemical, biological, and radiological (CBR) agents (http://www.fema.gov/library/viewRecord.do?id=1938).
- E155 and L156, "Building Design for Homeland Security." The purpose of E155 and L156 is to familiarize students with assessment methodologies available to identify the relative risk level for various threats, including explosive blast and CBR agents. Students are introduced to publications FEMA 426 and FEMA 452 and are asked to provide mitigation measures

for a range of human-made hazards. The primary target audience for these courses includes engineers, architects, and building officials (http://www.fema.gov/library/viewRecord.do?id=1939).

- FEMA 453, "Safe Rooms and Shelters—Protecting People Against Terrorist Attacks." The objective of this manual is to provide guidance for engineers, architects, building officials, and property owners to design shelters and safe rooms in buildings. This manual presents information about the design and construction of shelters in the workplace, home, or community building that will provide protection in response to human-made hazards (http://www.fema.gov/library/viewRecord.do?id=1910).

- FEMA 389, "Communicating with Owners and Managers of New Buildings on Earthquake Risk." FEMA 389 was developed to facilitate the process of educating building owners and managers about seismic risk management tools that can be effectively and economically employed during the building development phase—from site selection through design and construction—as well as the operational phase. The document provides guidance for identifying and assessing earthquake-related hazards during the site selection process, including the potential seismic hazards of ground shaking, surface fault rupture, soil liquefaction, soil differential compaction, landsliding, and inundation, as well as other potential hazards affecting building performance, vulnerable transportation, and utility systems (lifelines); the hazards posed by adjacent structures; the release of hazardous materials; and postearthquake fires (http://www.fema.gov/library/viewRecord.do?id=1431).

- FEMA 430, "Site and Urban Design for Security: Guidance Against Potential Terrorist Attacks." FEMA 430 provides information and design concepts for the protection of buildings and occupants from site perimeters to the faces of buildings. The intended audience includes the design community of architects, landscape architects, engineers and other consultants working for private institutions, building owners and managers, and state and local government officials concerned with site planning and design. FEMA 430 is one of a series that addresses security issues in high-population, private sector buildings. It is a companion to FEMA 426, which provides an understanding of the assessment of threats, hazards, vulnerability, and risk, and the design methods needed to improve protection of new and existing buildings and the people occupying them (http://www.fema.gov/library/viewRecord.do?id=3135).

- FEMA 427, "Primer for Design of Commercial Buildings to Mitigate Terrorist Attacks." This primer introduces a series of concepts that can help building designers, owners, and state and local governments mitigate the threat of hazards resulting from terrorist attacks on new buildings. FEMA 427 specifically addresses four high-population, private sector building types: commercial office, retail, multifamily residential, and light industrial. This manual contains extensive qualitative design guidance for limiting or mitigating the effects of terrorist attacks, focusing primarily on explosions but also addressing CBR attacks (http://www.fema.gov/library/viewRecord.do?id=1560).

- FEMA 428, "Primer for Design Safe Schools Projects in Case of Terrorist Attacks." The purpose of this primer is to provide the design community and school administrators with the basic principles and techniques to design a school safe from terrorist attacks (http://www.fema.gov/library/viewRecord.do?&id=1561).

Industry associations are an excellent source for guidelines to support security programs.

For example, ASIS International develops and publishes a range of guidelines that are available free of charge to its members and that may be purchased by nonmembers. Some of the subjects covered include (http://www.asisonline.org/guidelines/published.htm) the following:

- Business continuity
- Facilities physical security measures
- General security risk assessment
- Information asset protection
- Preemployment background screening
- Private security officer selection and training
- Threat advisory system response
- Workplace violence prevention.

The American Public Transportation Association also publishes a number of security-related guidelines, including the following:

- APTA SS-SEM-RP-001-08, "Recommended Practice for a Continuity of Operations Plan"
- APTA SS-SEM-RP-002-08, "Recommended Practice for First Responder Familiarization of Transit Systems"
- APTA SS-SEM-RP-003-08, "Recommended Practice: Security and Emergency Management Aspects of Special Event Service"
- APTA SS-SEM-RP-004-09, "Recommended Practice: General Guidance on Transit Incident Drills and Exercises"
- APTA SS-SEM-RP-005-09, "Recommended Practice: Developing a Contagious Virus Response Plan"
- APTA SEM-SS-RP-008-09, "Recommended Practice: Safe Mail and Package Handling"
- APTA SEM-SS-RP-009-09, "Recommended Practice: Emergency Communication Strategies for Transit Agencies"
- APTA SS-SEM-RP-012-09, "Recommended Practice: Responding to Threat Condition Levels"
- APTA SS-SIS-RP-002-08, "Recommended Practice for CCTV Camera Coverage and Field of View Criteria for Passenger Facilities"

- APTA RP-CCS-1-RT-001-10, "Securing Control and Communications Systems in Transit Environments, Part 1."

Care needs to be taken when reviewing guidelines for potential use in any given application to ensure that they do not conflict with any regulations or published standards that may be applicable. For example, the process for assessing security-related risks as defined in the ISO 31010 standard differs significantly from the "ASIS General Security Risk Assessment Guideline" described earlier. While each situation will need to be evaluated in the relevant contexts, as a general rule the following hierarchy of authority can be used as a guide:

1. Legislation/regulations
2. Standards (by recognized standards body)
3. Guidelines.

Regulators also routinely publish guidelines to assist organizations with compliance, and it is important to recognize that where such guidelines exist, they should be considered as a foundation for the applicable areas of the security program. Guidelines themselves do not in most cases have any statutory standing but may be referenced in separate regulatory instruments.

For example, the government of the State of Queensland in Australia has published crime prevention through environmental design guidelines (CPTED; http://www.police.qld.gov.au/programs/cscp/safetyPublic/). The Queensland CPTED guidelines are referenced by local governments in their policies and by laws, establishing a pseudo-regulatory role for the guidelines in this example. The CPTED guidelines are specifically mandated as a policy within the Southeast Queensland Regional Plan 2009–31 and the associated regulatory provisions (see Policy 6.3.4, p. 80). By referencing the CPTED guidelines in planning scheme policy, new developments can be assessed for compliance against practices nominated in the guidelines. Where deviations from the approaches described in the CPTED guidelines are identified, developers can be required to make the changes necessary for compliance.

Many guidelines developed by government agencies are not linked to regulatory requirements but still bear consideration when developing elements of a security program. For example, the "National Code of Practice for CCTV Systems for the Mass Passenger Transport Sector for Counterterrorism" includes recommendations for operational objectives and minimum storage requirements, but these have not been adopted as widely as the authors may have wished because of the cost of compliance. In the absence of regulatory compliance obligations or other compelling business risk, the guidelines in this case are little more than informative (http://www.coag. gov.au/coag_meeting_outcomes/2006-07-14/ docs/cctv_code_practice.rtf).

Standards bodies may develop guidelines as complementary documents to published standards. The *Australian Standards Handbook*, HB 167:2006, "Security Risk Management," outlines "a broad framework and the core elements that should be included in a security risk management process, and is consistent with the risk management principles of AS/NZS 4360: 2004" (https://infostore.saiglobal.com/store/details. aspx?ProductID=568733). This handbook is in turn referenced in the "Risk Management Kit for Terrorism" published by the Department of Transport in the Australian state of Victoria, which is "designed to assist operators of declared essential services (DES) to meet their legislative requirements under the Terrorism (Community Protection) Act 2003." This interweaving of statutory obligations, standards, and guidelines demands careful consideration and detailed review in managing compliance within the operational contexts that apply.

MANAGING COMPLIANCE

Every organization, regardless of size or sector of operations, can benefit from having a structured security management plan. The plan does not necessarily need to be complex, but it does need to recognize the range of risks to which the organization is exposed, including specific compliance-related risks. Inherently, the governance framework that overlays the security program needs to include mechanisms for monitoring compliance obligations and prioritizing decisions in relation to the management of related risks.

For example, the Sarbanes–Oxley Act 2002 (SOX), which is administered by the U.S. Securities and Exchange Commission, has significant implications for physical and information security programs. Managing SOX compliance requires a clear understanding of the range of risks that may lead to adverse audit outcomes and associated penalties. Given that records need to be retained for not less than 5 years, the SOX compliance element of the security program must consider the full range of strategies necessary to prevent the records from compromise through the following:

- Loss or destruction
- Denial of access
- Unauthorized modification or alteration
- Contamination.

The SOX legislation does not dictate how records are to be protected; it simply defines the outcome required. To some extent, this opens up a wide range of options for risk management but does not offer any guidance to support compliance management.

In contrast, some government agencies publish an extensive range of resources to support managing compliance with policy and regulatory obligations. For example, the "Australian Government Protective Security Policy Framework" is the means through which agencies are to achieve the mandatory requirements for protective security expected by government. To facilitate compliance management processes, a range of supporting documents are provided, including the following:

- "Protective Security Guidance for Executives"
- "Security Awareness Training Guidelines"

- "Australian Government Personnel Security Protocol"
- "Agency Personnel Security Guidelines"
- "Security Clearance Subjects Guidelines"
- "Procedural Fairness Guidelines"
- "Reporting Changes in Personal Circumstances Guidelines"
- "Contact Reporting Guidelines"
- "Personnel Security Practitioners Guidelines"
- "Personnel Security Adjudicative Guidelines."

Ultimately, compliance management requires a structured approach to understanding obligations and risks and facilitates defensible decisions based on a clear understanding of the implications for noncompliance in the context within which operational risks exist. While guidance may be available for some regulatory and policy compliance obligations, those responsible for managing security-related risks should ensure that all direct and indirect requirements are identified and that compliance management forms part of the overall governance framework.

If there are published standards that align with or support management of compliance with specific requirements, careful consideration should be given to drawing on those standards as the foundation from which strategies can be implemented. The ISO 28001:2007 standard, "Security Management Systems for the Supply Chain—Best Practices for Implementing Supply Chain Security, Assessments, and Plans—Requirements and Guidance," is a good example of a published standard that can be readily adapted for other applications. Although the title makes reference to the "supply chain," the principles embodied in the standard are substantially universal and could be used to guide protective security compliance within other sectors that do not have the same available resources.

It may appear obvious that a well-conceived and implemented program for managing security-related risks is essential for all private and public sector enterprises. The increasing frequency of litigation and regulatory prosecutions related to security risk management (or the lack thereof) highlights the need to have a defensible basis for your security program.

Where specific security program requirements form part of broader regulatory compliance obligations, these demands must be carefully considered in the context of the other security-related risks and must be managed in a proactive manner. Organizations should avail themselves for the resources available through regulatory agencies, standards bodies, and industry associations and ensure that the security program is able to respond to changes in the regulatory environment.

RESOURCES

A dedicated clearing house of information, resources, and links related to security standards, regulations, and guidelines is being established at http://clearinghouse.amtac.net to maintain the accuracy of links referenced in this chapter.

References

[1] NRC. Domestic safeguards regulations, guidance, and communications. 2004. Available at: http://www.nrc.gov/security/domestic/reg-guide.html.

[2] Queensland Department of Industrial Relations. Guide: personal security in the retail industry. 2004. Available at: http://www.deir.qld.gov.au/workplace/resources/pdfs/retailsec_guide2004.pdf.

[3] Legislative Assembly of Ontario. Bill 168, occupational health and safety amendment act (violence and harassment in the workplace). 2009. Available at: http://www.ontla.on.ca/web/bills/bills_detail.do?locale=en&BillID=2181&BillStagePrintId=4499&btnSubmit=go.

[4] Ministry of Labour, Ontario. Workplace violence and harassment: understanding the law. 2010. Available at: http://www.labour.gov.on.ca/english/hs/pubs/wpvh/index.php.

[5] International Standards Organization ISO31010:2009. Risk management—risk assess tech. 2009. Available at: http://www.iso.org/iso/iso_catalogue/catalogue_tc/catalogue_detail.htm?csnumber=43170.

[6] Canadian Standards Association CAN/CSA-Q850–97. Risk management: guideline for decision makers. 1997. Available at: http://shop.csa.ca/en/canada/risk-management/cancsa-q850-97-r2009/invt/27003271997/.

[7] SAI Global AS/NZS 4360: 2004. Risk management. 2004. Available at: http://infostore.saiglobal.com/store/Details.aspx?productID=381579.

[8] ACT. Bus services minimum service standards. 2009. Available at: http://www.tams.act.gov.au/__data/assets/pdf_file/0018/143019/BusAccreditationMSS_-_Part_3_-_Mar_09.pdf.

[9] New Zealand Privacy Commissioner. Privacy and CCTV: a guide to the privacy act for businesses, agencies and organisations. 2009. Available at: http://privacy.org.nz/privacy-and-cctv-a-guide-to-the-privacy-act-for-businesses-agencies-and-organisations.

[10] Attorney-Generals Department. Protective security policy framework downloads. 2010. Available at: http://www.ema.gov.au/www/agd/agd.nsf/Page/ProtectiveSecurityPolicyFramework_ProtectiveSecurityPolicyFrameworkDownloads.

18

Information Technology Systems Infrastructure*

Thomas Norman, CPP

This chapter provides a brief introduction to TCP/IP (Transport Control Protocol/Internet Protocol, the basic protocol of design systems) for the novice designer, with an overview of design, construction management, and system commissioning. The TCP/IP suite of basic protocols is explained, along with a detailed description of how TCP/IP works.

INTRODUCTION

This may be one of the most important sections in the book. The designer who does not thoroughly understand TCP/IP is at a severe disadvantage in design, in construction management, and in system commissioning. The designer is at the mercy of installers and physics, both of which can harm him or her. Not understanding TCP/IP is like not being able to read or write. This is not a comprehensive tome on TCP/IP. I suggest that the reader buys several other books on the subject. This description is intended for the novice designer.

BASICS OF TRANSPORT CONTROL PROTOCOL/INTERNET PROTOCOL AND SIGNAL COMMUNICATIONS

TCP/IP is the basic protocol of digital systems. From the understanding of that protocol, all knowledge about digital systems flows.

How Transport Control Protocol/Internet Protocol Works

The purpose of TCP/IP is to guide information from one place to another on a digital network. In the beginning, when computers were owned only by the government, military, universities, and really big business (banks and insurance companies), computers were not networked. Universities and the military held discussions on how to network their machines. The first network, called ARPANET, was developed in 1969 using Network Control Protocol, an early predecessor to TCP/IP. Although this permitted limited communications, several problems were evident, mainly that computers could only talk to other computers of the

---

*Originally from Integrated Security Systems Design. Thomas Norman : Butterworth-Heinemann, 2015. Updated by the editor, Elsevier, 2016.

Effective Physical Security, Fifth Edition
http://dx.doi.org/10.1016/B978-0-12-804462-9.00018-X

same manufacturer using the same operating system and software. This was not good since the whole idea was to allow communication, not to limit it. After several iterations, TCP/IP evolved. I will not go into the entire long story; you can look that up on Google under "TCP/IP history." TCP/IP is really two separate protocols. TCP is the Transport Control Protocol, and IP is the Internet Protocol. TCP was developed in 1974 by Kahn and Cerf and was introduced in 1977 for cross-network connections. TCP was faster, easier to use, and less expensive to implement. It also ensured that lost packets would be recovered, providing quality of service to network communications. In 1978, IP was added to handle routing of messages in a more reliable fashion. TCP communications were encapsulated within IP packets to ensure that they were routed correctly. On the receiving end, the TCP packets were unpacked from their IP capsules. Experts quickly realized that TCP/IP could be used for virtually any communication medium, including wire, radio, fiber, and laser, as well as other means. By 1983, ARPANET was totally converted to TCP/IP, and it became known as the Internet.

Transport Control Protocol/Internet Protocol Operates on Open Systems Interconnection Levels 3 (IP) and 4 (TCP)

One of the basic functions of networking involves the process of layering communications. Like making a sandwich, one cannot begin by spreading mayonnaise on one's hand. You have to put it on bread. Then you add the meat, lettuce, pickles, and so forth, and finally a last layer of bread. Network communications are like that. To send a packet of video, audio, or data, one must build up a series of layers. At the other end, those layers are taken off until the packet is ready for viewing or listening. There are seven layers to the Open Systems Interconnection (OSI) reference model. Each layer adds a protocol. Dick Lewis (Lewis Technology, www.lewistech.com/rlewis/Resources/JamesBondOSI2.aspx) uses an example of James Bond to describe how the seven layers work (Fig. 18.1). The following is his description:

> James Bond meets Number One on the seventh floor of the spy headquarters building. Number One gives Bond a secret message that must get through to the U.S. Embassy across town.

7 Layers of the OSI Model					
Layer #	Layer	Functions	Methods	Transmit	Receive
7	Application	Communication Partners Identified, Quality of Service Identified, User Authentication, Data Syntax	E-Mail, Network Software, Telnet, FTP	⬇	⬆
6	Presentation	Encryption	Encryption Software	⬇	⬆
5	Session	Establishes and Terminates Network Sessions between Devices and Software Requests	CPU Process	⬇	⬆
4	Transport	Error Recovery and Flow Control	CPU Process	⬇	⬆
3	Network	Switching and Routing, Network Addressing, Error Handling, Congestion Control, and Packet Sequencing	Switcher, Router	⬇	⬆
2	Data Link	Data Packets Encoded/Decoded into Bits	Media Access Control (MAC) and Logical Link Control (LLC)	⬇	⬆
1	Physical	Electrical, Light, or Radio Bit Stream	Cables, Cards, Ethernet, RS-232, ATM, 802.11a/b/g	⬇	⬆

FIGURE 18.1 OSI layers.

Bond proceeds to the sixth floor, where the message is translated into an intermediary language, encrypted, and miniaturized.

Bond takes the elevator to the fifth floor, where security checks the message to be sure it is all there and puts some checkpoints in the message so his counterpart at the U.S. end can be sure he's got the whole message.

On the fourth floor, the message is analyzed to see if it can be combined with some other small messages that need to go to the U.S. end. Also, if the message was very large it might be broken into several small packages so other spies can take it and have it reassembled on the other end.

The third-floor personnel check the address on the message and determine who the addressee is and advise Bond of the fastest route to the embassy.

On the second floor, the message is put into a special courier pouch (packet). It contains the message, the sender, and destination ID. It also warns the recipient if other pieces are still coming.

Bond proceeds to the first floor, where Q has prepared the Aston Martin for the trip to the embassy.

Bond departs for the U.S. embassy with the secret packet in hand. On the other end, the process is reversed. Bond proceeds from floor to floor, where the message is decoded.

The U.S. ambassador is very grateful the message got through safely.

Bond, please tell Number One I'll be glad to meet him for dinner tonight.

The important point to understand is that in any network today, each packet is encapsulated (enclosed) seven times and, when received, is decapsulated seven times. Each encapsulation involves checking and packaging to make the trip a sure and safe one for the data. Each decapsulation reverses that process:

- Data begin its trip at layer 7, the application layer, which includes software programs, Microsoft Word, and so forth.
- It is passed down to layer 6, the presentation layer, which adds data compression, encryption, and other similar manipulations of the data.

- It is then passed down to layer 5, the session layer, which provides a mechanism for managing the dialog between the two computers, including starting and stopping the communications and what to do if there is a crash.
- From there, it goes to layer 4, the transport layer (TCP), which ensures reliable communications between the machines. The packet changes from data to segments in the TCP layer.
- Down to layer 3, the network layer (IP), where error control and routing functions are described. The segments are combined or broken up into defined-sized packets at the IP layer. Routers are layer 3 devices.
- Down to layer 2, the data link layer, where functional and procedural means to transfer data between network entities and detection and correction of errors that could occur on the lowest layer take place. It is on this layer that the addressing of exact physical machines, each with its own media access control (MAC) address, is found. Each digital device attached to any network has its own unique MAC address, allowing sure identification that the device is authorized for connection to the communication or network. Network switches are layer 2 devices.
- Finally, down to layer 1, the physical layer, which includes cable, voltages, hubs, repeaters, and connectors.

TRANSPORT CONTROL PROTOCOL/USER DATAGRAM PROTOCOL/REAL-TIME PROTOCOL

One of the major advantages of TCP/IP is that it is able to fix bad communications. It does this by keeping track of packet lists for a given communication. Andrew G. Blank, author of

TCP/IP Foundations,[1] uses a wonderful illustration of a children's soccer team at a pizza parlor with an attached game arcade:

> Let's say that I take my son's soccer team to an arcade and restaurant for a team party. I have the whole team outside the arcade. My task is to get the team to the other side of the arcade, to my wife who is waiting for them in the restaurant. In this analogy, the team represents the complete file on one host, and each child represents a data packet. One of my goals is to lose as few of the kids as possible.

> While we are standing outside, it is easy to put the team in order; all the children are wearing numbered jerseys. I tell the kids that we will meet on the other side of the arcade in a restaurant for pizza and that they should all move as fast as possible through the arcade and to the restaurant.

> After I open the door and say "Go," the kids enter one at a time. Entering the arcade one at a time represents the fragmenting and sending of the file. Just as each of the kids has a numbered jersey, each packet has a number so that the receiving host can put the data back together.

> Now picture a dozen 6-year-olds moving through the arcade. Some of the children will take a short route; others will take a long route. Possibly, they'll all take the same route, though it is much more likely that they will all take different routes. Some will get hung up at certain spots, but others will move through faster. My wife is in the restaurant waiting to receive the team. As they start arriving at the restaurant, she can reassemble the children (packets) in the correct order because they all have a number on their backs. If any are missing, she will wait just a bit for the stragglers and then send back a message that she is missing part of the team (file).

> After I receive a message that she is missing a child (a packet), I can resend the missing part. I do not need to resend the entire team (all the packets), just the missing child (packet or packets).

> Please note, however, that I would not go look for the lost child; I would just put the same numbered jersey on a clone of the lost child and send him into the arcade to find the restaurant.

---

[1] This book is no longer available, but references to it still exist on a number of Internet web pages, most notably on www.wikipedia.com under the search string "OSI model."

TCP is designed to reconstruct lost packets so that an entire communication is intact. This is very important for files such as employee records, word processing files, and spreadsheets, where a missing packet can cause the whole file to be unreadable.

USER DATAGRAM PROTOCOL

For video and audio, another protocol is required. TCP can cause problems with audio and video files because its attempt to resend lost packets results in portions of the communication occurring out of place and therefore in the wrong sequence, making the video or audio communication intelligible. The human eye and ear are very good about rebuilding lost portions of communications. Imagine a restaurant in which you are overhearing a conversation at an adjacent table. You may not be able to hear the entire conversation—not every word because of the noise from others talking—but you can still follow what is being said.

Instead, what we need is a protocol that will send the data without error correction and without attempting to resend lost packets. That protocol is the User Datagram Protocol (UDP). UDP is called a connectionless protocol because it does not attempt to fix bad packets. It simply sends them out and hopes they arrive. The transmitting device has no way of knowing whether they do or not.

UDP and its partner, Real-Time Protocol (RTP), work together to ensure that a constant stream of data (hence the term "streaming data") is supplied for a receiving program to view or hear. RTP is used for audio and video. Typically, RTP runs on top of the UDP protocol.

As an industry default, all network data are called TCP/IP data, whether it is TCP/UDP or RTP. It is kind of like calling any tissue Kleenex or any copier a Xerox machine. It is not accurate; it is just that everyone does it.

Another important set of protocols that security designers will need to know about are unicast and multicast protocols. These are discussed in detail later in this chapter.

Transport Control Protocol/Internet Protocol Address Schemes

Each network device has a network card that connects that device to the network. The network interface card (NIC) has a MAC address and a TCP/IP address to identify itself to the network. The MAC address is hardware assigned at the factory when the device is manufactured. It can never be changed. The TCP/IP address is assignable, and it defines where in the network hierarchy the device is located. TCP/IP addresses are used to ensure that communication errors do not occur and that the address represents the logical location on the network where the device resides. TCP/IP addresses are like postal addresses, which identify where a house is on what street, in what neighborhood, in what city, in what state, and in what country. MAC addresses are like the name of the person who resides in the house. The MAC address will change if one replaces a computer with another, but the TCP/IP address can stay the same on the network for the user of the computer so that all messages to that user, worldwide, do not need a new MAC address to reach him or her.

There are two versions of TCP/IP addresses, which are known as IPv4 and IPv6. IP version 4 was the original version under which the whole Internet worked until it was determined that the number of available addresses would soon run out. So a larger array of numbers were defined, called IP version 6. IPv6 can accommodate a very large (virtually infinite) number of connected devices.

In IPv4, addresses are broken down into what is called decimal notation for the convenience of the user. Remember, each address is actually a series of binary data (ones and zeros), but they are grouped together in a fashion that is much easier to understand. Four groups are combined together, separated by decimals. Each group (byte) can be a number from 0 to 255 (a total of 256 numbers). This is an 8-bit value. A typical address can be from 0.0.0.0 to 255.255.255.255. IPv4 provides for in excess of 4 billion unique addresses. IPv6 replaces the 8-bit value with a 12-bit value (0.0.0.0 to 4095.4095.4095.4095). The IPv6 address range can be represented by a 3 with 39 zeros after it. It is a large number. IPv4 is still adequate for today's networks, but IPv6 is coming.

Briefly, the first one or two bytes of data, depending on the class of the network, generally will indicate the number of the network. The third byte indicates the number of the subnet and the fourth byte indicates the host (device) number on the network. The host cannot be either 0 or 255. An address of all zeros is not used because when a machine is booted that does not have a hardware address assigned to it, which provides 0.0.0.0 as it addresses until it receives its assignment. This would occur for machines that are remote booted (started up) or for those that boot dynamically using the Dynamic Host Configuration Protocol (DHCP). The part of the IP address that defines the network is called the network ID, and the latter part of the IP address is called the host ID.

Regarding the use of automatic or manual device addressing, we recommend manual addressing for security systems. DHCP incurs the possibility of security breaches that are not present with static addressing.

NETWORKING DEVICES

Security system digital networks are composed of five main types of network devices.

Edge Devices

Edge devices include digital video cameras, digital intercoms, and codecs. These are the devices that, for the most part, initiate the signals the rest of the system processes. One exception to this is that codecs can also be used to decode digital signals and turn them back into analog signals for viewing of digital video signals or listening to digital audio signals. The most common use of the decoding codec is for security intercoms, where an analog intercom module is a must to hear and speak from the console.

Communications Media

Digital signals are communicated along cable or wirelessly. The most common type of wired infrastructure is an Ethernet cabling scheme. Although other types exist (ring topology, etc.), none are prevalent. Ethernet is a wired scheme that allows many devices to compete for attention on the network. It is designed to handle collisions that occur when two or more devices want to talk simultaneously.

Devices contend for attention and are granted permission to speak while all other devices listen. Contention can slow a network, reducing its throughput. A network can be segmented by switches and routers to reduce contention and regain efficiency.

Ethernet is defined under IEEE[2] Standard 802.3. Ethernet classes vary by speed, with the slowest being 10Base-T [10 megabits per second (Mbps)]. Fast Ethernet is called 100Base-T and operates at 100 Mbps. Gigabit or 1000Base-T operates at 1 gigabit per second (Gbps). Wiring distances depend on wire type and speed. Ethernet is wired using unshielded twisted pair four-pair wiring on RJ-45 connectors. Category 5 or 5e (Category 5 Enhanced) wiring is used for 10Base-T, 100Base-T, and 1000Base-T (up to 328 ft). Category 6 wire is useful for 1000Base-T runs up to 328 ft. For 1000Base-T connections, all four pairs are used, whereas for 100Base-T connections, only two pairs of wires are used.[3]

Category 5, 5e, and 6 cables use four pairs, where the colors are the following:

- Pair 1—white/blue
- Pair 2—white/orange
- Pair 3—white/green
- Pair 4—white/brown.

The second most common type of wired infrastructure is fiber optic. These come in two types: single mode and multimode. When told that the difference between the two is the number of signals they can carry, newbies often think that the single mode will carry one and the multimode will carry more. In fact, just the opposite is true.

Single-mode fiber is based on a laser, whereas multimode may use either a laser or a light-emitting diode (LED) for a signal source (Fig. 18.2). Multimode fiber is typically plastic, whereas single-mode fiber is made of glass. Multimode fiber has a large cross-sectional area relative to the wavelength of the light transmitted through it, typically either 50 or 62.5 μm (micron) fiber diameter compared to 1.3 μm for 1300 nm modulated light frequency. Accordingly, multimode bounces the light off the inside of the fiber (Fig. 18.3). As the light bounces off the walls of the fiber, it takes many different paths to the other end, which can result in multiple signals at the other end. The result is a softening or rounding of the square digital signal. Over distance, the signal becomes more difficult to read at the receiver—thus the limited distance of multimode fiber.

Distance is also a factor of bandwidth. You can use multimode at longer distances with less speed. Fast Ethernet (100 Mbps) can travel farther than gigabit Ethernet (1000 Mbps). Check the manufacturer's specification sheets both for the fiber and transceivers you intend to use for exact limits based on speed.

---

[2] The Institute of Electrical and Electronics Engineers (IEEE) is the world's leading professional association for the advancement of technology.

[3] Hewlett-Packard, 1000Base-T gigabit Ethernet tutorial. September 15, 2000. Available at: http://www.docs.hp.com/en/784/copper_final.pdf.

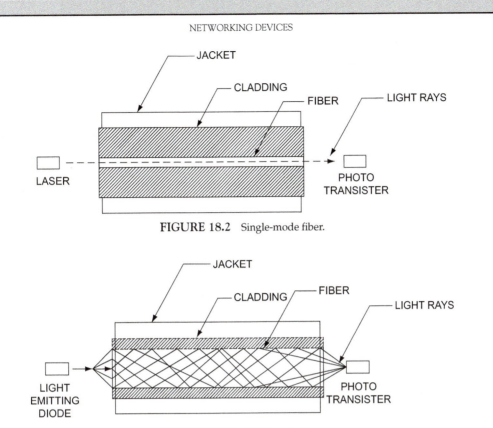

FIGURE 18.2 Single-mode fiber.

FIGURE 18.3 Multimode fiber.

Single-mode fiber is made of glass, and it pipes the laser directly down the middle of the glass tube like a waveguide.[4] This is because single-mode fiber has a small cross-sectional area (8 or 9 μm) relative to the frequency of the light

transmitted through it (1.3 μm at 1300 nm). The laser can carry multiple signals on its carrier.

The most commonly used frequencies are 1550, 1310, and 850 nm. The 1550 and 1310 nm frequencies are very common to single-mode fiber, and 850 nm is most commonly used in multimode fiber. The 1310 and 1550 nm frequencies are exclusively transmitted using lasers, and the 850 nm frequency is exclusively transmitted using LEDs. By using multiple frequencies (1310 and 1550 nm), it is possible to transmit and receive bidirectionally over a single fiber. Although this is not a common practice, some transceivers can accommodate two frequencies on a single fiber, especially with single-mode fiber. Typically, 1300 nm is used to send and 1550 nm is used to receive at one end and vice versa at the other end. More commonly, bidirectional communication is accommodated by

---

[4] A waveguide is a structure that guides very high-frequency radio waves (radar, microwave, etc.) down a tube from a transmitter to an antenna or from a receiving antenna to a receiver. Above normal radio frequencies, conventional wires are useless for carrying the signal because of the "skin effect." The skin effect is an effect of physics that results in radio waves traveling increasingly closer to the outside of a conductor as the frequency rises, eventually losing connection with the conductor altogether. Above that frequency, a waveguide must be used to contain the transmission because normal wiring is unusable. The low-frequency cutoff of a waveguide is half of the wavelength of the frequency being passed. Generally, waveguides are useful above 1 GHz.

using two separate fibers on the same frequency. No standard has been developed for multiple frequencies on a single fiber on multimode cable, but at least one security fiber optic company has developed a fiber optic media converter that can both transmit and receive on a single multimode fiber using two separate frequencies.[5]

Manufacturers have long since surpassed the IEEE 802.3z standard in terms of the distances served. Multimode fiber distances are typically limited to 1640 ft for fast Ethernet connections. Gigabit speeds are commonly limited to 1000 ft. Single-mode fiber distance limitations vary and can commonly be 43–62 miles with economical equipment;[6] much farther distances are possible (up to 500 miles) with more sophisticated media converters.[7] With commonly available equipment, it is possible to achieve distances of up to 93 miles with single-mode or multimode at 100Base-T speeds and 75 miles at 1000Base-T speeds.[8]

[5] The American Fibertek 47-LX series 1000Base-LX Ethernet Fiber Optic Media Converter uses a single multimode fiber and transmits and receives on two frequencies (1310 and 1550 nm). This company also makes a 100Base-LX converter "45-LX series." Both units use a laser to transmit and receive on a single multimode fiber. This company also makes LED two-fiber single-mode and multimode solutions, as do many other firms.

[6] Cisco Gigabit Interface Converter 1000Base-ZX GBIC media converter using premium single-mode fiber or dispersion shifted single-mode fiber.

[7] Goleniewski L. Telecommunication essentials: the complete global source for communications fundamentals, data networking and the Internet, and next generation networks. Reading, MA: Addison-Wesley; 2001.

[8] For example, FibroLAN TX/FX H.COM 10/100 provides 100Base-T speeds up to 93 miles (150 km) over single mode or multimode. Their GSM1000 and GSM1010 provide gigabit speeds up to 75 miles (120 km) over single mode or multimode. Prices vary from a few hundred to a few thousand dollars, depending on the range required.

Finally, single-mode transceivers and fiber are more costly than their comparable multimode equivalents. The cost delta can be vast. Use multimode for shorter distances (e.g., on a campus) or where cost is a factor. However, the cost delta can sometimes be worth it if there is available single-mode fiber in the ground on a campus and the only cost to mount up the system is that of the transceivers.

Gigabit switches and routers are usually supplied with single- or multimode fiber ports. This is the preferred connectivity method over the use of separate transceivers.

TCP/IP signals can also be communicated via radio, microwave, or laser. The most common type of radio communication network is in the 802.11 band. 802.11 is available in two major categories: backhaul or client service. The backhaul type is delivered by 802.11a, whereas client services are often provided by 802.11b/g/i. 802.11a makes available 10 channels, and with the correct antennas one can use all 10 channels in the same airspace. 802.11b/g/i are very similar but differ by the bandwidth provided and the level of security implemented. 802.11b provides 11 Mbps maximum, whereas 802.11g/i provide 54 Mbps. It is possible to find 802.11g devices that provide 108 Mbps. These are full-duplex devices that use a separate transmitter and receiver to double the bandwidth. This function is very common in 802.11a, which also provides 54 Mbps per available channel. 802.11b/g/i have 13 available channels, but cross-traffic is a problem. Do not plan to use more than six channels in a single airspace.

NETWORK INFRASTRUCTURE DEVICES

Network infrastructure devices comprise those devices that facilitate the movement of data along the communication media. Digital cameras and codecs connect to a digital switch to get on the network.

Hubs

The most basic type of network device is a hub. A hub is simply a device with Ethernet connectors that connects all devices together in parallel with no processing. A few hubs have power supplies and provide LEDs to indicate port activity but do not confuse this with active electronics. Hubs are dumb. Hubs have no ability to control the collisions that naturally occur in Ethernet environments, so when too many devices are connected together on a hub, the network throughput suffers due to delays caused by the collisions. It is inadvisable to use a hub for all but the simplest networks (less than eight devices). Hubs offer no security services, are OSI level 1 devices, and connect devices.

Switches

A switch is a smart hub. Unlike a hub that presents each signal to all connected devices, a switch is able to read the TCP/IP packet header and direct the signal to the appropriate port(s). Switches are OSI level 2 devices and control where data may go.

Routers

Routers are one step up from switches. In addition to directing the traffic of individual ports, they can in fact make decisions about data that are presented to them and can decide if that data belong to that section of the network. Routers can create subnets of the greater network. This allows functions and devices to be segmented into logical groups. Subnets reduce the overall amount of network traffic, making the network to operate more efficiently. Subnets can be used to separate different sites, campuses, and buildings and are sometimes even used to separate edge devices from client workstations. Routers control what data may go.

Firewalls

Firewalls are used with routers to deny inappropriate data traffic from another network. Firewalls can be configured in either hardware or software. Security systems that are connected to any other network should be connected through a firewall. Otherwise, a security system is not secure and thus, the facility will not be secure. Firewalls deny malicious data.

Intrusion Detection Systems

Intrusion detection systems (IDSs) can also be either hardware or software devices. They continuously monitor the traffic into and out of the network to detect any unauthorized attempt to gain access to the network. The IDS will warn the network administrator of the attempt and provide insight into how the attack attempt was executed to adjust the firewall to limit future attempts using that method. IDSs warn the system administrator about attempts to probe the network or insert malicious data.

SERVERS

Servers process and store data for use by workstations. For security systems, there are several possible types of servers. These may be combined on a single machine or may be distributed across several physical servers.

Directory Service Server

The directory service is an index for all workstations to use to find the data for which they are searching. It tells them where to find the correct camera, intercom, or archive stream. Additional functions may include Internet information services (IISs), domain name service (DNS), and other network management services.

Archive Service

The archive server stores data for future reference.

Program Service

The program service allows programs to reside on the server rather than on the workstation. This is not recommended because the few dollars saved results in a slower system.

FTP or HTTP Service

This is very useful for remote monitoring and retrieval of data from a remote site to a central monitoring station, for example, or for a manager to "look in" on a site.

E-mail Service

Servers can send or manage e-mail.

Broadcast Service

Servers can broadcast alerts or alarms to pagers, cell phones, loudspeakers, printers, and so forth.

Workstations

Workstations provide a human interface to the network. Workstations can be single purpose or multiuse, serving other types of programs and other networks. For large sites, it is often best to use single-purpose machines on a dedicated network. Workstations can support many video monitors to display digital video, alarm/access control, intercom, report and analysis software, browser, and so forth. We often design systems that have up to six monitors per workstation. It is also possible to operate more than one workstation with a single keyboard and mouse to support more functions than a single workstation can handle. This is often necessary for systems that do not prioritize intercom audio over video.

Printers

Printers can be connected to a workstation or directly to the network, where they can serve multiple workstations.

Mass Storage

Digital video systems can store a lot of data—much more data than any other type of system. It is not unusual for us to design systems with many terabytes of video storage. This amount of storage cannot be contained in a single server or workstation. There are two ways of extending the storage: network attached storage (NAS) and storage area networks (SANs). The names are so similar that they can be confusing, but the differences are extensive.

NAS units include a processor and many disk or tape drives (or a combination of both). They are typically configured to "look" like a disk drive to the system, and they connect directly to the network, just like a server or a workstation. This means that a large volume of data traffic is on the network to feed the NAS.

A SAN is on its own network to separate the vast amount of traffic it generates away from the common network. This is a good idea, even for small systems. SANs can be created easily by adding a second NIC to the archive server and connecting the SAN to that NIC.

NETWORK ARCHITECTURE

Simple Networks

The simplest networks connect two devices together on a cable (Fig. 18.4). Basic networks connect several devices together on a single switch. This creates a local area network (LAN) (Fig. 18.5). From there, tree architecture is common. There may be a single workstation/server (one computer serving both purposes) that is connected through one or more switches to a

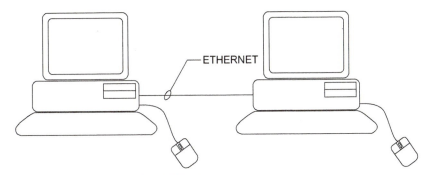

FIGURE 18.4   Simple network.

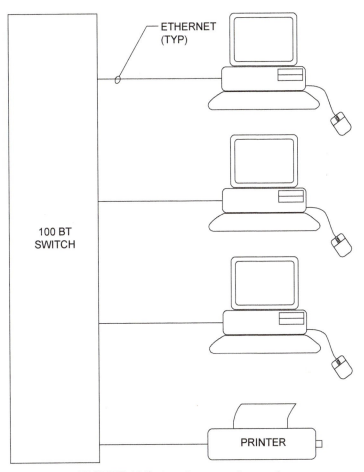

FIGURE 18.5   Switch connected network.

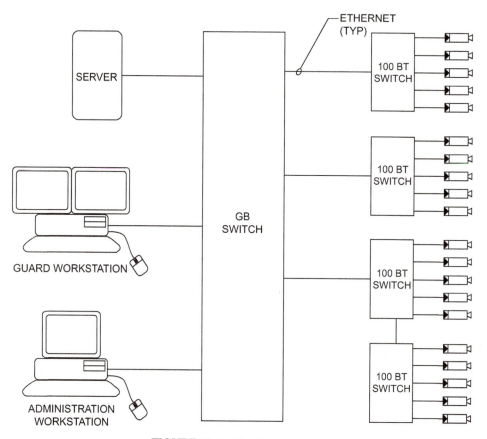

FIGURE 18.6 Simple tree network.

number of cameras, intercoms, codecs, access control panels, and so forth (Fig. 18.6).

Advanced Network Architecture

Backhaul Networks

Beyond simple tree architecture, as network size grows, it is common to create a backhaul network and a client network. This can be achieved in its simplest form with gigabit switches. A simple gigabit switch is equipped with a number of fast Ethernet (100 Mbps) ports to connect edge devices, such as cameras, codecs, intercoms, or access control panels, and a backhaul connection that supports gigabit (100 Mbps) speeds.

The result looks like an organization chart in which the server/workstation is at the top on the gigabit backhaul network and the edge devices (clients) are on the 100 Mbps ports of the switches (Fig. 18.7).

Subnets

A subnet is basically virtual LAN (VLAN) that is a logical subset of the overall LAN.

Subnets are used for several reasons, the most common of which are to limit network bandwidth to manageable levels or to minimize traffic that is not appropriate for certain devices, such as segregating buildings on a campus.

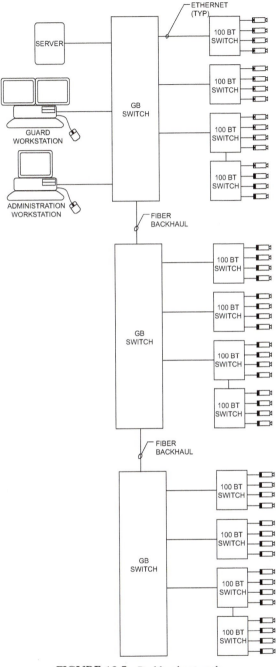

FIGURE 18.7 Backhaul network.

Subnets to Limit Network Traffic

As network bandwidth increases, it can task the switches to a point at which they begin to drop packets. I recommend that you do not pipe more than 45% of the rated bandwidth of any device because the rated bandwidths are based on normal network traffic, not streaming data such as video. Stay under 45% and you will not usually experience problems. A VLAN is created by joining two or more networks by routers.

Typically, routers are placed on the backhaul network, and they in turn may have their own backhaul networks that serve many edge devices. Architected thus, no single subnet will have too much traffic on it (Fig. 18.8).

Subnets to Segregate Network Traffic

When a security system serves many buildings on a campus, it is not useful to have the traffic of one building on the network of others. So each building can be joined to the main backhaul network through a router such that its traffic is limited only to data that are relevant to that building alone (Fig. 18.9).

The security system could be placed on the larger organization's network as a subnet. Subnets can be integrated onto a larger network in a way that would seem by their physical connections to be blending the two networks, whereas in fact they operate as completely segregated networks, totally isolated from each other by routers and firewalls. Be advised that enterprise security systems using large amounts of digital video can tax the bandwidth of virtually any organization's business network architecture to the breaking point.

It is often advisable to physically segregate the networks. Additionally, when the security system is placed on the organization's network, significant additional effort is required to secure the security system network from the organization's network, which will never likely be as secure as the security system network, notwithstanding the assertions of the organization's information technology department (Fig. 18.10).

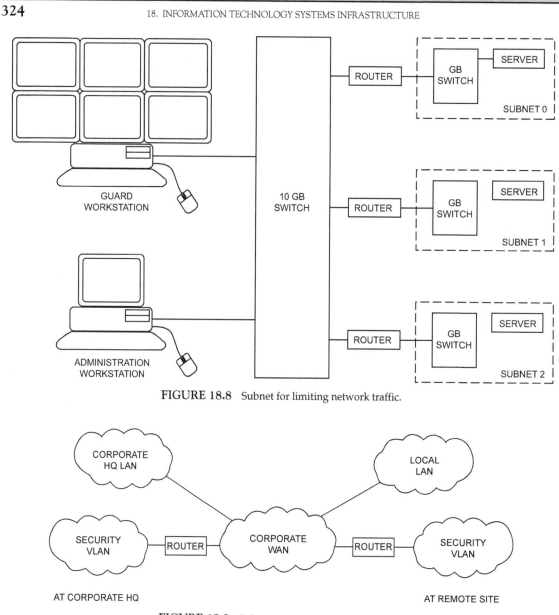

FIGURE 18.8 Subnet for limiting network traffic.

FIGURE 18.9 Subnet to segregate network traffic.

Virtually Local Area Networks

VLANs are global subnets. Like a subnet, a VLAN segregates a data channel for a specific purpose or group. Unlike a subnet, which is a hierarchical daughter of a physical LAN, a VLAN can coexist across the mother LAN as a VLAN as though there were two separate sets of hardware infrastructure. It does this by operating on a dedicated port to which only the VLAN has privileges. Therefore, cameras, intercoms, and access control system controllers can be plugged into the same managed switch with

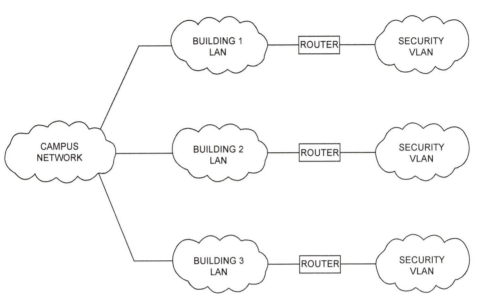

FIGURE 18.10   Subnet used to blend networks.

workstations and printers of the organization's business LAN, and when the security devices' ports are dedicated to a security VLAN, those devices will not be apparent or accessible to the users or the LAN. This is one of the best methods for sharing networks between security and business units.

NETWORK CONFIGURATIONS

A network is composed of a series of TCP/IP devices connected together. There are different ways to do this, and each has its own advantages and limitations.

Peer-to-Peer

The most basic network is a stand-alone peer-to-peer network. Peer-to-peer networks are created by connecting each device together through a hub or switch. Each computer, codec, or access control panel is equal in the eyes of the switch. This is adequate for very small networks (Fig. 18.11).

Client/Server Configuration

As network sizes expand, a client/server configuration is preferred. Major processing is performed in one or more servers, and the human interface is accommodated with client devices or workstations (Fig. 18.12). Cameras, intercoms, access control readers, locks, door position switches, request-to-exit devices, alarm-triggering devices, and so forth are all human interface devices, as are guard and lobby workstations, intercom master stations, and so forth.

Typically, the human interface devices are connected to processing devices that interface to the network via TCP/IP connection, usually Ethernet. These may include codecs and alarm/access control panels.

On larger networks, it is common to use multiple servers. Commonly, there will be multiple archive servers.

It is also common to use a second set of servers as a backup to the primary servers in case of a disaster that disables the primary servers. This allows for remote access to the data up to

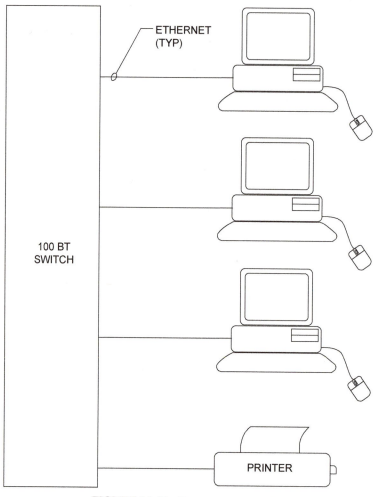

FIGURE 18.11   Peer-to-peer network.

the second of the disaster to analyze the event and to provide a business continuity record of all network data.

CREATING NETWORK EFFICIENCIES

One of the major advantages of enterprise security systems is the opportunity for remote monitoring of distant buildings. This often requires blending the security system network with the organization's business network.

The most common requirement is to monitor remote sites. It is not necessary to send all of the data from the monitored site to the site doing the monitoring. The monitoring center only needs to see the data it wants to look at. When you are watching a sports broadcast on TV on channel 11, you do not usually care much about the opera playing on channel 4. Likewise, it is advisable to attach the remote monitoring center only to those data that are relevant at the moment. You do not need to send the video of all the cameras all the time. Using this method, great efficiencies can be gained. Overall network bandwidth can

CLIENTS

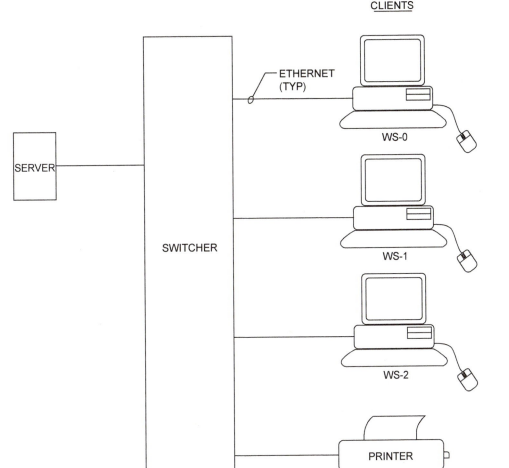

FIGURE 18.12 Client/server network.

be limited only to the cameras being monitored. I use cameras as an example here because they consume the most bandwidth.

There are two very efficient ways to remotely monitor over a business network: browser and virtual private network (VPN). A browser connection is quick, easy, and does not consume any bandwidth when it is not sending data. It consumes only what it displays. One can configure simple monitoring centers with browser connections to the remotely monitored sites. When one wants to see the site, one makes the connection; otherwise, the connection is closed. However, browser connections consume data even when minimized, whether or not the data are sent to the screen. This will consume both network bandwidth and workstation processing power. So it is advisable to close browsers when not being viewed. Alarms can be sent on a separate data link to alarm-monitoring software that is always open. These consume virtually no bandwidth, so they can stay open at all times. Browsers should be run under https rather than http (https is a higher security environment), and secure socket layer encryption is often

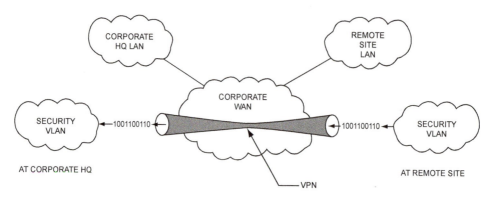

FIGURE 18.13   Virtual private network.

advisable to ensure the security of the system being monitored. Even so, browsers are not as secure as VPNs. Browser connections can be hacked.

A VPN can open and close like a browser, but it has vast advantages in terms of network security. A VPN is a tunnel between the server being monitored and the server that is requesting its data. That tunnel is firewalled and encrypted. It is as good as gold for security. It takes extremely high skill levels to hack a VPN. The disadvantage of VPNs is that they utilize a fixed bandwidth. When a VPN connection is open, that amount of bandwidth is in use regardless of the number of cameras being monitored.

That bandwidth is no longer available for the business network connection to that site (Fig. 18.13).

DIGITAL VIDEO

Cameras and Codecs

Digital video cameras are available in two types: digital cameras or analog cameras with digital codec converters. Digital cameras are an emerging trend. The predominance of cameras available are still analog, and to use them in a digital video system, one must add a codec.

Digital cameras do not provide a baseband video output (PAL or NTSC). They are equipped with either a USB or Ethernet connection. They issue digital images directly.

A codec is a device that converts analog to digital. There are different codec types, in the following categories:

Number of channels. Single-channel codecs support only one camera. Multiple-channel codecs support multiple cameras. Single-channel codecs are the best choice when the wiring infrastructure is predominantly digital, and multiple-channel codecs are a good choice when most of the wiring is analog. Multiple-channel codecs facilitate wiring a number of cameras to a single point where perhaps an analog video switch used to be, its space now being occupied by codecs.

Number of video data streams. Many codecs output only one data stream per camera. Some support two, which is better. Each data stream can typically be configured to adjust the frame rate and resolution. With two data streams, you can adjust one for live viewing and the second for archiving. You might adjust the live viewing data stream at, for example, 15 frames per second (fps) and at medium resolution and the second stream at 4 fps and high resolution. Generally, it is desirable for archiving retrievals to display higher resolution than for live viewing, since you are looking for detail rather than just a transient image.

Audio/no audio. Some codecs support an audio channel and some do not. The audio channel will be its own separate data stream, usually under the same TCP/IP address.

Input and output contacts. Many codecs also provide one or more dry-contact inputs and outputs. These are useful to control nearby devices or to cause some activation in the system. For example, they could be used to unlock a door or to cause an alert if a door opens.

Compression schemes. Different codecs use different compression schemes, which are discussed later.

A basic digital image such as a BMP (bitmap) is composed of a large number of picture elements called pixels, with each pixel having its own data attributes. These images take up a lot of data space. It is common for a single BMP image to require several megabits of data. These large files are not useful for network transmission because they use too much network bandwidth. The images can be compressed (made into smaller packets) literally by throwing away useless data.

There are two major types of digital video compression schemes: JPEG and MPEG. JPEG (Joint Photographic Experts Group) is a scheme that results in a series of fixed images, strung together like a movie. MPEG (Moving Pictures Experts Group) is a similar group that from its inception created compression algorithms specifically meant for moving pictures.

- MPEG-1 was the earliest format and produced video CDs and MP3 audio.
- MPEG-2 is the standard on which digital television set-top boxes and DVDs are based. This is very high-quality video.
- MPEG-3 (MP3) is an audio codec.
- MPEG-4 is the standard for multimedia for the fixed and mobile web.
- MPEG-7 and MPEG-21 also exist but are for future projects.

Digital video security codecs and cameras are typically MJPEG (a series of JPEG images strung together as a stream of data) or MPEG-4.

BMP images are resolution dependent; that is, there is one piece of data for each separate pixel.

JPEG compression basically replicates similar data rather than storing it. For example, if there were a picture of a flag, the red portion might only be stored in a single pixel, but there will be a note to replicate the red pixel everywhere it existed in its original BMP file. This can achieve very high compression compared to BMP files.

MPEG compression takes this process one step further. For a sequence of images, the first one is stored as a JPEG image, and each subsequent image stores only the differences between itself and the previous image. The first frame is called an "I-frame," and subsequent frames are called "P-frames." When too much updating is occurring, the process stores a new I-frame and starts the process all over again. The MPEG protocol results in very efficient file compression.

Advantages and Disadvantages

Each JPEG image is a new fresh image. This is very useful where the frame rate must be very low, such as on an offshore oil platform with a very low bandwidth satellite uplink, or where only a dial-up modem connection is available for network connectivity. I used JPEG on an offshore platform with only a 64 kb/s satellite connection available. MPEG is most useful where there is adequate data bandwidth available for a fast-moving image but where it is desirable to conserve network resources for future growth and for network stability.

DIGITAL RESOLUTION

Digital image resolution is the bugaboo of digital video. You can never have enough resolution. However, high resolution comes at a high price in network bandwidth usage and in hard disk storage space. There is always a

FIGURE 18.14   Fuzzy JPG image.

SQCIF 128 X 96	
QCIF - 176 X 120	
CIF - 352 X 240	
2CIF - 704 X 288	
4CIF - 704 X 488	

FIGURE 18.15   MPEG resolutions.

trade-off between resolution and bandwidth/ storage space. Thankfully, the cost of storage keeps dropping (I think we will soon see terabyte hard drives blister-packed for 99 cents), but I think that network bandwidth will always be a problem.

JPEG resolution is measured in pixels per inch (PPI). Proper resolution is required for good viewing. Ideally, you should be displaying one pixel of video image onto each pixel on the video monitor. If you display a JPEG image at a greater size on paper or screen than its native resolution, you will see a very fuzzy image (Fig. 18.14). Common file sizes are from 120×160 to 720×480. Larger sizes are available with even higher resolution.

MPEG resolution is measured in common intermediate format (CIF). In NTSC, CIF provides 352×240 pixels. In PAL, it provides 352×288 pixels. The lowest resolution MPEG image is a quarter CIF (QCIF) at 176×120 pixels, followed by CIF, 2CIF (704×240, NTSC), and (704×288, PAL), and finally 4CIF (704×480, NTSC) and (704×576, PAL). 16CIF will soon be available with very high resolution (1408×1152 for both formats), and there is also an amazingly low resolution SQCIF (128×96, NTSC). Most digital codecs provide CIF, 2CIF, and sometimes 4CIF resolutions (Fig. 18.15).

FRAME RATES

To see moving images, they have to move. Frame rate is the rate at which one frame of video is replaced by another. The speed at which this occurs is measured in frames per second (fps). Some unique applications result in very slow frame rates of seconds per frame.

The human eye can visualize real-time motion as low as 12 or 13 fps. A minimum frame rate of 15 fps is recommended for real-time images. Many users prefer 30 fps because that is what is displayed on analog video. However, that frame rate is not required unless objects are moving rapidly.

Like resolution, frame rates affect both bandwidth and storage capacity in direct proportion to the fps.

DISPLAY ISSUES

Display Parity

Display parity is one of the problems that the security industry has not dealt with yet. This is achieved when the number of pixels sent to a screen is exactly the same as the number of pixels on the screen.

If one is displaying nine cameras in a window on a 20 in. LCD high-resolution screen, one might have only 160 × 120 pixels available on the screen for each image. Why would one want to send a 4CIF image (704 × 480) to that number of pixels? Why indeed? What happens to all those extra pixels? They are wasted, thrown away. The problem is that they are thrown away on the screen. They occupy tons (if that is a measure of screen processing) of central processing unit (CPU) and video card processing power before it gets thrown away on the LCD monitor.

No problem you say? Who cares? You do, if you are smart. Here is the problem. A 4CIF image generates 337,920 pixels. Each individual pixel requires a great deal of CPU processing power and many more graphics processing units (GPUs). Both CPUs and GPUs are consumed for each pixel. The original supercomputer, the Cray-1 developed at Los Alamos National Laboratory in 1976, was capable of 80 megaflops of processing power. (Flops is a unit of CPU or video card processing effort; it is an abbreviation of floating point operations per second.) Although there is not a direct correlation between flops and pixel processing (there are approximately 40 variables involved in the calculation, making a calculation essentially meaningless), you can rely on the fact that it takes a lot of processing power to process video to the screen or to archive. At 30 fps, the computer is processing 10,137,600 pixels (10.1 megapixels) for each image at 30 fps. Remember, we were displaying nine images that calculates to 91.2 megapixels per second, and that is just for the video. You are also running the video application, and on larger systems you are also processing audio for the intercom, alarm/access control, and perhaps other data. One can easily exceed 100 megapixels being processed per screen on one's desktop. For 16 images, at 30 fps at 4CIF, the number exceeds 160 megapixels being processed in real time, and that is just on one screen. That will crash virtually any workstation regardless of processing power. High-resolution times high frame rate times many images can easily equal a computer crash. Additionally, pixels thrown away on the screen present a rough look

to the images. Without a doubt, display parity results in the best appearance.

The ideal process here is to have software in the server that disposes of unneeded pixels before they are sent to the workstation. This approach of pre rendering the video image has many advantages in quality of display and network throughput. However, to date, no software vendor that we know of is even thinking about this problem.

So what is a designer to do? Well, there are only three variables available to manage this problem: image resolution, frame rate, and processing power.

First, there is little need to display images at 4CIF or greater unless one is displaying at full screen. It is better to send live images to the screen at 2CIF because the extra pixels will just be thrown away and no good will be served by the extra resolution that is consuming unneeded network bandwidth and processing power.

Second, archived images do not usually need to be displayed at 15 or 30 fps. Use a slower speed and higher resolution for archived video. When one calls up archived video, one is usually interested in seeing as much detail in the image as possible. Use higher resolution and lower frame rate. There are a few applications in which this is not appropriate, such as for casino environments, where fast-moving hands hold the secret to cheating.

Finally, I usually design systems with lots of processing power, typically dual Xeon computers as workstations. Dual core processors better that. Expected advances will put teraflops of graphics processing power at hand.

Storage Issues

As with display, storage consumes lots of data and processing power. Unless there is a compelling reason otherwise, it is best to store data at a slower frame rate than for live viewing. This not only saves disk and tape space but also helps ensure growth capacity.

MANAGING DATA SYSTEMS THROUGHPUT

Network throughput management requires math, sometimes lots of math, but it is a good investment. I do not recommend running any network or network segment beyond 45% of its rated capacity. If there is a segment that has a capacity of 100 Mbps, keep traffic to 45 Mbps. If it is a gigabit backhaul segment, keep the traffic to 450 Mbps. If you have to exceed 450 Mbps, it is better to use multiple gigabit communications paths or a 10 GB path. Your client will not likely understand, but he or she will not sue you either.

There are two ways of managing network throughput: more capacity and network segmentation. The cost/benefit is usually in favor of network segmentation.

By segmenting the network into subnets or VLANs, one can manage the traffic to manageable levels. All traffic does not have to be everywhere. By recording video remotely rather than centrally, traffic is diminished. If a backup is needed, or if there is a concern about the loss of data in remote storage, centralized recording is possible at far greater cost in network traffic and infrastructure cost. An alternative is "neighborhood" archiving, where a few sites are gathered together for storage, limiting traffic on the enterprise network.

SYSTEM ARCHITECTURE

Servers

Servers provide the guidance and direction for the entire system and store its activities and history. A server can operate several applications simultaneously, and a server equipped with a dual-core CPU can also prioritize those services, ensuring that, for example, intercom calls always go through. Servers provide several basic services.

Directory Service

The directory service provides the routing information to locate cameras, intercoms, and archived video on demand. It also maintains the necessary information for all system devices to communicate effectively.

Directory services can be local or global. In an enterprise integrated security system, the directory service may be both, with a global directory service centrally controlled, and local servers may maintain their own subordinate automatic failover directory services in case of loss of communications with the global directory server.

Enterprise-integrated security systems also typically use an automatic failover server that runs parallel to the main server but in another location, ready to take over its activities immediately upon a failure of the main server.

Archiving Data

The server will typically archive alarm/access control, video, and intercom activity, indexing it by date and time and often correlating video and voice data to alarm and security events so that the operator has immediate access to appropriate video and voice as he or she views alarm activity. Enterprise systems also typically use an automatic failover archive server.

Remote Access Services

Web Access

A VPN helps ensure data integrity for off-site web service connections. Remote access from within the domain is often accommodated by use of a VLAN.

E-mail and Pager Notification Service

The server software may support e-mail and pager notification. These will require exchange server or similar software or a dial-up or web connection for a pager.

Hardware Configurations

Central Processing Units

Generally, it is appropriate to specify the fastest or nearly fastest CPU available for the server with significant cache memory and a very fast front side bus.

Memory

More is better. At least 2 GB of RAM should be considered in 2007 era terms. As this book ages, more memory should be considered. Fill the thing to capacity. You will not regret it, and memory is almost cheaper than candy bars.

Disk Storage

Operating Systems and Programs

All system servers should be equipped with multiple disks, including two mirrored automatic failover drives for operating systems and programs, complete with current configurations. These should be kept up to date so if one fails, the other takes over immediately. This is also less expensive than a full hot redundant off-site failover server and should be done even when a redundant server is used.

Additional disk slots should be dedicated to data archive up to the server's capacity. Disks are so inexpensive that it is almost always appropriate to specify the largest disks available. RAID-5 should be considered and configured to 500 GB segments for rapid searching of archived data.

Where additional disk capacity is necessary, external storage capacity should be considered. There are two methods of external storage.

Tape or Disk

External storage is available in both tape and disk. It is generally recommended to use both. Disks can store up to a given time depth. Beyond that, you can store endlessly on tape. For very large storage requirements, a tape carousel automatically handles the process of keeping fresh tapes loaded and used tapes stored and ready for use. The carousel can be expanded to store as much or as little as is appropriate based on network archive usage and the length of time storage is desired.

Network Attached Storage

NAS is external storage that is attached directly to the server switch. This is the least expensive option, but it has a negative effect on network throughput. Accordingly, I do not recommend NAS.

Storage Area Network

A SAN is a separate network on the backside of the server that is dedicated only to moving storage data between servers and the external storage media. There is a perception that SANs are unnecessarily expensive, but this does not have to be the case. A SAN can be created simply by placing an additional NIC in the server and porting archive data out the back to the external storage. Where multiple servers or multiple external storage units are required, a SAN switch handles the task. SANs make the best use of the primary data network over which live data are flowing. They place virtually no additional burden on the live data network, conserving its spare capacity for system growth. SANs are always recommended for external storage, even if there is only one server and one external storage unit.

Workstations

A workstation is a computer used by a person who operates the system. There are various basic workstation types.

Security Monitoring (Command) Workstations

Security command workstations are used in security command centers, typically in enterprise security systems. A security command center typically includes two or more security command workstations and may include an array of large-screen video monitors to support the joint viewing of images by operators at several consoles. These workstations typically include alarm/access control/digital video and security intercoms as well as report writing programs.

Guard or Lobby Desk Workstations

A guard or lobby desk workstation is a single computer dedicated to supporting a guard's desk duties in a lobby. These may include alarm/access control, digital video, and intercom.

Administrative Workstations

An administrative workstation supports management of an integrated security system, including system configuration, database management, and reports.

Photo ID Workstations

Photo ID workstations are used to create identification badges for use with the access control system. A photo ID workstation typically includes a camera, backdrop, light source, sitting chair, digital camera, and workstation and may include a posing monitor to help the subject pose to his or her satisfaction. On larger systems, there may be several photo ID workstations in a single area.

Access Verification Workstations

On high-security installations, an access verification workstation may be used in conjunction with a mantrap and card reader to ensure that the person passing into a secure area is indeed who he or she claims to be and that his or her credential is valid for the secure area. The access verification workstation displays a photo of the cardholder each time a card is presented. This allows a guard at the workstation to verify that the face is that of the valid cardholder.

Edge Devices

Edge devices include cameras, intercoms, card readers, alarm detection devices, electrified door locks, and request-to-exit detectors. These are the devices that interface with the user. On a typical integrated security system, the edge device connects with a data controller or codec, which converts its native signal (audio/video, dry contact, or data) to a uniform TCP/IP standard. Thus, controllers and codecs are also edge devices. The edge devices typically connect to the system through a data switch.

Infrastructure Devices

Between edge devices and servers/workstations is the digital infrastructure, which connects the system together and manages its communications rules.

Switches

Digital switches are the connection points for almost all system devices. A digital switch is a device that not only provides a connection point but also can manage how each device communicates with the system. A digital switch is like a mail carrier on a mail route, who ensures that each house gets the mail that is addressed to it.

Switches can segregate communications between devices and manage the priority and limit the bandwidth of the data of different devices. Switches generally have a number of RJ-45 eight-conductor modular jacks (typically 8–48) and can cascade communications in a ring or tree architecture. The switch must be specified to support the amount of data that is expected to go into its edge ports and out of its infrastructure ports. It is wise not to exceed more than 45% of the rated capacity of any switch for all signals combined, under worst-case conditions. Switches are OSI layer 2 devices, but better switches can also perform OSI layer 3 management functions. These are commonly called "managed" switches. Switches should be able to support IGMP querying and IGMP snooping to support video multicast. Ample memory is recommended (at least 100 KB per port), and the switch should be able to support VLAN operation. If the switch may need to become part of a trunk within a VLAN, then it should also be able to support 802.1Q protocol. For outdoor operation, a robust environmental tolerance is needed. The switch should be able to operate from well below freezing (−10°F/−23°C) to high temperatures (160°F/70°C is ideal). These are commonly called "hardened" switches. Redundant power supplies are also recommended.

Routers

Routers manage data traffic at a more global level and are OSI level 3 devices. An edge router is like a local post office that routes mail from one locale to another, where it will be handed off to the neighborhood postal worker (the switch). A router that manages traffic for an entire organization to the Internet is called a core router.

Routers are capable of segregating traffic into subnets and VLANs, creating logical separations of data and making communications within the network much more efficient and secure.

Firewalls

A network firewall is a computing device that is designed to prevent communications from and to some devices in support of an organization's network security policy.

Wireless Nodes

Wireless nodes are radio frequency transceivers that support network communications. Often, they also incorporate network switches, and sometimes they can incorporate routers and even firewalls. They also commonly encrypt data placed on the wireless link.

Network Communications Speeds

There are four common speeds of network communications:

- 10Base-T: 10 Mbps
- 100Base-T: 100 Mbps
- 1000Base-T: 1 Gbps
- 10,000Base-T: 10 Gbps.

Cabling

Network cabling can be wired or fiber optic. Fiber optic cabling types include single mode and multimode.

Wired Cabling

Category 5e and 6 cables are used for network cabling. Both have a native distance limit of 300 ft. Cat5e and Cat6 cables can support 10Base-T, 100Base-T, and 1000Base-T connections, with distance decreasing as the speed increases.

Fiber Optic

Fiber optic cabling can support faster speeds, longer distances, and simultaneous communications. Unlike wired cable, fiber only supports a single communication on a single frequency at one time.

Multimode

Multimode fiber uses inexpensive LEDs operating at 850 or 1500 nm to transmit data. Multimode fiber is made of inexpensive plastic. In multimode fiber, the light propagates through the fiber core, bouncing off its edges (thus multimode). Multimode fiber can support only one communication at a time on each frequency. Typically, two fibers are used together, one to transmit and one to receive.

Single Mode

Single-mode fiber uses more expensive lasers and optical glass. Single-mode communication is right down the center of the glass fiber, never bouncing (thus single mode). Single-mode fiber can stand higher power and thus yields longer distances.

Scaling Designs

Systems can be scaled by creating subnets, which can segregate the system based on function or location. This approach allows the master system to have oversight and observation of the activities of all of its subsystems while not allowing the subsystems to see or affect each other.

INTERFACING TO OTHER ENTERPRISE INFORMATION TECHNOLOGY SYSTEMS

Enterprise Local Area Network or Wide Area Network

The fundamental interface of the integrated security system is to the organization's enterprise LAN or wide area network (WAN). The recommended interface is to configure the enterprise security system as a VLAN on the enterprise LAN/WAN.

Remote monitoring from inside the enterprise LAN can be accomplished by placing the monitoring computer on the VLAN. If the monitoring computer must also be used on the business network, it should be equipped with two NICs to better segregate the VLAN from the LAN.

Remote monitoring over the Internet should be accomplished by use of a VPN.

Process Control Networks

Integrated security systems are classified as process control networks. A process control network differs from a business network in that it is a closed network, dedicated to a special purpose, and is segregated from the business network. The integrated security system may integrate with other types of process control networks, including building automation systems (BASs), elevators, telephony systems, fire alarm systems, parking management systems, and vending systems.

Building Automation Systems

BASs include controls for HVAC, lighting, signage and irrigation control, and the control of other building systems. BASs may interface to the integrated security system via RS-232 or TCP/IP. The common interface language is ASCII delimited files, although sometimes database integration is possible.

Elevators/Lifts

There is often good reason to integrate security systems with the elevator system of a building. This interface permits the control of who goes to what floor on which elevator at what time. Additionally, it is common to place video cameras and intercoms within elevators.

There are two basic types of elevators: traction and hydraulic. Traction elevators are used in high-rise buildings, and hydraulic elevators are commonly used in low-rise buildings and parking structures.

Access Control Interfaces

There are two common types of elevator access control interfaces: floor-by-floor control and hall call control. Hall call control simply enables or disables the hall call pushbuttons in the elevator lobby. Floor-by-floor control allows control over the selection of individual floors in each car for each cardholder. Floor-by-floor control components include a card reader in the elevator and an access control system controller that enables or disables each floor select button based on the authorizations for the individual card presented to the reader in the car.

More sophisticated floor-by-floor access control systems provide an indication of which floors the card can select by turning off the button lights to floor select buttons for which the cardholder is not valid and may also keep a record of which floor was actually selected. Today, those functions are handled in the programming of the elevator controller. For older elevators, as was done in the past, those functions can be accomplished with elegant relay logic programming.

Elevator control mechanisms affect the design of the elevator access control system. There are three common types: automated, relay, and on-the-car control. These are covered in detail elsewhere in this book.

Video cameras can be interfaced up the hoistway by using coax, ribbon cable, laser, or radio frequency methods.

Intercoms can be the direct ring-down type or dedicated intercom type. They must ring to a location that will always be answered and must never be unmanned, even for a few minutes.

Private Automatic Branch Exchange Interfaces

Private automatic branch exchange (PABX) systems facilitate the connection of a number of analog or digital station sets to a central switch. The PABX switch will accommodate a number of central office telephone lines (from a couple to hundreds) and a number of telephone station sets (from six to thousands). The PABX switch routes incoming calls to the correct extension and routes outgoing calls to an available central office line.

Additional features of PABX switches may include direct inward dialing so that certain extensions can be dialed directly from the outside without going through the switch, an automated attendant, call waiting, voice mail, and many other unique features. Internal intercom functions are usually standard.

Station sets may be simple or complicated. Simple station sets may look like a home phone, whereas more complicated sets may display time/date and incoming caller ID. The set also may have many speed-dial buttons and may also show the line status of frequently called internal numbers. An operator's station set may

display the status of every extension in the system by a field of lamps and select buttons or in software.

PABX systems are normally controlled by a dedicated computer located in the main telephone closet. They are capable of sophisticated interfaces to other systems, including security systems.

The security designer can use the PABX system as a security intercom system by utilizing door stations in lieu of standard station sets (depending on the manufacturer and model of the PABX system).

For almost every installation, it is important for the security console to be equipped with a direct central office telephone that is not routed through the PABX switch. This serves as an emergency communication link in case of total power or equipment failure.

Voice Over IP Systems

PABX switch systems are rapidly being replaced by Voice over IP (VoIP) systems. VoIP systems do not rely on central office telephone lines for their connection to the telephone company. Rather, they utilize the Internet for that connection.

The telephone station sets may be either conventional station sets with a VoIP converter or network devices.

VoIP phone systems are extremely flexible since all of their functions operate in software. However, they suffer from two major potential problems relating to the security of the organization they serve. VoIP systems are subject to Internet outages, which are much more common than central office line outages that operate on battery power from the central office. With central office lines, if electrical power fails, it is likely that the telephone lines will still work. This is not the case with VoIP phones. Additionally, VoIP phone systems are subject to intrusion by skilled hackers, making communications on a VoIP phone extremely unsecure.

VoIP phones are a natural for integration with other systems, although those interfaces have yet to be developed by the industry.

VoIP systems should easily accommodate integration with IP-based security intercoms and with pagers. Digital two-way radios are also a natural point of integration.

Fire Alarm Systems

Fire alarm systems are among the oldest of process control networks used in commercial buildings. These typically have their own proprietary infrastructure that may be unique to the manufacturer. However, they often interface to other systems by means of RS-232 serial data streams or TCP/IP Ethernet. Typically, the interface is an ASCII delimited data stream that identifies the change of state of a fire alarm zone. Occasionally, a designer may see access to a database that displays real-time status of all points in the system.

Public Address Systems

Public address systems can be configured with an analog or a digital infrastructure. The interface to a public address system will always be a one-way audio signal from the security system to the public address system for paging purposes.

Typically, the interface between the systems includes an audio signal and a zone selection, plus a push-to-talk momentary trigger. The interface may be analog or digital. Typically, analog interfaces are used on smaller public address systems, and larger systems may receive an analog or a digital interface for the audio stream.

Analog interfaces employ a microphone or line level input to the paging system and one or more dry-contact inputs to select one or more zones. Often, it is possible to select groups of zones or an "All Call" selection, in which all zones will be paged.

Digital interfaces employ a digitized audio feed and a data string that performs the zone selection. On larger systems, both analog and digital, multiple public address amplifiers may be used to support different areas of a building or different buildings on a campus. In such cases, the zone selections employ a hierarchical zone selection, in which one string may select the building, another selects the amplifier, and still another selects the zone on the amplifier.

We have also used the alarm/access control system to perform zone selections, controlling a single audio buss. This is an effective way to make a simple public address system operate like a very expensive one.

Parking Control Systems

Parking control systems perform a number of functions:

- Allow vehicles into a parking structure (car park) or parking lot.
- Direct cars within a parking structure to one area or another.
- Meter the number of cars in the structure.
- Display up/down count signage of available spaces to drivers of cars entering.
- Produce tickets for cash transactions.
- Read the tickets and facilitate cash transactions for parking.
- Use buried vehicle-sensing loops to verify the presence of a car at a card reader or in the path of a barrier gate, or to notify the gate that it can close after a car has passed through.
- Access control systems interface with parking systems to facilitate the entry of cars to the parking area.
- Access control readers may simply provide a dry-contact closure to notify the gate to open.

The parking system may also feedback a dry-contact signal that causes the card reader to refuse to read cards if the parking area is full. Access control card readers may be short range (6 in.) or long range (3 ft), or they may be overhead vehicle tag readers that do not require the driver to roll down the window.

The access control system may also be integrated with the parking monthly cash control system such that the card is enabled or disabled based on payment of a monthly fee. The card readers may also permit special privileged parking for handicapped people, expectant mothers, high-rent tenants, high-level executives, and so forth.

Vending Access Management Systems

Vending access management systems are a variation of access control systems that are interfaced with a product vending system to provide product in kind for a prepayment or a charge account. In effect, the access control system is used like a credit or debit card.

Vending systems may include fuel management and vending machines, or the card may be used at a school bookstore, and so forth. This requires a database interface between the access control system and the vending system such that the vending system has daily status on the validity of the card and it keeps a running database of credits and debits.

More Protocol Factors

Wired and wireless digital security systems both use unicast and multicast protocols to communicate. Unicast protocols, commonly TCP/IP, are meant to communicate a signal from one device to another. They ensure that the communication occurs by verifying the receipt of every packet of data. Unicast protocol is commonly used for pure data, such as alarm and access control data. Most networks are inherently based on TCP/IP protocol.

Multicast protocols such as UDP/IP and RTP/IP are used to broadcast data to any number of receiving devices. Unlike unicast TCP data, if a packet is not received, there is no mechanism or attempt to verify that and resend the packet. Multicast is widely used for video and audio data.

Do not confuse multicast protocol with multipath. It is the phenomenon caused by radio frequency reflections, and multicast is the distribution of a single digital signal to more than one destination using a single signal to which each receiving device signs up on a subscription.

Multicast can both reduce and increase network traffic, depending on how the network is configured. Multicast can reduce network traffic because there is no attempt to resend data. It is sent only once. Especially for radio frequency and satellite systems, where latency (circuit delays) can be a factor, the receiving computer can make many requests for unreceived packets. This has the effect of increasing data traffic for no good purpose because the video frame or audio signal cannot be received in time to be useful, since it has already been displayed or heard.

However, because multicast transmits to any device that will listen, it is important to configure the network to adapt to multicast protocol so that devices that do not need to process the data will not hear it. Otherwise, many devices are kept busy trying to process data that is of no use to them. On security systems, some devices have a capability of only 10Base-T (10 Mbps). Their input can be swamped by the signals of only a few video cameras, rendering them incapable of communicating. The effect is similar to a denial-of-service attack on a website, where it is flooded with unwanted traffic, bringing it down.

It is important to understand that multicast was designed for an entirely different application than to support distributed video cameras. It was designed to support a single source transmitting data to many destination devices. In video systems, there are many sources (cameras and intercoms) transmitting to a few destination devices (servers and workstations). This difference can have unintended consequences for the uninitiated. For example, in conventional multicast environments, the "edge" switches (those at the outermost devices) do not have to be managed switches. However, in distributed digital video systems, the outermost switches should be managed, because when multicast touches a device that cannot handle multicast protocol, and that device broadcasts a return message for each packet it sees, often bringing down the entire network. When managed edge switches are used, however, each individual port can be set up with IGMP snooping to prevent multicast signals from getting to unicast devices (e.g., alarm/access control system panels).

Multicast Anomalies

Additionally, be advised that multicast traffic can have unanticipated side effects even on systems that are properly configured for it. For example, adding a set of mirrored backup archive servers to a security system requires the system to operate in multicast mode since both the primary and the backup servers are receiving the data of all digital cameras at all times. On a typically configured digital video system, this can result in directing 200 Mbps of data traffic across the backhaul network to the backup servers. It is a little known fact that multicast data traffic can have an adverse effect on intercom codecs. I was once confronted with an enterprise security system that exhibited audio distortion in its intercoms when the backup servers were turned on. The additional data traffic was enough to cause the intercom talk codecs to distort the audio only when the archive servers were turned on (changing the system from unicast to multicast for all video signals). By reducing the volume setting of the talk intercoms, the "clipping" of audio signals was eliminated. This condition is especially obvious where audio converters are used to convert two-wire intercoms to four-wire for use with conventional audio codecs, because the two-/four-wire converter also inserts an additional volume control in series in the circuit.

Multicast is a very "user surly" environment. It is especially not friendly to radio traffic and should not be used on such by the unsophisticated designer. Many configuration settings are required to operate multicast on a wireless mesh network to ensure that the radios do not retransmit the multicast traffic endlessly, thus flooding the mesh with unnecessary traffic.

It is ideal to configure the digital video network into two distinct VLANs, where VLAN1 is the camera-to-server network and VLAN2 is the server-to-workstation network. Run VLAN1 (the cameras) in unicast and VLAN2 (clients) in multicast. Configure IGMP querying on a primary and backup core switch and configure all switches to support IGMP snooping to ensure that no unicast devices retransmit multicast signals. IGMP querying asks which switch ports want to sign up for multicast signals, and IGMP snooping sends those signals only to those ports. Utilize managed switches to ensure IGMP conformance.

SUMMARY

Understanding information technology infrastructure is the basis for a successful integrated security system design. The reader should carefully read and understand this chapter to succeed as a designer.

The TCP/IP suite of protocols is the basis for information technology networked systems. This chapter provides a detailed description of how TCP/IP works. The designer will not achieve success without a comprehensive understanding of TCP/IP.

TCP/IP operates on levels 3 and 4 of the OSI networking model. Data are encapsulated from the application program through the seven layers down to the network wire, sent across the network, and then decapsulated back up the seven layers to the application on the other end.

TCP protocol is able to fix bad communications. Other protocols in the TCP/IP family include UDP and RTP, which do not fix bad communications but are better suited for streaming data, such as video and audio.

TCP/IP is also an addressing scheme. Each network-connected device is assigned a TCP/IP address that identifies its location on the network. Addresses can be assigned automatically or manually.

Common wiring schemes include Ethernet and fiber optic cables. Ethernet is available on Cat5, Cat5e, and Cat6 cable at speeds of 10,

100, and 1000 Mbps or 10Base-T, 100Base-T, or 1000Base-T (gigabit Ethernet). Fiber optic runs can be on either single-mode or multimode fiber. Single-mode fiber can carry more data farther. Multimode cable and transducers are less expensive. Gigabit switches are often available with fiber connectors to link switches together over long distances, and RJ-45 connectors are used for short runs of Ethernet cables to local devices.

Edge devices include IP video cameras, IP intercoms, and codecs. Network infrastructure and wiring are connected using hubs, switches, routers, and firewalls. Hubs are rarely used today because they simply connect wires together and do nothing to handle network contention. Switches handle the connection of local devices. Routers control where network communications can go. Firewalls exclude unauthorized devices from gaining access to the network. IDSs monitor the network firewall to detect any attempt to intrude into the network.

Integrated security system network computers include servers and workstations. Servers can include directory service servers (Windows directory service), IISs, DNS, and other network management services. Other services may include archiving, application program service, ftp, http, e-mail, and broadcast services. Workstations provide the interface between users and the network. Printers and mass storage systems round out the network attached devices. Mass storage systems include NAS and SANs.

Network architecture includes simple networks, LANs, and WANs. Advanced network architecture includes backhaul networks, subnets, and VLANs. Network connection types include peer-to-peer and client/server configurations. Systems can be monitored remotely and safely using browser (http) or VPNs. Digital cameras can link directly to the network, whereas analog video cameras require a codec interface.

Typical video compression schemes include MJPEG, MPEG-2, and MPEG-4. MJPEG is a stream of individual images strung together to show movement, whereas MPEG schemes display a single image and then update subsequent frames only with the changes in the image.

Workstation types include security monitoring centers, guard or lobby desk workstations, administrative workstations, photo ID workstations, and access verification workstations.

Integrated security systems can interface to many other types of systems, including process control networks, BASs, elevators, PABXs, VoIP systems, fire alarm systems, public address systems, parking control systems, and vending systems.

Multicast protocol is sometimes used in digital video systems, but it is fraught with many nuances requiring special skills and knowledge. I recommend a thorough understanding before implementing multicast protocol.

Security Officers and Equipment Monitoring

Craig McQuate, CPP

INTRODUCTION

After basic training, a security officer will be assigned a specific post. Each post requires additional training, and that training starts with post orders. Post orders are written procedures on how a security guard is to perform his or her duties throughout the shift. Once written, policy, post orders, or procedures will be reviewed and approved by upper management of the organization. These policies tend to remain in place for a period of time, but the post orders/procedures need to be reviewed every 6 months. This is because procedures for carrying out the policy are subject to change to meet the changing demands of the business unit. Post orders are usually kept in both soft copy and hard copy for easy access.

Post orders should contain at least the following information:

1. Date of revision
2. What is confidentiality
3. Instructions on how to deal with public relations
4. Security staffing levels, hours of coverage, and specific functions and duties
5. Description of the building (floor plans if possible)

6. Specific instructions on handling of emergency situations
7. Emergency contact information including after-hours contact information
8. Code of ethics and standards of conduct

Security personnel should first be trained in the basic areas:

1. Security policy and procedure and protocols
2. Professionalism
3. Authority of a security officer and scope of responsibility
4. Relationships with law enforcement
5. Patrol procedures
6. Observation techniques
7. Challenging techniques
8. Investigations
9. Report writing
10. Emergency medical assistance, first aid, and the AED units
11. Workplace violence
12. Operation of security equipment.

One very important post for security is the command center. This is a center from which the security staff can view, record, and retrieve video from surveillance cameras also known as closed-caption television (CCTV). A command center should have a minimum of two security officers, who may be called command center operators or CCTV operators. A security office can be managed by one security guard. The center is a place where security officers can view images of video surveillance from hundreds or even thousands of cameras.

Something that always needs to be watched is the length of time the guard is viewing the CCTV. Periodic breaks are very important as the human body can only view something for so long before the eyes start to become tired. The ideal setup for a moderately sized center is two security guards. Each officer monitors the CCTV for 1 h and then they switch the monitoring responsibilities. This way there are always fresh eyes viewing the cameras.

The most important task for a command center operator is to uphold safety of staff members and the public and prevent any crime. One may joke that the only requirement to work as a command center operator is that you have unblinking eyes, but there are in fact many skills and traits that come in handy.

COMMAND CENTER

It is imperative for command center operators to have extraordinary attention to detail since they will be watching live pictures on an entire bank of monitors. Command center operators work in a central control room watching up to 15 screens at a time, receiving live feeds from more than 100 surveillance cameras. It is extremely important that every activity be closely observed to maintain safety and order. Shifts are scheduled tightly to make sure that there is no downtime during shift changes. Some command center operators work alone, while others work in teams. Command center operators have specific procedures to follow if they witness any illegal or suspicious activity and may often call or radio security staff or police.

To work successfully as a command center operator, it is important to have some specific skills. Two of the most important traits, of course, is excellent eyesight and attention to detail. It is also important to be able to react quickly in case of an emergency and be discreet. Discretion is important because operators must not ever relay what they have seen on the monitors to the public. Their ability to work unsupervised is also important since they are responsible for watching a lot of screens at once and then need to be able to make quick judgment calls about what they see.

Command center operators can operate the cameras from inside the control room, which can help them prioritize what they are watching. Certain areas may be more important to watch during certain times or in case of emergencies. For instance, if an alarm goes off in a building forcing security to check into the problem, the command center operator will monitor the area and communicate with security if he or she sees anything suspicious.

Command center operators are often in contact with other security staff and the police to report crimes such as theft and vandalism. Because command center operators can see what is happening live they are often able to aid in the capture of criminals before they leave the scene of the crime. In addition to the task of monitoring live footage, command center operators are responsible for maintaining the video recordings. All recordings are kept for a specific amount of time in case the police need them for an investigation. They must also keep a written log of all incidents they witness in case the police require that information as well.

The best practice for CCTV is to have a digital video system. The most commonly used are DVRs (digital video recorders). These have the ability to record and play back the images that the CCTV captured. Through the DVR network a command center operator can view other locations that are not local.

There are two types of cameras used by security departments: fixed cameras (static—they do not move) and PTZ (pan, tilt, and zoom). A fixed focal or variofocal lens is used with the camera to capture a defined field of view. A benefit associated with using a fixed camera is that the camera is always aimed at the desired view, which facilitates assessment. A PTZ camera is able to pan (move side to side) or tilt (move up and down). This is to help the operator to observe/access a much larger viewing area. Plus these cameras are available in HD, as are the monitors (Fig. 19.1).

The use of CCTV is only one element to a company's security plans, and CCTV can be installed for a small cost compared to adding security staff to cover its function. One or two security officers are able to watch many locations from one central location, meaning that these security officers can view and respond to a location by means of watching the CCTV from another building. They are also able to view the CCTV playback from another location, in case there is an incident that takes place and they are at another location and need to provide the police with video. The use of CCTV equipment is one way that a company can save money with the reduction of the security guard staff, which considerably lowers the cost of security.

FIGURE 19.1 Command center.

BEST LOCATIONS FOR CLOSED-CAPTION TELEVISION

Entrance and exit doors present your best chance of viewing and recording facial images that can be used for identification purposes. To capture a useful ID image, the security camera should be set to view an area of about 3 feet wide, that is, the width of the average door. Caution should be used when pointing cameras toward exterior doors. As the door opens, a sudden change in light will often cause the subject to go black. Instead of the facial image being captured, there will be nothing but a dark outline. In many cases the guard will have an easier time viewing an exit. The lighting will be more even since the security camera will be facing away from outside light. The design and scope of the physical assets protection management system is based on the size, nature, and complexity of the organization and site.

Targets

Targets include cash drawers, jewelry cabinets, safes, filing cabinets, or any area that a thief may target, as well as areas that may be considered *high risk*. In these areas, security cameras should be set up to capture as wide an image as possible. The idea here is not so much to identify a face as it is to review or respond to a crime. These are also areas where security cameras may be mounted relatively high so that they can see down into cabinets and drawers.

Secluded Areas

Parking lots and back alleys are also good locations for security cameras. The images captured in these areas are useful for investigating vandalism or violence. The deterrent value of a camera system also comes into play in these applications. Seeing a security camera staring at them, potential perpetrators may think twice about committing a criminal act. As part of the physical assets protection management system plan, guards should review the exterior light level (see Chapter 5).

Testing and Maintenance

I recently read in a security text to make sure exterior doors that have a portable alarm are tested annually. To my surprise, when we checked at our location, every battery was dead. My point is, *develop a maintenance program that includes all physical asset protection devices*, and in the maintenance program, require vendors to supply only qualified technicians.

INTRODUCTION TO ACCESS CONTROL AND BIOMETRICS

Perimeter barriers, intrusion-detection devices, and protective lighting provide physical-security safeguards; however, they alone are not enough. An access control system must be established and maintained to preclude unauthorized entry. Effective access control procedures prevent the introduction of harmful devices and components. They minimize the misappropriation; pilferage; or compromise of recorded information by controlling packages, materiel, and property movement. Access control rosters, personal recognition, ID cards, badge-exchange procedures, and personnel escorts all contribute to an effective access control system.

DESIGNATED RESTRICTED AREAS

The security manager is responsible for designating and establishing restricted areas. A restricted area is any area that is subject to special restrictions or controls for security reasons. This does not include areas over which aircraft flight is restricted.

Restricted areas may be established for the following reasons*:

- The enforcement of security measures and the exclusion of unauthorized personnel.
- Intensified controls in areas requiring special protection.
- The protection of classified information or critical equipment or materials.

Access control and biometrics will grant or deny admittance and ensure authorized access. Badges not used in 30 days must be deleted. These devices increase the level of protection with a high degree of reliability.

SUMMARY

The functions of a physical assets protection management system are to deter the occurrence of an undesirable event, delay an adversary from reaching his or her target/assets, detect an undesirable event or adversary attack, deny an adversary from reaching his or her target, and enable law enforcement/security to successfully respond to an undesirable event.

*This information is from Joseph Nelson, CPP, author of Chapter 16 of this book.

Video Technology Overview*

Herman Kruegle

This chapter introduces most of the current video technology and equipment as used for security purposes. Some key aspects listed are lighting, lenses, type of camera, and the analog or digital video signal transmission.

OVERVIEW

The second half of the 2000s witnessed a quantum jump in video security technology. This technology has manifested with a new generation of video components, such as digital cameras, multiplexers, digital video recorders (DVRs), and so forth. A second significant activity has been the integration of security systems with computer-based local area networks (LANs), wide area networks (WANs), wireless networks (WiFi), intranets, and Internet and the World Wide Web (WWW) communications systems.

Although today's video security system hardware is based on new technology that takes advantage of the great advances in microprocessor computing power, solid-state and magnetic memory, digital processing, and wired and wireless video signal transmission (analog, digital over the Internet, etc.), the basic video system still requires the lens, camera, transmission medium (wired cable, wireless), monitor, recorder, and so forth. This chapter describes current video security system components and is an introduction to their operation.

The primary function of any video security or safety system is to provide remote eyes for the security force located at a central control console or remote site. The video system includes the illumination source, the scene to be viewed, the camera lens, the camera, and the means of transmission to the remote monitoring and recording equipment. Other equipment often necessary to complete the system includes video switchers, multiplexers, video motion detectors (VMDs), housings, scene combiners and splitters, and character generators.

This chapter describes the technology used to (1) capture the visual image, (2) convert it to a video signal, (3) transmit the signal to a receiver at a remote location, (4) display the image on a video monitor, and (5) record and print it for permanent record. Fig. 20.1 shows the simplest video application requiring only one video camera and monitor.

The printer and video recorder are optional. The camera may be used to monitor employees,

*Originally from Kruegle H. CCTV surveillance. Boston: Butterworth-Heinemann; 2006. Updated by the editor, Elsevier, 2016.

Effective Physical Security, Fifth Edition
http://dx.doi.org/10.1016/B978-0-12-804462-9.00020-8

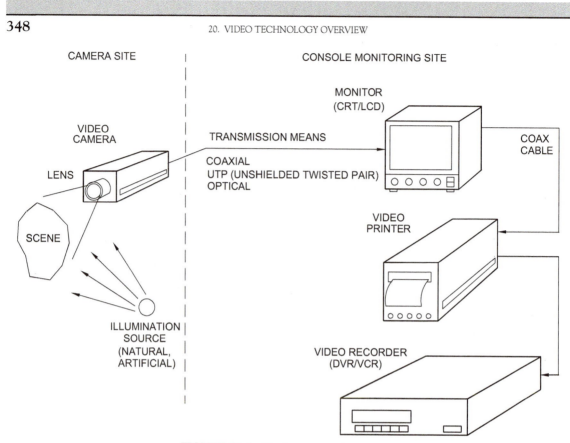

FIGURE 20.1   Single-camera video system.

visitors, or people entering or leaving a building. The camera could be located in the lobby ceiling and pointed at the reception area, the front door, or an internal access door. The monitor might be located hundreds or thousands of feet away, in another building or another city or country with the security personnel viewing that same lobby, front door, or reception area. The video camera/monitor system effectively extends the eyes, reaching from observer location to the observed location. The basic one-camera system shown in Fig. 20.1 includes the following hardware components.

- **Lens.** Light from the illumination source reflects off the scene. The lens collects the light from the scene and forms an image of the scene on the light-sensitive camera sensor.

- **Camera.** The camera sensor converts the visible scene formed by the lens into an electrical signal suitable for transmission to the remote monitor, recorder, and printer.
- **Transmission link.** The transmission media carries the electrical video signal from the camera to the remote monitor. Hard-wired media choices include: (1) coaxial, (2) two-wire unshielded twisted pair (UTP), (3) fiber-optic cable, (4) LAN, (5) WAN, (6) intranet, and (7) Internet network. Wireless choices include: (1) radio frequency (RF), (2) microwave, and (3) optical infrared (IR). Signals can be analog or digital.
- **Monitor.** The video monitor or computer screens [cathode ray tube (CRT), liquid crystal display (LCD), or plasma] display the camera image by converting the electrical

video signal back into a visible image on the monitor screen.

- **Recorder.** The camera scene is permanently recorded by a real-time or time lapse (TL) video cassette recorder (VCR) onto a magnetic tape cassette or by a DVR using a magnetic disk hard drive.
- **Hard-copy printer.** The video printer produces a hard-copy paper printout of any live or recorded video image, using thermal, inkjet, laser, or other printing technology.

The first four components are required to make a simple video system work. The recorder and/or printer is required if a permanent record is required.

Fig. 20.2 shows a block diagram of a multicamera digital video security system using these components plus additional hardware and options to expand the capability of the single-camera system to multiple cameras, monitors, recorders, and so forth, providing a more complex video security system.

Additional ancillary supporting equipment for more complex systems includes: camera switchers, quads, multiplexers, environmental camera housings, camera pan/tilt mechanisms, image combiners and splitters, and scene annotators.

- **Camera switcher, quad, multiplexer.** When a closed-circuit TV (CCTV) security system has multiple cameras, an electronic switcher, quad, or multiplexer is used to select different cameras automatically or manually to display the images on a single or

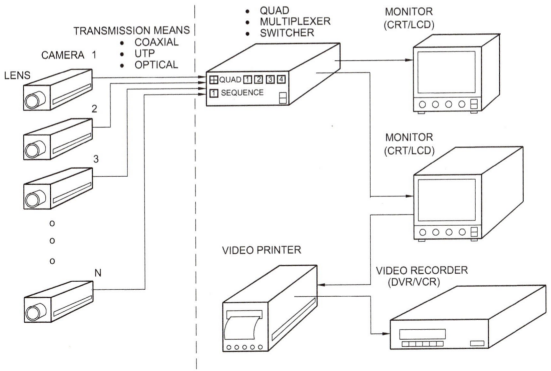

FIGURE 20.2 Comprehensive video security system.

multiple monitors, as individual or multiple scenes. The quad can digitally combine four cameras. The multiplexer can digitally combine 4, 9, 16, or even 32 separate cameras.

- **Housings.** The many varieties of camera/lens housings fall into three categories: indoor, outdoor, and integral camera/housing assemblies. Indoor housings protect the camera and lens from tampering and are usually constructed from lightweight materials. Outdoor housings protect the camera and lens from the environment such as precipitation, extremes of heat and cold, dust, dirt, and vandalism.
- **Dome housing.** The dome camera housing uses a hemispherical clear or tinted plastic dome enclosing a fixed camera or a camera with pan/tilt and zoom lens capability.
- **Plug and play camera/housing combination.** To simplify surveillance camera installations many manufacturers are now packaging the camera-lens-housing as a complete assembly. These plug and play cameras are ready to mount in a wall or ceiling and to connect the power in and the video out.
- **Pan/tilt mechanism.** When a camera must view a large area, a pan and tilt mount is used to rotate it horizontally (panning) and to tilt it, providing a large angular coverage.
- **Splitter/combiner/inserter.** An optical or electronic image combiner or splitter is used to display more than one camera scene on a single monitor.
- **Annotator.** A time and date generator annotates the video scene with chronological information. A camera identifier puts a camera number (or name such as Front Door, etc.) on the monitor screen to identify the scene displayed by the camera.

The digital video surveillance system includes most of the devices in the analog video system. The primary differences manifest in using digital electronics and digital processing within the video devices. Digital video components use digital signal processing (DSP), digital video signal compression, digital transmission, recording, and viewing. Fig. 20.3 illustrates these devices and signal paths and the overall system block diagram for the digital video system.

VIDEO SYSTEM

Fig. 20.4 shows the essentials of the CCTV camera environment: illumination source, camera, lens, and the camera–lens combined field of view (FOV), that is, the scene the camera–lens combination sees.

The Role of Light and Reflection

A scene or target area to be viewed is illuminated by natural or artificial light sources. Natural sources include the sun, the moon (reflected sunlight), and starlight. Artificial sources include incandescent, sodium, metal arc, mercury, fluorescent, infrared, and other man-made lights.

The camera lens receives the light reflected from the scene. Depending on the scene to be viewed the amount of light reflected from objects in the scene can vary from 5% or 10% to 80% or 90% of the light incident on the scene. Typical values of reflected light for normal scenes such as foliage, automobiles, personnel, and streets fall in the range of about 25–65%. Snow-covered scenes may reach 90%.

The amount of light received by the lens is a function of the brightness of the light source, the reflectivity of the scene, and the transmission characteristics of the intervening atmosphere. In outdoor applications there is usually a considerable optical path from the source to the scene and back to the camera; therefore, the transmission through the atmosphere must be considered. When atmospheric conditions are clear, there is generally little or no attenuation

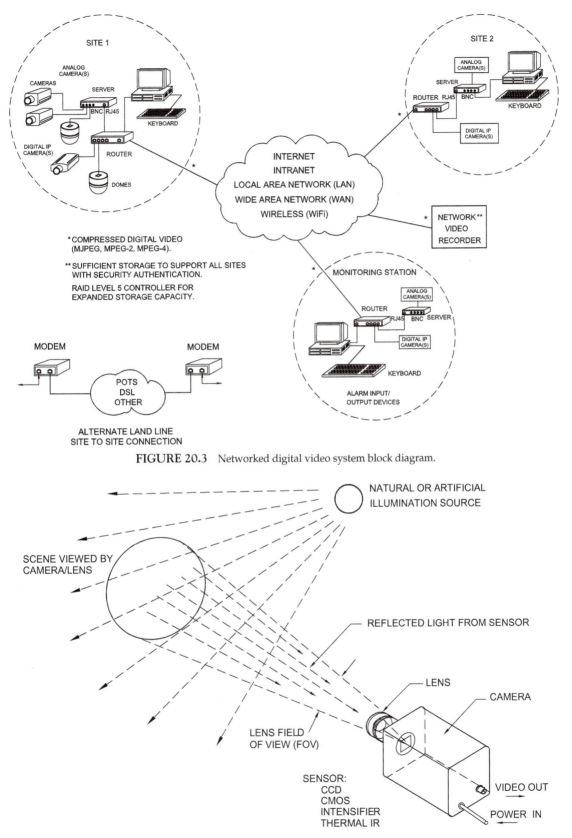

FIGURE 20.3 Networked digital video system block diagram.

FIGURE 20.4 Video camera, scene, and source illumination.

of the reflected light from the scene. However, when there is precipitation (rain, snow, or sleet, or when fog intervenes) or in dusty, smoky, or sand-blown environments, this attenuation might be substantial and must be considered. Likewise, in hot climates thermal effects (heat waves) and humidity can cause severe attenuation and/or distortion of the scene. Complete attenuation of the reflected light from the scene (zero visibility) can occur, in which case no scene image is formed.

Since most solid-state cameras operate in the visible and near-IR wavelength region the general rule of thumb with respect to visibility is that if the human eye cannot see the scene

neither can the camera. Under this situation, no amount of increased lighting will help; however, if the visible light can be filtered out of the scene and only the IR portion used, scene visibility might be increased somewhat.

This problem can often be overcome by using a thermal IR imaging camera that works outside of the visible wavelength range. These thermal IR cameras produce a monochrome display with reduced image quality and are much more expensive than the charge-coupled device (CCD) or complementary metal oxide semiconductor (CMOS) cameras. Fig. 20.5 illustrates the relationship between the viewed scene and the scene image on the camera sensor.

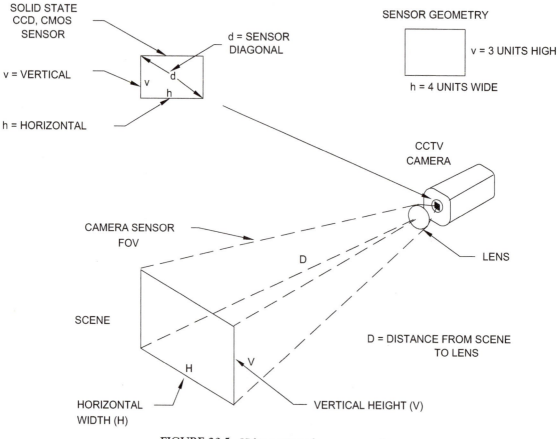

FIGURE 20.5 Video scene and sensor geometry.

The lens located on the camera forms an image of the scene and focuses it onto the sensor. Almost all video systems used in security systems have a 4×3 aspect ratio (4 units wide × 3 units high) for both the image sensor and the FOV. The width parameter is designated as h, and H, and the vertical as v, and V. Some cameras have a 16×9 unit's high definition television (HDTV or 1080 p) format.

Lens Function

The camera lens is analogous to the lens of the human eye (Fig. 20.6) and collects the reflected radiation from the scene much like the lens of your eye or a film camera. The function of the lens is to collect reflected light from the scene and focus it into an image onto the CCTV camera sensor. A fraction of the light reaching the scene from the natural or artificial illumination source is reflected toward the camera and intercepted and collected by the camera lens. As a general rule, the larger the lens diameter, the more the light will be gathered, the brighter the image on the sensor, and the better the final image on the monitor. This is why larger aperture (diameter) lenses, having a higher optical throughput, are better (and more expensive) than smaller diameter lenses that collect less light. Under good lighting conditions—bright indoor lighting, outdoors under sunlight—the large-aperture lenses are not required and there is sufficient light to form a bright image on the sensor by using small-diameter lenses.

Most video applications use a fixed-focal-length (FFL) lens. The FFL lens, like the human eye lens, covers a constant angular FOV. The FFL lens images a scene with constant fixed magnification. A large variety of CCTV camera lenses are available with different focal lengths (FLs) that provide different FOVs. Wide-angle, medium-angle, and narrow-angle (telephoto) lenses produce different magnifications and FOVs. Zoom and varifocal lenses can be adjusted to have variable FLs and FOVs.

EYE OR CAMERA SENSOR SCENE

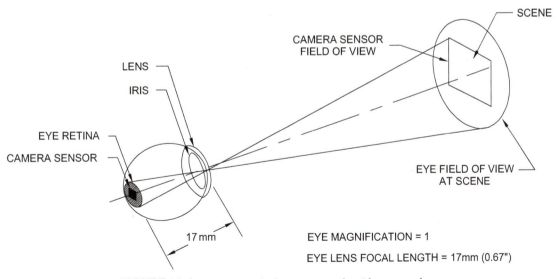

FIGURE 20.6 Comparing the human eye to the video camera lens.

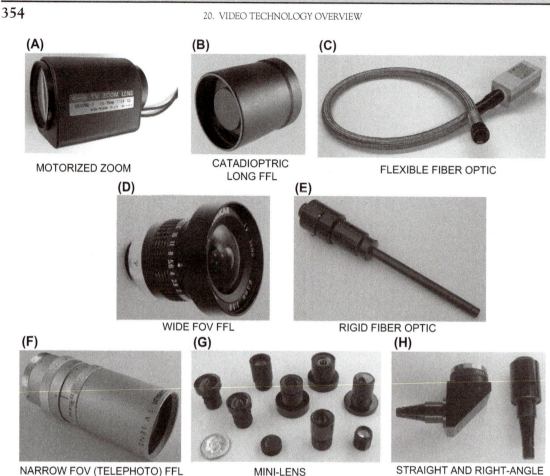

FIGURE 20.7   Representative video lenses.

Most CCTV lenses have an iris diaphragm (as does the human eye) to adjust the open area of the lens and change the amount of light passing through it and reaching the sensor. Depending on the application, manual- or automatic-iris lenses are used.

In an automatic-iris CCTV lens, as in a human eye lens, the iris closes automatically when the illumination is too high and opens automatically when it is too low, maintaining the optimum illumination on the sensor at all times. Fig. 20.7 shows representative samples of CCTV lenses, including FFL, varifocal, zoom, pinhole, and a large catadioptric lens for long-range outdoor use (which combines both mirror and glass optical elements).

CAMERA FUNCTION

The lens focuses the scene onto the camera image sensor, which acts like the retina of the eye or the film in a photographic camera. The video camera sensor and electronics convert the visible image into an equivalent electrical signal suitable for transmission to a remote monitor. Fig. 20.8 is a block diagram of a typical analog CCTV camera.

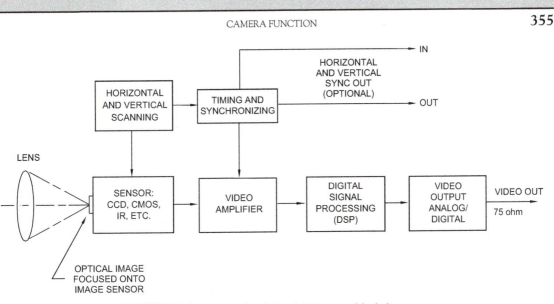

FIGURE 20.8 Analog closed-circuit TV camera block diagram.

The camera converts the optical image produced by the lens into a time-varying electric signal that changes (modulates) in accordance with the light-intensity distribution throughout the scene. Other camera electronic circuits produce synchronizing pulses so that the time-varying video signal can later be displayed on a monitor or recorder or printed out as hard copy on a video printer. Although cameras may differ in size and shape depending on specific type and capability, the scanning process used by most cameras is essentially the same. Almost all cameras must scan the scene, point by point, as a function of time (an exception is the image intensifier). Solid-state CCD or CMOS color and monochrome cameras are used in most applications. In scenes with low illumination, sensitive CCD cameras with IR illuminators are used. In scenes with very low illumination and where no active illumination is permitted (i.e., covert) low-light-level (LLL) intensified CCD (ICCD) cameras are used. These cameras are complex and expensive.

Fig. 20.9 shows a block diagram of an analog or digital camera with (1) DSP and (2) the all-digital Internet Protocol (IP) video camera.

In the early 1990s, the nonbroadcast, tube-type color cameras available for security applications lacked long-term stability, sensitivity, and high resolution. Color cameras were not used much in security applications until solid-state color CCTV cameras became available through the development of solid-state color sensor technology and widespread use of consumer color CCD cameras used in camcorders. Color cameras have now become standard in security systems and most CCTV security cameras in use today are color. Fig. 20.10 shows representative CCTV cameras including monochrome and color solid-state CCD and CMOS cameras, a small single board camera, and a miniature remote head camera.

Transmission Function

Once the camera has generated an electrical video signal representing the scene image, the signal is transmitted to a remote security monitoring site via some transmission means: coaxial cable, two-wire twisted-pair, LAN, WAN, intranet, Internet, fiber-optic, or wireless techniques. The choice of transmission medium

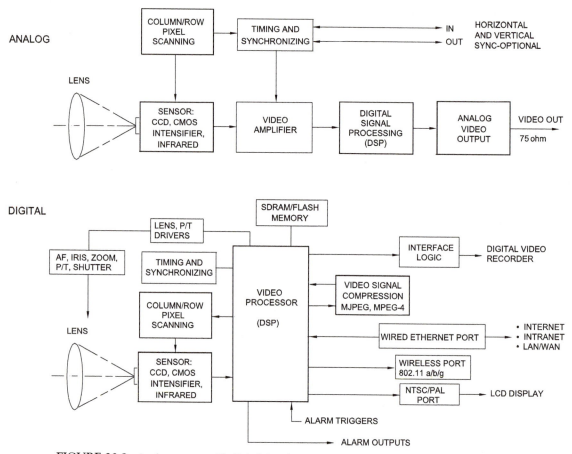

FIGURE 20.9 Analog camera with digital signal processing and all-digital camera block diagram.

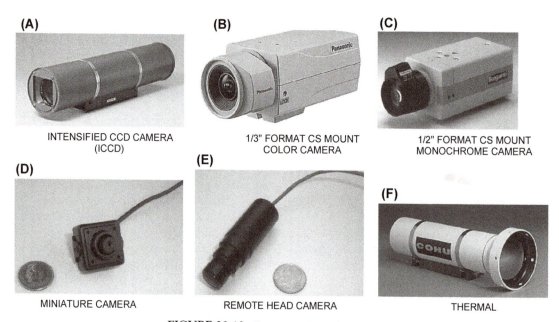

FIGURE 20.10 Representative video cameras.

depends on factors such as distance, environment, and facility layout.

If the distance between the camera and the monitor is short (10–500 ft), coaxial cable, UTP, and fiber optic or wireless are used. For longer distances (500 ft to several thousand feet) or where there are electrical disturbances, fiber-optic cable and UTP are preferred. For very long distances and in harsh environments (frequent lightning storms) or between separated buildings where no electrical grounding between buildings is in place, fiber optics is the choice. In applications where the camera and monitor are separated by roadways or where there is no right of way, wireless systems using RF, microwave, or optical transmission are used. For transmission over many miles or from city to city the only choice is the digital or Internet IP camera using compression techniques and transmitting over the Internet. Images from these Internet systems are not real time but sometimes come close to real time.

Monitor Function

At the monitoring site a CRT or LCD or plasma monitor converts the video signal back into a visual image on the monitor face via electronic circuitry similar but inverse to that in the camera.

The final scene is produced by a scanning electron beam in the CRT in the video monitor. This beam activates the phosphor on the CRT, producing a representation of the original image onto the faceplate of the monitor. Alternatively, the video image is displayed point by point on an LCD or plasma screen. A permanent record of the monitor video image is made using a VCR tape or DVR hard disk magnetic recorder and a permanent hard copy is printed with a video printer.

Recording Function

For decades the VCR has been used to record monochrome and color video images. The real-time and TL VCR magnetic tape systems have been a reliable and efficient means for recording security scenes.

Beginning in the mid-1990s the DVR was developed using a computer hard disk drive and digital electronics to provide video image recording. The availability of large memory disks (hundreds of megabytes) made these machines available for long-duration security recording. Significant advantages of the DVR over the VCR are the high reliability of the disk as compared with the cassette tape, its ability to perform high-speed searches (retrieval of images) anywhere on the disk, and absence of image deterioration after many copies are made.

SCENE ILLUMINATION

A scene is illuminated by either natural or artificial illumination. Monochrome cameras can operate with any type of light source. Color cameras need light that contains all the colors in the visible spectrum and light with a reasonable balance of all the colors to produce a satisfactory color image.

Natural Light

During daytime the amount of illumination and spectral distribution of light (color) reaching a scene depends on the time of day and atmospheric conditions. The color spectrum of the light reaching the scene is important if color CCTV is used. Direct sunlight produces the highest-contrast scene, allowing maximum identification of objects. On a cloudy or overcast day, less light is received by the objects in the scene resulting in less contrast. To produce an optimum camera picture under the wide variation in light levels (daytime to nighttime), an automatic-iris camera system is required. Table 20.1 shows the light levels for outdoor illumination under bright sun, partial clouds, and overcast day down to overcast night.

Scene illumination is measured in foot-candles (fc) and can vary from 10,000 to 1 (or more). This exceeds the dynamic operating range of most camera sensors for producing a good-quality video image.

TABLE 20.1   Light Levels Under Daytime and Nighttime Conditions

Condition (fc)	Illumination (lux)	Comments	
Direct saunlight	10,000	107,500	Daylight range
Full daylight	1000	10,750	
Overcast day	100	1075	
Very dark day	10	107.5	
twilight	1	10.75	
Deep twilight	0.1	1.075	
Full moon	0.01	0.1075	Low-light-level range
Quarter moon	0.001	0.01075	
Starlight	0.0001	0.001075	
Overcast night	0.00001	0.0001075	

1 lux = 0.093 fc.

After the sun has gone below the horizon and if the moon is overhead, reflected sunlight from the moon illuminates the scene and may be detected by a sensitive monochrome camera. Detection of information in a scene under this condition requires a very sensitive camera, since there is very little light reflected into the camera lens from the scene. As an extreme, when the moon is not overhead or is obscured by cloud cover, the only light received is ambient light from (1) local man-made lighting sources; (2) night-glow caused by distant ground lighting reflecting off particulate (pollution), clouds, and aerosols in the lower atmosphere; and (3) direct light caused by starlight. This is the most severe lighting condition and requires (1) ICCD, (2) monochrome camera with IR light-emitting diode (LED) illumination, or (3) thermal IR camera. Table 20.2 summarizes the light levels occurring under daylight and these LLL conditions and the operating ranges of typical cameras. The equivalent metric measure of light level (lux) compared with the foot-candle (fc) is given. One foot-candle is equivalent to approximately 9.3 lux.

Artificial Light

Artificial illumination is often used to augment outdoor lighting to obtain adequate video surveillance at night. The light sources used are tungsten, tungsten-halogen, metal-arc, mercury, sodium, xenon, IR lamps, and LED IR arrays. Fig. 20.11 illustrates several examples of these lamps.

The type of lighting chosen depends on architectural requirements and the specific application. Often a particular lighting design is used for safety reasons so that personnel at the scene can see better and for improving the video picture. Tungsten and tungsten-halogen lamps have by far the most balanced color and are best for color cameras. The most efficient visual outdoor light types are the low- and high-pressure sodium-vapor lamps to which the human eye is most sensitive. These lamps, however, do not produce all colors (missing blue and green) and therefore are not good light sources for color cameras. Metal-arc lamps have excellent color rendition. Mercury-arc lamps provide good security illumination but are missing the color red; therefore,

TABLE 20.2 Camera Capability Under Natural Lighting Conditions and Camera Requirement per Lighting Conditions

Illumination Condition (fc)	Illumination (lux)	Vidicon[a]	CCD	CMOS	ICCD	ISIT[a]
Overcast night	0.00001	0.0001075				
Starlight	0.0001	0.001075				
Quarter moon	0.001	0.01075				
Full moon	0.01	0.1075				
Deep twilight	0.1	1.075				
Twilight	1	10.075				
Very dark day	10	107.5		Operating range of typical cameras		
Overcast day	100	1075				
Full daylight	1000	10,750				
Direct sunlight	10,000	107,500				

CCD, charge-coupled device; *CMOS*, complementary metal oxide semiconductor; *ICCD*, intensified CCD; *ISIT*, intensified silicon intensified target.

[a] *For reference only.*

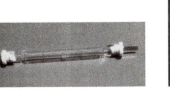

TUNGSTEN HALOGEN

FLUORESCENT
- STRAIGHT
- U

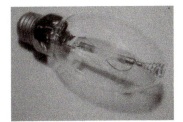

HIGH-PRESSURE SODIUM

TUNGSTEN PAR
- SPOT
- FLOOD

XENON LONG ARC

HIGH-INTENSITY DISCHARGE METAL ARC

FIGURE 20.11 Representative artificial light sources.

they are not as good as the metal-arc lamps at producing excellent quality color video images. Long-arc xenon lamps with excellent color rendition are often used in outdoor sports arenas and large parking areas.

LED IR illumination arrays mounted in monochrome video cameras or located near the camera are used to illuminate scenes when there is insufficient lighting. Since they only emit energy in the IR spectrum they can only be used with monochrome cameras. They are used at short ranges (10–25 ft) with wide-angle lenses (50–75 degree FOV) or at medium long ranges (25–200 ft) with medium- to narrow-FOV lenses (5–20 degree).

Artificial indoor illumination is similar to outdoor illumination, with fluorescent lighting used extensively in addition to the high-pressure sodium, metal-arc, and mercury lamps. Since indoor lighting has a relatively constant light level, automatic-iris lenses are often unnecessary. However, if the CCTV camera views a scene near an outside window or a door where additional light comes in during the day, or if the indoor lighting changes between daytime and nighttime operation, then an automatic-iris lens or electronically shuttered camera is required. The illumination level from most indoor lighting is significantly lower by 100–1000 times than that of sunlight.

SCENE CHARACTERISTICS

The quality of the video image depends on various scene characteristics that include: (1) the scene lighting level; (2) the sharpness and contrast of objects relative to the scene background; (3) whether objects are in a simple, uncluttered background or in a complicated scene; and (4) whether objects are stationary or in motion. These scene factors will determine whether the system will be able to detect, determine orientation, recognize, or identify objects and personnel. As will be seen later, the scene illumination—via

sunlight, moonlight, or artificial sources—and the actual scene contrast play important roles in the type of lens and camera necessary to produce a quality image on the monitor.

Target Size

In addition to the scene's illumination level and the object's contrast with respect to the scene background, the object's apparent size, that is, its angular FOV as seen by the camera, influences a person's ability to detect it (try to find a football referee with a striped shirt in a field of zebras).

The requirements of a video system are a function of the application. These include: (1) detection of the object or movement in the scene; (2) determination of the object's orientation; (3) recognition of the type of object in the scene, that is, adult or child, car or truck; or (4) identification of the object (Who is the person? Exactly what kind of truck is it?). Making these distinctions depends on the system's resolution, contrast, and signal-to-noise ratio. In a typical scene the average observer can detect a target about one-tenth of a degree in angle. This can be related to a standard video picture that has 525 horizontal lines (from the National Television System Committee; NTSC) and about 350 TV line vertical and 500 TV line horizontal resolution. Fig. 20.12 and Table 20.3 summarize the number of lines required to detect, orient, recognize, or identify an object in a television picture. The number of TV lines required will increase for conditions of poor lighting, highly complex backgrounds, reduced contrast, or fast movement of the camera or target.

Reflectivity

The reflectivity of different materials varies greatly depending on its composition and surface texture. Table 20.4 gives some examples of materials and objects viewed by video cameras and their respective reflectivity.

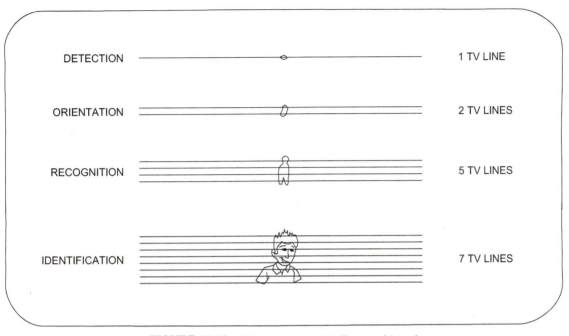

FIGURE 20.12   Object size versus intelligence obtained.

TABLE 20.3   TV Lines Versus Intelligence Obtained

Intelligence	Minimum TV Lines[a]
Detection	1 ± 0.25
Orientation	1.4 ± 0.35
Recognition	4 ± 0.8
Identification	6.4 ± 1.5

[a] One TV line corresponds to a light and dark line (one TV line pair).

Since the camera responds to the amount of light reflected from the scene, it is important to recognize that objects have a large range of reflectivity. The objects with the highest reflectivity produce the brightest images. To detect one object located within the area of another the objects must differ in reflectivity, color, or texture. Therefore, if a red box is in front of a green wall and both have the same reflectivity and texture, the box will not be seen on a monochrome video system. In this case, the total reflectivity in the visible spectrum is the same for the green wall and the red box. This is where the color camera shows its advantage over the monochrome camera.

The case of a color scene is more complex. Although the reflectivity of the red box and the green wall may be the same as averaged over the entire visible spectrum from blue to red, the color camera can distinguish between green and red.

It is easier to identify a scene characteristic by a difference in color in a color scene than it is to identify it by a difference in gray scale (intensity) in a monochrome scene. For this reason, the target size required to make an identification in a color scene is generally less than it is to make the same identification in a monochrome scene.

Effects of Motion

A moving object in a video image is easier to detect but more difficult to recognize than a stationary one provided that the camera

TABLE 20.4   Reflectivity of Common Materials

Material	Reflectivity (%)[a]
Snow	85–95
Asphalt	5
Plaster (white)	90
Sand	40–60
Trees	20
Grass	40
Clothes	15–30
Concrete—new	40
Concrete—old	25
Clear windows	70
Human face	15–25
Wood	10–20
Painted wall (white)	75–90
Red brick	25–35
Parking lot and automobiles	40
Aluminum building (diffuse)	65–70

[a] Visible spectrum: 400–700 nm.

can respond to it. LLL cameras produce sharp images for stationary scenes but smeared images for moving targets. This is caused by a phenomenon called "lag" or "smear." Solid-state sensors (CCD, CMOS, and ICCD) do not exhibit smear or lag at normal light levels; therefore, they can produce sharp images of both stationary and moving scenes. Some image intensifiers exhibit smear when the scene moves fast or when there is a bright light in the FOV of the lens.

When the target in the scene moves very fast, the inherent camera scan rate (30 frames per second, fps) causes a blurred image of this moving target in the camera. This is analogous to the blurred image in a still photograph when the shutter speed is too slow for the action. There is no cure for this as long as the standard NTSC television scan rate (30 fps) is used. However, CCTV snapshots can be taken without any blurring using fast-shuttered CCD cameras. For special applications in which fast-moving targets must be imaged and tracked, higher scan rate cameras are available.

Scene Temperature

Scene temperature has no effect on the video image in a CCD, CMOS, or ICCD sensor. These sensors do not respond to temperature changes or temperature differences in the scene. On the other hand, IR thermal imaging cameras do respond to temperature differences and changes in temperature in the scene. Thermal imagers do not respond to visible light or the very near-IR radiation like that produced by IR LEDs. The sensitivity of IR thermal imagers is defined as the smallest change in temperature in the scene that can be detected by the thermal camera.

LENSES

A lens collects reflected light from the scene and focuses it onto the camera image sensor. This is analogous to the lens of the human eye focusing a scene onto the retina at the back of the eye (Fig. 20.6). As in the human eye, the camera lens inverts the scene image on the image sensor, but the eye and the camera electronics compensate (invert the image) to perceive an upright scene. The retina of the human eye differs from any CCTV lens in that it focuses a sharp image only in the central 10% of its total 160 degree FOV. All vision outside the central focused scene is out of focus. This central imaging part of the human eye can be characterized as a medium FL lens that is 16–25 mm. In principle, Fig. 20.6 represents the function of any lens in a video system.

Many different lens types are used for video surveillance and safety applications. They range from the simplest FFL manual-iris lenses to the more complex varifocal and zoom lenses, with an automatic iris being an option for all types.

In addition, pinhole lenses are available for covert applications, split-image lenses for viewing multiple scenes on one camera, right-angle lenses for viewing a scene perpendicular to the camera axis, and rigid or flexible fiber-optic lenses for viewing through thick walls, under doors, and so forth.

FFL Lens

Fig. 20.13 illustrates three FFL or fixed-FOV lenses with narrow (telephoto), medium, and wide FOVs and the corresponding FOV obtained when used with a 1/3-in. camera sensor format.

Wide-FOV (short-FL) lenses permit viewing a very large scene (wide angle) with low magnification and therefore provide low resolution and low identification capabilities. Narrow

FOV or telephoto lenses have high magnification with high resolution and high identification capabilities.

Zoom Lens

The zoom lens is more versatile and complex than the FFL lens. Its FL is variable from wide-angle to narrow-angle (telephoto) FOV (Fig. 20.14).

The overall camera/lens FOV depends on the lens FL and the camera sensor size as shown in Fig. 20.14. Zoom lenses consist of multiple lens groups that are moved within the lens barrel by means of an external zooming ring (manual or motorized), changing the lens FL and angular FOV without having to switch lenses or refocusing. Zoom FL ratios can range from 6:1 to 50:1.

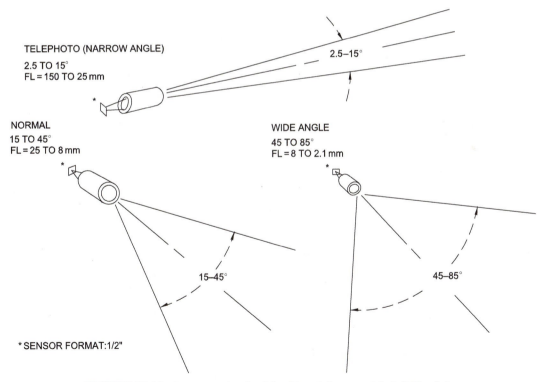

FIGURE 20.13 Representative fixed-focal-length lenses and their fields of view.

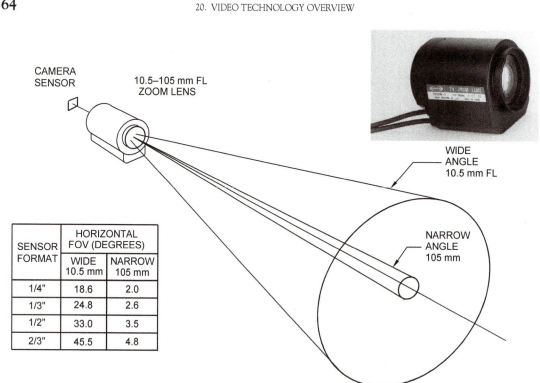

FIGURE 20.14   Zoom video lens horizontal field of view.

SENSOR FORMAT	HORIZONTAL FOV (DEGREES)	
	WIDE 10.5 mm	NARROW 105 mm
1/4"	18.6	2.0
1/3"	24.8	2.6
1/2"	33.0	3.5
2/3"	45.5	4.8

Zoom lenses are usually large and used on pan/tilt mounts viewing over large areas and distances (25–500 ft).

Varifocal Lens

The varifocal lens is a variable FL lens used in applications where an FFL lens would be used. In general, they are smaller and cost much less than zoom lenses. Like the zoom lens, the varifocal lens is used because its FL (angular FOV) can be changed manually or automatically, using a motor, by rotating the barrel on the lens. This feature makes it convenient to adjust the FOV to a precise angle when installed on the camera. Typical varifocal lenses have FLs of 3–8, 5–12, and 8–50 mm. With just these three lenses FLs from 3 to 50 mm (91–5 degree horizontal FOV) can be covered on a 1/3-in. format sensor. Unlike zoom lenses, varifocal lenses must be refocused each time the FL and the FOV are changed. They are not suitable for zoom or pan/tilt applications.

Panoramic 360 degree Lens

There has always been a need to see "all around," that is, an entire room or other location, seeing 360 degree with one panoramic camera and lens. In the past, 360 degree FOV camera viewing systems have only been achieved by using multiple cameras and lenses and combining the scenes on a split-screen monitor.

Panoramic lenses have been available for many years but have only recently been combined with digital electronics and sophisticated mathematical transformations to take advantage of their capabilities. Fig. 20.15 shows two lenses having a 360 degree horizontal FOV and a 90 degree vertical FOV.

(A)

(B)

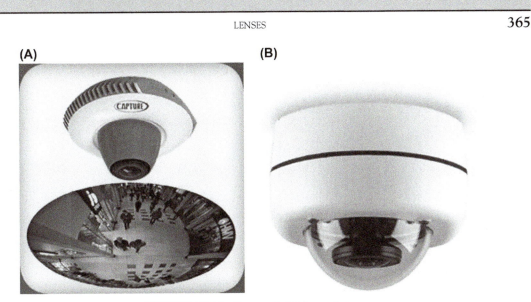

FIGURE 20.15 Panoramic 360 degree lens.

(A)

(B)

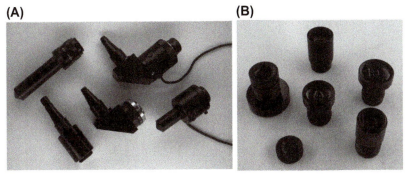

PINHOLE LENSES   MINI-LENSES

FIGURE 20.16 Pinhole and mini-pinhole lenses.

The panoramic lens collects light from the 360 degree panoramic scene and focuses it onto the camera sensor as a donut-shaped image. The electronics and mathematical algorithm convert this donut-shaped panoramic image into the rectangular (horizontal and vertical) format for normal monitor viewing.

Covert Pinhole Lens

This special security lens is used when the lens and CCTV camera must be hidden. The front lens element or aperture is small (from 1/16 to 5/16 of an inch in diameter). Although this is not the size of a pinhead, it nevertheless has been labeled as such. Fig. 20.16 shows examples of straight and right-angle pinhole lenses used with C or CS mount cameras. The very small mini-pinhole lenses are used on the low-cost, small board cameras.

Special Lenses

Some special lenses useful in security applications include split image, right angle, relay, and fiber optic (Fig. 20.17).

(B)

(A)

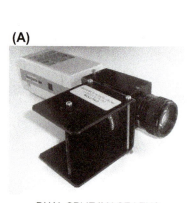

(C)

DUAL SPLIT IMAGE LENS

TRI SPLIT IMAGE LENS

RIGHT ANGLE LENS

(E)

(F)

(D)

RIGID FIBER OPTICS

RELAY LENS

FLEXIBLE FIBER OPTICS

FIGURE 20.17   Special video lenses.

The dual-split and tri-split lenses use only one camera to produce multiple scenes. These are useful for viewing the same scene with different magnifications or different scenes with the same or different magnifications. Using only one camera can reduce cost and increase reliability. These lenses are useful when two or three views are required and only one camera was installed.

The right-angle lens permits a camera using a wide-angle lens installed to view a scene that is perpendicular to the camera's optical axis. There are no restrictions on the FLs so they can be used in wide- or narrow-angle applications.

The flexible and rigid coherent fiber-optic lenses are used to mount a camera several inches to several feet away from the front lens as might be required to view from the opposite side of a wall or in a hazardous environment. The function of the fiber-optic bundle is to transfer the focused visual image from one location to another. This may be useful for (1) protecting the camera and (2) locating the lens in one environment (outdoors) and the camera in another (indoors).

CAMERAS

The camera lens focuses the visual scene image onto the camera sensor area point by point and the camera electronics transforms the visible image into an electrical signal. The camera video signal (containing all picture information) is made up of frequencies from 30 cycles per second, or 30 Hz, to 4.2 million cycles per second, or 4.2 MHz. The video signal is transmitted via a cable (or wireless) to the monitor display.

Almost all security cameras in use today are color or monochrome CCD with the rapid emergence of CMOS types. These cameras are available as low-cost single printed circuit board cameras with small lenses already built in, with or without a housing used for covert and overt surveillance applications. More expensive cameras in a housing are larger and more rugged and have a C or CS mechanical mount for accepting any type of lens. These cameras have higher resolution and light sensitivity and other electrical input/output features suitable for multiple camera CCTV systems. The CCD and CMOS cameras with LED IR illumination arrays can extend the use of these cameras to nighttime use. For LLL applications, the ICCD and IR cameras provide the highest sensitivity and detection capability.

Significant advancements in camera technology have been made in the last few years, particularly in the use of DSP in the camera and development of the IP camera. All security cameras manufactured between the 1950s and 1980s were the vacuum tube type, vidicon, silicon, or LLL types using silicon intensified target (SIT) and intensified SIT. In the 1980s the CCD and CMOS solid-state video image sensors were developed and remain the mainstay in the security industry. Increased consumer demand for video recorders using CCD sensors in camcorders and the CMOS sensor in digital still frame cameras caused a technology explosion and made these small, high-resolution, high-sensitivity, monochrome and color solid-state cameras available for security systems.

The security industry now has both analog and digital surveillance cameras at its disposal. Up until the mid-1990s analog cameras dominated, with only rare use of DSP electronics, and the digital Internet camera was only being introduced to the security market. Advances in solid-state circuitry, the demand from the consumer market, and the availability of the Internet were responsible for the rapid use of digital cameras for security applications.

The Scanning Process

Two methods used in the camera and monitor video scanning process are raster scanning and progressive scanning. In the past, analog video systems have all used the raster scanning technique; however, newer digital systems are now using progressive scanning. All cameras use some form of scanning to generate the video picture. A block diagram of the CCTV camera and a brief description of the analog raster scanning process and video signal are shown in Figs 20.8, 20.9, 20.18, and 20.19.

The camera sensor converts the optical image from the lens into an electrical signal. The camera electronics process the video signal and generate a composite video signal containing the picture information (luminance and color) and horizontal and vertical synchronizing pulses.

Signals are transmitted in what is called a *frame* of picture video, made up of two *fields* of information. Each field is transmitted in 1/60 of a second and the entire frame in 1/30 of a second, for a repetition rate of 30 fps. In the United States, this format is the Electronic Industries Association (EIA) standard called the NTSC system. The European standard uses 625 horizontal lines with a field taking 1/50 of a second and a frame 1/25 of a second and a repetition rate of 25 fps.

Raster Scanning

In the NTSC system the first picture field is created by scanning 262½ horizontal lines. The second field of the frame contains the second 262½ lines, which are synchronized so that they fall between the gaps of the first field lines thus producing one completely interlaced picture frame containing 525 lines. The scan lines of the second field fall exactly halfway between the lines of the first field resulting in a 2-to-1

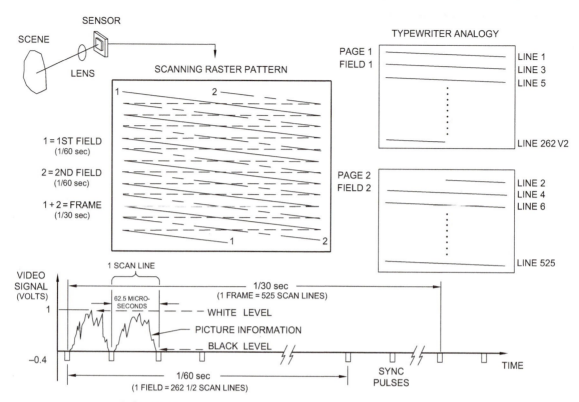

FIGURE 20.18 Analog video scanning process and video display signal.

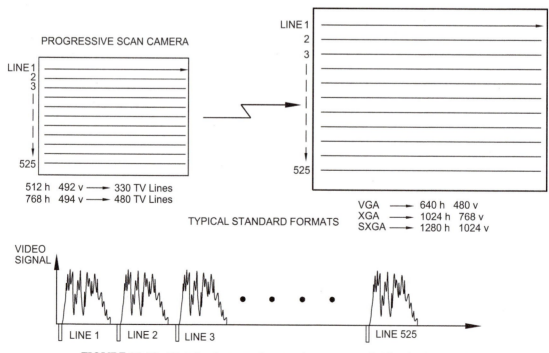

FIGURE 20.19 Digital and progressive scanning process and video display signal.

interlace system. As shown in Fig. 20.18, the first field starts at the upper left corner (of the camera sensor or the CRT monitor) and progresses down the sensor (or screen), line by line, until it ends at the bottom center of the scan.

Likewise the second field starts at the top center of the screen and ends at the lower right corner. Each time one line in the field traverses from the left side of the scan to the right it corresponds to one horizontal line as shown in the video waveform at the bottom of Fig. 20.18. The video waveform consists of negative synchronization pulses and positive picture information. The horizontal and vertical synchronization pulses are used by the video monitor (and VCR, DVR, or video printer) to synchronize the video picture and paint an exact replica in time and intensity of the camera scanning function onto the monitor face. Black picture information is indicated on the waveform at the bottom (approximately 0 V) and the white picture information at the top (1 V). The amplitude of a standard NTSC signal is 1.4 V peak to peak. In the 525-line system the picture information consists of approximately 512 lines. The lines with no picture information are necessary for vertical blanking, which is the time when the camera electronics or the beam in the monitor CRT moves from the bottom to the top to start a new field.

Random-interlace cameras do not provide complete synchronization between the first and the second fields. The horizontal and the vertical scan frequencies are not locked together, therefore, fields do not interlace exactly. This condition, however, results in an acceptable picture, and the asynchronous condition is difficult to detect. The two-to-one interlace system has an advantage when multiple cameras are used with multiple monitors and/or recorders in that they prevent jump or jitter when switching from one camera to the next.

The scanning process for solid-state cameras is different. The solid-state sensor consists of an array of very small picture elements (pixels) that are read out serially (sequentially)

by the camera electronics to produce the same NTSC format—525 TV lines in 1/30 of a second (30 fps)—as shown in Fig. 20.19.

The use of digital cameras and digital monitors has changed the way the camera and monitor signals are processed, transmitted, and displayed. The final presentation on the monitor looks similar to the analog method, but instead of seeing 525 horizontal lines (NTSC system) individual pixels are seen in a row and column format. In the digital system the camera scene is divided into rows and columns of individual pixels (small points in the scene) each representing the light intensity and color for each point in the scene. The digitized scene signal is transmitted to the digital display, be it LCD, plasma, or other, and reproduced on the monitor screen pixel by pixel, providing a faithful representation of the original scene.

Digital and Progressive Scan

The digital scanning is accomplished in the 2-to-1 interlace mode as in the analog system, or in a progressive mode. In the progressive mode each line is scanned in linear sequence: line 1, then line 2, line 3, and so forth. Solid-state camera sensors and monitor displays can be manufactured with a variety of horizontal and vertical pixels' formats. The standard aspect ratio is 4:3 as in the analog system, and 16:9 for the wide screen. Likewise, there are many different combinations of pixel numbers available in the sensor and display. Some standard formats for color CCD cameras are 512 h × 492 v for 330 TV line resolution and 768 h × 494 v for 480 TV line resolution, and for color LCD monitors it is 1280 h × 1024 v.

Solid-State Cameras

Video security cameras have gone through rapid technological change during the last half of the 1980s to the present. For decades the vidicon tube camera was the only security camera available. In the 1980s the more sensitive and rugged silicon-diode tube camera was the best available. In the late 1980s the invention and development of the digital CCD and later the CMOS cameras replaced the tube camera. This technology coincided with rapid advancement in DSP in cameras, the IP camera, and use of digital transmission of the video signal over LAN, WANs, and the Internet. The two generic solid-state cameras that account for most security applications are the CCD and the CMOS.

The first generation of solid-state cameras available from most manufacturers had 2/3-in. (sensor diagonal) and 1/2-in. sensor formats. As the technology improved, smaller formats evolved. Most solid-state cameras in use today are available in three image sensor formats: 1/2, 1/3, and 1/4 in. The 1/2-in.89 format produces higher resolution and sensitivity at a higher cost. The 1/2-in. and smaller formats permitted the use of smaller, less expensive lenses as compared with the larger formats. Many manufacturers now produce 1/3 and 1/4-in. format cameras with excellent resolution and light sensitivity. Solid-state sensor cameras are superior to their predecessors because of their (1) precise, repeatable pixel geometry, (2) low power requirements, (3) small size, (4) excellent color rendition and stability, and (5) ruggedness and long life expectancy. At present, solid-state cameras have settled into three main categories: (1) analog, (2) digital, and (3) Internet.

Analog

Analog cameras have been with the industry since CCTV has been used in security. Their electronics are straightforward and the technology is still used in many applications.

Digital

Since the end of the 1990s there has been an increased use of DSP in cameras. It significantly improves the performance of the camera by (1) automatically adjusting to large light level changes (eliminating the automatic-iris),

(2) integrating the VMD into the camera, and (3) automatically switching the camera from color operation to higher sensitivity monochrome operation, as well as other features and enhancements.

Internet

The most recent camera technology advancement is manifest in the IP camera. This camera is configured with electronics that connects to the Internet and the WWW network through an Internet service provider. Each camera is provided with a registered Internet address and can transmit the video image anywhere on the network. This is really remote video monitoring at its best. The camera site is viewed from anywhere by entering the camera Internet address (ID number) and proper password. Password security is used so that only authorized users can enter the Website and view the camera image. Two-way communication is used so that the user can control camera parameters and direct the camera operation (pan, tilt, zoom, etc.) from the monitoring site.

LLL-Intensified Camera

When a security application requires viewing during nighttime conditions where the available light is moonlight, starlight, or other residual reflected light, and the surveillance must be covert (no active illumination like IR LEDs), LLL-intensified CCD cameras are used. The ICCD cameras have sensitivities between 100 and 1000 times higher than the best solid-state cameras. The increased sensitivity is obtained through the use of a light amplifier mounted in between the lens and the CCD sensor. LLL cameras cost between 10 and 20 times more than CCD cameras.

Thermal Imaging Camera

An alternative to the ICCD camera is the thermal IR camera. Visual cameras see only visible light energy from the blue end of the visible spectrum to the red end (approximately 400–700 nm). Some monochrome cameras see beyond the visible region into the near-IR region of the spectrum up to 1000 nm. This IR energy, however, is not thermal IR energy. Thermal IR cameras using thermal sensors respond to thermal energy in the 3–5 and 8–14 µm range. The IR sensors respond to the changes in heat (thermal) energy emitted by the targets in the scene. Thermal imaging cameras can operate in complete darkness as they require no visible or IR illumination whatever. They are truly passive nighttime monochrome imaging sensors. They can detect humans and any other warm objects (animals, vehicle engines, ships, aircraft, warm/hot spots in buildings) or other objects against a scene background.

Panoramic 360 degree Camera

Powerful mathematical techniques combined with the unique 360 degree panoramic lens have made a 360 degree panoramic camera possible. In operation the lens collects and focuses the 360 degree horizontal by up to 90 degree vertical scene (one-half of a sphere; a hemisphere) onto the camera sensor. The image takes the form of a "donut" on the sensor (Fig. 20.20).

The camera/lens is located at the origin (0). The scene is represented by the surface of the hemisphere. As shown, a small part (slice) of the scene area (A, B, C, D) is "mapped" onto the sensor as a, b, c, d. In this way the full scene is mapped onto the sensor. Direct presentation of the donut-ring video image onto the monitor does not result in a useful picture.

That is where the use of a powerful mathematical algorithm comes in. Digital processing in the computer using the algorithm transforms the donut-shaped image into the normal format seen on a monitor, that is, horizontal and vertical.

All of the 0–360 degree horizontal by 90 degree vertical images cannot be presented on a monitor in a useful way—there is just too much picture "squeezed" into the small screen area. This condition is solved by computer software by looking at only a section of the entire scene at any particular time.

The main attributes of the panoramic system include: (1) capturing a full 360 degree FOV, (2) the ability to digitally pan/tilt to anywhere in the scene and digitally zoom any scene area, (3) having no moving parts (no motors, etc., that can wear out), and (4) having multiple operators that can view any part of the scene in real time or at a later time.

The panoramic camera requires a high-resolution camera since so much scene information is contained in the image. Camera technology has progressed so that these digital cameras are available and can present a good image of a zoomed-in portion of the panoramic scene.

TRANSMISSION

By definition, the camera must be remotely located from the monitor and therefore the video signal must be transmitted by some means from one location to another. In security applications, the distance between the camera and the monitor may be from tens of feet to many miles or, perhaps, completely around the globe. The transmission path may be inside buildings, outside buildings, above ground, underground, through the atmosphere, or in almost any environment imaginable. For this reason, the transmission means must be carefully assessed and an optimum choice of hardware made to satisfactorily transmit the video signal from the camera to the monitoring site. There are many ways to transmit the video signal from the camera to the monitoring site. Fig. 20.21 shows some examples of transmission cables.

The signal can be analog or digital. It can be transmitted via electrical conductors using coaxial cable or UTP, by fiber optic, by LAN or WAN, and intranet or Internet.

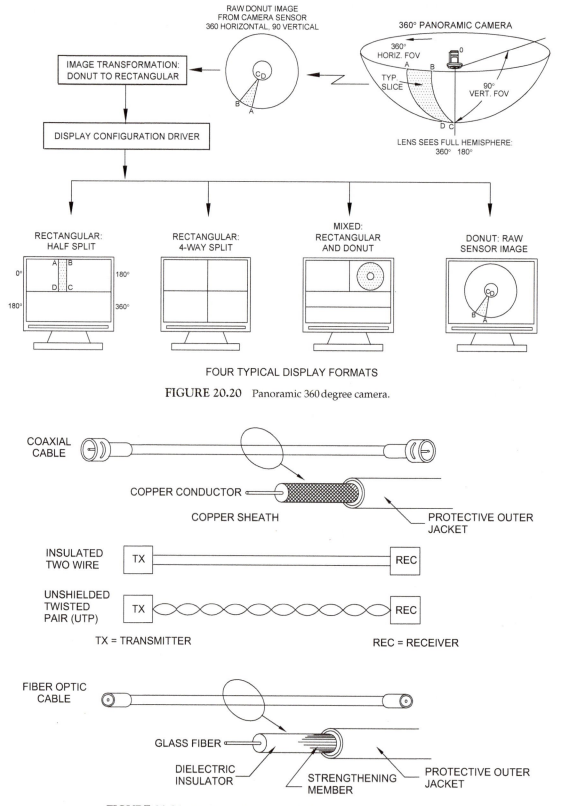

RAW DONUT IMAGE
FROM CAMERA SENSOR
360 HORIZONTAL, 90 VERTICAL

360° PANORAMIC CAMERA

IMAGE TRANSFORMATION:
DONUT TO RECTANGULAR

360°
HORIZ. FOV

TYP.
SLICE

90°
VERT. FOV

LENS SEES FULL HEMISPHERE:
360° 180°

DISPLAY CONFIGURATION DRIVER

RECTANGULAR:
HALF SPLIT

RECTANGULAR:
4-WAY SPLIT

MIXED:
RECTANGULAR
AND DONUT

DONUT: RAW
SENSOR IMAGE

FOUR TYPICAL DISPLAY FORMATS

FIGURE 20.20   Panoramic 360 degree camera.

COAXIAL
CABLE

COPPER CONDUCTOR

COPPER SHEATH

PROTECTIVE OUTER
JACKET

INSULATED
TWO WIRE

TX

REC

UNSHIELDED
TWISTED
PAIR (UTP)

TX

REC

TX = TRANSMITTER

REC = RECEIVER

FIBER OPTIC
CABLE

GLASS FIBER

DIELECTRIC
INSULATOR

STRENGTHENING
MEMBER

PROTECTIVE OUTER
JACKET

FIGURE 20.21   Hard-wired copper and fiber-optic transmission means.

Particular attention should be paid to transmission means when transmitting color video signals, since the color signal is significantly more complex and susceptible to distortion than monochrome. There are advantages and disadvantages of all of the transmission means and the hardware available to transmit the video signal.

Hard Wired

There are several hard-wired means for transmitting a video signal: coaxial cable, UTP, LAN, WAN, intranet, Internet, and fiber-optic cable.

Fiber-optic cable is used for long distances and when there is interfering electrical noise. LANs and Internet connections are digital transmission techniques used in larger security systems and where the signal must be transmitted over existing computer networks or over long distances.

Coaxial Cable

The most common video signal transmission method is the coaxial cable. This cable has been used since the inception of CCTV and is still in use today. The cable is inexpensive and easy to terminate at the camera and monitor ends, and it transmits a faithful video signal with little or no distortion or loss. It has a 75-Ω electrical impedance, which matches the impedance of the camera and monitor, ensuring a distortion-free video image. This coaxial cable has a copper electrical shield and center conductor that works well over distances up to 1000 ft.

Unshielded Twisted Pair

In the 1990s UTP video transmission came into vogue. The technique uses a transmitter at the camera and a receiver at the monitor with two twisted copper wires connecting them. Several reasons for its increased popularity are that (1) it can be used over longer distances than coaxial cable, (2) it uses inexpensive wire, (3) many locations already have two-wire twisted-pair installed, (4) it uses a low-cost transmitter and receiver, and (5) it has higher electrical noise immunity as compared

with coaxial cable. The UTP using a sophisticated electronic transmitter and receiver can transmit the video signal 2000–3000 ft.

LAN, WAN, Intranet, and Internet

The evolution of the LAN, WAN, intranet, and Internet revolutionized the transmission of video signals in a new form (digital), which significantly expanded the scope and effectiveness of video for security systems. The widespread use of business computers and consequent use of these networks provided an existing digital network protocol and communications suitable for video transmission. The Internet and WWW attained widespread use in the late 1990s and truly revolutionized digital video transmission. This global computer network provided the digital backbone path to transmit digital video, audio, and command signals from anywhere on the globe.

The video signal transmission techniques described so far provide a means for real-time transmission of a video signal, requiring a full 4.2-MHz bandwidth to reproduce real-time motion. When these techniques cannot be used for real-time video, alternative digital techniques are used. In these systems, a non-real-time video transmission takes place, so that some scene action is lost. Depending on the action in the scene, the resolution, from near real time (15 fps) to slow scan (a few fps) of the video image is transmitted. The digitized and compressed video signal is transmitted over a LAN or Internet network and decompressed and reconstructed at the receiver/monitoring site.

Wireless

In legacy analog video surveillance systems, it is often more economical or beneficial to transmit the real-time video signal without cable (wireless) from the camera to the monitor using an RF or IR atmospheric link. In digital video systems using digital transmission, the use of wireless networks (WiFi) permits routing the video and control signals to any remote location. In both the analog and the digital systems some form of video scrambling or encryption is often used to remove the possibility of eavesdropping by unauthorized personnel outside the system. Three important applications for wireless transmission include: (1) covert and portable rapid deployment video installations, (2) building-to-building transmission over a roadway, and (3) parking lot light poles to building. The Federal Communications Commission (FCC) restricts some wireless transmitting devices using microwave frequencies or RF to government and law enforcement use but has given approval for many RF and microwave transmitters for general security use. These FCC-approved devices operate above the normal television frequency bands at approximately 920 MHz and 2.4 and 5.8 GHz. The atmospheric IR link is used when a high-security link is required. This link does not require an FCC approval and transmits a video image over a narrow beam of visible light or near-IR energy. The beam is very difficult to intercept (tap). Fig. 20.22 illustrates some of the wireless transmission techniques available today.

Fiber Optics

Fiber-optic transmission technology has advanced significantly in the last 5–10 years and represents a highly reliable, secure means of transmission. Fiber-optic transmission holds several significant advantages over other hard-wired systems: (1) very long transmission paths up to many miles without any significant degradation in the video signal with monochrome or color; (2) immunity to external electrical disturbances from weather or electrical equipment; (3) very wide bandwidth, permitting one or more video, control, and audio signals to be multiplexed on a single fiber; and (4) resistance to tapping (eavesdropping) and therefore a very secure transmission means.

Although the installation and termination of fiber-optic cable requires a more skilled technician, it is well within the capability of qualified security installers. Many hard-wired installations requiring the optimum color and resolution rendition use fiber-optic cable.

SWITCHERS

The video switcher accepts video signals from many different video cameras and connects them to one or more monitors or recorders. Using manual or automatic activation or an alarming signal input, the switcher selects one or more of the cameras and directs its video signal to a specified monitor, recorder, or some other device or location.

Standard

There are four basic switcher types: manual, sequential, homing, and alarming. Fig. 20.23 shows how these are connected into the video security system.

The manual switcher connects one camera at a time to the monitor, recorder, or printer. The sequential switcher automatically switches the cameras in sequence to the output device. The operator can override the automatic sequence with the homing sequential switcher. The alarming switcher connects the alarmed camera to the output device automatically, when an alarm is received.

Microprocessor Controlled

When the security system requires many cameras in various locations with multiple monitors and other alarm input functions, a microprocessor-controlled switcher and keyboard is used to manage these additional requirements (Fig. 20.24).

In large security systems the switcher is microprocessor controlled and can switch hundreds of cameras to dozens of monitors, recorders, or video printers via an RS-232 or other communication control link. Numerous manufacturers

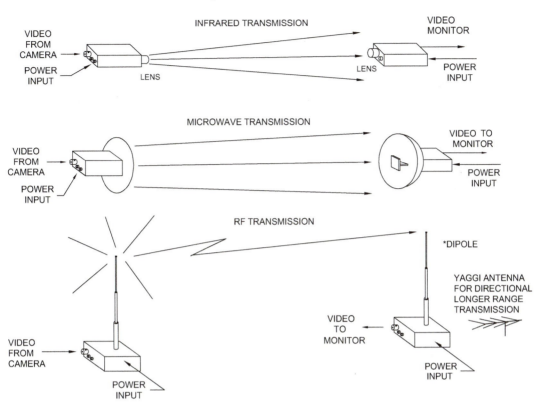

FIGURE 20.22   Radio frequency, microwave, and infrared video transmission links.

make comprehensive keyboard-operated, computer-controlled consoles that integrate the functions of the switcher, pan/tilt pointing, automatic scanning, automatic preset pointing for pan/tilt systems, and many other functions. The power of the software-programmable console resides in its flexibility, expandability, and ability to accommodate a large variety of applications and changes in facility design. In place of a dedicated hardware system built for each specific application, this computer-controlled system can be configured via software for the application.

QUADS AND MULTIPLEXERS

A quad or a multiplexer is used when multiple camera scenes need to be displayed on one video monitor. It is interposed between the cameras and the monitor, accepts multiple camera inputs, memorizes the scenes from each camera, compresses them, and then displays multiple scenes on a single video monitor. Equipment is available to provide 2, 4, 9, 16, and up to 32 separate video scenes on one single monitor. Fig. 20.25 shows a block diagram of quad and multiplexer systems.

The most popular presentation is the quad screen showing four pictures. This presentation significantly improves camera viewing ability in multicamera systems, decreases security guard fatigue, and requires three fewer monitors in a four-camera system. There is a loss of resolution when more than one scene is presented on the monitor with resolution decreasing as the number of scenes increases. One-quarter of the resolution of a full screen is obtained on a quad display

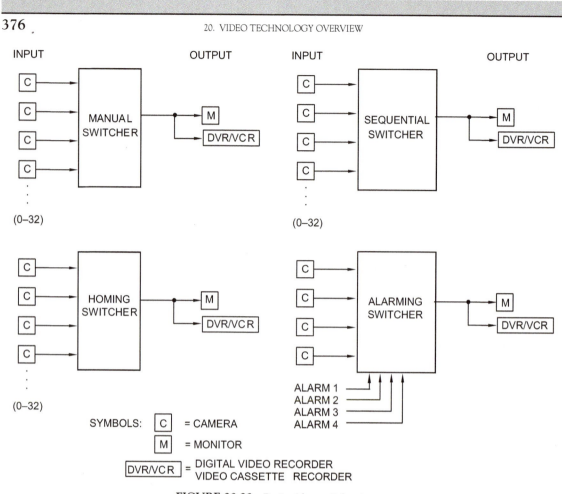

FIGURE 20.23　Basic video switcher types.

(half in horizontal and half in vertical). Quads and multiplexers have front panel controls so that: (1) a full screen image of a camera can be selected, (2) multiple cameras can be displayed (quad, nine, etc.), or (3) the full screen images of all cameras can be sequentially switched with dwell times for each camera, set by the operator.

MONITORS

Video monitors can be divided into several categories: (1) monochrome, (2) color, (3) CRT, (4) LCD, (5) plasma, (6) computer display, and (7) high definition. Contrary to a popular misconception, larger video monitors do not necessarily

have better picture resolution or the ability to increase the amount of intelligence available in the picture. All US NTSC security monitors have 525 horizontal lines; therefore, the vertical resolution is about the same regardless of the CRT monitor size. The horizontal resolution is determined by the system bandwidth. With the NTSC limitation the best picture quality is obtained by choosing a monitor with resolution equal to or better than the camera or transmission link bandwidth. With the use of a higher resolution computer monitor and corresponding higher resolution camera and commensurate bandwidth to match, higher resolution video images are obtained. Fig. 20.26 shows representative examples of video monitors.

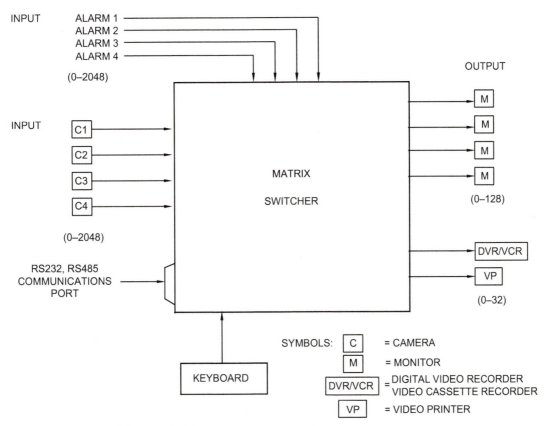

FIGURE 20.24 Microprocessor-controlled switcher and keyboard.

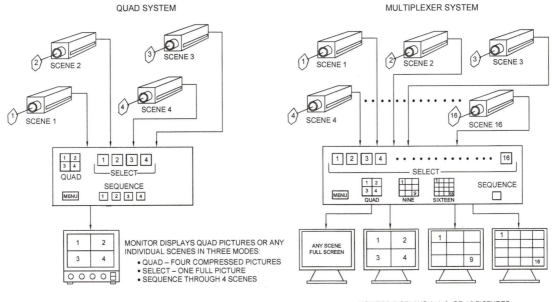

FIGURE 20.25 Quad and multiplexer block diagrams.

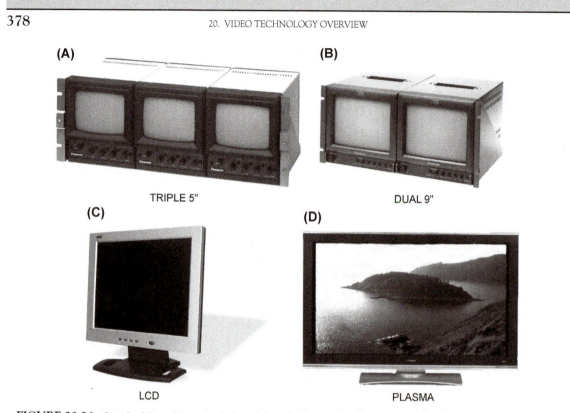

FIGURE 20.26 Standard 5- and 9-in. single/multiple cathode ray tube, liquid crystal display, and plasma monitors.

Monochrome

Until the late 1990s the most popular monitor used in CCTV systems was the monochrome CRT monitor. It is still used and is available in sizes ranging from a 1-in. diagonal viewfinder to a large 27-in. diagonal CRT. By far the most popular monochrome monitor size is the 9-in. diagonal that optimizes video viewing for a person seated about 3 ft away. A second reason for its popularity is that two of these monitors fit into the standard EIA 19-in. wide rack-mount panel. Fig. 20.26(B) shows two 9-in. monitors in a dual rack–mounted version. A triple rack–mounted version of a 5-in. diagonal monitor is used when space is at a premium. The triple rack–mounted monitor is popular, since three fit conveniently into the 19-in. EIA rack. The optimum viewing distance for the triple 5-in. diagonal monitor is about 1.5 ft.

Color

Color monitors are now in widespread use and range in size from a 3- to 27-in. diagonal and have required viewing distances and capabilities similar to those of monochrome monitors. Since color monitors require three different colored dots to produce one pixel of information on the monitor, they have lower horizontal resolution than monochrome monitors. Popular color monitor sizes are 13-, 15-, and 17-in. diagonal.

CRT, LCD, Plasma, HD, 1080p Displays

The video security picture is displayed on three basic types of monitor screens: (1) CRT, (2) LCD, and, most recently, (3) the plasma display. The analog CRT has seen excellent service from the inception of video and continues as a strong contender providing a low-cost, reliable security monitor. The digital LCD monitor is growing in popularity because of its smaller size (smaller depth)—2–3 in. versus 12–20 in. for the CRT. The LCD is an all solid-state display that accepts the VGA computer signal. Most small (3- to 10-in. diagonal) and many large (10- to 17-in. diagonal) LCD monitors also accept an analog video input. The most recent monitor entry into the security market is the digital plasma display. This premium display excels in resolution and brightness and viewing angle and produces the highest quality image in the industry. It is also the most expensive. Screen sizes range from 20 to 42 in. diagonal. Overall depths are small and range in size from 3 to 4 in. They are available in 4:3 and HDTV 16:9 format.

Audio/Video

Many monitors have a built-in audio channel with speakers to produce audio and video simultaneously.

RECORDERS

The video camera, transmission means, and monitor provide the remote eyes for the security guard, but as soon as the action or event is over the image disappears from the monitor screen forever. When a permanent record of the live video scene is required a VCR, DVR, network video recorder, or optical disk recorder is used (Fig. 20.27).

The video image can be recorded in real time, near real time, or TL. The VCRs record the video signal on a magnetic tape cassette with a maximum real-time recording time of 6h and near real time of 24h. When extended periods of recording are required (longer than the 6-h real-time cassette), a TL recorder is used. In the TL process the video picture is not recorded continuously (real time), but rather "snapshots" are recorded. These snapshots are spread apart in time by a fraction of a second or even seconds so that the total elapsed time for the recording can extend for hundreds of hours. Some present TL systems record over an elapsed time of 1280h.

The DVR records the video image on a computer magnetic hard drive (HD) and the optical disk storage on optical disk media. The DVR and optical disk systems have a significant advantage over the VCR with respect to retrieval time of a particular video frame. VCRs take many minutes to fast forward or fast rewind the magnetic tape to locate a particular frame on the tape. Retrieval times on DVRs and optical disks are typically a fraction of a second. The VCR cassette tape is transportable and the DVR and optical disk systems are available with or without removable disks. This means that the video images (digital data) can be transported to remote locations or stored in a vault for safekeeping. The removable DVR and optical disks are about the same size as VHS cassettes.

SINGLE CHANNEL DVR   16 CHANNEL DVR   32 CHANNEL NVR

FIGURE 20.27 Digital video recorder and network video recorder video disk storage equipment.

Video Cassette Recorder

Magnetic storage media have been used universally to record the video image. The VCR uses the standard VHS cassette format. The 8-mm Sony format is used in portable surveillance equipment because of its smaller size. Super VHS and Hi-8 formats are used to obtain higher resolution. VCRs can be subdivided into two classes: real time and TL. The TL recorder has significantly different mechanical and electrical features permitting it to take snapshots of a scene at predetermined (user-selectable) intervals. It can also record in real time when activated by an alarm or other input command. Real-time recorders can record up to 6h in monochrome or color. TL VCRs are available for recording time lapse sequences up to 720h.

Digital Video Recorder

The DVR has emerged as the new generation of magnetic recorder of choice. A magnetic HD like those used in a microcomputer can store many thousands of images and many hours of video in digital form. The rapid implementation and success of the DVR has resulted from the availability of inexpensive digital magnetic memory storage devices and the advancements made in digital signal compression techniques. Present DVRs are available in single channel and 4 and 16 channels and may be cascaded to provide many more channels.

A significant feature of the DVR is the ability to access (retrieve) a particular frame or recorded time period anywhere on the disk in a fraction of a second. The digital technology also allows many generations (copies) of the stored video images to be made without any errors or degradation of the image.

Optical Disk

When very large volumes of video images need to be recorded, an optical disk system is used. Optical disks have a much larger video image database capacity than magnetic disks given the same physical space they occupy. These disks can record hundreds of times longer than their magnetic counterparts.

HARD-COPY VIDEO PRINTERS

A hard-copy printout of a video image is often required as evidence in court, as a tool for apprehending a vandal or thief, or as a duplicate record of some document or person. The printout is produced by a hard-copy video printer, which is a thermal printer that "burns" the video image onto coated paper or an ink-jet or laser printer. The thermal technique used by many hard-copy printer manufacturers produces excellent quality images in monochrome or color. Fig. 20.28 shows a monochrome thermal printer and a sample of the hard-copy image quality it produces. In operation, the image displayed on the monitor or played back from the recorder is immediately memorized by the printer and printed out in less than 10s. This is particularly useful if an intrusion or unauthorized act has occurred and been observed by a security guard. An automatic alarm or a security guard can initiate printing the image of the alarm area or of the suspect and the printout can then be given to another guard to take action. For courtroom uses, time, date, and any other information can be annotated on the printed image.

ANCILLARY EQUIPMENT

Most video security systems require additional accessories and equipment, including: (1) camera housings, (2) camera pan/tilt mechanisms and mounts, (3) camera identifiers, (4) VMDs, (5) image splitters/inserters, and (6) image combiners. The two accessories most often used with the basic camera, monitor, and

(A)

(B)

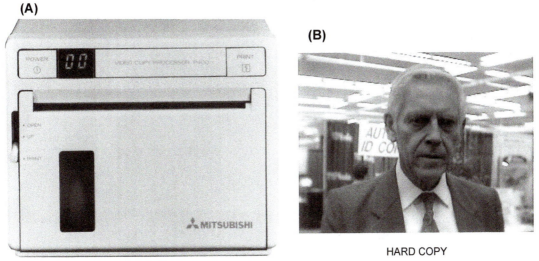

HARD COPY

PRINTER

FIGURE 20.28 Thermal monochrome video printer and hard copy.

transmission link are camera housings and pan/tilt mounts. Outdoor housings are used to protect the camera and lens from vandalism and the environment. Indoor housings are used primarily to prevent vandalism and for aesthetic reasons. The motorized pan/tilt mechanisms rotate and point the system camera and lens via commands from a remote control console.

Camera Housings

Indoor and outdoor camera housings protect cameras and lenses from dirt, dust, harmful chemicals, the environment, and vandalism. The most common housings are rectangular metal or plastic products, formed from high-impact indoor or outdoor plastic, painted steel, or stainless steel (Fig. 20.29). Other shapes and types include cylindrical (tube), corner-mount, ceiling-mount, and dome housings.

Standard Rectangular

The rectangular-type housing is the most popular. It protects the camera from the environment and provides a window for the lens to view the scene. The housings are available for indoor or outdoor use with a weatherproof and tamper-resistant design. Options include heaters, fans, and window washers.

Dome

A significant part of video surveillance is accomplished using cameras housed in the dome housing configuration. The dome camera housing can range from a simple fixed monochrome or color camera in a hemispherical dome to a "speed-dome" housing having a high-resolution color camera with remote-controlled pan/tilt/zoom/focus. Other options include presets and image stabilization. The dome-type housing consists of a plastic hemispherical dome on the bottom half. The housing can be clear, tinted, or treated with a partially transmitting optical coating that allows the camera to see in any direction. In a freestanding application (e.g., on a pole, pedestal, or overhang), the top half of the housing consists of a protective cover and a means for attaching the dome to the structure. When the dome housing is mounted in a ceiling, a simpler

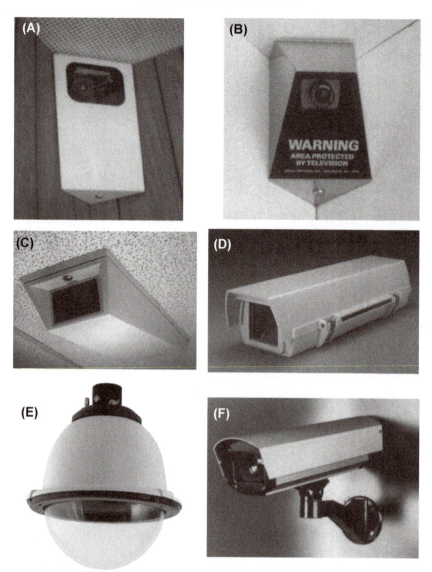

FIGURE 20.29 Standard indoor/outdoor video housings: (A) corner, (B) elevator corner, (C) ceiling, (D) outdoor environmental rectangular, (E) dome, and (F) plug and play.

housing cover is provided and mounted above the ceiling level to support the dome.

Specialty

There are many other specialty housings for mounting in or on elevators, ceilings, walls, tunnels, pedestals, hallways, and so forth. These special types include explosion-proof, bulletproof, and extreme environmental construction for arctic and desert use.

Plug and Play

In an effort to reduce installation time for video surveillance cameras, manufacturers have combined the camera, lens, and housing in one assembly ready to be mounted on a ceiling, wall, or pole and plugged into the power source and video transmission cable. These assemblies are available in the form of domes, corner mounts, ceiling mounts, and so forth, making for easy installation in indoor or outdoor applications.

Pan/Tilt Mounts

To extend the angle of coverage of a CCTV lens/camera system a motorized pan/tilt mechanism is often used. Fig. 20.30 shows three generic outdoor pan/tilt types: top mounted, side mounted, and dome camera.

The pan/tilt motorized mounting platform permits the camera and lens to rotate horizontally (pan) or vertically (tilt) when it receives an electrical command from the central monitoring site. Thus the camera lens is not limited by its inherent FOV and can view a much larger area of a scene. A camera mounted on a pan/tilt platform is usually provided with a zoom lens. The zoom lens varies the FOV in the pointing direction of the camera/lens from a command from the central security console. The combination of the pan/tilt and zoom lens provides the widest angular coverage for video surveillance. There is one disadvantage with the pan/tilt/zoom configuration compared with the fixed camera installation.

When the camera and lens are pointing in a particular direction via the pan/tilt platform, most of the other scene area the camera is designed to cover is not viewed. This dead area or dead time is unacceptable in many security applications; therefore, careful consideration should be given to the adequacy of their wide FOV pan/tilt design. Pan/tilt platforms range from small, indoor, lightweight units that only pan, up to large, outdoor, environmental designs carrying large cameras, zoom lenses, and large housings. Choosing the correct pan/tilt mechanism is important since it generally requires more service and maintenance than any other part of the video system.

Video Motion Detector

Another important component in a video surveillance system is a VMD that produces an alarm signal based on a change in the video scene. The VMD can be built into the camera or be a separate component inserted between the camera and the monitor software in a computer.

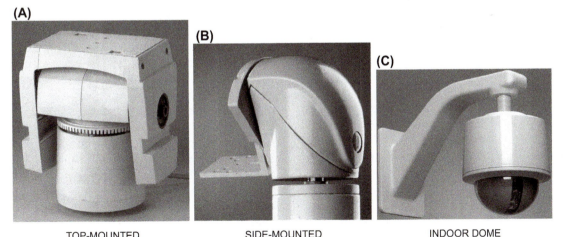

(A)

(B)

(C)

TOP-MOUNTED   SIDE-MOUNTED   INDOOR DOME

FIGURE 20.30 Video pan/tilt mechanisms.

The VMD electronics, analog or digital, store the video frames, compare subsequent frames with the stored frames, and then determine whether the scene has changed. In operation the VMD digital electronics decides whether the change is significant and whether to call it an alarm to alert the guard or some equipment, or declare it a false alarm.

Screen Splitter

The electronic or optical screen splitter takes a part of several camera scenes (two, three, or more), combines the scenes, and displays them on one monitor. The splitters do not compress the image. In an optical splitter the image combining is implemented optically at the camera lens and requires no electronics. The electronic splitter/combiner is located between the camera output and the monitor input.

Camera Video Annotation

Camera ID

When multiple cameras are used in a video system some means must be provided to identify the camera. The system uses a camera identifier component that electronically assigns an alphanumeric code and/or name to each camera displayed on a monitor, recorded on a recorder, or printed on a printer. Alphanumeric and symbol character generators are available to annotate the video signal with the names of cameras, locations in a building, and so forth.

Time and Date

When time and date is required on the video image, a time/date generator is used to annotate the video picture. This information is mandatory for any prosecution or courtroom procedure.

Image Reversal

Occasionally video surveillance systems use a single mirror to view the scene. This mirror reverses the video image from the normal left-to-right to a right-to-left (reversed image). The image reversal unit corrects the reversal.

SUMMARY

Video surveillance serves as the remote eyes for management and the security force. It provides security personnel with advance notice of breaches in security, including hostile and terrorist acts, and is a part of the plan to protect personnel and assets. It is a critical subsystem for any comprehensive security plan. In this chapter an introduction to most of the current video technology and equipment has been described.

Lighting plays an important role in determining whether a satisfactory video picture will be obtained with monochrome and color cameras and LLL ICCD cameras. Thermal IR cameras are insensitive to light and only require temperature differences between the target and the background.

There are many types of lenses available for video systems: FFL, varifocal, zoom, pinhole, panoramic, and so forth. The varifocal and zoom lenses extend the FOV of the FFL lens. The panoramic 360 degree lens provides entire viewing of the scene. The proper choice of lens is necessary to maximize the intelligence obtained from the scene.

Many types of video cameras are available, such as color, monochrome (with or without IR illumination), LLL intensified, thermal IR, analog and digital, simple and full featured, and daytime and nighttime. There are cameras with built-in VMD to alert security guards and improve their ability to detect and locate personnel and be alerted to activity in the scene.

An important component of the video system is the analog or digital video signal transmission means from the camera to the remote site and to the monitoring and recording site. Hard wire or fiber optics is best if the situation permits. Analog works for short distances and digital for long distances. The Internet works globally.

In multiple camera systems the quad and multiplexers permit multicamera displays on one monitor. Fewer monitors in the security room can improve guard performance.

The CRT monitor is still a good choice for many video applications. The LCD is the solid-state digital replacement for the CRT. The plasma display provides an all solid-state design that has the highest resolution and brightness and largest viewing angle, but at the highest cost.

Until about the year 2000 the only practical means for recording a permanent image of the scene was the VCR real-time or TL recorder. Now, new and upgraded systems replace the VCR with the DVR recorder with its increased reliability and fast search and retrieval capabilities to distribute the recorded video over a LAN, WAN, intranet, or Internet or wirelessly with WiFi using one of the 802.11 protocols.

Thermal, ink-jet, and laser hard-copy printers produce monochrome and color prints for immediate picture dissemination and permanent records for archiving.

All types of camera/lens housings are available for indoor and outdoor applications. Specialty cameras/housings are available for elevators, stairwells, public facilities, casinos, shopping malls, extreme outdoor environments, and so forth.

Pan/tilt assemblies for indoor and outdoor scenarios significantly increase the overall FOV of the camera system. Small, compact speed domes have found widespread use in many indoor and outdoor video surveillance environments.

Plug and play surveillance cameras permit quick installation and turn-on and are available in almost every housing configuration and camera type.

The video components summarized above are used in most video security applications including: (1) retail stores, (2) manufacturing plants, (3) shopping malls, (4) offices, (5) airports, (6) seaports, (7) bus and rail terminals, and (8) government facilities. There is widespread use of small video cameras and accessories for temporary covert applications. The small size and ease of deployment of many video components and the flexibility in transmission means over short and long distances has made rapid deployment equipment for portable personnel protection systems practical and important. It is clear that the direction the video security industry is taking is the integration of the video security function with digital computing technology and the other parts of the security system: access control, intrusion alarms, fire, and two-way communications. Video security is rapidly moving from the legacy analog technology to the digital automatic video surveillance technology.

GLOSSARY FOR CCTV

Many terms and definitions used in the security industry are unique to CCTV surveillance; others are derived from the electro-optical-optical and information-computer industries. This comprehensive glossary will help the reader better understand the literature, interpret manufacturers' specifications, and write bid specifications and requests for quotation. These terms encompass the CCTV, physical computer and communications industries, basic physics, electricity, mechanics, and optics.

1. Serves as a deterrent
2. Records as a witness various events
3. Recognition and detection
4. Connect active usage
5. Capable of watching many areas at same time
6. Records and transmits
7. Camera can pan and tilt, zoom, and be in color
8. Return on Investment makes it worthwhile

Understanding Layers of Protection Analysis

Mark Beaudry, Ph.D., CPP

INTRODUCTION

The usage of risk analyses has been adopted by security professionals around the world as a best practice. This risk analysis typically begins with an assessment that determines the likelihood of an unfortunate event that may possibly occur. A risk analysis may or may not require some type of quantitative data in the event or likelihood that an event will occur. It also assesses this likelihood and provides a comparative analysis to determine the probability that the existing protection layers will or will not operate as required (sometimes technology, procedures, or human behavior may not act or perform as predetermined). In addition, a risk is the result of any deviation from the expected operation, process design, failed procedures, or a lax (possibly a nonexistent) site safety and security culture. The risk analysis seeks to identify these deviations and to develop a plan to reduce or mitigate an event should one occur. Once the results of each deviation have been measured and analyzed, the design and previous performance should be included as part of the holistic posture. This of course may result in some of the event deviations being significant enough that a

serious hazard may be likely. However, by using the layers of protection analysis (LOPA) concept a security professional can reduce or mitigate the risk as low as reasonably manageable.

Any business or agency that has implemented and uses a risk-ranking procedure do so to support a risk matrix, which compares the frequency and consequence priorities. The risk-ranking procedure is used to determine both the priority and criticality posture for the security professional to make recommendations that will additionally reduce or mitigate a risk of any deficiencies specifically within the safety and security measures. In addition, a security professional is then able to provide the rankings of the consequence severity by considering the hazardous situation posed by the event. It is important that the consequence severity ranking be based on the harm that results when everything that could go wrong, either has gone wrong or may go wrong (training, testing, and any simulations that can be done will assist with finding any deviations). Also, sometimes the historical data can be used to determine previous incidents or difficulties that security professionals may have experienced. Determine if there are any incident records including any safety and security

Effective Physical Security, Fifth Edition
http://dx.doi.org/10.1016/B978-0-12-804462-9.00021-X

operation safeguards that can reduce the potential harm caused by varied types of hazardous situations (i.e., such as an armed intruder or a failed emergency response procedure). As stated previously, any type of consequence modeling or simulations, role playing, or realistic training that can be practiced and can be used to better understand the hazardous situation and impact zones where the situation has or may possibly occur moving forward [4].

Layers of Protection Analysis

The security professional also may use varied levels of a risk analysis to provide estimates that the event likelihood technique called LOPA. The LOPA also allows the risk to be estimated along various points throughout the incident sequence. In addition, it can provide quantitative estimates of the risk, which LOPA can be applied to hazardous events that have a consequence severity involving any type of scenario:

- Any facility or equipment damage or failures that may cause harm (i.e., may be either an internal or external explosion, or a detonation within the facility perimeter);
- Significant operations interruption (i.e., possibly a bomb threat, workplace violence incident, threat via the mail, etc....);
- Serious injury or fatality of an employee or staff (i.e., active shooter/active assailant, etc....);
- Any external injury or fatality to the community at large;
- Significant environmental impact that affects everyone (i.e., gas or chemical exposure).

When LOPA is used by the security professional, they will begin with examining how causes lead to process deviations (or initiating events), this will assist with understanding how they propagate (also called "chain reaction" or domino effect). Hopefully, the security professional is able to determine if any enabling conditions (root causes) were critical to understanding the

failed event, i.e., any inappropriate process deviation. In addition, the risk rank procedure that is performed will use a risk matrix for calculation purposes, and then the event risk is compared to the operations risk to determine whether additional risk reduction or mitigation techniques is required. According to Ref. [3], who argue that when the process risk does not satisfy the chosen risk criteria then an independent protection layer (IPL) is used to close the gap by reducing or mitigating the hazardous or harmful event frequency [1]. Initially, the main purpose of IPLs is to stop propagation of the hazardous event (think of it as a time-delayed mechanism) and any probable harm that may result from the event. Generally, most security professionals will utilize an onion skin concept (sometimes referred to as lines of defense or defense in depth), used to illustrate the typical order of IPL deployment. Should a scenario progress through the onion skin of IPLs, it is designed to prevent or reduce the impact on the process operation. Also, a key element of using these types of lines of defense, it will cause time delays, or difficulties, or the propagation (sometimes called a hard target versus a soft target that does not use layers of protection). Using LOPA is exactly represented by the layers of an onion skin, sometimes called "lines of defense" (Fig. 21.1). The objective is to implement barriers

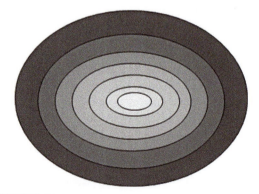

FIGURE 21.1 Typical lines of defense when designing layers of protection.

that will result in time delays for the offender to get to a targeted area.

Ultimately, the primary goal of any layers of protection design is to implement a plan that will add value to preventing or delaying (reduce or mitigate) any attempts to breaching a business environment successfully. Typically, most designs lack an overall full proof plan. However, LOPA will assist the security professional to design a safer environment that adds key lines of defense with manageable access control and supervisory procedures or measures (checks and balance technique). In addition, the LOPA design creates preventive and mitigation layers that add to mitigating events from occurring. In addition, a well-designed posture that proactively reduces or mitigates any type of hazardous event can have a high certainty of effectiveness.

Since risk is a function of frequency and consequence, the frequency estimation and the LOPA concept can provide different techniques in evaluating its acceptability. Typically, the consequence severity is used by security professionals to conduct an assessment of the potential likelihood of events for more strict frequency analysis. As mentioned previously, many security professionals may rely on the assessment of operating experience and incident history to make their determination, and they may use holistic factors that influence the severity (i.e., crime rates, types of crime data, etc....), including operating practices, layers of protection, and conditional modifiers that can alert or monitor a situations events. Historically, during the assessments, the security professional may consider reactive and response layers, i.e., actions that facility personnel must take to reduce or mitigate harm, this will sometimes be in addition to the proactive layers (i.e., closing and locking a door from the inside of an office or room). One other important issue to keep in mind is that each layer provides protection independent of each other, the use of these layers and the conditional modifiers are critical, since they are often interrelated. For example, an alarm annunciator system may be used to initiate evacuation of personnel or a lockdown situation for occupants.

Using Layers of Protection Analysis

When using risk analysis, the LOPA can also be incorporated to improve implementation of consequence estimation tools (Summers, 2010). In addition to the consequence estimation tool, the risk analysis is also dependent on the estimated frequency of the hazardous event. Additionally, any error associated with the consequence severity estimate directly impacts the risk reduction measures. Most security professionals will find that using the LOPA is easy and flexible. When attempting to determine priorities based on the estimate of the hazardous event frequency, look carefully at those root causes of events that lead to the hazardous event and the possibility that the safety and security measures may fail. Security professionals will use experience to determine the right types of protection layers to utilize and use best practices to demonstrate the risk reduction or mitigation techniques that have worked when conducting previous risk analysis. Security professionals will need to determine the root causes (or initiating causes) and analyze those enabling conditions that result in process deviations (or initiating events). This is a critical part of a risk analysis since understanding the likelihood of the types of hazards that may occur and the conditions that enable them, security professionals can then estimate the initiating event frequency.

In LOPA, the security professional may recommend IPLs based on the hazard or threat. Also, an IPL can be a best practice that is known to provide the risk reduction (i.e., fences, gates, guards, police, CCTV, alarms, etc....). Generally, all of the aforementioned best practices used, however, alarms are typically identified as safety and security tools that are used as an input to identification and notification systems. Basically, these types of alarms are defined as "an audible and/or visible means of indicating to the operator an equipment malfunction, process deviation, or abnormal condition *requiring a response*," which is different than a safety alarm, "an alarm that is classified as critical to process safety or to the protection of human life" [2].

Using the IPL risk reduction method also allows the security professional to estimate the hazardous event frequency based on information and incident data that corresponds to key performance indicators (i.e., it could be alarm logs, CCTV usage determined to view incidents, police reports, staff or visitor information, etc....). Once again, security professionals will find that LOPA is a superb tool for assessing a wide variety of critical threat scenarios, as well as being able to apply the appropriate protection layers and design measures. In addition, LOPA can be utilized as a semiquantitative analysis as mentioned earlier with key performances, which will also allow for efficient evaluation of the threat or vulnerability. Realistically, the more that organizations progress with using and implementing LOPA throughout different schools, it will invariably result in similar usage, comparisons, and questions asked on implementation. When similar threats or vulnerabilities are compared from school to school, the LOPA will become more constant, and staff, will see the variation in the risk estimate for similar threats. Fortunately, LOPA procedures have well-defined methods that security professionals can implement when estimating any type of hazardous event frequency. In addition, it will assist with understanding the inconsistency in the risk estimate that is generally due to a variation in the estimated consequence severity.

CONCLUSION

As security professionals attempt to get consistency in the LOPA methodology by providing business with varied types of LOPA scenarios, the safety and security measures will improve and eventually reduce or mitigate events. This can be a challenge to organizations with large campus-type locations, as well as global structures. Many of the LOPA template scenarios can be useful by providing specific guidance to a business safety and security measures. In many cases, the LOPA best practices utilized by security professionals have guidance on not only the risk analysis but also the means for risk reduction and mitigation. Finally, there are varied models that represent a LOPA template, and end users will need to determine which model best fits your business environment.

References

[1] CCPS/AIChE. Layer of protection analysis: Simplified process risk assessment. New York: Concept Series; 2001.
[2] Stauffer T, Sands NP, Dunn DG. Get a life (cycle)! Connecting alarm management and safety instrumented systems. In: ISA safety & security symposium (April, 2010). http://www.isa.org.
[3] Summers AE, Hearn WH. Risk criteria, protection layers and conditional modifiers. SIS-TECH; 2010.
[4] Summers A, Vogtmann B, Smolen S. Consistent consequence severity estimation. In: Spring meeting, 6th global congress on process safety, San Antonio, Texas, March 22–24. American Institute of Chemical Engineers; 2010.

Fire Development and Behavior

Inge Sebyan Black, B.A., CPP, CFE, CEM, CPOI, CCIE

INTRODUCTION

This chapter discusses the stages of fire, as well as fire prevention, fire safety, and fire classifications. Recognizing the stages of fire development and the burning regime allows the firefighters to better assess what might happen next if no action is taken. Although firefighters can easily observe many of the basic fire indicators, fire behaviors indicators encompass a wide range of factors that firefighters might see, hear, or feel.

Fire is defined as the state, process, or moment of combustion in which substances combine chemically with oxygen from the air and give off light, heat, and smoke. To break the definition down further, lets discuss the four stages of fire.

STAGES OF FIRE

1. **Germinal or incipient (ignition)**: Fuel, oxygen, and heat join together in a sustained chemical reaction. At this stage, a fire extinguisher can control the fire. Some critical fire behavior indicators are building factors, air tract, heat, flame, and

smoke. It is important to integrate these factors into the process when reviewing the fire as a dynamic risk assessment. Note: depending on the size of the space and the ventilation provided, there may only be a limited indication, if any, from the exterior of the building that an incipient stage fire is burning inside the space, no smoke at this point.

2. **Flame stage**: With the initial flame as a heat source, additional fuel ignites. Convection and radiation ignite more surfaces. The size of the fire increases and the plume reaches the ceiling. Hot gases collecting at the ceiling transfer heat, allowing all fuels in a room to come closer to their ignition temperature at the same time. Smoke and flames are visible, and heat is at a minimal.

3. **Smoldering stage**: Fire has spread over much if not all the available fuel; temperatures reach their peak, resulting in heat damage. Oxygen is consumed rapidly. Smoke is visible.

4. **Heat stage**: The fire consumes available fuel, temperatures decrease, and the fire gets highly intense, heat is intense and building up.

Effective Physical Security, Fifth Edition
http://dx.doi.org/10.1016/B978-0-12-804462-9.00022-1

HOW FIRE SPREADS

Fire spreads by transferring the heat energy from the flames in three different ways.

- **Conduction**. The passage of heat energy through or within a material because of direct contact, such as a burning wastebasket heating a nearby couch, which ignites and heats the drapes hanging behind, until they too burst into flames.
- **Convection**. The flow of fluid or gas from hot areas to cooler areas. The heated air is less dense and rises, while cooler air descends. A large fire in an open area produces a plume or column of hot gas and smoke high into the air. But inside a room, those rising gases encounter the ceiling. They travel horizontally along the ceiling forming a thick layer of heated air, which then moves downward.
- **Radiation**. Heat traveling via electromagnetic waves, without objects or gases carrying it along. Radiated heat goes out in all directions, unnoticed until it strikes an object. Burning buildings can radiate heat to surrounding structures, sometimes even passing through glass windows and igniting objects inside.
- **Ionization detectors**. They identify a fire in its incipient stage before any smoke is visible.

The following two simple decisions will give you and your family the life-saving advantage of time if fire starts in your home:

1. **Decide to have working smoke alarms to warn at the first sign of fire**. Dead or missing batteries mean no alarm will sound if a fire starts. Regularly test batteries to ensure the alarm is ready to sound. Replace batteries each year—January 1 and Halloween are popular annual change dates. State requirements vary, but the NFPA recommends a working smoke alarm on every level of the home, inside each bedroom, and outside each sleeping area. Will your fire insurance company pay up on a claim if smoke alarms were absent, of insufficient number, or not working?

2. **Decide to create a fire escape plan and share it with your family and overnight guests**. Think about it. Fire drill practice regularly occurs at work and school. Why do you think you are safe at home without fire drills and escape plans? Because you know the place so well? Not true if you or your children have less than 2 min to get out of any room, on any floor.

    a. NFPA suggests you walk through your home and inspect all possible exits and escape routes. Consider drawing a floor plan of your home, perhaps with help from your children, which indicates *two ways out of each room, including windows and doors. Add smoke alarm locations.*

    b. Commit to these two life-saving decisions—install working smoke alarms and make escape plans with your family—and you have made one huge choice: to give everyone in your home the advantage of time and forethought, so they will not become a fire statistic like the thousands who die each year.

FOUR WAYS TO PUT OUT A FIRE

1. Cool the burning material.
2. Exclude oxygen.
3. Remove the fuel.
4. Break the chemical reaction.

Fire Extinguishers

After extinguishers have been installed, a regular annual program of inspection and maintenance must be established. A good policy is for security personnel to check all devices visually once a month and to have the extinguisher service company inspect them twice a year. In this process, the serviceman should retag and if necessary recharge the extinguishers and replace defective equipment.

High-Quality Fire Extinguishers

Whether you need a new extinguisher, an inspection, or testing, we can replace parts for extinguishers from any manufacturer. You will have a peace of mind knowing that you, your family, and your property are protected.

Pressurized Water Models

They are appropriate for use on Class A fires only. These must never be used on electrical or flammable liquid fires.

Carbon Dioxide

These extinguishers contain pressurized liquid carbon dioxide, which turns to a gas when expelled. These models are rated for use on Class B and C fires but can be used on a Class A fire. Carbon dioxide does not leave a residue.

Dry Chemical Extinguishers

These are either stored-pressure models or cartridge-operated models. The stored-pressure models have a lever above the handle for operation. The cartridge-operated models require two steps: Depress the cartridge lever and then squeeze the nozzle at the end of the hose. The dry chemicals leave a residue that must be cleaned up after use.

Ammonium Phosphate

This is a dry chemical that can be used on Class A, B, and C fires but should never be used on a fire in a commercial grease fryer because of the possibility of reflash and because it will render the fryer's automatic fire-protection system less effective.

Sodium Bicarbonate

This is a dry chemical, suitable for fighting Class B and C fires, is preferred over other dry chemical extinguishers for fighting grease fires. Where provided, always use the extinguishing system first. This also shuts off the heat to the appliance.

Potassium Bicarbonate

Potassium bicarbonate, urea-base potassium bicarbonate, and potassium chloride—dry chemicals that are more effective and use less agent than sodium bicarbonate on the same fire.

Foam (or AFFF and FFFP) Extinguishers

This coats the surface of a burning flammable liquid with a chemical foam. When using a foam extinguisher, blanket the entire surface of the liquid to exclude the air.
http://www.gorhamfire.com/quincy-ma-fire-extinguishers.htm.

CLASSIFYING FIRE

Fire classifications based on fuel type:

Class A. This includes ordinary combustible materials, such as wood, cloth, paper, rubber, and many plastics. They burn with an ember and leave an ash. They extinguish by cooling the fuel to a temperature that is below the ignition temperature. Water and other extinguishing agents are effective.

Class B. It includes flammable liquids (burn at room temperature) and combustible liquids (require heat to ignite). Petroleum greases, tars, oils, oil-based paints, solvents, lacquers, alcohols, and flammable gases are some examples. They are high fire hazard; water may not extinguish. They extinguish by creating a barrier between the fuel and the oxygen, such as layer of foam.

Class C. This includes fuels that would be A or B except that they involve energized electrical equipment. They require special techniques and agents to extinguish, most commonly carbon dioxide or dry chemical agents. Use of water is very dangerous because water conducts electricity.

Class D. This includes combustible metals, such as magnesium, titanium, zirconium, sodium, lithium, and potassium. Most cars contain numerous such metals. Because of extremely high flame temperatures, water can break down into hydrogen and oxygen, enhancing burning or exploding. They extinguish with special powders based on sodium chloride or other salts and also clean dry sand.

Class K. This includes fires in cooking appliances that involve combustible cooking media (vegetable or animal oils and fats).

- During an emergency, the actual shut-down of equipment should be assigned to people familiar with the process.
- Plan ahead! If a fire breaks out in your home or office, you may have only a few minutes to get out safely once the smoke alarm sounds. Everyone needs to know what to do and where to go if there is a fire.

Some of the most widely used codes are the following:

- NFPA 1, Fire Code: Provides requirements to establish a reasonable level of fire safety and property protection in new and existing buildings.
- NFPA 54, National Fuel Gas Code: The safety benchmark for fuel gas installations.
- NFPA 70, National Electric Code [1]: The world's most widely used and accepted code for electrical installations.
- NFPA 85: Boiler and Combustion Systems Hazards Code.
- NFPA 101, Life Safety Code: Establishes minimum requirements for new and existing

buildings to protect building occupants from fire, smoke, and toxic fumes.
- NFPA 704, Standard System for the Identification of the Hazards of Materials for Emergency Response: Defines the colloquial "fire diamond" used by emergency personnel to quickly and easily identify the risks posed by hazardous materials.
- NFPA Standards:
  - NFPA 70—National Electrical Code
  - NFPA 70B—Recommended Practice for Electrical Equipment Maintenance
  - NFPA 70E—Standard for Electrical Safety in the Workplace
  - NFPA 72—National Fire Alarm and Signaling Code
  - NFPA 101—Life Safety Code
  - NFPA 704—Standard System for the Identification of the Hazards of Materials for Emergency Response (four-color hazard diamond)
  - NFPA 921—Guide for Fire and Explosion Investigations
  - NFPA 1001—Standard for Fire Fighter Professional Qualifications
  - NFPA 1123—Code for Fireworks Display, 2014
  - NFPA 1670—Standard on Operations and Training for Technical Search and Rescue Incidents
  - NFPA 1901—Standard for Automotive Fire Apparatus, 2016

UL STANDARD 217, 268 AND NFPA 72

UL Standard 217, "Single and Multiple Station Smoke Alarms," allows for dual-sensor alarms so long as each sensor is primarily a smoke sensor and the design meets the standard. The alarm logic is an {OR} type such that the alarm is activated if either the photoelectric sensor or ionization sensor alarm threshold is met. The individual sensor sensitivities are not tested separately. Therefore, manufacturers have the freedom to set each sensor's sensitivity separately. Since an individual sensor can be set to meet all current sensitivity standards, it is not obvious what overall benefit is achieved from a dual alarm with an additional sensor technology that could be more or less sensitive than what would be found in a stand-alone unit employing such a sensor. Additionally, another potential benefit of a dual-sensor alarm may be realized by adjusting each sensor's alarm threshold to reduce nuisance alarms. Thus, the sensitivity of each sensor factors into the overall performance of a dual alarm.

Table 22.1 shows the distributions of ionization, photoelectric, and dual alarm times in histograms with the median and mean alarm times indicated. These particular distributions arise in part from the variation of the fire sources and locations of the alarms.

Since individual sensor sensitivities were not known, an estimate of which ionization and photoelectric sensor was more sensitive was made (either the ionization alarm or the ionization sensor in the dual alarm, and either the photoelectric alarm or the photoelectric sensor in the dual alarm). To make this judgment, the following logic was considered. Between the ionization and photoelectric alarm, the ionization alarm was the first to respond in 18 of the 54 instances, responding 83 s faster on average than the photoelectric alarms. Considering those 18 instances, the dual alarm responded first in 17 of those instances and responded 81 s faster on average than the ionization alarm (SD = 158 s), with a median response 19 s faster. In addition to the aforesaid detectors, there are also obscuration detectors, which due to smoke, light is decreased; thermal detectors used in the detection of *predetermined* temperature; and infrared flame detectors, in which the emission from the flame trips the infrared [2].

WATER SUPPLY FOR SPRINKLERS AND TANKS [3]

For automatic sprinklers to operate, there must be a supply of water to the sprinkler that opens to extinguish or control fire and prevents it from spreading. This water may come from a variety of sources such as public water systems, usually considered the principal or primary water supply, and storage tanks of different types (see NFPA 13, Standard for the installation of Sprinkler Systems).

Gravity tanks are tower or roof mounted and is used in high-rise buildings. Suction tanks are equipped with automatically operated fire pump(s), pressure tanks are pressurized water reservoirs used to supply a limited amount of water, and a fire pump (some fire pumps are called booster pumps because they boost the pressure) is a mechanical device for improving the water supply pressure.

The types of automatic sprinkler systems are as follows:

- Wet pipe systems
- Dry pipe systems
- Preaction systems

The types of stand pipe systems are as follows:

- Automatic wet systems
- Automatic dry systems
- Semiautomatic dry systems

TABLE 22.1 Average Alarm Times for NRC Canada Test Series

Alarm Type	Average Alarm Time (s)	Standard Deviation (SD) (s)
Ionization alarm	1205	1102
Photoelectric alarm	666	537
Dual alarm	587	450

All were initially smoldering fires.
Conclusion: Remember smoke detectors older than 10 years must be replaced.

The automatic wet stand pipe system is most commonly installed in modern high-rise buildings with a fixed water supply not exposed to freezing.

Certification is an important credential that is evident of a person's skills in their practice specialty. Available certification programs are as follows:

Certified Electrical Safety Worker (CESW)
Certified Electrical Safety Compliance
  Professional (CESCP)
Certified Fire Protection Specialist (CFPS)
Certified Fire Inspector I (CFI)
Certified Fire Inspector II (CFI-II)
Certified Fire Plan Examiner I (CFPE).

References

[1] NFPA website, www.nfpa.org.
[2] Presented at the Fire Protection Research Foundation's 13th annual Suppression and Detection Research and Applications Symposium (SUPDET 2009), February 24–27, 2009, Orlando, FL.
[3] Craighead G. High-rise security and fire life safety. 3rd ed. 2009. Waltham (MA).

APPENDIX: A FIRE SAFETY INSPECTION

Michael Stroberger, CPP

The following inspection is designed to be the basis of a revised and property-specific inspection program. Some of the entries refer to functions performed with a "reasonable frequency." In reviewing your specific property or location, care should be taken to consider the nature of the structure, geographic location, intended use, and actual use. In many cases, functions that are best performed on a daily basis in one environment can be reasonably performed on a weekly or possibly monthly basis in a different environment.

In addition, note that every application is unique in some manner. As such, what might be prudent for one location, however seemingly similar, might be insufficient at another location. While benchmarking of a similar program is highly recommended, this also should be seen as simply a basic guideline in the creation of a customized, location-specific program.

Some sections pose inspection inquiries that reference a large number of possible locations or items to be reviewed. One example would be the inspection of sprinkler heads. In designing the actual checklist for such an inspection, it is often desirable to break down the physical layout of the facility into reasonable and manageable zones. Identifying sets of sprinkler heads by the room in which they are installed allows the person performing the inspection to review them as a set and make comments in reference to that area of coverage. In cases such as fire doors, it might be reasonable to identify them with a location number, which could be included not only on the inspection form but also a numbered tag, on the hinge-side edge of the door, for later identification.

ADMINISTRATIVE AND PLANNING PHASE

- Are copies of all locally enforced codes maintained on site for reference?
- Does the facility meet requirements of locally enforced building code?
- Does the facility meet requirements of locally enforced fire prevention code?
- Does the facility meet requirements of locally enforced life safety code?
- Does the facility have a written and appropriately distributed Fire Prevention and Response Plan? Is this plan known to all employees? Is training provided to those with defined responsibilities? Is all training documented and securely filed? Is the plan reviewed annually, updated as required, and redistributed?
- Does the facility maintain a fire brigade? Is the fire brigade training documented and

securely filed? Is the fire brigade training conducted in conjunction with the local fire department? Is the fire brigade comprised of persons, or positions, that are present or represented at all times?

- Are all inspection reports retained for a reasonable number of years, as defined by local codes, insurance requirements, or industry standards? Are inspection reports filed in a secure location?
- Are all employees trained in basic fire prevention concepts and fire event response procedures? Is the content of this training consistent and reasonably inclusive? Is this training documented and securely filed? Is annual refresher training conducted? Is annual refresher training documented and securely filed?

GENERAL PHYSICAL INSPECTION PHASE

- Are all fire exit routes clearly marked? Are all exit routes unobstructed at all times? Are all exit routes and egress hardware items in compliance with the Americans with Disabilities Act (ADA) requirements?
- Are all fire doors and egress hardware items in proper working order?
- Are service areas secured against unauthorized entry when not in use?
- Are all areas free of loose or disorganized combustible items (such as rags or empty boxes)?
- Are all storage areas well organized to allow ease of access in emergency situations?
- Are flammable or combustible items properly stored to protect against accidental ignition?
- Are flammable or combustible items properly stored to protect against unauthorized usage or tampering?

- Are all fire lanes clearly marked? Are fire lanes maintained in an unobstructed condition at all times?
- Are master keys available for fire department use at all times?
- Are all electrical panels accessible at all times? Are all panels clearly marked to facilitate emergency power disconnection?
- Are gas line shutoff valves accessible at all times?
- Are all gas-operated pieces of equipment inspected for wear and damage with reasonable frequency? Are inspections documented and filed in a secure location?
- Are all heat-generating devices (such as boilers, furnaces, and dryers) provided a reasonable clear zone, based on levels of heat output, where storage of any kind is prohibited?
- Are all ducts inspected regularly and cleaned as required?
- Is the use of extension cords discouraged in all areas?
- Are all electrical cords and electrically operated items inspected for wear or damage with reasonable frequency? Are such inspections documented?
- Are designated smoking areas clearly defined and at a proper minimum safe distance from any common or identified ignition threats? Are appropriate ash and cigarette receptacles available for use in these areas? Are they per state laws?

EXTINGUISHER INSPECTION PHASE

- Have all extinguishers been inspected and serviced as required by a licensed vendor or trained technician within the past 12 months?
- Are all extinguishers of a type appropriate for most probable types of fires in the immediate area?

- Are specialty extinguishers available in those areas that would require them?
- Are persons trained in the use of the extinguishers available in the areas where they are typically present? Is this training documented and filed in a secure location?
- Are extinguishers inspected with reasonable frequency (daily, in most cases) to ensure that they are present and have not been tempered with or discharged? Is each extinguisher inspection fully documented and securely filed?

STAND PIPE, FIRE HOSE, AND CONTROL VALVE INSPECTION PHASE

- Do tamper switches, linked to an alarm system, monitor all control valves?
- Are all control valves inspected and tested annually by a licensed vendor or trained technician?
- Are all stand pipes, control valves, and fire hoses accessible at all times?
- Are fire hoses inspected, per manufacturer recommendations, for wear and decay?

SPRINKLER SYSTEM INSPECTION PHASE

- Are all flow switches inspected and tested annually by a licensed vendor or trained technician?
- Are all sprinkler heads of a type appropriate for the location in which they are installed?
- Are all sprinkler heads installed and maintained within the manufacturers' recommendations?
- Are all sprinkler heads provided with a clear area of operation in compliance with local fire codes?

- Does the sprinkler system have a pressure maintenance pump? If so, is this pump inspected and tested with reasonable frequency (weekly, in most cases) by a licensed vendor or trained technician?
- Are all areas requiring sprinkler system coverage, per the local fire code, provided with such coverage?

HAZARDOUS MATERIALS INSPECTION PHASE

- Are proper warning placards utilized in areas of chemical storage and usage?
- Is proper personal protective equipment (PPE) provided for initial response to fire and emergency situations related to any hazardous materials that are maintained or utilized on site? Is training provided in the use of this PPE? Is such training documented and filed in a secure location?
- Is the fire department made aware of storage areas, use areas, and large arriving or departing shipments of hazardous materials?
- Is all appropriate containment, standoff distance, and warning signals utilized in storage areas?
- Are MSDS books on file and accessible 24/7?

ALARM SYSTEM INSPECTION PHASE

- Is the system monitored by a licensed, off-site monitoring service?
- Is the system inspected and tested annually by a licensed vendor or trained technician?
- Is this inspection documented and filed in a secure location?
- Is the area of coverage broken down into identified zones?
- When activated, does the alarm system clearly identify the location of the potential fire?

- Are audible alarms heard in all areas of a zone when activated? Is the system designed to warn adjacent zones, inclusive of floors above or below?
- Are strobes visible in all areas of a zone when activated? Is the system designed to warn adjacent zones, inclusive of floors above or below? Are there any ADA complaints?
- Does the alarm system record activation and use history? For what length of time is this history retained?
- Does the system's audible signal include a prerecorded advisory message? If so, does this message recommend a route or method of egress? If so, does this message advise against the use of elevators if any are present?
- Does the system automatically recall or drop elevators on activation? Are override keys available for fire department use?
- Are detector types installed as appropriate for the specific location of installation? If the intended use of a given area is altered, is the type of detector also reviewed and changed to match the updated intended use of that area?

Alarms Intrusion Detection Systems*

Frank Davies, CHS-IV, CIPS, CVI

INTRODUCTION

This chapter discusses various types of intrusion detection systems with a focus on how technology has enhanced the level of safety and security over the years. Also discussed are the types of alarm systems and ways to select the right one for your home or organization.

Burglary is a big business. Moreover, crime figures show a staggering rate of increase for burglaries of private homes. It is no wonder then that many homeowners and business owners are giving serious consideration to electronic alarm protection. Alarm operators are in the market to make a fast dollar, and the unwary customer who buys what seems to be a bargain too often ends up being cheated.

FALSE ALARMS

There are four hard-core reasons for false alarms, and the secret to reducing them is to clearly identify the cause and make proactive corrections:

1. Lack of proper education on how to enter and exit the complex, such as improper arming and disarming of the keypad
2. Weather

3. Equipment failure (dead batteries) and poor installation problems
4. User error (forgetful or unknowledgeable homeowners or roaming pets).

Research tells us that false burglar alarms are not evenly distributed. Some alarm systems experience no false alarms, and others, many. One study suggests that 20% of alarm systems trigger 80% of false alarms. As a result, officers responding to false alarms are often spending time away from locations where crime and disorder are occurring.

The Costs of False Burglar Alarms: Each false alarm requires approximately 20 min of police time, usually for two officers. This costs the public as much as $1.5 billion per year in police time.

In the vast majority of jurisdictions, the cost of responding to false alarms is not recouped through fines. Jurisdictions that try to recoup costs generally omit the lost-opportunity costs, potentially a significant part of the equation. Typical costs include:

- personnel costs of police call-takers and dispatchers;
- personnel, equipment, and training costs of responding officers, along with those of any backup personnel;

*This material was originally compiled by Lawrence J. Fennelly, Mike Rolf, and James Culley.

- personnel costs associated with analyzing false alarms;
- software, hardware, office space, and equipment costs for false alarm management;
- administrative and staff costs of notifications, permitting, billing, and education programs;
- costs of developing, printing, and distributing publications to educate the public and alarm companies about false alarms;
- lost-opportunity costs, since police are unavailable to work on actual crime problems; and
- costs associated with call displacement, because other 911 calls take longer to respond to.

The selection of a proper alarm system is not a simple matter, because the needs of each homeowner or business owner are different, like a set of fingerprints. Some factors that determine the requirements of an individual alarm system and the questions that must be answered when selecting a system include:

1. The threat or risk. What is the system to protect against?
2. The types of sensors needed. What will be protected?
3. What methods are available to provide the level of protection needed?
4. The method of alarm signal transmission. How is the signal to be sent and who will respond?

Most of the confusion regarding intrusion detection systems is a result of the variety of methods available to provide the protection needed. The combinations of detection methods are in the thousands. An intrusion detection system may deter a would-be intruder. However, the primary function of the alarm system is to signal the presence of an intruder. An intrusion detection system can be just a portion of the overall protection needed. Many large businesses supplement these systems with security

guards and other security personnel. The successful operation of any type of an alarm system depends on its proper installation and maintenance by the alarm installing company and the proper use of the system by the customer.

COMPONENTS OF ALARM SYSTEMS

Sensing devices are used in the actual detection of an intruder (Figs. 23.1 and 23.2). Each has a specific purpose and can be divided into three categories: perimeter protection, area/space protection, and object/spot protection.

Perimeter Protection

Perimeter protection is the first line in the defense to detect an intruder. The most common points equipped with sensing devices for premise perimeter protection are doors, windows, vents, skylights, or any opening to a business or home. Since over 80% of all break-ins occur through these openings, most alarm systems provide this type of protection. The major advantage of perimeter protection is its simple design. The major disadvantage is that it protects only the openings. If the burglar bursts through a wall, comes through the ventilation system, or stays behind after closing, perimeter protection is useless.

1. **Door switches**. These are installed on a door or window in such a way that opening the door or window causes a magnet to move away a contact switch, which activates the alarm. They can be surface mounted or recessed into the door and frame. A variety of types of switches are manufactured for all types of doors and windows. The switches are both wide gap type and magnetic standard type.
2. **Glass break detectors**. These detectors are attached to the glass and sense the breakage of the glass by shock or sound. Glass breakage sensors use microphone transducers to detect

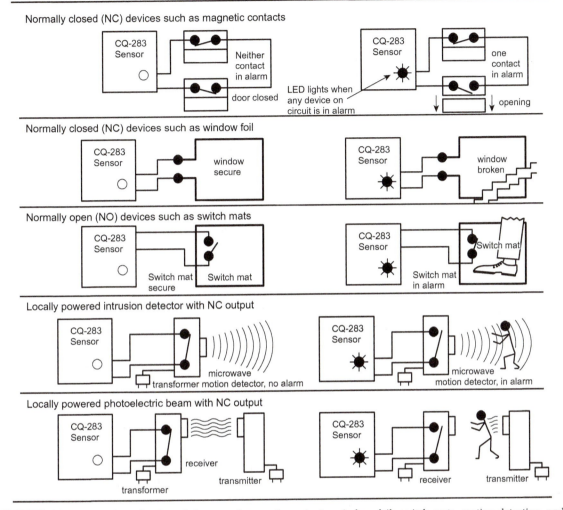

Normally closed (NC) devices such as magnetic contacts

CQ-283 Sensor — Neither contact in alarm — door closed

CQ-283 Sensor — one contact in alarm — opening

LED lights when any device on circuit is in alarm

Normally closed (NC) devices such as window foil

CQ-283 Sensor — window secure

CQ-283 Sensor — window broken

Normally open (NO) devices such as switch mats

CQ-283 Sensor — Switch mat | Switch mat — Switch mat secure

CQ-283 Sensor — Switch mat — Switch mat in alarm

Locally powered intrusion detector with NC output

CQ-283 Sensor — microwave transformer motion detector, no alarm

CQ-283 Sensor — microwave motion detector, in alarm

Locally powered photoelectric beam with NC output

CQ-283 Sensor — receiver — transmitter — transformer

CQ-283 Sensor — receiver — transmitter

FIGURE 23.1 Typical application of the use of magnetic contacts, window foil, switch mats, motion detection, and photoelectric beam. *Courtesy of Aritech Corporation.*

the glass breakage. A ceiling sensor over a window covers a 30-degree radius.

3. **Wooden screens**. These devices are made of wooden dowel sticks assembled in a cage-like fashion no more than 4 inches from each other. A very fine, brittle wire runs in the wooden dowels and frame. The burglar must break the doweling to gain entry and thus break the low-voltage electrical circuit, causing the alarm. These devices are used primarily in commercial applications.

4. **Window screens**. These devices are similar to regular wire window screens in a home except that a fine, coated wire is a part of the screen. When the burglar cuts the screen to gain entry, the flow of low-voltage electricity is interrupted and causes the alarm. These devices are used primarily in residential applications.

5. **Lace and panels**. The surfaces of door panels and safes are protected against entry by installing a close lace-like pattern of metallic

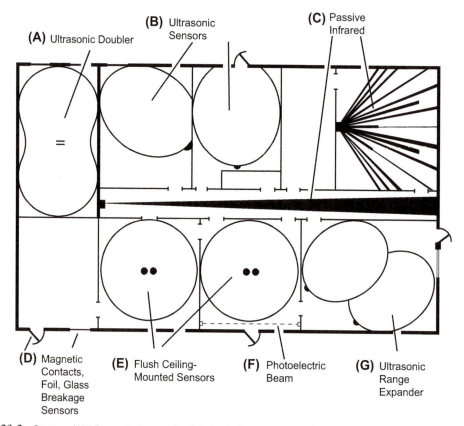

(A) Ultrasonic Doubler
(B) Ultrasonic Sensors
(C) Passive Infrared
(D) Magnetic Contacts, Foil, Glass Breakage Sensors
(E) Flush Ceiling-Mounted Sensors
(F) Photoelectric Beam
(G) Ultrasonic Range Expander

FIGURE 23.2 Sensors. (A) Ultrasonic doubler: back-to-back ultrasonic transceivers provide virtually double the coverage of single detectors at almost the same wiring and equipment cost. With more than 50×25 feet of coverage, the doubler is the best value in space protection. (B) Ultrasonic sensors: easy to install, no brackets needed. Can be mounted horizontally, vertically, or in a corner; surface, flush, or with mounting feet on a shelf. Each UL-listed sensor protects a three-dimensional volume up to 30 feet wide and high. (C) Passive infrared: for those zones where the lower-cost ultrasonic sensor is inappropriate, there is no need to buy a complete passive infrared system as both ultrasonic and passive infrared can be used in the same system. (D) Magnetic contacts, foil, glass breakage sensors: the building's perimeter protection detectors can be wired into the system via universal interface sensor. There is no need for running a separate perimeter loop. (E) Flush ceiling-mounted sensors: only the two small 2-inch-diameter transducer caps are visible below the ceiling tiles. Designed for where minimum visibility is needed for aesthetic or security purposes. (F) Photoelectric beam: the universal interface sensor allows the connection of any NO or NC alarm device into the system for zoned annunciation. It can be used with photoelectric beams, switch matting, microwave motion detectors, and many other intrusion detectors. (G) Ultrasonic range expander: adding an ultrasonic range expander can increase the coverage of an ultrasonic sensor by 50–90%, depending on where it is positioned and the surrounding environment. *Courtesy of Aritech Corporation.*

foil or a fine brittle wire on the surface. Entry cannot be made without first breaking the foil or wire, thus activating the alarm. A panel of wood is placed over the lacing to protect it.

6. **Interior sensors**. They come in many shapes and sizes depending upon the application, for example, interior motion detector units and proximity and boundary penetration.

Area/Space Protection

Area/space protection devices (Table 23.1) protect the interior spaces in a business or home. They protect against intrusion whether or not

TABLE 23.1 Motion Sensor Survey Checklist

Environmental and Other Factors Affecting Sensor Usage	Effect on Sensor			Recommendation and Notes
Circle one	Ultrasonics	Microwave	Passive IR	
If the areas to be protected are enclosed by thin walls or contain windows, will there be movement close to the outside of this area?	Yes No	None	Major	None	Avoid using a microwave sensor unless it can be aimed away from thin walls, glass, etc., which can pass an amount of microwave energy
Will the protection pattern see sun, moving headlamps, or other sources of infrared energy passing through windows?	Yes No	None	None	Major	Avoid using a PIR sensor unless the pattern can be positioned to avoid rapidly changing levels of infrared energy
Does the area to be protected contain HVAC ducts?	Yes No	None	Moderate	None	Ducts can channel microwave energy to other areas; if using a microwave sensor, aim it away from duct openings
Will two or more sensors of the same type be used to protect a common area?	Yes No	None	None (see Note)	None	Note: Adjacent units must operate on different frequencies
Does the area to be protected contain fluorescent or neon lights that are on during the protection-on period?	Yes No	None	Major	None	Microwave sensor, if used, must be aimed away from any fluorescent or neon light within 20 feet
Are incandescent lamps cycled on and off during the protection-on period included in the protection pattern?	Yes No	None	None	Major	If considering use of a PIR sensor, make a trial installation and, if necessary, redirect the protection pattern away from incandescent lamps
Must the protection pattern be projected from a ceiling?	Yes No	None, but only for ceiling heights up to 15 feet	Major	Major	Only ultrasonic sensors can be used on a ceiling, but height is limited to 15 feet; at greater ceiling heights, use rigid ceiling brackets to suspend the sensor to maintain the 15-foot limitation or, in large open areas, try a microwave sensor mounted high on a wall and aimed downward

Continued

TABLE 23.1 Motion Sensor Survey Checklist—cont'd

Environmental and Other Factors Affecting Sensor Usage	Effect on Sensor				
	Yes No				
Is the overall structure of flimsy construction (corrugated metal, thin plywood, etc.)?	Yes No	Minor	Major	Minor	Do not use a microwave sensor; where considerable structural movement can be expected, use a rigid mounting surface for an ultrasonic or PIR sensor
Will the protection pattern include large metal objects or wall surfaces?	Yes No	Minor	Major	Minor (major if metal is highly polished)	Use an ultrasonic sensor or use a PIR sensor
Are any radar installations nearby?	Yes No	Minor	Major when radar is close and sensor is aimed at it	Minor	Avoid using a microwave sensor
Will the protection pattern include heaters, radiators, air conditioners, or the like?	Yes No	Moderate	None	Major when rapid changes in air temperature are involved	Use an ultrasonic sensor, but aim it away from sources of air turbulence (desirable to have heaters, etc., turned off during protection-on period), or use a microwave sensor
Will the area to be protected be subjected to ultrasonic noise (bells, hissing sounds)?	Yes No	Moderate, can cause problems in severe cases	None	None	Try muffling the noise source and use an ultrasonic sensor, use a microwave sensor, or use a PIR sensor
Will the protection pattern include drapes, carpet, racks of clothing, or the like?	Yes No	Moderate, reduction in range	None	Minor	Use an ultrasonic sensor if some reduction in range can be tolerated or use a microwave sensor
Is the area to be protected subject to changes in temperature and humidity?	Yes No	Moderate	None	Major	Use an ultrasonic sensor unless changes in temperature and humidity are severe or use a microwave sensor
Is there water noise from faulty valves in the area to be protected?	Yes No	Moderate, can be a problem	None	None	If noise is substantial, try correcting faulty valves and use an ultrasonic sensor; use a microwave sensor, or use a PIR sensor

Question					Remedy
Will the protection pattern see moving machinery, fan blades, or the like?	Yes No	Major	Major	Minor	Have machinery, fans, and the like turned off during the protection-on period, carefully place an ultrasonic sensor, or use a PIR sensor
Will drafts or other air movement pass through the protection pattern?	Yes No	Major	None	None, unless rapid temperature changes are involved	If the protection pattern can be aimed away from air movement or air movement can be stopped during the protection-on period, use an ultrasonic sensor, use a microwave sensor, or use a PIR sensor
Will the protection pattern see overhead doors that can be rattled by wind?	Yes No	Major	Major	Minor	If the protection pattern can be aimed away from such doors, use an ultrasonic sensor or use a PIR sensor
Are there hanging signs, calendar pages, or the like that can be moved by air currents during the protection-on period?	Yes No	Major	Major	Moderate, can be a problem	Use an ultrasonic sensor, but aim the pattern away from objects that can move or remove such objects, or use a PIR sensor
Are adjacent railroad tracks used during the protection-on period?	Yes No	Major	Minor	Minor	A trial installation is required if using an ultrasonic sensor
Can small animals (or birds) enter the protection pattern?	Yes No	Major	Major	Major (particularly rodents)	Install a physical barrier to prevent intrusion by animals or birds
Does the area to be protected contain a corrosive atmosphere?	Yes No	Major	Major	Major	None of these sensors can be used

HVAC, heating, ventilating, and air conditioning; IR, infrared, PIR, passive infrared detector.
False Burglar Alarms Problem-Oriented Guides for Police Problem-Specific Guides Series No. 5 2016 by Rana Sampson.

the perimeter protection was violated. It is particularly effective against a stay-behind intruder or the burglar who cuts through the roof or breaks through a block wall.

Space protection devices are only a part of the complete alarm system. They should always be supplemented with perimeter protection. The major advantage of space protection devices is that they provide a highly sensitive, invisible means of detection. The major disadvantage is that improper application and installation by the alarm company can result in frequent false alarms.

The types of area/space protection include:

1. **Photoelectric eyes (beams)**. These devices transmit a beam across a protected area. When an intruder interrupts the beam, the beam circuit is disrupted and the alarm initiated. Photoelectric devices use a pulsed infrared beam that is invisible to the naked eye. Some units have a range of over 1000 feet and can be used outdoors, although they are rarely used today.

2. **Ultrasonic**. They (although rarely used today) work on a low-frequency sound wave projected from the unit. The frequency is in kilohertz (23–26) and its area of coverage can be anywhere from 5 to 40 feet in length. The pattern is volumetric and cannot be aimed, although the pattern may be directed by the use of deflectors. Deflectors come in 90-degree or 45-degree angles. A doubler type uses two 45-degree angles back to back. Ultrasonics work on a change in frequency, called the *Doppler effect*. A motion detector has two transducers; the transmitter sends out a signal that is bounced back to the receiver by immobile objects in the protected area. If an intruder moves toward or away from the unit, the change in its reflected frequency signals an alarm. Ultrasonic may be found as stand-alone units or part of what is called a *master system*. The stand-alone units compare the reflected

signal within the unit and trip the control panel by opening or closing a relay contact. Master systems work by sending the signal back to a main processing unit. The main processing unit compares the signal and trips the relay contacts of the processor. False alarms result from three types of sources:

   a. **Motion**. Objects that move in the path of protection and air turbulence are seen as motion because of the frequency of the unit.

   b. **Noise**. Ultrasonic noise is present when audible noises are heard; hissing (such as from high-pressure air leaking or steam radiators) or bells ringing can be a source of these noises.

   c. **Radio or electrical interference**. Induced electrical signals or radio frequency (RF) interference from radio transmitters can cause false alarms.

3. Grounding and shielding are both very important in a master system. If an earth ground is required, it should be a cold water pipe. The length of the ground wire should be as short as possible and with a minimum number of bends. Potential problems include:

   a. Turbulence and draft, hanging displays, moving draperies, and small pets.

   b. Noise caused by air hissing, bells, and telephones.

   c. Temperature or humidity can affect range of the ultrasonic unit.

4. Carpets, furniture, and draperies may absorb some of the signal, decreasing the unit's sensitivity. Ultrasonic energy does not penetrate most objects. The signal may be reflected off some smooth surfaces.

5. **Microwave**. Microwave detectors are a volumetric type of space protection and are based on a Doppler shift. They detect intruders by the use of a radiated RF electromagnetic field. The unit operates by sensing a disturbance in the generated RF field, called the Doppler effect.

The frequency range is between 0.3 and 300 GHz (1 GHz = 1 billion cps). Any type of motion in the protected area creates a change in frequency, causing an alarm condition. Because the power output from the unit is relatively low, the field radiated is harmless. Microwave energy penetrates most objects and reflects off of metal. One of the most important considerations in placement of these units is vibration. The microwave must be mounted on a firm surface: Cinder block, brick, or main support beams are ideal mounting locations. Never mount two microwave units with identical frequencies in the same room or area where the patterns may overlap. This could cause cross talk between the units, causing false alarms. Microwave units draw excessive current, so the proper gauge of wire should be used and the length of the wire run should also be taken into consideration. Current readings should be taken at the end of an installation or while troubleshooting units to ensure that the maximum current of the control panel has not been exceeded. Fluorescent lights may be a problem because the radiated ionization from the lights may be seen as motion by the detector. Potential problems include:

a. Vibrations or movement of mounting surfaces, or mounts on a wall, sense change in electrical current.
b. Reflection of pattern or movement of metal objects in a protected area, such as moving fan blades or movement of overhead doors.
c. Penetration of thin walls or glass is a potential problem if motion or large metal objects, such as trains or cars, are present.
d. RF interference, radar, or AC line transients in severe cases can be a problem.
e. Water movement in plastic or PVC storm drains is a potential interference

if located close to the unit. Most microwave units provide a test point, where the amplifier output voltage can be read. By following the manufacturer's recommended voltage settings, the microwave can be set up properly and the unit environment examined.

6. **Passive infrared motion detectors**. These detectors are passive sensors, because they do not transmit a signal for an intruder to disturb. Rather, a source of moving infrared radiation (the intruder) is detected against the normal radiation/temperature environment of the room. Passive infrared detectors (PIRs) detect a change in the thermal energy pattern caused by a moving intruder in the field of view of the detector. The field of view of an infrared unit must terminate on an object to ensure its proper operation and stability. An infrared unit should never be set up to look out into midair. Potential problems include:

   a. Turbulence and drafts are a problem if the air is blowing directly on the unit or causes a rapid change in temperature of objects in the path of protection.
   b. Stray motion (i.e., drapes blowing, hanging objects or displays, small animals).
   c. Changing temperatures (i.e., hotspots in machinery, sunlight) may cause false alarms. The temperature of the background infrared level may also affect the unit's sensitivity: PIRs become less sensitive as the temperature increases.
   d. Lightning or bright lights, such as halogen headlights. The infrared radiation pattern is blocked by solid objects as it is unable to penetrate most objects. The pattern of protection may also be affected by reflection off smooth surfaces.

7. **Pressure mats**. These mats are basically mechanical switches. Pressure mats are most frequently used as a backup system to

perimeter protection. When used as traps they can be hidden under the carpet in front of a likely target or in hallways where an intruder would travel.

8. **Sound sensors**. These sensors detect intrusion by picking up the noise created by a burglar during an attempt to break into a protected area. These sensors consist of a microphone and an electronic amplifier/processor. When the sound level increases beyond the limit normally encountered, the unit signals an alarm. Some units have pulse-counting and time-interval features. Other types can actually listen to the protected premises from a central monitoring station.

9. **Dual-technology sensors**. Dual-technology sensors, commonly referred to as *dual-techs*, are a combination of two types of space-protection devices. The principle of the unit is that both sections of the detectors must be tripped at the same time to cause an alarm. A dual-tech unit could be a combination passive/microwave or a combination passive/ultrasonic. By using a dual-technology device, an installer can provide space protection in areas that may have presented potential false alarm problems when a single-technology unit was used. Repair people can replace units sending false signals because of environment or placement. Dual-techs are not the solution to all false alarm problems, and unless careful consideration is used in installing or replacing a device, the false alarm problems may persist. Since these contain two different types of devices, there is much more to consider. Dual-techs draw much more current than conventional detectors. Current readings are essential and additional power supplies may be necessary to provide enough operating current and standby power. Until recently, if one section of the unit stopped working or was blocked off in some way by the end user, the unit was rendered inoperable. Manufacturers are only now working on supervising the microwave section of these units. If the unit is located or adjusted so that one section of the unit is continuously in an alarm condition, the dual-technology principle is worthless.

10. **Interior sensors**. These are generally active or passive, covert or visible, or volumetric or line applications.

Emerging trends in the past 5 years:

1. IT infrastructure protection planning
2. IT infrastructure as a single strategic plan
3. Mitigation strategies
4. IP video and digital video
5. IP security provisions
6. Security IP edge device
7. HD cameras and monitors
8. Video analytics
9. Visible light cameras
10. Thermal imaging and cameras
11. Thermal imaging sensors
12. Perimeter protection
13. Layers of protection analysis
14. Visitor management systems
15. Mass notification
16. Active shooter/active assailants
17. Cloud storage and computing for security
18. Advancement of CPTED
19. Contractor prequalification
20. Emergency management and planning for disasters
21. Software for physical security maintenances
22. Laser communication
23. Drones becoming a safety issue
24. Encryption
25. Critical thinking
26. Soft targets versus target hardening
27. Establishment of countermeasures and deterrents
28. Embracing the beast
29. Social media monitoring software
30. Active Shooter/Active Assailant Initiative

APPLICATION

For all practical purposes, the reason we use space protection is as a backup to the perimeter system. It is not necessary to cover every inch of the premises being protected. The best placement is as a trap in a high-traffic area or spot protection for high-value areas. The worst thing an installer can do is overextend the area being protected by an individual unit (e.g., trying to cover more than one room with a detector or trying to compensate for placement or environment by over adjusting the sensitivity). By using a little common sense and checking for all possible hazards, you can ensure a trouble-free installation. Make sure that the units have adequate power going to each head and the standby batteries are working and charging properly. Be sure to adjust for pets and brief customers and any problems they may create, such as leaving fans or machinery on, and not to open windows in the path of protection. Before leaving an installation, make sure that all units have been walk-tested and the areas in question have been masked out. One of the most important considerations in setting up a number of space protection devices is zoning. Never put more than two interior devices in one zone if at all possible. The majority of false alarms are caused by interior devices. Breaking up the interior protective circuits as much as possible gives the service person a better chance of solving a false alarm problem (even with two heads in one zone you have a 50/50 chance of finding the trouble unit). Zoning a system correctly helps with troubleshooting, makes the police department feel better about the company and the company feel better about the installer, and ensures good relations with the customer.

Object/Spot Detection

Object/spot detection is used to detect the activity or presence of an intruder at a single location. It provides direct security for objects. Such a detection method is the final stage of an in-depth system for protection. The objects most frequently protected include safes, filing cabinets, desks, art objects, models, statues, and expensive equipment. The types of object/spot protection are:

1. **Capacitance/proximity detectors**. The object being protected becomes an antenna, electronically linked to the alarm control. When an intruder approaches or touches the object/antenna, an electrostatic field is unbalanced and the alarm is initiated. Only metal objects can be protected in this manner.
2. **Vibration detectors**. These devices utilize a highly sensitive, specialized microphone called an *electronic vibration detector* (EVD). The EVD is attached directly to the object to be protected. It can be adjusted to detect a sledgehammer attack on a concrete wall or a delicate penetration of a glass surface. It sends an alarm only when the object is moved, whereas capacitance devices detect when the intruder is close to the protected object. Other types of vibration detectors are similar to tilt switches used in pinball machines.

The types of IDS devices that are used to detect intrusions:

- Position detection devices—usually a magnet that detects when one part of the device is moved away from the other (door position switch).
- Motion detector—creates an alarm when the static conditions of the protected area change (microwave detectors, infrared detectors, ultrasonic detectors, beam detectors).
- Sound detectors—transmit an alarm when sounds outside a selectable ambient range are received by the detector (vault).
- Vibration sensors—react to motions such as shaking or physical shocks (tool attacks).
- Heat sensors—trigger alarms when the air or surface temperature changes.

- Temperature sensors—trigger alarms when the air or surface temperature changes occur outside of predetermined limits.
- Capacitance devices—detect changes in electrical capacitance (safes and vaults).
- Impact sensors—detect sudden changes in air pressure.
- Glass break sensors—detect the impact that causes glass to break, the sound frequencies of breaking glass or broken glass hitting the floor.

Duress/panic alarms—employed to protect personnel by transmitting assistance alarms—highest priority level.

The intrusion detection alarm should be monitored by a reliable company available 24/7, and when there is an incident, the alarm company contacts the security desk before dispatching first responders.

Many alarms consist of position switches, vibration sensors, glass break sensors, and duress/panic alarms and motion detectors.

- Alarm transmissions, monitoring, and notification mediums should be supervised to better detect occurrences of tampering or interception. Regular tests/audits should be performed to assure accuracy and timeliness of transmitted information, as well as response by security personnel.
- Intrusion detection sensors can add an extra layer of protection when they are interfaced/integrated with access control, security surveillance systems, and lighting.

Alarm Controls

All sensing devices are wired into the alarm control panel that receives their signals and processes them. Some of the most severe burglary losses are caused not by a failure in equipment but simply by someone turning off the alarm system. The type of control panel needed depends on the sophistication of the overall intrusion alarm system. Some control panels provide zoning capabilities for separate annunciation of the sensing devices. Others provide the low-voltage electrical power for the sensing devices.

Included in the control panel is the backup or standby power in the event of an electrical power failure. Batteries are used for standby power. Some equipment uses rechargeable batteries; the control has a low-power charging unit (a trickle charger) and maintains the batteries in a fully charged condition.

Modern control panels use one or more microprocessors. This allows the control panel to send and receive digital information to the alarm station. An alphanumeric pad can display zone information as well as supervisory conditions. Each user can also have a unique code, allowing restriction during specified times or limiting access into certain areas. By using individual code numbers, the alarm control panel can track activity as well as transmit this information off-site.

If the alarm control panel is connected to a central monitoring station, the times that the system is turned on and off are recorded and logged. When the owner enters the building in the morning, a signal is sent. If this happens at a time prearranged with the central station, it is considered a normal opening. If it happens at any other time, the police are dispatched.

The owner or other authorized persons can enter the building during the closed times. The person entering must first call the central station company and identify himself or herself by a special coding procedure. Records are kept at the central station company for these irregular openings and closings.

Tamper protection is a feature that generates an alarm signal when the system is compromised in any way. Tamper protection can be designed into any or all portions of the alarm system (control panel, sensing devices, loop wiring, alarm transmission facilities).

Alarm Transmission/Signaling

The type of alarm transmission/signaling system used in a particular application depends on the location of the business or residence, the frequency of police patrols, and the ability of the customer to afford the cost. Remember, after deterrence, the purpose of an alarm is to summon the proper authorities to stop a crime during its commission or lead to the apprehension of the intruder. It is very important that the response by proper authorities to the alarm comes in the shortest possible time. Two types of alarm signaling systems are in general use:

1. **Local alarm**. A bell or light indicates that an attempted or successful intrusion has taken place. The success of the system relies on someone hearing or seeing the signal and calling the responsible authorities. The local alarm also notifies burglars that they have been detected. This may be advantageous in frightening off the less-experienced intruder.
2. **Central station system**. The alarm signal is transmitted over telephone lines to a specially constructed building called the central station. Here, trained operators are on duty 24 h a day to supervise, record, and maintain alarms. On receipt of an alarm, the police are dispatched and, in some cases, the alarm company guard or runner. The record-keeping function and guard response ensure thorough documentation of any alarm signal. There are seven types of alarm transmissions to the central station. Each type of transmission has certain advantages and disadvantages that must be considered in determining the risk. Transmission of an alarm signal to the Underwriters Laboratories (UL)-listed central station is generally regarded as the most reliable method for reducing the burglary losses.
   a. **Direct wire systems**. High-risk locations (banks, jewelers, furriers) are generally protected with a direct wire system. A single dedicated telephone line is run from the protected premises to the central station or police station, where a separate receiver supervises only that alarm. A fixed DC current is sent from the central

station to the protected premises and read on a meter at the central station. The advantage of a direct wire system is that problems can be traced very quickly to a specific alarm system. This makes compromising the alarm signal by a professional burglar more difficult. The disadvantage of such a system is the higher cost of leased telephone lines. This becomes a more serious economic factor as the distance from the central station to the protected premises increases. Proper transmission of the alarm signal to the central station is essential. Problems can result on these telephone lines from shorts and broken wires. Most central stations expect these problems and are well equipped to rapidly make repairs. However, some of today's burglars are more sophisticated. They know they can prevent the transmission of the alarm signal to the central system by shunting or jumpering out the leased telephone line. Special methods are used by the alarm company to protect against jumpering of the alarm signal. Alarm systems having this special line security are classified as AA Grade Central Station alarms by UL.
   b. **Circuit (party line) systems**. Alarm signals transmitted over circuit transmission systems can be compared to a party line where several alarm customers defray the cost of the telephone line by sharing it. With a circuit transmission system, as many as 15 alarm transmitters may send alarm signals to a single receiving panel at the central station over the same line or loop. The alarm signals at the central station are received on strips of paper. Each alarm has a distinct code to identify it from others. The advantage of a circuit-loop alarm transmission system is the lower telephone line cost. Thus, a central station can make its services available to more customers by subdividing the cost of the

telephone line among different users. The disadvantage of circuit-loop alarm transmission systems is that problems on a leased telephone line are more difficult to locate than with a direct wire system.

c. **Multiplex systems**. The multiplex system is designed to reduce leased telephone line charges while providing a higher degree of line security than circuit-loop alarms. Multiplex systems introduced data processing (computer-based techniques) to the alarm industry.

d. **Digital communicators**. This computer-based type of alarm transmission equipment sends its signal through the regular switch line telephone network. The alarm signal transmitted is a series of coded electronic pulses that can be received only on a computer terminal at the central station.

e. **Radio signal transmission**. This method takes the alarm signal from the protected premises and sends it via radio or cellular phone to either a central station or police dispatch center. Additionally, the alarm signal can be received in a police patrol car.

f. **Video verification**. Along with standard alarm transmissions, video images are sent to the central station. This provides for a higher level of protection while helping to eliminate false alarms by allowing central station operators to see what is happening inside the protected area. With the increase of the false police dispatches, video verification is playing a major role in the battle against false alarms.

Alarms Deter Crime

False alarms waste police resources and alarm company resources. The police and alarm industry are acutely aware of this, and both have initiated efforts across the country to relieve the dilemma.

The National Crime Prevention Institute has long endorsed alarm systems as the best available crime deterrent. This education institution realizes that most criminals fear alarm systems; they much prefer to break into an unprotected building rather than risk capture by a hidden sensor.

Problem deterrence is the alarm business, a field that, in fact, extends far beyond protecting premises from burglary. The crisis prevention duties of alarm firms range from monitoring sprinkler systems and fire sensors and watching temperature levels in buildings to supervising industrial processes such as nuclear fission and the manufacturing of dangerous chemicals.

To alarm companies, deterrence is a sophisticated, specialized art. In the area of crime prevention, companies take pride in spotting potential weaknesses in a building and designing an alarm system that confounds the most intelligent criminals.

Crime prevention is the area where police need the most help. The rise in burglary and other crimes has often put police officers in a response posture.

False Alarms

The full crime prevention potential in alarm systems has yet to be realized. Relatively speaking, the number of premises not protected by alarms is great, although those businesses and residences holding the most valuable goods are thoroughly guarded by the most sophisticated sensor systems.

Yet the main drag on the potential of alarms, as industry leaders and police are aware, remains the false alarm problem. A modern instance of the boy who cried "wolf," false alarms erode the effectiveness of alarm systems. They are costly to alarm companies and police agencies.

It is a fact that alarm systems prevent crime. These electronic and electrical systems deter burglars, arsonists, vandals, and other criminals. They are both the most effective and most economical crime prevention tool available.

Police budgets have been reduced in most locales and frozen in others, whereas private investment in alarm security is growing yearly.

The National Burglary and Fire Alarm Association (NBFAA) asked its members to rank their priorities on association activities. The outstanding response asked for a comprehensive program to help member companies reduce false alarms. Moreover, while researching possible programs, the NBFAA learned that many members had already embarked on significant reduction efforts.

Some police departments initiated a written letter program from the police chief to those who have an excessive number of alarm runs. Others have the crime prevention officer make a follow-up visit to the business or residence. After the other steps have failed, many police departments are assessing false alarm fines.

By protecting such places as hospitals, office buildings, and schools, alarm systems free up police resources and enable patrol officers to spend more time in areas with high crime rates and fewer premises protected by alarm systems. Police may also dedicate more officers to apprehending criminals. In this manner, police and alarm companies work together, complementing one another and waging a mutual war on crime.

ALARM EQUIPMENT OVERHAUL

A California alarm station undertook a major overhaul. The effort began with a false alarm inventory, in which subscribers whose systems produced four or more false alarms per week were weeded out. Service workers then replaced—virtually reinstalled—the alarm systems for those subscribers. New sensors, new batteries, new wiring, and new soldering jobs were required in many instances. The process was costly, but it paid off in the long run. The office then had fewer service calls and an improved relationship with the local police that increased business.

Many NBFAA member companies instituted training programs for their sales, installation, and service personnel. Also, subscribers are educated on the operation of their systems three times: by salespeople, by installers, and by supervisors when they inspect newly installed systems.

One member company weeded out and entirely rebuilt its problem systems. This approach is the most feasible way for smaller firms to attack the problem. Lacking sufficient capital to initiate a comprehensive program, such companies can, nevertheless, cut down the number of false alarms by renovating the relatively few systems that cause the majority of problems.

Police chiefs and crime prevention officers working in areas troubled by false alarms should meet with the heads of the firms in their areas and discuss reduction programs like these.

ADDITIONAL RESOURCES

NBFAA members have a guide in the form of a comprehensive quality control manual outlining measures they can undertake to alleviate false alarms. To provide an idea of what is inside the *False Alarm Handbook*, an outline of it follows:

1. Determine false alarm rate and causes.
2. Form an alarm equipment evaluation committee.
3. Institute equipment testing procedures.
4. Develop equipment training facilities.
5. Know how to plan and make alarm installations.
6. Be familiar with sensor zoning procedures.
7. Inspect installations.
8. Educate the subscriber.
9. Cooperate with local law enforcement officers.

The theory behind the handbook is evident in the section titles. Companies are encouraged to begin with a series of statistical studies, from the general false alarm rate per total alarms and systems to causes distinguishing among equipment, user, telephone line, and environmental problems. A separate study helps companies determine how much money false alarms cost them.

The results of these studies should then be reviewed by the company's alarm equipment evaluation committee. That committee, made up of the chief engineer and plant, sales, and general managers, next decides which systems to keep, which to drop, and which to study further.

Sections 3 and 4 are self-explanatory, and are both aimed at eliminating equipment-related problems through further testing and by education of all personnel on equipment operations. Note that salespeople particularly are urged to go through the training process.

The next two parts cover installation procedures. Service workers are warned about environmental hazards that can affect different sensors. Such hazards include heat, static electricity, vibration, and electromagnetic interference from radio waves. The zoning section tells companies how they may set up their installations to isolate faults in different sensors and pieces of equipment.

Under subscriber education, firms are urged to inundate their customers with training films, brochures, seminars, and whatever else it takes to teach them how to operate their alarm systems properly.

The NBFAA also developed a separate booklet to educate alarm subscribers. It incorporates a discussion of alarm system fundamentals along with procedures that customers may undertake to reduce mistakes by their employees who operate the systems.

Last, the *False Alarm Handbook* asks alarm companies to work closely with the local police on this problem. Here, the NBFAA endorses companywide research and forming a local private security advisory council to oversee efforts.

Both the alarm company and the police must recognize that they need each other. Like surgeons and other medical specialists who need sophisticated drugs and instruments to prevent diseases, the law enforcement community needs the alarm industry. Prevention, the reason for alarm protection, must lead the war on crime.

At the same time, the alarm industry must remove from its ranks the flimflam-selling of placebos and faulty systems. Users must be taught to care for their security.

Police should take action against such companies and customers when they aggravate the false alarm problem. If some friendly arm-twisting fails to stop such practices, then police should meet with responsible alarm firms, and together they should develop programs and, if necessary, ordinances to penalize negligent subscribers and deceitful companies.

CONCLUSION

As we enter the 21st century and look back, we have seen a lot of changes occur, with many changes for the better. Passive infrared units are widely used and ultrasonic motion detectors are rarely used. Foil is no longer placed on glass windows being replaced by a properly placed PIR. Home and commercial applications of PIR units come in all shapes and sizes as well as all necessary patterns for proper coverage. Smoke detectors come with remote maintenance reporting to reduce false alarms (two-wire detectors only). Keypads are now hardware, and two-way voice modules and wireless and control panels (UL listed) are in single- and multizone panels.

The growth in technology will continue as will the need for updated technology.

APPENDIX 23A: SMOKE DETECTORS

Q: I have heard a lot of controversial comments about the use of ionization-type smoke detectors versus photoelectric-type smoke detectors. Where would one specifically choose to use ionization-type smoke detectors?

A: Proper selection of a type of detector begins with an understanding of the operating principles of each type of detector.

In an ionization smoke detector, "a small amount of radioactive material is used to ionize the air between two differently charged electrodes to sense the presence of particles. Smoke particles entering the ionization volume decrease the conductance of the air by reducing ion mobility. The reduced conductance signal is processed and used to convey an alarm condition when it meets present criteria."

In a photoelectric light-scattering detector, "a light source and photosensitive sensor arranged so that the rays from the light source do not normally fall onto the photosensitive sensor. Then smoke particles enter the light path; some of the light is scattered reflection and refraction onto the sensor. The light signal is processed and used to convey an alarm condition when it meets preset criteria."

The appendix further explains that photoelectric light-scattering detectors respond more to visible particles, larger than 1 μm in size, produced by most smoldering fires. They respond somewhat less to the smaller particles typically produced by flaming fires. They also respond less to fires yielding black or darker smoke, such as fires involving plastics and rubber tires.

Ionization detectors tend to exhibit somewhat opposite characteristics. In a fire yielding "invisible" particles of size less than 1 μm, an ionization detector will more likely respond than will a photoelectric light-scattering detector. Particles of this size tend to more readily result from flaming fires. Fuel in flaming fires burns "cleaner," producing smaller particles.

Thus, the answer to whether you should use one type of detector over another lies in understanding the burning characteristics of the particular fuel. An ionization-type smoke detector will likely detect a fire that produces flaming combustion more quickly, and a photoelectric-type detector will likely detect a low-energy fire that produces larger particles during combustion more quickly.

Finally, keep in mind that both types of smoke detectors successfully pass the same battery of tests at the nationally recognized testing laboratories. For example, UL-listed ionization smoke detectors and UL-listed photoelectric smoke detectors pass the same tests under UL 268, Standard for Safety for Smoke Detectors for Fire Protection Signaling Systems.

APPENDIX 23B: ALARM CERTIFICATE SERVICES GLOSSARY OF TERMS CERTIFICATE TYPES

The Fire Alarm System Certificate Types are:

- Central Station (NFPA 71 or 72)—Central Station Fire Alarm System Certificate
- Local (NFPA 72)—Local Fire Alarm System Certificate
- Auxiliary (NFPA 72)—Auxiliary Fire Alarm System Certificate
- Remote Station (NFPA 72)—Remote Station Fire Alarm System Certificate
- Proprietary (NFPA 72)—Proprietary Fire Alarm System Certificate

The Burglar Alarm System Certificate Types are:

- Central Station—Central Station Burglar Alarm System Certificate
- Mercantile—Mercantile Burglar Alarm System Certificate
- Bank—Bank Burglar Alarm System Certificate
- Proprietary—Proprietary Burglar Alarm System Certificate
- Residential—Residential Burglar Alarm System Certificate
- National Industrial Security—National Industrial Security System Certificate

STANDARDS

- UL 681—Installation and Classification of Burglar and Holdup-Alarm Systems
- UL 827—Central Station Alarm Services
- UL 1023—Household Burglar-Alarm System Units
- UL 1076—Proprietary Burglar-Alarm Units and Systems
- UL 1641—Installation and Classification of Residential Burglar-Alarm Systems
- UL 1981—Central Station Automation Systems
- UL 2050—National Industrial Security Systems for the Protection of Classified Materials
- NFPA 71: Standard for the Installation, Maintenance and Use of Central Station Protective Signaling Systems for Watchman Fire Alarm and Supervisory Service http://catalog.nfpa.org/Search. aspx?k=NFPA+71#sthash.oKAyZZq9.dpuf
- NFPA 72—Standard for the Installation, Maintenance, and Use of Protective Signaling Systems (2016). The traditional role of fire alarm systems is rapidly evolving. Now, the benchmark for fire alarm systems has changed to give designers, engineers, contractors, installers, and inspectors rules that reflect the current state of the field. An industry milestone, the 2016 edition of *NFPA 72: National Fire Alarm and Signaling Code* has the most advanced provisions ever developed for the application, installation, location, performance, and inspection, testing, and maintenance of fire alarm and emergency communications systems, including Mass Notification Systems.

New *NFPA 72* facilitates interconnections using networks.

- See more at: http://catalog.nfpa.org/ NFPA-72-National-Fire-Alarm-and- Signaling-Code-P1198.aspx?order_ src=B487&gclid=CO3-1dqS8MoCFcGPHwod Jh0AkQ#sthash.1qnyyD4c.dpuf

APPENDIX 23C: FIRE CLASSIFICATIONS

A fire is very dangerous, but it can be even more so if the wrong equipment is used in fighting it. Because of this, a fire classification system has been established that has made it easy to match the correct fire extinguisher to the correct type of fire.

Fires are divided into five types. It is important to use the correct fire extinguisher in combating the blaze. The five classifications include:

1. **Class A**: This fire is distinguishable by the fact that it leaves an ash. Some of the materials that burn in a Class A fire are wood, cloth, leaves, and rubbish (e.g., this is the class of fire that people have in their fireplaces).
2. **Class B**: This fire is ignited by flammable liquids. Examples are gasoline, oil, and lighter fluid (e.g., a charcoal grill is started by Class B fires).
3. **Class C**: These are electrical fires. They are common in fuse boxes.
4. **Class D**: Metals that are flammable cause Class D fires. Examples are sodium, magnesium, and potassium.
5. **Class K**: In recent years studies have found that some cooking oils produce too much heat to be controlled and extinguished by traditional Class B extinguishing agents. Class K fires and extinguishers deal with cooking oil fires.

USE OF FIRE EXTINGUISHERS

When combating a fire, the extinguisher used must be the same class as the fire. If a Class A extinguisher is used to put out a Class C fire, it could cause an explosion if the electrical current is still flowing. The following is an explanation of the contents and purposes of each type of extinguisher.

- **Class A Extinguishers** will put out fires in ordinary combustibles, such as wood and paper. The numerical rating for this class of fire extinguisher refers to the amount of water the fire extinguisher holds and the amount of fire it will extinguish.
- **Class B Extinguishers** should be used on fires involving flammable liquids, such as grease, gasoline, oil, and so forth. The numerical rating for this class of fire extinguisher states the approximate number of square feet of a flammable liquid fire that a nonexpert can expect to extinguish.
- **Class C Extinguishers** are suitable for use on electrically energized fires. This class of fire extinguishers does not have a numerical rating. The presence of the letter C indicates that the extinguishing agent is nonconductive.
- **Class D Extinguishers** are designed for use on flammable metals and are often specific for the type of metal in question. There is no picture designator for Class D extinguishers. These extinguishers generally have no rating and there is no multipurpose rating for use on other types of fires.
- **Class K Extinguishers** are suitable for cooking oil fires. Studies have found that some cooking oils produce too much heat to be controlled and extinguished by traditional Class B extinguishing agents. Class K extinguishers are a polished stainless steel cylinder, and these wet chemical extinguishers are the best restaurant kitchen appliance hand-portable fire extinguishers you can purchase. At Computershare we have such units in the kitchen.

Appendix 1: Glossary of Terms

Terms and Definitions for Doors and Windows Security

Access control A method of providing security by restricting the movement of persons into or within a protected area.

Accessible window (1) Residential, any window located within 3.7 m (14 feet) of grade or a building projection and (2) commercial, any window located within 4.6 m (18 feet) of grade or within 3 m (10 feet) of any fire escape or other structure accessible from public or semipublic areas (check local codes).

Ace lock A type of pin tumbler lock in which the pins are installed in a circle around the axis of the cylinder that move perpendicularly to the face of the cylinder. The shear line of the drive and bottom tumblers is a plane parallel to the face of the cylinder. This type of lock is operated with a push key.

Active door (or leaf) The leaf of a double door that must be opened first. It is used in normal pedestrian traffic. This leaf is usually the one in which a lock is installed.

ADA Americans with Disabilities Act.

Anchor A device used to secure a building part or component to adjoining construction or to a supporting member (see also **floor anchor**, **jamb anchor**, and **stud anchor**).

Antifriction latch A latch bolt that incorporates any device, which reduces the closing friction between the latch and the strike.

Applied trim A separately applied molding used as the finishing face trim of a frame.

Apron The flat member of a window trim placed against the wall immediately beneath the windowsill.

Architectural hardware See **finish builders' hardware**.

Areaway An open subsurface space adjacent to a building that is used to admit light or to provide a means of access to the building.

Armored front A plate or plates that is secured to the lock front of a mortised lock by machine screws to provide protection against tampering with cylinder set screws. Also called armored face plate.

Auxiliary lock A lock installed on a door or window to supplement a previously installed primary lock. Also called a secondary lock. It can be a mortised, bored, or rim lock.

Back plate A metal plate on the inside of a door that is used to clamp a pin or disc tumbler rim lock cylinder to the door by means of retaining screws. The tail piece of the cylinder extends through a hole in the back plate.

Backset, flush bolt A distance from the vertical centerline of the lock edge of a door to the centerline of the bolt.

Backset, hinge On a door, the distance from the stop face to the edge of the hinge cutout. On a frame, the distance from the stop to the edge of the hinge cutout.

Backset, lock The horizontal distance from the vertical centerline of the face plate to the center of the lock cylinder keyway or knob spindle.

Backset, strike The distance from the door stop to the edge of the strike cutout.

Baffle See **guard plate**.

Balanced door A door equipped with double-pivoted hardware designed to cause a semicounterbalanced swing action when it is opened.

Barrel key A key with a bit projecting from a round, hollow key shank that fits on a post in the lock.

Barricade bolt A massive metal bar that engages large strikes on both sides of a door. Barricade bolts are available with locking devices and are completely removed from the door when not in use.

Bevel (of a door) The angle of the lock edge of the door in relation to its face. The standard bevel is 0.32 cm in 5.1 cm (1/8″ in 2″).

Bevel (of a latch bolt) A term used to indicate the direction in which a latch bolt is inclined: regular bevel for doors opening in, reverse bevel for doors opening out.

Bevel (of a lock front) The angle of a lock front when not at a right angle to the lock case, allowing the front to be applied flush with the edge of a beveled door.

Bicentric pin tumbler cylinder A cylinder having two cores and two sets of pins, each having different combinations. This cylinder requires two separate keys, used simultaneously, to operate it. The cam or tail piece is gear operated.

Bit A blade projecting from a key shank that engages with and actuates the bolt or level tumblers of a lock.

Bit key A key with a bit projecting from a round shank. It is similar to the barrel key but with a solid rather than hollow shank.

Bitting See **cut**.

Biometrics A method of providing a higher level of security to an area by way of solid core doors.

Blank An uncut key or an unfinished key as it comes from the manufacturer, before any cuts have been made on it.

Blind stop A rectangular molding, located between the outside trim and the outside sashes, used in the assembly of a window frame. This serves as a stop for storm, screen, or combination windows as well as resisting air infiltration.

Bolt That part of a lock which, when actuated, is projected (or "thrown") from the lock into a retaining member, such as a strike plate, to prevent a door or window from moving or opening (see also **dead bolt**, **flush bolt**, and **latch**).

Bolt attack A category of burglary attack in which force, with or without the aid of tools, is directed against the bolt in an attempt to disengage it from the strike or to break it.

Bolt projection (bolt throw) The distance from the edge of the door, at the bolt centerline, to the furthest point on the bolt in the projected position.

Bored lock (or latch) A lock or latch whose parts are intended for installation in holes bored in a door (see also **key-in-knob lock**).

Bottom pin One of the pin tumblers that determines the combination of a pin tumbler cylinder; it is directly contacted by the key. They are varied in length and usually tapered at one end, enabling them to fit into the "V" cuts made in a key. When the proper key is inserted, the bottom pins level off at the cylinder core shearline, allowing the core to turn and actuate the lock.

Bottom rail The horizontal rail at the bottom of a door or window connecting the vertical edge members (stiles).

Box strike A strike plate that has a metal box or housing to fully enclose the projected bolt and/or latch.

Builders' hardware All hardware used in building construction, but particularly that used on or in connection with doors, windows, cabinets, and other moving members.

Bumping A method of opening a pin tumbler lock by means of vibration produced by a wooden or rubber mallet.

Burglar-resistant glazing A type of hinge with matching rectangular leaves and multiple bearing contacts. It is designed to be mounted in mortises in the door edge and in the frame.

Butt hinge A type of hinge with matching rectangular leaves and multiple bearing contacts. It is designed to be mounted in mortises in the door edge and in the frame.

Buttress lock A lock that secures a door by wedging a bar between the door and the floor. Some incorporate a movable steel rod that fits into metal-receiving slots on the door and in the floor. It is also called police bolt/brace.

Cabinet jamb A door frame in three or more pieces usually shipped knocked down for field assembly over a rough buck.

Cam The part of a lock or cylinder that rotates to actuate the bolt or latch as the key is turned. The cam may also act as a bolt.

Cam, lazy A cam that moves less than the rotation of the cylinder core.

Cam lock See **crescent sash lock**.

Cane bolt A heavy cane-shaped bolt with the top bent at right angles. It is used on the bottom of doors.

Case The housing in which a lock mechanism is mounted and enclosed.

Casement hinge A hinge for swinging a casement window.

Casement window A type of window that is hinged on the vertical edge.

Casing Molding of various widths and thicknesses used to trim door and window openings at the jambs.

Center-hung door A door hung on center pivots.

Center rail The horizontal rail in a door usually located at lock height to separate the upper and lower panels of a recessed panel-type door.

Chain bolt A vertical spring-loaded bolt mounted at the top of a door. It is manually actuated by a chain.

Chain door interviewer An auxiliary locking device that allows a door to be opened slightly but restrains it from being fully opened. It consists of a chain with one end attached to the doorjamb and the other attached to a keyed metal piece that slides in a slotted metal plate attached to the door. Some chain door interviewers incorporate a keyed lock operated from the inside.

Change key A key that will operate only one lock or a group of keyed-alike locks, as distinguished from a master key (see also **keyed-alike cylinders** and **master key system**).

Changes The number of possible key changes or combination changes to a lock cylinder.

Checkrails They are the meeting rails of double-hung windows. They are usually beveled and thick enough to fill the space between the top and bottom sash due to the parting stop in the window frame.

Clearance A space intentionally provided between components, either to facilitate operation or installation, to ensure proper separation, to accommodate dimensional variations, or for other reasons (see also **door clearance**).

Clevis A metal link used to attach a chain to a padlock.

Code An arrangement of numbers or letters used to specify a combination for the bitting of a key or the pins of a cylinder core.

Combination doors or windows They are storm doors or windows permanently installed over the primary doors or windows. They provide insulation and summer ventilation and often have self-storing or removable glass and screen inserts.

Common entry door (of a multiple dwelling) Any door in a multiple dwelling that provides access between the semipublic, interior areas of the building, and the out-of-doors areas surrounding the building.

Component A subassembly that is combined with other components to make an entire system. Door assembly components include the door, lock, hinges, jam/strike, and jamb/wall.

Composite door A door constructed of a solid core material with facing and edges of different materials.

Connecting bar A flat metal bar attached to the core of a cylinder lock to operate the bolt mechanism.

Construction master keying A keying system used to allow the use of a single key for all locks during the construction of large housing projects. In one such system, the cylinder cores of all locks contain an insert that permits the use of a special master key. When the dwelling unit is completed, the insert is removed and the lock then accepts its own change key and no longer accepts the construction master key.

Continuous hinge A hinge designed to be the same length as the edge of the moving part to which it is applied. It is also called a piano hinge.

Coordinator A mechanism that controls the order of closing of a pair of swing doors used with overlapping astragals and certain panic hardware that requires that one door close ahead of the other.

Core See **cylinder core**.

CPTED The design or redesign of a building or place to reduce crime opportunity and fear of crime through the specific application of strategies and tactics to reduce crime opportunity through environmental design. These strategies involve surveillance, access control, territoriality, maintenance, and place management. The tactics of CPTED are further specified into natural, mechanical, and procedural components. CPTED plans are best developed and implemented by multidisciplinary teams.

Crash bar The crossbar or level of a panic exit device that serves as a push bar to actuate the lock (see also **panic hardware**).

Cremone bolt A surface-mounted device that locks a door or sash into the frame at both the top and bottom when a knob or lever is turned.

Crescent sash lock A simple cam-shaped latch that does not require a key for its operation, usually used to secure double-hung windows. It is also called a cam lock.

Cut An indention made in a key to make it fit a pin tumbler of a lock. Any notch made in a key is known as a cut whether it is square, round, or V-shaped. It is also called bitting.

Cylinder The cylindrical subassembly of a lock, including the cylinder housing, the cylinder core, the tumbler mechanism, and the keyway.

Cylinder collar See **cylinder guard ring**.

Cylinder core (or plug) The central part of a cylinder, containing the keyway, which rotates to operate the lock bolt.

Cylinder guard ring A hardened metal ring, surrounding the exposed portion of a lock cylinder, that protects the cylinder from being wrenched, turned, pried, cut, or pulled by attack tools.

Cylinder housing The external case of a lock cylinder, which is also called the cylinder shell.

Cylinder lock A lock in which the locking mechanism is controlled by a cylinder. A double cylinder lock has a cylinder on both the interior and exterior of the door.

Cylinder, mortise type A lock cylinder that has a threaded housing that screws directly into the lock case with a cam or other mechanism engaging the locking mechanism.

Cylinder, removable core A cylinder whose core may be removed by the use of a special key.

Cylinder, rim type A lock cylinder that is held in place by tension against its rim applied by screws from the interior face of the door.

Cylinder ring See **guard ring**.

Cylinder screw A set screw that holds a mortise cylinder in place and prevents it from being turned after installation.

Cylindrical lock (or latch) See **bored lock**.

Dead bolt A lock bolt that does not have an automatic spring action and a beveled end as opposed to a latch bolt, which does. The bolt must be actuated to a projected position by a key or thumb turn and when projected is locked against return by end pressure.

Dead latch A spring-actuated latch bolt having a beveled end and incorporating a feature that automatically locks the projected latch bolt against return by end pressure.

Disc tumbler A spring-loaded, flat plate that slides in a slot that runs through the diameter of the cylinder. Inserting the proper key lines up the disc tumblers with the lock's shear line and enables the core to be turned.

Dogging device A mechanism that fastens the crossbar of a panic exit device in the fully depressed position, and retains the latch bolt or bolts in the retracted position to permit free operation of the door from either side.

Dogging key A key-type wrench used to lock down, in the open position, the crossbar of a panic exit device.

Door assembly A unit composed of parts or components that make up a closure for a passageway through a wall. It consists of the door, hinges, locking device or devices, operational contacts (such as handles, knobs, push plates), miscellaneous hardware and closures, the frame including the head and jambs, the anchorage devices to the surrounding wall, and the surrounding wall.

Door bolt A rod or bar manually operated without a key, attached to a door to provide a means of securing it.

Door check (door closer) A device used to control the closing of a door by means of a spring and either hydraulic or air pressure or by electrical means.

Door clearance The space between a door and either its frame or the finished floor or threshold or between the two doors of a double door (see also **Clearance**).

Door frame An assembly of members surrounding and supporting a door or doors and perhaps also one or more transom lights and/or sidelights (see also **integral frame**).

Doorjambs The two vertical components of a door frame called the hinge jamb and the lock jamb.

Door light See **light**.

Door opening The size of a doorway measured from jamb to jamb and from floor line to sill to head of frame. The opening size is usually the nominal door size and is equal to the actual door size plus clearances and threshold height.

Door stop The projections along the top and sides of a door frame against which a one-way swinging door closes (see also **rabbeted jamb**).

Double-acting door A swinging door equipped with hardware that permits it to open in either direction.

Double-bitted key A key having cuts on two sides.

Double cylinder lock See **cylinder lock.**

Double door A pair of doors mounted together in a single opening (see also **active door** and **inactive door**).

Double egress frame A door frame prepared to receive two single-acting doors swinging in opposite directions, and both doors are of the same hand.

Double glazing Two thicknesses of glass, separated by an air space and framed in an opening, designed to reduce heat transfer. In factory-made double glazing units, referenced to as insulating glass, the air space between the glass sheets is desiccated and sealed airtight.

Double-hung window A type of window composed of upper and lower sashes that slide vertically.

Double-throw lock A bolt that can be projected beyond its first position, into a second, or fully extended one.

Double-throw lock A lock incorporating a double-throw bolt.

Driver pin One of the pin tumblers in a pin tumbler cylinder lock, usually flat on both ends, that is on line with and pushes against the flat ends of the bottom pins. They are projected by individual coil springs into the cylinder core until they are forced from the core by the bottom pins when the proper key is inserted into the keyway.

Drop ring A ring handle attached to the spindle that operates a lock or latch. The ring is pivoted to remain in a dropped position when not in use.

Dry glazing A method of securing glass in a frame by use of a preformed resilient gasket.

Drywall frame A knocked down door frame for installation in a wall constructed with studs and gypsum board or other drywall facing material after the wall is erected.

Dummy cylinder A mock cylinder without an operating mechanism used for appearance only.

Dummy trim This is trim only, without lock; usually used on the inactive door in a double door.

Dutch door A door consisting of two separate leaves, one above the other, which may be operated either independently or together. The lower leaf usually has a service shelf.

Dutch door bolt A device for locking together the upper and lower leaves of a Dutch door.

Dwelling unit entry door Any door giving access to a private dwelling unit.

Electric strike An electrically operated device that replaces a conventional strike plate and allows a door to be opened by using electric switches at remote locations.

Escutcheon plate A surface-mounted cover plate, either protective or ornamental, containing openings for any or all of the controlling members of a lock such as the knob, handle, cylinder, or keyhole.

Exit device See **panic hardware.**

Expanded metal An open mesh formed by slitting and drawing a metal sheet: It is made in various patterns and metal thicknesses, with either a flat or an irregular surface.

Exterior private area The ground area outside a single family house, or a ground floor apartment in the case of a multiple dwelling, which is fenced off by a real barrier, is available for the use of one family, and is accessible only from the interior of that family's unit.

Exterior public area The ground area outside a multiple dwelling that is not defined as being associated with the building or building entry in any real or symbolic fashion.

Exterior semiprivate area The ground area outside a multiple dwelling that is fenced off by a real barrier and is accessible only from the private or semiprivate zones within the building.

Exterior semipublic area The ground area outside a single family house or multiple dwelling that is accessible from public zones but is defined as belonging to the house or building by symbolic barriers only.

Face (of a lock) See **face plate.**

Face glazing A method of glazing in which the glass is set in an L-shaped or rabbeted frame, the glazing compound is finished off in the form of a triangular bead, and no loose stops are employed.

Face plate The part of a mortise lock through which the bolt protrudes and by which the lock is fastened to the door.

Fast pin hinge A hinge in which the pin is fastened permanently in place.

Fatigue Structural failure of a material caused by repeated or fluctuating application of stresses, none of which is individually sufficient to cause failure.

Fence A metal pin that extends from the bolt of a lever lock and prevents retraction of the bolt unless it is aligned with the gates of the lever tumblers.

Fidelity loss A property loss resulting from a theft in which the thief leaves no evidence of entry.

Filler plate A metal plate used to fill unwanted mortise cutouts in a door or frame.

Finish builders' hardware Hardware that has a finished appearance as well as a functional purpose and that may be considered as part of the decorative treatment of a room or building. It is also called finish hardware and buildings' finish hardware.

Fire stair Any enclosed stairway that is part of a fire-resistant exitway.

Fire stair door A door-forming part of the fire-resistant fire stair enclosure and providing access from common corridors to fire stair landings within an exitway.

Floor anchor A metal device attached to the wall side of a jamb at its base to secure the frame to the floor.

Floor clearance The width of the space between the bottom of a door and the rough or finished floor or threshold.

Flush bolt A door bolt so designed that when installed, the operating handle is flush with the face or edge of the door. It is usually installed at the top and bottom of the inactive door of a double door.

Flush door A smooth-surfaced door having faces that are plain and conceal its rails and stiles or other structure.

Foot bolt A type of bolt applied at the bottom of a door and arranged from foot operation. Generally the bolt head is held up by a spring when the door is unbolted.

Forced entry An unauthorized entry accomplished by the use of force upon the physical components of the premises.

Frame The component that forms the opening of and provides support for a door, window, skylight, or hatchway (see also **door frame**).

Frame gasket Resilient material in strip form attached to frame stops to provide tight closure of a door or window.

Front (of a lock) See **face plate**.

Gate A notch in the end of a lever tumbler that when aligned with the fence of the lock bolt allows the bolt to be withdrawn from the strike.

General circulation stair An interior stairway in a nonelevator building that provides access to upper floors.

Glass door A door made from thick glass, usually heat tempered, with no structural metal stiles.

Glazing Any transparent or translucent material used in windows or doors to admit light.

Glazing bead A strip of trim or a sealant such as caulking or glazing compound, which is placed around the perimeter of a pane of glass or other glazing to secure it to a frame.

Glazing compound A soft, dough-like material used for filling and sealing the spaces between a pane of glass and its surrounding frame and/or stops.

Grand master key A key designed to operate all locks under several master keys in a system.

Grating, bar type An open grip assembly of metal bars in which the bearing bars, running in one direction, are spaced by rigid attachment to crossbars running perpendicular to them or by bent connecting bars extending between them.

Grout Mortar of such consistency that it will just flow into the joints and cavities of masonry work and fill them solid.

Grout frame A frame in which all voids between it and the surrounding wall are completely filled with the cement or plaster used in the wall construction.

Guard bar A series of two or more crossbars, generally fastened to a common back plate, to protect the glass of screen in a door.

Guard plate A piece of metal attached to a door frame, door edge, or over the lock cylinder for the purpose of reinforcing the locking system against burglary attacks.

Hand (of a door) The opening direction of the door. A right-handed door (RH) is hinged on the right and swings inward when viewed from the outside. A left-handed door (LH) is hinged on the left and swings inward when viewed from the outside. If either of these doors swings outward, it is referred to as a right-hand reverse door (RHR) or a left-hand reverse (LHR) door, respectively.

Handle Any grip-type door pull (see also **lever handle**).

Hasp A fastening device consisting of a hinged plate with a slot in it that fits over a fixed D-shaped ring or eye.

Hatchway An opening in a ceiling, roof, or floor of a building large enough to allow human access.

Head Top horizontal member of a door or window frame.

Head stiffener A heavy-gauge metal angle or channel section placed inside, and attached to, the head of a wide door frame to maintain its alignment. It is not a load-carrying member.

Heel of a padlock That end of the shackle on a padlock that is not removable from the case.

Hinge A device generally consisting of two metal plates having loops formed along one edge of each to engage and rotate about a common pivot rod or "pin," used to suspend a swinging door or window in its frame.

Hinge backset The distance from the edge of a hinge to the stop at the side of a door or window.

Hinge edge or hinge stile The vertical edge or stile of a door or window to which hinges or pivots are attached.

Hinge pins They come in two types: removable pins and nonremovable pins for higher security.

Hinge reinforcement A metal plate attached to a door or frame to receive a hinge.

Holdback feature A mechanism on a latch that serves to hold the latch bolt in the retracted position.

Hollow core door A door constructed so that the space (core) between the two facing sheets is not completely filled. Various spacing and reinforcing materials are used to separate the facing sheets; some interior hollow core doors have nothing except perimeter stiles and rails separating the facing sheets.

Hollow metal Hollow items such as doors, frames, partitions, and enclosures that are usually fabricated from cold-formed metal sheet, usually carbon steel.

Horizontal sliding window A type of window, composed of two sections, one or both of which slide horizontally past the other.

Impression system A technique to produce keys for certain types of locks without taking the lock apart.

Inactive door (or leaf) The leaf of a double door that is bolted when closed; the strike plate is attached to this leaf to receive the latch and bolt of the active leaf.

Integral frame A metal door frame in which the jambs and head have stops, trim, and backbends all formed from one piece of material.

Integral lock (or latch) See **preassembled lock**.

Interior common-circulation area An area within a multiple dwelling that is outside the private zones of individual units and is used in common by all residents and the maintenance staff of the building.

Interior private area The interior of a single family house; the interior of an apartment in a multiple dwelling; or the interior of a separate unite within a commercial, public, or institutional building.

Interior public area An interior common-circulation area or common resident-use room within a multiple dwelling to which access is unrestricted.

Interior semipublic area An interior common-circulation area or common resident-use room within a multiple dwelling to which access is possible only with a key or on the approval of a resident via an intercom, buzzer-reply system.

Invisible hinge A hinge so constructed that no parts are exposed when the door is closed.

Jalousie window See **louvered window**.

Jamb The exposed vertical member of either side of a door or window opening (see also **doorjambs**).

Jamb anchor A metal device inserted in or attached to the wall side of a jamb to secure the frame to the wall. A masonry jamb anchor secures a jamb to a masonry wall.

Jamb depth The width of the jamb measured perpendicular to the door or wall face at the edge of the opening.

Jamb extension The section of a jamb that extends below the level of the wash floor for attachment to the rough floor.

Jamb peeling A technique used in forced entry to deform or remove portions of the jamb to disengage the bolt from the strike (see **jimmying**).

Jamb/strike The component of a door assembly that receives and holds the extended lock bolt. The strike and jamb are considered a unit.

Jamb/wall The component of a door assembly to which a door is attached and secured by means of the hinges. The wall and jamb are considered a unit.

Jimmying A technique used in forced entry to pry the jamb away from the lock edge of the door a sufficient distance to disengage the bolt from the strike.

Jimmy pin A sturdy projecting screw, which is installed in the hinge edge of a door near a hinge, that fits into a hole in the doorjamb and prevents removal of the door if the hinge pins are removed.

Key An implement used to actuate a lock bolt or latch into the locked or unlocked position.

Key changes The different combinations that are available or that can be used in a specific cylinder.

Keyed-alike cylinders Cylinders that are designed to be operated by the same key. (Not to be confused with masterkeyed cylinders.)

Keyed-different cylinders Cylinders requiring different keys for their operation.

Keyhole The opening in a lock designed to receive the key.

Key-in-knob lock A lock having the key cylinder and the other lock mechanism, such as a push or turn button, contained in the knobs.

Key plate A plate or escutcheon having only a keyhole.

Keyway The longitudinal cut in the cylinder core. It is an opening or space with millings in the sides identical to those on the proper key, thus allowing the key to enter the full distance of the blade (see also **warded lock**).

Knifing See **loiding**.

Knob An ornamental or functional round handle on a door; it may be designed to actuate a lock or latch.

Knob latch A securing device having a spring bolt operated by a knob only.

Knob shank The projecting stem of a knob into which the spindle is fastened.

Knocked down (KD) It is disassembled one and designed for assembly at the point of use.

Knuckle The enlarged part of a hinge into which the pin is inserted.

Laminate A product made by bonding together two or more layers of material.

Laminated glass A type of glass fabricated from two layers of glass with a transparent bonding layer between them. Also called safety glass.

Laminated padlock A padlock, the body of which consists of a number of flat plates, all or most of which are of the same contour, superimposed and riveted or brazed together. Holes in the plates provide spaces for the lock mechanism and the ends of the shackle.

Latch (or latch bolt) A beveled, spring-actuated bolt that may or may not include a deadlocking feature.

Leading edge See **lock edge**.

Leaf, door An individual door used either singly or in multiples.

Leaf hinge The most common type of hinge, characterized by two flat metal plates or leaves, which pivot about a metal hinge pin. A leaf hinge can be surface mounted or installed in a mortise (see also **butt hinge** and **surface hinge**).

Lever handle A bar-like grip rotated in a vertical plane about a horizontal axis at one of its ends designed to operate a latch.

Lever lock A key-operated lock that incorporates one or more lever tumblers, which must be raised to a specific level so that the fence of the bolt is aligned with the gate of the tumbler to withdraw the bolt. Lever locks are commonly used in storage lockers and safety deposit boxes.

Lever tumbler A flat metal arm pivoted on one end with a gate in the opposite end. The top edge is spring loaded. The bitting of the key rotates against the bottom edge, raising the lever tumbler to align the gate with the bolt fence. Both the position of the gate and the curvature of the bottom edge of the lever tumbler can be varied to establish the key code.

Light A space in a window or door for a single pane of glazing. Also, a pane of glass or other glazing material.

Lintel A horizontal structural member that supports the load over an opening such as a door or window.

Lip (of a strike) The curved projecting part of a strike plate that guides the spring bolt to the latch point.

Lobby That portion of the interior common area of a building that is reached from an entry door and provides access to the general circulation areas, elevators, and fire stairs and from these to other areas of the building.

Lock A fastener that secures a door or window assembly against unauthorized entry. A door is usually key operated and includes the keyed device (cylinder or combination), bolt, strike plate, knobs or levers, trim items, and so forth. A window lock is usually hand operated rather than key operated.

Lock clip A flexible metal part attached to the inside of a door face to position a mortise lock.

Lock edge The vertical edge or stile of a door in which a lock may be installed. Also called the leading edge, the lock stile, and the strike edge.

Lock edge door (or lock seam door) A door that has its face sheets secured in place by an exposed mechanical interlock seam on each of its two vertical edges. See also **lock seam**.

Lock faceplate See **face plate**.

Locking dog (of a padlock) The part of a padlock mechanism that engages the shackle and holds it in the locked position.

Lock-in-knob See **key-in-knob lock**.

Lock pick A tool or instrument, other than the specifically designed key, made for the purpose of manipulating a lock into a locked or unlocked condition.

Lock rail The horizontal member of a door intended to receive the lock case.

Lock reinforcement A reinforcing plate attached inside of the lock stile of a door to receive a lock.

Lock seam A joint in sheet metal work formed by doubly folding the edges of adjoining sheets in such a manner that they interlock.

Lock stile See **lock edge**.

Locks Come in different shapes and styles, for example: pin tumbler, the most widely used; warded lock was the first developed (see warded lock); level lock was used in cabinets, lockers, desk drawers; dial combination, a dial with combination instead of a key, is used to open the lock.

Loiding A burglary attack method in which a thin, flat, flexible object such as a stiff piece of plastic is inserted between the strike and the latch bolt to depress the latch bolt and release it from the strike. The loiding of windows is accomplished by inserting a thin, stiff object between the meeting rails or stiles to move the latch to the open position, or by inserting a thin stiff wire through openings between the stile or rail and the frame to manipulate the sash operator of pivoting windows. Derived from the work "celluloid." Also called knifing and slip-knifing.

Loose joint hinge A hinge with two knuckles. The pin is fastened permanently to one and the other contains the pinhole. The two parts of the hinge can be disengaged by lifting.

Loose pin hinge A hinge having a removable pin to permit the two leaves of the hinge to be separated.

Louver An opening with a series of horizontal slats so arranged as to permit ventilation but to exclude rain, sunlight, or vision.

Louvered window A type of window in which the glazing consists of parallel, horizontal, movable glass slats. Also called a jalousie window.

Main entry door It is the most important common entry door in a building and provides access to the building's lobby.

Maison keying A specialized keying system, used in apartment houses and other large complexes, that enables all individual unit keys to operate common-use locks such as main entry, laundry room, and so forth.

Master disc tumbler A disk tumbler that will operate with a master key in addition to its own change key.

Master key system A method of keying locks that allows a single key to operate multiple locks, each of which will also operate with an individual change key. Several levels of master keying are possible: a single master key is one that will operate all locks of a group of locks with individual change keys, a grand master key will operate all locks of two or more master key systems, and a great grand master will operate all locks of two or more grand master key systems. Master key systems are used primarily with pin and disk tumbler locks, and to a limited extent with lever or warded locks.

Master pin A segmented pin, used to enable a pin tumbler to be operated by more than one key cut.

Meeting stile The vertical edge member of a door or horizontal sliding window, in a pair of doors or windows, which meets with the adjacent edge member when closed. See also **checkrails**.

Metal mesh grille A grille of expanded metal or welded metal wires permanently installed across a window or other opening to prevent entry through the opening.

Mill finish The original surface finish produced on a metal mill product by cold rolling, extruding, or drawing.

Millwork Generally, all building components made of finished wood and manufactured in millwork plants and planning mills. It includes such items as inside and outside doors, window and door frames, cabinets, porch work, mantels, panel work, stairways, moldings, and interior trim. It normally does not include flooring, ceiling, and siding.

Molding A wood strip used for decorative purposes.

Mono lock See **preassembled lock**.

Mortise A rectangular cavity made to receive a lock or other hardware; also, the act of making such a cavity.

Mortise bolt A bolt designed to be installed in a mortise rather than on the surface. The bolt is operated by a knob, lever, or equivalent.

Mortise cylinder See **cylinder, mortise type**.

Mortise lock A lock designed for installation in a mortise, as distinguished from a bored lock and a rim lock.

Mullion (1) A movable or fixed center post used on double door openings, usually for locking purposes. (2) A vertical or horizontal bar or divider in a frame between windows, doors, or other openings.

Multiple dwelling A building or portion of a building designed or used for occupancy by three or more tenants or families living independently of each other (includes hotels or motels).

Muntin A small member that divides a glass or openings of sash or doors.

Mushroom tumbler A type of tumbler used in pin tumbler locks to add security against picking. The diameter of the driver pin behind the end in contact with the bottom pin is reduced so that the mushroom head will catch the edge of the cylinder body at the shear line when it is at a slight angle to its cavity (see also **spool tumbler**).

Night latch An auxiliary lock having a spring latch bolt and functioning independently of the regular lock of the door.

Nonremovable hinge pin A type of hinge pin that has been constructed or modified to make removing it from the hinge difficult or impossible.

Offset pivot (or hinge) A pin-and-socket hardware device with a single bearing contact by means of which a door is suspended in its frame and allowed to swing about an axis that normally is located about 1.9 cm (3/4 in) out from the door face.

One-way screw A screw specifically designed to resist being removed, once installed (see also **tamper-resistant hardware**).

Opening size See **door opening**.

Operator (of a window sash) The mechanism, including a crank handle and gear box, attached to an operating arm or arms for the purpose of opening and closing a window. It is usually found on casement- and awning-type windows.

Overhead door A door that is stored overhead when in the open position.

Padlock A detachable and portable lock with a hinged or sliding shackle or bolt, normally used with a hasp and eye or staple system.

Panel door A door fabricated from one or more panels surrounded by and held in position by rails and stiles.

Panic bar See **crash bar**.

Panic hardware An exterior door-locking mechanism that is always operable from inside the building by pressure on a crash bar or lever.

Patio-type sliding door A sliding door that is essentially a single, large transparent panel in a frame (a type commonly used to give access to patios or yards of private dwellings); "single" doors have one fixed and one movable panel and "double" doors have two movable panels.

Pin (of a hinge) The metal rod that serves as the axis of a hinge thereby allowing the hinge (and attached door or window) to rotate between the open and closed positions.

Pin tumbler One of the essential, distinguishing components of a pin tumbler lock cylinder, more precisely called a bottom pin, master pin, or driver pin. The pin tumblers, used in varying lengths and arrangements, determine the combination of the cylinder (see also **bottom pin, driver pin**, and **master pin**).

Pin tumbler lock cylinder A lock cylinder employing metal pins (tumblers) to prevent the rotation of the core until the correct key is inserted into the keyway. Small coil compression springs hold the pins in the locked position until the key is inserted.

Pivoted door A door hung on pivots rather than hinges.

Pivoted window A window that opens by pivoting about a horizontal or vertical axis.

Plug retainer The part often fixed to the rear of the core in a lock cylinder to retain or hold the core firmly in the cylinder.

Preassembled lock A lock that has all the parts assembled into a unit at the factory and, when installed in a rectangular section cutout of the lock edge, requires little or no assembly. It is also called integral lock, mono lock, and unit lock.

Pressed padlock A padlock whose outer case is pressed into shape from sheet metal and then riveted together.

Pressure-locked grating A grating in which the crossbars are mechanically locked to the bearing bars at their intersections by deforming or swaging the metal.

Privacy lock A lock, usually for an interior door, secured by a button, thumbturn, and so forth, and not designed for key operation.

Push key A key that operates the Ace type of lock.

Quadrant See **Dutch door bolt**.

Rabbet A cut, slot, or groove made on the edge or surface of a board to receive the end or edge of another piece of wood made to fit it.

Rabbeted jamb A doorjamb in which the projecting portion of the jamb that forms the door stop is either part of the same piece as the rest of the jamb or securely set into a deep groove in the jamb.

Rail A horizontal framing member of a door or window sash that extends the full width between the stiles.

Removable mullion A mullion separating two adjacent door openings that is required for the normal operation of the doors but is designed to permit its temporary removal.

Restricted keyway A special keyway and key blank for high-security locks with a configuration that is not freely available and must be specifically requested from the manufacturer.

Reversible lock A lock that may be used for either hand of a door.

Rim cylinder A pin or disc tumbler cylinder used with a rim lock.

Rim hardware Hardware designed to be installed on the surface of a door or window.

Rim latch A latch installed on the surface of a door.

Rim lock A lock designed to be mounted on the surface of a door.

Rose The part of a lock that functions as an ornament or bearing surface for a knob and is normally placed against the surface of the door.

Rotary interlocking dead bolt lock A type of rim lock in which the extended dead bolt is rotated to engage with the strike.

Rough buck A subframe, usually made of wood or steel, that is set in a wall opening and to which the frame is attached.

Rough opening The wall opening into which a frame is to be installed. Usually, the rough opening is measured inside the rough buck.

Sash A frame containing one or more lights.

Sash fast A fastener attached to the meeting rails of a window.

Sash lock A sash fast with a locking device controlled by a key.

Screwless knob A knob attached to a spindle by means of a special wrench, as distinguished from the more commonly used side screw knob.

Screwless rose A rose with a concealed method of attachment.

Seamless door A door having no visible seams on its faces or edges.

Secondary lock See **auxiliary lock**.

Security glass or glazing See **burglar-resistant glazing**.

Setback See **backset**.

Shackle The hinged or sliding part of a padlock that does the fastening.

Shear line The joint between the shell and the core of a lock cylinder; the line at which the pins or discs of a lock cylinder must be aligned to permit rotation of the core.

Sheathing The structural exterior covering, usually wood boards or plywood, used over the framing studs and rafters of a structure.

Shell A lock cylinder, exclusive of the core. It is also called housing.

Shutter A movable screen or cover used to protect an opening, especially a window.

Side light A fixed light located adjacent to a door within the same frame assembly.

Signal sash fastener A sash-fastening device designed to lock windows that are beyond reach from the floor. It has a ring for a sash pole hook. When locked, the ring lever is down; when the ring lever is up, it signals by its upright position that the window is unlocked.

Sill The lower horizontal member of a door or window opening.

Single-acting door A door mounted to swing to only one side of the plane of its frame.

Skylight A glazed opening located in the roof of a building.

Slide bolt A simple lock that is operated directly by hand without using a key, a turnpiece, or other actuating mechanism. Slide bolts can normally only be operated from the inside.

Sliding door Any door that slides open sideways.

Sliding metal gate An assembly of metal bars jointed so that it can be moved to and locked in position across a window or other opening to prevent unauthorized entry through the opening.

Slip-knifing See **loiding**.

Solid core door A door constructed so that the space (core) between the two facing sheets is completely filled with wood blocks or other rigid material.

Spindle The shaft that fits into the shank of a door knob or handle and that serves as its axis of rotation.

Split astragal A two-piece astragal, one piece of which is surface mounted on each door of a double door and is provided with a means of adjustment to mate with the other piece and provide a seal.

Spool tumbler A type of tumbler used in pin tumbler locks to add security against picking. It operates on the same principal as the mushroom tumbler.

Spring bolt See **latch**.

Spring bolt with antiloading device See **dead latch**.

Stile One of the vertical edge members of a paneled door or window sash.

Stool A flat molding fitted over the windowsill between the jambs and contacting the bottom rail of the lower sash.

Stop (of a door or window frame) The projecting part of a door or window frame against which a swinging door or window closes or in which a sliding door or window moves.

Stop (of a lock) A button or other device that serves to lock and unlock a latch bolt against actuation by the outside knob or thumb piece. Another type holds the bolt retracted.

Stop side That face of a door that contacts the door stop.

Store front sash An assembly of light metal members forming a continuous frame for a fixed glass store front.

Storm sash, window, or door An extra window or door usually placed on the outside of an existing one as additional protection against cold or hot weather.

Strap hinge A surface hinge of which one or both leaves are of considerable length.

Strike A metal plate attached to or mortised into a doorjamb to receive and hold a projected latch bolt and/or dead bolt to secure the door to the jamb.

Strike, dustproof A strike that is placed in the threshold or sill of an opening, or in the floor, to receive a flush bolt and is equipped with a spring-loaded follower to cover the recess and keep out dirt.

Strike, interlocking A strike that receives and holds a vertical, rotary, or hook dead bolt.

Strike plate See **strike**.

Strike reinforcement A metal plate attached to a door or frame to receive a strike.

Strike, roller A strike for latch bolts having a roller mounted on the lip to reduce friction.

Stud A slender wood or metal post used as a supporting element in a wall or partition.

Stud anchor A device used to secure a stud to the floor.

Subbuck or subframe See **rough buck**.

Surface hinge A hinge having both leaves attached to the surface and thus is fully visible.

Swing See **hand**.

Swinging bolt A bolt that is hinged to a lock front and is projected and retracted with a swinging rather than a sliding action. It is also called hinged or pivot bolt.

Tail piece The unit on the core of a cylinder lock that actuates the bolt or latch.

Tamper-resistant hardware Builders' hardware with screws or nut-and-bolt connections that are hidden or cannot be removed with conventional tools.

Template A precise detailed pattern used as a guide in the mortising, drilling, and so forth of a door or frame to receive hardware.

Template hardware Hardware manufactured within template tolerances.

Tension wrench An instrument used in picking a lock. It is used to apply torsion to the cylinder core.

Three-point lock A locking device required on "A-label" fire double doors to lock the active door at three points. The normal position plus top and bottom.

Threshold A wood or metal plate forming the bottom of a doorway.

Throw See **bolt projection**.

Thumb piece (of a door handle) The small pivoted part above the grip of a door handle, which is pressed by the thumb to operate a latch bolt.

Thumbturn A unit that is gripped between the thumb and forefinger and turned to project or retract a bolt.

Tolerance The permissible deviation from a nominal or specified dimension or value.

Transom An opening window immediately above a door.

Transom bar The horizontal frame member that separates the door opening from the transom.

Transom catch A latch bolt fastener on a transom that has a ring by which the latch bolt is retracted.

Transom chain A short chain used to limit the opening of a transom; it is Susually provided with a plate at each end for attachment.

Transom lift A device attached to a door frame and transom by means of which the transom may be opened or closed.

Trim hardware See **finish builders' hardware**.

Tryout keys A set of keys that includes many commonly used bittings. They are used one at a time in an attempt to unlock a door.

Tumbler A movable obstruction in a lock that must be adjusted to a particular position, as by a key, before the bolt can be thrown.

Unit lock See **preassembled lock**.

Vertical bolt lock A lock having two dead bolts that move vertically into two circular receivers in the strike portion of the lock attached to the doorjamb.

Vision panel A fixed transparent panel of glazing material set into an otherwise opaque wall, partition, or door; it is a nonopening window (see also **light**).

Ward An obstruction that prevents the wring key from entering or turning in a lock.

Warded lock A lock containing internal obstacles that block the entrance or rotation of all but the correct key.

Weather stripping Narrow or jamb-width sections of flexible material that prevent the passage of air and moisture around windows and doors. Compression weather stripping also acts as a frictional counterbalance in double-hung windows.

Wet glazing The sealing of glass or other transparent material in a frame by the use of a glazing compound or sealant.

Window frame See **frame**.

Window guard A strong metal grid-like assembly, which can be installed on a window or other opening.

Windows Designed to provide ventilation, illuminative, visual access, or any combination. They come in different shapes, sizes, strengths, and appearance.

Wire glass Glass manufactured with a layer of wire mesh approximately in the center of the sheet.

References

[1] U.S. Green Building Council. LEED Green Building Z Rating System for new construction and major renovation version 2.1. November 2002. Available from: http//www.usgbc.org.

[2] Crowe TD. CPTED. Boston: Butterworth-Heinemann; 2000. p. 3–54.

[3] Bernard R. What is a security infrastructure? Secur Technol Exec 2010:6.

Index

'Note: Page numbers followed by "f" indicate figures, "t" indicate tables and "b" indicate boxes.'